Independent Kashmir

MANCHESTER
1824

Manchester University Press

Independent Kashmir

An incomplete aspiration

Christopher Snedden

Manchester University Press

The right of Christopher Snedden to be identified as the author of this work has been asserted by him in accordance with the Copyright, Designs and Patents Act 1988.

The views and opinions expressed in this book are Christopher Snedden's own. The facts, as reported by him, have been verified to the extent possible, and the publishers are not in any way liable for the same.

Published by Manchester University Press
Altrincham Street, Manchester M1 7JA
www.manchesteruniversitypress.co.uk

British Library Cataloguing-in-Publication Data
A catalogue record for this book is available from the British Library

ISBN   978 1 5261 5614 3   hardback

First published 2021

The publisher has no responsibility for the persistence or accuracy of URLs for any external or third-party internet websites referred to in this book, and does not guarantee that any content on such websites is, or will remain, accurate or appropriate.

Typeset
by New Best-set Typesetters Ltd

For Diane – enough said

Contents

Tables

Acknowledgements

Research and writing are solitary pastimes and this has been a long project. In particular, I would like to thank Dr Smruti Pattanaik and Dr Priyanka Singh, at the Manohar Parrikar Institute for Defence Studies and Analyses, New Delhi, for some thoughtful and stimulating conversations – which they may not remember – in 2017 about the concept, and practice, of *azadi* (independence). One of these conversations with Smruti partially instigated this book. I would like to thank various libraries and librarians, including the State Library of Victoria, Melbourne; the National Library of Australia, Canberra; the Hamilton Library at the University of Hawaii, Honolulu; and Tami Rosado, Mary Ellen Haug and Gayle Yoshikawa at the library at the Daniel K. Inouye Asia-Pacific Center for Security Studies (APCSS), Honolulu, where I worked from 2014–19. Accessing their extensive physical and electronic South Asia collections has been invaluable. I also wish to thank some former colleagues at APCSS, particularly Dr Mohan Malik and Dr Christopher Harmon, for their collegiality, moral support, encouragement and many interesting and beneficial discussions. I particularly enjoyed our luncheon conversations, which were always stimulating, productive and enjoyable. Similarly, I thank three Australian colleagues based in Melbourne for their ongoing friendship, support and encouragement: Professor Robin Jeffrey, Dr Thomas Weber and Professor Kama Maclean. Further afield, I thank Asma Khan Lone for her encouragement and help securing some contacts with Kashmiris. I thank Mr Zafar Khan, Head of Diplomatic Affairs at the Jammu Kashmir Liberation Front (JKLF), who kindly supplied me with some material from, and about, the JKLF. I thank Ramachandra Guha for sending me some articles and the timely and invaluable July 2020 report by The Forum for Human Rights in Jammu and Kashmir, of which he is a member. A number of Kashmiris both in Kashmir and in India also have been very helpful and informative, though they wish to remain anonymous.

Acknowledgements

I thank the entire team at Manchester University Press for their professional and personable help, particularly Rachel Evans, Humairaa Dudhwala and the cartographer, Don Shewan, who drew the excellent maps in this book. Apart from these people and institutions, I wish to deeply thank my wife and editor, Diane Barbeler, for her generosity, perceptiveness and perseverance over the last four intense years. I could not have written this book without her. I dedicate this book to Diane.

Abbreviations

9/11	Terrorist attack in the United States, 11 September 2001 (which term uses the US date format: September 11, 2001)
AISPC	All-India States Peoples' Conference
APHC	All Parties Hurriyat [Freedom] Conference
BJP	Bharatiya Janata Party (Indian People's Party)
ISI	Inter-Services Intelligence Directorate, Pakistan
JKLF	Jammu Kashmir [sic] Liberation Front
J&K	Jammu and Kashmir
LOC	Line of Control
NC	National Conference
NWFP	North-West Frontier Province (now Khyber-Pakhtunkhwa)
OHCHR	Office of the United Nations High Commissioner for Human Rights
Pt.	Pandit
Rs	rupees
UNCIP	United Nations Commission for India and Pakistan
UNSC	United Nations Security Council
USSR	Union of Soviet Socialist Republics; also called the Soviet Union

Glossary

biradari	brotherhood, clan or tribe
Britisher	a term often used by Indians and Pakistanis for their colonial 'masters'
crore	ten million
Dewan	Prime Minister
Dogra	An ethnic group who largely populate the Jammu area of J&K, particularly its eastern parts; the ruler of J&K was always a Dogra
durbar	administration
gaddi	throne
hartal	strike
jathas	bands of demonstrators
J&K-ites	Author's term for the people who populate J&K
katcha	unmetalled (road)
lakh	100,000
Muslims	Also called, on occasions, Mohammedans/Mohammadans
Praja Sabha	People's House
tehsil	sub-district
wazarat	district
wazir	head (of a district)

USSR

AFGHANISTAN

0   km   200

N

Chitral   Yasin   Ishkuman

Gilgit Agency

Hunza

CHINA

Kuh Ghizar   Punial

Nagar

Sinkiang

Gilgit

Gilgit
Leased
Area

Indus

FRONTIER
DISTRICTS
PROVINCE

North-West
Frontier
Province

Chilas

Astore   Skardu   Skardu Tehsil

Hazara
District

KASHMIR
PROVINCE

Baramulla
District

Kargi

Ladakh   District

Muzaffarabad   Muzaffarabad
District

Sopore

Kar3li Tehsil   Leh

Abbottabad

Baramulla

Uri   Srinagar

Murree

Poonch
Jagir   Poonch

Anantnag
District

Ladakh Tehsil

Tibet

Rawalpindi

Rawalpindi
District

Mirpur
District   Reasi District

Rajauri

Anantnag

Udhampur
District

Kishtwar

Indus

Mirpur

JAMMU PROVINCE

Chenani Jagir

Punjab

Jhelum

Sialkot

Jammu
District

Jammu

Kathua
District

Chamba

Chenab

Sialkot
District

Gurdaspur
District

Pathankot

Punjab

Gurdaspur   Kangra

Lahore   Amritsar

INDIA

·············· International border ———— Province or Princely
State border ············ District/Tehsil border

═══════ Jhelum Valley Road ··············· Banihal Cart Road

Jammu and Kashmir on 15 August 1947

xiii

Jammu and Kashmir: current situation

Introduction

This book examines the topic of an internationally independent 'Kashmir' and why this political aspiration to be self-governing and free from coerced subordination to another nation has never been achieved. There have been many interesting books written about either Jammu and Kashmir (J&K) – or 'Kashmir', as the state was popularly called – or about the India–Pakistan dispute over this entity, the so-called 'Kashmir dispute'. Most have sought to detail, explain and discuss this diverse state, including its people and their politics, and/or the India–Pakistan dispute over J&K. This book takes a different approach. It focuses on how Maharaja Hari Singh, Sheikh Mohammad[1] Abdullah and Muslim Kashmiris have envisioned or sought independence for J&K, or for their particular region within this disputed entity. Singh and Abdullah were the two most significant figures in J&K in the twentieth century. In 1988, militant Muslim Kashmiris surprisingly began a violent anti-India uprising that continues to pose challenges for India. By concentrating on these two men and this insurgency, the book provides a focused and in-depth history of J&K from around the mid-1920s, when Hari Singh became ruler of the princely state, to the present time, when many disenchanted Kashmiris still crave what they call *azadi* (independence or freedom) from India. While an 'independent Kashmir' is a long envisioned but incomplete aspiration, this book also discusses how feasible either an independent J&K or an independent Kashmir (i.e., the Kashmir Valley) would actually be.

Through this book's examination of the issue of independence, it also discusses three longstanding disputes or issues that concern, or involve, Jammu and Kashmir. The first is the intractable Kashmir dispute, 'one of the thorniest political issues of modern times'.[2] Because of its 'thorniness', this bitter dispute is unlikely to disappear soon. Indeed, it is unlikely to be resolved as long as the combative nations of 'secular' India and 'Islamic' Pakistan exist in their present structures and formats.

Imbued with their unaddressed historical baggage and limited by their intense geo-political rivalry, they lack any significant desire to engage with each other in meaningful ways. Only when something happens to shatter this seemingly permanent India–Pakistan shibboleth is the Kashmir dispute likely to be resolved. Otherwise, this issue provides a conundrum: which nation should possess the former princely state of Jammu and Kashmir – or, since the late 1950s, how and where should India and Pakistan divide this disputed entity?

The second longstanding issue concerns India and its (now former) state of Jammu and Kashmir and this state's integration, or otherwise, into India. This Indian state was also called 'Jammu and Kashmir' as it was the successor entity to Hari Singh's princely state of the same name. However, given that Singh's former state has been physically divided between India and Pakistan since late 1947 – China also holds some territory – a clearer term for the Indian-controlled portion might be 'Indian J&K'. Until 2019, it comprised three regions: Jammu, Kashmir and Ladakh. Indian J&K now comprises the Union Territory of Jammu and Kashmir and the Union Territory of Ladakh.[3] (On the other side of the Line of Control (LOC) that divides J&K into Indian and Pakistani sectors, 'Pakistan-Administered J&K' comprises two regions: Azad (Free) Jammu and Kashmir, popularly called 'Azad Kashmir', and the Northern Areas, renamed Gilgit-Baltistan in 2009. China-controlled J&K comprises two regions: Aksai Chin and the Shaksgam Valley.) The major challenge in this second longstanding dispute has been trying to agree how much autonomy Indian J&K should, or should not, have, with the chief instigators of this issue being Sheikh Abdullah and Jawaharlal Nehru, (post-British) India's initial, and influential, Prime Minister. Abdullah wanted maximum autonomy for his state; Nehru wanted its full integration into India. Over time, to the chagrin of some in Indian J&K, particularly Muslim Kashmiris, India increasingly has integrated this state into the Indian Union. Seemingly, the Indian Government fully and finally resolved this issue in August 2019 by removing some special constitutional provisions that had only applied to Indian J&K and by bifurcating Indian J&K into the two Union territories of J&K and Ladakh. It remains to be seen whether these steps have worked.

The third longstanding dispute concerning or involving J&K exists among people who live in the geo-political sub-region of Indian J&K that comprises Kashmir, i.e., the Kashmir Valley. This local matter involves severely disenchanted Kashmiris struggling to decide whether their region should remain with India, try to unify with Pakistan, or strive to become independent from both nations. Seemingly, the latter option is most popular with Kashmiris, despite the challenges of securing, then possibly maintaining, such an independent state given its potential geo-strategic circumstances and the penchant of India and Pakistan to meddle. As part of their struggle, Muslim Kashmiris and other 'foreign' Muslim extremists operating in the Kashmir Valley have been opposing India and its security forces since 1988. This anti-India insurgency continues. Even so, one of India's advantages is that Kashmiris are very disunified in their anti-India activities and in their aspirations for their region. Should Kashmiris ever become unified, motivated by a liberation ideology and/or well organised, then India may confront some really serious challenges in Kashmir.

These three disputes are interrelated. Indeed, they operate in a vicious cycle: because the Kashmir dispute is unresolved, India (and Pakistan) wants to control – New Delhi would call it defend – its part of J&K closely; because India controls Indian J&K closely, this seriously antagonises Kashmiris, who consider this control heavy handed; the Kashmiris' severe disgruntlement with India, in turn, offers Pakistan opportunities to interfere in Kashmir and its surrounds; because Pakistan meddles in Kashmir, India refuses to deal with its neighbor until it ceases doing so; because India refuses to talk with Pakistan, the Kashmir dispute continues; because the Kashmir dispute continues, India wants to control Indian J&K closely etc., etc. At any point, New Delhi could intervene to try to change, or break, this vicious cycle, but it rarely chooses to do so. Similarly, Islamabad could stand back and allow India a free hand in J&K, but this is impossible as Pakistan must take every opportunity that it can to weaken its more powerful neighbor. Some Pakistanis call this strategy 'death by a thousand cuts'. Supposedly, Pakistan also feels incomplete without 'Kashmir', by which it means the Kashmir Valley with its almost overwhelmingly Muslim population. This vicious cycle is going to continue for some time: neither nation has any great need, or compulsion, to resolve the Kashmir dispute, nor to improve their relations. Both have long functioned effectively with minimal contacts with each other. Indeed both, seemingly, have enjoyed their poor-to-parlous relations. Meanwhile, life remains somewhat uncertain and difficult for many people in J&K (who I refer to as 'J&K-ites'), if only because their international status has not been fully resolved and because they are stifled by excessive metropolitan control.

Although India and Pakistan have failed to resolve the Kashmir dispute since 1947, they have dismissed a third possibility for J&K that might offer one way to resolve this dispute: independence. Vicariously, this option might also resolve the other two disputes. An internationally independent J&K is not a new proposition. Rather, it is a lapsed or superseded one. When Maharaja Hari Singh acceded to India on 26 October 1947, J&K ostensibly had been independent for seventy-two days. I say 'ostensibly' as the princely state had not been fully or genuinely independent in the sense of having complete sovereignty, total control over its own affairs, and being responsible for its own defence and external affairs. Rather, it was de facto independence as J&K was then a state in political limbo. The J&K ruler was trying to determine his state's future international status during a tenuous time of political and social upheaval as the newly created dominions of India and Pakistan severed, suffered and sorted themselves out after, and due to, the British division of British India on 15 August 1947. Being unsure of what to do, Maharaja Hari Singh, the empowered decision maker, remained in Srinagar, his summer capital, pondering his options. Should he keep J&K independent of both dominions or should he accede to one of them, as many people expected him to do? While Singh's preferred option may have been for J&K to continue to be independent, by mid-to-late October 1947 circumstances would compel him to make an accession.

On 26 October 1947, Maharaja Hari Singh finally acceded to India. I say 'finally' as, over time, this increasingly looked more likely to be the option that he would take. Singh hadn't rushed into his decision, however. Before his accession, the otherwise distracted leaders of India and Pakistan had been trying to ascertain whether he would join J&K with Pakistan or India. (I put Pakistan first as many subcontinentals then expected that J&K should, and would, join this dominion.) More pointedly, these politicians were trying to determine, or influence, when, and how, such unification might take place. At the same time, motivated J&K-ites had been taking their own actions to ensure that J&K joined their dominion of choice. Few J&K-ites, it seems, then favoured independence for J&K. Soon after partition, pro-Pakistan Muslims in Poonch, in southwestern J&K, instigated a major anti-Maharaja uprising. In September–October, pro-India Hindus and Sikhs and pro-Pakistan Muslims engaged in serious inter-religious violence throughout J&K's southern Jammu Province.[4] These actions by J&K-ites were little reported, partly as subcontinental attention, if it had time to focus on J&K at all, was then focused on Srinagar and Maharaja Hari Singh. While Singh may have been interested in J&K continuing to exist as an independent entity, the invasion of Kashmir Province by Pukhtoons from Pakistan on 22 October 1947 ended this aspiration. Needing military assistance to defend his state, a desperate Hari Singh asked India for help. New Delhi would only provide assistance if he acceded to India, which Singh duly did on 26 October 1947.

Maharaja Hari Singh's accession to India should have ended the matter of J&K's international status, but it didn't. Similarly, it should have killed the concept of an

4

independent J&K, but it didn't. Apart from Hari Singh, another possible supporter of independence was the 'paradoxical figure', Sheikh Mohammad Abdullah, the leading politician in J&K during 1931–82.[5] In 1947, this Muslim ethnic Kashmiri, who also was a practitioner of secular politics, had supported Singh's accession to India. Thereafter, however, Abdullah on occasions – he was far from consistent – supported either full autonomy for J&K or for it to remain apart from both India and Pakistan but with good relations with both. To 'remain apart' essentially amounted to independence – to being self-governing and free from coerced subordination to another nation. Problematically, however, what Sheikh Abdullah actually meant by 'Kashmir' was not always clear. Did he mean all of the former princely state or did he mean only the Kashmir Valley? To some extent, Abdullah's meaning depended on his audience. Equally, his vagueness about 'Kashmir' reflects one of the challenges of the Kashmir dispute: terminology. This is discussed further below.

In 1953, Sheikh Abdullah was dismissed as Prime Minister of Indian-controlled J&K. Thereafter, he was detained for long periods by the Government of J&K or by the Government of India. When not incarcerated, Abdullah was often a lone voice in pursuing an autonomous or independent status for J&K. Arguably, what he wanted was maximum autonomy for his beloved Kashmir from which region he hailed. In 1963, Prime Minister Jawaharlal Nehru apparently also seriously considered independence for J&K. Nehru did so after being approached by Lord Louis Mountbatten, the last British Viceroy of India and the first Governor-General of (post-British) India. Nehru, nearing the end of his life, was trying to resolve the Kashmir conundrum. By then, however, the idea of an independent J&K was untenable with Nehru's colleagues,[6] and with Pakistan. In 1975, Sheikh Abdullah returned from the political wilderness to again lead Indian J&K. In order to assume power again, he had agreed to confirm J&K's accession to India. In other words, he agreed that J&K was an integral part of India. Finally, it seemed, the concept of independence for 'Kashmir' had ended. However, it hadn't.

In 1988, the concept of an independent J&K re-emerged suddenly, and violently. It did so when members of the Jammu Kashmir Liberation Front (JKLF) instigated an anti-India, pro-independence uprising in the Kashmir Valley.[7] These militants called for the political and physical reunification of the former princely state of J&K and for this reunified entity to be granted independence. The JKLF's stance was popular with Muslim Kashmiris, many of whom thought that independence was 'just around the corner'. However, this possibility was not popular with all J&K-ites: Hindu Kashmiris (called Pandits), some Muslim Kashmiris, and many people located in Jammu or Ladakh strongly wanted J&K to be with India. Some

Muslims in the Kashmir Valley and in Jammu wanted J&K to join Pakistan. Similarly, J&K-ites in Pakistan-Administered J&K wanted to be with Pakistan. In the early-to-mid 1990s, pro-Pakistan insurgent groups such as the Hizbul Mujahideen (Party of Holy Warriors; whose fighters predominantly comprise ethnic Muslim Kashmiris) and India's security forces brutally attacked and severely weakened the JKLF. Nevertheless, it continues to operate on both sides of the LOC, although it now functions at the political level using non-violent methods.[8] JKLF members still desire an independent J&K free from India and Pakistan.

The anti-India agitation that Muslim Kashmiris began in 1988 continues. The idea of independence for 'Kashmir' is still popular among some, perhaps many, J&K-ites, particularly Muslim Kashmiris. I use the terminology 'some, perhaps many, J&K-ites' as nobody knows for certain what international status these people want for their state or for their particular region. J&K-ites have never been asked such questions in any inclusive or meaningful ways. That said, the Kashmir Valley appears to be the only region in J&K where people are severely dissatisfied with their international status. Many Muslim ethnic Kashmiris, who comprise the great bulk of Kashmir's population, dislike what they see as intrusive and excessive Indian rule. Their disenchantment was increased in August 2019 when the Indian Parliament officially abrogated Article 370 of the Indian Constitution, which had supposedly, but largely unsuccessfully, guaranteed J&K's autonomy. This also led to the abrogation of Article 35-A, which had allowed only State Subjects (i.e., locals) to purchase immoveable property (i.e., land) in J&K. Concurrently, J&K was demoted in stature by dividing it into two territories. Neither is now self-governing, a factor that allows New Delhi to impose its will largely unhindered in both of these strategically important entities. Also concurrently, New Delhi imposed draconian security measures on Kashmir, including stringent curfews and severely limiting telecommunication services and internet access. Seemingly, these changes have resolved New Delhi's legal and administrative issues with this recalcitrant state that had formerly enjoyed a 'special' status. Similarly, its residents supposedly have now become ordinary Indians.

Whether these legal changes have lessened Kashmiris' desire either for *azadi* or for autonomy remains to be seen, although this would seem unlikely. Given a choice, it seems that many Muslim Kashmiris now almost certainly want to be free from India. What status they want thereafter is uncertain. Some want independence for Kashmir. Some want Kashmir to join Pakistan, although this nation is not universally popular with all Muslim Kashmiris, despite its Islamic connections. Some consider that Pakistanis have, on occasions during the Kashmiris' anti-India uprising, appeared to be more interested in obtaining Kashmiris' lands, than in supporting or securing their welfare. For them, India and Pakistan 'both want the land, but they don't want the people'.[9] (Conversely, Hindu ethnic Kashmiris, many of whom tragically fled Kashmir in 1990 because they felt severely threatened by anti-India militants, want their own separate 'Panun Kashmir' (Our Own Kashmir) homeland created in the Kashmir Valley, to which they eventually could return, should they ever feel secure enough to do so.[10] For some Kashmiris, chiefly Muslim Kashmiri politicians, the Kashmir Valley is 'incomplete' without its Pandit minority.) Whether an independent 'Kashmir' could ever come into being, how this might happen, and whether such an entity would be viable and able to withstand meddling neighbours, are challenging questions to answer. This book attempts to do so.

Three factors stimulated me to write this book. The first was a desire to investigate the concept of an independent J&K, as was suggested in 1947–48 by various people, including Maharaja Hari Singh, India's Defence Committee of the Cabinet, and India's United Nations representative. Equally, I wanted to clarify some catchy, but incorrect, Pakistani terminology about the Kashmir dispute being the 'unfinished agenda of partition' or 'the unfinished business of Partition'.[11] In 1947, the British 'transfer of power' was made directly to India and Pakistan.[12] Otherwise, each empowered ruler of a princely state, over which the British had only ever ruled indirectly, had to make their own decision about whether to join India or Pakistan. Therefore, the Kashmir dispute is actually the 'unfinished business of the decolonisation of India's princely states'. The second factor was a desire to understand the Kashmiri identity and why Kashmir and Kashmiris have always 'hogged the limelight' in J&K and the Kashmir dispute before and after 1947 – factors that Indians have also long wrestled with. The third, and final, factor was to understand what *azadi* actually means for J&K-ites, with this possibly meaning securing more and/or genuine autonomy within India, unifying with Pakistan, or irrevocable independence from India.

In brief, this book discusses the topic of an independent 'Kashmir', actual or envisaged, and why this aspiration remains incomplete. Chapter 1 discusses relevant aspects of the rapid British decolonisation of their Indian Empire and the possibilities for India's major princes and politicians. Chapter 2 looks specifically at Maharaja Hari Singh, the international status that he wanted for India's largest princely state, and his efforts to obtain this status. Chapter 3 discusses the significance of the politically important Kashmir region, nationalism in J&K, and the inherent Kashmiri identity that India has found difficult to integrate. Chapter 4 examines the development of Kashmiri nationalism from around 1925, including the rise of Sheikh Abdullah as a major political figure in J&K. Chapter 5 discusses the significant 1947–53 period when Abdullah was powerful in J&K, with New Delhi supporting him almost unequivocally until he was deposed in 1953. Chapter 6 continues to discuss Sheikh Abdullah and his wavering attitudes to independence, autonomy or self-determination for J&K from 1953 until his death in 1982. Chapter 7 discusses Muslim Kashmiris' anti-India uprising since 1988 and what they mean by the vexed term *azadi*. This includes the major constitutional and administrative changes imposed by India on Indian J&K in 2019. The book ends with a Conclusion, after which follows three appendices that provide some additional information about J&K.

Before ending this Introduction, it is worth noting that the terms 'Kashmir' and 'Kashmiris' cause significant confusion. When people talk about 'Kashmir', it is often unclear whether they are referring generally to the state of Jammu and Kashmir or specifically to the Kashmir Valley region. When people talk about 'Kashmiris', they may be referring generally to citizens of the princely state of 'Kashmir' or specifically to ethnic Kashmiris who largely, but not totally, populate the Kashmir Valley. The 'real' Kashmir refers to the Kashmir Valley, also called the 'Vale of Kashmir', or, in 1931, the 'Valley of Kashmir'.[13] People living in this region call it 'Kashir'.[14] Additional confusion arises because the princely state of Jammu and Kashmir, which came into being in 1846, was popularly, and simply, often called 'Kashmir', even though its rulers actually were ethnic Dogras from Jammu. This was due to the fame and prestige of Kashmir (i.e., the Kashmir Valley), the most high-profile and prized part of this large princely domain and which, because of these factors, provided the princely state with its popular name of 'Kashmir'. Apart from when they are talking about 'the Kashmir dispute', Indians and Pakistanis often use the term 'Kashmir' differently. Generally, Indians use the term 'Kashmir' to refer specifically to the Kashmir Valley, which area is populated largely by ethnic Kashmiris. Generally, Pakistanis use the term 'Kashmir' to refer to the former princely state of Jammu and Kashmir that was popularly called 'Kashmir' and which was populated by people popularly called 'Kashmiris'. The context may provide clarity, but often their usage is unclear or misleading.

I use the term 'Kashmir' to refer specifically to the Kashmir Valley. To reduce confusion, I may, on occasions, use the term 'the Kashmir Valley', rather than just the word 'Kashmir'. The only exception is when I use 'Kashmir' in the term 'the Kashmir dispute'. Similarly, I use the term 'Kashmiris' when talking about the ethnic group who largely populate the Kashmir Valley. I use the term 'J&K' to refer to all of the former princely state of Jammu and Kashmir, while I use the term 'J&K-ites' to refer to all of the people who populated, or still populate, this now imagined and never-likely-to-be-reunified entity. On occasions, I use the term 'Kashmir Province', which administrative entity in 1947 was one of J&K's three provinces, along with Jammu Province and the Frontier Districts Province. In 1947, the Kashmir Valley, which comprised the districts of Anantnag and Baramulla, was located wholly within Kashmir Province. India claims all of J&K because Maharaja Hari Singh acceded to it in 1947. Roughly, it directly controls two-thirds of J&K's three former provinces in the successor state of Jammu and Kashmir. For clarity, I use the term 'Indian J&K' for this Indian-controlled entity. Also, given that most of this book was written *before* J&K and Ladakh were made Union Territories, when I use the abbreviation 'J&K' in the text, unless stated otherwise, I am referring either to the former princely state of Jammu and Kashmir or to the now former Indian state of Indian J&K. The context should provide clarity.

This is my third book about Jammu and Kashmir and aspects of its history and geo-politics.[15] While carrying out my research, I have been excited by the array of material now available electronically. This includes a considerable amount of older material about British rule of India. To be able to read documents such as an 1854 Gazetteer of 'Native States'[16] or the *Census of India, 1901*, or the 1846 edition of *The Times*, all in electronic formats has been enlightening.[17] Whether this book makes me a 'Kashmirologist' or not remains to be seen.[18] Either way, I take full responsibility for any errors, omissions and commissions.

1

Decolonisation and the departure of the British from India

1947 was a tumultuous year on the Indian subcontinent. Thoughts of independence were everywhere. On 20 February, the British Government announced that it 'would grant Indian independence no later than June 1948'.[1] This was significant. The British had been the only people ever to unify the entire Indian subcontinent into a single political entity – 'their' Indian Empire, or Raj. By 1947, however, these dispirited foreigners were 'scuttling'. They wanted to decolonise their vast, disparate and increasingly unruly 'possession' – rapidly.[2] At the time of its announcement, the British Government had not resolved how it would fully and finally disengage from India. Ultimately, this 'savage disentanglement' would involve the clinical partitioning, or dividing, of the parts of their Indian Empire that the British directly administered ('British India') into two new political entities.[3] The larger of these two entities, (post-British) India, would consist of territory that made up the bulk of British India. The other entity, (Muslim) Pakistan, would comprise two wings, East and West Pakistan, located on either side of the subcontinent. Almost unbelievably, certainly in retrospect, these two Pakistani portions would be separated by a thousand miles of Indian territory. This circumstance would eventually prove to be untenable.

In 1947, the British imperialists also left behind many confused, uncertain and equally dispirited princely protégés, some of whom also had been thinking about independence. The British, in their role as the paramount power and guarantor of the Indian princes' autocratic regimes, had maintained superiority and power over some 562 rulers for nearly ninety years via various treaties and other arrangements. These would end, or lapse, after the British departure. Thereafter, some princely rulers, along with the leaders of the soon-to-be-created political entity of Pakistan, believed that the princely states ('Princely India') would be independent. That is, they would not have to join either India or Pakistan. Maharaja Hari Singh, the ruler of the princely state of Jammu and Kashmir, was one such 'believer'. He had enjoyed British support and, as some saw it, 'power without responsibility' since securing the J&K *gaddi* (throne) in 1925 following the death of his childless uncle, Maharaja Pratap Singh.[4] How these supposed future independent princely entities, many of which were landlocked and/or physically separated from each other, would survive was unclear. More realistically, therefore, the British, along with the new leaders of India – but not, initially, of Pakistan – encouraged, and expected, each legally empowered major ruler to take a decision to join his state with either India or Pakistan. Formally, this decision was called an accession. Each ruler was supposed to make an accession before 15 August 1947, the date that the British would depart India and bring the new dominions of (post-British) India and Pakistan into being. In 1947, some 140 princes, including Maharaja Hari Singh, were legally empowered to make an accession to either dominion.[5]

This chapter examines the British Indian Empire, relevant aspects of its administrative structure, and the positions of India's politicians and princes in the hasty and purgative – for the British, at least – decolonisation processes of 1947. It explains that, during 1947, there were differing ideas about the Indian princes' legal positions and post-British options, including in relation to independence or otherwise, considerable politicking by politicians – all of whom were Indians until 15 August 1947 – and much uncertainty and upheaval for many subcontinentals, including J&K-ites. One of the most significant of these J&K-ites was Maharaja Hari Singh, the person charged, and empowered, to decide J&K's post-British future by making an accession. As this chapter explains, the British decolonisation of their substantial Indian Empire in 1947 enabled him to seriously contemplate and envisage independence for J&K

The paramount power's empire

In 1947, the British directly and indirectly controlled all of India. The areas under their direct control and administration were referred to as British India; the areas under their indirect control were referred to as Princely India[6] or the 'Indian States'.[7] British India comprised roughly two-thirds of the Indian Empire divided into eleven provinces and with a population in 1941 of 296 million.[8] In this directly controlled section of their empire, the departing colonial rulers were leaving behind two new dominions: Pakistan, which would comprise almost all of the subcontinent's Muslim-majority areas, but, significantly, not all of the subcontinent's Muslims; and India, which would comprise the remaining non-Muslim-majority areas. The basis for the establishment of these two new legal entities was the rapidly enacted Indian Independence Act of 18 July 1947. It stated that 'As from the fifteenth day of August, nineteen hundred and forty-seven, two independent Dominions shall be set up in India, to be known respectively as India and Pakistan'.[9] So, even though Pakistanis actually celebrate 14 August as their nation's independence day, Pakistan did not legally come into being until 15 August 1947. While self-governing and essentially independent, the two new dominions of India and Pakistan would become fully independent of the United Kingdom after each instituted their respective constitution: in 1950 for India; in 1956 for Pakistan.

Reflecting the fact that the major religious group in (post-British) India was Hindus, some people, chiefly Pakistanis, referred to the new Dominion of India as 'Hindustan' (the land of Hindus). They may have used this name to emphasise the Hindu character of India.[10] Conversely, some Indians called their nation 'Bharat', an ancient term for India. Members of the Indian National Congress ('Congress'), such as Jawaharlal Nehru,[11] whose political party had long fought for Indian independence, and (post-British) Indians considered their state to be the post-partition/post-British and residual Indian entity. It was the successor state to British India, not the seceding state, which was Pakistan.[12] For these Indians, Bharat inherited the 'international personality of India' that previously had been under British control, including many of this entity's offshore assets, responsibilities, and membership of international bodies.[13] This was an important distinction. Due to this 'inheritance', India already belonged to the United Nations in 1947, as British India had been admitted as a member on 30 October 1945. Newly created Pakistan, however, had to apply for membership of the United Nations. It was admitted on 30 September 1947.[14] Some Indians also considered that Congress, which would form the new Indian Government, was 'the *de facto* successor to [British] para-mountcy'.[15] Congress did not accept that, after the British had left India, paramountcy would revert, or be retroceded, to India's princely rulers,[16] or that each prince would then become 'an autocratic and independent sovereign'.[17] Rather, most rulers necessarily would need to have a subordinate relationship with India, which essentially would act as the post-British paramount power. Invariably, India's princes disagreed with this position. Few hereditary rulers were keen to submit themselves to being controlled by elected politicians, a position the princes had enunciated as early as 1929, as the Indian States Committee's report had noted. The issue of paramountcy therefore was an 'old vexed question'.[18]

Paramountcy was the 'vague and undefined' feudatory system whereby the British, as the suzerain power, dominated and controlled India's princely rulers.[19]

Collectively, these Indian rulers and their lands under British suzerainty comprised Princely India. British dominance and control was achieved in two ways. First, by direct 'treaty relationships' with 40 larger Indian states, whose total population amounted to about two-thirds of Princely India's total population. Second, by 'engagements and *Sanads*' with the smaller princely states that bound them to the paramount power.[20] (A sanad was a legal instruction or decision, an 'acknowledgement of concession or authority or privileges generally coupled with conditions proceeding from the Paramount Power'.)[21] These 'loyal collaborators of the Raj' were 'afforded [British] protection in exchange for helpful behavior in a relationship of tutelage, called paramountcy'.[22] This arrangement enabled British control of India's princely states in three areas or ways: '(1) external affairs; (2) defence and protection; (3) intervention', when necessary, to ensure good governance in the princely state.[23] These controls came out of the 'two great principles' that the British had followed since the 1860s in dealing with India's States:

(1) the integrity of the states should be preserved by perpetuating the rule of the Princes whose power to adopt heirs was recognized by sanads granted in 1862;
(2) flagrant misgovernment must be prevented or arrested by [the] timely exercise of intervention.[24]

Generally, Indian princes did not suffer from actual British interference in their specific state unless this was required to protect or advance British interests.[25]

In 1947, a significant concern for the Government of (post-British) India was that, while British paramountcy would end, it needed to ensure that there was no 'vacuum or anarchy in any part of India'.[26] The entire process of the British withdrawal was 'a violent blow' to India's 'political, economic and geographical integrity'.[27] However, the partition of British India confirmed that 'the essential transfer of power [wa]s between Britain and British India'.[28] Apart from transferring political power to the new Governments of India and Pakistan, the British also determined their borders. Similarly, they divided and supervised the transfer of various local assets, such as railways and military forces, to each new entity. Newly empowered, the post-partition leaders of India and Pakistan became potent local authorities, serious powerbrokers and decision makers, and strident new nationalists. Despite the brutal months surrounding the actual partition, these leaders did, indeed, largely ensure that there were no major power vacuums or ongoing anarchic situations. Significantly, the final British Viceroy, Lord Louis Mountbatten, despite his royal blood, a factor of importance to some Indian princes, helped this process by ensuring that almost all rulers of princely states had acceded to India or to Pakistan before, or on, 15 August 1947.

The Indian Independence Act, 1947, provided the legal basis for the creation of post-British India and Pakistan. Apart from establishing both dominions,[29] this Act established Constituent Assemblies for each. These bodies would then determine, finalise and legally institute each dominion's constitution. In the interim, the 1947 Act, along with the Government of India Act, 1935, would govern the administrations of India and Pakistan until their constitutions came into being. The 1935 Act, which was the 'longest piece of parliamentary legislation on the British statute book',[30] was important. It had envisaged a 'federation of India' that was to comprise both the Indian Provinces (i.e., where the British ruled directly) and the Indian States (which Indian princes ruled). It therefore had 'provided for a constitutional relationship between the Indian States and British India on a federal basis'.[31] This was not a new concept: the Montagu-Chelmsford Report in 1919 first proposed the idea of an Indian Federation.[32] The 1935 Act talked of accession by Indian States to this envisaged Federation, although, seemingly, it did not mention what would, or should, happen to States that chose not to accede to it – that is, if they chose to be independent.[33] This accession would be voluntary and subject to limitations, as specified by the ruler in his accession,[34] a factor that may have influenced princely rulers, including Maharaja Hari Singh, in later decisions. The intervention of World War II in 1939 'postponed',[35] or actually prevented, the establishment of the federation of India, if only because the British were significantly distracted by the need to defend their own nation than to seriously contemplate a future Indian political structure. Additionally, many senior Congressmen were being detained for not supporting the British war effort, while India's hereditary rulers and elected officials had not been able to agree on an Indian federation. By 1947, things had changed and British decolonisation was assured. This made Indians contemplate their options.

The Indian or princely states

Concurrent with their direct control of British India in 1947, the British also indirectly controlled and oversaw the administration of Princely India, which comprised some 562 Native or Indian States. I say 'some' as the exact number of princely states that existed is difficult to determine. As the *Report of the Indian States Committee, 1928–1929* noted, 'The term Indian State is, in fact, extremely elastic as regards both size and government'.[36] And, as Walter Lawrence, who worked as

Viceroy Curzon's Private Secretary from 1899–1903,[37] noted: 'Very little is known about the Indian States'.[38] Certainly, there was confusion about how many princely states actually existed. Lawrence states that there were 'some six hundred and seventy-five States in India'.[39] An Indian advocate, K. R. R. Sastry, states there were 601, although, confusingly, he provides figures that total 562.[40] George MacMunn, a senior British Army officer, believed there were 585 princely states, divided into fifteen classes 'of which 149 are major states and 436 [are] minor or non-salute states'. These figures included Bhutan and Sikkim, both of which were 'In Immediate Political Relations with the Government of India' and were important because of their position on the frontier with Tibet.[41] I have settled on the lesser number of 562 princely states, as per the *Report of the Indian States Committee, 1928–1929* presented by the Secretary of State for India to the British Parliament in March 1929.[42] This official report would appear to be authoritative.

In 1921, India's princely states comprised 598,000 square miles and had a population of 69 million people. This amounted to 'about two-fifths of the area and one-fifth of the population' of all of India.[43] By 1941, the population of Princely India had increased to 93 million.[44] In 1947, India's 562 princely states were scattered throughout the subcontinent like a patchwork quilt. Generally, they were located in 'the least favoured areas of the subcontinent', a factor that may have helped their political survivability during British times but which probably hindered their economic development and political advancement.[45] Many princely states were small or even tiny: 'The area of 178 states [wa]s from ten to [one] hundred square miles each; two hundred and two states have each an area of less than 10 square miles'.[46] Many were landlocked or were 'islands within India',[47] with individual states, or groups of states such as the Rajputana Agency, which comprised thirteen princely states,[48] usually separated from each other by territory that comprised British India. Significantly, their locations were a factor that favoured the new Dominion of India, with almost all princely states prospectively located within, or adjacent to, its ultimate boundaries. British-controlled or British-managed roads and railways, the bulk of which the new dominion of India also would inherit, connected many princely states or groups of states.

Politically, the Indian States were administered separately from British India. The semi-autonomous ruler of each major state invariably was 'advised' – that is, overseen or supervised – by a Resident. This British official worked for the small, British-run, Political Department, the elite sub-set of the Indian Civil Service that looked after the Indian States and which, according to one Indian, had 'unfettered discretion … to intervene in their internal affairs'.[49] As one British official put this circumstance in relation to J&K: 'the whole State is ruled over by a Maharaja. It is one of what are known as the Native States of India, – States which are ruled by their own Chiefs, but feudatory to the British Government, whose interests are represented by a British Resident at the capital.'[50] This powerful Political Agent, Political Officer or Resident 'might be deceived, or cajoled, but he was rarely disobeyed'.[51] Significantly, Residents, or 'Politicals' as they also were called, coveted appointments to the princely state of Jammu and Kashmir, or to Rajputana. The Resident in J&K 'led an agreeable existence based at Srinagar, moving up to the lovely hills of Gulmarg ... in the summer and gravitating to Sialkot in the Punjab for the winter'.[52] This was a relatively new position. J&K had only had a Resident since 1885 when the British finally were able to impose their representative on the new J&K ruler, Maharaja Pratap Singh. However, the British later made a major concession to Pratap's successor, Maharaja Hari Singh, J&K's fourth and final ruler. Hari Singh was able to insist that, during the winter months, the British Resident would reside outside J&K at Sialkot, located nearby in neighbouring, British-ruled, Punjab. This gave Singh a little distance from this important Britisher. During Pratap's (and possibly Hari's) time, the Assistant Resident would remain in Srinagar when the ruler and the Resident departed this city in winter.[53]

According to the *Report of the Indian States Committee, 1928–1929*, there were three divisions of Indian states:[54]

- *[Division] 'I. States the rulers of which are members of the Chamber of Princes in their own right: 108'.*

Members of the First Division were large, 'fully empowered', Salute States that comprised rulers of princely states who enjoyed 'permanent dynastic salutes of eleven guns and over' and 'other States who exercised such full powers as, in the opinion of the Viceroy, qualified them for individual membership' of the Chamber of Princes.[55] The salute involved 'the firing on all formal occasions' of a number of rounds of a cannon or artillery piece, depending on the ruler's status.[56] Also called 'fully jurisdictional states',[57] First Division States were largely autonomous in all matters except defence, foreign affairs and communications. Five states known as the 'five great states' or 'the big five' were 'In Immediate Political Relations with the Government of India': Hyderabad, Mysore, Baroda, Jammu and Kashmir, and Gwalior.[58] In their combined area, the 108 Division I states comprised 514,886 square miles. They had a population of almost 60 million people and a combined revenue of Rs 42.16 crores.[59] (A crore is ten million.) Many rulers in First Division states lived opulent lifestyles. Allegedly, each enjoyed an 'Average of eleven titles, 5.8 wives, 12.6 children, 9.2 elephants, 2.8 private railway cars, 3.4 Rolls Royces and 22.9 tigers killed'.[60]

- *[Division] 'II. States the rulers of which are represented in the Chamber of Princes by twelve members of their order elected by themselves: 127'.*

Members of the Second Division were Non-Salute States. They were smaller, 'semi-jurisdictional states',[61] whose rulers enjoyed limited autonomy within their states, with British officials essentially ruling, managing and overseeing administrative matters: 'the Crown Representative exercised certain powers and jurisdiction'.[62] In their combined area, the 127 Division II states comprised 76,846 square miles. They had a population of just over 8 million people and a combined revenue of Rs 2.89 crores.[63]

- *[Division] 'III: Estates, Jagirs and others …: 327', of which 286 were located in 'Kathiawar and Gujerat [sic]', with some 'amounting in extent to a few acres only' and 'yield[ing] a revenue not greater than that of the annual income of an ordinary artisan'.*[64]

Members of the Third Division were 'petty', 'non-jurisdictional states',[65] with their 'rulers' largely comprising hereditary landowners of estates in which Political Agents of the Government of India administered all civil and criminal jurisdiction, supposedly on their behalf. They were 'relatively of very little consequence, and only exist[ed] independently as the result of an historical accident'.[66] The combined area of these 327 Division III entities was 6,406 square miles. They had a population of only 802,000 people and a combined revenue of Rs 0.74 crores.[67] On average, each state was 'about 20 square miles' in area, had a population of 'about 3,000' and an average annual revenue of 'about Rs. 22,000'.[68]

The abovementioned Chamber of Princes was a representative body for India's princes. The British, in post-World War I reforms, had established this Chamber in 1921 to operate as a 'deliberative, consultative and advisory body' for senior Indian princes.[69] The rulers of all Division I States were entitled to membership; rulers of Division II States elected twelve representatives; Division III States were not entitled to any representation. The Chamber's decisions were non-binding collectively or individually on princes.[70] The Chamber of Princes was India's third chamber in 'Council House (Parliament House)', New Delhi, along with the Central Legislative Assembly and the Council of State. This Chamber ceased functioning in 1947.[71] The Central Legislative Assembly later became the Lok Sabha (Lower House) in India's post-British Parliament, while the Council of State became its Rajya Sabha (Upper House).

Apart from the British Resident's often intrusive 'tutelage' of 'his' local ruler, the British interfered little in First Division states unless there was 'gross misgovernment' or the need to preserve the dynasty or state. Major British intervention occurred three times in J&K. The first was in mid-1846, soon after J&K came into existence following the Treaty of Amritsar whereby the British sold Jammu and Kashmir to Maharaja Gulab Singh, a native of Jammu. This new ruler, who apparently had 'desired to conquer [neighbouring Kashmir] from his boyhood', had been actively involved in 1819 capturing this region for Emperor Ranjit Singh.[72] The Sikh Empire then ruled Kashmir until 1846, when the British obtained this region from the defeated Sikhs in war reparations. Gulab Singh needed British military assistance to impose his regime over rebellious Kashmiris in his newly purchased Kashmir Valley.[73] The second British intervention in J&K was from 1889 to 1905. A British-led Council of State 'temporarily deposed' J&K's third ruler, Maharaja Pratap Singh, and administered the state because his maladministration had bankrupted it.[74] Equally, the British were concerned about some alleged attempts by Pratap to communicate with foreign governments, particularly Russia.[75] The Council of State was effective: by 1900, 'there was no State in India more prosperous' than J&K.[76] The third British intervention in J&K occurred in 1931. British regiments from Jullundur, Punjab, provided military assistance 'in Mirpur and surrounding area' to help quell 'communal clashes' and a major 'political agitation in the State'. This shored up Maharaja Hari Singh's regime.[77] These 'Imperial Troops' were in J&K from November 1931 until October 1932 when J&K State Forces replaced them.[78]

Maharaja Gulab Singh and his great grandson, Maharaja Hari Singh, respectively welcomed the first and third British interventions in J&K. Each intervention clearly helped to secure (for Gulab) or to support (for Hari) their respective regime. The third intervention was particularly significant as it involved controlling 'communalism', an ongoing issue both in India and J&K. (As Park succinctly defines it, 'Communalism, in Indian terms, denotes political action motivated primarily by religious considerations'.[79] Arguably, the British partition of its empire into India and Pakistan based on religion provides the 'best', and most extreme, example of communalism in the subcontinent in recent times.) In relation to the second British intervention, J&K's ruler, Maharaja Pratap Singh, while loyal to the British Crown, did not like being usurped. This empowered his ambitious younger brother,

Raja Amar Singh, who was Hari Singh's father and an apparently 'brilliant man'[80] but who engaged in 'family intrigues' with Pratap.[81] By 1891, Pratap Singh may also have been perturbed by a report in the *Amrita Bazar Patrika* newspaper that talked of the British annexing J&K and ruling it directly.[82] This did not come to pass. Significantly, all three British interventions, or the ongoing possibility of British intervention, to support the J&K regime made it difficult for aspiring anti-maharaja elements to oppose Dogra rulers.[83] (The term 'Dogra' referred to the ruler's ethnicity, with people in their home region of Jammu in southern J&K 'known generally as Dogras, whatever their origin'.)[84] The removal of British support for J&K rulers in August 1947 partially explains why Maharaja Hari Singh's autocratic, and by then essentially independent, regime disappeared so quickly.

The British departure in 1947 meant that the rulers of the more important, or 'viable', princely states would be able to decide their state's post-British international status. A viable state was one entitled to separate representation in the Indian Constituent Assembly proposed during the pre-1947 period when the British seriously tried to leave behind a unitary and unified Indian nation.[85] In 1947, according to the Secretary of India's States Department, there were 140 empowered princely states entitled to make a full accession.[86] While each empowered ruler signed the highest type or form of Instrument of Accession, there also were two other versions. Seventy 'intermediate rulers' signed a lesser Instrument of Accession which ensured that they 'did not exercise higher powers' than they had before the British left. Rulers of the small '*estates* and *talukas* [*tehsils* or sub-districts] ... numbering over 300' signed a third form of Instrument of Accession 'suitable for their [lesser] status and requirements' that 'vested all the residuary powers and jurisdiction in the Central Government'.[87]

Chiefly, viable states comprised those princely states who were members of the First Division. Collectively, in area and population, this comprised the bulk of Princely India (see Table 1.1). However, not all viable states potentially had the wherewithal to become independent. The 1946 Cabinet Mission identified nineteen such states that might: 'Baroda, Gwalior, Hyderabad, Jammu and Kashmir, Mysore, Bhopal, Indore, Kolhapur, Travancore, Udaipur, Bikaner, Cochin, Jaipur, Jodhpur, Kotah, Patiala, Rewa, Alwar, and Mayurbhanj'.[88] Sir Conrad Corfield, Political Adviser to the Viceroy and head of the Political Department, thought that 'only about ten or twelve [princely states] had inherent survival [value]' and that 'the only units which could afford temporary independence were those which had or could negotiate an outlet to the sea'. India's first Prime Minister, Jawaharlal Nehru, apparently agreed with Corfield.[89] Of the Cabinet Mission's nineteen viable states, only Baroda, Travancore and Cochin had direct access to the sea. Mysore and Mayurbhanj were relatively close, but both were landlocked, as were the other fourteen princely states, including J&K.

Writing in 1975, Corfield identified sixteen states that he felt could have survived as independent, post-British entities: Hyderabad, J&K, Mysore, Travancore, Baroda, Gwalior, Kolhapur, Indore, Jaipur, Jodhpur, Udaipur, Bhopal, Bahawalpur, Kalat, Manipur and Cooch Behar.[90] Of these, five were large and/or wealthy 21–gun Salute States: Hyderabad, J&K, Mysore, Baroda and Gwalior; six were influential 19–gun Salute States: Travancore, Kolhapur, Indore, Udaipur, Bhopal and Kalat; three were large 17–gun states: Jaipur, Jodhpur and Bahawalpur; Cooch Behar was a 13–gun state; Manipur was an 11–gun state. Udaipur also was 'the leading Rajput State' in Rajputana due to having long maintained Rajput honour against invasive Muslim rulers.[91] Baroda and Travancore had access to the Indian Ocean. Jodhpur and Jaisalmer bordered Pakistan. Kalat and Bahawalpur had become part of Pakistan, due to their location in the northwest of the subcontinent and their Muslim-majority populations. Two states had international borders (apart from with Pakistan), which gave them greater strategic significance: Manipur, with Burma; J&K, with Afghanistan, Tibet and Sinkiang – both of which China did not control in 1947. Apart from its size, population and prestige, these international borders made J&K a potential candidate for independence.

Table 1.1   *Jammu and Kashmir State in relation to Princely India, 1921*

Entity	Total					
	Area (square miles)	% of Indian States	% of Div. I States	Population	% of Indian States	% of Div. I States
Total Indian States: 562	598,138	100		68,652,974	100	
Division I States: 108	514,886	86		59,847,186	87	
Division II States: 127	76,846	13		8,004,114	12	
Division III States: 327	6,406	1		801,674	1	
Jammu and Kashmir State	84,258[a]	14.1	16.4	3,320,518	4.8	5.6

Source: (1) *Report of the Indian States Committee, 1928–1929*, London, His Majesty's Stationery Office, 1929, p. 10 (which took its figures from the *Census of India, 1921*); (2) *Census of India, 1921*, Volume XXII [Jammu and] Kashmir, Part I, Lahore, Khan Bahadur Chaudhri Khushi Mohammed, Director of Census Operations, 1923, p. 6.
Note: [a] In the *Census of India, 1931*, J&K's area had increased to 84,471 square miles due to 'more accurate measurements' (*Census of India, 1931*, Part I – Report, pp. 7–8).

The issue of independence

Importantly, under the Indian Independence Act, 1947, each ruler of a viable princely state theoretically would be independent after the British departed the subcontinent on 15 August 1947. This supposed freedom was to do with the ending of British paramountcy. The Indian Independence Act described the ending of this British overlordship as the lapsing of 'the suzerainty of His Majesty over the Indian States'.[92] However, the princely states' post-paramountcy status was a contentious issue. It was not fully clear what status these states would have, or be entitled to, with some senior princes wanting an independent, post-British status. Certainly, the British withdrawal and the lapse of paramountcy 'seemed to the Maharaja of J&K – and to some of his advisors – to open the way to an independent Kashmir'. Maharaja Hari Singh 'fondly believed that with the help of the Dogra forces he might achieve this end'.[93] While independence for such a major political entity theoretically may have been possible, there would be practical challenges. In order to survive economically, each princely state would, at the very least, need some sort of post-British arrangement with either India or Pakistan, or both in J&K's case. Therefore, while a major princely state might obtain '*technical* independence' when British paramountcy lapsed,[94] this would have been 'a precarious independence'.[95] As early as 1929, the Indian States Committee had recognised the seeming impossibility of Indian States surviving on their own. Its report noted that 'The India States have no international life. They cannot make peace or war or negotiate or communicate with foreign states'.[95] While somewhat prescient, the Committee highlighted a major challenge for major princely states contemplating post-British independence: they lacked international expertise and connections.

Corfield considered that 'No State could have preserved *actual* independence for very long'. This was because India had 'been welded by the exercise of paramountcy into too firm a structure'[97] in which a 'mutually useful relationship … [had] developed between British India and the Indian States'.[98] Both entities were so closely bound together that it was simply impossible for an Indian State, be it Hyderabad or Travancore, Kashmir or Bhopal, to lead a life completely cut off from the rest of India'.[99] Before partition, the princely states had been economically integrated with British India, particularly landlocked states that had few, if any, other trade, travel or transport options. Each state's economic situation, along with its relative military vulnerability, was compounded because, by severing paramountcy, the Indian Independence Act made each state an isolated entity. Before this Act, the British had looked after each princely state's foreign policy, as well as their individual and collective defences. As a result, few, if any, princely states had sufficient armed forces to guarantee – or, if necessary, to fight for – their own independence. And, even though the Indian Army was to be divided between post-British India and newly created Pakistan, these dominions' reconstituted armed forces would be considerably larger, more capable and more experienced than most armed forces that then existed in any single princely state.[100] In 1948, Hyderabad, India's wealthiest and most prestigious princely state, would realise this deficiency to its detriment after Indian forces militarily secured the princely state for India.

On 3 June 1947, Lord Mountbatten, the final British Viceroy, officially announced the plan to partition British India into the dominions of India and Pakistan.[101] Thereafter, the British, along with the leaders of the new dominion of India, but not the leaders of Pakistan, expected all entitled princely rulers to join India or Pakistan. Each prince would do so via an Instrument of Accession duly signed before 15 August 1947. The British had made it clear to all princes that, after that date, the United Kingdom would only have relations with the dominions of India or Pakistan, and not with any individual princely state. The British also stated that dominion status was not possible for any princely state. This was significant. Dominion status meant membership of the Commonwealth, then a small, exclusive, somewhat attractive group of seven relatively advanced, economically strong, influential 'white'-led nations. These comprised Australia, Canada, Ireland, New-foundland, New Zealand, South Africa and the United Kingdom.[102] Membership of the Commonwealth offered India and Pakistan 'preferential advantages', including in defence and economic matters.[103] Conversely, the British insistence on not having relations with any individual princely state clearly suggested to each princely ruler that he had one option only: to join one or the other dominion. This factor, plus Princely India's geographic disparateness, rulers' self interest in preserving their individual dynasty, and the lack of political unity, made it difficult for India's princes to organise a 'third dominion' comprising princely states.[104] Circumstances were just too difficult for this potential but disjointed 'Third Force'[105] to create an independent 'Princestan' or 'Stateistan'.[106]

The British and Indian positions about the future of India's princely states were confirmed the day after the partition plan was officially announced. On 4 June 1947, Mountbatten noted that, after paramountcy lapsed, 'the States could do what they wished, but they could not enter the Commonwealth as Dominions'.[107] More firmly, the Congress-dominated All India States People's Conference, a body formed in December 1927, declared that: 'at the lapse of Paramountcy, the sovereignty rested in the people of the State ... Any Ruler declaring his State independent would thereby express his hostility not only to the Indian Union, but to his own people. Such an act would naturally be resisted.'[108] This declaration may not have endeared the future dominion of India to Indian princes. However, it certainly made clear the position of the body that represented popular politicians residing and operating in the Indian States. One of those was the imprisoned Kashmiri, Sheikh Abdullah, then leader of the secular National Conference, a major rival of Maharaja Hari Singh and, despite being detained, President of the All India States People's Conference.[109] The declaration also reinforced a statement made by Jawaharlal Nehru on 18 April 1947 at the annual session of the All India States People's Conference. Nehru stated that 'any [Indian] State which did not come into the [Indian] Constituent Assembly would be treated by the country [i.e., India] as a hostile State'. Any such state 'would have to bear the consequences of being so treated.'[110] This effectively was India's position: it expected all empowered princely rulers to make an accession, most probably to it.

Despite these clear positions by the British and Indians, some princely rulers wavered or equivocated with their choice for the post-British future of their state. Wavering rulers included Bhopal, Hyderabad, Indore, Jaisalmer, Jodhpur, Kashmir and Travancore, in relation to joining India, and Kalat, in relation to joining Pakistan. Seven maritime Kathiawar States comprising Jamnagar, Bhavnagar, Gondal, Porbandar, Morvi, Dhrangadhra and Junagadh, apparently discussed creating an independent 'Union of Kathiawar', but nothing came of it.[111] Some princes decided to try to ensure that their princely state became, then remained, an independent entity. This appeared to be the preferred option for the Nizam of Hyderabad, the Khan of Kalat, the Maharaja of Jammu and Kashmir, and, briefly, for the Maharaja of Travancore. Indeed, on 20 June 1947, *The Statesman* reported that, when British paramountcy lapsed, Travancore and Hyderabad would declare their independence.[112] Soon after, the Travancore *Dewan* (Prime Minister), Sir C. P. Ramaswami Iyer, seriously alarmed Congress leaders by publicly proclaiming that Travancore would 'be independent' when paramountcy lapsed.[113] Independence was feasible as this prestigious southern princely state had a long coastline, sea frontage and more people than Australia.[114] On 17 July, Iyer proclaimed that Travancore's independence was a 'fait accompli'.[115] The next day, a representative of Hyderabad delivered a similar announcement.[116] This made senior Congressmen, particularly the influential Nehru and the powerful Sardar Vallabhbhai Patel, India's Home Minister, Minister for States and de facto deputy Prime Minister, nervous. They were concerned that the sentiments of these southern rulers might be contagious and provoke others, including Maharaja Hari Singh, to try and obtain independence. Any such moves by princely states, should they have been successful, would have fragmented India, robbing it of a number of large and prestigious princely states, their populations and revenues. This could have decimated, or even devastated, the new nation of India.

In 1947, therefore, Indians wanted to obtain the accession of princely states such as J&K, Hyderabad and Travancore. They had no interest in obtaining the remote Kalat State, which, post-partition, almost certainly would be surrounded by Pakistani territory and beyond India's physical reach. However, India's leaders also did not encourage an independent Kalat. They did not want to start a trend whereby any prince or princes would pursue independence for their state or states, a process that could have fragmented post-British India. Such a 'Balkanisation of India' was possible if, for example, 'an Independent Sikhistan' comprising a number of Sikh-ruled states in Punjab came into existence.[117] Such Indian concerns were explained by the Government of India's *White Paper on Hyderabad, 1948* (which subject matter equally applied to J&K):

> The approach of the Government of India to the problem of Hyderabad has been governed by their general policy towards the Indian States. India is not a mere geographical expression but an economic and political entity. The States are an integral part of India. ... The Indian Independence Act relieved the States from all their obligations to the Crown and in consequence India's unity was seriously threatened with disintegration. The Government of India sought to avert this grave threat by negotiating [a] constitutional relationship with the Indian States on the basis of their accession to the Dominion of India on the three subjects of defence, foreign affairs and communications. This was no emotional approach nor any expansionist policy, nor power politics. Highly practical reasons of geography, all-compelling defence and internal security requirements and the other equally strong considerations rendered India's organic unification imperative.[118]

India needed the princely states to ensure its national coherence. It therefore needed, and wanted, to secure the accession of as many of the empowered princely states as it could obtain.[119] This included the large, wealthy, prestigious and strategically important states of Hyderabad and J&K, without which India would have been a smaller, less populous, entity.

Leading up to 15 August 1947, Lord Mountbatten and Sardar Patel used a combination of tactics to ensure the princes' individual and collective agreement to join their state with India. These included: pressure; appeals to patriotism, to logic and/or to pragmatism; displays of respect for the royal rulers; and veiled threats, on occasions. Travancore and Hyderabad were examples of princely states that aspired to independence being put under pressure. On 27 July 1947, after an intimidating physical attack by pro-India elements against the Dewan, Travancore publicly acceded to India. While the attackers may have been self-motivated, there was little popular support for Travancore's independence 'except that which could be coerced'.[120] However, writing in December 1947, one commentator thought that Travancore's accession had been 'for certain limited purposes' only. The Dewan might have been playing a 'waiting game' to see whether the new state of India could successfully stabilise itself and institute an acceptable constitution that 'would only involve very limited interference with the sovereignty of the States'. If these two things happened, Travancore would remain in the Indian Union. If they didn't, then Travancore would 'prefer independence'.[121] While possibly so, Travancore's public accession to India in 1947, which seemingly ended any private desire for independence, 'had a distinct effect on other rulers who were still wavering'.[122]

In 1947, Hyderabad was playing a waiting game.[123] This prestigious princely state had a Muslim ruler, Nizam Sir Mir Osman Ali Khan, who ruled over an overwhelming Hindu-majority population. The Nizam wanted either independence for India's wealthiest, most populous and second largest princely state, or for it to join Pakistan. Either option was difficult for this landlocked state. Ultimately, as India's *White Paper on Indian States, 1950*, noted, 'Hyderabad did not accede to the Dominion of India'.[124] Rather, in September 1948, India militarily secured this state after serious instability within it caused Indian armed forces to invade. According to India's Prime Minister, India's forces entered to 'restore peace and tranquility inside the State and a sense of security in the adjoining Indian territory', as was India's right and, more importantly, its responsibility.[125] Thereafter, on 18 November 1948, the Nizam sent a letter to the Government of India, followed by a *firman* (or proclamation) on 23 November 1949, stating that the Indian Constitution would provide 'a suitable basis' for his state to enter into 'a constitutional relationship with the Indian Union'.[126] The Nizam had few, if any, other genuine options. This effectively ended Hyderabad's bid to remain independent, an ambition that had been confined largely to a small Hyderabadi elite only.[127]

Realistically, therefore, apart from joining India or Pakistan, and given their state's geo-economic compulsions, princely rulers had no other viable international options, a factor that most of them ultimately grasped. Between 2 August and 15 August 1947, at least 114 empowered rulers acceded to India.[128] They could not do so beforehand as the States Department had only formalised the Instrument of Accession document on 31 July 1947.[129] After a flurry of activity, pressure and persuasion, 'all the States [with]in the geographical limits of India had acceded to the Indian Dominion' by 15 August,[130] except J&K, Junagadh and Hyderabad, where 'special factors' had affected 'the course of events' in each.[131] For Pakistan, J&K and Kalat similarly had not acceded to it, as had been expected. Apart from J&K (discussed in detail in Chapter 2), the other three 'recalcitrant' princely rulers were Junagadh, Hyderabad and Kalat. We have already discussed Hyderabad. In Junagadh, the Muslim Nawab of this Hindu-majority princely state, Sir Mahabthakhan Rasulkhanji, acceded to Pakistan on 15 August 1947, the day that this new dominion officially came into being. While surrounded by Indian territory on land, Junagadh theoretically could access Pakistan across the Arabian Sea. However, Nawab Rasulkhanji's intention to join his state with Pakistan was unexpected,[132] and ultimately unsuccessful. Indian forces entered Junagadh in September 1947, then conducted a vote in February 1948 in which the population voted to join India. Pakistan disputed this process, but there was little that it could do about the pro-India confirmation. In Kalat, the Muslim Khan, Mir Ahmad Yar Khan, wanted his Muslim-majority princely state to be independent. Despite Pakistan initially accepting this status,[133] Karachi compelled Kalat to join it in March 1948.[134] Totally surrounded by Pakistani territory, Kalat had little other choice.

Ultimately, India triumphed by acquiring almost all of 'its' Princely States in their entirety. The exception was J&K, which India acquired legally in 1947 thanks to Maharaja Hari Singh's accession, but which it didn't gain full possession of physically, politically or even emotionally. The issue of J&K's accession was always contentious. Even before Hari Singh finally acceded to India, Muslims living in Poonch and Mirpur in southwestern J&K had been fighting to ensure that their respective area joined 'Muslim' Pakistan, not 'Hindu' India. Post-accession, so also did Muslims living in the Gilgit and Baltistan areas of northern J&K. Nevertheless, India's 'bloodless revolution', as Patel called it in January 1948, in acquiring all bar ten princely states was a significant achievement.[135] (The other ten joined Pakistan.) The princes who joined India delivered 'their states ... cash and investments amounting to something like 95 crores [rupees] (£74½ million)'. In return, they 'received privy purses that cost the Government of India 580 lakhs [rupees] (£4 million) in the first year and less with each succeeding year'.[136] This was a net gain of some £70 million for (post-British) India. The two Indians chiefly responsible for this acquisitive feat were the strong and strategic Sardar Patel and V. P. Menon, his agile, able and experienced Secretary of the States Department, which had been established on 25 June 1947 to replace the British Political Department.[137]

The pragmatic Patel had done his arithmetic. Due to partition, India 'lost an area of 364,737 square miles' and 81.5 million people to Pakistan. By integrating its '554' princely states, India acquired 'nearly 500,000 square miles' and 86.5 million people.[138] An official publication put India's acquisitions as '584' princely states amounting to 645,000 square miles, 91 million people, 50.5 per cent of India's territory and 23.8 per cent of India's population.[139] These figures did not include J&K, which respectively would have added an additional 84,471 square miles and 4,021,616 population.[140] Patel and Menon had been clever, capable and strong.

Jinnah and the legal issue of independence

While India's position on the princely states was clear, Pakistan's position differed. In 1947, the future leader of Pakistan, Mohammad Ali Jinnah, a politician as well as a highly capable lawyer, considered that India's princely states would be theoretically and actually independent after British paramountcy ended on 15 August. It is impossible to know if he genuinely believed this to be the legal case or whether it was a ploy to try to weaken India, which, due to geography, stood to gain the most number of princely accessions. In June 1947, Pakistan's future leader noted that:

> Constitutionally and legally the Indian States will be independent sovereign States on the termination of Paramountcy and they will be free to decide for themselves to adopt any course they like. It is open to them to join the Hindustan Constituent Assembly or the Pakistan Constituent Assembly, or decide to remain independent.[141]

In a press statement released in July 1947, Jinnah reiterated this stance and mentioned J&K:

> I have already made it clear more than once that the Indian States are free to join either the Pakistan Constituent Assembly or the Hindustan Constituent Assembly or remain independent. I have no doubt that the Maharaja and the Kashmir Government will give their closest attention and consideration to this matter and realize the interests not only of the ruler but also of his people. We have made it clear that we are not going to coerce, intimidate, or put any pressure on any State making its choice. ... Those who wish to declare their complete independence may do so.[142]

This was clear and unequivocal.

Two other lawyers concurred with Jinnah. Possibly both were employing Jinnah's unofficial 'weaken India' ploy. As early as April 1947, Liaquat Ali Khan, the senior

Muslim League leader who would become Pakistan's initial Prime Minister, indicated the possibility of independence for princely states:

> When the decision regarding the future of British India has been announced, the Indian States will be free to negotiate agreements with Pakistan or Hindustan as considerations of contiguity or their own self-interest may dictate, or they may choose to assume complete and separate sovereign status for themselves.[143]

Similarly, a British bureaucrat, Sir Walter Monckton, an advisor to the Nizam of Hyderabad, opined in early August 1947 that Congress would not 'object in principle to a State remaining independent for some time after 15 August'. Surprisingly, he also informed some British colleagues that Congress was 'ready to acquiesce in the independence of Kashmir'.[144] Rather than knowing what was actually happening with J&K, Monckton was probably reflecting his brief to secure independence for Hyderabad. However, two later sources partially support Monckton's claim. First, the Indian Defence Committee's decision on 27 October 1947 when accepting Maharaja Hari Singh's accession, to offer a 'reference to the people',[145] later called a plebiscite, with 'three choices: to join India, to join Pakistan, or to remain independent', with Nehru observing that India would not mind J&K remaining independent 'provided that it were within India's sphere of influence'.[146] Second, the statement by N. Gopalaswami Ayyangar (also Aiyangar, Iyengar) in the United Nations Security Council (UNSC) in January 1948 about whether J&K should stay with India, accede to Pakistan 'or remain independent' and seek UN membership.[147]

Such statements about possible independence for princely states were not necessarily helpful or useful. Indeed, for some nervous Congressmen, they were alarming. In May 1947, Nehru had been the first Indian to see Lord Mountbatten's 'final' partition plan whereby 'any [British-ruled] province or kingdom [i.e., princely state] could choose to join India or Pakistan – or to declare independence after the British left'.[148] Nehru had objected violently to Mountbatten's plan because, if implemented, lots of princes declaring independence could have seriously weakened post-British India. It is not known what impact Jinnah's statements supporting independence for princely states had on Maharaja Hari Singh. Perceptive pro-Pakistan elements, however, disliked Jinnah's policy of 'absolute non-intervention' in princely affairs, or allowing princes to follow 'any course they like', including independence.[149] One pro-Pakistani stated in August 1947 that Jinnah's policy meant that 'Kashmir can join Hindustan and Quaid-i-Azam [Jinnah] cannot have any objection to it, though geographically Kashmir may be contiguous to Pakistan'. Concurrently, some J&K-ites considered that 'the Muslim League stands for the sovereignty of rulers whereas the Congress stands for sovereignty of the people', with such a 'disinterested' Muslim League stance having 'terribly demoralized' pro-Pakistan Muslims in J&K.[150] In March 1948, Jinnah clearly abrogated his position of princely states being independent when Pakistan forcibly incorporated Kalat into Pakistan.[151]

Ultimately, Jinnah's pragmatic ploy to encourage India's princes to pursue independence in order to weaken India was ineffectual. When the India–Pakistan borders were announced on 17 August 1947, Pakistan had only ten princely states that clearly were located within, or were contiguous with, its borders and whose accessions Pakistan could expect to obtain. These comprised Amb, Bahawalpur, Chitral, Dir, Kalat, Khairpur, Kharan, Las Bela, Makran, and Swat.[152] Geographically, all ten were associated with West Pakistan, not East Bengal (later renamed East Pakistan). Controversially, Pakistan also accepted the Nawab of Junagadh's accession, although ultimately this state became part of India. Two other Muslim rulers located in the Gilgit Agency 'acceded' to Pakistan in November 1947: the *Mirs* (rulers) of Hunza and Nagar. Legally, Karachi could not accept these accessions as both rulers were under the suzerainty of the Maharaja of J&K and only he could make, and by then had made, an accession. Instead, Karachi chose only to acknowledge the Mirs' allegiance. Had Pakistan decided to accept the 'accessions' of these two 'lesser' or subordinate local rulers, this could have fragmented J&K and weakened Pakistan's aim to obtain this princely state in its entirety.[153] It was 'all or nothing' for Pakistan, with Karachi hoping that a 'reference to the people', which the democrat idealist, Nehru, had promised when accepting Hari Singh's accession,[154] and which the United Nations later reiterated as a plebiscite, would deliver J&K to Pakistan. Conversely and ambitiously, India tried to gain possession of Chitral, which princely state supposedly had been under the Maharaja of J&K's suzerainty since 1854. However, while Chitral was contiguous with J&K's northwestern border, J&K had never actually administered this smaller princely state. Rather, Chitral had been part of the British-controlled Malakand Agency.[155] On 6 October 1947, it was reported that Chitral had 'passed out of the suzerainty of Kashmir State' and had 'acceded to Pakistan without previous consultation with the Maharajah's government in Kashmir'.[156] This may have inspired other J&K-ites nearby, particularly Gilgitis, to later rebel and opt for Pakistan.

Seemingly, Jinnah was either relaxed about the future legal status of India's princely states or he felt that, inevitably, few would survive the difficulties of being independent. Certainly, in relation to Jammu and Kashmir, Jinnah judged that it eventually would join, or would be compelled by circumstances to join, its Muslim neighbour of Pakistan. Indeed, he believed that 'J&K would fall into Pakistan's "lap like a ripe fruit" once the Maharaja realised his and the people's interests and acceded to Pakistan'[157] Thus, while he was suggesting that J&K could be independent, he did not actually think this would happen. Pre-partition, Pakistan's future leader apparently told some Muslim Conference politicians from J&K, whose party essentially was aligned with his Muslim League, that 'Kashmir is in my pocket'.[158] Jinnah may have believed this because, in June 1944, he had drawn a crowd of 100,000 to hear him speak at Srinagar's main mosque, the Jamia Masjid, during the Muslim Conference's annual session.[159] For Jinnah, J&K joining Pakistan also seemed obvious and logical: apart from its Muslim-majority population, the princely state's most significant physical, historical, economic, social and cultural links were with Muslim-majority areas of the subcontinent that, almost certainly, would become Pakistan after the British left. These factors later became the basis of Pakistan's irredentist interest in J&K becoming part of Pakistan: 'that J&K, for reasons of religion (Islam) and the supposed shared common culture, ethnicity, geography and/or history of Pakistanis and J&K-ites, should be with Pakistan'.[160]

J&K-ites, such as Sheikh Abdullah, were well aware of J&K's geo-economic situation, even dependence, in relation to Pakistan. However, such ethnic Kashmiris felt a strong desire to preserve their identity, a factor that Jinnah did not seem to appreciate. He apparently found Kashmiris excessively 'quarrelsome' and difficult,[161] while he considered their campaign against princely rule to be 'a movement engineered by some malcontents'. Such attitudes disenchanted senior Kashmiris.[162] Some of them, such as Abdullah, rejected J&K joining Pakistan as, among other things, they felt that Punjabis, who were 'ethnically and culturally different from the Muslims of Kashmir', would dominate this new dominion.[163] Jinnah also confused matters by publicly advocating that J&K could be independent, despite the word 'Pakistan' being an acrostic in which the 'k' stood for 'Kashmir', by which was meant the princely state of Jammu and Kashmir. Hence, among Pakistanis, both prospective (i.e., before 15 August 1947 when they were still Indians) and actual (after 15 August 1947 when Pakistan had actually come into being), there was a strong expectation that J&K should, and would, join Pakistan, not become independent. Indeed, given the acrostic Pakistan, this new dominion would have been incomplete, perhaps even untenable, if it did not include 'Kashmir'. Seemingly, Jinnah and his ilk wanted it both ways.

Apart from Jinnah's certainty that J&K would join Pakistan, the Muslim League leader's role in relation to J&K is interesting. It seems that he and Hari Singh never met, either in mainland India or in J&K.[164] This is somewhat surprising given

Jinnah's national stature, given Singh's regal importance, given J&K's Muslim-majority population, and given the senior pro-India politicians who Singh had met. Jinnah visited J&K at least three times: first, possibly as early as 1924,[165] but certainly some time before 1929 as he was accompanied on his initial visit to Kashmir by his wife, Rattanbhai, who died that year;[166] second, in 1936;[167] and third in 1944.[168] If Jinnah's first visit to J&K was made in 1924, then this was before either he or Hari Singh enjoyed significant, uncontested public status: Jinnah was not yet the unassailable leader of the Muslim League; Raja Hari Singh only ascended the J&K *gaddi* in 1925. On Jinnah's second visit to Kashmir in 1936, he met various locals in J&K, including members of the Muslim Conference. On both of these visits, the British departure from India was still very much in the political distance.

Jinnah's third visit to Kashmir in 1944 was for about two months.[169] This was his most significant visit. With the idea of Pakistan growing in popularity and strength, Jinnah had become a high-profile political figure as a leader of India's Muslims. The Muslim League leader attempted to see Maharaja Hari Singh, but was unable to do so. The Dogra ruler had just returned from serving in the War Cabinet in London and was not available, possibly because he was unwell.[170] This slight made Jinnah 'rather angry'.[171] He angered a fellow Muslim leader, Sheikh Abdullah, by engaging in local politics in Kashmir. This occurred when Jinnah made a speech in Srinagar in 1944 to Muslim Conference members that criticised the National Conference and its notion of uniting J&K-ites 'under one national banner'. In response, Abdullah said that he had wanted 'Kashmir politics to be free from outside interference' but unfortunately Jinnah 'willed it otherwise and brought the evil germs of British Indian politics here' by his 'unwarranted' speech. Abdullah appealed to Jinnah to keep his 'Hands off Kashmir'.[172] One week later, 'disavowing communal separatism', Abdullah said that the National Conference 'envisages free and full development of cultural units and the principle of self-determination on the basis of nationality as a solution of the problems'.[173] Thereafter, the two politicians seemingly had little in common or much to do with each other, a circumstance advantageous to pro-India elements.

In the significant year of 1947, Jinnah again tried to meet Maharaja Hari Singh, sending some personal requests through Singh's 'British Military Secretary'. Apart from being interested in J&K's international future and with rumours that J&K might join India, Jinnah was ill and had been advised to spend the summer recuperating in Kashmir. He planned to visit J&K in mid-September. However, Maharaja Hari Singh declined Jinnah's visit, stating that he could not 'make suitable arrangements with all the necessary formalities for the stay of the Governor-General of a neighbouring State in his territory'. This rejection possibly also 'enraged Jinnah'.[174] Equally, Singh chose either to avoid, or to ignore, the Pakistani leader, despite some senior officials advising him to discuss his state's future with both India and Pakistan. Corfield, for example, believed that, had Hari Singh negotiated with Pakistan's Governor-General, 'Jinnah would never have allowed the frontier tribes to invade Kashmir' on 22 October 1947.[175] Almost certainly, the Pukhtoon invaders, whose aim was to capture Kashmir for Pakistan, had the 'blessing' of Jinnah and his Prime Minister, Liaquat Ali Khan, although, utilising 'plausible deniability', Jinnah disclaimed knowledge of the Pukhtoons' actions. Liaquat, however, almost indisputably, played an active part organising the first of Pakistan's (many) proxy efforts in J&K.[176] Khan Abdul Qayyum Khan, originally a J&K-ite from the Baramulla area who was then Chief Minister of the North-West Frontier Province (NWFP), was also heavily involved.[177] Apart from wanting to secure J&K for Pakistan, Qayyum possibly 'aspired to become the ruler of Kashmir'.[178] He also may have inspired the rapacious Pukhtoon tribesmen to invade Kashmir by suggesting that they would receive support locally or that 'the ruler and his people were well-off' and exploitable.[179]

Options other than India and Pakistan

Apart from joining India or Pakistan, Indian princes had a few other options. One was to play politics, which is what the Nizam of Hyderabad, encouraged by Pakistan, did until Indians tired of this and militarily acquired his princely state in September 1948. Another was to vacillate and do nothing, which is what Maharaja Hari Singh did until 26 October 1947 when circumstances finally compelled him to make an accession. The vacillation by the Hindu ruler of J&K was significant as J&K was India's largest princely state and it had a Muslim-majority population. In mid-1947, press reports had suggested that Hari Singh was contemplating an independent status for J&K. In response, Lord Mountbatten and Mahatma Gandhi met this 'politically very elusive' ruler in Srinagar and counselled, or possibly warned, him not to make any declaration of independence.[180] After meeting Singh, Gandhi noted publicly 'that on August 15 legally the State of Kashmir and Jammu would be independent'. Presciently or forewarned, Gandhi was 'sure that the state would not remain in that condition for long. It had to join either the Union of India or Pakistan.'[181]

In October 1947, with a Pukhtoon gun figuratively, and potentially literally, at his head, Maharaja Hari Singh contentiously chose to join India. Singh acceded utilising the highest type of Instrument of Accession, which was the same as that used by other fully empowered princely rulers. For Sheikh Abdullah, however, Singh's accession was conditional: it had only been for the subjects of defence, foreign affairs and communications, as envisaged by List 1 of Schedule VII of the Government of India Act, 1935.[182] J&K retained all other subjects. The 1935 Act 'formed the basis' of this 'conditional accession'.[183] It allowed a 'limited accession', with the ruler specifying these limitations.[184] This issue would later become important for Sheikh Abdullah. Apart from the 1935 Act, he also considered that the accession's 'conditionality' referred to India's promise to allow J&K's unification with India to be settled via a plebiscite. This promise adhered to India's 'democratic political philosophy', an important factor that had influenced him towards J&K joining this secular nation and away from 'Islamic' Pakistan.[185] Maharaja Hari Singh's only son, Dr Karan Singh, importantly also noted that his father acceded to India for the three subjects of defence, foreign affairs and communications, signing 'the same Instrument of Accession that all other princely states signed'. However, while all other princely states 'subsequently merged' into India, 'J&K did not merge'. Therefore, 'from the very beginning, J&K, rightly or wrongly, has been given a special position' in the Indian Union.[186] This 'specialness' would later become important for J&K. Conversely, India considered that the 'accession of the States on "defence" … secured [it] the right of entry into a State whenever internal security was threatened', an important point Abdullah may have been unaware of. By ceding communications, India also considered that it gained control of 'maritime shipping and navigation', a matter that may have impacted on J&K's long-cherished ability to collect customs duties.[187]

When Maharaja Hari Singh finally chose India in 1947, it was 'Hobson's choice', although things might have been different. For one Kashmiri author, Singh's 'cardinal mistake was not to remain in touch with his people'.[188] Being aloof, the Dogra enjoyed little popular support for J&K's independence, or otherwise. Pakistan, on the other hand, claimed that the Maharaja and Indian leaders had long been plotting to get J&K to join India and were just waiting for the right time to announce this arrangement. Pakistan therefore rejected Hari Singh's accession to India, claiming that it was 'based on fraud and violence':[189] 'The accession of Kashmir to India is a fraud perpetrated on the people of Kashmir by its cowardly Ruler with the aggressive help of the India [sic] Government'. For Pakistan, the fraud was underhanded Indian activity to obtain Singh's accession. This involved the J&K ruler releasing Sheikh Abdullah from jail in late September,[190] despite his conviction for 'high treason' and despite keeping Muslim Conference leaders incarcerated. Abdullah's major political rival, Chaudhri Ghulam Abbas, was only released from jail on 2 March 1948, some five months, and many major incidents, after Abdullah's release.[191] For Pakistan, the violence was the Indian Army's post-accession intervention in J&K. On 2 November 1947 while promising J&K-ites a plebiscite, Nehru agreed that there had been 'fraud and violence in Kashmir', but he questioned who was responsible for this.[192] For him, Pakistan's underhanded invasion of J&K had been the 'fraud and violence'. After Hari Singh's accession to India, Jinnah no longer talked of independence for J&K.

There were other options in 1947 for princely rulers apart from an either/or accession to India or Pakistan. A third option was for a ruler to try to ascertain the popular desire of his subjects in relation to the future of 'their' respective princely state. Accustomed to ruling autocratically, many princes found such an option difficult to contemplate, let alone implement. A fourth option was to seek the support or protection of an external power, such as China or the Soviet Union (USSR). China was contiguous with J&K; the Soviet Union was located close by. Between 1911 and 1920, J&K's trade with Central Asia had been 'flourishing', chiefly via Ladakh to Sinkiang, with political refugees 'probably responsible' for this 'short lived revival'. By 1939–40, however, trade had 'dwindled to practically nothing' due to instability and a 'hostile attitude' among elements in Sinkiang Province and other areas of Central Asia.[193] Apart from lacking good contacts in the subcontinent, World War II had severely weakened China and the Soviet Union. In 1947, both nations also were distracted. The USSR, which had gained admiration due to its heroic fight against Nazi fascism, was desperately trying to rebuild. It was yet to re-emerge as an insidious bogey.[194] China was trying to conclude a civil war and did not control the Sinkiang and Tibetan borderlands adjacent to J&K. Concerns existed that the 'communist menace' might impact on J&K, including via Communists seeking to infiltrate from Central Asia, as was feared when some Kazakhis entered Ladakh in 1942,[195] or in other ways, with the Communists' aim being to destabilise post-British India and/or Pakistan.[196] Concerns also existed that some Kashmiri politicians were Communists,[197] and had been, or would be, influenced by this assertive ideology.[198] People pointed to the National Conference's 1944 *Naya Kashmir* (New Kashmir) manifesto that, almost certainly, Soviet Communism had inspired.[199] Peoples' and governments' fears about the influence of Communism did not fully disappear from national and international affairs until the Soviet Union's demise around 1990.

A fifth option was for rulers and politicians to contemplate possibilities other than a princely state joining only India or Pakistan. In relation to J&K, most of this contemplation was undertaken after 1947. In February 1948, for example, Sheikh Abdullah apparently suggested to Britain's Commonwealth Secretary, Patrick Gordon-Walker, that 'Kashmir', by which he meant J&K, 'should accede to both Dominions' of India and Pakistan.[200] Abdullah's idea was that J&K would look after its own internal affairs, but that India and Pakistan would jointly guarantee its autonomy and control its defence and foreign policy. This 'dual accession' (my term) was necessary because J&K's larger markets were with India, a progressive nation, and because Abdullah's great friend, political supporter and 'Kashmirophile', Jawaharlal Nehru, for whom Kashmir 'and its people, and their welfare [would] ever remain a first priority',[201] was an Indian. Equally, the quickest and easiest route for J&K's trade with India was via Pakistani territory, while 'a hostile Pakistan would be a constant danger' to J&K Abdullah supposedly had the agreement for his dual accession of Nehru and his former Muslim Conference political opponents, while he could guarantee the support of 'his' party, the National Conference. He apparently sought to approach Pakistanis with this idea at the United Nations in 1948 when he was a member of the Indian delegation. However, 'there was such arrogance and hostility toward him that the Pakistani representatives would not even talk to him'.[202] Seemingly, Abdullah had been thinking about this idea for some time. In New Delhi in July or August 1947, he told the American journalist, Phillips Talbot, that he was seeking 'an arrangement by which Kashmir could have normal relations' with both India and Pakistan.[203]

Another idea that people have contemplated as a way to resolve the dispute over J&K's international status was/is the partition of J&K, most probably along religious lines. In 1947, Talbot met 'a man who works at [the] policy level', possibly V. P. Menon, who personally favoured the partition of J&K.[204] According to *The Times*, as early as December 1947, the Joint Defence Council for India and Pakistan, which included the prime ministers of both dominions, also discussed J&K's partition. However, this proposal was 'popular with no one' and an 'alternative … canvassed' for J&K was 'independent status under a joint guarantee from both Dominions with moral support from Great Britain' or a referendum with three choices: 'accession to either India or to Pakistan, or neutrality towards both'.[205] In August 1948, Sheikh Abdullah 'and some leading Indian spokesmen' reportedly 'unofficially' suggested partitioning J&K 'as the solution of the Kashmir imbroglio'.[206] Later in October, Nehru apparently made an offer to Liaquat to partition J&K along 'the current front lines', which the Pakistani leader rejected.[207] In 1948, Abdullah suggested partitioning J&K to members of the United Nations Commission for India and Pakistan (UNCIP). Presciently, he stated that if 'the division' of J&K

wasn't achieved, India and Pakistan would 'prolong the quarrel indefinitely'.[208] When later challenged, Abdullah quickly rejected the press's allegation that he had suggested partitioning J&K as 'utterly wrong and preposterous'.[209] By 1968, Abdullah's attitude had changed. Pragmatically, he stated that J&K had 'already been partitioned and partition is certainly a reality'. The question for Kashmiris to consider was 'where their future lies'.[210]

Others, including some Britishers, also considered partition of J&K to be a viable option. Mountbatten's biographer states that Mountbatten told two British officials in January 1948 that 'he believed' that J&K's partition was the only solution. However, Mountbatten stated that 'He had not personally been able to advocate this, because he would have been hounded out of India immediately'.[211] According to the Britisher, Hodson, who had access to Mountbatten's personal papers, India would have accepted 'a solution by partition' in May 1948 to its dispute with Pakistan over J&K. Apparently, 'partition maps were all marked up' and had been discussed by Nehru and the Chief of the Indian Army.[212] In 1949, in answer to a question, Nehru said that 'partition cannot be ruled out or something of that kind, because modification of boundaries etc., cannot be ruled out'.[213] In 1949, an article in *Pakistan Horizon* by a 'Study Group' also seriously discussed partition as a possible solution to the Kashmir dispute. Perhaps not surprisingly given Pakistan's desire to obtain all of J&K, the Study Group concluded (falsely) that there were 'no geographical, economic, strategic or practical considerations to recommend it' and that 'a fair plebiscite, under neutral supervision' should be held for the people of J&K.[214]

There were also later proposals that J&K be partitioned. In 1950, the United Nations Representative for India and Pakistan, Sir Owen Dixon, suggested to Nehru and Liaquat a partition of J&K 'outright, or combined with a partial plebiscite limited to an area which included the valley of Kashmir'.[215] In 1953, there was talk of dividing J&K, possibly along the ceasefire line.[216] Nehru wrote to his Pakistan counterpart, Mohammad Ali Bogra, in August suggesting that 'some kind of a division of the State had to be made'. Such a partition 'should only be done after the plebiscite of the entire State', as this would provide 'the necessary data for this decision'. For Nehru, J&K would be appropriately divided depending 'primarily on the result of the plebiscite' and how each region voted.[217] In 1955, Nehru apparently suggested to Pakistani leaders that J&K be partitioned along the ceasefire line.[218] However, some Pakistanis considered that India needed 'to offer the districts of Baramulla and Sopore inclusive of the Wullar Lake to make the partition attractive'.[219] In the 1980s, Karan Singh believed that 'the only rational solution' was 'a peaceful partition of his [father's] State between the new nations'.[220] Ultimately, the idea of partitioning J&K came to nothing. India–Pakistan relations were too poor and with too much mistrust. While relations were difficult from the outset, they worsened after India learnt that the Pakistan Army had officially entered J&K in May 1948,[221] a major factor that changed the nature of the conflict in the state. Thereafter, India and Pakistan effectively 'partitioned' J&K between them, albeit militarily and often illogically, into Indian and Pakistani portions. The ceasefire line of 1949 agreed by the Indian and Pakistan armies essentially formalised this arrangement.

While partitioning J&K along religious lines might have been a feasible concept, the challenges would have been to ensure the total cooperation of the various powerbrokers and to determine where to draw the actual dividing line. This may not have been as problematic as it seems. The *Census of India, 1931* stated that religion could provide one basis for such a division. It noted that the

> fate of the country seems at present inextricably bound with religion … it is but natural that the people have become habituated to class themselves under religious labels instead of economic or social divisions.
>
> In view of the above difficulties in the way of selection of a better substitute[,] religion will have to be retained as a basis of classification as it still exercises an irresistible sway over the public mind and is one of the clearest and distinctive marks of differenciation [sic] of mankind.[222]

In 1931, J&K-ites were able to self-identify, a factor that would still have been present, even more so, in the religiously polarising and divisive year of 1947.

Equally, however, there were no clear-cut religio-demographic lines. If the division of J&K was based purely on each province's majority religion, then this meant that Muslim-majority provinces of Jammu, Kashmir and the Frontier Districts all would have gone to Pakistan – in other words, the whole state. If the division was based on districts, Pakistan would have retained these three provinces minus Jammu Province's eastern Hindu-majority districts of Jammu, Kathua, Udhampur and Chenani Jagir, and possibly Ladakh District's southern Buddhist-majority Ladakh Tehsil.[223] However, the proposition of Kashmir going to Pakistan may not have been acceptable to Muslim Kashmiris under the sway of their secular leader, Sheikh Abdullah, nor to the Kashmirophile, Jawaharlal Nehru. In 1947, some, perhaps many, of these Muslim Kashmiris – no one knows exactly how many – possibly favoured J&K joining India, not Pakistan. Certainly, many of their Kashmiri Hindu Pandit brethren and Kashmiri Sikhs, who respectively comprised almost 5 per cent and 1.5 per cent of the Kashmir Valley's population, wanted J&K to join India.[224] However, Phillips Talbot's unknown Indian interlocutor was (unrealistically) only interested in 'yielding the divisions of Poonch and Mirpur to Pakistan and keeping the rest'.[225] This may have been because, when Maharaja Hari Singh finally acceded to India on 26 October 1947, the bulk of these two districts was already under the physical control of pro-Pakistan forces. Conversely, Pakistan held considerable territory in the Gilgit area after Muslims there staged an anti-Maharaja uprising, established a Provisional Government, and asked Pakistan to send an administrator, which Karachi did soon after.[226]

Pakistan and 'Kashmir' in 1947

In 1947, potential, then actual, Pakistanis had certain perceptions and expectations about J&K's post-British future. One leading Pakistani academic considers that, according to the 'rules [sic] of Partition' whereby 'Muslim-majority areas were to go to Pakistan, Hindu-majority ones to India', such a division of J&K along religious lines would have been appropriate.[227] His view is partly explicable, given Mountbatten's use of similar terminology to compel the recalcitrant Maharaja of Jodhpur to accede to India: 'the principle underlying the partition of India [was] on the basis of Muslim and non-Muslim majority areas'.[228] A rule has more standing than a principle. However, if there was any 'rule' for princely rulers in 1947, it was that the ruler himself had to decide and make an accession to India or to Pakistan. Thereafter, the ruler's state, in its entirety, would join either dominion; partition of his state was not a possibility; religion did not necessarily come into his decision. Despite the Pakistani perception that the 'partition rule' for the division of British India supposedly was applicable to princes in Princely India, it did not stop Pakistan in 1947 from accepting the accession of Hindu-majority, but Muslim-ruled, Junagadh. Similarly, pre-partition, future Pakistanis sought to obtain the accessions of Hindu-majority, Hindu-ruled Jodhpur and Jaisalmer, both of which princely states almost certainly would be contiguous with Pakistan.[229] Similarly, they were happy to provide 'moral support' to Muslim rulers of Hindu-majority states that almost certainly would not be contiguous to Pakistan, such as Bhopal and Rampur, and to support Muslim-ruled and Hindu-majority Hyderabad to become independent. Interestingly, Karachi's acceptance of Junagadh's accession to Pakistan, which acceptance actually repudiated the 'two-nations' theory,[230] was a factor that made it possible for ambivalent Indians, such as Sardar Patel, to later strongly accept the accession of Muslim-majority J&K to secular India.[231]

Apart from J&K being a Muslim-majority state, Pakistanis also had expectations that J&K would join their nation because of the term 'Pakistan' itself. Ironically, although the concept of a subcontinental homeland for Muslims and the actual term of 'Pakistan' were relatively new, both had Kashmiri connections. In 1930, the influential Indian, Sir Muhammad Iqbal, who had Kashmiri forebears,[232] first suggested the concept of a 'consolidated North-West Indian Muslim State'.[233] In 1933, in a pamphlet titled 'Now or Never', some Indian students in England built on Iqbal's thinking and coined the term 'Pakstan'. By this, they meant 'the five Northern units of India, Viz.: Punjab, NWFP (Afghan Province), Kashmir, Sind and Baluchistan'.[234] From the outset, therefore, this invented term included Kashmir. Some time later, the letter 'i' was added to make 'Pakstan' easier to pronounce. Conveniently, this revised term 'Pakistan' also meant 'land of the pure' in Sindhi, Persian and Urdu, the language that became Pakistan's national language. This suggested that Pakistan enjoyed unanimity of religious belief in 1947, which it didn't (and still doesn't). The term also suggested that Pakistani Muslims had already attained ritual purity or, if you like, God's blessings, something that their karmic-ridden Hindu 'brothers' were still striving to achieve. Thus, while these Pakistani Muslims were already pure, the 'impure' Indian Hindus were still striving to become pure and thereby secure *moksha* (liberation) from the long and difficult cycle of birth and rebirth through which each individual journeys in order to reunite their *atman* (soul) with the *Brahman* (the Godhead). For Pakistanis, Pakistan was already a more homogenous and superior entity to India, a claim totally rejected by many Hindus.

More specifically, the acrostic 'Pakistan' was composed of the following elements:

- 'P' for 'Punjab', i.e., the British-administered province;
- 'a' for 'Afghania', i.e., ethnic Pukhtoons residing in the British administered NWFP (Khyber Pakhtunkhwa since 2010) who had strong links with Pukhtoons/Pushtoons located in Afghanistan;[235]
- 'k' for 'Kashmir', by which was meant the princely state of Jammu and Kashmir, the popular name for which was Kashmir (although Pakistanis have long craved obtaining the real Kashmir, i.e., the Kashmir Valley);
- ['i' had no meaning, although some Pakistani revisionists now claim that 'i' stands for the 'Indus River', conveniently forgetting that this long river, much of which flows through Pakistan also rises in Tibet, which region is under China's control, and then flows through Ladakh, in Indian J&K];
- 's' for 'Sindh'; i.e., the British-administered province;
- 'tan' for 'Baluchistan', i.e., the Baluchistan Agency which comprised British-administered areas and the Kalat princely state.

It is not known what Maharaja Hari Singh thought of the term 'Pakistan', in which the k was so significant, if only because it stood for 'his' state. It is also not known if Singh was consulted about whether he wanted, or would actually allow, or even liked, his princely state being involved with this term. Such consultations seem unlikely, given Singh's aloofness and his reluctance for J&K to join Pakistan. In my research activities since 1984, I also don't recall seeing or hearing anyone, J&K-ite or otherwise, mount any objections to the inclusion of the 'k' for 'Kashmir' in the term 'Pakistan'. Pre-partition, most subcontinentals, including Indians, appear to have adopted the term 'Pakistan' fairly quickly and uncritically. The actual creation of Pakistan was, of course, an entirely different matter.

While initially only an aspiration, the acrostic 'Pakistan' had five interesting aspects to it. First, it contained no 'b' for 'Bengal', a fact that partly explains why East Pakistan violently broke away from West Pakistan in 1971 and became Bangladesh. Importantly, the Muslim Bengalis' uprising confirmed that Islam was not a monolith. For secular Kashmiri Muslims, it partially vindicated their stance that membership of a shared religion was not a sufficient basis for J&K to join 'Islamic' Pakistan in 1947.[236] Second, it contained no 'm' for *mohajirs*, or refugees, by which term was meant Muslims from India who moved to Pakistan in, or after, 1947, and their descendants. These Muslims remain very influential in Karachi and Hyderabad, Sind. Third, the composition and explanation of the term 'Pakistan' changed briefly, possibly in an attempt to influence the departing British to maximise the area to be granted to the new state of Pakistan. This occurred in 1947 when Rahmat Ali, one of the students who created the term 'Pakstan', claimed more expansively that 'the word *Pakistan* was composed in the following manner: *P*unjab, *A*fghania (NWFP), *K*ashmir, *I*ran, *S*indh (including Kachch and Kathiawar), *T*ukharistan, *A*fghanistan and Balochista*N*'.[237] The inclusion of Afghanistan, Iran, Kachch and Kathiawar as part of Sindh, and Tukharistan, which roughly equated to Turkestan, was ambitious and unrealistic. Significantly, however, the 'k' still stood for 'Kashmir'.

Fourth, the term 'Pakistan' was, and still is, an aspirational term. It reflected what Muslim leaders, before partition, hoped the future international state of Pakistan would comprise, including all of British-administered Punjab and all of the princely state of Jammu and Kashmir. Their hopes were dashed in 1947 when the British partitioned Punjab on the basis of religion into two Punjabs: Pakistani Punjab in the west, which was predominantly Muslim, and Indian Punjab in the east, which predominantly comprised Hindus and Sikhs. Similarly, Pakistan only secured part, but not all, of 'Kashmir' comprising Azad Kashmir and the Northern Areas (renamed Gilgit-Baltistan in 2009). Pakistan's possession of these two regions remains *de facto*, not *de jure*. For Islamabad, this will continue to be the case until a United Nations-supervised plebiscite finally allows the people of J&K to determine whether their state, in its entirety, will join India or Pakistan. The problem with this stance is that India is totally uninterested in having this poll held. Should it ever be held and regardless of which nation 'wins' – the result is not a foregone conclusion – the outcome almost certainly will cause a refugee problem as thousands of disgruntled 'losers' flee to the nation for whom they voted, but which 'lost' the poll.

Fifth, although the creation of Pakistan seemed unstoppable by mid-1947, a large number of the subcontinent's Muslims were nevertheless still not in favour of a separate homeland for Muslims. For example, secular politicians in Muslim-majority J&K in a straight choice of J&K joining India or Pakistan – that is, without any option of independence – favoured J&K joining India. Similarly, many Muslims living in what became post-partition India had no desire to leave their homelands, inhabited by their forebears for centuries, for Pakistan and/or they simply could not afford to move to this new and supposed homeland for Muslims. Consequently, after partition, India ended up numerically with roughly the same number of Muslims as lived in West Pakistan. In 1947, prospective Pakistani Muslims also had divisions. In British India's NWFP, which had an overwhelming Muslim-majority population, a referendum was conducted in July 1947 to determine whether electors wanted NWFP to join India or Pakistan. Although only 50.49 per cent of the electorate voted, the referendum was 'won' overwhelming by pro-Pakistan proponents.[238] By then, a very popular local NWFP leader and Congressman, Khan Abdul Gaffar Khan, the so-called 'Frontier Gandhi' whose disenchanted followers boycotted the poll, was possibly in favour of an independent Pukhtunistan nation for Pukhtoons living in NWFP and southeastern Afghanistan. On the other side of British India in the tea-growing district of Sylhet, in Assam Province in northeastern India, 56.6 per cent of people voted to join Pakistan.[239] These were not overwhelming votes of Muslims in favour of Pakistan. Like the loss of East Bengal/Bangladesh in 1971, they countered the false assumption that Islam is a monolith.

A final factor worth mentioning is that it is possible that the actual meaning of 'Pakistan' had changed by 1944.[240] In 1940, the Muslim League had stated in a resolution agreed at Lahore after much discussion that, in any future constitutional plan for India, it wanted separate 'Independent States' created 'in the North-Western and Eastern zones of India' where Muslims comprised the majority populations.[241] The resolution was not in any way geographically specific about these zones, nor did it use the actual term 'Pakistan'. Nevertheless, this is what it amounted to. The

Indian press thereafter called this resolution the 'Pakistan Resolution'.[242] In 1944, Gandhi asked Jinnah about whether the term 'Pakistan' still bore its 'original meaning – the Punjab, Afghanistan [sic], Kashmir, Sind, and Baluchistan – ... How are Muslims under the Princes to be disposed of as a result of this scheme?' In reply, Jinnah told Gandhi that 'The word [Pakistan] has now become synonymous with the Lahore resolution ... [which, in terms of territory] is only confined to British India'.[243] There was no Muslim League aspiration or expectation that any state in Princely India, including J&K, would join, should join, or would be joined with, Pakistan, despite the acrostic. For Jinnah, the potential nation of 'Pakistan' hoped, but did not supposedly aspire or expect, to obtain the princely state of J&K. This may partially explain why Maharaja Hari Singh seemingly did not object to the acrostic 'Pakistan'.

Given the above circumstances, and given that Pakistan has never obtained all of 'Kashmir', I consider that there is a more realistic and updated explanation for the acrostic 'Pakistan'. It now appears that the 'P' stands for Punjab; the 'a' stands for Azad Kashmir and Gilgit-Baltistan, both of which were formerly part of J&K; the 'k' stands for Khyber Pakhtunkhwa; the 'i' for immigrants from India and their descendants (i.e., *mohajirs*); the 's' stands for Sind; and, the 'tan' represents the troubled state of Balochistan, which is enduring the fifth phase of an anti-Pakistan insurgency that began as early as 1948. While my revision of this acrostic reflects today's composition of this Islamic Republic, I expect many Pakistanis will reject it, if only because it removes any suggestion of Pakistani interest in the prized Kashmir Valley.

The indisputable truth

In 1947, there was much confusion in the first half of the year about India's princely states and their potential post-British international status. Would these states be legally and actually independent or would they be compelled to join India or Pakistan? As 1947 progressed, one thing became indisputable. The British, along with the leaders of India, and eventually of Pakistan, made it abundantly clear that it was the right and responsibility of every fully empowered ruler to determine his state's future international status. For the British and the leaders of (post-British) India, the ruler needed to make an accession before 15 August 1947. The future, then actual, leaders of Pakistan were far less rigid and binary. Before partition, they considered that it was a viable option for a prince to seek independence for his princely state. Whatever the options, Maharaja Hari Singh needed to make a decision in 1947 on J&K's future international status. In doing so, and although it was a not legal requirement, he was encouraged to consider the popular will and political desires of his subjects. Ultimately, the autocrat did not do so. He was neither politically equipped, nor emotionally inclined, to engage in any such plebeian activities. Rather, the Dogra ruler was elusive and aloof. As a result, it is difficult to know what he actually thought throughout 1947 about the uncertain and volatile decolonisation of the subcontinent and the possibility of independence for his state. Similarly, it is difficult to know what, if any, matters Maharaja Hari Singh may have considered before he was finally compelled by circumstances to accede to India on 26 October 1947. As we shall discover in Chapter 2, we know little about this man, about his personality, and about what his political and international aspirations for J&K were in the highly significant and pivotal year of 1947.

2

Maharaja Hari Singh and his accession issue

In 1947, Jammu and Kashmir was significant and desirable for at least eight reasons. First, J&K was India's largest princely state. It was larger than the Province of Bengal, one and half times larger than nearby Nepal and six times the size of Switzerland. Second, based on revenues, J&K was one of India's wealthiest princely states.[1] Third, J&K was India's most strategically important princely state, the 'Shield of [the] Empire',[2] due to it having international borders with Afghanistan, Tibet and Sinkiang (both of which in 1947 were not under Communist China's control), and due to it being located close to the militarily and ideologically provocative Soviet Union. Fourth, and relatedly, J&K was located at the top edge or crown, literally in terms of geography and figuratively in terms of prestige, of the British Indian Empire. Advantageously for J&K, it was not surrounded by territory directly controlled by British India, as most other princely states were. Fifth, J&K was India's most populous Muslim-majority princely state, a factor that meant Muslim Pakistan expected this entity to join it, although India felt that there was a place for this princely state in secular India. Sixth, some of India's largest rivers flowed through J&K, particularly the Indus River from which India and the Indian subcontinent take their names. Seventh, and possibly most importantly, the Kashmiri Pandit (Hindu) forebears of India's future prime minister, 'Pandit' Jawaharlal Nehru, came from the Kashmir Valley region from which J&K took its popular name of 'Kashmir'. While Nehru's forebears arrived in mainland India long before the victorious British constructed the princely state of J&K then sold it to Raja Gulab Singh in 1846, Nehru's love of Kashmir ensured that he remained involved emotionally with this state – excessively, as it turns out. Eighth, Jammu and Kashmir was the only major princely state that had a three-word title; all other princely states had a one-word title, e.g., Udaipur. The significance of J&K's name was that it pointed to some of the challenges that this disparate princely state comprising three different provinces would have trying to cohere as a unified entity after the British had departed.

In 1947, Maharaja Sir Hari Singh was the ruler of Jammu and Kashmir State. He confronted the most momentous and atypical decision of his 22–year reign: to decide the future international status of his premier princely entity. Singh was uncertain due to finding himself in an 'anomalous position'.[3] Should he join his Muslim-majority state with Pakistan, a homeland being created on the subcontinent for Muslims? Should he seek to unite J&K with India where fellow Hindus were establishing a secular state in which Hindus nevertheless would be dominant? Should he pursue independence, given that J&K was India's largest princely state and one of its most prestigious, with international borders? It was a challenging choice, made more difficult by the politico-religious complexion of his diverse and politically divided state, by his own 'almost fatal indecisiveness',[4] and by his lack of popularity and inability to consult his subjects in any serious or inclusive way. In 1934, a publication about India's princes had noted that 'Considering the outstanding importance of Kashmir and his own personality', Sir Hari Singh 'will be one of the Princes who will have great influence in India in the future'.[5] Less than 15 years later, this turned out to be the case, although not in the way that the 1934 publication had positively envisaged.

This chapter examines Maharaja Hari Singh, his personality and influence, his regime and administration, and his options for J&K's status in 1947. In particular, it looks at the option of independence for J&K and Hari Singh's (non-)efforts to obtain this status, as well as the personalities and factors that ultimately ensured that he acceded to India in 1947.

Hari Singh: the person

Despite the unparalleled British decolonisation of India that Maharaja Hari Singh confronted and was seriously involved with in 1947, little has ever been written by, or specifically about, him. Apart from some hagiographies,[6] only a small amount has been written about his role as a princely ruler or his standing as an influential Indian. Additionally, this aloof ruler said little publicly, or to the press via interviews or press releases, or to others, in 1947. His 1952 'Memorandum' to the President of India, Rajendra Prasad, which was later published by his son, Karan Singh,[7] supposedly was 'the only time' that Hari Singh 'put forward his point of view, his difficulties and his grievances' in relation to J&K and his accession.[8] Until Karan Singh published it, however, it was a restricted document. Overall, therefore, it is difficult to understand this important man, his personality, and his thinking and actions in relation to his significant accession in 1947.

Some of what we know about Maharaja Hari Singh is as follows. 'Lieutenant-General His Highness Raj Rajeshwar Maharajadhiraj Maharaja Sri Harisinghji Bahadur, Indar Mahindar, Sipar-i-Saltanat-i-Inglishia, G.C.S.I., G.C.I.E., K.C.V.O., LL.D., Maharaja of Jammu and Kashmir State', was born on 30 September 1895.[9] A Hindu by birth, he ascended the J&K throne on 23 September 1925,[10] stating that his religion was 'justice'.[11] Hari Singh was the only son of Raja Amar Singh, who died in 1909 after having been a powerful, even dominant,[12] rival to his elder brother, Maharaja Pratap Singh, for the attention of the British, particularly their Resident stationed in J&K. This Britisher dominated the J&K regime for 'over a dozen years' after Pratap Singh was sidelined as J&K ruler in 1889,[13] a circumstance that Hari Singh may later have reflected on. In 1903, Hari Singh served as a page to Viceroy Curzon at the Delhi Durbar event.[14] In 1908, he attended Mayo College, Ajmer, a school established to educate the Indian elite, including young Indian princes.[15] In 1915, he was made Commander-in-Chief of the J&K State Forces.[16] In 1918, he was appointed an 'Honorary Captain', presumably in the British Army.[17] In January 1922, he was inducted as the Senior Member of the new J&K State Council. Thereafter, with his uncle Pratap ailing, Hari Singh did 'most of the work' in J&K.[18] He was gazetted as a Colonel in the British Army in 1926, made Aide-de-Camp to the 'King Emperor' in 1931, and promoted to Major-General in 1935.[19] During his life, Hari Singh had four wives, with the first three being childless.[20] His final wife, Maharani Tara Devi, gave birth to his only son and heir, 'Yuvraj Shree Karansingh Ji Bahadur' (i.e., the abovementioned Karan Singh), on 9 March 1931.[21] In subcontinental parlance, Maharaja Hari Singh was often called, or was simply known as, 'Kashmir', which was the popular name for his princely state of Jammu and Kashmir, and therefore for him.

While there is little primary source information about Hari Singh, some reports provide insights into his personality. Writing for a Melbourne newspaper, 'One Who Knows Him' described Raja Hari Singh as 'strikingly tall and handsome, well over six feet in height with a ... distinguished appearance'. He was 'a magnificent polo-player, and an all-round athlete, very much persona grata with the Anglo-India ladies who flock to ... Sir Hari's parties, polo ponies and motor-cars'. Perhaps best of all for 'One Who Knows Him', the ethnic Dogra was 'an Englishman – at least by aspiration and in hope ... with a high degree of civilisation'.[22] Some Britishers who met Hari Singh in the late 1920s similarly described him as 'one of the most broad-minded and enlightened of the Indian ruling princes'. He was a 'highly educated, admirably informed man ... holding his own in any conversation.[23] According to *The Times* in 1925, 'Sir Hari Singh' was 'popular both with the Kashmiri Moslems and with the Dogra soldier-caste who form the efficient Kashmiri Army'. The former claim re 'Kashmiri Moslems' was then possible, but questionable; the latter claim was most likely. For *The Times*, the young Dogra also was 'best qualified' to fill the late Maharaja's place 'with success'. However, there was also a note of uncertainty: 'If he has bought experience dearly, he has won many friends both in India and in this country, and it would be unfortunate if official or religious disapproval of youthful errors were to prevent his succession to the Throne or to diminish his popularity as its occupant.' Nevertheless, Maharaja Pratap Singh supposedly had 'regarded' him and 'trained [him] as his heir'.[24]

The 'youthful errors' that *The Times* spoke of had become publicly known in 1924. That year, Raja Hari Singh became internationally famous as 'Mr. A' in a thirty-nine-day civil court case in London that threw 'more light upon Kashmir and its rulers than the world would have learnt in a decade from ordinary reading'.[25] The case involved Singh's blackmail in Paris by an English prostitute, his astonishing £300,000 payment as 'hush money', and British attempts to suppress the true identity of Mr. A.[26] Singh's 'incident' had occurred during a trip to Europe in 1919 during which this 'respected and trusted man ... [with] gentle manners, [who is] refined and reserved and speaks English fluently ... is widely travelled and well read', efficient militarily and well connected, apparently spent £950,000 on racehorses and polo ponies.[27] This suggests Hari Singh was rich, which he was. In 1947, his 'yearly income' was 'said to be at least £2,250,000'. Additionally, he supposedly had 'a vast fortune tucked away in London and elsewhere', while he owned a private plane 'finished in silver inside and out, sumptuously appointed, and well armed'.[28] In 1946, *The New York Times* stated that 'the pleasure-loving Maharaja is among the principal race-horse owners in India and he has a passion for buying planes and building palaces'.[29] Nevertheless, despite his European 'folly', in which Hari Singh apparently 'was more sinned against than sinning' but which also caused him to become an 'object of international mirth',[30] he became the ruler of J&K in 1925. The London court case had not impinged on his royal career.

One useful source about Maharaja Hari Singh's proclivities and intentions is his only son, Karan Singh. Considered a 'scholar-prince',[31] his *Autobiography* is one of the best sources of information about the J&K ruler.[32] When the British departed the subcontinent, Karan Singh was an impressionable sixteen-year old who had little directly to do with J&K affairs. However, as Yuvraj (Heir Apparent or Crown Prince), he was physically close to, and necessarily emotionally involved with, Maharaja Hari Singh. Indeed, despite enduring an undemonstrative relationship with his father,[33] Karan Singh spent more personal and intimate time with Hari Singh than anyone else who has written about this former J&K ruler. He provides many interesting insights into, and observations about, his experiences with Hari Singh and about J&K's ultimate accession to India. Writing in the 1980s, Karan Singh claimed that, without reading his *Autobiography*, 'you cannot write accurately the history of Jammu and Kashmir'.[34] While this is stretching things somewhat, his book is interesting, insightful, and a good source of information about the last of the Dogra rulers of J&K.

In his *Autobiography*, Karan Singh mentions or names his father more than one hundred times, in various contexts. From a close analysis of his account of J&K, a few words and terms stand out in relation to summarising Maharaja Hari Singh, the person. These words are more negative than positive. For Karan Singh, his father was feudal, aloof, difficult, formal, moody, a poor loser, and essentially vindictive. But, positively and rather contradictorily, the younger Singh considered his father to be 'highly intelligent', 'progressive' and 'generally an enlightened ruler', although, equally, Hari Singh was 'happier racing than administering the State' and was 'understandably jealous of his [own] authority and prestige as Maharaja'.[35] Most positively, Karan Singh considered the last J&K Maharaja to be meticulous and a good organiser, although such traits did not necessarily make him a good or popular ruler. Indeed, popularity was an issue for Hari Singh. To survive as the ruler of J&K in post-British India, he needed popularity and political skills, not just in J&K, but also in New Delhi. However, by training and inclination, Hari Singh was neither popular nor a politician, nor would he ever be, unlike the man who would later allow him to be deposed: Jawaharlal Nehru.

Interestingly, Karan Singh's book suggests that he was motivated more by Jawaharlal Nehru and serving India than by loyalty to his 'feudal' and seemingly out-of-touch or disinterested father. This factor appears to colour the younger Singh's analysis: 'I had admired this man [Nehru] ever since I was a schoolboy, and it was a fascinating experience to be near him and to listen to him. ... How different this was from the constricted viewpoints that I heard in my father's circle and the all-pervasive atmosphere of tension and intrigue at home.'[36] Furthermore, Karan Singh 'tried to function not so much as a Dogra but as an Indian'. For him, securing and advancing the larger entity of post-British, post-partition India and its interests were always more important than ensuring the continuance of Dogra rule in the 'lesser' entity of J&K. By 1949, Karan Singh had realised that the hereditary Dogra rulership 'had gone, never to return'. However, this created 'an even more exciting opportunity of doing something in the broader national interest, and at the behest of one of the greatest leaders of our times [Nehru]'.[37]

Poignantly, Karan Singh appears somewhat disinterested in his father and his political survival. Seemingly, this arose because, in 'the post-Independence generation … we judge men and ideas by their post- rather than pre-Independence performances'. Pre-Independence, and unlike Jawaharlal Nehru, his father supposedly had neither understood, nor contemplated, the major changes that were coming to India.[38] Equally, however, as Karan Singh himself notes, he possibly was negative about his father because he simply was craving his father's love and attention: 'He was always a formidable character, [an] almost titanic figure in my consciousness. A distinguished reviewer … perceptively remarked that I was craving for my father's love. I am sure he loved me, but yet I could wish that he had done so as I love my own sons, without inhibition or restraint.'[39] This analogy is interesting, given that the 'unsinkable' Titanic did actually sink – as did the previously impregnable Dogra dynasty soon after its backers, the British, left India.

Two other people who worked closely with Maharaja Hari Singh and have written about him were Ramchandra Kak and Mehr Chand Mahajan. Both were former prime ministers of J&K. Kak, a Kashmiri Pandit, was J&K Prime Minister from June 1945 to August 1947. According to him,

> The Maharaja had a very quick understanding and was receptive to suggestion and advice where his prejudices were not involved. This unfortunately was, however, the case only too often. He could be unbelievably vindicative [sic], even when he must have had glimmerings that the pursuit of his [con]viction to the bitter [e]nd might prove as much of a catastrophe to himself as to the object of his vengeance.
>
> Though on occasion generous, as a rule, he was close-fisted and inconsiderate of other people's feelings. While he expected unquestioning loyalty from all who served him or were in any way connected with him, it did not occur to him that loyalty is a two-way traffic in that one has to give as well as to take in one's relations with other people. This, in fact, is the chief reason why even in cases where benefits flowed from him, the beneficiary seledom [sic] felt grateful for long. Added to this, there was in him a deeply ingrained streak of superstition which on occasions paralysed and petrified his natural intelligence.[40]

Kak's assessment is significant: this 'insider' served in the J&K administration for 33 years. During this time, he often saw Hari Singh in action, including closely when he served as Singh's Prime Minister during the challenging period when the ruler was contemplating his state's post-British future. Kak also appeared to have been trusted. As early as 1933, he represented the J&K Government at a meeting of the United Kingdom Parliament's Joint Select Committee on Indian Constitutional Reforms.[41] In July 1946, he met with the Chancellor of the Chamber of Princes, the Nawab of Bhopal, and had 'informal discussions' with the Congress President, Dr Maulana Azad, and with Sardar Patel.[42] He met senior Indians on the Maharaja's behalf.

Mehr Chand Mahajan, J&K's Prime Minister from 10 October 1947 to 6 March 1948,[43] does not directly comment on Maharaja Hari Singh's personality. However, he does state that, during his short career in J&K, Hari Singh treated him with 'kindness, love and affection'. Furthermore, the Maharaja 'reposed implicit faith in my judgement and not once did he decline to accept my advice. ... I have had the highest respect for the Maharaja and the friendly relations thus started between us continued till his death.'[44] Although Mahajan spoke Dogri,[45] which was widely spoken by ethnic Dogras in Jammu, he was nevertheless an 'outsider' from Kangra, a district to J&K's east in Punjab Province. This was not necessarily a shortcoming as Hari Singh's final wife came from Kangra, while he also had major cohnections with this district. Significantly, Mahajan had the support of the influential Sardar Patel, a politician Hari Singh respected and who had 'practically ordered' Mahajan to take the job in J&K.[46] Initially, Mahajan was appointed J&K Prime Minister for eight months, having been given leave from the East Punjab High Court for that period.[47] Most of his tenure occurred in the difficult times after Hari Singh had determined his accession. Interestingly, Singh, Kak and Mahajan all disliked or distrusted Sheikh Abdullah, Hari Singh's major political rival since 1931 and with whom Mahajan also would have problems.

While Karan Singh considered that his father was 'generally an enlightened ruler' and 'a progressive ruler', he has made comments about Hari Singh that warrant further investigation. Singh stated that his father was 'not able to grasp the historic dimensions of the changes that were around the corner' in India in 1947. He 'seemed to be blissfully unaware of the tremendous forces that were on the move in the subcontinent', or that 'the end of Dogra rule was fast approaching'.[48] These statements suggest that Hari Singh may not have been well informed about events in the subcontinent. Such regal ignorance or indifference seems unusual for a ruler who 'enjoyed absolute power [but who] conducted himself like a constitutional monarch'. Being such a monarch requires the ruler to be reasonably well informed about his subjects, their hopes and desires, and, most importantly, their political aspirations and possibilities. Karan Singh's claims also are surprising given the 'hair-raising situation' that existed in India during July and August 1947 and given Hari Singh's relatively weak, and rapidly weakening, position.[49] They certainly contradict what some Britishers thought about the Maharaja. The penultimate Viceroy of India, Archibald Wavell, considered Maharaja Hari Singh, whom he liked, to be 'one of the shrewdest of the Princes – well informed, a man of the world, and with liberal ideas – for an Indian Prince'. He had 'the right idea about his State and his duties' but, was 'not prepared to work really hard or to put himself out in support of them'. For Wavell, this was a 'pity' as he considered that Singh's 'abilities are much above the average'.[50] Despite Karan Singh's claim that his father could not 'grasp' the 'historic … changes' confronting India in 1947,[51] there is considerable evidence to suggest otherwise.

Hari Singh's 'grasp' of events in 1947

In 1947, Maharaja Hari Singh almost certainly understood that historic change was coming to India, or at least that Indians were fervently hoping for, and were expecting, change to occur. His experiences show that this ruler had been well informed about some previous political developments concerning India and its eventual post-British future. He had, for instance, been a member of the Standing Committee of the Chamber of Princes that met with British officials who conducted an enquiry into the Indian States throughout Princely India and in London in 1928, and which also visited Kashmir.[52] Similarly, he was a representative in the Indian States Delegation that attended the First Round Table Conference in London in 1930–31 and which seriously contemplated some sort of an Indian federation.[53] Shortly before this trip, Hari Singh had made a public statement, reported by *The Times of India* on 4 November 1929, that backed statements by 'several highly placed princes … supporting the national [Indian] demand for dominion status'.[54] Similarly, in London, he called for 'India's enjoyment of a position of honour and equality in the British Commonwealth'.[55] Concurrently, various Indian princes made a declaration stating that they were prepared to enter into an Indian federation. This declaration was 'not made by only one or two [princely rulers], but by a very powerful conservative State such as Hyderabad, by a progressive State like Mysore, by Kashmir, and by the group of States represented by Bikaner and Bhopal'.[56] Their seniority was significant.

The J&K State's *Administration Report* suggests that Maharaja Hari Singh understood that historic change was coming to India. 'Issued under the authority of His Highness's Government', Hari Singh had final control over this report, particularly in relation to matters about him.[57] In 1944, the *Administration Report* stated that:

> His Highness has played an important part in the joint effort concerning the political future of British India and the Indian States. ... His Highness kept in touch with the subsequent conferences in London [after the first Round Table conducted in 1930–31], and other deliberations held from time to time in connection either with the States or with India as a whole. Before the commencement of the talks of Sir Stafford Cripps with Indian leaders towards the end of March last [1942], His Highness issued an historical statement, in the course of which he said that it was the duty of the Princes to show that as patriots, they were desirous that their countrymen should feel themselves the equals of nationals anywhere in the world. ... His Highness urged that the Princes could not logically object to dealing with a Central Government in India which the Crown might constitute in future, and they had no reason to assume that they would not get a square deal from such a Government.[58]

Similarly, Hari Singh made a 'farsighted observation' via a statement in March 1942 about India after British decolonisation: 'Logically ... it would seem that the Princes cannot object to having dealings with a [post-British] Central Government of India which the Crown may continue.'[59] While both statements predated a number of later important developments, they suggested that Hari Singh was then thinking about a future, post-British India.

During World War II, Maharaja Singh continued to be informed about other developments concerning India. In 1941, he visited the Middle East, where he inspected 'his own as well as other Indian troops' stationed there and broadcast a message calling upon people in J&K 'to put forth efforts in the war ... [to ensure] the ultimate triumph of justice'.[60] In 1943, he established a 'Post-war Reconstruction Committee' that examined a number of schemes in various sectors in J&K. Starting in April 1944, he served as 'a representative of India in the War Cabinet' in London for three months, possibly in part because '45,000 recruits had been enlisted in the Indian Army from the [J&K] State'.[61] Equally, his participation in the War Cabinet may have been 'one of those elaborate farces at which the imperial British excelled'.[62] However, Hari Singh did have some military experience, having been Commander-in-Chief of J&K State Forces since 1915, an appointment bestowed upon him by Maharaja Pratap Singh before Hari Singh was twenty years old.[63] According to an English newspaper, *The Daily Chronicle*, the 'efficiency' of these forces apparently was 'largely due to his personal care'.[64] Hari Singh's role in the War Cabinet involved him representing India, along with another Indian, Firoz Khan Noon, and the Secretary of State for India, L. S. Amery. This included participating in talks held in May 1944 about 'vital subjects connected with the future conduct of the war and affecting the commonwealth [sic]'.[65] Commonwealth leaders who attended were Winston Churchill (United Kingdom), John Curtin (Australia), McKenzie King (Canada), Peter Fraser (New Zealand), Jan Smuts (South Africa) and Godfrey Huggins (Southern Rhodesia). According to Hari Singh, his role in the War Cabinet did not include 'particular discussions' about India or its future, although there was 'considerable interest in Indian affairs'.[66]

Other activities informed Hari Singh. On his way home to India from London in 1944, he visited the front line in Italy, after which he visited J&K troops serving in Iran. In 1945, he celebrated the Allied victory in Europe 'with great enthusiasm'.[67] In the same year, Viceroy Wavell informed Lord Pethick-Lawrence, Secretary of State, India Office, that the rulers of Hyderabad and Kashmir, would be consulted formally about the composition of the [Preliminary] Conference [on the Constitution Making Body] and informally as regards the draft agenda'.[68] Importantly, this gave him input into the development of India's future constitution. In April 1946, Maharaja Hari Singh had lunch with the Cabinet Mission whose members were staying in State guest-houses while holidaying in Kashmir during Easter.[69] He also had a conversation with its senior member, Lord Pethick-Lawrence, about paramountcy in which the Maharaja 'expressed certain views on the Indian structure'.[70] According to the record of conversation, Hari Singh had been thinking about post-British India and 'the transfer of power to Indian hands'. He stated that:

> it is difficult to conceive that States whose incomes are less than a crore of rupees annually would be able to establish adequate administrative standards. The only satisfactory solution would be to attach smaller States to larger ones so as to build up units with sufficient revenues. The progress of the States will, however, follow their own lines, though there is no doubt that such development will be greatly influenced by happenings in British India. ... for the future of India the worst thing that could happen is for administrations to allow themselves to be coerced by obstreperous elements. It is essential to ensure stability and orderly advancement.[71]

Later, Hari Singh would pursue his idea to 'build up units with sufficient resources' by trying to establish an independent 'Dograstan' or 'Dogristan', as discussed below. By 'obstreperous elements', he may have had in mind his difficult political rival, Sheikh Abdullah. In 1947, Maharaja Hari Singh's Publicity Department concluded its *Handbook* by repeating verbatim the ruler's 1944 *Administration Report* statement in which Maharaja Hari Singh 'urged' India's Princes to deal with any future Central Government in India and that 'they had no reason to assume that they would not get a square deal from such a Government'. This was the final sentence of the *Handbook*.[72]

By 1947, Maharaja Hari Singh had a network that comprised various Indians who presumably also informed his thinking and knowledge of what was going on in India. Apart from fellow former students from Mayo College, Hari Singh had received training from 1908 at the Imperial Cadet Corps, Dehra Dun.[73] He was friends with other princely rulers, such as the Maharaja of Jodhpur and the Nawab of Palanpur, while 'several Ruling princes' attended his coronation in 1926.[74] Similarly, 'a galaxy of Indian princes and other personages would come up every summer' to Kashmir, some as Hari Singh's guests,[75] as was regularly reported in the 'Distinguished guests and visitors' section of the J&K State's *Administration Reports*. In winter, he took holidays in Bombay 'for several months of the year' and engaged in various pursuits, particularly horseracing. Invariably he would have heard, or possibly actively sought, gossip about British plans for India, if only because he, like many Indians, was uncertain of the British and their intentions.[76]

According to Karan Singh, Hari Singh was 'a patriot',[77] not a 'stooge'.[78] Nevertheless, he 'genuinely distrusted' his British 'masters'. He knew how they had sidelined his uncle when Pratap Singh was ruler – although he seemingly also overlooked his own father's role in Pratap's circumvention. The embarrassing Mr. A case may have made him wary of the British, even though some British officials had tried to hide his involvement. Whatever the reasons, Maharaja Hari Singh wanted 'to shake off the British yoke'.[79] After becoming the ruler of J&K in 1925, he successfully persuaded the British to move their Residency from its winter location in Jammu City, J&K's winter capital, to Sialkot,[80] nearby in Punjab. He began this process as early as 1928.[81] However, Hari Singh's assertiveness did not necessarily help his relations with the British. In 1931, after serious popular political disturbances occurred in J&K, he came to believe that these disturbances 'were in fact masterminded by the British'. Supposedly, they did so in order to teach him a lesson for having made an earlier 'remarkably patriotic speech urging the British to respect the aspirations of the Indian people' at the first Round Table Conference in London.[82] Others also felt that the British 'engineered' the 1931 agitation, but they did so because they 'took exception to Hari Singh's haughty temperament which he … displayed in his dealings with them', including by trying to regain control of the strategic Gilgit Agency area that the British then controlled.[83] For Singh, the British became 'openly hostile' to him.[84]

While possibly distrusting the British, Hari Singh publicly and privately took other stances. On 12 April 1944, he proclaimed his interest in England on his arrival in London in 1944 to serve on the War Cabinet. That day, according to *The Times*, Hari Singh publicly stated that it was 'a great honour and a great responsibility' to serve on the War Cabinet, that he had 'admire[d England] from afar' during the seven years since his previous visit, and that he hoped that he would be 'uplifted' by the British 'cheerfulness' and 'undaunted spirit'. Additionally, *The Times* noted that Singh was 'among the most generous of India's contributors to the war effort'.[85] Hari Singh was also happy to leave his son in the care of 'a series of British guardians' until Karan Singh 'went to public school at the age of eleven'.[86] One of these was the British Officer, Capt. R. G. Wreford, 'Census Commissioner' for J&K in 1941.[87] According to Karan Singh, 'Captain (Reggie) Wreford' and his wife, Katherine, were their 'favourites among the British'.[88] Karan Singh states that, during World War II, however, J&K's ruling family 'were all secretly rooting for the Germans, and would jump around gleefully whenever there was news of British reverses'.[89] The royal Singhs appeared to enjoy a love-hate relationship with the British.

Other sources kept Hari Singh informed. He had access to reporting by 'I.P.A.', the Indian Press Association. He read *The Civil & Military Gazette* and the *Tribune*, two Lahore-based newspapers that reported political developments in India, which circulated in J&K,[90] and which were delivered regularly to his residence.[91] His own State's *Administration Report* for 1941–43 suggested that he knew about current affairs, including in relation to India's political future and possible bifurcation. It noted that the (not yet finalised) 'Pakistan scheme met with severe criticism from all sections of Hindus in the State. The National Conference also opposed the scheme.'[92] Similarly, his State's *Administration Report* for 1943–44 mentioned the term 'Pakistan' in its 'Political' section three times, none of them positive.[93] By June 1944, the partition of India 'had become a burning issue', including in J&K,[94] where people were already agitating for or against J&K joining Pakistan.[95] This was three years before the actual partition of British India. It is unlikely that Hari Singh remained unaware of such passions and politicking among his people.

Post-World War II

After World War II, things changed dramatically for India and Indians. The exhausted British indicated that they would leave India, with the date and the post-British political arrangements to be determined. Following elections in British India in January 1946, in which the Muslim League secured a 'resounding victory' in Muslim-majority seats everywhere except the North-West Frontier Province, it became almost impossible for the British Government to ignore the demand of Indian Muslims for Pakistan. 'This much was obvious to even the meanest understanding.'[96] The Muslim League's victory was significant for J&K. It had a 77 per cent Muslim-majority population, with some, perhaps many, of these Muslims desiring J&K's unification with Pakistan, the potential homeland for Muslims.[97] Soon the Maharaja would be compelled to make a choice. At that stage, independence seemed to be the preferred option, as later indicated by Hari Singh's final British 'Chief of State Military Forces',[98] Major-General Sir Henry Lawrence Scott, who had served in J&K from 1936 until 29 September 1947.[99] Briefing British diplomats in Lahore in October 1947 soon after leaving J&K, Scott stated that 'the majority of Kashmiris have no strong bias for either India or Pakistan and prefer to remain independent of either Dominion', although, equally, Kashmiris understood that 'a hostile Pakistan could seriously disrupt Kashmir's economy'.[100] As for the Maharaja, he had a 'pro-independence attitude', although he was surrounded by a 'coterie ... [that] strongly favoured union with India'.[101]

Post-World War II, Maharaja Hari Singh was forced to consider the United Kingdom's changed, but uncertain, intentions towards its Indian Empire. Sir Stafford Cripps' visit to India in 1942 and his unsuccessful plan to devolve some power to Indians had already suggested some sort of future autonomous political entity for Indian Muslims. The 'Cripps Mission' also injected into some princes 'the discomforting realization' that the link between them and the British might be severed irrevocably, probably not to their advantage, with the question being what would replace this relationship?[102] The visit to India in March–April 1946 by the three-man Cabinet Mission, which included Cripps again, similarly considered India's political future and probable self-government. It sought, in conjunction with the Viceroy and Indian leaders, elected and unelected (i.e., Indian princes), to determine the process to formulate a new political constitution for India. The Nawab of Bhopal, as Chancellor of the Chamber of Indian Princes, represented the princes, along with five rulers on the Chamber's Standing Committee. In separate meetings with Bhopal and with the five princes, discussions involved India's political future and the important issue of paramountcy. By the time the Cabinet Mission left India in May 1946, it had become clear that British paramountcy would lapse when India received its new post-British Government, or Governments. This meant that 'the rights of the States which flowed from their relationship to the Crown would no longer exist, and that all the rights surrendered by the States to the paramount power would return to them'.[103] Essentially, each prince would become independent, although the Cabinet Mission's memorandum did not specifically mention this.[104] Significantly, Maharaja Hari Singh met the Cabinet Mission, whose members visited Kashmir for Easter in April 1946. They also met Prime Minister Ramchandra

Kak[105] and 'two leading politicians': Sheikh Abdullah, leader of the National Conference, and Chaudhri Ghulam Abbas, leader of the Muslim Conference.[106]

In late 1946, the Government of India sought J&K's 'views on the subject of accession'. By then supposedly 'the issue of Partition had not arisen except as a remote contingency, and accession was envisaged only with reference to the newly to-be-created Dominion of India'.[107] In autumn 1946, Sir Conrad Corfield, the Viceroy's Political Adviser, discussed J&K's future post-British status with Maharaja Hari Singh. Writing retrospectively, Corfield states that he 'advised' Maharaja Hari Singh 'to make it clear to both Jinnah and Nehru that he would accept a standstill agreement with both and then begin negotiations for the new links without which his State could not survive'. When Corfield departed Kashmir in 1946, he 'was satisfied that the Maharaja would be reasonable and offer to negotiate with both Dominions'. Hari Singh's 'Chief [i.e., Prime] Minister', Ramchandra Kak, agreed with this stance.[108] Despite such sensible advice to negotiate with Jinnah and Nehru, Maharaja Hari Singh did not do so. Seemingly, he was more motivated by Corfield's point that 'the Maharaja had of course the right to choose which Dominion he would join'.[109] It was the ruler's decision, and his decision only. Equally, Corfield's claims may be uncertain as the creation of Pakistan had not been finally decided in autumn 1946.

Maharaja Hari Singh's experienced and 'shrewd' senior bureaucrat, Pandit Ramchandra Kak, kept the ruler informed about potential political changes for India.[110] Prime Minister Kak, at the height of his powers in 1947, was 'practically unapproachable' and supposedly had the J&K ruler under his sway.[111] Kak and his 'Kakistocracy ... dominated the whole administration of the State'.[112] A fellow Kashmiri Pandit described Kak as being 'egoistic, ambitious, conceited and [a] reactionary of the worst type'.[113] For Karan Singh, his former guardian (Kak) was 'in many ways a remarkable man, arrogant but unflinching in his adherence to the principles in which he believed'.[114] Born in 1893, this capable ethnic Kashmiri Hindu served as J&K Prime Minister from 30 June 1945 to 11 August 1947. Kak was intelligent and productive, having written at least three books, with his *Ancient Monuments of Kashmir* 'favourably received by the British, foreign, and Indian press' in 1934.[115] He was also diligent, having worked his way up the ranks after joining J&K's Archaeological Department in August 1914. In 1919, he became Superintendent of this organisation. In 1926, he was made Assistant Private Secretary to 'Maharaja Bahadur'. In 1929, he was promoted to Foreign and Political Secretary. Importantly, in 1931 and 1932, Kak was deputed to attend the Second and Third Round Table Conferences on Indian Constitutional Reforms in London and to give evidence to the Joint Select Committee of the United Kingdom Parliament in 1933.[116] This gave him considerable understanding about India's possible future, as well as some useful connections.

After serving as 'Minister-in-Waiting and Army Minister' from November 1940,[117] Kak became J&K's Prime Minister in June 1945. He replaced the jurist, Sir Benegal Rau. According to one of Sheikh Abdullah's biographers, 'Hari Singh presumably appointed him because he [Kak] favoured independence for the state'.[118] This is possible. As early as 15 January 1945, Olaf Caroe, a British official serving as the Government of India's Foreign Secretary, reported that Hari Singh and Kak had 'a growing inclination "to obtain a [post-British] status" as near as possible to independence'.[119] However, British observers such as Caroe were wary of Kak. Viceroy Wavell, for example, who judged Kak to be 'clever, plausible, and quite unreliable in a crisis',[120] visited J&K in October 1945 and saw some real 'possibilities of political trouble' there due to 'the intentions' of Ramchandra Kak.[121] Similarly, in 1946, *The New York Times* saw the princely state with its 'tangled political situation' as being 'a potential source of trouble'.[122] Jawaharlal Nehru, a fellow Kashmiri Pandit, considered that Kak had Maharaja Hari Singh 'frightened' and 'isolated'[123] and that Kak had a 'habit of intrigue'.[124] Mohammad Ali Jinnah accused the 'Pandit ring', which he believed Kak led, of running a 'Raj of Goondaism' (thuggery).[125] While controversial, Ramchandra Kak nevertheless had some skills and useful experience. And, if nothing else, he was a State Subject of J&K, not an outsider like many former prime ministers of J&K. Having that indigenous status, however, did not automatically make him popular with other Kashmiris, particularly Muslims.

Early inclinations

Evidence shows that, as early as 14 November 1946, Maharaja Hari Singh had started to contemplate J&K's international future, including the possibility of J&K becoming independent. On that day, Lieutenant-Colonel Webb, the British Resident in J&K, reported to the Political Department, New Delhi, that he was 'inclined to think that the Maharaja and [his Prime Minister] Kak are seriously considering the possibility of Kashmir not joining the [Indian] Union if it is formed'. An enclosure provided to the Resident by Prime Minister Kak stated that 'those who are likely to assume the reins of government in India in future are not disposed to ... the State ... and unless satisfactory assurances are forthcoming that interference in its internal affairs in any shape or form will in future not be made, [J&K] may even decide to decline to join the Indian Union should it materialise'.[126] Kak confirms this statement: in 1946, 'the Kashmir Government's decision not to accede was communicated to the Government of India through the Resident'. He did not want J&K to join an entity that would be dominated by the disruptive Indian National Congress, a party that had caused 'breaches of [the] peace' in J&K, 'considerable embarrassment' to the J&K Government and 'deep resentment amongst those sections of the people of the State, who had not thrown in their lot with Sheikh Abdullah'.[127] Despite the uncertainty, politicking and volatility occurring in the subcontinent around that time, for many Indian princes the proposition of their state potentially becoming independent was exciting.

Matters changed in February 1947 when Lord Mountbatten arrived as Viceroy. They changed even more with his decision on 3 June to partition British India into two dominions: India and Pakistan. Thereafter, the J&K Government's 'feelings with regard to non-accession [became] more pronounced'. Given the future creation of an independent India and an independent Pakistan, a 'matter of choice' for J&K now became 'a matter of necessity'.[123] On 25 July, Mountbatten, in his capacity as Crown Representative, discussed the princes' potential post-British options when he addressed the Chamber of Princes for his first and only time.[129] Being a cousin of King George VI, he enjoyed credibility with India's princes because of his Royal blood. Unexpectedly, however, Mountbatten diminished any such aspirations for independence that many of these seemingly naive rulers suffering from 'the paralysis of Princely uncertainty' and with 'quite a high proportion of thick skulls' may have had.[130] Dressed in his full naval uniform and the 'apogee of persuasion',[131] Mountbatten addressed the 'audience of hereditary shepherds in the unenviable position of lost sheep'.[132] He 'advised the rulers to accede to the appropriate Dominion in regard to three subjects of "defence", "external affairs", and "communications". He pointed out that "defence" was a matter which a State could not conduct for itself; "external affairs" was something that no State had dealt with before. The continuity of communications necessitated their accession on this subject also'.[133] For Mountbatten, an accession to India or Pakistan would give each princely ruler 'all the practical independence that they could possibly use and made them free of those subjects which they could not possibly manage on their own'. This would not 'involve any financial liability'; 'there would be no encroachment on their sovereignty'.[134] Many princes, whose questions of him Mountbatten thought 'had been incredibly unrealistic',[135] apparently accepted the Crown Representative's argument.

Concurrently, Ramchandra Kak remained influential, representing the Maharaja at discussions with the British, Indians and prospective Pakistanis. On 3 June 1947, 'Rai Bahadur Ramchandra Kak',[136] or 'Kak of Kashmir', was a member of the high-powered, sixteen-man 'States Negotiating Committee', which comprised the 'cream of the Princely counsellors'.[137] They met with Viceroy Mountbatten and four of his officials in the Viceroy's New Delhi residence. This was before Mountbatten's official radio announcement that night stating that the subcontinent would be partitioned into the dominions of India and Pakistan, both with 'strong central governments'.[138] The States Negotiating Committee had previously met 'many times' with the 'Negotiating Committee of the Constituent Assembly' to determine post-British political arrangements. In March 1947, on the basis of 'one representative for every million people', 'Kashmir' had been allocated four of ninety-three seats for Indian States in the prospective Constituent Assembly then envisaged for a unified India.[139] On 23 April, a 'Kashmir Government spokesman' told the press that 'no final decision had yet been taken' about J&K participating in the Constituent Assembly.[140]

In July 1947, senior J&K-ites began to indicate that J&K would remain independent. In early July, Prime Minister Kak non-committedly informed Lord Mountbatten about J&K: 'linking ourselves from the Military point of view with either one or the other of the Dominions or of sending representatives to a Constituent Assembly. A decision on these matters will be taken when we see how things turn out and in the light of circumstances as they develop.'[141] One developing 'circumstance' was the 'fever resulting from the [potential] partitioning of India and the division of certain Provinces [that] has thrown most people off balance'.[142] There was considerable angst and much nervous anticipation among Indians living both in British India and Princely India. As July progressed, J&K's position on its post-British status seemed to solidify. Between 23 July and 27 July, Kak met Sardar Patel, Mahatma Gandhi and Mohammad Ali Jinnah and informed each of them that J&K did not want to accede to either dominion.[143] It would seek to remain independent. When Kak returned to Srinagar, he 'conveyed to the Maharaja all that happened in New Delhi and sent him a note in confirmation.'[144] It seems inconceivable that Maharaja Hari Singh would have allowed his Prime Minister to make such an important (or provocative) statement to three of India's most senior, and influential, Indians without Kak first having obtained his approval. Seemingly, Hari Singh had made up his mind. Perhaps this is why Singh vacillated in making an accession.

Maharaja Hari Singh's vacillation

Despite the inevitable and significant changes that would result from the British withdrawal from India, Maharaja Hari Singh apparently developed a 'Micawberish frame of mind, hoping for the best while continuing to do nothing … [and] toying with the idea of an "Independent Jammu and Kashmir".[145] ('Micawber: An idle optimist; a person who trusts in the future to provide.')[146] Although circumstances and various influential individuals were pressuring Singh to decide J&K's future international status, he seemingly was doing little in terms of making a decision. Why did Hari Singh vacillate, or, as one Kashmiri rather kindly put it, decide to 'remain uncommitted'?[147] Was it because he was ambitious and genuinely wanted independence for J&K and hoped that this simply would fall into his lap? Or was there some other reason, such as the real possibility that he would become increasingly redundant after he had made his accession and joined one of the new dominions (which, indeed, is what happened after he acceded to India)? Was it his personal disinterest in joining 'Muslim' Pakistan while, conversely, senior Congress politicians, including Nehru and Patel, were reluctant to support him? These two senior Indians had publicly pledged to liberate the Indian provinces *and* the Indian states from British rule and were openly against the 'dangerous void pompously called "Sovereign Independence".[148] Nehru, who disliked Hari Singh, had hinted ominously in December 1945 at the Indian States Peoples' Conference in Udaipur, itself a princely state, that 'In dealing with the States, therefore, we deal with the British Government in another guise. As soon as that Government goes from India, the problem changes completely.[149] More pointedly, at the same body's conference held in Gwalior, also a princely state, in April 1947, Nehru said that any princely state that did not join the Indian Constituent Assembly 'would be considered hostile, and accordingly dealt with.[150] In the same month, Nehru presciently informed Viceroy Mountbatten that 'he felt that the future of Kashmir might produce a difficult problem'.[151]

Karan Singh, quite reasonably, states that his father may have vacillated because he confronted a 'once-in-a-millennium historical phenomenon'. This comprised four elements, each of which Maharaja Hari Singh was 'on hostile terms with': the British, whom he had long mistrusted and whom 'he never really believed until the very end' would actually leave India, but, rather, would 'preside over India's destiny for decades to come';[152] the anti-J&K Indian National Congress, one of whose leaders, Jawaharlal Nehru, was close to Hari Singh's 'arch enemy Sheikh Abdullah'; the Muslim League, whose 'aggressive Muslim communalism' this Hindu ruler could not 'stomach'; and the National Conference, led by Sheikh Abdullah, who, while concurring with the ruler's anti-Pakistan inclination,[153] Hari Singh (correctly) saw as being 'the major threat to his throne and Dogra rule'.[154] Apart from these four elements, the Hindu Maharaja, Hari Singh, was 'carrying the burden of religious diversity' with a 'substantial majority' of his subjects belonging to 'another faith', i.e., to Islam.[155] Additionally, Singh was impaired by a personal affliction: the 'feudal virus' of 'disinclination to take a firm decision one way or the other'.[156] Ramchandra Kak put it differently: Hari Singh was 'hag-ridden by superstition … and was unable to make up his mind firmly in any matter'.[157] 'Indecisive by nature, he merely played for time.'[158]

Of the various post-British options available to Maharaja Hari Singh, it is difficult to determine why he vacillated about making a choice. One practical explanation is that he realised that, regardless of the choice he made, it would not please everyone. Indeed, it would displease many. So, it was better, or easier, not to take any decision. That said, Singh's choice was actually a tough one because, unlike almost every other princely state under British paramountcy, J&K had the geo-economic option of joining either Muslim Pakistan or secular India. Almost certainly, J&K would be neighbours with both new dominions, although the exact borders would not be known until mid-August. Most other princely states, including Hyderabad, would be largely, or even completely, surrounded by territory that strongly 'suggested' to which dominion the ruler should accede: India mainly, or Pakistan for ten or so princely states. Additionally, J&K was large, prestigious, strategically important, desirable and desired. It had major rivers that rose and/ or flowed through it: the Indus, Jhelum and Chenab, with the Ravi nearby to J&K's east. These rivers provided water to the world's largest irrigation area located downstream in Punjab. As Mahatma Gandhi noted shortly before partition, 'Kashmir was a big State and had the greatest strategic value perhaps in all India.'[159] Conversely, these factors possibly suggested to Hari Singh that, realistically, J&K could be independent. Equally, he confronted two genuine accessional options, both very different. This set of circumstance created considerable stress, both for the tentative J&K ruler, but also for his uncertain, yet expectant, subjects.

A further reason for Hari Singh's vacillation was his difficult mix of personal emotions. Ignoring the theoretical possibility of J&K obtaining independence, his choice about J&K's international status was really simple, but stark: J&K must join Pakistan or India. It wasn't that simple for Hari Singh, however. He was a 'Dogra Hindu Rajput',[160] or, more correctly, a Hindu ethnic Dogra from the Jamwal Rajput clan or *biradari* (brotherhood, clan or tribe; kinsmen),[161] many of whose members lived in eastern parts of Jammu Province. Walter Lawrence, a former 'Settlement Commissioner' during Maharaja Pratap Singh's rein,[162] called the 'ruling family … Mian Rajputs' and Pratap Singh 'a Jamwal Rajput of the 'Dogra hills'.[163] These Dogras were 'found chiefly … around the foot of the mountains to the south of the [Kashmir] valley'.[164] The *Census of India, 1941*, described Maharaja Hari Singh as the 'head' of the 'Dogra Hindu-Rajput community',[165] with his lineage possibly descended from Maharaja Sundarshan of Ayodhya, the ruler of Rama's supposed birthplace around 1,600 BC.[166] The significance of this ethnicity and lineage was that Hari Singh 'was enough of a Hindu' to strongly dislike the Muslim League's 'aggressive Muslim communalism',[167] even though his state had a Muslim-majority population and despite 'tempting offers' from this soon-to-be Muslim-majority dominion.[168] Hari Singh also may have believed (unrealistically) that, if he acceded to Pakistan, 'not even a single hindu [sic] will be allowed to survive',[169] a thought possibly provoked by the serious inter-religious violence that occurred in Calcutta in 1946, throughout Punjab in 1947, and which later occurred internally within Jammu Province in September–October 1947. Additionally, Hari Singh may have feared that 'he would be dethroned by Jinnah for religious reasons' if he joined Pakistan.[170]

The British also may have induced, or furthered, Hari Singh's accessional trepidation. In December 1946, a Britisher informed the Resident in J&K that there were two important factors to remember about J&K that he could use in discussions with Prime Minister Kak, who presumably would then advise the Maharaja:

(1) That Kashmir is economically so dependent on India that it cannot afford to alienate India

(2) That Kashmir is strategically of such importance to India as a whole that India cannot afford to alienate a Kashmir in which Ruler and subjects are united.[171]

The first point was pertinent, although by 'India' the Britisher meant the unified, pre-partition entity. The second point might have stimulated Hari Singh's thinking, although the 'Ruler and [his] subjects' were far from united, even pre-partition. Another remark by a Britisher, Lord Mountbatten, in late June 1947 directly suggested that Hari Singh could prevaricate. He advised Singh and Kak that 'Kashmir should not decide about joining any constituent assembly until the Pakistan Constituent Assembly had been set up and the situation before them was a bit clearer'.[172] In response, Hari Singh told Mountbatten that he (Singh) 'would make up his mind about joining one side or the other as soon as he could see what the respective constitutions were going to be like and could gauge the feelings of his people'.[173] This gave him even more time to prevaricate – or to be far sighted – given that India's constitution came into being on 26 January 1950 while Pakistan's only came into being on 23 March 1956.

A further factor added to the situation. From 18–23 June 1947, Lord Mountbatten visited the 'very elusive' Hari Singh in J&K.[174] Extraordinarily, this was the only princely state that the Viceroy had the time, or made the time, to make an extended visit to before 15 August 1947. While in Srinagar, Mountbatten met Hari Singh and Prime Minister Kak and obtained a commitment from them 'not to make any independence declaration for the present' and, instead, 'to give serious consideration' to J&K joining India or Pakistan.[175] Mountbatten's statement confirms that J&K's two most senior officials were seriously considering independence for J&K. Surprisingly, however, Mountbatten also may have suggested to Hari Singh that J&K should accede to Pakistan. According to Singh:

> Lord Mountbatten stressed the dangerous situation in which Kashmir would find itself if it lacked the support of one of the two Dominions by the date of the transfer of power. The impression which I gathered from my talks with Lord Mountbatten who explained the situation with plans and maps was that, in his opinion, it was advisable for me to accede to Pakistan.[176]

While not necessarily an attractive option for Hari Singh, as a consequence, he thought (in retrospect) that 'it was advisable to have Standstill Agreements with India and Pakistan and get breathing time to decide which accession would be in the interests of the State'.[177]

Nevertheless, Maharaja Hari Singh didn't rush into approaching the leaders of India and prospective Pakistan to ensure the continuance of the provision of services to J&K. On 12 August 1947, the Prime Minister of J&K sought Standstill Agreements with India and Pakistan.[178] Pakistan accepted J&K's offer 'very quickly and willingly'[179] on 15 August, when this new dominion came into existence.[180] India did not accept J&K's offer. New Delhi wanted to consider fully any agreement before signing it, a stance that India has made a virtue out of. As Hari Singh saw things, however, India 'dealt' with the matter 'in a half hearted and desultory manner'.[181] According to Sheikh Abdullah, India 'could not accept such an agreement until it had the approval of the [J&K] people', which was a stretch.[182] In reality, land-locked J&K was then largely dependent on Pakistan, with which it had almost all of its major geo-economic links, including road, rail and postal services. Additionally, Karachi was the port for J&K. On 15 August, J&K had minimal physical links with India, including 'no effective road', as Sardar Patel perceptively noted.[183]

At the end of August 1947, Lord Ismay, Mountbatten's Chief of Staff in India, visited Kashmir for a 'much-needed rest'. Given the 'uncertain and dangerously unstable position' there, Mountbatten asked Ismay to try to get the

Maharaja to 'make up his vacillating mind and accede without further delay'.[184] By that time, as Hari Singh (retrospectively) saw things, his difficulties were that:

1. The People of the State were divided in several groups, each group having its own ideas about accession;
2. The Border Feudatory Territories such as Hunza, Nagar and Chitral and the District of Gilgit, where British influence was supreme were definitely for accession to Pakistan and were pressing me to accede to Pakistan without delay and threatening me with dire consequences if I did not act according to their suggestion;
3. The Muslim population of the State was also divided into groups with divergent views. Muslims from parts of Jammu such as, Mirpur, Poonch, Muzaffarabad, were for accession to Pakistan because of Pakistan propaganda inside the State. Muslims of Kashmir and some Muslims of Jammu who were led by Sheikh Abdullah and the leaders of the National Conference did not want the question of accession to be decided at that stage but wanted me to part with power in their favour so that they could decide the question independently of me. ...;
4. Hindus of Jammu and all the people of Ladakh were for affiliation with or accession to India;
5. A portion of the population of Kashmir was also for accession to Pakistan.

Thus, there was a sharp division of opinion. The Partition aggravated the situation and unhinged and unbalanced the minds of the people with the result that the people of the State were not in a position to give any considered opinion if I chose to consult them.[185]

This was a fairly accurately assessment.

However, J&K's future international status also offered significant opportunities, along with some divisive challenges. Writing in 1952, Singh stated that:

The position of my State was very difficult, situated as it was in contiguity to India and Pakistan as also to Afghanistan, Tibet and Russia. The situation therefore required to be dealt with more tact and foresight than in the case of other states. Mahatma Gandhi and the Prime Minister [Nehru] were anxious that I should not make a declaration of Independence. ... Lord Mountbatten chose to visit the State in June 1947 and we had several talks. Lord Mountbatten then urged me and my Prime Minister, Kak, not to make any declaration of Independence but to find out in one way or another, the will of the people of Kashmir as soon as possible and to announce our intention by the 14 August to send representatives accordingly to one Constituent Assembly or the other. Lord Mountbatten further told us that the newly created States Department [for post-British India] was prepared to give an assurance that if

Kashmir went to Pakistan, it would not be regarded as an unfriendly act by the Government of India.[186]

This last point was important.

According to Lord Mountbatten, therefore, had Maharaja Hari Singh made an accession before the British left India, the leaders of both post-British India and Pakistan would have accepted his decision, regardless of which dominion Singh chose to join. Already, Jinnah had acknowledged that any decision on J&K's future was Hari Singh's alone and that he (Jinnah) would accept Singh's choice. Presumably, this was because Jinnah seriously expected that J&K would choose to join Pakistan or to become independent – not to join India. Similarly, Sardar Patel, 'Free India's first Deputy Prime Minister and Minister for States',[187] who was then in charge of all matters to do with post-British India's princely states, would have accepted Singh's decision.[188] However, Prime Minister Nehru soon sidelined Patel from all matters to do with J&K, an action that some J&K-ites believed greatly weakened India's position in relation to J&K.[189] Patel was hardnosed, pragmatic, calm and able to 'manage' the volatile Kashmiri politician, Sheikh Abdullah. He was also unemotional about J&K and the Kashmir Valley – unlike Nehru. In Nehru's defence, Patel's sidelining may have happened anyway after India took the Kashmir dispute to the United Nations, after which the issue 'became the concern of the External Affairs Ministry', which was Nehru's portfolio.[190] That said, Nehru, who valued his friendship with Abdullah, felt very strongly, and almost irrationally, about Kashmir. Had Hari Singh chosen to join Pakistan, it is unlikely that Nehru would have dispassionately accepted this decision. As Nehru told Mahajan, 'it would be a tragedy … if Kashmir went to Pakistan'.[191]

The will of the people

When Lord Mountbatten met Maharaja Hari Singh in June 1947, he advised Singh to try to determine 'the will of the people of Kashmir'. In late August, he asked Lord Ismay to get the Maharaja to make an accession 'without further delay to whichever Dominion he and his people desire'.[192] Determining what J&K-ites wanted re J&K's accession would have been difficult for Maharaja Hari Singh. He had an entrenched autocratic mindset, as evidenced by his 1952 Memorandum. In this missive, Hari Singh does not mention anywhere that he had directly sought, or was interested in directly seeking, in any way his subjects' pre-accession opinion on J&K's future status, despite Mountbatten's urging him to assess 'the will of the people of Kashmir as soon as possible'.[193] The *Praja Sabha* (People's House) that Hari Singh had reluctantly granted to J&K in 1934 was exclusive, not inclusive. Only about 5 per cent of J&K-ites comprising suitably qualified subjects were entitled to elect candidates to an assembly that was, in truth, only advisory.[194] Seemingly, Hari Singh already knew his subjects' 'will': they were 'divided in their opinion' about J&K's future, which is why he sought Standstill Agreements with Pakistan and India 'in order to have time for things to settle down'.[195] Mountbatten was aware of J&K's democratic shortcomings. He suggested to Singh that, while a plebiscite had not been practicable, the Maharaja 'could have held public meetings with a show of hands' to gauge people's accessional desires.[196] While an easy, though highly unscientific and non-secret, way of assessing popular opinion, nothing came of it.

Mahatma Gandhi also spoke of the people's will. He met Hari Singh in Srinagar in early August 1947 on his one and only visit to J&K during which, surprisingly, some protesting Muslim Conference Kashmiris shouted for him to 'Quit Kashmir'.[197] After meeting Singh on 6 August, Gandhi publicly stated that 'the will of the Kashmiris should decide the fate of Kashmir and Jammu, and the sooner it was done, the better', a point the Maharaja had 'readily acknowledged'.[198] In 1952, Nehru, in a strongly worded critique of Hari Singh's Memorandum, informed Singh that he had been advised 'repeatedly … in 1946 and 1947' that 'the people's will must prevail'. Nehru considered that Singh 'had not sense[d] the spirit of the times and the revolutionary changes that were coming over India and the world' and he and his 'then advisers pursued a mistaken policy that led to the grievous development of subsequent days'.[199] (Nehru informed Karan Singh that his father's Memorandum was 'rather an angry and tendentious document' and that the Maharaja did 'not seem to realize at all that the world has changed and is changing rather rapidly'. He used similar words in a note to Rajendra Prasad.)[200]

In terms of ascertaining the 'people's will', Maharaja Hari Singh confronted another difficulty: his aloofness. He was 'shy and uneasy in public'[201] and found it challenging to meet or relate to his subjects. This prevented him from discovering what J&K-ites truly thought about the accession. According to Karan Singh's mother, who was Hari Singh's last wife: 'Your father never meets the people', she would complain, 'that's the trouble. He just sits surrounded by fawning courtiers and favourites, and never really gets to know what is going on outside.'[202] Viceroy Wavell, a taciturn individual himself, considered that Hari Singh

suffers from a dislike of personal contacts, and is disinclined to see people; I understand that it is quite difficult for his Ministers, or the Resident, or other influential persons to get interviews with him. Nor does he show himself enough to his subjects, amongst whom he enjoys considerable prestige and influence. I tried to encourage him to come out of his shell more, but I doubt whether it will have much effect. He … is genial and quite amusing in company; but he cannot be bothered with people whom he thinks may be troublesome or importunate.[203]

Similarly, in 1946, Nehru considered Hari Singh, whom he had not then met but who had the reputation of 'being a fairly decent man', as one who was 'really not interested in public affairs at all' and who was 'rather timid and keeps more aloof from people than most Indian rulers'.[204] On 1 March 1948, Singh's former Prime Minister Ayyangar, who was by then India's Minister for States, suggested to Hari Singh that he should shed his 'usual reserve, come out in the open and put [him] self at the head of [his] people, both Muslims and non-Muslims'.[205] Hari Singh did not act on any of this advice.

Maharaja Hari Singh faced other problems in order to determine the people's will. His large, disparate and disjointed state, with its difficult terrain and remote populations, also lacked electoral rolls inclusive of all adults. The existing electoral system effectively disenfranchised most peasants, workers and people without prestige, property or qualifications. The Praja Sabha, to which Hari Singh appointed thirty-five of the seventy-five members, reflected his opinions, given that elite or wealthy members of J&K society elected the other forty members, with electorates skewed in favour of non-Muslims.[206] In terms of consulting popular leaders, by 1947, Maharaja Hari Singh had imprisoned the leaders of the National Conference (Sheikh Abdullah), Muslim Conference (Chaudhri Ghulam Abbas) and Kisan Mazdoor Conference (Prem Nath Bazaz). While each wanted to end Hari Singh's rule of J&K and secure J&K for their nation of choice, probably in that order, these politicians may have been helpful to Singh in determining, or ensuring, the people's will in relation to his accession. By 1952, Singh finally seemed prepared to engage in a popular political contest against Sheikh Abdullah. To support his contention that he would be more popular, Singh claimed that, during his rule of J&K, 'the administration of the State in the matter of efficiency and organization was better than even in some of the Provinces of British India'. He could say 'without fear of contradiction, that the people of my State were content and had no cause for grievances against me or the administration of the State'.[207] Many political leaders in both India and J&K, as well as many J&K-ites, would have disagreed with him, except possibly for some Hindu co-religionists and some Jammu Dogras.

For Bhagwan Singh, Maharaja Hari Singh's last Private Secretary, obtaining the people's will was actually a major factor in the Maharaja's vacillation. Writing in

1973, he stated that this obligation imposed on Hari Singh by people such as Mountbatten and Gandhi,[208] to be done by 14 August 1947, was an 'impossible condition'. Hari Singh had been 'too willing to accede to India' but 'was prevented from doing so by this 'impracticable condition … laid down by the Indian Government'.[209] As Bhagwan Singh noted, 'ascertaining the will of the people' of J&K was no easy task: this process 'baffled India, Pakistan, and the United Nations, for the last twenty five years' when they tried to organise a plebiscite for J&K-ites.[210] Therefore, it was 'extremely unfair to blame [the] Maharaja for the delay' in acceding in 1947. For Bhagwan Singh, a further factor that worked against Hari Singh concerned the Standstill Agreement offered to Pakistan and India. Pakistan signed reasonably quickly, but India refused to sign 'Until it had the approval of the people's representatives'. This popular but difficult-to-achieve requirement also explained 'the much talked of delay on the part of the Maharaja to come to a decision about accession'.[211]

The India option

While Maharaja Hari Singh may not have been enamoured with J&K joining Pakistan, to accede to India also posed challenges. For a start, Singh knew that it would be challenging for J&K to physically access this dominion. While the exact borders of the future dominions of India and Pakistan were not known on 15 August 1947, the major pre-partition arterial routes into J&K were from areas that, post-partition, probably would be in Pakistan. Chiefly, these were the Jhelum Valley Road from Rawalpindi, via Murree and Domel, near Muzaffarabad, to Srinagar, and the road and railway from Sialkot, Punjab, to Jammu City. Rawalpindi also was important because of its rail connections, with this cantonment city being the 'warehouse' for goods traversing to, or from, the Kashmir Valley.[212] Apart from J&K's Muslim-majority population, these geo-economic links also suggested that J&K should join Pakistan. Conversely, J&K lacked viable rail or road connections with India, thereby making accession to this dominion difficult, but not impossible, to contemplate. Hari Singh was clearly aware of this shortcoming. Pre-partition, he had begun trying to create an alternative land option to India in order to lessen the prospect of J&K's almost total dependence on Pakistan – as well as to make an accession to India feasible and possible. On 29 July, *The Civil & Military Gazette* reported that the J&K Government intended to metal the 'fair-weather'[213] Kathua Road and hopefully 'thus connect Jammu State' with the future post-British India 'through Pathankot', a town about seventeen miles to Kathua's east.[214] The 1941

Census had suggested that 'An all-weather motor road from Jammu to Kathua will be a tremendous gain to the whole area served by the road'. While important, this was a difficult route, with the Ujh River impassable after rains. At such times, 'a traveller from Jammu to Kathua had to go by train [from Jammu via Sialkot] to Pathankote [sic] and then back to Kathua by tonga or foot'.[215] Pathankot was in Gurdaspur District, Punjab. Pathankot Tehsil had a Hindu majority, which made some observers think that it would end up with India. Importantly, Pathankot was also a rail terminus. By as early as mid-1947, therefore, J&K's connectivity with post-British India had become a significant factor.

The India–Pakistan borders were announced on 17 August 1947. However, little had happened by then to physically connect J&K with India. On 14 September, *The Civil & Military Gazette* stated that the J&K Government was (still) contemplating metalling this road and that it was actively considering building a bridge 'over the river Ravi with a view to linking Jammu with India'.[216] On 17 October, Hari Singh complained to a visitor, Guru M. S. Golwalker, head of the (Hindu) Rashtriya Swayamsevak Sangh (National Self-Service Society) since 1940, that J&K lacked road, rail and air links with India.[217] Singh then probably knew that others had been considering his state's connectivity with India. Just before partition, Sardar Patel had directed that the Madhopur-Kathua Road be improved. (Madhopur was located north of Pathankot and just east of the Ravi River that separated Indian Punjab and J&K.) As Patel and Hari Singh both knew, this link would reduce J&K's dependence on Pakistan, as well as provide a possible link from India to J&K, should the future India–Pakistan border enable this. Much work upgrading this road and bridging the Ravi River had apparently been done by the time of 'the events of October 1947', i.e., the Pukhtoon invasion of J&K on 22 October 1947 and Maharaja Hari Singh's subsequent accession to India on 26 October 1947.[218]

In mid-1947, the Boundary Commission's deliberations on the future India–Pakistan borders therefore became important. On 17 July, V. P. Menon stated in a note that, although J&K presented some difficulties because it was

> claimed by both the Dominions ... It is possible that a predominantly Muslim State like Kashmir cannot be kept away from Pakistan for long ... [However, u]nlike Hyderabad [which was surrounded by India], it does not lie in the bosom of Pakistan and it can claim an exit to India, especially if a portion of the Gurdaspur district goes to East Punjab.[219]

Menon, an influential civil servant with 30 years experience,[220] was either being strategic, prescient or was trying to influence the Boundary Commission. Similarly, in his report discussing the last 'week of British rule in India', Mountbatten noted that Maharaja Hari Singh had decided to sack his Prime Minister, Kak, and was talking of holding a referendum to decide whether J&K should join Pakistan or India, 'provided that the Boundary Commission gives him land communications between Kashmir and India'.[221] Mountbatten also was either being strategic, prescient or was trying to pressure the Boundary Commission. Some Pakistanis suggest the latter, given that the Boundary Commission did, indeed, provide a land communication between J&K and India via 'a portion of the Gurdaspur district'.

On 17 August 1947, the officially announced Radcliffe Awards revealed the new India–Pakistan borders. These awards were the result of the deliberations of Sir Cyril Radcliffe, the Chairman of the Boundary Commissions for Punjab and for Bengal. He had been assisted by two Congress appointees and two Muslim League appointees. Their appointees' ideological leanings made them largely unhelpful. Radcliffe had been tasked to determine 'the contiguous majority areas of Muslims and non-Muslims … [and] other factors' and then to decide where the India–Pakistan borders should be located.[222] When finally announced, the Punjab Boundary Commission gave India three of the four tehsils in Gurdaspur District: Batala, Gurdaspur and Pathankot. This was problematic for Pakistanis as, overall, Gurdaspur District had a Muslim majority, a factor that suggested to them that Pakistan should have received this district in its entirety. However, Gurdaspur's Muslim majority was only slight. Based on figures in the *Census of India, 1941*, Gurdaspur District had a 51 per cent Muslim-majority population. Tehsil-wise, Batala's population was 53 per cent Muslim; Gurdaspur Tehsil's population was 52 per cent Muslim; Shakargarh was 51 per cent Muslim; Pathankot, the least populous tehsil by a long way, was only 39 per cent Muslim, thereby making it a Hindu-majority tehsil.[223] Supposedly, India was awarded the three tehsils of Batala, Gurdaspur and Pathankot to ensure that Amritsar District, an important religious centre for Sikhs to Gurdaspur's south, was not geographically isolated.[224] Fortuitously, obtaining these tehsils, particularly Pathankot, gave India land access to J&K, and vice versa.

The Boundary Commission's final award favouring India with most of Gurdaspur District was not totally unexpected, including by some Pakistanis. Viceroy Wavell had suggested to London as early as February 1946 such an arrangement to prevent Amritsar's isolation.[225] According to Radcliffe's British Secretary, Christopher Beaumont, from the outset, Radcliffe had apparently always intended to award Gurdaspur to India.[226] Importantly, this award of territory to India made J&K's Kathua District, in the far southeastern corner of Jammu Province, contiguous with India. Thus, J&K obtained a narrow land corridor from Kathua to India's Pathankot Tehsil, where a railhead and a road to mainland India were located. This reduced J&K's almost total reliance on Pakistan, although this dependence did not lessen immediately due to the poor state of the Kathua-Pathankot road. This award of Pathankot also meant that India could access J&K's Jammu Province and the much desired Kashmir Valley beyond, by land. Without these three tehsils of Gurdaspur District, India would have needed to construct a new road through the hilly-to-mountainous terrain to Gurdaspur District's north. This road via Bhaderwah, Kishtwar, Chamba and Dalhousie could have connected J&K with India.[227] Embittered Pakistanis, feeling 'betrayed' as Pakistan had not obtained Gurdaspur District, possibly started to 'contemplate unorthodox, and unofficial courses of action' to obtain J&K for Pakistan.[228] Ultimately, these led to the Pukhtoon invasion of Kashmir Province in October. (Some Indians were similarly displeased as the Chittagong Hill Tracts, which had a Buddhist-majority population, ended up in East Pakistan, not India.)

An independent J&K?

The possibility of an independent J&K may have appealed to Hari Singh. This was the easiest option because it did not require him to actually take a decision. However, Singh was also encouraged to consider this option by Swami Sant Dev, the alleged 'Rasputin of [the] Kashmir Court'.[229] The Swami had appeared 'around 1944' and had become Rajguru (spiritual guide to the ruler) in 1946.[230] A positive personal influence on Hari Singh but politically 'disastrous', Swami Sant Dev allegedly planted in the ruler's 'mind visions of an extended kingdom sweeping down to Lahore'.[231] One possibility was an independent 'Dograstan',[232] or 'Dogristan',[233] which would include J&K, nearby Kangra, and some other princely states of the Punjab Hills. Kak states that Dogristan would have included J&K, 'the districts of Kangra and the States and areas now mostly included in the [sic] Himachal Pradesh', the new political state created by India in 1950. Indeed, Maharaja Hari Singh apparently went as far as creating a 'draft agreement' that 'defined the aims and objectives of the proposed federation and the safeguards in relation to dynastic matters of the ruling families'.[234] These rulers included the Maharaja of Sirmur and the Rajas of Mandi and Jubbal, all three of whom had stayed with the Maharaja as his guests in June 1947.[235] On 18 July, *The Statesman* reported that a merger of J&K and the Punjab Hill States of Sirmur, Mandi and Jubbal had been discussed in Srinagar on 10 July, with the aim being to form a union 'to attain security and maximum possible development of a large geographic and economically homogenous tract'.[236] Nothing eventuated from these discussions.

A potential 'Dogristan' state made some sense. First, creating this entity would have enabled J&K, in theory, to access India in the event that the Boundary Commission did not give this dominion any major land link to J&K. Some discussions about the possibility of Dogristan took place, with the Viceroy's 'Personal Report' in August noting that two Punjab Hill States had been negotiating with Kashmir.[237] Second, Hari Singh, like his forebear Gulab Singh,[238] saw himself as a leader of his Dogra and Rajput 'kinsmen'. Thus, when World War II began in September 1939, Hari Singh had made a patriotic appeal to 'all Dogras, Hindu or Muslim' within J&K and to those 'outside my State whom I claim as my kinsmen'.[239] (This was noted in Prem Nath Bazaz's 1941 book, *Inside Kashmir*, which the Maharaja had proscribed.)[240] These 'kinsmen' included people in nearby Kangra.[241] Third, Hari Singh had meaningful connections with Kangra. While most Dogras in his state were 'indigenous to the area', some were from Kangra and other adjacent districts in Punjab.[242] His wife, Maharani Tara Devi, was originally a commoner from this district, as was her elder brother, Thakur Nachint Chand, who had 'great influence' over her but was unpopular at court until he became the 'main courier' between Swami Sant Dev and the Maharaja after 1946.[243] The J&K State Forces had a regiment in which half of the soldiers were Kangra Rajputs.[244] Hari Singh's regime had a 'Kangra faction',[245] which was strengthened when he made two men from Kangra senior officials in 1947. The first was General Janak Singh, a 'close relation of the ruling family'[246] and a long term member of the administration from 'a respectable family of Katoch Rajputs of Kangra'.[247] He had joined the J&K State administration in 1901 as a Naib Tehsildar (assistant to a District revenue officer) and had served in civilian and military positions, including in the three-man J&K Cabinet that administered the state while the Maharaja attended the 1930 Round Table Conference in London.[248] In Srinagar in 1931, as 'Army and Public Works Minister', he announced that Karan Singh had been born in Cannes, France.[249] The second was Mehr Chand Mahajan, who became J&K's Prime Minister in early October 1947 after a suggestion made by Patel to Hari Singh in September.[250] Additionally, J&K's Deputy Prime Minister, Ram Lal Batra, a Punjabi, had served 'in one of the tiny hill states of north India',[251] possibly in the nearby Punjab Hill States or Simla Hill States.

Maharaja Hari Singh asked Prime Minister Ramchandra Kak for his opinion about the proposed new Dogristan political entity. The Kashmiri informed the ruler that he thought the idea was 'futile and impracticable'. It was 'utterly unrealistic ... for anybody to imagine that the forces which had compelled the British to leave India, would allow the creation of a new empire in their midst'.[252] For Kak, those 'forces' comprised the senior, and increasingly politically powerful, Congressmen, such as Gandhi, Nehru and Patel, who – unlike the senior, supposedly non-interventionist, Muslim League leaders – had spent many years and much energy opposing the British politically and physically. This included spending considerable time confined in Indian jails for their efforts to liberate India from British rule. Being imprisoned for one's political beliefs and principles gave one 'an aura of great respectability'.[253] Kak continued: the best Hari Singh could hope for was 'the survival' of J&K 'as already constituted and ... any move in the direction contemplated by the Maharaja and his guests was [a] sure invitation to disaster'.[254] The views of Kak, who some thought was 'the tail wagging the dog',[255] were not well received by Swami Sant Dev, nor by Hari Singh, who allegedly had already 'prepared a new crown of diamonds and emeralds for his coronation as the ruler of the new empire'.[256] Consequently, the Swami started to intrigue against Kak, as a result of which the Hindu Pandit Prime Minister eventually lost his job.

Nevertheless, Kak was a 'supporter' of independence for J&K. For him, however, independence was not necessarily anything grandiose or expansive like Maharaja Hari Singh envisaged. Rather, by independence, Kak meant that J&K would not accede to either India or Pakistan. The state would remain aloof from both dominions, but hopefully with good relations with them. Kak's independence, therefore, was essentially a neutral non-accession rather than a pro-active, genuine pursuit of stand-alone freedom from external rule. The 'Kashmir Government's decision not to accede' – that is, not to make any accession to any post-British political entity (or entities, as events later transpired) – had been conveyed to the Government of India, via the Resident, as early as late 1946.[257] Similarly, according to Kak, he notified Lord Mountbatten in June 1947 in Srinagar that 'since Kashmir would not accede to Pakistan, it could not accede to India'. Between 23 July and 27 July, Kak told Jinnah that 'the State's decision not to accede [to either dominion] was definite'. Jinnah was prepared to concede this option, so long as J&K 'did not accede to India'.[258] Kak reiterated this stance after talking with Mahatma Gandhi on 3 August when, on being asked if J&K intended to join India or Pakistan or remain independent, Kak replied 'We are – and want to be – friendly with everybody'.[259]

Kak apparently also was aware that it would be difficult for J&K to remain independent should Pakistan be hostile or should India be indifferent. His perception was confirmed by the British Resident to J&K, Lieutenant-Colonel Webb, on 13 August 1947:

> His Highness, Dogras and Hindu communities incline towards India but [the] bulk of [the] population are Moslem and if consulted would probably favour Pakistan especially Mirpur, Poonch and Muzaffarabad area. Kak, although [a] Hindu clearly saw [the] implication and felt that if Kashmir joined either Dominion especially India it would mean serious trouble. … it is apparent that they are not likely to join either Dominion at present. Kashmir Government are [sic] in a grave dilemma as a decision to join either Dominion will result in serious trouble that might have repercussions outside [the] State.[260]

Indeed, according to Kak, for J&K, given its long border with Pakistan and its 77 per cent Muslim-majority population, 'the only safe and possible course, short of proceeding to Pakistan, was, in the circumstances then prevailing, to remain outside the arena' of both nations' control.[261] Hence, J&K would accede to neither new dominion. However, if independence was not possible, Kak apparently favoured J&K joining Pakistan. Indeed, some of his rivals considered him to be pro-Pakistan.[262] Possibly, this was 'to save his skin' as he did not get on with Nehru or Abdullah.[263] Some Indians also perceived that Kak, along with his European wife and the two British chiefs respectively of the J&K Military Staff and the J&K police had 'conspired' in a 'secret pact between Kashmir and Pakistan' to hand over J&K to this new dominion. For such Indians, 'Pandit Kak and his group in J&K, in whose hands the Maharaja was only a tool, were about to have the State of Jammu and Kashmir annexed to Pakistan'. Kak and Co. would allow this to happen because Pakistan was prepared to recognise Maharaja Hari Singh as the 'sovereign ruler' of J&K.[264] Such perceptions almost certainly were incorrect.

Initially, and significantly, some local political parties publicly encouraged Maharaja Hari Singh to pursue independence for J&K, with him as a constitutional figurehead. These were the Jammu and Kashmir Rajya Hindu Sabha,[265] the Muslim Conference and the Kisan Mazdoor Conference. Based in Jammu Province, the Rajya Hindu Sabha believed that 'a Hindu State' like J&K 'should not merge its identity into secular India'.[266] This related to the J&K rulers' Hindu religion and their support for some Hindu practices, such as banning cow slaughter and building temples. While the first three Dogra rulers were all considered to be devout Hindus,[267] Hari Singh was generally more eclectic, secular and 'far from being a religious person'.[268] The Muslim Conference similarly called for an independent J&K. This stance was in line with Jinnah's position that princes would be independent after British paramountcy ended. Equally, it may have been a ploy to woo the

Maharaja away from India. According to Chaudhri Hamidullah, acting President of the Muslim Conference, the idea was 'to allay the fears and suspicions of the minorities'.[269] (Hamidullah was acting President because the actual President, Chaudhri Ghulam Abbas, was in jail.) Equally, and importantly, the Muslim Conference and the Rajya Hindu Sabha distrusted and disliked 'leaders of the Kashmir region'.[270] This term was shorthand for Sheikh Abdullah and his National Conference. In September, the Kisan Mazdoor Conference passed a resolution that called on Maharaja Hari Singh to 'declare the independence of the State and that simultaneously he should introduce complete responsible government'.[271] For Maharaja Hari Singh, being a 'Constitutional Head' in a 'State of Full Responsible Government' was not a new concept. He had seriously considered this option in 1945, but the departure of his then Prime Minister, Benegal Rau, along with some 'intrigues' and British reluctance, apparently prevented this change from happening.[272]

Over time, the Muslim Conference's stance changed. In May 1947, Hamidullah had 'urge[d] the Maharaja to declare Kashmir an independent sovereign State immediately', suggesting that Muslims would 'readily acclaim him as the first constitutional king of a democratic and independent Kashmir'.[273] Soon after, Hamidullah stated that 'Kashmir has enough resources to become an independent State and we shall maintain cordial relations with Hindustan and Pakistan'.[274] On 28 May, he repeated his call for independence for J&K at a press conference in a Jammu hotel.[275] On 22 June, while still urging the 'Maharaja to declare Kashmir's independent status', Hamidullah also reportedly warned Hari Singh against acceding to India because Muslims would revolt if he did so.[276] Two weeks later, the President of the Muslim Conference Co-ordination Organization, New Delhi, telegrammed 'Heartiest congratulations on the reported independence decision' to the Maharaja.[277] Later that month (July), a *Dawn* editorial titled 'Whither Kashmir?' encouraged the Maharaja to do 'some hard thinking' and decide J&K's future. It mentioned that independence for J&K had neither been confirmed nor announced, after which the editorial suggested that 'The only sensible course for Kashmir is … to join the Pakistan Dominion … We trust that Sir Harri [sic] Singh will soon make his choice and come down on the right side of the fence on which he has so long been occupying an uncertain and precarious perch.'[278] The very next day (29 July), however, all pro-independence forces received a jolt. Under considerable pressure from New Delhi, Travancore confirmed that it would join the Indian Union. Independence for any princely state was beginning to look less possible and less likely.[279]

From 22 July 1947 – less than four weeks before the transfer of British power to the new dominions of India and Pakistan – the Muslim Conference's stance on J&K's international status changed totally. Through a resolution 'passed unanimously' on this day,[280] this party now considered that J&K's accession to Pakistan was 'absolutely necessary'. It considered that

> in view of its geographical position, means of communication, facilities of import and export of [the] necessities of life, racial and cultural affinities, contiguity of frontiers as well as the fact that Muslims constitute 85 per cent of the population, the only proper course for the State is to join Pakistan. … [The resolution also warned] the authorities that if this friendly advice is ignored and if the Kashmir Government joins the Indian Union, the Muslims of the State will strongly oppose and condemn such a step.[281]

By the end of July, some J&K Muslims were seriously concerned that Maharaja Hari Singh might accede to India.

Consequently, even though Hari Singh had not publicly made up his mind about his accession, Muslims in the Poonch and Mirpur areas of western Jammu Province started to politically and militarily oppose him. Rather than seeking independence for J&K, they sought to make parts of their areas *azad* (free) from the Maharaja's control, which they successfully did. These rebels also wanted to unify J&K with Pakistan, which they failed to do.[282] One week after the Muslim Conference's unanimous pro-Pakistan resolution, *Dawn*'s 'Whither Kashmir' editorial provided an ominous warning for J&K. It stated that if Pakistan's 'repeated gestures of friendliness and generosity fail to make any impression on the powers that be [in J&K], other means will have to be devised to carry good sense where it is found so conspicuously lacking.'[283] Even before the British had left the subcontinent, pro-Pakistan elements were hinting at trouble for J&K if it didn't join Pakistan.

It is difficult to determine how serious Maharaja Hari Singh or Ramchandra Kak were about obtaining independence for J&K in 1947. In early July, *The Civil & Military Gazette* reported that 'the Kashmir State has finally decided to declare independence after the lapse of paramountcy next month'.[284] In July in Kashmir, Hari Singh apparently told the Viceroy that he didn't want to accede to Pakistan 'on any account'. Mountbatten replied 'then you must join India', to which Singh said: 'No … I don't wish to join India either. I wish to be independent.'[285] On 4 August, *The New York Times* noted that 'Kashmir is one of several states that may remain independent after Aug. 15.'[286] A concurrent Indian publication stated that 'It is expected that Bhopal, Kashmir and perhaps Indore will also announce their decision to become independent.'[287] By October, J&K certainly had a dedicated

'Minister, External Affairs, Jammu and Kashmir, Srinagar'. He sent telegrams to 'Foreign, Karachi' on 3 October and 22 October and to 'Governor-General, Pakistan, Karachi' on 22 October.[288] Previously, this position had been 'Foreign and Commerce Minister'.[289] According to Menon, Hari Singh contemplated an 'Independent Jammu and Kashmir', even though Mountbatten told him this was not feasible and that the British Government would not recognise J&K as a dominion.[290] In his letter that accompanied his accession, Maharaja Hari Singh stated that 'I wanted to take time to decide to which Dominion I should accede, or whether it is not in the best interests of both the Dominions and my State *to stand independent*'.[291] In a note to Nehru soon after, Mountbatten stated that he 'knew the Maharaja was most anxious to remain independent, and nothing but the terror of violence could have made him accede to either Dominion'.[292] This 'terror of violence' was the Pukhtoons' invasion of Kashmir Province. In 1997, Karan Singh confirmed that 'the tribal incursion … [had] forced his father to abandon the idea of an independent Kashmir'.[293]

Seemingly, Prime Minister Ramchandra Kak also had seriously contemplated independence for J&K. In his note of 1956, Kak asked 'Could J&K have survived if it had not acceded' to either India or Pakistan?[294] Economically, Kak claimed that under his stewardship J&K had achieved a surplus and it would be able to 'live on its own resources and within its own means'. Similarly, in terms of internal security, he believed that 'Peace within the State was firmly established and remained so until 11th August 1947' when he lost office. In terms of external security or 'danger from outside', Kak didn't think that the J&K Army, which comprised 9,100 men in 1939,[295] could 'withstand for any length of time, an organised invasion by a really powerful army'. Equally, neither could India or Pakistan. Presumably, Kak was thinking of the Soviet Union's Red Army or, perhaps by the time he wrote his article in 1956, the People's Liberation Army of China, both of which militaries then potentially posed serious defense issues for India, Pakistan and many other nearby nations. For Kak, 'The only other quarter from which danger to Kashmir could have arisen, would be India or Pakistan', about which threats he did not offer any assessment of J&K's ability to resist. Interestingly, Kak stated that 'The prospect of Kashmir's security in the immediate future did not present so gloomy a picture in the middle of 1947 as some people seen [sic] to think'.[296] In this he was probably correct, given that, in 1947, the strategic and security situation beyond the tumultuous subcontinent was much more benign than in 1956: the post-war Cold War was just beginning, while the Communists had not yet achieved victory over the Nationalists in mainland China.[297]

Becoming in favour of India

From around early August 1947, Maharaja Hari Singh seemed to slowly come around to favouring J&K joining India. There were a number of reasons for this. Many of his brother princes, most of whom were Hindus and some of whom were personal friends, were acceding to India. After Gandhi's visit to Srinagar, and probably because of it, Hari Singh 'unceremoniously' sacked Pandit Ramchandra Kak as his Prime Minister on 11 August,[298] ostensibly because Kak was impeding J&K's accession to India. There had been rumours in early July 'that the deep-seated desire of the Maharaja and the people of the State for entry into the Indian Union is being frustrated by the Prime Minister'.[299] Indeed, *The Civil & Military Gazette* reported on 2 July that, according to 'reliable Kashmir sources', Kak 'may be relieved from his office soon'.[300] This was five weeks before his final dismissal. The next day, the same paper editorialised that Kak was frustrating the Maharaja's accessional desire for India.[301] Stephens, the editor of *The Statesman*, confirms that, in early July, rumours were reaching his newspaper that Maharaja Hari Singh 'was privately seeking pretexts for acceding to India'.[302] Kak therefore had to go.

For Kak, his termination may not have been unexpected. Apart from various rumours, including in the press, Nehru had suggested to Mountbatten on 17 June that, before J&K could join 'the Constituent Assembly of India', one of the 'immediate steps' needed was 'the removal of Mr. Kak from the Prime Ministership'.[303] While the press thereafter reported that Kak had 'retired',[304] Kak himself stated that he had 'relinquished the office of Prime Minister'.[305] Possibly, he did so because he knew that Maharaja Hari Singh had decided to accede to India.[306] According to the British Resident in Kashmir, Kak 'asked for permission to retire as he felt he had lost [the] confidence of [the] Ruler who he found had been corresponding with Congress through other channels'.[307] Equally, Kak's dismissal possibly came about because of the 'indecision of His Highness to make up his mind either to join one or other Dominion'. It was a 'grave dilemma' that may have provoked 'serious trouble ... [and] repercussions'.[308] Whatever the reason, Kak was sacked four days before partition, which suggested something was afoot, although it was not then certain what. The day after Kak's dismissal, his replacement, General Janak Singh, actively sought Standstill Agreements with India and Pakistan.[309] This may have been due to Kak's removal; equally, it may have been a coincidence. In the final analysis, Kak's demise may have been the result of a basic choice for the Maharaja: 'to choose between his Swami and his Prime Minister. Inevitably, Hari Singh chose the Swami.'[310]

Kak's dismissal was significant. According to Karan Singh, his father sacked 'the one man who had the intellectual capacity to make some coherent effort towards an acceptable settlement' of the accession issue.[311] Secondly, the timing of it shortly after, and possibly because of, Gandhi's visit and just before partition 'sent a deep wave of apprehension among Muslims' that Hari Singh had decided to opt for India.[312] Kak was replaced by the 'septuagenarian'[313] loyalist Janak Singh who had a 'brilliant administrative and military record',[314] was steady and was trusted, although, according to Karan Singh, his father 'had a strange tendency ... that was ultimately to prove his political undoing – his inability to trust anyone for any length of time'. (The one possible exception was Gopalaswami Ayyangar, who served as J&K Prime Minister for six years.)[315] Seemingly, Janak Singh was not of the same caliber as the 'moderate' Pandit.[316] This low-profile loyalist served as a stopgap prime minister for two months until Mehr Chand Mahajan became Prime Minister of J&K on 10 October.[317] Kak did not rate Janak Singh highly: 'Loyalty is a great virtue, but as the Maharaja soon found, it [did] not compensate for lack of ability'.[318] As for Mahajan, Sardar Patel had been involved organising for this pro-India jurist to be appointed J&K's Prime Minister. As well as being from Kangra, Mahajan had previously served as a member of the Radcliffe-led Punjab Boundary Commission that granted three of Gurdaspur District's four tehsils to India on 17 August.[319] His specific role, if any, in this windfall for India is not known. While somewhat new to J&K, Mahajan nevertheless had connections with the state: his wife was from Mirpur, while her father and brother worked for the J&K Government.[320] With Mahajan in place, all of the senior officials who led the J&K administration during the state's short post-British period of independence – Prime Ministers Janak Singh and Mahajan and Deputy Prime Minister Batra – were non-J&K-ites. This may have been helpful in ensuring that J&K joined India.

Kak's dismissal also appeared to mark the beginning of the end of whatever aspirations Maharaja Hari Singh had for an independent J&K. It also suggested that Singh wanted, or felt compelled, or was starting to prepare, to join India.[321] With Janak Singh's appointment, 'the uncertainty about the future of the State was removed and it became clear that the Maharaja and his government ... had lined up with the Congress', a situation that caused 'grave tension in the State'.[322] According to Karan Singh, his 'father's court' then comprised a 'circle of small-minded men ... a coterie of time-servers and yes-men hanging around interminably'.[323] Hari Singh apparently instituted 'wholesale change in the administration' that included replacing many experienced officers with 'others of little experience and ability' who were loyal to the ruler.[324] These newcomers included the Prime Minister, a loyal retainer brought out of retirement as a 'temporary' replacement,[325] the Deputy Prime Minister, Chief Secretary, Deputy Political Secretary, Chief of State Military Forces, Inspector-General of Police, Director-General of Civil Supplies, and the Director-General of Medical Services.[326] However, these major changes in personnel may not have improved the J&K administration. Kak considered that Singh's policy of loyalty over ability 'emasculated [the] State Government' while, after his prime ministership, 'Peace within the State' ended.[327] Thereafter, Muslims instigated a pro-Pakistan uprising in Poonch, while serious inter-religious violence began, then intensified, in Jammu Province. While both events were coincidental with Kak's dismissal, they almost certainly were inspired far more by the creation of the new dominions of India and Pakistan – and by J&K-ites' differing desires for J&K to join one of these entities. It is a vexed question as to whether Ramchandra Kak, or anyone else for that matter, would have been able to maintain law and order throughout J&K in the volatile and emotional circumstances of mid-1947, particularly once the British departed the subcontinent. Kak later confronted a Commission of Inquiry into 'certain allegations' against him.[328] Then, in October, he was prevented from leaving J&K because his departure 'might prove prejudicial to the interest of the State and the existing good relations between the Kashmir Government and other Governments'. With the Maharaja 'unable to make up his mind firmly on any matter' except seemingly about sacking Kak, it was 'No wonder then that the [J&K] ship foundered'.[329]

By September, the J&K Government was becoming increasingly uneasy about Pakistan. In early September, it accused Pakistan of infiltrating armed men into J&K, claiming that Pakistan and/or Pakistanis, some of whom were active servicemen, were creating security problems along the J&K-Pakistan border and in J&K's Poonch Jagir and Mirpur District. (In those days, it was easier to travel from Poonch City to Jhelum Town, via Kotli and Mirpur, than to Jammu City.)[330] While Pakistan and Pakistanis may have been doing so, Poonchis and Mirpuris also had their own martial capabilities, as Lieutenant-General Hari Singh was well aware. Men from both districts of Jammu Province had served in his armed forces and, more particularly, in large numbers in the British Indian Army during World War II. Hari Singh had been reminded of these Muslims' martial capabilities when, from 21–25 April 1947, he toured western Jammu and Poonch, where the bulk of these ex-servicemen lived.[331] In early October, the J&K Government accused Pakistan of withholding vital supplies to J&K in what amounted to an economic blockade, despite the J&K-Pakistan Standstill Agreement.[332] These supplies included quantities of rice, gram, cloth, salt and petrol.[333] Karachi claimed that the instability then wracking the subcontinent was preventing the delivery of supplies to J&K,[334] which was plausible. However, the severing of railway services between Sialkot and Jammu in mid-September did nothing to help J&K.[335] These factors made Pakistan even more unappealing for Maharaja Hari Singh.

Also in mid-September 1947, *The Civil & Military Gazette* carried a story titled 'Kashmir to Join Indian Union'.[336] As early as 3 July, the same newspaper had reported that Singh's 'deep-seated desire' was for J&K to join India;[337] similarly, *The Times* stated on 1 August that Hari Singh 'would like to accede to India'.[338] On 20 September, *The Civil & Military Gazette* quoted a 'special dispatch' first published in *The Pakistan Times* on 13 September which stated that 'The Kashmir Government has arrived at an understanding with the Indian Union and an announcement about Kashmir joining the Indian Union is expected shortly'. The J&K Government denied this 'unauthenticated' report, which didn't mean that it was incorrect.[339] J&K then appeared to be moving away from Pakistan – although not necessarily towards India – with Hari Singh rejecting on 17 September Mohammad Ali Jinnah's request made on 5 September to visit J&K 'in a private capacity'.[340] (Singh may have been distracted around that time by the 'splendid treble for Kashmir' won by his racehorses at Poona races on 6 September.)[341] Jinnah's visit may have been in relation to the possible purchase of 'a vacation houseboat' in Srinagar,[342] the 'City of the Sun' where 'summer or winter the sun smiles and sparkles'.[343] Equally, the Governor-General of Pakistan may have been prompted to visit J&K by a note forwarded by Liaquat Ali Khan on 23 August from the Publicity Secretary, Muslim Conference. It stated that the local Congress newspaper was forecasting that 'Kashmir [was] definitely joining [the] Indian Union'.[344] Jinnah may have wanted to meet Singh to try to change this possibility.

In early October 1947, the Maharaja's intentions became a little clearer. On 3 October, *The Civil & Military Gazette* reported that Sheikh Abdullah's recent release from jail 'was indicative of the [J&K] State's decision to accede to the Indian Union, which, it is understood, Sheikh Abdullah will support'.[345] Hari Singh may have released Abdullah after pressure from Indian leaders, particularly Jawaharlal Nehru, Abdullah's good friend. Nehru disliked Hari Singh; however, he could, and wanted to, work with Abdullah and he understood the need to have Abdullah 'on the streets' in Kashmir because of his popularity and leadership skills. Nevertheless, on 11 October, J&K's Deputy Prime Minister, R. L. Batra, contradicted such reporting, stating that 'strict neutrality' described J&K's policy towards India and Pakistan. J&K was waiting 'until a calmer atmosphere conducive to balanced thinking prevailed', after which the State would determine which dominion it would join.[346]

Such 'strict neutrality' was questionable: while Abdullah had been released, his major pro-Pakistan rival, Chaudhri Ghulam Abbas, was kept in detention. (Abbas was not released until early March 1948.) Three days later, Batra continued with the theme of neutrality. He was reported as saying that 'we have no intention of either joining India or Pakistan. ... The Maharaja has told me that his ambition is [for] ... a State that is completely neutral'.[347] J&K's newly appointed Prime Minister, Mahajan, reiterated such evenhandedness at his first press conference two days later. He stated that 'whether it is decided that the State will remain independent or will accede to either of the two Dominion[s,] it will always remain on the friendliest of terms with both'.[348] At that (late) stage and despite rumours about joining India, independence was still seemingly a serious option being considered for J&K.

For Hari Singh, the biggest problem about joining India was, arguably, Jawaharlal Nehru, with whom he was 'hardly the best of friends'.[349] According to Karan Singh, his father 'was hostile [to Congress] mainly because of Jawaharlal's close association with his [father's] arch enemy Sheikh Abdullah'.[350] Certainly, Hari Singh strongly disliked India's new Prime Minister whom he had arrested in June 1946 when Nehru attempted to enter J&K to legally assist his friend and political colleague, Sheikh Abdullah, who had been arrested for instituting his anti-Maharaja 'Quit Kashmir' campaign (discussed in Chapter 4). The Maharaja's regime had charged Abdullah with the serious crime of sedition, for which he later received a sentence of three years' rigorous imprisonment. Abdullah's Quit Kashmir campaign had sought to compel the Dogra 'dictator', whose forebear, Gulab Singh, had purchased large parts of J&K, including the Kashmir Valley, from the British, to 'quit', or leave, Kashmir. The National Conference would then replace Hari Singh's autocratic rule with popular and responsible rule, presumably under its leadership. An accession to India almost certainly would have meant that Hari Singh would come under the control of the disliked Nehru, while Singh's rival and Nehru's friend, Sheikh Abdullah, would obtain political power in J&K. Neither politician would provide guarantees about the Maharaja's future or the future of his princely state. Both the ruler and his realm were in jeopardy.

Coincidentally, Hari Singh's pro-India feelings got stronger the longer he vacillated – and as circumstances became more difficult for J&K due to actions involving, or instigated by, Pakistan. Karachi allegedly had been making 'tempting offers',[351] including a 'blank cheque'. This meant that Hari Singh could write his own accession terms which, regardless of what these might be, would be acceptable to the unassailable Mohammad Ali Jinnah. He apparently had offered the same 'blank cheque' to the young Maharaja of Jodhpur to try to obtain his accession,[352] even though Jodhpur had a small Muslim population (about 8.4 per cent).[353] Jodhpur's accession to Pakistan was feasible as the border of this princely state almost certainly would be contiguous with this new dominion when it came into being. Pressured by Mountbatten, however, Jodhpur chose India. Seemingly, Hari Singh was not tempted by Jinnah's blank cheque offer. (Interestingly, Jinnah was somewhat similar to Singh: both were aloof and difficult to approach. Both had never obtained the freedom fighter's 'badge of honour': imprisonment by the British. However, Jinnah's advantages were his strong intellect, focus and determination, which some saw as intransigence, and his prestige as the undisputed leader of Indian Muslims.)

Visits by senior Indians in 1947 also influenced Hari Singh. Before partition, Congress President J. B. Kripalani visited, as did Mahatma Gandhi and the Maharajas of Patiala, Kapurthala and Faridkot.[354] Gandhi's visit was particularly influential given that Ramachandra Kak was sacked as Prime Minister five days later.[355] On 18 October, the Rashtriya Swayamsevak Sangh's Supreme Leader, M. S. Golwalker, made a significant visit facilitated by Mahajan.[356] Considered the 'principal ideologue of Hindu nationalism',[357] Golwalker told Maharaja Hari Singh that he was a 'Hindu Raja. To accede to Pakistan means your Hindu subjects will have to struggle for their existence. It is correct that at present there is no rail, road or air link with India but within a short time these will be available to your state. It is in your interest as well as the interest of your state that you should join the Indian Union.'[358] Certainly, the Kathua-Pathankot road was being taken care of. Sardar Patel informed Maharaja Hari Singh on 2 October that he was 'expediting as much as possible the linking of the State with the Indian Dominion by means of telegraph, telephones, wireless and roads'.[359] This included significantly upgrading the sixty-five-mile Jammu-Pathankot road.[360] Otherwise, Hari Singh's response to Golwalker appears to have been positive. Golwalker's appeal to 'Hindu' factors may have resonated with Singh, who by then was also under the influence of his Rajguru. Importantly, this 'god man', Swami Sant Dev, was 'in touch' with some Congress leaders.[361] One of these was Jawaharlal Nehru who, by his own admission, was 'an old friend' of the Swami.[362] Supposedly, Golwalker's visit finally changed Maharaja Hari Singh's 'rigid thinking to remain independent or to join Pakistan'.[363]

The accession to India

On 26 October 1947, J&K's status as an ostensibly independent entity ended after seventy-two days. On this day, Maharaja Hari Singh finally made an accession – to

India. The Pukhtoons' invasion of Kashmir Province on 22 October had compelled him to seek defensive assistance from this new dominion. India would only provide help if Maharaja Hari Singh acceded to it. While Singh finally chose to join India, it is impossible to know what status he *actually* desired for his princely state. Karan Singh states that, for his father, 'the prospect of becoming an independent ruler after the British withdrawal [from India] was an alluring one'.[364] Similarly, the former J&K Prime Minister, Mahajan, states that the Maharaja and his advisers 'would have been happy if such a consummation [of independence] had taken place. They entertained dreams of an independent Kashmir, a Switzerland in Asia'.[365] Seemingly, Abdullah also regarded Switzerland 'as a model' for J&K, although he wanted the people of J&K, or their elected representatives, to take the decision, not the ruler.[366] Hari Singh's Deputy Prime Minister Batra told the Indian press on 12 October 1947 that 'Despite constant rumours, we have no intention of joining either India or Pakistan'. No decision would be taken until there was 'peace on the [Punjab] plains', which then were expecting major communal violence and upheaval. Batra continued that 'The Maharaja has told me that his ambition is to make Kashmir the Switzerland of the East – a State that is completely neutral'.[367] Batra later told the Indian press that 'The only thing that will change this [non] decision is if one side or other decides to use force against us'.[368] Given what subsequently happened with the Pukhtoons' invasion, Batra either was prescient or the J&K Government knew that Pakistan was planning something. As Mahajan confirmed, the latter was the case: 'His Highness got information about this contemplated attack on the State a month before it actually came'. Provided by 'a loyal friend', the regime seemingly ignored this.[369]

Significantly, the Indians also knew beforehand about the Pukhtoons' invasion. On 27 September 1947, Nehru wrote to Patel that he was aware that the Muslim League in Punjab and NWFP were 'making preparations to enter Kashmir in considerable numbers'.[370] The intruders would enter Kashmir Province via the Jhelum Valley Road 'by the end of October or, at the latest, the beginning of November'. The 'Pakistan strategy is to infiltrate into Kashmir now and to take some big action as soon as Kashmir is more or less isolated because of the coming winter'.[371] On 2 October, Patel wrote to Maharaja Hari Singh stating that he was 'expediting' telegraph, telephone, wireless and roads links between J&K and India as 'we fully realize the need for despatch and urgency'.[372] Patel, it appears, was preparing for Singh's alignment with, or accession to, India, something Nehru suggested on 27 September should be achieved 'as rapidly as possible'.[373] On 5 October, Nehru again wrote to Patel. He enclosed a report about J&K from

Dwarkanath Kachru, Secretary of the All-India States Peoples' Conference, who had been in Srinagar (again) for four days.[374] (In mid-1946, Kachru had delivered a letter from Nehru to the Maharaja.)[375] Kachru reported that the National Conference had 'decided for the Indian Union', although its decision was yet to be announced. Additionally, Kachru discussed 'the utter collapse of [J&K's] administrative and government machinery', which alerted India that it needed options re J&K's future. On 7 October, Home Minister Patel wrote to India's Defence Minister, Sardar Baldev Singh, asking him to immediately send arms and ammunition to J&K, by air if necessary. For Patel, there was 'no time to lose', as the Pakistani intervention was 'going to be true to [the] Nazi pattern' – presumably swift, overwhelming and conclusive.[376]

Interestingly, on 23 October 1947, a Pakistan representative, Major Shah, 'Joint Secretary, Ministry of Foreign Affairs', spoke with J&K's Prime Minister, Mahajan, in Srinagar about agreeing a 'satisfactory solution' to the accession issue.[377] The Pakistani allegedly warned of possible 'serious consequences' if J&K did not join Pakistan. Ironically, Shah's meeting with Mahajan took place one day after the Pukhtoons had invaded Kashmir Province. It is not known if Mahajan and Singh – or, indeed, Shah – then knew of this actual invasion, which certainly amounted to 'serious consequences'. Probably they did. Hari Singh apparently had returned that morning from touring areas of Jammu Province affected by inter-religious violence. On his arrival in Srinagar, he had been informed about the Pukhtoons' invasion. Consequently, the same day, Batra possibly was sent to New Delhi with a letter dated 23 October and signed by Maharaja Hari Singh stating that Batra could sign an accession to India on Singh's behalf, provided (inexplicably) that the terms were the same as those for Hyderabad.[378] After Mahajan briefed the ruler about his meeting with Major Shah, Hari Singh stated that he 'was now of the view that Kashmir should not accede to Pakistan', even if this required building the Bhaderwah-Kishtwar-Chamba-Dalhousie route to connect J&K with India. Belligerently, Hari Singh said that he would build this new and difficult road 'rather than let it [J&K] go to Pakistan'.[379] Seemingly, the negative Mahajan-Shah meeting was a major turning point in Hari Singh's attitude about acceding to India. The Pukhtoons' invasion of Kashmir Province around the same time was probably the greater incentive or compulsion, however.

The invasion was a close run thing. Had the Pukhtoons, who apparently 'had been promised booty as their reward for fighting in Kashmir',[380] not got sidetracked by looting and pillaging, especially in Baramulla, Kashmir may have been 'lost' to India. The 'calamity' of the invasion began at 4.30 a.m. on 22 October. By the evening of 24 October, 'vague', yet chaos-inducing, reports of the invasion reached Srinagar. That day, people in Srinagar were celebrating two festivals: Hindu Dussehra (death of Ravan) and Muslim Id (end of Ramadan).[381] *The Times* also reported that 'armed raiders consisting of several hundred Pathans from Hazara' were supporting the pro-Pakistan, anti-maharaja 'rebel peasantry' who had gained control of Muzaffarabad District.[382] Kashmiris realised something was afoot the next day when the Mahura hydro-electric plant, to Srinagar's west, stopped transmitting power. On 27 October, the Indian Army started arriving in Srinagar. After securing the airfield, it started to engage with the invaders and repel them from Kashmir, albeit very slowly initially. On 6 November, Indian forces engaged in 'comparatively heavy fighting' with the invaders 4.5 miles west of Srinagar.[383] On 9 November, Indian forces recaptured Baramulla.[384] This was the beginning of the Indian Army ejecting the Pukhtoons from the Kashmir Valley. It may have pushed the Pukhtoons totally out of J&K, except that New Delhi ordered troops to go south to protect Poonch City, which Azad Kashmir forces then were seriously threatening.

The invaders, or raiders, as reporters often labelled them, comprised a 'mixed lot', with their exact number and composition not known. Apparently, the Pukhtoons felt some 'affinity with Kashmir', with this possibly relating to Afghan Durrani rule of Kashmir from 1752 to 1819.[385] *The Times'* correspondent estimated that, in terms of the invasion force, there were from 'several hundred to 10,000, but probably it does not exceed 3,000'. The invaders supposedly comprised: 'Muslim League agents and agitators from Pakistan'; deserters from the J&K State Forces; pro-Pakistan, anti-maharaja rebels from southwestern J&K; and, 'Pathan tribesmen who have joined the rebels partly from religious sympathy and partly for loot'.[386] A British diplomat, C. B. Duke, who visited Abbottabad in mid-November 1947, the 'nerve centre' in NWFP for the J&K operations, considered that 'Mahsuds were the dominant component of the tribal forces, but that Afridis, Mohmands, Wazirs, migratory tribes and others were also present'.[387] The Pukhtoons' destruction impacted almost exclusively on Kashmir Province and largely on Kashmiris – of all religions. Many were killed or had to flee for their lives.

The supposed primary purpose of the Pukhtoon invaders was to capture J&K for Pakistan. From the outset, however, their undisciplined invasion was perverted. Instead of rushing to capture Srinagar and Maharaja Hari Singh, the tribesmen focused on satisfying their legendary pecuniary desires. They violently looted, pillaged, raped and killed people located along the Jhelum Valley Road, all of whom, regardless of their religion, the Pukhtoons seemingly saw as either exploitable objects or expendable enemies. The British diplomat, Duke, noted that they were considered 'wolves – rapacious, quarrelsome and dangerous'.[388] Hari Singh's weakened and severely dispersed State Forces did try to oppose and delay the Pukhtoons in places, including at Uri, midway between Muzaffarabad and Baramulla, where Dogra troops destroyed 'a key bridge' over the Jhelum River. However, apart from those 'rearguard actions',[389] the Muslim Pukhtoon invaders attacked Kashmiris unable to flee – or not expecting to have to flee – regardless of their individual or collective religious persuasions. In other words, the Pukhtoons also attacked fellow Muslims. Emotionally, therefore, the invasion was a direct threat to the Kashmiris' personal security, particularly as some Kashmiris, including Sheikh Abdullah, believed that 'anything up to 200,000 Pathan tribesmen and Punjabi Muslims were gathered in training camps along the Pakistan side of the border ready to invade Kashmir territory'.[390] This was why Kashmiris in Srinagar, under National Conference leadership, quickly organised their own volunteer militia to defend themselves. Had the Pukhtoons arrived in Srinagar, these Kashmiris were prepared to have 'resisted strongly' and defended themselves.[391]

Tactically, the Pakistanis erred by invading Kashmir Province. First of all, they chose to use highly undisciplined proxy forces who were motivated more by plundering as many Kashmiris as possible than in capturing J&K for Pakistan. As a result of the Pukhtoons' brutality and rapaciousness, Pakistan quickly lost the moral high ground to India. The Pakistanis also chose the wrong area to invade. While the route to Srinagar was much closer for the Pukhtoons, and while sending them to Kashmir Province distracted and kept these marauders from looting (non-Pukhtoon) Pakistanis, as Karachi and NWFP administrators possibly feared might happen, Pakistan should have invaded Jammu Province. This was, after all, where Hindus and Sikhs allegedly had been massacring Muslims, a circumstance that had upset some Pukhtoons. An attack by pro-Pakistan forces from Pakistan's Sialkot District to the Jammu sector of the J&K-Pakistan border would have been made across much easier terrain by forces located logistically much closer to Pakistan. Such an attack very quickly could have severed the important, but then rudimentary, Jammu-Pathankot road. Such a severance would have caused J&K and India serious logistical and communication challenges. Furthermore, after securing a foothold in Jammu, the pro-Pakistan forces could have advanced towards the Kashmir Valley, although this may have been challenging if they chose to go via eastern Jammu Province where people clearly were pro-India. However, apart from using aircraft in J&K, which was difficult as the nearest Indian Air Force base was in Ambala, India then would have had few other options but to attack Pakistan directly and try to reopen the Jammu-Pathankot road or to construct the Bhaderwah-Kishtwar-Chamba-Dalhousie road to J&K from India. Alternatively, India could have gone to all-out war with Pakistan, which would have been difficult on 22 October as Maharaja Hari Singh had not then acceded to India. Ultimately, however, the Pukhtoons did more harm than good for Pakistan. As one Britisher wryly put it: the tribesmen's 'outstanding achievement … was to make up the Maharaja's mind for him'.[392] Their invasion also galvanised Patel and Nehru, who pre-invasion would have accepted J&K's accession to Pakistan, reluctantly in Nehru's case, but who after the Pukhtoons invaded, were not interested in any compromise in relation to J&K being Indian.[393]

After the accession

While J&K joined India in October 1947, this did not totally end the issue of independence for J&K. In 1947–48, some people in India still thought that it might be the best option for J&K. In late October 1947, the Indian Defence Committee – whose senior member was Lord Mountbatten in his role then as India's Governor-General – when considering whether to accept Maharaja Hari Singh's accession had apparently suggested that a possible plebiscite for J&K-ites 'should be on three choices: to join India, to join Pakistan, or to remain independent'. Prime Minister Nehru apparently responded that the 'Government of India would not mind Kashmir's remaining an independent country provided that it were within India's sphere of influence'.[394] Similarly, around the same time, Nehru apparently informed his sister on 28 October 1947 that he 'would not mind if Kashmir [became] more or less independent'.[395] According to Sheikh Abdullah, some time in 1948, the *Hindustan Times*, a leading Indian daily, also 'had advocated, in an editorial independence for Kashmir'.[396]

Perhaps most significantly, in January 1948, India's representative at the United Nations, Gopalaswami Ayyangar,[397] an old J&K 'hand', stated that:

> The question of the future status of Kashmir *vis-à-vis* her [sic] neighbours and the world at large, and a further question, namely, whether she should withdraw from her accession to India, and either accede to Pakistan or remain independent, with a right to claim admission as a Member of the United Nations – all this we have recognized to be a matter for unfettered decision by the people of Kashmir, after normal life is restored to them.[358]

That a senior Indian official suggested publicly that J&K might 'remain' independent was surprising. Presumably, as India's representative, he had New Delhi's approval to make such a statement. Soon after Ayyangar's statement, however, the choices for J&K-ites would only ever be binary: J&K could join either India or Pakistan. The so-called 'third option' of independence was never offered to the people of J&K by India or Pakistan or the United Nations in any way, including via an 'unfettered decision by the people of Kashmir', which soon would be called a 'plebiscite'. Interestingly, it was Sheikh Abdullah who had first proposed a plebiscite for the people of J&K in 1946. However, his call was to do with whether the 'present regime' of Maharaja Hari Singh should either continue in J&K or 'Quit Kashmir'.[399] Also interestingly, Pakistan initially may not have been in favour of having a plebiscite for J&K-ites. It feared that, to its detriment, J&K's restricted franchise 'confined to property owners and literate subjects who are mainly Hindu or members of the "National Conference"' would be used as the 'electoral list'.[400] This was reasonable except that there weren't many National Conference voters so enfranchised.

While it is unclear whether Maharaja Hari Singh actually wanted independence for J&K, the princely state certainly was independent from 15 August to 26 October 1947: that is, for a total of seventy-two days. This was not full independence in the sense that J&K was fully autonomous and self-governing with a set of foreign relations with, and having its own diplomatic missions located in, various other nations. Maharaja Hari Singh had not emulated the Maharaja of Travancore, for example, whose Dewan had started to instigate diplomatic relations with Pakistan when his ruler seriously sought to make his princely state independent.[401] So too had Hyderabad, which had established diplomatic relations with Pakistan and was apparently seeking them with the United States and the United Kingdom.[402] Rather, J&K had quasi independence in the sense that the new dominions of India and Pakistan largely, and seemingly ambivalently, were keeping their hands off, and out of, the princely state. Their stances were hardly surprising. The governments of both dominions were heavily pre-occupied with their own array of major post-partition problems and issues. These included accommodating the flood of refugees while trying to maintain law and order and the (vitriolic) dividing of the post-British assets, with particular emphasis on ensuring that they received their fair share. Indians and Pakistanis, particularly, then had little time, nor the capacity, to focus on Jammu and Kashmir. Thus, J&K's independence was not about its ruler actively strutting the world stage as an independent sovereign ruler with standing and stature utilising his worldwide diplomatic service and with capable armed forces able to deter potential intruders. Rather, he and his state were independent by default, not by design. Interestingly, for some J&K-ites, particularly Jammuites, the experience of J&K being independent had been 'too harrowing to inspire confidence'. Even though 'the Maharaja had aspired for independence of the State', J&K's actual independence had created a severe 'sense of uncertainty'.[403] The invasion of J&K by Pukhtoon intruders from across the border in Pakistan showed how vulnerable an independent J&K would be to external forces and influences located on or near its borders.

Why J&K did not obtain independence

It is impossible to know how keen Maharaja Hari Singh actually was in 1947 for J&K to be independent. His stance essentially was 'non-accession': to not make an accession to either dominion or, to use a Jinnahism, to hope that independence would 'fall into his lap like a ripe fruit'. This he did for seventy-two days. However, there are few indications that the Maharaja was positively pursuing independence for J&K. Beyond vaguely discussing Dogristan with some royal 'fellow travellers', he made no substantive public declaration of J&K's post-British independence. As *The Times* noted as late as 10 October, 'Kashmir has remained remote and silent in its mountain fastness. … The Maharaja has remained silent about the future of his State.'[404] For *The Economist*, Maharaja Hari Singh was 'sitting on the fence – or on the elephant's trunk, if a more Indian simile may be used'.[405] Perhaps the only thing certain is that this Hindu ruler never seriously contemplated joining his princely state with Muslim Pakistan, whose 'aggressive Muslim communalism' he disliked.[406] By being indecisive, however, Hari Singh set himself up to fail. By doing nothing about J&K's status, he achieved nothing; by saying nothing about this matter, he encouraged rumours; by meeting more Indians than Pakistanis, he fueled resentment; by being aloof, he endeared himself to few people; by not making an accession, he encouraged others to take their own actions to ensure that J&K joined their dominion of choice. Consequently, there would be no independent 'Switzerland of the East'.

Despite Hari Singh's personal inertia and inabilities, for him to have secured independence for J&K in such tumultuous times would have been a major achievement. That said, the time was actually ripe for a brave and bold ruler to assert himself and proclaim independence for his state. The British had left the subcontinent; Indian and Pakistani leaders were heavily distracted trying to establish their own nations; the world was entering an extended phase of decolonisation supported, even encouraged, by the world's most powerful nation, the United States. It would have been interesting to see what both dominions could, and would, have done had Maharaja Hari Singh actually declared an independent

Jammu and Kashmir State. Certainly, India and Pakistan would have continued to compete over J&K – if only to deprive it from the other's control or sphere of interest. Hari Singh did have 'Bahadur' (brave, in Persian) in his princely title, which suggested that he might be prepared to be bold about J&K's status. However, he not only proved unwilling to assert himself in the uncertain political circumstances and opportunities that 1947 offered him and his regime, but also he severely vacillated. This was because the Maharaja of Jammu and Kashmir State was more of a 'regal-utionary' than a revolutionary. He was an aristocratic autocrat neither able, nor prepared, to 'get his hands dirty' by taking a major political risk to pro-actively pursue independence for J&K. In this sense, he was the total opposite of his ruthless and opportunistic forebear, Gulab Singh. When seriously challenged by the circumstances of 1947, Hari Singh proved to be highly deficient, after which his regime crumbled rapidly and he equally quickly was sidelined.

Ultimately, it was Maharaja Hari Singh's vacillation that disempowered him. He 'took just as much time to decide about [his] accession as was necessary to bring his downfall'.[407] Wooed beforehand by Indians and Pakistanis, potential then actual after 15 August 1947, and counselled and supported by Britishers, he could have asserted himself and negotiated a position of power or influence in India or Pakistan. After he made his accession, however, he rapidly lost power, prestige and usefulness, although, interestingly, the concept of an independent Jammu and Kashmir did not end. On 20 June 1949, Maharaja Hari Singh appointed Yuvraj Karan Singh as Regent of J&K. Concurrently, he left J&K, never to return. Hari Singh apparently had long been waiting for his son 'to be twenty-one so that he could hand over the State responsibilities and then do the things he loved – shoot, fish, cook, race and build'.[408] Thereafter the former ruler lived in Bombay. His partial compensation was to receive a privy purse which the Government of India actually had to pay as Sheikh Abdullah, his former rival now in power in J&K, refused to do so.[409] On 14 November 1952, Dogra rule of J&K was officially terminated.[410] Thereafter, Maharaja Hari Singh essentially became, if it was possible, just another Indian citizen.

3

The significance of Kashmir and Kashmiri identity in J&K

This chapter provides important historical and social background about J&K and its administrative structure, as well as some geo-political observations about this princely state. It explains why Jammu and Kashmir was popularly, but confusingly, called 'Kashmir' not 'Jammu', and why the Kashmir region was the most important and popular region in J&K in 1947. The chapter's other observations chiefly concern the Kashmir region and Kashmiri Muslims, their relationships with other J&K-ites, and why people have always focused on them. This dynamic is important to understand as it helps to explain why Kashmir enjoyed greater status and was more significant politically in 1947 than either the Jammu region or the Frontier Districts region. In this tumultuous year, the major ramification of Kashmir's importance was that subcontinental politicians desired Kashmir and wooed Kashmiris far more than other J&K-ites. Indeed, they focused almost exclusively on this region and its residents; the other areas of J&K appeared to be peripheral. Additionally, in 1947 and thereafter, Kashmir and Kashmiris quickly came to dominate politics in J&K and in relation to the Kashmir dispute. To the chagrin of other J&K-ites, particularly Jammuites and Ladakhis, and also many Indians, Kashmiris' higher profile in J&K continues to be the case – and a major challenge for India.

This chapter also comprehensively explores the significant and ongoing issues of Kashmiri identity and Kashmiri nationalism and why these are important factors within J&K. Who or what actually comprises a nation is difficult to determine, including in relation to Kashmir. Much of it involves individuals' self-perceptions. For the *Dictionary of International Relations*, a nation is 'a vague notion which refers to a social collectivity, the members of which share some or all of the following: a sense of common identity, a history, a language, ethnic or racial origins, religion, a common economic life, a geographical location and a political base. However, these criteria and characteristics are often present in different degrees and combinations. ... Nations can exist without a political identity (e.g., the Jewish nation during the Diaspora)'.[1]

Out of the term 'nation' comes the important term nationalism. This comprises 'Devotion to one's nation'.[2] If you actively support your nation, you are a 'nationalist' engaging in 'nationalism'. A further aspect is that 'groups claiming treatment as nations, [feel] deserving of their own nations. ... [they] dream of a more perfect alignment of identity and territory'.[3] A shorter definition states that 'Nationalism is an ideology based on the belief that a people with common characteristics such as language, religion or ethnicity constitutes a separate and distinctive political community',[4] or nation.

Kashmir and Kashmiris comprise such a community or nation. As this chapter discusses, Kashmiris have long believed in, and been devoted to, a Kashmir 'nation' – the 'Kashmiri *quom*' (or *quam*).[5] In 1947, a major challenge for subcontinental politicians was how to accommodate Kashmiris' broad and narrow aspirations, in the form of nationalism, within the emerging and broader Indian or Pakistani nationalisms, and indeed within the politically and physically disintegrating J&K state itself. As Sheikh Abdullah put it, the issue was about accommodating 'a great nation questing and struggling after its identity', a struggle that he could say 'with certainty' would 'continue into the future too'.[6] In this, he proved to be correct.

Important antecedents in J&K

Although Maharaja Hari Singh ended his aspirations for independence by acceding to India on 26 October 1947, some important antecedents are worth discussing, particularly in relation to Kashmir, Kashmiris and Kashmiri nationalism. The first concerns how Jammu and Kashmir came into being. In 1846, all Kashmiris came under the control and domination of the Dogra 'southerners' from Jammu. This had important consequences for Kashmiris – and later for the 1947 decolonisation of the British Raj. From 1846 to 1947, four Hindu Dogra Maharajas ruled J&K. Maharaja Gulab Singh, who founded both J&K and its Dogra dynasty, ruled from 1846 to 1856.[7] His third son, Ranbir Singh, ruled from 1856 to 1885. (Ranbir's two elder brothers had predeceased him.) Ranbir's eldest son, Pratap Singh, ruled from 1885 until 1925, but with some 'assistance' between 1889 and 1905 from a British-dominated Council of State (or Regency) and his ambitious younger brother, Raja Amar Singh. The paramount power imposed this Council on Maharaja Pratap Singh due to his alleged disorganisation and 'serious maladministration'.[8] However, he was also in a weaker situation than his Dogra forebears as, by 1889, the British had consolidated, and entrenched, their rule of Punjab and, indeed, of India. During the Council of State's rule, three important strategic developments took place: a British Resident dominated J&K; the British took control of the Gilgit Agency; and, the Jhelum Valley Highway was constructed. Supposedly 'highly respected' by his subjects,[9] Pratap Singh's powers were partially restored in 1905 and fully restored in 1921. In 1925, Hari Singh, Gulab Singh's great grandson and the nephew of the childless Pratap, became ruler of J&K. The fourth and final Dogra ruler, Maharaja Hari Singh ruled until 20 June 1949, when he appointed his son, Karan Singh, Regent. On 14 November 1952, the Government of Indian J&K officially ended Dogra rule of J&K.[10]

Dogra rule came to J&K following the British defeat of the Sikhs in the first Anglo-Sikh War in 1846. (British forces also won the second Anglo-Sikh War in 1849.) The victorious East India Company then concluded two consecutive treaties. The first was the Treaty of Lahore on 9 March, which, amongst other matters, imposed reparations on the losers. The second, exactly a week later, was the Treaty of Amritsar with Raja Gulab Singh who, in 1846, assisted the British against the Sikhs.[11] According to the Frenchman, Victor Jacquemont, who met Gulab Singh in 1831, he 'was a soldier of fortune and a usurper'.[12] Along with his younger brothers, Dhyan and Suchet, these three Singh brothers from Jammu had enjoyed considerable influence and notoriety at Emperor Ranjit Singh's Lahore Court until his death in 1839. Dhyan, who became Ranjit Singh's Prime Minister in 1828, and Suchet, were particular favourites of the Emperor.[13] In the post-Ranjit political turmoil, their power and status diminished when Dhyan was assassinated in 1843 and Suchet was killed in 1844. Gulab remained alive, but possibly with some blood on his hands. Allegedly, Gulab was 'inferior ... in talent' to his younger brothers, particularly Dhyan.[14] Nevertheless, most Britishers generally considered him to be very capable, although some disliked him, even though, or possibly because, he perfidiously assisted the British to defeat the discombobulated Sikhs. Herbert Edwardes, for example, who had been Gulab Singh's political advisor in 1846,[15] considered the Dogra ruler to be 'a bad king, a miser, and a liar! If he is not all this, and a thousand times worse (for he is the worst native I ever came in contact with).'[16] Edwardes' boss, Henry Lawrence,[17] a signatory with Gulab Singh on the Treaty of Amritsar, considered the Dogra to be 'a bad man' and 'a man of indifferent character', although, pragmatically, 'there are few princes who were any better'.[18] While the character of their ally, Gulab Singh, left a lot to be desired, the British at that stage had little choice but to be involved with this Jammuite as they then knew few, if any, Kashmiris. By 1846, less than ten Europeans had ever visited Kashmir.[19]

As a result of the Treaty of Amritsar, which flowed from the Treaty of Lahore, the British ratified Gulab Singh's control of Jammu. More importantly, they sold the territory that comprised Kashmir, along with its entire residential population of Muslims, Hindus and Sikhs, to the Dogra. As a consequence, the princely state of Jammu and Kashmir came into being. The British agreed the Treaty of Amritsar to reward the wily Gulab and his capable forces for their neutrality – or treachery – during the first Anglo-Sikh War against Singh's former overlords, the Sikhs. The non-participation of these Jammu forces significantly helped, even enabled, the British to win their first war against the militarily strong Sikhs who had expected that General Gulab Singh would fight with, and, indeed, would direct, their military forces. For his services to the British, Gulab Singh secured the indefeasible (i.e., not forfeitable) title to 'Jammu and Kashmir'. As a result, he became the owner of all of the lands there, as well as the absolute ruler over all of the people there.[20]

The British provided assistance to Maharaja Gulab Singh to enable him to establish his rule over the unruly Kashmiris, led by the popular, Sikh-appointed Governor, Sheikh Ghulam Mohi-ud-Din, who briefly opposed the imposition of Dogra rule in Kashmir. However, with British military support, the Jammuite soon became the ruler of the newly created political entity of Jammu and Kashmir. In 1857, Gulab Singh died. By about 1861, his son, Maharaja Ranbir Singh, had consolidated J&K. The final area that he incorporated into J&K was the large, strategically important Frontier Districts Province in J&K's north and northeast. It comprised the vast, remote and lightly populated, but mountainous and difficult-to-access, regions of Gilgit and Baltistan. Gulab Singh had possessed Baltistan, along with Ladakh, since 1842, when General Zorawar Singh had captured them for him. The British permitted Gulab and Ranbir to add the Gilgit area, and its various sub-districts, located north of the Indus River, to their domain. This went beyond the original terms of the Treaty of Amritsar by which the British had 'made over' to Gulab Singh 'all the hilly or mountainous country with its dependencies situated to the eastward of the River Indus.'[21] Despite such largesse, the strategically nervous British nevertheless decided to directly administer the frontier areas via the Gilgit Agency, from 1889, and the Gilgit Leased Area, from 1935. This was due to their strategic sensitivity.

Dogra rule had some important impacts on the Kashmiri psyche. For the first time in their long history, Kashmiris and their lands were not directly captured by an external force, as had happened when the Mughals, Afghans and Sikhs each militarily seized the Kashmir Valley. Instead, Kashmiris were traded – sold is more accurate – by the victorious British in what essentially was a real estate transaction. The 'consideration' for this transaction amounted to some Rs 7.5 million, with 'fifty lakhs to be paid on ratification of this treaty and twenty-five lakhs [to be paid] on or before the first October 1846'.[22] This 'deal' satisfied the mercantile victors' need to obtain reparations from the defeated Sikhs to cover the costs of their war. The Kashmiris, therefore, were merely the booty of war. They had no say in the sale or transfer of their lands, and of themselves, to Gulab Singh's control. As Sheikh Abdullah has noted, they were part of a 'sale deed, this instrument of subjugation, handed by the East India Company agents to a bunch of Dogras'.[23] (Abdullah's critics claim that this was a binding, non-abrogable treaty made between two equal parties, although these critics also forget that the British had no qualms unilaterally abrogating the Treaty of Amritsar in 1947.)[24] At his formal investiture as the ruler of J&K on 15 March 1846, Maharaja Gulab Singh confirmed the mercantile nature of his deal with the British. He expressed his gratitude to the British Viceroy' and informed him 'without however any ironical meaning, that he was indeed his Zurkhureed or gold-boughten slave'.[25] Gulab Singh had purchased, not captured, Kashmir.

Second, Dogra rule over Kashmiris meant that Kashmiris continued to be subjects of, and supplicants to, an external ruler. Equally, this relationship bound Jammuites to Kashmir and Kashmiris. Despite British attempts, on occasions, to limit or curtail the Dogras' power and influence, the Jammuites dominated J&K's administration and its politics from 1846 until late 1947. They had a significant advantage over previous external rulers of J&K: they were much closer geographically to Kashmir than the Mughals, Afghans or Sikhs had been. Indeed, they were contiguous or 'just down the road', so to speak. Their home region of Jammu was situated immediately south and southwest of the Kashmir Valley, just beyond the natural boundary of the Pir Panjal Range. This closeness enabled the Dogras to successfully intrude politically, administratively and militarily into Kashmir. From 1872, it also enabled the regime to emulate the British tradition of having two capitals between which the *durbar* (administration) moved each year in order to enjoy the better weather in each locale.[26] Up until 1872, Jammu City had been 'the capital of the whole country', i.e., J&K.[27] Thereafter, the J&K durbar operated in Jammu City in winter, and in Srinagar in summer. Dogra rule also facilitated trade between the two provinces. Jammu Province imported 'charas [an intoxicating preparation made from a species of hemp], rice and other crops, seeds, fruits, ghee, wool and wollens [sic], cotton clothes, hides, drugs, leather, namadas [pieces of felt], dyeing material and so on'.[28] Kashmir Province imported 'turmeric, grains and pulses, oils, seeds, ghee, wool, cotton piece goods, livestock, sugar, opium, silk, spices, silver, apparels, metals, provisions and tobacco and so on'.[29]

Third, Jammuites arguably understood Kashmir and Kashmiris better than any previous external rulers. This made it more difficult for Kashmiris to throw off this foreign yoke. Though neighbours, Kashmiris and Jammuites were culturally different, with varying languages, dress, housing, habits and religious practices. Indeed, Jammuites had more in common with Punjabis than with Kashmiris. Nevertheless, men from Jammu, in particular Gulab Singh, had campaigned in Kashmir as early as 1813 when the Sikhs first attempted to capture the region from the Afghan Durranis and/or had served in Kashmir when the Sikhs had ruled this province after 1819. Indeed, Ranjit Singh had sent Gulab Singh and another 'trusted lieutenant' to capture Kashmir in 1819. In 1842, at the 'fag end' of the Sikh Empire's control, Raja Gulab Singh was again ordered there to deal with an uprising in the province.[30] Just prior to that, General Zorawar Singh had captured Ladakh and Baltistan for the Jammu Raja, on behalf of the Sikh Empire. This extended the Jammu kingdom's borders across the Himalayas into Tibet and made Gulab Singh the first Indian ruler for some time to actually expand India's geo-political boundaries.[31] Knowing much about Kashmir, the commercial term *caveat emptor* (let the buyer beware) did not apply in 1846 to Raja Gulab Singh: he knew exactly what he was 'purchasing' from the British. Indeed, Gulab's knowledge of Kashmir and Kashmiris enabled him to dominate and govern Kashmiris and to suppress any Kashmiri nationalism that had been temporarily alive in 1846.

Fourth, even though J&K's population was strongly Muslim, the Dogra rulers actually favoured Hindus. As a result, Muslim Kashmiris essentially became third-class 'citizens', or subjects, to non-Muslims, particularly Hindu J&K-ites from Jammu, then to Hindu Kashmiri Pandits. In 1947, the regime considered J&K to be a Hindu state, even though it actually, and contradictorily, had a Muslim-majority population. Indeed, 'The "Hindu-ness" of the state became a critical element in its legitimacy'.[32] (Surprisingly, Sheikh Abdullah, who generally had little positive to say about Hari Singh, states that the Maharaja 'always appeared to be free from religious prejudices' and was 'close to his Muslim courtiers'.)[33] In 1945, most senior officials, or courtiers, were Hindus, with only seventeen of sixty-six (26 per cent) listed 'Chief Officers' being non-Hindus: five British; twelve Muslims.[34] Beneath them, Muslims 'formed about 40 per cent' of 'the total strength of the civil services'.[35] In the 'superior service', there were 525 Gazetted officials, of whom 159 were Muslims (30 per cent). Below them were 13,790 non-Gazetted officials, of whom 5,070 were

Muslims (37 per cent). In the 'inferior service' in 1945, there were 7,934 officials, of whom 3,760 were Muslims (47 per cent). Muslims were heavily under represented in the J&K administration.

Hindus dominated J&K in other ways. They were dominant in the J&K State Forces, although Major General H. L. Scott, a Britisher, was the Chief of the Military Staff from 1936 to 1947.[36] Of the 9,100 J&K soldiers in 1939, Muslims comprised a maximum of 25 per cent.[37] Partly, this was because Kashmiris were debarred from military service in the 'Jammu army'[38] as they were 'considered a non-martial race'.[39] Of the non-Muslim soldiers, about 63 per cent were Hindus from the Maharaja's own Dogra community,[40] which 'look[ed] upon itself as a royal clan'[41] and upon J&K as 'sort of Rajput oligarchy'.[42] This circumstance made it difficult for Pandit Kashmiris who, while Brahmans not Rajputs, traditionally had been prevalent in the J&K administration. While their prevalence was partly because they were Hindu co-religionists with the Dogras, Pandits also were intelligent, well educated and skilled. Thus, Dogra domination was not as bad for Kashmiri Pandits, many of whom actively participated with, or in, the Dogra regime. There was some 'logic' for this. Traditionally Hindu Kashmiris consisted of two groups that, essentially, had consolidated during Kashmir's Sultanate period in response to Kashmir increasingly coming under the sway of Islam. The majority *karkun* faction 'specialized in the secular sphere … and undertook administrative employment', and particularly had 'a tradition of government service', while *bhasha bhatts* were usually priests who 'engaged in ritual practices requiring knowledge of Sanskrit'.[43] Zutshi similarly identifies them as Karkun Pandits, who were 'largely identifiable with a quill-driver, while a Gour Pandit was a priest'.[44] The former group was numerically 'preponderant', economically 'better off' and socially superior. This was mainly because of their 'long traditions as administrative servants' for various Kashmiri and external rulers.[45]

Under Maharaja Pratap Singh, however, the Pandits' position weakened after the Council of State made an edict that Urdu, not Persian, would be the state language and after the regime started employing Urdu-speaking Punjabis. This agitated the Pandits, few of whom then spoke Urdu. As early as 1910, they began an anti-Punjabi agitation in J&K. Later, they similarly agitated when Maharaja Hari Singh continued this 'Rajput oligarchy' that favoured Jammuites, many of whom the Pandits considered to be 'mediocre' or sycophantic.[46] Indeed, Hari Singh's 'partiality for the Rajputs … left the Kashmiris much dissatisfied'.[47] Consequently, from 1925 to 1931, educated Kashmiri Pandits began a 'Kashmir for Kashmiris' campaign in which they sought better access to public positions, freedom of the press and of association, and a representative legislature.[48] These Hindu Kashmiris were not seeking independence from their Dogra co-religionists, just more economic 'freedom' and wellbeing, including at the expense of Kashmiri Muslims, if necessary. While this movement was confined to the Kashmiri Hindu Pandit community, it was an early attempt to revive Kashmiri nationalism, albeit narrow. Hindu Kashmiris therefore 'stole a march' on their Muslim Kashmiri brethren.[49] Their campaign, which was motivated by 'resentment against outsiders', was the 'first expression of the popular Movement [sic] in Kashmir'.[50]

The structure of Jammu and Kashmir in 1947

Another antecedent worth examining is the actual structure and composition of Jammu and Kashmir in 1947. Significantly in 1947, J&K had a Muslim-majority population. According to the 1941 Census, an invaluable source of information (see Table 3.1), J&K had a population of 4,021,616. However, the state's ethnic and social composition was complex, although the Census did not actually use the terms 'ethnic' or 'ethnicity'. Instead, people described themselves, or Census collectors classified them, as: Dogras, Rajputs, Brahmans (or Brahmins), Thakkars, Jats, Untouchables, Gujjars, Bakarwals, Poonchis, Syeds, Afghans, Punjabis, Maliks, Mians, Sikhs, Kashmiris, Pandits, Bodhs, Baltis, Shins and Yashkins.[51] In terms of religion, Muslims comprised 3.1 million people or 77 per cent of the state's population; Hindus comprised 20 per cent, or 823,000 people.[52] These percentages had not changed since 1931, when J&K's population was 3.6 million, of whom 2.8 million, or 77 per cent, were Muslims.[53] Of J&K Muslims, the most populous, homogenous and important group were Muslim Kashmiris.

While J&K's Muslim-majority religious demography suggested that the state should join Pakistan, the matter was not that simple. Significantly, the people of J&K were not unified in 1947 in their political aspirations for J&K's post-British status. Hindus in Jammu Province and Buddhists in Ladakh, in the south of the Frontier Districts Province, wanted the princely state to join India. Many Muslims in both of these provinces, however, wanted J&K to join Pakistan. Contradictorily, many Muslims in the Kashmir Valley, which sub-region's population comprised the bulk of J&K's third province, Kashmir Province, probably favoured J&K joining India. Equally, Kashmiris confusingly often displayed photos in their houses or businesses of Sheikh Abdullah, Allama Iqbal and Mohammad Ali Jinnah, whose aspirations for Kashmir differed.[54] Possibly, this was because, broadly speaking, Kashmiris were relatively secular. Correctly, Sheikh Abdullah noted that Jinnah

Muslim League's party was 'primarily represented' by 'powerful [Muslim] landlords', a particularly unattractive factor for him and many suppressed rural Kashmiris.[55] However, had J&K Muslims been unified in 1947 in their desire for J&K to join Pakistan, it would have been almost impossible for Maharaja Hari Singh to accede to India. The sheer compulsion of such an overwhelming majority would have been telling, particularly as the bulk of these pro-Pakistan elements would have been located closer to Pakistan than to India and would have had existing geo-economic and social links with this new dominion. J&K's pro-India elements, on the other hand, were located east of the Chenab River that flowed through (and roughly divided) Jammu Province, or were located in southern parts of the remote Frontier Districts Province.

In 1947, another important factor to note in relation to J&K was the regime's lack of popularity. The four Hindu Dogras who had ruled this Muslim-majority princely state for 101 years were disdainful of public opinion. With the benefit of British backing, these autocrats had never sought, nor seen the need, to popularise their rule or to develop the notion of a unified or supportive J&K citizenry. As a result, the Dogras from Jammu were not universally popular with non-Jammuites and Muslims, particularly Kashmiri Muslims. There was no 'strong personal link between the Raja [ruler] and his people', as Walter Lawrence, a Britisher who knew J&K and India well, believed existed positively among rulers and their subjects in many other Indian states.[56] Indeed, in 1947, Hari Singh's chief aspiration appeared to be to ensure the continuation of Dogra rule over 'his' state and 'his' subjects.[57] Consequently, lacking the affection of his subjects, but also lacking any ability or meaningful way to garner, or indeed marshal, the support of J&K-ites, Hari Singh stood alone. He could not rely on the unequivocal support of 'his' subjects, whatever accession he finally decided to make. Additionally, he confronted popular political rivals with a clear vision for J&K's post-British future. Locally, these were Sheikh Abdullah and Chaudhri Ghulam Abbas; externally, they chiefly were Jawaharlal Nehru and Mohammad Ali Jinnah. Seemingly, Hari Singh was disinterested in all of them. This reluctance to engage gave him a semblance of appearing to be even-handed regarding India's future and the possible creation of Pakistan. In reality, his non-engagement was more likely due to his regal aloofness.

A further factor in relation to J&K in 1947 was that J&K Muslims did not suffer from a 'minority complex' as did other Muslims living as minorities throughout India. To attempt to assuage Muslims' fears of being politically subjugated by the more populous Hindu community, the departing British had finally agreed to establish Pakistan. The most anxious subcontinental Muslims, and the ones 'more vehemently' in favour of the creation of Pakistan, were often those 'hemmed in by the Hindu majority'.[58] As one Kashmiri put it, though, 'The minority complex, which gave birth to the Muslim League's two-nation theory, was not the Kashmiris' malaise'.[59] Muslims were the majority population everywhere in J&K, except in eastern parts of Jammu Province. The certainty of the British departure in 1947 nevertheless unleashed massive emotions and expectations amongst J&K-ites. Increasingly, people began to strongly, and publicly, identify as 'Muslims' or 'Hindus', with this usually reflecting the dominion they wanted J&K to join. Many Muslims wanted J&K to join 'Muslim' Pakistan. Most non-Muslims (Hindus, Sikhs, Jains, Untouchables, Christians, etc.) wanted J&K to join secular India, which dominion nevertheless would have a majority population of (disparate and amorphous) Hindus. As J&K-ites wrestled with their future throughout 1947, their biggest challenge was to determine, then to satisfy, their personal aspirations for J&K's future status.

In 1947, J&K's three provinces were all different. Table 3.1 provides each province's area, population and religious composition. Of note, Jammu Province was J&K's second largest and most populous province. Kashmir Province was J&K's smallest but second most populous province. The Frontier Districts was J&K's largest, but least populated, province, comprising an area five times larger than Jammu Province but with a population roughly one-sixth the size. Of J&K's total population, there were 2.1 million males and 1.9 million females.[60] This gender imbalance was due to high levels of 'infantile and maternal mortality' and the prevalence of female infanticide.[61] It was reflected in J&K's political and administrative situations, which men thoroughly dominated.

Challengingly, J&K was 'one of the most mountainous countries [sic] in the world'.[62] All of it was mountainous except for a 'comparatively small area' bordering Punjab and the Kashmir Valley's flatlands. Many of these mountains were in the Frontier Districts Province, which was a remote, vast and 'sparsely populated mountainous waste'.[63] Four mountain ranges met and merged in the Gilgit area: Hindu Kush, Pamirs, Karakorams and western Himalayas. This province was difficult to access, with 'no roads worth the name' in the Frontier Districts.[64] Conversely, Jammu Province was part of the greater Indo-Gangetic plain, with its 'natural position' being in Punjab,[65] a factor that essentially made Jammu 'part and parcel' of mainland India, from which it was relatively easy to access. The province was flattish and irrigable, apart from the arid 'Kandi' foothills that rose to 2,000 feet above sea level in northern parts of the province.[66] Jammu City was 1,200 feet above sea level; by comparison, nearby Sialkot, the closest

Table 3.1   The princely state of Jammu and Kashmir in 1941

Province	Area (square miles)	Population	Religious composition	
			Percentage	Number
Jammu	12,378	1,981,433	61.19 Muslims	1,212,405
			37.19 Hindus	736,862
			1.41 Sikhs	27,896
			0.21 Others (Jains, Christians, Buddhists, etc.)[a]	4,270
Kashmir	8,539	1,728,705	93.48 Muslims	1,615,928
			4.95 Hindus	85,531
			1.56 Sikhs	27,001
			0.01 Others[a]	245
Frontier Districts	63,554	311,478	86.86 Muslims	270,539
			12.89 Buddhists	40,164
			0.25 Hindus, Unspecified Others and Sikhs[b]	775
State total	84,471	4,021,616	77.06 Muslims	3,098,872
			20.46 Hindus	822,955
			1.37 Sikhs	54,975
			1.01 Buddhists	40,684
			0.10 Unspecified Others	4,130

Source: *Census of India, 1941*, Volume XXII, *Jammu & Kashmir State*, Part III: Village Tables, Srinagar, R. G. Wreford, Editor, Jammu and Kashmir Government, 1942.
Notes: [a] Breakdown of figures not provided; [b] Only the Ladakh District had Hindus, Sikhs or Unspecified Others.

town in (British, later Pakistani) Punjab, was 829 feet above sea level.[67] Kashmir Province was also known as the 'Jhelum Valley division'.[68] The Kashmir Valley was wholly within this province. With an 'altitude of about 5,600 feet', this valley comprised relatively flat, fertile agricultural land encircled by mountains, with the large city of Srinagar, at its centre.[69] It was some '84 miles long by 20 to 25 miles broad'.[70]

While only 5.6 per cent of J&K was cultivable, agriculture was 'by far the most important industry' in J&K.[71] The next most important industries of 'forest exploitation, sericulture and fruit growing' were also 'closely allied with agriculture and the State must be described as almost entirely agricultural'.[72] Of J&K's land, 18 per cent of Jammu Province was cultivable, 19 per cent of Kashmir Province was cultivable, but little of the Frontier Districts was cultivable: less than 1 per cent of Gilgit District, and a miniscule 0.28 per cent of Ladakh.[73] Of this cultivable land,

15 per cent was double cropped each year, 35 per cent was irrigable. This comprised 50 per cent of Kashmir Province's cultivable land and 14.4 per cent of Jammu Province's;[74] the Frontier Districts had some localised water channels.[75] Adequate rainfall therefore was a matter of 'prime importance'. In spite of J&K's size, there was 'serious overcrowding of the land'.[76] In 1941, J&K's overall population density was forty-eight persons per square mile. Specifically, Kashmir Province had 202 persons per square mile, Jammu had 160 persons per square mile, and the Frontier Districts had five persons per square mile.[77] When based on 'cultivated' or 'purely agricultural areas',[78] the population density exceeded 1,000 persons per square mile in most districts. In some areas of Anantnag District, in Kashmir Province, and in the Frontier Districts Province, the population density approached 2,000 persons per square mile.[79] Not surprisingly, most non-agricultural industries were located on the flatter lands in and around the cities of Jammu and Srinagar and around the towns of Anantnag and Baramulla in the Kashmir Valley.[80]

A further important factor was that, while the Dogra regime legally possessed all of J&K, British support was the 'glue' that had compelled the state to adhere.[81] When this support was withdrawn, J&K confronted serious challenges. Until August 1947, the J&K Government directly controlled Jammu Province, Kashmir Province, which included Astore (geographically in the Frontier Districts Province), and Ladakh District.[82] The Maharaja directly governed with the assistance of a 'Council of Ministers' presided over by his appointed Prime Minister and which, in 1945, included Ministers for Development, Revenue, Public Works, and Home.[83] The administration of J&K was

> divided into districts and tehsils under the executive control of the Revenue Department at the head of which is the Revenue Minister who is assisted by a Revenue Commissioner and a Director of Land Records. The senior revenue officer in each of the two provinces of Jammu and Kashmir is called the Governor of the Province. District officers are called Wazirs, tehsil officers, Tehsildars and the latter's assistants, Naib-Tehsildars.[84]

As the Revenue Department's name implied, its primary function was to collect revenue, chiefly from land use. The senior revenue officer in Jammu and Kashmir provinces was designated as its governor, with their respective headquarters in Jammu City and Srinagar. The senior official for Ladakh District was the Wazir-i-Wazarat (Head of Administration) based in Leh.[85] He reported directly to the Revenue Minister.[86] In 1931, the average area of a district in J&K was 6,501 square miles. If the huge Frontier Districts Province was excluded from calculations, the average district size diminished in area to a more manageable 2,400 square miles.[87]

Challengingly, four parts of J&K were outside the Maharaja's direct control: Poonch, Chenani, Gilgit Agency, and Gilgit Leased Area. All except Chenani would cause him serious problems in 1947. Poonch and Chenani were jurisdictional jagirs (hereditary estates) subject to the Maharaja's 'overlordship'.[88] The Muslim-dominant Poonch Jagir (1,627 square miles; population 422,000)[89] was situated in western Jammu Province. The Raja of Poonch was a distant cousin of the Maharaja, as Poonch's forebear, Dhyan Singh, had been given possession of the Poonch region. Poonch had a small administration, a small army, limited powers and was totally under his cousin's suzerainty, a situation Hari Singh had ensured after becoming J&K's ruler in 1925.[90] Hindu-majority Chenani Jagir (ninety-five square miles;[91] population 12,000),[92] surrounded entirely by Jammu Province's Udhampur District, was inconsequential.[93] In J&K's far north, the Government of India (i.e., the British) directly administered Gilgit Agency (15,000 square miles; population 77,000) and Gilgit Leased Area (1,500 square miles; population 22,000).[94] The British controlled the strategic Gilgit Agency from 1877 to 1881 and from 1889 in order to limit Russian (later Soviet) or Chinese influence. In 1947, this Agency comprised Chilas, Hunza, Ishkuman, Kuh-Ghizar, Nagar, Punial and Yasin.[95] From 1935, the British controlled Gilgit Leased Area, which was focused on territory on 'the right bank of the Indus' and on Gilgit town,[96] after leasing the 'Trans-Indus portion of the Gilgit Wazarat' (district) from J&K for sixty years.[97] For the J&K Government, its nominal possession of these two northern areas comprised the 'Trans-Indus *Illaqa*' (region).[98]

A British Political Agent, supported by a local British-officered militia called the Gilgit Scouts, maintained 'absolute control of both Gilgit areas. Significantly, on 1 August 1947, exactly twelve years after first leasing Gilgit Leased Area,[99] the British publicly retroceded it and the Gilgit Agency to J&K.[100] Both areas added to J&K's (post-British) strategic attractiveness – and to its challenges.[101] From early August, Hari Singh's (Hindu) Governor, Brigadier Ghansara Singh, sought to re-establish (Hindu) Dogra rule over Muslims who had been living under the religiously benign British administration. To ensure continuity, Ghansara Singh continued to have two British officers oversee the Gilgit Scouts, whose members were all Muslims.[102] Problematically, these British officers turned out to be pro-Pakistan.

By 15 August 1947, J&K was again administratively 'whole' and under Maharaja Hari Singh's control. Concurrently, however, his rule was weakening. In Poonch, pro-Pakistan Muslims had begun an anti-ruler agitation soon after partition. This insurgency quickly severed western parts of Jammu Province from Hari Singh's control, particularly large parts of Poonch Jagir and Mirpur District. In September–October, there was serious inter-religious violence between pro-Pakistan Muslims and pro-India Hindus and Sikhs, which killed or dislocated thousands. On 22 October, Pukhtoons invaded Kashmir Province. Two days later, rebel Muslim Poonchis announced that they had formed a Provisional Azad (Free) Government for J&K in the 'liberated' or freed areas, to which they also added much of Muzaffarabad District. Their announcement was made two days before Maharaja Hari Singh acceded to India. This Azad Kashmir 'government' supposedly was 'assuming the administration of the [entire] state'.[103] Despite such ambitions, Pakistan did not grant this entity *de jure* recognition. Indeed, Pakistan's 'Heads of Agreement' with Azad Kashmir leaders in April 1949 downgraded this government to a 'local authority' and confined its activities to Azad Kashmir.[104] This reflected the United Nations Commission for India and Pakistan's resolution of August 1948 that had not mentioned Azad Kashmir but which, instead, had talked of 'local authorities' administering the territory to be 'evacuated by the Pakistani troops'.[105] In Gilgit, Governor Ghansara Singh survived politically until early November 1947 when various locals, possibly encouraged by the two British military officers overseeing the Gilgit Scouts,[106] staged an uprising and sought to join Gilgit, and its various districts, with Pakistan. Soon after, Pakistan sent an administrator to this area.

The significance of Kashmir in J&K in 1947

Despite these various actions, political attention in 1947 was focused predominantly on the Kashmir Valley. One obvious, and significant, reason for this was because Maharaja Hari Singh, the person deciding J&K's political future, was in residence in Srinagar contemplating his options. More notably, the Kashmir region had compactness, a large and fairly homogenous population, and prestige, factors that were important (and which remain so). In area, Kashmir (i.e., the Kashmir Valley) was approximately 6,100 square miles. It comprised the districts of Anantnag (2,800 square miles; population 852,000) and Baramulla (3,300 square miles; population 612,000). These two districts, along with the smaller, less populous Muzaffarabad District to their west (2,400 square miles; population 265,000), comprised Kashmir Province.[107]

Within J&K, Kashmir (i.e., the Kashmir Valley) was the most popular and politically significant region. As Table 3.2 below suggests, its population had 'critical mass'. Based on figures in the 1941 Census, Muslims living in the Kashmir Valley comprised a third of all J&K-ites, 44 per cent of the state's entire Muslim population,

Table 3.2 *The Kashmir Valley: area, population and religious mix*

District	Area (square miles)	Population
Anantnag District: tehsils of Anantnag, Khas, Kulgam, Pulwama	2,814	851,606
Baramulla District: tehsils of Baramulla, Sri Pratapsinghpura, Uttarmachhipura	3,317	612,428
Total	6,131	1,464,034

Religious mix	Number	Percentage
All Muslims in KV	1,369,620	34.06 of all J&K-ites 44.20 of all J&K Muslims 93.55 of KV population
Kashmiri Muslims in J&K	1,270,261	31.59 of all J&K-ites 40.99 of all J&K Muslims
Kashmiri Muslims in KV	1,110,327	27.61 of all J&K-ites 35.83 of all J&K Muslims 87.41 of all Kashmiri Muslims 81.07 of all Muslims in KV 75.84 of KV population
Other (non-Kashmiri) Muslims living in KV	240,129	5.97 of all J&K-ites 5.16 of all J&K Muslims 17.53 of all Muslims in KV 16.40 of KV population
Unidentified Muslims living in KV	19,164	0.48 of all J&K-ites 0.62 of all J&K Muslims 1.40 of all Muslims in KV 1.31 of KV population
Kashmiri Hindu Pandits living in KV	76,171	1.89 of all J&K-ites 5.20 of KV population

Source: (1) *Census of India, 1941*, Volume XXII, Jammu & Kashmir State, Part II: Tables, Srinagar, R. G. Wreford, Editor, Jammu and Kashmir Government, 1942, various pages; (2) Appendix II: Kashmir Valley Muslims in J&K and their numerical dominance.

and 94 per cent of the Kashmir Valley's population. More specifically, people 'describing themselves as Kashmiri Muslims' comprised over 80 per cent of all Muslims living in the Kashmir Valley.[133] The other 20 per cent were Muslims who called themselves Sheikhs, Gujjars, Hajjams, Hanjis, Syeds, etc., all of whom presumably would have identified closely with Muslim Kashmiris, particularly if it was a binary Hindu or Muslim 'equation' or choice.[109] These Muslims in Kashmir, of whom about 90 per cent were of the Sunni persuasion, had 'the confident perception of a majority community'.[110] Whoever could successfully woo them would be well placed to receive their political support in the accession or any future plebiscite.

In the tumultuous times of 1947, therefore, Kashmiri Muslims were politically significant because of their numbers. Additionally, their popular leader, Sheikh Abdullah, who had mass support and considerable influence among Muslim Kashmiris, was more inclined towards J&K joining secular India than 'Islamic' Pakistan. His practice of secularism was significant as, co-located in the Kashmir Valley, was a small, influential and 'vital' Hindu minority and an even smaller community of Sikhs. Many people within both groups probably favoured J&K joining India. Most Hindus living in Kashmir comprised Kashmiri Pandits, who were 'from the same stock' as Kashmiri Muslims.[111] They comprised 5.20 per cent of Kashmir's population, with about 85 per cent of Pandits living in Anantnag District, which included Srinagar, and 15 per cent living in Baramulla District. All of these Kashmiri Pandits were Hindus and Brahmans,[112] from which community, significantly, Jawaharlal Nehru's forebears had come. The small community of Sikhs in Kashmir comprised 1.6 per cent of Kashmir Province's population. About half (13,000) lived in the Muzaffarabad Tehsil of Muzaffarabad District, a factor that caused them major problems when the Pukhtoons invaded in 1947.[113] The Sikhs in J&K had been 'introduced' to Kashmir when Ranjit Singh's Sikh Empire had controlled this region.[114]

In 1947, Kashmir was also significant because its largest city, Srinagar, was J&K's summer capital each year from May to October. At that time of the year, the region was climatically attractive, given the much hotter summers in Jammu Province and the Indian plains. Srinagar was also one of India's oldest and largest cities. With a population of 208,000, it was the largest city north of Lahore, the capital of Punjab Province, which had a population of almost 700,000. Srinagar also was more populous than the important British cantonment of Rawalpindi, population 181,000,[115] which was the warehouse and most significant rail destination for Srinagar.[116] Jammu City was J&K's winter capital from November to April, when Srinagar's cold weather and Jammu's milder temperatures made it a more attractive destination for the J&K ruler. Srinagar was four times more populous than Jammu City, which was Jammu Province's most populous city,[117] with a population of 50,379.[118] Jammu City was also crowded; in 1931, 'with an area of only 1 square mile' it was home to 38,000 people. By comparison, Srinagar's population density in 1931 was 16,000 persons per square mile.[119] Politically, Srinagar's size, coupled with the surrounding population in the Kashmir Valley for which 'Srinagar was an important centre of exchange',[120] meant that it was easier for politicians to draw a large audience to meetings held in this region than anywhere else in J&K. This was a further advantage for Kashmir and Kashmiris in 1947.

Despite their seemingly superior geo-political position, the influence of Kashmiri politics and politicians did not spread far beyond the Kashmir Valley.[121] Within Kashmir, however, they were paramount. Most Kashmiris remained aloof from active involvement in subcontinental politics before 1947.[122] Partly, this was because they had neither the means, nor the inclination, to engage with other parts of the subcontinent in any way, except possibly economically. While the National Conference represented 'Kashmiri nationalism',[123] as late as 1944, there was 'no representative body for all the Hindus of the State',[124] the vast majority of whom, almost 90 per cent, lived in Jammu Province.[125] The main rival to the National Conference was the 'Jammu-based' Muslim Conference.[126] However, as its name suggests, the Muslim Conference sought, first and foremost, to advance Muslim causes. In the Frontier Districts Province, there did not appear to have been much, if any, pre-partition political activity. The British closely monitored local political activity there, much of which centred on local rulers and various appointed senior officials, particularly the Muslim *Mirs* (rulers) of Hunza and Nagar, who were under the Maharaja's suzerainty. In Ladakh, which was even more geographically remote and isolated than British-controlled Gilgit, the Ladakh Buddhist Association 'on behalf of the People of Ladakh' wanted either Maharaja Hari Singh's rule of Ladakh to continue, or for the region to join with the Hindu-majority areas of Jammu, or East Punjab. Most importantly, Ladakhis wanted Ladakh to be separated from Kashmir.[127] This was to shed Kashmiri domination.[128] Due to the Frontier Districts Province's size, difficult terrain and the poor or non-existent roads and communications, Muslims and Buddhists invariably had little contact with each other.

So, in 1947, Kashmir was better known than other parts of J&K, and Kashmiris enjoyed a higher profile than other J&K-ites. There was, however,

> colossal ignorance among leaders and intellectuals of Kashmir about the heroes of Jammu, freedom fighters (directed more against British rule and much less against rule of the Dogra monarch, as was the case in Kashmir) … Unfortunately, the Jammu region did not attract a galaxy of foreign or Indian scholars to record its history as Kashmir did. … The same is true about Ladakh.[129]

Indeed, Ladakh had an even lower profile than Jammu. No member of the ruling Dogra dynasty had ever visited this remote and seemingly Dogra-free region,[130] despite Maharaja Hari Singh's title being 'Maharaja of Jammu and Kashmir Tibetadipati', with 'Tibetadipati' meaning Ladakh,[131] which title appeared in his official 'Instrument of Accession'.[132] Ladakh's isolation was partly because wheeled vehicles could not travel on the few mountain roads to the Frontier Districts Province, nor on the 'bridle paths' therein.[133] Therefore, politically speaking, the Frontier Districts Province was J&K's forgotten province in 1947. Both the Ladakh District and the other areas of the province (Astore, Gilgit Agency, Gilgit Leased Area) did not appear to be important to Indian politicians, including to those living and operating in J&K. Therefore, the discussion of the Frontier Districts Province hereafter will be limited. Instead, Kashmir will dominate the narrative.

Because Muslim Kashmiris numerically comprised the most populous and most important political grouping in J&K, they received the most external attention in 1947. They and their political leaders were considered to be 'a determining factor in State politics'.[134] Newspaper reporting in 1947 of mainstream political activities that occurred in J&K focused on Kashmir, particularly Srinagar, and on Kashmiris, particularly Muslim Kashmiris. Hari Singh's home region of Jammu and its residents were much lower profile than Kashmir and its 'self-respecting community', whose self-respect partly arose because Muslims numerically dominated Kashmir. Apart from the ruling Dogras and their armed forces, which largely comprised Hindus, there was no minority community that Kashmiri Muslims physically had to fear. This was vastly different from many other parts of mainland India where Indian Muslims were an increasingly nervous minority throughout 1947.

Why Kashmir was more important than Jammu: history

In 1947, the Kashmir region enjoyed significant 'hegemony' and political appeal over other parts of J&K.[135] It, rather than Jammu, was the focus of subcontinental attention. Examining the Kashmir region's history helps to understand this important dynamic. Kashmir is an old, long-established and famous region, nation or country. It has enjoyed renown and a high profile for centuries. This is partly because Kashmir has long been a coherent geo-political entity. Historically, the writer Kalhana has traced a line of Kashmiri kings back to at least 1182 BC.[136] Invariably, the political and geographic heart of these Kashmiris' kingdoms was the Kashmir Valley. However, Kashmiris also once had empires that extended into northern India. These included Lalitaditya-Muktapida in the 700s and Sultan Shihab-ud-Din in the 1300s. Buddhism and monistic Shaivite Hinduism prepared the way for the arrival of monotheistic Sunni Islam,[137] which started coming to Kashmir from the late 1000s and was seriously established there by the 1200s. From 1339 to 1586, under Muslim rulers, each independent kingdom of Kashmir was called the 'Sultanate of Kashmir'.[138] These were independent from rulers with kingdoms in mainland India.

In 1586, Kashmiris lost both their independence and their geographic isolation that often, but not always, had helped to protect and preserve their distinct identity. This occurred when the third, and most famous, Mughal Emperor, Akbar, finally captured Kashmir from Yusuf Shah Chak, whose family had ruled Kashmir as *sultans* since 1555.[139] The highly capable Mughals had long coveted Kashmir. Akbar's grandfather, Babur, who founded the Mughal Dynasty in 1526, initially had tried to conquer it in 1527. His son, Humayan, also tried but failed. Akbar had first tried to capture Kashmir in 1561.[140] He succeeded in 1586 when Kashmiris, weakened by sectarian in-fighting, were no longer able to resist the aggressive, expansive and persistent Mughals. Akbar's capture of Kashmir allegedly involved some deceitful tactics, a factor that seemingly 'Kashmiris never forgot'.[141] Thereafter, he re-integrated the Kashmir region, and its people, politically and administratively into northern India.

The Mughals also effectively subjugated the sovereign Kashmiri 'nation' that had long existed in the Kashmir Valley under Srinagar-based rulers – although these outsiders also partially kept the Kashmir entity alive by retaining it as an administrative province in their empire. Overall, however, Mughal rulers subdued Kashmiris. They did not recruit Kashmiris into their armies.[142] Possibly, they imposed the loose fitting item of clothing, the *pheran*, on Kashmiri men to destroy their manliness,[143] or at least to stifle their significant martial spirit: it is difficult to draw a sword while wearing a pheran. As a result, Kashmiris supposedly became 'ease loving' people,[144] 'cowardly' people,[145] or 'not high spirited people of an independent or resolute temper'.[146] Mughal subjugation was partially agreeable for Muslim Kashmiris because at least Akbar and his courtiers were fellow Sunni Muslims. The previous Chak rulers had been Shia Muslims, which is one reason why some Kashmiri fifth columnists had invited Akbar to conquer and rule Kashmir in the first place. With the Muslim Mughals being religious brethren, Kashmiri Muslims enjoyed personal religious rights. Equally, they lost their independence, with Kashmir no longer ruled by 'a son of the soil', i.e., by a local person.[147] (Hindu Kashmiris lost their freedom and independence in 1320 when the Ladakhi, Rinchan Shah, first established Muslim rule in Kashmir,[148] or certainly by 1339 when Shah Mir consolidated Muslim rule in Kashmir.)[149]

According to Sheikh Abdullah, Kashmiris 'did not like the Mughal hegemony'.[150] Rather ambitiously, he considered that the Kashmiris' 'freedom movement … started the day Kashmir lost freedom at the hands of the Mughals'.[151] Thereafter, outside rulers – not just Mughals, but also Afghan Durranis, Punjabi Sikhs and Jammu Dogras – suppressed Kashmiris, the Kashmiri nation and Kashmiri nationalism. Perhaps not surprisingly, then, an important factor embedded deeply in Kashmiri psyches is dislike or 'distrust of the outsider'.[152] This included nearby 'outsiders' such as the Dogras from Jammu, but also possibly Punjabis, with whom Kashmiris had significant geo-political and economic links, including in 1947. That year, Sheikh Abdullah had a distinct choice: he could advocate for J&K's joining either 'a Muslim nation whose leadership would surely be Punjabi, a people whom Kashmiris feared and distrusted and who were unlikely to respect the[ir] distinct religious tradition and identity' or secular India 'where Kashmiris would be free to live a life of their own choosing'.[153] More on this stark choice later, suffice it to say that, ironically, Pakistan has had few leaders who have been ethnic Punjabis.

Fortuitously for Kashmiris, the Muslim Mughals generally, and genuinely, liked and enjoyed Kashmir. For about two hundred years, Kashmir was their summer residence.[154] The Mughal emperors liked its beauty and its relatively benign summer climate.[155] Emperor Jehangir was 'so enamoured of the vale of Kashmir' that he visited this region eight times.[156] Reflecting the opportunities offered by the Mughal Empire, some Kashmiris, in what has been a long tradition, moved to the Indian plains seeking advancement or better living conditions. Such Kashmiris included Nehru's forebears. Mughals ruled Kashmir as a province of their empire until 1752. That year, Afghan Durranis from Kandahar seized Kashmir from the coddled and much weakened Mughals. These Afghans ruled Kashmir until 1819. Although they were fellow Muslims, the Afghans exploited, brutalised and suppressed all Kashmiris, regardless of their religion. It was a dark period for the Kashmir Valley during which both Hindu and Muslim Kashmiris suffered.

Punjabi Sikhs followed the Afghans. The powerful and unifying Sikh ruler, Emperor Ranjit Singh, and his empire controlled Kashmir from 1819 to 1846. (Singh died in 1839.) Following the Afghans' brutal rule, Kashmiris, particularly Hindu Kashmiris, may have hoped for better times. However, the Sikhs similarly engaged in subjugation and exploitation of all Kashmiris. Possibly because of this exploitation, Kashmir was the Sikh Empire's second richest of its eight provinces.[157] The other seven provinces were Gujrat, Jalandhar (Jullundur), Jammu, Kangra, Lahore, Multan and Peshawar.[158] The Sikh Empire therefore administratively connected the two provinces of Jammu and of Kashmir. Importantly, senior officials of the Sikh Empire, such as Raja Gulab Singh, served both in Jammu Province and in Kashmir Province.[159] A major change, not to the betterment of Muslim

Kashmiris, occurred in 1846 when Gulab Singh and his Dogras assumed control of J&K. Thereafter, they became the absolute rulers of this state.

By about 1889, the princely state of J&K had been consolidated. According to the 1901 Census, it comprised the areas of '1. Jammoo [sic] Province. 2. Kashmir Province. 3. Frontier Districts.'[160] Despite being officially called 'Jammu and Kashmir', within ten years of J&K coming into existence in 1846, people were using the term 'Kashmir' as the shorthand name for this princely state. The first major census of J&K in 1901 similarly shortened the official name to 'Kashmir', as displayed on its front cover.[161] This term seemingly diluted, or perhaps accommodated, any existing or outstanding Kashmiri nationalism. Equally, it may have expanded the geo-political 'consciousness' of some Kashmiris. So too did devastating natural calamities such as earthquakes, cholera outbreaks, fires, floods and famines. The latter, on occasions such as the 1877–79 famine, apparently killed three-fifths of the Kashmir Valley's population, although 'with good administration', that figure might have been avoided.[162] Consequently, some Kashmiris moved to the Indian plains in search of better living conditions, employment opportunities, or less repressive regimes. Such times of trouble or of external rule, including the 'strong and stern' Dogra rule of J&K,[163] suppressed Kashmiri nationalism. Nevertheless, it was sufficiently resolute and resilient that it didn't ever fully disappear.

Why Kashmir was more important than Jammu: reputation

Significantly, the rulers of J&K, who came from Jammu, allowed, and were happy for, their princely state to be called 'Kashmir' and not 'Jammu'. This section explains why this was so. Much of the documentation that I have accessed refers to the state of Jammu and Kashmir and/or to its ruler simply as 'Kashmir'.[164] There were exceptions. The former Settlement Commissioner for J&K, Walter Lawrence, called the princely state for which he worked in 1895 'Kashmir and Jammu'.[165] (By 1928, however, Lawrence was using 'Jammu and Kashmir'.)[166] In 1947, Mahatma Gandhi also called J&K 'Kashmir and Jammu'.[67] Predominantly, however, the princely state was simply called 'Kashmir', not 'Jammu', including by some Jammuites, on occasions. For example, in 1936, a letter to *The Times* was signed by 'B. J. Dalal, Jammu Tawi, Kashmir, India'.[168] (Jammu Tawi is another name for Jammu City, which is located astride the Tawi River.) Similarly, on 5 April 1939, 'the Maharaja of Kashmir and the Viceroy of India' wished 'Godspeed' to a new Royal Navy destroyer named 'Kashmir'.[169] The Kashmir region had always enjoyed a much higher profile than the Jammu region. This partly explains why subcontinental politicians in 1947 were more interested in the Kashmir Valley and Kashmiris, than in other areas of J&K or in other J&K-ites.

The use of the single word nomenclature of 'Kashmir' for J&K occurred early in the princely state's history. As early as 1854, a Gazetteer used 'Cashmere' (Kashmir) as shorthand for Jammu and Kashmir. It described 'Cashmere' as: 'The name now given to the extensive tract of country in Northern India, constituting the dominions of Gholab [sic] Singh ... Within its limits are included the valley of Cashmere [sic], the provinces of Jamu [sic; Jammu], Bulti [sic; Balti] or Iskardoh [sic; Skardu], Ladakh, Chamba, and others of less consequence.'[170] In relation to Jammu, the same Gazetteer only had a listing for the town, not the region: 'Jamoo [sic], a considerable town in the north of the Punjab ... is still held by Gholab [sic] Singh as part of his dominions, although the position of this prince has been greatly altered by the transfer to him of Cashmere [sic] and the adjacent hill country.'[171] For this Gazetteer, the town 'Jamoo' was still part of Punjab while, seemingly, the region of Jammu was either unknown or not significant.

An Englishman, Frederic Drew, provided an explanation for the use of Kashmir as shorthand for J&K. In 1875, he noted the following about the Maharaja of J&K: 'By the Panjabis [sic] he is most commonly called after the former place, by English-men after the latter. It is this last practice which has led Englishmen at home to confound 'Kashmir' with the whole of the territories. ... [rather than] restricting the use of the word 'Kashmir' to the very defined tract that from time immemorial has borne the name.'[172] That 'defined tract' was the Kashmir Valley. Drew also noted that the J&K Maharaja's title was 'not complete as denoting all the territories ruled by him; for these include, besides the Jummoo [sic] districts and Kashmir, the more distant countries of Ladakh, Baltistan, and Gilgit.'[173] To use a title that accurately reflected all of the J&K ruler's geographic possessions would have been long and convoluted. It was understandable, certainly in J&K's early days, that Punjabis would call the Maharaja of J&K 'Jammu', rather than 'Kashmir': they were geographically closer to J&K than the majority of Britishers. Equally, Gulab Singh may have been happy to move away from his former Punjabi connections and reputation by adopting the new name of 'Kashmir'. 'Jammu' had negative connotations about him and his perfidious role in the Sikh Empire's downfall.

Ultimately, the use of the term 'Kashmir' as shorthand for Jammu and Kashmir was because of the fame and prestige of the Kashmir Valley and its ancient civilisation – that 'far-famed country which lies in [J&K's] midst'.[174] The 1854 Gazetteer described Kashmir as follows: 'The grandeur and splendour of Cashmirian [sic] scenery ... the mildness of the climate, and the fertility of the soil, make Bernier conclude that it was actually the site of the garden of Eden.'[175] Bernier, a Frenchman, was the first European traveller 'known to have visited Kashmir', which he did in 1664, long before Dogra rule.[176] He waxed lyrical about Kashmir, which was then under Mughal control:

> In truth, the kingdom [of Kashmir] surpasses in beauty all that my warm imagination had anticipated. It is probably unequalled by any country of the same extent, and should be, as in former ages, the seat of sovereign authority, extending its dominion over all the circumjacent mountains, even as far as *Tartary* and over the whole of *Hindoustan* [sic], to the island of *Ceylon*.[177]

Two hundred and fifty years later, Younghusband, the British Resident in Kashmir in 1908, coincidentally concurred: 'I have seen many visitors to Kashmir, and my experience is that the bulk of them are of the same view as the … Frenchman', Bernier. For Younghusband's various visitors, 'the reality [of Kashmir] has, with most, exceeded the expectation'.[178] Similarly, the 1901 Census noted that Kashmir was 'the gem of the *riasat* [state] … [to which] Every gentleman, European or a native of Hindustan, is eager to pay homage'.[179] For Lawrence, Kashmir was 'an emerald set in pearls'.[180] For a long time, people had spoken highly of Kashmir.

Kashmir's fame also was enhanced by Jammu's lack of fame. The 'region' of Jammu lacked Kashmir's geographic cohesiveness, distinctiveness and reputation for history and beauty. While possibly ancient, the Jammu 'region' was apparently not mentioned in any major documents until the eleventh century. This included not being mentioned in Kalhana's *Rajatarangini*, the chronicle of Kashmiri kings, which caused 'considerable surprise' to Hutchison and Vogel. They believed that this oversight was possibly because the Jammu region's name previously had been 'Durgara', while its capital had been known as 'Bahu'.[181] While possibly so, it was Raja Gulab Singh who actually consolidated Jammu into a political entity. He did so by unifying twenty-two 'hill principalities' that had previously been in 'perpetual conflict with each other',[182] but which 'generally recognized the supremacy of the Rajas of Jammu'.[183] Under Gulab Singh, Jammu became part of, and was under the suzerainty of, the Sikh Empire. Nevertheless, Jammu's fame was always lesser than Kashmir's, if only because Kashmir Province was richer.[184]

Why Kashmir was more important than Jammu: geo-economy

Examining Kashmir's geo-economic situation explains this politically important region's advantages, hegemony and appeal politically over other parts of J&K in 1947. Generally speaking, the Kashmir Valley was easy to access. It comprised an arena-like longitudinal valley that had much fertile land and a relatively homogenous population.[185] In 1941, 'what is usually known as the Kashmir Valley' comprised seven tehsils: Anantnag, Khas (which included Srinagar),[186] Kulgam and Pulwama, in Anantnag District, and Baramulla, Sri Pratapsinghpura and Uttarmachhipura, in Baramulla District.[187] The 1931 Census called these districts 'Kashmir South', 'Kashmir North' and 'Pahar District'.[188] (Pahari was 'the language of people dwelling in the mountains', of which Muzaffarabad District had many.)[189] Similarly, a Kashmiri author considered that Kashmir comprised '*Kamraj* (North Kashmir) and *Maraj* (South Kashmir)'.[190] Kashmir was located between, and was surrounded by, the Zanskar and Pir Panjal ranges. The former range separated the Frontier Districts Province and Kashmir; the latter separated Jammu Province and Kashmir.[191]

Historically, Kashmir had been an area physically separate from J&K's more lowland parts (Jammu Province) or highland parts (Frontier Districts). This separateness was partly because the Kashmir region had been difficult to access. Before the opening of the Jhelum Valley Road in 1890, Kashmir had often been physically isolated in winter. (Most areas in the Frontier Districts Province were similarly isolated every year. Indeed, this province's ruggedness and remoteness made it even more difficult to access than Kashmir.) On occasions, such isolation had been administratively enforced. An Indian observer associated with an early visit to J&K in 1846 by officials from the East India Company noted that Kashmiris were 'kept in a kind of involuntary prison, none being allowed to go to or from without a passport from the [local] authorities'.[192] Such control was relatively easy to arrange and maintain then because there were only six major routes into or out of the Kashmir Valley. These comprised: the Banihal Pass route from Jammu, to the south; the old Mughal Road from Rajauri, in western Jammu Province, to the southwest; the Tosamaidan Pass route from Poonch, to the west; the Jhelum Valley Road from Muzaffarabad, also to the west, but further north of the Poonch route; the Zoji La route from Ladakh, to the east; and, the Burzil Pass route to Gilgit and Skardu, to the north.

Generally, transport links were poor throughout J&K. This made urban areas more significant, particularly in Kashmir, as the region was relatively easier to move around physically due to its smaller area and flatter ground. These factors, plus Srinagar's size, made Kashmir a more attractive destination for a politician to access and potentially draw a crowd or for a journalist to report from. In 1947, the two most important roads into Kashmir were the Jhelum Valley Road and the Banihal Pass route, also called the Banihal Cart Road. Considered to be 'excellent motor roads',[193] they importantly allowed relatively easy access for Kashmiris to or from Punjab, particularly the all-weather Jhelum Valley Road, sometimes called 'the Rawalpindi Road'.[194] Opened in 1890 after British engineers[195] constructed it along the 'furious and boisterous'[196] Jhelum River below Baramulla,[197] the 196–mile Jhelum Valley Road went from Srinagar to Domel near Muzaffarabad. At Domel, there was a Customs House for 'the registration [and control] of visitors',[198] while the Jhelum River, into which the Kishenganga River converged, was also crossed by a strategic bridge. After Domel, a traveller had two options, both of which ultimately connected with the Indian (later Pakistani) rail network: the more northerly fifty-eight-mile all-weather road via Abbottabad to the railhead at Havelian;[199] or, the eighty-five-mile road to Rawalpindi, via Murree, with the Jhelum River crossed again at Kohala, twenty-one miles west of Domel. From Srinagar, it usually took about six hours to reach Rawalpindi, although, unlike the Abbottabad road, snow often closed the Rawalpindi Road in winter.[200] The Banihal Cart Road was completed in 1922, but was only opened to motor vehicles registered outside J&K in 1935.[201] This 203–mile road went from Jammu City via the 'Banihal Pass at an altitude of 9,000 feet', after which it dropped into the Kashmir Valley 'which has a uniform level of over 5,000 feet'.[202] Apart from being snowbound in winter, this road was sometimes blocked by landslides.[203] This road also connected Jammu with Sialkot, in Punjab.

According to the 1941 Census, the 'main artery' in, and through, J&K comprised the 'Sialkot-Jammu-Srinagar-Rawalpindi-Abbottabad' route.[204] The Jammu-Srinagar section of this route comprised the Jhelum Valley Road and the Banihal Cart Road, which met at Srinagar. This arterial route traversed, or passed nearby, a number of major urban centres in J&K. These comprised (from south to north) the cities of Jammu and Srinagar and the towns of Udhampur, Anantnag, Baramulla, Uri and Muzaffarabad. For J&K rulers, this road was strategically important as it connected Jammu Province and Kashmir Province. It also allowed these autocrats, who distrusted the 'intrusive' British, to access their winter or summer capital without having to traverse British-controlled territory in India (Punjab, North-West Frontier Province),[205] including avoiding nearby Sialkot. This British-free route was not as silly as it sounds. The British apparently had 'designed [Sialkot] chiefly to observe Jummoo' (Jammu).[206] In 1931, the British had also moved troops from the Sialkot cantonment into southwestern J&K to help Maharaja Hari Singh quell an internal uprising in J&K.

Since 1890, the Jhelum Valley Road had become the easiest way to access Srinagar. Importantly, this negated Kashmiris' geo-economic dependence on Jammu,[207] lessened their isolation from Punjab, and provided an easier way to access the extensive Indian rail system than going via Jammu Province. In 1947, J&K was devoid of railways, apart from a sixteen-mile stretch that connected Jammu City, via Suchetgarh, situated on the Punjab border, with Sialkot, twenty-seven miles away.[208] There was a Customs House at Suchetgarh, and at Jammu Tawi.[209] Sialkot, in turn, was on a branch line of the North Western Railway. However, this Sialkot-Jammu branch line was not 'of very considerable importance', chiefly because it needed to be extended 'right into the Kashmir Valley',[210] although it did make the popular Vaishno Devi shrine 'comparatively accessible' for devotees.[211] Extending the railway line to Kashmir would have been challenging and expensive as the terrain beyond Jammu City was very difficult, being uphill and subjected to landslides. In 1887, British and J&K engineers instead contemplated constructing a railway that followed the Jhelum Valley to Srinagar,[212] with electricity generated by this river supplying the 'motive power'.[213] This line was never built as there was disagreement about who should pay for its construction. There was also no strategic 'urgency': the 'Northern Frontier' was quiet, with no need to move 'a large force' into J&K for 'defensive or offensive' operations.[214] Kashmir Province and Srinagar had also been able to function satisfactorily without any railway, particularly after the Jhelum Valley Road was opened.[215] Indeed, by 1936, this road had economically 'transformed [Srinagar] beyond recognition'.[216]

The influence and impact of Punjab, Punjabi politics and Punjabis on all of J&K was significant. All of J&K had substantial geo-economic and cultural links with this British-controlled Indian province. Historically, many J&K-ites with ambition, or out of necessity due to impoverishment or the effects of natural calamities such as epidemics or famines, or disliking tyrannical rulers, moved to Punjab and its better opportunities. In 1931, Punjabis were influential in a serious anti-Maharaja uprising.[217] Punjab Province and its capital, Lahore, located 105 miles away from Jammu City,[218] was the British-administered 'neighbouring country' to which J&K-ites looked to for education, news or recreation. Until 1947, 'Panjab' University was the only 'examining institute' for J&K-ites seeking a Matriculation qualification.[219] Newspapers from Punjab, such as *The Civil & Military Gazette* or *The Tribune*, reported J&K politics. These were available in areas of J&K located close to, or easily accessible from, Punjab: chiefly, urban areas like Mirpur and Jammu City in Jammu Province, and Baramulla and Srinagar in Kashmir Province. For many J&K-ites, it was (and still is) easier to access other parts of J&K by travelling via Punjab.

Significantly, Punjab was also the location to which J&K-ites mostly went in winter for sustenance, trade or to obtain temporary work.[220] The 1931 Census noted that 94,448 J&K-ites, both male and female, temporarily 'emigrated' from the state for about five months in winter. The bulk of them (90,505) went either to Punjab (79,691), NWFP (8,263) or Baluchistan (2,551).[221] (Slightly greater numbers moved internally within J&K during winter months, usually seeking employment.)[222] These 'emigrants' undertook labour and semi-permanent employment that included working as timber cutters, 'cooks, water-bearers, apprentices in workshops and coolies'.[223] Most appear to have been from Jammu Province, which partly was due to its proximity and ease of access to Punjab. Equally, as the Census of India, 1921, had noted, Kashmiris and Ladakhis found it too hard to live in the 'much warmer climate of the plains' and generally only migrated when 'driven by sheer necessity'. (It also noted that 167,695 'Mussalman Kashmiris' were permanently settled in Punjab, chiefly in Rawalpindi, Lahore, Amritsar, Ludhiana and other minor towns and 'along the train line'.)[224] In terms of religion, most temporary emigrants from Kashmir and the Frontier Districts Provinces were Muslims, with those from Jammu Province mostly Hindus, except for Muslims from Mirpur District. Apart from Lahore, J&K-ites also went to Sialkot, Gujranwala and Gujrat. Only 470 emigrated to Delhi,[225] which then had a similar population to Lahore (700,000)[226] but was 360 miles away and less important.

Until the actual creation of Pakistan on 15 August 1947, therefore, the majority of J&K-ites living in Jammu and Kashmir provinces, and even the remote Frontier Districts Province, invariably looked southwards towards undivided Punjab for economic opportunities, religious sympathy or political inspiration. However, post-partition, a combination of three events encouraged, then compelled, J&K-ites to move their vision away from Lahore and western Punjab towards India and New Delhi. Concurrently, Jammu's geographic influence also increased. First, the Radcliffe Boundary Awards on 17 August 1947 that gave India the 'boon' of the bulk of Gurdaspur District made geographic access to India feasible, particularly for Jammuites living in eastern Jammu.[227] Second, the Pukhtoons' invasion of Kashmir Province on 22 October 1947 effectively and permanently closed the Jhelum Valley Road, thus denying Kashmiris access to the (by then Pakistani) 'mainland'. Thereafter, Kashmiris accessed India via Jammu and Pathankot in (Indian) Punjab, where a railhead was located. Ironically, this made the Jammu area more geo-economically important in J&K, although Kashmir retained its superior prestige and political position. Third, Maharaja Hari Singh's accession to India on 26 October 1947 exacerbated fighting in J&K, after which India–Pakistan relations rapidly deteriorated further. Indeed, because India–Pakistan relations fluctuated from poor-to-parlous virtually from day one of the two dominions' creation, this state of affairs reduced the option of J&K-ites physically accessing Pakistan. The India–Pakistan war finally and totally eliminated this physical access in 1965. Had there been goodwill between these two new entities from their political instigation in August 1947, accessing Lahore and (Pakistani) Punjab might still have been possible, and significant, for J&K-ites, particularly Jammuites and Kashmiris. However, with its access to (Pakistani) Punjab gone, life became more difficult for all people in Indian J&K.

In 1947, Kashmir had other 'advantages' over Jammu and the Frontier Districts. Due to the mountainous nature of J&K and the long distances involved, 'communications were difficult and scanty within the State'.[228] Srinagar had a landing strip for planes, albeit untarmaced and without fuelling or servicing facilities.[229] There was no airport of any description in Jammu Province,[230] although by 1943, one was 'under contemplation'.[231] Invariably, post and telegraphic links followed the state's major road links. Because Kashmir was smaller with a heavier population, this region often had better, or at least shorter, internal communications than the remainder of J&K. Certainly, word-of-mouth and rumours would have travelled quicker. Additionally, 85 per cent of Kashmir Province's residents, almost 1.5 million people, lived in the two districts of Anantnag and Baramulla. By 1947, Srinagar was well connected to mainland India. There was a Jammu–Srinagar mail service that had begun during Gulab Singh's rule;[232] a trunk line telephone service between Srinagar and Jammu 'linked up with the British Indian system';[233] a telegraph service ran between Sialkot, Jammu and Srinagar, and from 'Kashmir to Gilgit and from Astore to Askaradu [Skardu]'.[234] This latter was an important strategic link for the British. Equally, these factors made it easier for journalists to send reports from Kashmir than from the other regions of J&K.

Nevertheless, replicating restrictions in place in British India, the J&K Government tightly controlled the local press,[235] as a result of which its tone 'was on the whole satisfactory'.[236] In 1943–44, 'representatives of the press agencies and outside newspapers' were present in J&K, while sixty-three newspapers and periodicals reportedly were being published in the state, of which fifty were in Urdu, a popular language in Kashmir, five were in English, three were in Hindi, and one was in Gurmukhi. Publication of newspapers in the state had only been allowed since 1932,[237] but three daily newspapers existed, at least one of which was produced in Kashmir Province. One significant Urdu weekly journal was *Hamdard*, which had been started collaboratively in August 1935 by the Kashmiris Prem Nath Bazaz, a Pandit, and Sheikh Abdullah, who were then politically aligned.[238] In August 1943, the All-Jammu and Kashmir Editors' Conference had been held in Srinagar.[239]

This, along with the number of Urdu publications, suggested that the news focus was more on Kashmir Province than on Jammu Province. It was another matter as to whether J&K-ites could actually read the various publications available in 1947. Literacy rates were low: 7 per cent for J&K.[240] Specifically, 4 per cent of J&K Muslims (111,000 people) were literate; 15 per cent of Hindus (107,000); 32 per cent of Sikhs (18,000); and, 5 per cent of Buddhists (1,900).[241] In 1939, the J&K Educational Reorganisation Committee noted this 'alarmingly low percentage of literacy', which was partly due to low levels of spending.[242] In 1931, the 'backwardness of Muslims' had been identified as a major concern, particularly in Kashmir where Muslims predominated. Their low levels of literacy were due to 'their concentration on the soil which does not permit the agriculturist to devote sufficient time and energy for his personal education or the education of his children'.[243] Equally, the community that had 'evinced the keenest interest in augmenting its ranks of literates is beyond doubt the Kashmiri Muslim'.[244]

Because of J&K-ites' low levels of literacy, oral communications continued to be important. Therefore, leaders and politicians who could orate publically, particularly in the popular languages of Urdu or Kashmiri, had a huge advantage over people who could not, or would not, speak in public in these languages. Of the nine major languages spoken in J&K, Kashmiri and its sub-dialects had 1.4 million speakers, or 'about 2/5ths of the population of the state'. The next major language groups, Pahari and Dogri, respectively had 596,000 and 550,000 speakers. Even so, Urdu was 'the common language of the State ... understood and spoken by people in various parts'. Written in the Persian script, it was the lingua franca for J&K, although, surprisingly, no census actually counted how many J&K-ites specifically spoke this language.[245] Thus, Sheikh Abdullah, who spoke both Kashmiri and Urdu and had a 'melodious voice',[246] had a significant advantage over his political rivals, Maharaja Hari Singh, who apparently was fluent in Kashmiri but chose not to speak it publicly,[247] and Ghulam Abbas, who could not speak Kashmiri.

Apart from its geographic advantages, the Kashmir region enjoyed a considerably higher profile than either Jammu or the Frontier Districts. This was due to Kashmir's more favourable circumstances. As the 1931 Census noted, Kashmir Province was 'blessed with copious boons of Nature and enjoys a decided superiority over the sister province of Jammu'.[248] It continued:

> The fertility of the Kashmir soil, its temperate climate, its natural water-courses, navigable rivers, productive lakes, rich forests, abundance of fruits, its numerous handicrafts and manufactures all combine to give it precedence over any spot on the

face of the earth not to speak of the province of Jammu or the Frontier Districts. The salubrious climate, natural scenery, beautiful springs, pleasure grounds and health resorts annually attract a large number of European and Indian visitors who constitute a ready market for the products of Kashmir. Instead of the Kashmir manufactures [sic] going in search of the market it is the market itself which annually comes to Kashmir to carry away the products of the country.[249]

Perhaps not surprisingly, two Kashmiris had written the 1931 Census.

A final aspect of Kashmir's higher geo-economic profile in J&K concerned the number of people who visited Kashmir. The summer visitor 'season' ran from 15 April to 15 October.[250] During this time, Srinagar's population increased by 'many thousands' as 'visitors flock[ed] to Kashmir'.[251] In 1940, this 'flock' comprised '29,292' visitors, a significant increase from the 1931 figure of '8,404'. Visitors went to 'Kashmir famous for its salubrious climate, beautiful valleys and magnificent scenery not for generations but for centuries'.[252] Indeed, Kashmir had long been 'earning a handsome living off its beauty',[253] chiefly via tourism although, equally, the 'complete failure' of tourist traffic in any year 'would mean ruin to many small industries, shopkeepers and house boat owners and semi-starvation to many thousands ... dependent on the visitor'.[254] In 1941, many visitors travelled along the Jhelum Valley Road, where car traffic had increased by 'about 35 per cent' and lorry transport by 'about 40 per cent' since the 1931 Census. Others came via the Banihal route, where car and lorry traffic had increased by 20 per cent since 1931.[255] These tourist figures confirmed Kashmir's 'decided superiority over ... Jammu'.[256] In 1947, Kashmir was the region people were focused on.

J&K's diverse identities and nationalisms

Jammu and Kashmir has been, and remains, ethnically and religiously complex and disparate. Many 'nations', 'nationalities' and 'nationalisms' have existed, or still exist, in J&K. These involve and include various J&K-ites. The mix of 'nations' or social collectives – a better word may be 'grouping', or possibly 'community' – in J&K is numerous. Apart from Muslim Kashmiris, who will be discussed in the next section, these groupings in J&K include:

- the independent J&K 'nation' based on the princely state, as once desired by Maharaja Hari Singh and as still propagated by groups such as the Jammu Kashmir Liberation Front;
- the Jammu 'nation', as supported by Jammuites of various ethnic, political and/ or religious 'shades', particularly when Dogras from Jammu ruled J&K;

- the Hindu or non-Muslim 'nation' that appeals to non-Muslims in J&K;
- the Hindu Pandit 'nation' whose adherents desire a 'Panun Kashmir' ('Our Own Kashmir') so that these supposed 'aborigines of Kashmir do not become extinct in their own land',[257] but whose desire for a separate homeland has largely appeared since the anti-India uprising began in Indian J&K's Kashmir Valley in 1988 (although Sheikh Abdullah states that Pandits requested 'a separate homeland in the Kolgam [Kulgam?] region' of southern Kashmir during Maharaja Hari Singh's rule);[258]
- the pro-Pakistan 'nation', almost all of whose supporters comprise Muslims;
- the pro-India 'nation', many, but not all, of whose adherents comprise non-Muslims, chiefly Hindus and Buddhists, but also mainstream Kashmiri politicians and possibly also J&K Shias in the Kargil area;
- the Buddhist Ladakhi 'nation' which has geo-cultural and religious similarities with the neighbouring 'nation' of Tibet;
- the 'nation of the Northern Areas'[259] or the Gilgit-Baltistan 'nation', proponents of which see this 'region' as having a 'separate political identity';[260]
- and, importantly, given that Islam is far from being a monolith in J&K, the 'nation' that Muslims other than Kashmiris, such as Jammu Muslims or Gilgit Muslims, might desire, if only to avoid domination by ethnic Kashmiri Muslims.

Various minorities and sub-nations also exist in J&K. These include Dogras (Hindu and/or Muslim), Kashmiri Pandits, Buddhists, Sikhs, Shias, Harijans, etc.[261] Sub-nations comprise communities of ethno-religious brotherhoods, clans or tribes, or *biradari*,[262] and/or like-minded people, who exist in this diverse and disparate former princely state. Such *biradari*, in the broad sense of this term, include Poonchis, Kargil Shias, Gujjars, Bakerwals, Baltis, Paharis and Gilgitis. Each of the many different groupings of J&K-ites has their own particular desire for the political and international future of 'their' state, region and/or community. Satisfying all of these varying and conflicting desires, differences and 'nationalities' remains one of the greatest challenges to resolving the Kashmir dispute.

Apart from the various minorities and sub-nations in J&K, there has also been some religious vagueness in the state, on occasions. For example, Sikhs were sometimes considered a sect of Hinduism, as confusingly noted in the 1931 Census: the 'Brahman' category included 11,723 'followers of Sikhism'.[263] One Britisher even described Maharaja Ranbir Singh as 'eminently religious, and in faith is an orthodox Sikh, being generally considered at the present time the head of this sect of the Hindus'.[264] Others, however, described Ranbir as a 'strict Hindu' whose 'ambition

[was] that Jammu should rival Benares in its number of temples', a tradition that his son, Pratap, who was one of the most devout of Indian princes,[265] sought to continue. Such religious or identity 'fuzziness' was not then unusual.[266] Similarly, in 1941, Kashmir Province also had 1,675 'Arya Samajists'.[267] These Hindu reformers, among other things, sought the 'abolition of caste restrictions' in marriage and were 'ready to accept converts'.[268] Almost unbelievably, at least for the data collectors, Srinagar had two female atheists 'who gave no details by which their real community could be decided'.[269] Not surprisingly, there was no specific category for atheists.

Karan Singh has indicated a further noteworthy challenge in relation to J&K-ites' identity that caused him difficulties when he served as the Head of the State for Indian J&K. This might be called the 'local-versus-nation' issue. It partially explains why India and Indians continue to have serious issues with Muslim Kashmiris in the Kashmir Valley. Both he and Sheikh Abdullah were State Subjects of the Jammu and Kashmir State but each had a differing perspective on their specific relationship with the new post-British entity of India in which they found themselves. For Singh, while Sheikh Abdullah 'looked upon himself as a Kashmiri who happened to find himself in India, I considered myself an Indian who happened to find himself in Kashmir'.[270] This observation is important. Geographically, ethnic Kashmiris were generally more focused on their own (more autonomous) region than on northern India – unlike Jammuites, whose region essentially was more integrated into northern India. Also, people came in larger numbers to Kashmir than Kashmiris ventured outside. In other words, relatively speaking, Kashmiris were more insular in their travel activities and awareness of mainland India than Jammuites. This local-versus-nation issue continues to be a significant factor among J&K-ites. In particular, it is a serious issue among many Muslim Kashmiris living in the Kashmir Valley: they struggle to be Indians. Indeed, many oppose being Indians or considering themselves to be Indians. (India shouldn't feel disheartened: many Muslim Kashmiris seemingly also do not want to be with Pakistan nor see themselves as Pakistanis.)

For non-Muslims, their first or uppermost identity invariably is as Indians. Many Jammuites (such as Karan Singh) and Ladakhis see themselves as Indians first and foremost, then possibly as Jammuites or Ladakhis and/or as Hindus/Muslims or Buddhists/Shia Muslims. Similarly, Kashmiri Pandits see themselves as Indians first, then as Kashmiris and/or as Hindus. In Indian J&K, therefore, people have had at least three distinct, and different, politico-religious identities. Across the Line of Control, differences also exist in Pakistan-Administered J&K. Many Azad Kashmiris and people from Gilgit-Baltistan (GBians) see themselves as Pakistanis first, then as Muslims and/or as Azad Kashmiris or GBians. However, some Azad Kashmiris favour an independent J&K, while some GBians favour an independent Balawaristan ('*Balawar*' means 'mountain people')[271] that would comprise Gilgit, Baltistan and Ladakh, along with Chitral and Kohistan from neighbouring Khyber-Pakhtunkhwa Province. Surprisingly, some GBians do not even see themselves as J&K-ites at all. For them, Gilgit-Baltistan 'is not part of J&K but [is] part of the Kashmir dispute', which holds them 'hostage': 'GB's accession to Pakistan [in 1947] is deferred' and its ability to become a 'full part of Pakistan' can only happen 'after the final solution of the Kashmir issue'.[272]

To this complex mix of identities and nationalisms for J&K and J&K-ites, we must add the differing stances of India and Pakistan on J&K's international future. Both perceive only two nationalities for J&K-ites: either Indian or Pakistani. That said, some Indians see only one nationality for J&K-ites: they and their lands are 'an integral part of India', a position that supposedly is 'well known'.[273] Even so, Indians have never set foot in or controlled four areas of J&K: Azad Kashmir; Gilgit-Baltistan; and Chinese-controlled Aksai Chin and Shaksgam.[274] It is hard to imagine that people living in these four areas feel themselves to be 'an integral part of India'. Conversely, Pakistan wants the UN plebiscite held to enable J&K-ites to decide whether J&K joins Pakistan or India. In 1953, Sheikh Abdullah made an interesting observation about the poll for J&K-ites: 'It is the Muslims who have to decide [the] accession with India and not the non-Muslims as the latter have no place in Pakistan and therefore their only choice is India.'[275] Problematically, J&K Muslims have never been unified in their political aspirations for J&K. Their first challenge – which creates a politico-strategic opportunity for India – is to establish a strongly unified Muslim 'brotherhood'. Equally, accommodating J&K's fractious Muslim community has always been difficult for India. Meanwhile, legally for the people of J&K, their political identity and nationalism remain in dispute and undecided. One ramification of this is that Azad Kashmiris and GBians travel on Pakistani passports, even though they are not legally or actually Pakistani citizens. This is because Pakistan is only 'administering' Azad Kashmir and Gilgit-Baltistan, and the residents therein, until the UN plebiscite is held to determine J&K's 'fate'.

The Kashmiri identity and nationalism

In 1947, Kashmiris, apart from being the most populous and homogenous group in J&K, also had the strongest sense of identity. Part of their challenge that year was to try to determine whether this identity would better survive and thrive in

125

India, with its secular and 'asymmetrical federal model',[276] or in Pakistan, with its more narrow religious and 'capitalist feudal ideology'.[277] On the other hand, the challenge for Indians and prospective Pakistanis was to appeal to this group at the forefront of J&K politics.

The Kashmiri identity is an old one. However, there is no 'monolithic' Kashmiri, and Kashmiri society is 'by no means egalitarian or unpatriarchal'.[278] For Alexander Evans, an astute observer of J&K, Kashmir and Kashmiris were *uniquely different*, or exceptional', although, equally, such a belief 'in most cases ... is a conceit'.[279] One aspect of this Kashmiri exceptionalism may be 'a tragic one: history happens to Kashmiris ... rather than Kashmiris deciding history'.[280] Since 1586, Kashmiris have been subjugated and exploited by other Muslims (Mughals; Afghans), Sikhs and Hindu Dogras, with this process often being brutal. Partly because of their subjugation, Kashmiris have suffered and banded together, making them think that their ethnic group is unique and special – if only because its members have all been equally oppressed. For Kashmiris, they are exceptional because they have suffered and have had to fight to retain their identity.

Over the years, the Kashmiri identity also has 'acquired an exclusivist character' and now largely reflects the community of Kashmiri-speaking Muslims who live in the Kashmir Valley.[281] The significant and formerly influential minority community of Hindu Pandit Kashmiris seemingly has been excluded. This is because many Pandits have left Kashmir, or felt compelled by militants' violence and antipathy against them to leave, since Muslim Kashmiris began their anti-India uprising in 1988. While many Muslim Kashmiris find this loss sad and unacceptable, the discussion of the Kashmiri 'nation' and 'nationalism' now focuses largely on the Muslim Kashmiri population. This group has dominated politics in J&K since 1931 when the allegedly 'great nation' of Kashmir began seriously 'questing and struggling after its identity'.[282] It continues to dominate Kashmir, with its 'language of nationalism' now 'about the injustice done to Kashmiris by Indians or Pakistanis'.[283]

Kashmir has often been a political or administrative entity. This has resulted in Kashmiris sharing, and displaying, a common identity based on various shared characteristics. One of these is Kashmiris' use of Koshur (or Kashmiri), the language spoken by Kashmiris, which 'is perhaps the principal defining feature of Valley Kashmiri identity'.[284] Apart from being spoken widely in Kashmir, Koshur/Kashmiri is spoken in northern parts of Jammu, particularly around Kishtwar, in far northern parts of Azad Kashmir, and among members of the Kashmiri Diaspora living in mainland India, Pakistan and overseas. While the Koshur language was a unifying factor, it nevertheless had dialects and 'rival' languages. Dialects of Koshur were Kamrazi, spoken in northwestern parts of the Valley; Marazi, spoken in the Valley's south; Yamrazi, spoken around Srinagar; and, the 'distinct dialect'[285] of Kishtwari.[286] The 1931 Census also distinguished between 'Musalmani Kashmiri and Hindu Kashmiri … [with] the former having borrowed words from Persian while the latter is free from any such admixture'.[237] Although these dialects of Koshur/Kashmiri were probably mutually understandable to Kashmiri speakers, the language was certainly different from, and unintelligible to, other J&K-ites who spoke various other languages including Dogri, Punjabi, Pahari, Gojri, Bhotia and Shina.[288] The 1941 Census noted that, while the state language was Urdu, 'Hindustani is the usual medium of conversation between those having a different mother tongue and not knowing Kashmiri' in J&K.[289] Urdu and Hindustani were similar languages, but with some differences, particularly in their written forms, with Urdu using a Perso-Arabic script and Hindustani using a Devnagari script.

Religion has been one unifying factor for the majority 'community' of Muslims in Kashmir, with this community's identity supposedly 'based on Islam'.[290] Significantly, Muslims brought Islam to Kashmir peacefully, not as foreign conquerors.[291] Kashmiris therefore became Muslims by choice, not by compulsion. However, various interpretations of Islam can be found in J&K, including Sunni, Shia, Sufi and Islamist.[292] There also are various practices, including venerating saints, shrine worship and revering the Moe-e-Muqaddas (Hair of the Prophet) artifact at Hazratbal. According to some Kashmiri believers, 'Whosoever has seen the sacred hair of Muhammad, [h]as had in reality the vision of the Prophet'.[293] Importantly, there also is an inclusive Islamic 'strand of mysticism' propagated by Kashmir's revered patron saint, Sheikh Noor-ud-Din or Nund Rishi (1377–1438).[294] He was informed and inspired by the 'mysticism and collectivism' of an earlier Kashmiri whom he apparently met: the famous and revered Hindu Shaivite, Muslim Sufi, and 'first mystic poet' of Kashmir, Lala Arifa, more commonly called Lal Ded.[295] An important early figure in Kashmir. Lal Ded lived during a period of 'social and political turmoil' in the fourteenth century as both Islam and the new Sultanate of Kashmir were consolidating themselves. Her 'simple Kashmiri verse … suffused with a sense of the fluidity of religious boundaries, and … interpreted as a manifestation of the Kashmiri ethos of tolerance' and inclusivity inspired, and still inspires, Kashmiris.[296] Similarly, Sheikh Noor-ud-Din lived, taught and inspired people of all religions in Kashmir in the late fourteenth to early fifteenth centuries.[297] Partly as a result of his teachings and saintly example, the 'great mass' of Kashmiris had accepted Islam by the end of the fifteenth century.[298] Arguably, both Nund Rishi and Lal Ded were major proponents of the syncretic and pluralistic concept later called Kashmiriyat that is discussed below.

While most Kashmiris had accepted Islam as their personal faith, Kashmiri Muslims also were 'riven by schisms'. In the 1930s, they were divided into 'so many sects such as *Hanafis, Ahle Hadith, Ahmadiyas, Ahle Sunnah, Shiites* and *Sunnis.* … Even Hanafis within their sect had got further split into *Tsecha* and *Kotta*', with the former following the 'senior' Kashmiri Muslim religious leader, Mirwaiz Yusuf Shah, and the latter following his religious 'junior', Mirwaiz Hamadani.[299] Both 'Maulvies' had been serious rivals for control of Srinagar's mosques until 1921, when the Governor of Kashmir, Khan Bahadur Chaudhri Khushi Mohammad, divided Srinagar's mosques between them, then obtained an 'undertaking' from both 'not to preach in the mosques allotted to the other'.[300] The 1931 Census similarly noted various 'Muslim sects' among J&K Muslims: 'Suni [sic]' (Sunni), 'Shia', 'Molayi Shia' (Maulias, Ismailis), 'Nur Bakshi', 'Ahl-i-Hadis' (Ahl-i-Hadith), 'Hanfi [sic]' (Hanafi), 'Sufi', 'Ahmadi', and 'Qadiani'.[301] The 1941 Census also noted various types of Muslims living in Kashmir. These were identified as Arain, Bafinda, Bakarwal, Balti, Dhund, Gujjar, Hajjam, Hanjis, Jat, Kashmiris, Kumiar, Lohar, Machi, Moghal, Pathan, Rajput, Sheikh, Sudhan, Syed, Tarkhan, and Teli.[302] Given these interpretations and schisms, Islam may not be an absolute unifier of Kashmiris. History suggests this. In Kashmir's Muslim 'community', Sunnis and Shias had not always co-existed peacefully. On occasions, they clashed, with the last major outburst of Sunni-Shia violence appearing to have occurred in 1872. This involved a 'fierce clash' during a downturn in the shawl industry between 'impoverished' Sunni weavers and 'rich' Shia merchants and traders.[303] More recently, there was some Sunni-Shia conflict 'at several places, resulting in terrorism' during the 1977 elections held in J&K.[304]

While Islam has been very important for Muslim Kashmiris, there has always been another greater, higher or even more important factor. This has been their unique, geographically-based, Kashmiri identity that gives Kashmiris great 'love and devotion for their mother land (*Mouj Kashir*)', the Kashmir Valley.[305] One consequence of this identity is that Kashmiris are 'unlikely to submerge their Kashmiri identity in the name of Islam'.[306] Indeed, for the Indian scholar, Navnita Chadha Behera, Kashmiris 'disavowed their *religious identity* long ago in favour of a *Kashmiri identity*. And they were prepared to defend this in the face of coercion.'[307] This means that many Muslim Kashmiris have considered themselves, or may still consider themselves, to be Kashmiris first, Muslims second, and possibly Indians third. (That said, since the Kashmiris' anti-India uprising, more rigidly

Islamist Muslim Kashmiris may see themselves as Muslims first, then Kashmiris, but never as Indians.) This is an important concept. As Sheikh Abdullah put it in his later years, Kashmiris 'are not fighting so much for territory as for the preservation of certain values that we have inherited through traditions going back over several centuries'.[308] Therefore, rather than wanting first to protect Islam, Muslim Kashmiris have wanted first to protect, maintain and ensure their Kashmiri identity. This issue of preserving the Kashmiri identity is possibly the key to resolving the tortuous relationship between the Kashmir Valley and New Delhi.

Protecting the Kashmiri identity was important for Muslim Kashmiris in 1947. It explains why many of them did not find the possibility of J&K joining Muslim Pakistan fully appealing. Amongst other things, Pakistan's 'monolithic structure … did not recognize any identity other than that based on religion'.[309] This was both a disadvantage and a disincentive for identity-strong Kashmiris. Many believed that, had J&K joined Pakistan, their unique Kashmiri identity would have been quickly submerged, subjugated and subsumed in the greater Pakistani identity. As Sheikh Abdullah saw things, the concept of Pakistan also was a 'slogan of escapism': everywhere in (pre-partition) India there also were 'Muslim monuments, habitations, mosques and holy places, burial places, signs of immortal achievements, academic and mundane'. Therefore, how could Muslims 'quit from any part of India?', he queried.[310] Certainly, in October 1947, 'Islamic' Pakistan proved to be far from benign for Kashmiris. On 22 October, marauding Pukhtoon tribesmen from Pakistan invaded Kashmir Province, brutalised the towns and people of Muzaffarabad, Uri and Baramulla, regardless of their religion, and then threatened Srinagar. These Pukhtoons also were Muslims. Nevertheless, they made no concessions to any J&K-ites, including fellow Muslims, Kashmiri or otherwise, many of whom opposed the Pukhtoons and their raping, pillaging and murderous behaviour.

Conversely, the matter of their identity explains why joining India was more appealing for many Muslim Kashmiris in 1947. They perceived that India would support an inclusive, secular approach that would have accepted, perhaps even encouraged, many different entities within this broad and diverse nation. This included a separate Kashmiri identity and Kashmiri nationalism. Pragmatically, the Kashmir community with its many artisans and traders also may have found the markets of India more appealing than Pakistanis' call to 'the brotherhood of Islam'.[311] Equally, secular but Hindu-dominant India may have been appealing, or at least acceptable, to Muslim Kashmiris because of their innate tolerance, inclusivity, even 'Hinduness'. Muslim Kashmiris were not fundamentalists, to use a term that suggests rigid, hardline beliefs and practices. As an Arab preacher apparently told

Lawrence in the late nineteenth century, 'in their hearts the Kashmiris of the Valley', the majority of whom were Muslims, 'were as Hindu as were the Brahmans of the Capital', Srinagar.[312] The Census of India, 1911, similarly noted that 'Saint worship is more prevalent here [in J&K] among the Sunnis than is the case in the Punjab or elsewhere; and as to Kashmir, there it is carried to extremes'.[313] Lawrence also spoke with 'holy men from Arabia' who spoke 'with contempt of the feeble flame of Islam which burns in Kashmir'.[314] While contestable and not necessarily a bad characteristic, Lawrence's statements had some credence, given his service in J&K from 1889 to 1895, and his understanding of this state's complexity as a result.[315] And while J&K may have changed by 1947,[316] the Hindu Kashmiri, Prem Nath Bazaz, similarly noted in 1954 that a Kashmiri Muslim 'shares in common with his Hindu compatriots many inhibitions, superstitions, idolatrous practices as well as social liberties and intellectual freedoms which are unknown to Islam'. Such Kashmiri 'sharings' had come about due to the influence of the 'Religious Humanism' of Lal Ded and Nund Rishi.[317]

In 1947, Kashmiris shared another important characteristic: many apparently identified with the concept of Kashmiriness, or 'Kashmiriyat', which latter term is derived from Persian and Arabic. Kashmiriyat projects 'a common cultural heritage among Kashmiri Hindus and Muslims', as well as 'papering over their religious and social dissimilarities'.[318] Put another way, Kashmiriyat describes 'a culture and politics which emphasized Hindu-Muslim solidarity'.[319] This supposedly exceptional or unique concept comprises a 'harmonious blending of religious cultures' that stresses 'a united, syncretic Kashmiri cultural identity'.[320] This was/is 'Religious Humanism'[321] or, as one Kashmiri scholar states, 'it appears that this concept has been largely used to denote communal harmony, multiculturalism, and the tolerance that the majority community displays toward the minority community'. It is the 'integral personality of Kashmir'.[322] For another Kashmiri, it is 'a spirit of independence and willing espousal of a secular ideology'.[323] One important aspect of Kashmiriyat therefore includes 'the acceptance and tolerance of all religions among Kashmiris'.[324] They are 'pluralists'.[325] (Equally, however, some people now consider Kashmiriyat to be 'a myth', with 'so much hatred and mistrust around: between Kashmiri Pandits and Kashmiri Muslims; between Jammu and Kashmir; between India and Pakistan'.)[326]

Supposedly, therefore, there were few divisions and little antipathy historically between Kashmiri Muslims and Kashmiri Pandits in the Kashmir 'nation'. Indeed, Bazaz (surprisingly) claims that 'If there was any communalism, it existed among the upper classes; the general mass of people were entirely free from it'. Kashmiri

Muslims and Pandits were of the same ethnicity or 'stock'. They used the same or a very similar language. Both groups had endured repressive rulers. They enjoyed a type of 'cultural pluralism', as a result of which both groups celebrated each other's religious figures and festivals, they ate 'halal' mutton but not beef or pork, which were unacceptable respectively to Hindus and Muslims, and they were not particular about 'defilement or pollution by touch'.[327] As Bazaz put it, 'Racially, culturally and linguistically the Hindus and Muslims living in Kashmir [were] practically one. ... Only their religions differ'.[328] This overstates the situation, as the historian, Ishaq Khan, has suggested. There was 'remarkable affinity between Hindus and Muslims in Kashmir', but both communities had 'dual identities' culturally, as well as 'dual social orders'.[329] The communities were similar, but not the same.

Certainly, Kashmiris were different from other communities dispersed throughout J&K. In southwestern J&K, many J&K-ites congregated in clans or tribes (*biradari*) and were connected with, or heavily influenced by, Punjab and Punjabis. J&K-ites, on the other hand, located in Gilgit, Baltistan and Ladakh, had more links with Central Asia, Chinese Sinkiang and/or Tibet. Kashmir had connections with both Punjab and Central Asia, which, arguably, made it J&K's most international region. Nevertheless, some of these were fluid. For example, trade routes that traversed these areas often converged on Srinagar, which had long been a meeting point for traders from Yarkand, Bukhara, Badakhshan, Khotan, Kashgar, Turkistan, China, Ladakh, Tibet and Baltistan,[330] not to mention traders from Punjab and Pukhtoon areas. In Srinagar, Central Asian traders and travelers rested in the 'Yarkandi Serai', on the left bank of the Jhelum River. This trade had been significant. However, it was interrupted by World War II, then ended in 1949 after the Chinese Communists incorporated Xinjiang into their republic.[331] Many Kashmiris felt different from, and engaged in different ways with, other J&K-ites, especially the Hindu ruler, with whom they were compelled to be involved as his subjects but who, equally, did not permit them to join his armed forces at all, or his administration in numbers that reflected their ethno-numerical dominance. The only exception was the J&K administration, in which Kashmiri Pandits had long worked as an intelligent and 'privileged class'.[332] This situation was not always to the benefit of other Kashmiris, particularly Kashmiri Muslims, whom some Kashmiri Pandit administrators exploited via 'crushing exactions', on occasions.[333]

While Kashmir may have comprised a self-perceived, unified nation, the broader princely state of Jammu and Kashmir did not enjoy any such perception or status. In many people's minds, it was only ever a princely realm or entity. J&K had identifiable geographic boundaries, organised administrative regions and a quantifi-able population, but insufficient of its residents shared 'common characteristics such as language, religion or ethnicity'.[334] Indeed, religion was, arguably, the major dis-unifying factor in J&K throughout 1947, with many, but by no means all, Muslims considering or tending to identify with 'Muslim' Pakistan, while Hindus, Buddhists and Sikhs were identifying with 'Hindu' India. As noted, however, Islam was not monolithic in J&K. According to the 1941 Census, most J&K Muslims were Sunnis (2,821,247 people). There also were 280,000 Shias living in J&K, of whom 74,000 were located in Gilgit Agency, in the Frontier Districts Province.[335] J&K's Shia population amounted to about 9 per cent of the princely state's total Muslim population. Ismailis (followers of the Aga Khan) also lived throughout the Frontier Districts Province, mainly in Gilgit Agency. Uncounted, and perhaps uncountable, were the many Kashmiri Muslims, and some Hindu Pandits, who were inspired by Sufism and/or by the local and inclusive Rishi mystical tradition. Also unquantifiable was the supposed circumstance that Muslims in Kashmir Province and Jammu Province apparently did 'not like each other and they frankly express[ed] it'.[336] Similarly, Hindus could be classified by differing beliefs, practices and caste allegiances, with the ruling Dogra family and the major portion of the J&K State Army comprising Kashatriyas (Dogra Rajputs), while many of the ruler's administrators were Brahmans (Kashmiri Pandits).

Kashmiri Muslims appear generally to have disliked Maharaja Hari Singh. He was unpopular, partly because his 'clan', the Dogras, considered Kashmir to be 'conquered country' in which, and from which, the ruler and his clansmen could, and did, benefit most of all.[337] The Dogras were 'the ruling class over the whole of the territories that comprise the so-called Kashmir kingdom'.[338] However, Kashmiris considered the Dogras to be 'aliens' or 'foreigners' who imposed 'a sort of Dogra imperialism in the State' in which Kashmiris were 'inferiors'. As one Kashmiri noted: 'politically, we might be equal in theory but in actual practice we are looked down upon as a conquered race or, worse still, as people who were purchased. We are not therefore trusted on [sic] positions of responsibility and are not recruited in the Army.'[339] This 'rule by externals' brought many Kashmiris 'nothing but misery, thralldom, physical and mental deterioration', particularly during early Dogra rule when Kashmiris 'suffered great misery'.[340] This 'misery' included the imposition of heavy taxation, with Knight observing in 1895 that the Maharaja governed J&K 'primitively' using 'grasping official middlemen' to 'plunder the peasant', the majority of whom were Muslims.[341] A manifesto published in August 1938 by 'twelve prominent Hindu, Muslim and Sikh leaders' noted the 'ever-growing menace of unemployment amongst ... the illiterate masses in the country, the incidence of numerous taxes, [and] the burden of exhorbitant [sic] revenue' by the J&K Government.[342] A further imposition, and a source of corruption, was the State's use of *begar*: forced unpaid labour by men used as coolies, particularly along the notorious Gilgit Road. While an old and brutal tradition that long pre-dated Dogra rule, this J&K regime 'had made an art of obtaining it [begar] for free'. Conversely, trying 'to escape begar was a constant preoccupation for the Kashmiri cultivator', most of whom were Muslims.[343] Begar was abolished in 1920.[344]

Dogra rule further alienated the Kashmiri Muslim and Hindu *bourgeoisie* (middle class) who had lost direct power when the Mughals captured Kashmir but who had nevertheless enjoyed some indirect power and influence under the Mughals, Afghan and/or Sikh rulers. This loss particularly applied to Muslim Kashmiris after the Dogras took over in 1846: 'Speaking generally and from the *bourgeois* point of view, Dogra rule ... [was] Hindu Raj'.[345] Consequently, upper-class and upper-caste Hindus, chiefly Dogras from Jammu, dominated the J&K regime. With long memories, the loss of Muslim rule in Kashmir, which long predated the Dogras, was 'grievance No. 1' for Kashmiri Muslims.[346] Equally, however, Kashmiri Pandits felt threatened by Jammu Dogras. These Kashmiri Hindus struggled, in particular, because of Maharaja Pratap Singh's increasing use of Punjabi Hindus in government positions in the early 1900s after, and because, Urdu replaced Persian as the state language. Kashmiri Hindus then were fluent in Persian, not Urdu, a factor that advantaged the Punjabis and disadvantaged them. Maharaja Hari Singh finally resolved this issue in 1927 by creating the 'State Subject' status. It had four classes. Class I comprised all persons resident in J&K before 1885. Class II were those who came to J&K between 1885 and 1911. Class III comprised those who came to J&K after 1911 and before 31 January 1927 and who had obtained a concession or permission to purchase immoveable property. Class IV State Subjects related to companies.[347] Basically, as a result of the State Subject status, only people who had this status could live in J&K, or work for the J&K administration, or buy immoveable property (i.e., land). This status was one of the few factors that all J&K-ites had in common in 1947 and, indeed, thereafter – although no longer. Pakistan withdrew State Subject status from Gilgit-Baltistanis in 1974; India withdrew it from Jammuites, Kashmiris and Ladakhis in 2019. These changes may be making some Kashmiris ponder whether their identity can still survive and thrive in India or might be better off in Pakistan or perhaps it should be free from both nations.

The significance of Kashmir's 'superior' position in J&K

In 1947, Kashmir, by virtue of its reputation, population and politicians, was at the centre of J&K politics. The high-profile local politician, Sheikh Abdullah, conducted many of his political activities in his Kashmir homeland. As a result, he attracted visits by other high-profile politicians to the Kashmir Valley, particularly Jawaharlal Nehru, who Abdullah first met in January 1938 and with whom he had a long, strong and secular friendship.[348] Others visitors attracted to Kashmir included the Pukhtoon politician, Khan Abdul Ghaffar Khan, Mahatma Gandhi and Mohammad Ali Jinnah, whom Sheikh Abdullah found difficult. Although Abdullah and many others seemingly had little interest in, or knowledge about, political issues in Jammu or the Frontier Districts, the political, economic and social issues that invariably existed in other parts of the princely state differed little from those that existed in Kashmir. Mostly, these issues concerned securing people's socio-economic uplift and obtaining some meaningful participation for them in J&K's largely autocratic administrative and political processes.

Perhaps the major difference between J&K's three provinces in 1947 was determining what role the Hindu Dogra rulers should play in future in the princely state. Kashmiri Muslims in particular were much more interested in limiting the ruler's role than many other J&K-ites, particularly Jammuites, both Hindu, and in some cases, Muslim. The post-partition actions of Poonch Muslims and Gilgit Muslims also showed that they were politically active at the local level in favour of J&K joining Pakistan, although their actions were little reported at the time. Instead, the media's focus was then on the Kashmir Valley and two of its residents: Maharaja Hari Singh and Sheikh Abdullah. While popular in Kashmir, this Kashmiri politician and other Kashmiri leaders had serious credibility problems in Jammu. For example, one Jammuite believed that all that Abdullah wanted was 'removal of the Maharaja, perhaps to pave the way for a Sultanate for himself, after establishing a mini-Pakistan within India'.[349] A later writer suggested that Abdullah wanted to establish 'an independent "Sheikhdom"'.[350] Similarly, for 'the communal Hindu press', Abdullah desired to replace the Maharaja as 'the Sultan of Kashmir',[351] with 'a crown installed and ready in a mosque' awaiting Abdullah's coronation 'at an opportune time'.[352] While many Kashmiris disliked the Jammuite Maharaja, many Jammuites equally disliked the Kashmiri political leader.

In 1947, Mohammad Ali Jinnah and Jawaharlal Nehru both understood the importance of Kashmir and Kashmiris. For Jinnah, the appeal of the Kashmir community was that it largely comprised Muslims, most of whom he assumed, not unreasonably, would want J&K to join 'Muslim' Pakistan after the British departure. Also, the 'k' in the acrostic 'Pakistan' represented 'Kashmir', i.e., the princely state of Jammu and Kashmir. The future leader of Pakistan therefore hoped, and even expected, that Pakistan would obtain possession of J&K. For Nehru, the Kashmiris and their region were appealing because of his own heritage as a 'Kashmiri settled in the heart of Hindustan',[353] and because of his abiding friendship with Sheikh Abdullah. He also felt that 'Kashmir is a definite historical, cultural and linguistic unit, and it was natural for a popular movement to spread there first without producing the same effect on Jammu'.[354] While almost smitten with Kashmir, Nehru did not rate Jammu. In a lopsided report to the Viceroy about J&K, he dismissed Jammu as 'largely a continuation of the Punjab',[355] which, geographically, was true. Similarly, Jinnah seemingly had little interest in that province. The focus of these two major politicians certainly suggested Kashmir's greater importance than Jammu in 1947. Ironically, however, there was more to Jammu Province than met the eye, given the political actions and religious upheavals that occurred there soon after partition while Kashmir remained relatively quiet. However, Kashmir really 'hogged the limelight' again after, and because, of the Pukhtoons' invasion in October.

An older, irrepressible identity

In 1947 and beforehand, the Kashmir Valley region situated within the princely state of Jammu and Kashmir was this state's pre-eminent, most socio-religiously cohesive and important region. Kashmir had prestige and standing. It was the part of J&K that was easiest to access. It was the part that both Indians and prospective Pakistanis wanted. It was the region they politicked in, and over. Even though Jammu Province was larger and more populous and the Frontier Districts Province was larger and strategically more important, Kashmir Province had one major advantage: it housed the famed, but relatively compact, Kashmir region with its old, large and fairly homogenous, Muslim population. Significantly, the Maharaja of 'Kashmir' was also in Kashmir's capital, the populous and important Srinagar, during the summer of 1947 trying to decide his state's future. However, Hari Singh's influence was waning in conjunction with the departure from the subcontinent of his imperial backers, the British. Concomitantly, Kashmiri nationalism and Kashmiris' political aspirations had been rising. By the time Hari Singh acceded to India, these had become so strong and virulent that Kashmiri nationalists, and a number of other factors, were directly threatening Hari Singh's power, influence and ongoing rule in, and of, J&K. He was slowly being divested of his disparate, diverse and politically divided state.

Following the violent events preceding, and surrounding, Maharaja Hari Singh's accession to India, including the anti-ruler insurgency in Poonch, inter-religious violence throughout Jammu Province and the Pukhtoons' invasion of Kashmir, the greater Jammu region contracted in size and population. Concurrently, demographic dominance and political power shifted from Jammu to Kashmir and from the Dogra ruler to Kashmiri politicians, never to return. This permanent shift was completed in June 1952 when the Dogra dynasty was abolished. Kashmiri nationalism under Sheikh Abdullah's leadership had risen powerfully and without any major regional or ethnic rivals. After 1947 and perhaps not surprisingly, the India–Pakistan dispute over possession of J&K slowly, but increasingly, became a dispute to see which nation could possess the desirable, and desired, Kashmir region only. The other parts of J&K appeared to be less attractive or of less interest, partly because their status seemingly, or de facto, was settled. At the same time, Kashmiri leaders sought to ensure that their 'nation' survived and thrived as much as possible within India. As the entity controlling Kashmir since 1947, India has wrestled long and hard with the strong and seemingly irrepressible Kashmiri identity and with the issue of how to accommodate, control or even repress, Kashmiri 'nationalism' and Kashmiri nationalists. For Indians, these tasks have been challenging, possibly because the identity of the modern, post-colonial nation of India is considerably younger than the Kashmiri identity or the Kashmir 'nation'.

4

The rise of Kashmiri aspirations, 1924–47

This chapter examines the rise of Kashmiri political aspirations from around 1924 until 1947 and, in particular, the overwhelming rise and influence of one of its major proponents and political leaders, the ethnic Muslim Kashmiri, Sheikh Abdullah. Essentially, Kashmiri nationalism 're-awoke' in 1931, partly, but not only, because of his significant actions, which made him a leader of Kashmir Muslims. Sixteen years later, when it was certain the British would be leaving India, Abdullah had become recognised as the undisputed leader of Kashmiris. He was then the most significant and, arguably, the most popular politician in J&K. Abdullah remained significant until his death in September 1982. He enjoyed great prestige and popularity amongst Muslim Kashmiris, both urban and rural. However, he was not as popular with non-Kashmiris and/or with non-Muslims, especially Jammuites and Ladakhis, and particularly after J&K joined India in 1947. Partly, this was because, as one Jammuite put it, Sheikh Abdullah was 'the leader of the struggle for the assertion of Kashmiri identity'. He 'symbolised the aspirations of regional nationalism of Kashmir' and often 'behaved as a leader of Kashmir and not of the whole State'.[1] His political assertiveness would cause him problems on a number of occasions after J&K joined India on 26 October 1947.

The rise of Kashmiri political aspirations and the rise of Sheikh Abdullah were inextricably intertwined with Maharaja Hari Singh and his regime. When Singh became ruler of J&K in 1925, Kashmiri nationalism was beginning to stir. Following an uprising in 1931, he grudgingly granted some limited political rights to some J&K residents. Three years later, a Legislative Assembly known as the *Praja Sabha* (People's House) began. It was heavily under Hari Singh's control and domination, if only because he appointed forty-two of its seventy-five members. Over time, some J&K-ites became frustrated by their lack of genuine political involvement in J&K. In May 1946, an agitated Sheikh Abdullah had the gall to demand that the J&K ruler 'Quit Kashmir' (i.e., abdicate). Some J&K-ites called for the establishment of a republic, possibly with the Maharaja as a constitutional head of state.[2] Abdullah's unexpected and inflammatory demand did not amount to him wanting independence for J&K, however. Indeed, for much of the period that this chapter covers, during which J&K was heavily under British influence, Abdullah had no desire whatsoever for independence for J&K. Rather, he wanted J&K-ites to be empowered so that they could determine their state's political future, not the Maharaja. The thought of an independent J&K would only start to form when it became clear that the British would be leaving the subcontinent and that Pakistan was likely to come into being.

Sheikh Abdullah: an introduction

Sheikh Abdullah was born on 5 December 1905 into a 'middle-class family' in Kashmir.[3] His 'average' shawl-making family was 'neither rich nor poor'.[4] After a challenging upbringing due to the death of Abdullah's father shortly before his birth, and some subsequent rivalry with his half-siblings,[5] he received a BSc (Bachelor of Science) from Islamia College, Lahore, and an MSc (Master of Science) from Aligarh Muslim University in 1930. These qualifications were then very unusual for a Kashmiri Muslim to obtain, chiefly as this community was 'not interested in education at all',[6] as the 1931 Census noted.[7] According to Abdullah, he was the first Kashmiri ever to receive an MSc.[8] Significantly, while studying in Lahore, Abdullah befriended the famous poet, influential Indian and 'old' Kashmiri, Sir Muhammad Iqbal, who apparently 'took [a] keen interest in affairs relating to Kashmir', while 'the plight of Kashmiri Muslims caused him great spiritual and mental agony'.[9] Abdullah witnessed the Kashmiris' 'plight' both in Kashmir and in nearby Lahore,[10] the city Kashmiris naturally gravitated to when looking for work and other opportunities. While at Aligarh, Abdullah heard Mahatma Gandhi speak. One of his teachers there also 'spiritually fortified' him by telling him to 'fear none' and to struggle for Kashmiri rights 'with unflinching courage and confidence'. Abdullah apparently remembered his teacher's advice thereafter 'at every ordeal of my life'.[11]

Around March 1929, Sheikh Abdullah made his 'first uninhibited attempt to engage in politics'. He had a letter published in *Muslim Outlook*, Lahore, that supposedly 'exposed the insidious designs of the Kashmir government', thereby countering some Muslim apologists' views in support of Maharaja Hari Singh.

For Abdullah, this had 'a cathartic effect' on his psyche and he 'felt galvanised into action'.[12] On 12 April 1930, Abdullah returned to Kashmir. Unable to obtain meaningful employment in Srinagar, disenchanted with the regime's discrimination in favour of Hindus, and irate that it could reject a Muslim candidate for a government job 'without assigning any reasons for the rejection', Abdullah 'smelled a rat' and contemplated taking action.[13] However, some time after his return, he took a job as science teacher at the State High School, Srinagar.[14] In July 1931, he was to be transferred to Muzaffarabad, the 'Siberia' of J&K,[15] but he resigned, or was dismissed, from 'the chains of service'.[16] Concurrently, he had become an increasingly high-profile Muslim activist whose political star was rising, which was why the authorities had attempted to transfer him from Srinagar. In resigning, Sheikh Abdullah told the J&K Director of Education that 'the be-all and end-all of his life' was 'to liberate my community from their ignominy and poverty'.[17] Equally, the Kashmiri and some of his colleagues felt that the time was right 'to give up the smoke screen of service' and, instead, 'strike at the autocratic regime'. Abdullah announced his resignation to a 'huge public meeting' held in the important Khanqah-i-Mualla mosque, Srinagar, during which he gave 'a highly emotional speech that electrified the crowd'.[18]

The political rise of Sheikh Abdullah therefore began in Kashmir in 1931. He was a major participant, and an increasingly high-profile leader, in a serious anti-Maharaja agitation in J&K that ultimately resulted in Maharaja Hari Singh receiving some British military support and in him granting a limited legislature to J&K-ites. Concurrent with Abdullah's rise was an awakening in Kashmiri nationalism, which had been starting to stir in the previous five or so years. In 1932, a Punjabi observer of Kashmir, Wali Ullah Zain-ul-abidin, stated that Kashmiris, after the Mughals' capture of Kashmir, 'who were considered as dead for three centuries have arisen again and now are a living nation'.[19] They were no longer 'tongue-tied'.[20] However, the Kashmiris' struggle in 1931 was not about ending Dogra rule or about obtaining independence for J&K. Rather, it was about changing or, if possible, limiting or reducing Maharaja Hari Singh's role, power and privileges in exchange for empowering J&K-ites. As Sheikh Abdullah put it: 'Ours was actually a struggle for the restoration of Kashmir's erstwhile identity' of being free from outside control and controllers.[21] Or, more realistically: the Kashmiris' 'fight' was 'for the toiling people of our beautiful homeland against the heartless ranks of the socially privileged'.[22] It was about lessening Dogra domination and obtaining some socio-economic and political rights for J&K-ites, particularly Kashmiris. Until mid-1946, these were the major Kashmiri aspirations.

The Dogra regime and the start of political activism in J&K

From the 1920s, Kashmiri nationalism, asleep since the Mughals' capture of Kashmir in 1586, started to re-awaken, albeit slowly, as Kashmiris engaged in political activism. Despite then having been ruled by Jammuites for around seventy-five years, Kashmiris 'had hardly reconciled themselves to the Dogra rule'.[23] Consequently, they started seeking more rights for themselves, wanting 'liberty in political, social, economic and intellectual spheres in accordance with the commonly established standards of the time'.[24] Before the 1920s, some community organisations may have formed in the princely state, although these were not political. Possibly as early as 1905, a socio-religious body called the Anjuman-i-Nusrat-ul-Islam was formed. Apolitical, it was concerned with Muslim education, not with Muslims' political rights.[25] The Kashmiri scholar, Ishaq Khan, states that this body was formed in 1921 when the Dogra Government renounced its 'ban on the formation of societies' and 'very unwillingly' permitted the 'Anjuman' to teach the Quran, but not to engage in 'political matters'.[26] Two years later, the J&K Government gave permission to the (Hindu) 'Sanatan Dharam [sic] Sabha' to open in Srinagar on the same non-political terms.[27] The formation of other similar bodies followed: the Muhammadan Youngmen's Association,[28] the Anjuman-i-Hamdard Islam and, for Kashmiri Pandits, the Yuvak Sabha. In Jammu, the Young Men's Muslim Association appeared, as did the Arya Samaj for Hindus and the Dogra Sabha for Dogra loyalists.[29] Formed in the mid-1920s, the Dogra Sabha was possibly J&K's first party organised on a secular basis.[30] All of these bodies did not challenge the ruler's authority or take part in political activities. Rather, they 'passed resolutions and sent memorials to him couched in respectful terms'.[31] No similar socio-religious bodies appear to have been formed or instigated concurrently in the remote Frontier Districts Province.

Significant Kashmiri political activity started in 1924 with two events. First, in July, a major strike occurred in the Government-owned Reshamkhana silk factory in Srinagar,[32] 'believed to be the biggest in the world',[33] with workers seeking better pay and conditions and less oppression. This was not the first such strike. In 1847, 'grossly under-paid' shawl workers in Kashmir had gone on strike, while 4,000 workers had 'set out for Lahore'[34] in 'migration marches' in what, possibly, was the first such 'class struggle' event in India.[35] In April 1865, confronting famine conditions, some shawl industry workers in Kashmir had demonstrated against 'extreme forms of exploitation'.[36] *The Times* considered these demonstrations to be a 'spontaneous mutiny' by Kashmiris over the lack, and cost, of food.[37] In 1877 and 1886, there had also been some 'agrarian discontent' amongst Kashmiris.[38] However, the 1924 action was significant because the sericulture industry was a state monopoly,[39] while the strike occurred at a time when Indian nationalists increasingly were demanding that Indians consume *swadeshi* (i.e., Indian made, as against foreign) goods.[40] Apart from these factors, shawl manufacturing had always been an important industry under the Dogras, employing as many as 120,000 workers on some 20,000 looms at its peak in the nineteenth century.[41] Local authorities suppressed the poorly led 1924 strike with some loss of life.[42]

The second major event in 1924 occurred in October when some leading Kashmiri Muslims gave the visiting Viceroy, Lord Reading, a seventeen-point memorandum that asked for an improvement to their 'utterly deplorable' conditions.[43] This memorandum was partly inspired by the regime's heavy-handed response to the earlier silk workers' strike. The petitioners' demands included property rights for peasants, greater Muslim representation in the J&K administration where there was an 'extreme inadequacy of Muslim representation', a Muslim Governor for Kashmir (or an Englishman if no suitable Muslim was available), and better education for Muslims, including compulsory primary education.[44] Indeed, the Muslim petitioners 'implored' the Government of India to propagate education for Kashmiri Muslims.[45] However, these dissident Kashmiri Muslims had not sought the permission of Maharaja Pratap Singh to present their memorandum to the Viceroy,[46] which they opportunistically had done when this highest British official in India 'visited a shop to see local handcrafts'.[47] Nor, possibly, did their protest resonate fully or emotively with 'the masses', who had not been involved in the protesters' 'confabulations'. Consequently, their protest made 'no impact' on 'ordinary' people,[48] although it may have affected a very young Sheikh Abdullah.[49] For their efforts, the 'greatly incensed' Maharaja Pratap Singh jailed some of the offenders or banished them from J&K, banned them all from engaging in political activity, and forced them to apologise.[50]

A third activity during Pratap Singh's reign was the 'Kashmir for Kashmiris' agitation. In the 1920s, even though J&K was a princely state beyond direct British control, outside events influenced politically aware J&K-ites. They were inspired by the Indian National Congress and 'luminous' personalities such as Mahatma Gandhi and Jawaharlal Nehru[51] and their earlier non-cooperation activities against the British, including the Khilafat Campaign that had supported the retention of the Islamic Caliphate in Turkey.[52] (Jinnah and the Muslim League seemingly then had little or no influence in J&K.) Equally, the previous activities by disgruntled Muslim Kashmiris had occurred near the end of a significant long-term local agitation undertaken by Hindu Kashmiri Pandits that had begun as early as 1910. Their 'Kashmir for Kashmiris' agitation was against Maharaja Pratap Singh's use in his administration of educated Hindus from neighbouring Punjab. It arose because, in 1907, the Maharaja had changed the language used at his court from Persian to Urdu, in which latter language Punjabis were proficient, while locals were not.[53] Since 1890, Punjabis had 'thronged the state' for economic and political reasons after the Jhelum Valley Road was opened. Thereafter, adroit and better-financed Punjabi traders apparently gained control of Kashmir's export trade.[54] Pratap Singh's change of the official language impacted on Kashmiri Pandits who, encouraged by the great and inclusive Kashmiri ruler, Sultan Zain-ul-Abidin, had mastered Persian 'over a century prior to [the Mughals'] decision to make Persian the court language' in 1582.[55] In 1907, however, few Pandits spoke Urdu to the level required administratively. They were significantly disadvantaged, therefore, and disenchanted.

These three agitations by Kashmiris all took place in the twilight of Maharaja Pratap Singh's reign: he would die on 25 September 1925, thus leaving the problems to his thirty-year-old nephew, Raja Hari Singh. The younger Dogra ascended the J&K throne on 23 September 1925, thereby becoming Maharaja of Jammu and Kashmir and one of the most important and influential of India's princes. While his ascension was considered 'a harbinger of [a] number of social and political measures of sweeping importance',[56] Hari Singh himself was somewhat controversial. For a start, he had not been his childless uncle's first choice as successor. Born in 1895, Hari Singh was the son of Pratap's younger brother and rival for British attention, Raja Amar Singh, whose untimely death in 1909 was possibly due to having been poisoned.[57] Pratap had had a trying relationship with Amar. Chiefly, the Dogra brothers' angst was in relation to Pratap's supposed maladministration of his domain and Amar's proactive role in the establishment in 1889 of a British-dominated Council of State. Sidelining Pratap, this Council administered J&K until 1905, with the capable Amar's assistance as Foreign Minister. In 1906, reflecting this brotherly antagonism, Pratap had adopted as his legal heir and potential successor Sukhdev Singh, the son of his distant cousin, Raja Baldev Singh of Poonch, a then semi-autonomous feudatory state under J&K's indirect control. Pratap's and Baldev's grandparents, respectively Gulab Singh and Dhyan Singh, had been brothers. However, the British thwarted Pratap's plan as they refused to recognise the Poonch prince as Pratap's legal successor, although Sukhdev Singh was allowed to be Pratap's spiritual heir, which gave Sukhdev certain religious rights and responsibilities only. This succession issue created bad blood between

J&K's Amar Singh line, particularly Hari Singh, and the Poonch royal family. Maharaja Hari Singh would 'correct' this circumstance soon after Raja Sukhdev Singh died in October 1927.[58]

Hari Singh had further interesting 'history'. He had helpful administrative experience, having been the 'Senior Member' of the J&K State Council since 1922, a position that gave him involvement running, and supposedly reforming, J&K.[59] Seemingly, Hari was more liberal than his 'intensely religious' and cricket loving uncle, Pratap.[60] However, like Pratap, Hari was also wealthy, although, unlike Pratap, Hari was ostentatious. A British newspaper in 1946 described Hari Singh as a man 'whose wealth is so great that even he cannot compute it'.[61] A Kashmiri did, however, compute it, claiming in 1941 that Maharaja Hari Singh and his family 'appropriated' a 'fabulous amount' of Rs 4,100,000, which amounted to about 16 per cent of the J&K State's revenues and most of which, unlike his uncle's income, was not spent in J&K.[62] Certainly, official figures in 1938 showed that the ruler's 'Privy Purse and Allowances' amounted to Rs 3,046,000 out of a total state expenditure of Rs 25,916,000. This meant that the ruler received a healthy 11.75 per cent of state revenues.[63] Either percentage suggested that, unlike the 'indebtedness in many villages throughout the State' where people's expenditures often exceeded their incomes and which acted 'as a millstone around the necks of the majority' of J&K-ites, Maharaja Hari Singh did not experience poverty.[64] One of his high-profile assets was a saloon 'silver aeroplane' built for his personal use in 1934 after an 'extended stay' in England during which he 'frequently chartered aeroplanes for his excursions'.[65] The Dogra prince had also been able to pay an astonishing £300,000 as 'hush money' to blackmailers, as a court case in London in 1924 revealed.[66] Possibly based on this negative judicial experience, the new ruler of J&K announced that his only religion would be 'justice', by which he meant that he would 'not permit any discrimination against any class of my people on the grounds of religion'.[67] Despite such lofty aims, Maharaja Hari Singh promulgated a new 'Constitutional Act' in March 1927 that actually increased his political powers.[68] From 1925, he had been operating under Maharaja Pratap Singh's British-influenced Constitution,[69] which may have been developed as early as 1905.[70]

On becoming ruler of J&K, Maharaja Hari Singh inherited a state administration, a police force and an army that helped him to administer J&K and control his subjects. Non-Muslim J&K-ites generally dominated these three entities. According to the 1931 Census, there were 15,073 people whose 'occupation' was given as 'service of the state'. Of these administrators in the State Service, 9,180 people, or 61 per cent of them, were Hindus and 5,052 people, or 34 per cent of them, were Muslims.

The other administrators were Buddhists (seventy-five), Jains (six), Sikhs (712) and Christians (forty-eight). The 1941 Census provided gross figures for people working in Public Administration, but without any religious breakdown. However, by April 1945 'according to [unidentified] government sources', the percentage of Muslims in the J&K administration had increased to 40 per cent.[71] According to the J&K Administration Report for 1934, the J&K police force comprised 3,090 men. Of these, 2,934 people, or 95 per cent, were 'Constables' (2,450 men), 'Selection Grade Constables' (ninety-four men) or 'Head Constables' (390). The Administration Report did not provide any ethno-religious details. However, according to figures provided in the 1931 Census, there were 3,390 people whose 'occupation' was identified as 'Police'. Of this total, 1,644 people, or 49 per cent, were Muslims and 1,634 people, or 48 per cent, were Hindus.[72] Of the thirty-seven men holding senior police positions of inspector and ranks above, only two were Muslims.[73]

Maharaja Hari Singh's predecessor had developed a significant 'State Army' of some 8,600 soldiers.[74] According to the J&K Administration Report for 1934, the J&K Army comprised some 7,770 'First Line Troops', divided into 7,000 combatants and 770 non-combatants, and an 'Auxilliary Service' of 828 members, divided evenly between combatants and non-combatants. The State Army was divided into four cavalry units, comprising a 'Body Guard Cavalry Artillery' and three mountain batteries, eight infantry units of which one was a 'Training Battalion', and auxiliary troops, comprising military transport, forts and a State band. The military was manned by 'Rajputs, Dogras, Kangra Rajputs, Gurkhas and Sikhs'; J&K Muslims were excluded from this 'Jammu army', as one Britisher called it,[75] as they were considered 'docile and passive' and a 'non-martial race'.[76] Partially reflecting this ethno-religious composition, two-thirds of the J&K forces (5,850 men) were stationed in Jammu Province, about 22 per cent (1,870) were in Kashmir Province, and 880 were in the Gilgit area. On occasions, State Forces were used for law and order duties. In 1936, for example, troops were 'immediately despatched [sic] from Jammu' to Poonch after the 'Wazir of Poonch' sought 'Military aid' to control Muslims agitated at the burning down of a mosque. Their arrival in the Poonch area 'was sufficient to bring the situation under control'.[77]

After his enthronement, one of Maharaja Hari Singh's first positive acts was to sort out the 'Kashmir for Kashmiris' issue. This was significant as it empowered J&K-ites over 'foreigners'. On 31 January 1927, he sanctioned an official notification that defined a 'Hereditary State Subject'.[78] This severely limited and controlled the ability of outsiders, chiefly Punjabi Hindus but also 'Kashmir Mohammadans domiciled in the Punjab',[79] to live in J&K and work in state employment. There

144

were four classes,[80] a hierarchy that meant that a higher-class State Subject would receive preference over a lesser-class State Subject in obtaining a position in the State Service or a scholarship, or in being able to purchase land for agriculture or housing.[81] The creation of the J&K State Subject status seemingly ended the significant local unease about the intruding Punjabis, even though it chiefly benefitted educated J&K-ites. Most of these were Hindus, particularly Dogras and Pandits, not Muslims, who generally were poorly educated. Thereafter, the Maharaja continued to predominantly use these educated J&K Hindus in his administration, particularly at higher levels, rather than 'foreign' Punjabis or local Muslims. He also used his Hereditary State Subject notification to control land in J&K. After 1928, only State Subjects could purchase 'immovable property' (i.e., land) in the princely state.

After Maharaja Hari Singh's enthronement, events in J&K seem to have gone reasonably well for him until about 1929 when a former Prime Minister of the princely state made a surprising statement about it. In March 1929, Sir Albion Banerji (or Banerjee), 'in a statement to the Press', said that

> Jammu and Kashmir State is labouring under many disadvantages with a large Mohammedan population, absolutely illiterate, labouring under poverty and very low economic conditions of living in the villages and practically governed like dumb-driven cattle. There is not much touch between the Government and the people, no suitable opportunity for the representation of their grievances and the administrative machinery itself requires over-hauling from top to bottom to bring it up to modern conditions of efficiency. It has at present little or no sympathy with the people's wants and grievances. … there is hardly any public opinion in the State. As regards the Press it is practically non-existent with the result that the Government is not benefited to the extent that it should be by the impact of healthy criticism.[82]

This statement was significant: as a former Prime Minister of J&K from 1927 to 1929, Banerji knew what he was talking about. As a 'senior Bengali officer of the Government of India', he also had considerable standing.[83]

Banerji's statement was interesting for two reasons. First, during his previous tenure as Prime Minister of J&K, he apparently 'had at no time … either officially or informally, drawn the attention of the Government to what he called the deplorable condition' of the Maharaja's 'Mohammadan' subjects.[84] Perhaps he felt that he didn't need to state the obvious. The second interesting factor was Banerji's mention of cattle in relation to Muslim J&K-ites. This was not a new analogy. During Sikh rule of Kashmir, 'The Sikhs seem[ed] to look upon the Kashmirians [sic] as little better than cattle'.[85] Additionally, the cow was sacred to Hindus and legally was unable to be killed in, or exported from, J&K. Consequently, there was no shortage of cattle in J&K. Indeed, there was 'an excess so large as to constitute a serious problem ... aggravated by the fact that most of the cattle [were] of very poor quality', underfed, ill-nourished and subject to 'every outbreak of disease'. The 'obvious remedy' to J&K's problem was a 'reduction in the number of useless cattle and the improvement of the breed'.[86] Was Banerji hinting that the regime felt the same politically in relation to Kashmiri Muslims?

Banerji's statement, along with other events occurring around the same time, apparently motivated J&K Muslims. Some were inspired to pursue political and, more particularly, economic justice for themselves and their state. In 1929, there was a 'Mohammadan agitation', with Muslims seeking more educational scholarships and positions in the State Service.[87] The following year (1930), some Kashmiris founded the 'Fateh Kadal Reading Room' in Srinagar. Attendees discussed 'the current topics of the day' and Muslim grievances, particularly their lack of employment in the J&K Government. An 'absolutely unknown', but active and 'earnest member', was 'S. M. Abdullah',[88] who was elected the organisation's secretary.[89] In September 1930, the young Kashmiri's profile rose when he was one of two Reading Room representatives to meet the three-man Cabinet administering J&K in Maharaja Hari Singh's absence at the Roundtable Conference in London. In particular, the Reading Room representatives sought (unsuccessfully) to have Muslims recruited into the J&K administration without conditions, as occurred for members of other J&K communities.[90] This seemingly was Abdullah's first major outing as a political representative.

Around the same time, or perhaps earlier, an All-India Kashmir Muslim Conference was founded in Lahore, with one prominent member being Sir Muhammad Iqbal, who in 1931 was banned from entering J&K.[91] In 1926, 'the Kashmir Muslim Conference ... had taken up the cause of the Mohammadans of Kashmir', including by attempting (unsuccessfully) to present a memorial to Maharaja Hari Singh.[92] This body also provided 'material and emotional support' to Kashmiri Muslims.[93] In 1929–30, a body called the *Majlis-e Ahrar-e Islam-e Hind* was founded, also in Lahore. While ostensibly 'fighting British imperialism', it began to organise demonstrations in Kashmir.[94] Its 'Kashmir Chalo' ('Let's go to Kashmir') slogan proved so successful that the J&K Government had to ask the Punjab Government to control the border in order to reduce the inflow of Ahrars into J&K.[95] In 1927, an organisation called the 'Gujar-Jat Conference' succeeded in securing state subject status in J&K for 'all sedentary Gujar', most, if not all, of whom were Muslims. Fours year later, 'all nomadic Gujar' achieved the same status. In 1935, a branch of the Gujar-Jat Conference was formed in J&K.[96] J&K Muslims were beginning to stir, or be stirred.

The 1931 uprising

The year 1931 was an extraordinary one in J&K. During the year, 'conditions remained abnormal' and volatile in the princely state,[97] Muslims were in a 'sullen mood',[98] and a major agitation marked the significant re-emergence of Kashmiri activism, even nationalism. On 13 July 1931, J&K-ites, particularly Muslims, engaged in serious rioting, which caused, involved or provoked 'communal clashes', 'political agitation' and 'much stir throughout the country', i.e., throughout J&K.[99] This quickly developed into an impromptu anti-Maharaja uprising. For one Jammuite, this anti-Maharaja agitation marked the 'beginning of the modern political movement in Kashmir'.[100] For a Kashmiri, the 1931 uprising 'shook the whole State, including the Administration' and seriously 'unnerved the Maharaja'.[101] On 14 July, he appointed a three-man 'official committee' to enquire into the causes of the previous day's 'disturbances' and actions taken to deal with them. Five days later, the ruler added two non-official members to the committee, a Hindu and a Muslim.[102]

The Riot Enquiry Committee reported in September 1931. In a section on the 'Circumstances Leading to Recent Disturbances', the Committee concluded that a number of factors caused the 1931 disturbances. These included: Maharaja Hari Singh's 'forced absence' from J&K 'on State business in September 1930' and the consequent lack of 'promptness and foresight' in the state, coupled with the 'want of harmony in the Cabinet' that administered J&K during his absence; official 'tolerance' of a preceding agitation by Muslims in Jammu and the later 'mishandling' in Srinagar of a delegation from Jammu; external help given to J&K Muslims by people, organisations and newspapers from outside the princely state, particularly Punjab; and, some 'tragic and accidental happenings' that appeared to be anti-Islamic that occurred in Jammu Province then in Kashmir Province. Importantly, this last factor provided 'the agitators', who included the now unemployed Sheikh Abdullah, with an opportunity to influence negatively, even 'inflame', 'the minds of the Mohammadan masses'.[103] However, the Riot Enquiry Committee also noted that 'the paucity of Mohammadens in State services' and an associated Muslim desire 'for a much larger share' in this service were factors that led to the 1931 disturbances. Importantly, this Muslim 'grievance' became 'more acute' when Muslims found 'that they have no ability to satisfy their natural desire for a voice in the Government of the State'. Their 'dissatisfaction' was a 'perpetual source of embitterment' to the

Muslim intelligentsia 'and an incentive to them to excite the masses by illusive religious grievances'.[104]

A number of other factors motivated the 1931 uprising. Muslims were provoked by powerful rallying slogans such as the 'easy cry of religion in danger',[105] or the even more specific 'Islam in Danger'.[106] In 1930, Iqbal suggested that Muslims unify and create a separate and 'consolidated North-West Indian Muslim State', a suggestion that amplified religious slogans being used in J&K.[107] In March 1931, the death occurred of the moderate and moderating, pro-Maharaja Muslim religious leader, Mirwaiz Ahmad Ullah.[108] This was followed by a huge funeral procession in Srinagar, involving 100,000 mourners, in which Reading Room members were 'conspicuous ... honouring the dead and arranging the procession'.[109] Thereafter the Kashmir Muslim community's youthful leaders, particularly Mirwaiz Yusuf Shah and 'Master Abdullah' (i.e., Sheikh Abdullah) from the Reading Room,[110] assertively competed for leadership of Kashmiri Muslims. These two men would become long-term rivals, with Abdullah being more progressive and Shah more conservative. Another factor was the growing unease and unrest among the Muslim *bourgeoisie*,[111] particularly Muslim Kashmiris who had obtained an education outside J&K then returned to the state but who could not secure government employment.[112] Prior to their return, some of these former students possibly may have formulated plans for a mass movement in Kashmir.[113]

Some other external events also motivated J&K-ites in 1931. The first was the 1929 'All India Congress' held at Lahore under Jawaharlal Nehru's presidency. Attended by 'a large number of politically-minded Kashmiri youngmen [sic]', it called for 'complete independence – *Purna Swarajya* – as its goal' for India.[114] Second, the anti-government and India-wide Civil Disobedience Movement that followed in 1930 had 'very far-reaching repercussions on the popular struggle in Kashmir, of 1931'.[115] J&K-ites were motivated by Mahatma Gandhi's provocative Salt March, which effectively protested against the British monopoly on salt. To support Gandhi's march, some J&K-ites had also undertaken a complete *hartal* (strike) in Jammu City, while others staged a large demonstration in Srinagar.[116] The worldwide depression was another factor as it had 'disastrous consequences' for J&K, particularly for its tourist and export sectors, many of which were located in the Kashmir Valley.[117] Given these various factors, by 1931, many J&K-ites were agitated and motivated.

Initially, and somewhat atypically in terms of many of J&K's later protests, the largely spontaneous 1931 uprising began in the Maharaja's home province of Jammu. This involved some incidents in April in which Muslims protested about their (lack of) rights[118] and some serious unrest because a Hindu police sergeant allegedly 'profaned' a Koran belonging to a Muslim policeman.[119] These two incidents were significant as Hindu-Muslim antagonism was 'said to be far more bitter [in Jammu] than in Srinagar'.[120] Trouble then spread to Kashmir, where Muslims were aggrieved and insulted after some pages of a Koran were allegedly found in a Srinagar latrine.[121] On 21 June, a visiting and 'non-descript outsider', Abdul Qadeer, who was the butler for one 'Major Abbott, an Englishman', gave an inflammatory and allegedly seditious speech in which he implored Kashmiris to 'Arise and take on your oppressors!'[122] His speech followed an extraordinary cross-factional meeting at the Khanqah-i-Mualla mosque, Srinagar, that the Reading Room had convened and which was attended by 'about fifty thousand people'.[123] With 'sectional differences … relegated to the background', with positive affirmations of solidarity made publicly and with widespread cries of 'Zindabad',[124] excited, even euphoric, Kashmir Muslims elected seven representatives to present their demands to the Maharaja. A Britisher, George Wakefield, who was then Prime Minister of J&K, had suggested such a meeting would be possible. These representatives included Mirwaiz Yusuf Shah, his traditional rival, Mirwaiz Hamadani, and the young Sheikh Abdullah.[125] Following Qadeer's 'inflammatory speech',[126] which was delivered impromptu after the various Kashmiri leaders had left the mosque, he was arrested and later put on trial for disturbing the peace. Interestingly, Qadeer apparently had met Sheikh Abdullah some time earlier in Srinagar.[127]

Kashmiri Muslims were agitated by Qadeer's arrest. His trial in-camera at Srinagar Central Jail on 13 July 1931 'greatly excited the Mohammedan public opinion'.[128] Some ill-prepared jail guards and police clashed with a large group of protesting Kashmiris, who, among other activities, pelted the Governor with stones, an old way (still in use) in J&K for people to show their displeasure with authority.[129] In response, a panicked police battalion fired on the crowd, killing as many as twenty-two people and injuring many more.[130] The Riot Enquiry Committee stated that 'the firing was not prolonged beyond what was necessary', that it was against a restive, agitated and 'advancing crowd … not a retreating crowd' numbering some 7,000 people, and that, 'as far as could be ascertained 10 men were killed by the firing at the Jail'.[131] After these deaths, looting and communal rioting 'paralyzed' Srinagar for a week,[132] with this city 'thrown into panic' and uncertainty.[133] *The Statesman* reported that the attack on the jail killed nine people, after which 'grave communal disturbances' followed, but 'by midnight, complete order was restored'.[134] The same newspaper followed up later stating that this 'first serious outbreak' of communal violence 'in a hundred years' had resulted in sixteen dead and sixty-five wounded in 'rioting' in Srinagar, with 'the principal basis of the present disturbances' being that the Maharaja had given the majority of official positions to Hindus.[135]

Violence continued into August and September, then again in November, 1931. On 14 August, a Kashmir Committee led by Iqbal directed that this day be celebrated as Kashmir Day. Protests and strikes erupted throughout J&K.[136] On 16 August, after receiving a strongly worded telegram from the Viceroy, Maharaja Hari Singh met some Kashmiri Muslim representatives. Nevertheless, further agitations occurred in September, culminating in Sheikh Abdullah's arrest in Srinagar on 21 September for not keeping the peace. Thereafter, rioting erupted in Srinagar, Islamabad (now Anantnag) and Shopian, as a result of which twenty-seven people were killed[137] in what amounted to 'mob violence'.[138] On 24 September, the J&K Government promulgated a draconian ordinance called 19–L. It was withdrawn due to negative public opinion on 6 October 1931, but re-imposed on 1 June 1933. According to Nehru, speaking in 1939 as the President of the All-India States Peoples' Conference (AISPC), 'Hundreds of arrests were made under this Notification during the first two civil disobedience agitations and during 1938'.[139] Essentially, 19–L imposed martial law on Kashmir.[140] It is one reason why Nehru started to take an interest in J&K affairs.[141] During the first week of November 1931, there were further 'disturbances' in 'Jammu and its environments'.[142] Fourteen people, comprising four Hindus and ten Muslims were killed.[143] Soon after these disturbances began, the British intervened militarily in 'Mirpur and other places' to assist Maharaja Hari Singh[144] retain his somewhat shaky six-year-old throne and, more importantly, to maintain control of his state.

These autumn disturbances were serious enough to warrant another official post-event 'inquiry' and report, with a British officer in the Punjab Government,[145] L. Middleton, undertaking both activities. (Hari Singh ignored an offer from the Nawab of Bhopal to 'act as a mediator'.)[146] Middleton reported in late February 1932. He found both 'the authorities' and 'Moslem leaders' at fault in September. Had there been better planning, coordination and supervision of the crowds, there would not have been a need to resort to military intervention.[147] For Bazaz, some of the turbulence in 1931 had a 'communal-cum-economic shape. It was a war of Muslim peasantry against the Hindu money-lenders'.[148] For Middleton, the Muslims' agitation was 'directed entirely against the [J&K] Government and not against the Hindu community or against the Ruling House'.[149] Seemingly, there was no coordination between Kashmiri Muslims and Jammu Muslims. Indeed, according to one Dogra author, the 'muslims [sic] of Jammu had little sympathy for those from the valley'.[150] Kashmiri Muslims possibly harboured similar sentiments in relation to

Jammu Muslims. Nevertheless, there is some evidence that the unrest in one location may have inspired action in the other. Certainly during a later period of agitation in Kashmir in 1933, Jammu Muslims supposedly for a time 'remained neutral', then, 'anxious to show their communal loyalty', they started a 'civil disobedience' campaign.[151]

More was to come. On 21 January 1932, J&K security forces fired on and killed twenty-five Muslim worshippers in Jammu, which led to 'another popular upsurge'.[152] Concurrently, there was 'grave rioting on the Kashmir border' as *jathas* and others from Punjab sought again to influence or stir up events in J&K.[153] (A jatha was a 'cohort of unarmed men, who seek to attain their object by organising obstruction to the authorities'.[154] The previous year, Punjabi jathas arriving via Suchetgarh had seriously disrupted trade and other activities in southern Jammu Province, with 1,400 arrested in November 1931 at the Punjab-J&K border, 4,600 being held at Satwari,[155] near Jammu City, and 869 detained at Udhampur.)[156] In 1932, in Reasi and Rajouri, residents were 'rising in rebellion', with Hindus being targeted as a result of 'the pernicious teaching of certain persons from the Panjab [sic]'.[157] In early February 1932, there was 'communal conflict' around Mirpur.[158] The situation became so bad that the (Muslim) Nawab of Bhopal, a senior and respected Indian ruler, offered to act as a mediator between 'the Kashmir Durbar and the Moslem population there'.[159] By the end of February 1932, however, the situation in J&K had apparently been brought under control.[160] Some serious violence and destruction had occurred. The Administration Report of 1933 stated that, in the Mirpur and Rajouri areas, the J&K Government had rebuilt 677 houses of non-Muslims 'which had been destroyed by Muslim rioters' in 1932, at a total cost of 'three lakhs' (300,000 rupees), while local Muslims 'suspected of having been instrumental in destroying them' rebuilt 'two hundred houses'.[161] The Administration Report did not mention Hindu violence against Muslims, of which, according to Middleton, there had also been some in 1931–32.[162]

In 1933, there were occasional sporadic outbursts of violence and the occasional death or two, often due to fighting between rival Muslim gangs supporting Mirwaiz Yusuf Shah or Sheikh Abdullah. This 'religious rivalry between two sections of Muslims'[163] was causing 'affrays', death and the destruction of property.[164] In late May, the leader of one of the factions, Sheikh Abdullah, was arrested, after which, in June, some of his colleagues sought to have him released or else they proposed to take 'direct action' against the J&K regime.[165] Arrested on 23 May 1933, Abdullah was released two months and eighteen days later.[166] In June 1933, the J&K Government imposed the powerful Ordinance 19-L, after which 'the tempo of the agitation began to slow down.[167] Nevertheless, major disturbances occurred thereafter in response to this imposition, with seven leaders exiled, hundreds arrested, and riots in Pulwama and Bijbehara in February 1934, in which ten people were killed.[168] A short 'civil disobedience' campaign in Jammu to support the Kashmiris followed, but it was unsuccessful[169] and quickly 'fizzled out'.[170]

By January 1934, popular support for civil disobedience had waned to such an extent that Sheikh Abdullah decided that 'it was time to come to ... an agreement with the authorities in the Kashmir State'. Abdullah's popularity was plummeting, with his placatory stance partially reflecting his controversial and, for many Kashmiri Muslims, unacceptable alleged status as a practicing Ahmadiyya (or Ahmadi). (According to a Kashmiri biographer, Abdullah was 'an extremely devout and highly orthodox (Hanifite) Muslim'.)[171] Followers in the Ahmadiyya sect considered their founder to be a prophet, a belief unacceptable to most Muslims. Other militating factors in J&K included the poor and unempowered masses' general fatigue and weariness with political and economic dislocation, repression by the Maharaja's forces, and strong British control of external elements, particularly in Punjab.[172] With his standing diminished, Sheikh Abdullah declared in late 1934 that he was withdrawing from politics for a time in order to undertake 'legal study' in England.[173] In 1935, according to the J&K Government, 'The efforts of Sh. Mohammad Abdulla [sic] ... to start a national movement with the object of presenting a united demand for a responsible Government did not make much head-way'.[174] In 1936, Abdullah returned to politics in J&K a seemingly more moderate and inclusive figure.[175] Later the same year, the Viceroy, Lord Linlithgow, briefly visited J&K and witnessed the supposed 'manifold improvements' made in the 'administration of the State'.[176]

A serious undertaking

The 1931 uprising in Kashmir, which continued into early 1932 and sporadically into 1933, was a significant undertaking. It was the first time that J&K-ites seriously challenged Dogra control of J&K. As Bazaz saw things, it marked the beginning of the struggle by J&K-ites to obtain some political and socio-economic rights. Equally, he notes that the 1931 struggle had a strong communal aspect,[177] with people in J&K of differing religions, usually Muslims and Hindus, acting separately. In terms of casualties and property damage, this 'major revolt', which involved 'three years of turmoil' was possibly 'the most serious communal outbreak in India between the Moplah rebellion of 1921 [in south India] and the Calcutta riots of

1946'.[178] Indeed, it was serious enough that the (British) Indian Government, after a request by Maharaja Hari Singh,[179] sent an 'Indian infantry battalion',[180] possibly even a brigade,[181] to Jammu Province from 3 November 1931 to October 1932 to 'quell' an uprising being supported by Muslim jathas from the British-administered Punjab Province.[182] 'Owing to the communal nature of the trouble', these were British troops.[183] They were considered less likely to succumb to communalism. The J&K Government also closed the important bridge at Kohala on the Jhelum Valley Road that allowed the entry of people, including possible Muslim jathas, into Kashmir Province.[184]

As one senior Britisher put it in early 1932: 'serious trouble has been experienced in Kashmir, where the Moslem population has become restive under the oppression, real or imaginary, of the Hindu rule'.[185] Writing slightly earlier, *The Statesman's* 'Special Correspondent' had been more specific: J&K Muslims 'bitterly resent[ed] a Hindu despotism in a State adjoining an independent Moslem country [Afghanistan] and British Indian Provinces which will shortly enjoy autonomy with Moslem majorities in power'. Importantly, he also noted that the 'Durbar turns a deaf ear even to Hindu representatives of embarrassing truths'. One 'embarrassing truth' was that 'It is perfectly obvious that that feeling – the huge majority's objection to the despotism of a very small alien majority – is the fundamental cause of all of the State's troubles of the past eight months'.[186] Because of the number of people killed or injured on 13 July 1931, Kashmiris, other J&K-ites and pro-J&K-ites living in other locations (e.g., Pakistan) have continued to commemorate this day as 'Martyrs' Day',[187] usually with 'great devotion'.[188] Conversely, Kashmiri Pandits have observed it as a 'black day' due to the 'large-scale burning and looting of property belonging to members of the minority community' (i.e., Hindu Pandits) that occurred.[189]

For Maharaja Hari Singh, the 'trouble' that started in J&K in 1931 'was engineered by elements outside the State under the instigation of the British'. This was because he had tried to 'shake off the British yoke', but, in doing so, had 'incurred the wrath of the British who thenceforth became openly hostile'.[190] Karan Singh similarly believed that events in J&K in 1931 'were in fact masterminded by the British' to teach his father a lesson for having made a 'patriotic speech' at the first Round Table Conference in London in 1930–31.[191] Other authors made similar claims about Hari Singh's 'faux pas' that seemingly 'incensed the British' who began 'to doubt his loyalty' and to scheme against him.[192] One of Hari Singh's hagiographers, for example, saw British treachery in 1931 simply because a Britisher, George Wakefield, who was then serving as Prime Minister of J&K, 'was acting as the agent [in J&K] of the British Government in Delhi'. Therefore, 'Was there any doubt as to who had orchestrated the sending of the *jathas* in the first place!'[193] Similarly, the fact that the provocateur, Abdul Qadeer, was employed by a Britisher provided another reason for people to allege that the British were involved fomenting the 1931 uprising.[194] While extraordinary claims, a book about the British 'Raj' suggested that 'One of Britain's favourite ways of dealing with an errant ruler was to diminish his prestige'. Although the author lists six examples where this happened overtly to Indian princes, these examples do not include any actions taken against the ruler of J&K. Possibly, this was because any British actions in J&K would have been undertaken covertly and would have been difficult to detect.[195]

While events in 1931 may have had a communal aspect, J&K Muslims were not united. Contributing to the tense environment in Srinagar in 1931 was a 'religious controversy' between the hereditary leaders of Srinagar's two main mosques: Mirwaiz Yusuf Shah from the Jamia Masjid and Mirwaiz Hamadani from the Khanqah-i-Mualla.[196] They had been 'actively promoting the spirit of hooliganism'.[197] Apart from their personal rivalry and ambitions, there was an issue of the religious acceptability and political involvement of Ahmadiyya Muslims in J&K politics. This occurred after Mirwaiz Hamadani allowed a senior Ahmadiyya cleric to speak in the Khanqah-i-Mualla. Thereafter, both men's feud moved beyond whether Ahmaddiya Muslims were apostates to such an extent that it 'thoroughly polarized' the Kashmir Muslim community. Their rivalry also quickly came to heavily influence politics in the Kashmir Valley, with Hamadani 'act[ing] in sympathy with Abdulla's [sic] political party' while Yusuf Shah supported Abdullah's opponents.[198] According to Abdullah, Shah may have instituted the Ahmadiyya issue to try to dent Abdullah's rising popularity.[199] However, for Saraf, this was 'factually, absolutely incorrect': Abdullah 'all along has remained a follower of the Sunni Hanafi sect'.[200] Nevertheless, there was some evidence to show that the Ahmadiyya 'Khalifa' (head), Mirza Bashir-ud-din Mahmud Ahmad, using Abdullah as a channel, supported the Youngmen's Association, for which Abdullah was its 'most gifted orator', with propaganda and funds and that 'the Sheikh was a practising Ahmadiyya'. Abdullah being an Ahmadiyya supposedly was confirmed in 1933 via an intercepted letter that the Kashmiri wrote to Mahmud Ahmad and after which 'Abdullah's popularity plummeted'.[201] His status as 'a good Muslim' would be in doubt for some years.

Significantly, the 1931 agitation physically involved, and partially was 'emboldened' by,[202] elements from Punjab Province, which was contiguous with J&K and easily accessible via the all-weather Jhelum Valley Road. Punjabi Ahrars and Ahmadiyyas saw J&K as a place in which to expand their activities and followers. Their involvement was not surprising as Punjabi politics impacted on J&K-ites, and vice versa. The Government of India noted this circumstance in its report to the British Parliament in 1933, stating that a 'serious communal riot [that] occurred in Srinagar on the 13th July' 1931 had 'received the very sympathetic attention of their [Muslim] co-religionists not only in Punjab, but also in other parts of India'.[203] Similarly, 'bitter relations in Punjab between the two communities', Hindu and Muslim, 'were given a peculiar and unexpected turn by events in Kashmir. … the riot at Srinagar on the 13th July excited widespread sympathy among Indian Muslims with the claims of their Kashmiri co-religionists. This feeling was rekindled by renewed disturbances in Kashmir towards the end of September.'[204] In late 1931, the Punjab Government had been granted power to deal with jathas in Punjab who 'were organized for the purpose of entry into Kashmir territory with the object of bringing pressure on the [J&K] Durbar'. Equally, the Maharaja of J&K 'was urged to deal firmly with [the] Muslim agitation and there was some talk of retaliatory Hindu action in Muslim states'. Such 'communal feeling' throughout northern India then caused governments 'much anxiety'.[205]

By 1936, the 'Ahrar-Ahmadi controversy … had faded into insignificance'. Mainly, this was because of the 'sudden reversal of conditions in the Punjab' due to the Shaheed Ganj 'mosque dispute' in Lahore, which involved competing Sikhs and Muslims. Consequently, the joint efforts of Sheikh Abdullah and Pandit Jia Lal Kilam 'to start a national movement … for a responsible Government did not make much head-way'.[206] By 1936, Abdullah and his ilk also had long sought to distance themselves from the unacceptable Ahmadiyyas, if only to make themselves smaller political targets with their Muslim opponents, particularly Mirwaiz Yusuf Shah and his supporters. By 1936, the Mirwaiz was also clashing with Hindus, unlike Abdullah who had started to work with them. Shah 'took objection' to a speech by Pandit Shiv Narayan Fotedar in which Fotedar allegedly stated that 'he had the same veneration for the cow as the Muslims had for their Prophet'. After some serious clashes with police, Shah was arrested, convicted, then later acquitted on what appeared to be a face saving appeal due to 'a flaw in the institution of the prosecution'.[207] The Abdullah–Shah rivalry suggested that the struggle in J&K was against not only the autocratic Dogra regime but also against other Muslims. This struggle did not involve any aspiration for the ending of Dogra rule or for independence for J&K. These aspirations would come much later.

Outcomes from the 1931 uprising: the Praja Sabha

One major impact of the 1931 anti-Maharaja uprising in J&K was that Maharaja Hari Singh was compelled to try and determine the causes of this disturbance. In doing so, he and his regime were subjected to significant scrutiny. Soon after the uprising, the ruler appointed the Srinagar Riot Enquiry Committee to investigate the 'circumstances which led to the recent disturbances' and the 'sufficiency' of the response.[208] The Committee comprised Chief Justice Barjor Dalal and two other judges from the J&K High Court: B. R. Sawhny and Abdul Qayoom. They 'examined' 112 witnesses, but not Sheikh Abdullah, who declined to be involved, then reported on 24 September 1931.[209] The Committee was clear that the 'main desire of the Mohammadans is to have a larger representation in the State services' and that this was 'a legitimate grievance'.[210] Equally, however, it noted that the Muslims' 'exclusion from the higher service is due to their backwardness in education', a point that Ramchandra Kak had also made in November 1931 in his then position as 'Political Secretary, Kashmir State'. Kak had noted that 'the Mohamedans [sic], in spite of all the inducements held out to them, did not take to education'.[211] Consequently, 'dissatisfaction is a perpetual source of embitterment of the Mohammadan intelligentsia and an incentive to them to excite the masses by illusive religious grievances'.[212]

A British official in the Indian Political Department, B. J. Glancy, also was lent to the J&K Government to head an enquiry, the Grievances Enquiry Commission. Glancy possessed 'intimate knowledge of the conditions prevailing in the Kashmir State' as he had been 'First Assistant to the Resident for several years'.[213] The Commission was to look into the 'various complaints of a religious or general nature' in J&K,[214] including apostasy,[215] 'the grievances of the State's subjects' and suggesting 'measures for the closer association of the people with the Government'.[216] It reported in April 1932.[217] Glancy's enquiry included four non-officials: two Hindus and two Muslims who had been nominated by their respective Jammu or Kashmir communities.[218] These representatives were Prem Nath Bazaz (Hindu) and G. A. Ashai (Muslim) from Kashmir Province; Chaudhri Ghulam Abbas (Muslim) and Lok Nath Sharma (Hindu) from Jammu Province.[219] In December 1931, Sharma resigned from the Commission because it was 'unable to exclude from the scope of its enquiry questions relating to the Hindu Law of inheritance'.[220] The Grievances Enquiry Commission, or Glancy Commission, as it came to be known, also sought and received a submission from Ladakhi Buddhists, although it ostensibly was 'the work of a very small group of Kashmiri Pandits'.[221]

The Glancy Commission, along with the Srinagar Riot Enquiry Committee, confirmed 'beyond doubt that real grievances existed [in J&K] which needed redress'.[222] Most of these grievances related to Muslims, particularly Kashmiri Muslims, who 'in the matter of State employment' were 'inadequately represented': 'Out of a total of 763 gazetted posts, Muslims held 135 while Hindus held 628 posts. Kashmiri-speaking Muslims held only ten posts.'[223] A dissenting member of the Glancy Commission, Ghulam Abbas, along with the Commission's other Muslim member, G. A. Ashai, called for greater representation for Muslims in the J&K administration within ten years.[224] By March 1933, the recently formed Muslim Conference was demanding 'that *all* future vacancies should be filled up by Muslims'.[225] The Glancy Commission's recommendations did result in more J&K Muslims being appointed to positions in the State Service 'in all ranks and grades', although their empowerment displeased Hindu Pandits.[226] Significantly, the Commission's recommendations also resulted in J&K-ites being granted proprietary rights in 1933.[227]

Maharaja Hari Singh sought to partially rectify the identified shortcomings through some political and administrative changes. As a result of these two bodies' reports, he agreed to grant some of his subjects, about ten per cent of them,[228] some limited representation through a legislative body and processes that he heavily controlled. This was the seventy-five member Legislative Assembly, or Praja Sabha. Its consisted of sixteen State Councillors, twelve officials, thirty-three elected members (twenty-one Muslims, ten Hindus and two Sikhs), and fourteen Hindus, Muslims, Sikhs and Buddhists 'nominated from constituencies in which election is impossible'. These latter members included two representatives from the *Megh* community (i.e., Untouchables), two Ladakhi Buddhists and 'one domiciled Hindu from Srinagar'.[229] Excluding the official members, the supposed minimum numbers of Muslims would be thirty-two, while the supposed maximum number of Hindus would be twenty-five, a proportion that still nowhere near reflected J&K's Muslim-majority religious demography. The Assembly would last for three years, although State Councillors would be appointed for 4.5 years.[230] The first President was Sir Barjor Dalal,[231] the Chief Justice who had sat on the Srinagar Riot Enquiry Committee.

On 17 October 1934, the Praja Sabha was finally inaugurated.[232] This legislature was the culmination of the ruler's appointment in May 1932 of a Franchise·Committee chaired by B. J. Glancy.[233] It delimited constituencies and formulated electoral rolls.[234] However, Hari Singh was still reluctant to instigate the Praja Sabha. It only happened after much stalling, inertia and political protests, including a serious demand made by a frustrated Muslim Conference in mid-December 1933 that an assembly be established before the end of the year.[235] While the instigation of the Praja Sabha was the 'most noteworthy event of the year', this body was not the first consultative arrangement that had existed in J&K.[236] For some time, an 'annual conference of representatives' had taken place 'with a view to keep the administration in close contact with the people'. One representative 'from each Tehsil from the rural areas' of the provinces of Jammu and Kashmir – seemingly, the Frontier Districts Province and urban areas were not involved – were 'summoned through the Revenue Minister' to either Srinagar or Jammu City. Treated as 'State guests', these rural representatives met with 'Ministers and Heads of Departments' where 'matters' were 'fully and freely discussed'. The Ministers then sent 'representations' to the Maharaja 'with their recommendations on each point'. He discussed the issues 'in detail with the representatives in person', then issued 'orders to his Government on each point'.

Maharaja Hari Singh's aim in creating the Praja Sabha was 'to give effect to His Highness's desire to associate his people with the administration of the State'.[237] As he proclaimed and explained in 1939, his purpose was 'to plant the feet of Our beloved subjects on the path of solid progress and achievement'.[238] Using the royal and inclusive 'we', his aim was to associate 'Our people closely in Our counsels',[239] a point he had also made in 1934.[240] In the penultimate paragraph of his 1939 Proclamation, the ruler stated that 'We have been led to issue these commands' to re-establish a Praja Sabha and a Council of Ministers presided over by a Prime Minister, by the 'hope' that:

> Our state will provide an inspiring example of cultural, economic and political development – so that the love of their motherland and their attachment to Our Person will be deepened in the hearts of Our people and contentment with Our efforts for their welfare and appreciation for the steady improvement in their lot will be writ large on the body politic.[241]

In the final paragraph of his Proclamation, Hari Singh called on 'Omniscient God' for wisdom and assistance,[242] a call that was not unusual in his day and age but which also possibly suggested that he was unsure of his own localised power and popularity.

While such language by Maharaja Hari Singh was not surprising, the point was that he only wanted to 'associate' J&K-ites with his administration, not give them any meaningful power or control. The Praja Sabha was a limited body that the ruler controlled and dominated. The minimum voting age for those entitled to vote was twenty-one years. Only 'about 6 per cent of the population, including a number of women,'[243] were entitled to vote.[244] This was less than the 10 per cent ratio of the population that the British 'adopted as the working rule in British India' for suffrage.[245] Those with the 'right of [sic] vote' were

> village officials like Zaildars and Numberdars, to Imams, Qazia, Muftis, Adishstatas and other ministers of religious denominations, to those who had rendered services to the State or British India, to lawyers, doctors as well as Hakims, Vaids and school masters, and to all those who had passed the Middle School Examination or any higher Examination. Those paying land revenue or grazing fees of Rs. 20 a year or owning an immoveable property of Rs. 600 were also included among the voters.[246]

Maharaja Hari Singh himself also selected many representatives to the Praja Sabha. Due to the qualification requirement, many invariably ended up coming from the J&K elite. As a result, as *The Statesman* noted, the 'problems of the peasants and artisans, who formed the bulk of the [J&K] population, remain untouched'.[247]

The first Praja Sabha in 1934 therefore comprised seventy-five members. Apart from the forty-two nominated members, which was over half of this body's members, a limited franchise electorate of landed, wealthy and/or educated persons elected the other thirty-three members. Of these electable seats, Muslims were allotted twenty-one seats, Hindus ten seats and Sikhs two.[248] In September 1934, in the first elections ever conducted in J&K, twenty-eight of thirty-three candidates were elected unopposed: all twelve candidates for non-Muslim seats and sixteen of the twenty-one candidates for Muslims seats. There were actual contests only in Srinagar, with these between Muslim Conference and Azad Conference candidates. The Muslim Conference won all five seats,[249] giving it a total of fourteen of the twenty-one Muslim seats in the Praja Sabha.[250] Sheikh Abdullah was not an electoral candidate: he was not entitled to stand having been jailed previously.[251] Nevertheless, for Bazaz, Abdullah's 'supreme self-abnegation was really commendable', especially as he 'could have been elected unopposed from any Muslim constituency in Kashmir'.[252]

In 1939, Maharaja Hari Singh promulgated a new constitution for J&K, which increased the number of elected members from thirty-three to forty, out of seventy-five seats. Possibly, the ruler made this change after all elected members of the Praja Sabha except one walked out in 1936 because the Government was 'unsympathetic towards the public demands' and because this 'toy legislature', as *The Tribune*, Lahore, called it, had consultative powers only.[253] Popular 'Responsible Government Day' rallies held throughout J&K on 8 May 1936 may also have influenced the ruler, partly as the rally leaders and participants significantly were from the Hindu, Sikh and Muslim communities.[254] Various meetings passed resolutions stating that the

Praja Sabha was 'inadequate and unrepresentative' and demanding a legislature 'to which the Government should be fully responsible'.[255] In the 1938 elections, the Muslim Conference won nineteen of twenty-one seats allocated to Muslims.[256] This showed this party's strong influence among J&K Muslims, although their overall numbers mattered little given that the majority of representatives in the Praja Sabha favoured the ruler and his administration.[257]

In a further limitation to its functioning, the Praja Sabha did not actually sit much. In 1935, which was a significant year because London passed the Government of India Act that envisaged an Indian federation, the Praja Sabha held two sessions. These comprised one session of thirteen days in Jammu from 30 March to 11 April during which three bills were passed, and a second session of nineteen working days in Srinagar from 14 October to 13 November during which five bills were passed.[258] While eight bills did not amount to a lot of legislation, the Praja Sabha did, on the other hand, answer 566 questions in its Jammu session, while the President allowed 780 questions (of 924 posed) to be answered at its Srinagar session.[259] Such questioning was limited, however. The Praja Sabha could not discuss anything to do with the Maharaja, his family or household, relations with India or other states, frontier policy, the State Army, or the provisions or rules of the Constitution Act as a result of which this body functioned.[260] Despite Hari Singh's aim, the Praja Sabha did little to meaningfully associate J&K-ites closely with the Maharaja or his 'counsels'.

The Praja Sabha was therefore a limited body. Indeed, as the 1941 Census importantly noted, regardless of the constitutional reforms that the ruler had made, including supposedly empowering some of his people and involving them in the state's administration, his reforms 'in no way impair the inherent powers of His Highness the Maharaja Bahadur'.[261] Similarly, the State *Handbook* while describing 'The system of Government' in J&K, stated unequivocally in 1947 that 'The Ruler is the source of all authority and power in the State'. It acknowledged the J&K Constitution, the five-member Executive Council whose members the ruler appointed, the legislature and the judiciary, and noted that the administration was 'carried on through well organized departments'.[262] However, as late as 1947, the ruler of J&K was still only talking of 'associating' his subjects with the administration of the State, not about devolving any genuine power or authority to any of them.[263] J&K was far from being an inclusive constitutional monarchy, or of having any aspiration to achieve that end. Maharaja Hari Singh was in effective, almost total, control and he wanted, and expected, this system of rule to continue.

Other implications of the 1931 uprising

Apart from its spontaneity and severity, the 1931 uprising was significant for three other reasons. First, it saw the rise of the young Kashmiri, Sheikh Mohammad Abdullah, as an inspiring orator, firebrand and, importantly, as a political leader of Kashmiris. As a result of his political actions and bravery in 1931, Abdullah quickly became known as 'Sher–e–Kashmir', the 'Lion of Kashmir'.[264] As early as September 1931, he 'was perhaps the second most influential Muslim in Srinagar after the Mir Waiz', Yusuf Shah.[265] *The Times* described him as 'one of the most active of the Moslem [sic] campaign' whose arrest in 1931 had caused 'much excitement amongst the Moslems [sic]'.[266] Soon after, *The Times* 'Special Correspondent' described Abdullah as 'the Kashmir Moslem [sic] leader'.[267] Abdullah's rise had been spectacular. As he later saw things: 'My political life in the real sense starts with this firing on the people' on 13 July 1931. Abdullah was 'greatly influenced by this incident':

> I felt as if the bullets were penetrating *my* heart. … A number of Kashmiris were killed or wounded and as I was helping a wounded man, he cried, 'Abdullah, I have done my duty. Now it is for you to go on with our mission.' I was greatly influenced by this incident. I felt that nothing could stop me after this.

The new Kashmiri leader quickly realised otherwise: on 21 September 1931, he was arrested, imprisoned and effectively stopped politically for the period of his initial incarceration. He would be arrested and imprisoned in each of the next three years.[268]

Second, the 1931 uprising raised J&K-ites' political awareness and resulted in the creation of political parties in J&K. In particular, on 4 June 1932, by which time 'Abdullahites and Usuf [sic; Yusuf] Shahis' were temporarily reconciled,[269] J&K Muslims formed the All-Jammu and Kashmir Muslim Conference. (This party was not directly connected with the All-India Kashmir Muslim Conference formed in 1926, although its formation may have been influenced by the Lahore-based body.)[270] The Muslim Conference, as it invariably was called, held its first annual session in October 1932, in Srinagar. Sheikh Abdullah was elected President.[271] Thereafter, until 1938, the party held annual sessions respectively in Mirpur, Sopore, Srinagar, Poonch and Jammu. (No annual session was held in 1936.)[272] Abdullah would dominate the Muslim Conference, presiding over four of these six annual sessions.[273] Only the third and fourth sessions were chaired by others: respectively Mian Ahmad Yar, from Muzaffarabad,[274] and Ghulam Abbas, from Jammu.[275] Between 1932 and 1938, the party's struggle was undertaken by 'middle and upper class Muslims ... for the achievements of their rights, especially in the matter of [the] distribution of State services'.[276] This struggle included members contesting elections to the limited Praja Sabha.

Initially, the Muslim Conference was 'communal in name ... but national in essence': supposedly, it stood 'for the rights of all communities', not just Muslims. Perhaps not surprisingly then, on 11 June 1939, in 'a painful process',[277] the Muslim Conference morphed via a vote of '176 delegates from all districts of the State'[278] into the secular National Conference. The aim was to transcend 'the purely religious basis of identity formation'[279] and make the party truly representative of the J&K 'nation': that is, less communal, less religious, and more inclusive of all communities in J&K.[280] For one Kashmiri, this morphing process was a 'unique feat in the political history of Kashmir'.[281] Equally, it 'brought politics into the forefront of discussions' about communalism and secularism[282] and marked the beginning of the formal division of the J&K Muslim 'community' into religious or secular elements and/or into Jammu Province or Kashmir Province Muslims. This division within J&K reflected the increasing division in India between the secular Congress and the religious Muslim League. Locally, Sheikh Abdullah was considered to be responsible for this 'tragic schism'. Conversely, as one critic noted, it was 'an irony of fate' to call Abdullah 'a secular national leader when his activities were restricted to his [Kashmir Muslim] community and to one section of the population of the State', i.e., Kashmir.[283] While a little harsh, Abdullah did concentrate his attention and activities more on Kashmir and Kashmiris than on other areas of J&K or on other J&K-ites.

Arguably, secularism was appealing to Kashmiris because of their adherence to Kashmiriyat, the 'common cultural heritage among Kashmiri Hindus and Muslims'.[284] While this may, or may not, be the case, as early as July 1932, two Kashmiris, Sheikh Abdullah, a Muslim, and Prem Nath Bazaz, a Hindu, apparently met and agreed that 'the Kashmir Freedom Movement will be conducted on secular, progressive and democratic lines'.[285] The Muslim Conference itself had first tried unsuccessfully in 1933 to involve non-Muslims in its organisation.[286] A two-week agitation in 1934 that sought to have the Glancy Commission's report implemented 'as it related to the Muslim proportion in [J&K] Government service' but which was quickly suppressed, was a factor that encouraged the Muslim Conference's conversion into the National Conference. Members began to realise 'that they must carry with them the goodwill of the minorities in political matters'.[287] Equally, they realised that even though non-Muslims had most government positions, all J&K-ites' 'woes were not lessened [and] It was the system which needed a change, not its personnel'.[288] Despite such logic, it was not an easy process to secularise the party and make it more inclusive. Abdullah faced significant opposition that amounted, in his colourful language, to 'being pulverized, caught in the obscurantist grinding mill-stones of the Hindus and the Muslims'.[289] 'Floury' stuff.

Nevertheless, on 11 June 1939, the All-Jammu and Kashmir National Conference officially came into being. After all the angst and politicking, it was almost a unanimous decision: only four of 176 delegates voted against what for Abdullah was an inclusive and 'revolutionary act'.[290] Nevertheless, in 1941, some dissident Muslims led by the Jammuite, Ghulam Abbas, re-formed the Muslim Conference. They were disenchanted with the National Conference's secularity, by its move towards a seeming semi-alliance with the Indian National Congress, and by Abdullah's perceived intolerance and 'lust for power and fame'.[291] The dissident Muslims' claims had some relevance, given Nehru's friendship with, and increasing influence on, Sheikh Abdullah. Similarly, Hari Singh claimed that the Muslims leading the National Conference adopted this name to 'gain sympathy and cooperation from those fighting for freedom from the British yoke in British India', including the Indian National Congress, and that, in British India, the National Conference was known as 'the National Movement in the Jammu and Kashmir State'.[292] Also in 1941, Prem Nath Bazaz and 'many others' left the National Conference, partly, it seems, due to Abdullah's autocratic ways of operating and partly because of anti-Pandit sentiments among some National Conference members.[293] Thereafter, as J&K's two major political parties, the Muslim Conference would compete with the National Conference for influence and popularity among J&K-ites. Generally speaking, the Muslim Conference was more popular in Jammu; the National Conference in Kashmir. Neither seemingly had any presence or influence in the Frontier Districts Province.

The 1931 uprising was significant for a third reason: as a result of this major event, Maharaja Hari Singh took the opportunity to enact or upgrade some significant notifications and legislation before the consultative Praja Sabha actually commenced its operations in 1934. He also raised a new and seventh infantry unit for the J&K State Forces, based in Jammu.[294] The Maharaja's significant notifications and legislation were: 'The Special Powers Notification, 1988. Notification No. 19–L, dated 8th Assuj/24th September 1931';[295] 'The Press and Publications Act, 1989 (… dated 25th April 1932)';[296] and, 'The Jammu and Kashmir State Ranbir Penal Code (… dated 6th August 1932)'.[297] The Special Powers Notification, which was more commonly known as the draconian Ordinance 19–L, was a direct response to the 'emergency' of 1931. It allowed 'the conferment of special powers' upon certain of the Maharaja's officers 'for the suppression of disorder and the restoration and maintenance of law and order'.[298] While inspired by the events of 1931, 19–L was, as we have seen, used in J&K to control and quell civil disturbances.

Initially, the Special Powers Notification was to cover Srinagar and was to 'come into operation immediately'. However, it could be 'extended to any other area within [the Maharaja's] rule by a notification'.[299] It enabled: 'arrest without warrant'; the keeping in custody in 'Jail in Srinagar' of an arrested person for up to a month; for 'a competent authority' to appoint 'persons as Special Police Officers'; to 'require any person to assist in the restoration or maintenance of law and order in such manner and within such limits as the competent authority may prescribe'; and, the seizure of land, property and goods.[300] In a catch all, 19–L also stated that:

> If any person disobeys or neglects to comply with an order made, direction given, or condition prescribed in accordance with the provisions of this notification or of the rules made ... the authority ... may take or cause to be taken such action as it thinks necessary to give effect thereto.[301]

In terms of punishment, an offender who disobeyed an order could be imprisoned for up to three years, flogged up to 'thirty stripes', or be fined up to 1,000 rupees.[302] Additionally, if a fine was imposed 'on any person under the age of 21', it could 'be recovered from his father or guardian' as if the fine had been imposed on them.[303] It was a very powerful act with no provisions for any appeals.

'The Press and Publications Act, 1989' was similarly empowering of the Maharaja. The main thrust was to control who printed material, with only State Subjects allowed to do so,[304] and to prevent any printed material from inciting violence or 'bring[ing] into hatred or contempt His Highness the Maharaja Bahadur or the Government' or 'promot[ing] feelings of enmity or hatred between different classes' of J&K-ites.[305] Likewise was the Ranbir Penal Code, under which Sheikh Abdullah would later be tried, and convicted, for violating its Section 124-A. This section stated that:

> Whoever by words, either spoken or written, or by signs, or by visible representation, or otherwise brings or attemps [sic] to bring into hatred or contempt, or excites or attempts to excite disaffection towards His Majesty or His Highness or the Government established by law in British India or in Jammu and Kashmir State shall be punished with imprisonment for life to which [a] fine may be added, or with imprisonment which may extend to three years, to which [a] fine may be added, or with [a] fine.
>
> Explanation I. – The expression 'disaffection' includes disloyalty and all feelings of enmity.[306]

Two other 'explanations' allowed people to express 'disapprobation' with the Government or its actions provided they did not 'excite hatred, contempt or disaffection'. However, given the broadness of 'Explanation I', it would have been very easy to convict any State Subject of J&K for 'disaffection'. There also did not appear to be any way someone convicted under Section 124-A could appeal their conviction or sentence. All power rested with the Maharaja and his regime.

The rise and rise of Sheikh Mohammad Abdullah

The brave and well-publicised efforts of Sheikh Mohammad Abdullah during 1931 made him both the Lion of Kashmir and the de facto leader of Kashmiri Muslims. Significantly, the Srinagar Riot Enquiry Committee's comprehensive report spoke of a 'Mr Mohammad Abdullah, M. Sc', who had refused, along with two other Muslims, to communicate with, or to appear as a witness before, the Committee, and of a 'Maulvi Mohammad Abdullah', a 'man of influence at the Bar and also among his co-religionists' but about whom the Commission seemed somewhat circumspect.[307] Almost certainly, 'Mr Mohammad Abdullah, M. Sc.' was a reference to Sheikh Abdullah, given that the Kashmiri did actually have a Master of Science degree. Most likely, 'Maulvi Mohammad Abdullah' was not him. Although Sheikh Abdullah was increasingly renowned for his ability to melodiously recite the Koran, he was not a 'man of influence at the Bar'. However, he certainly had influence over Kashmiris. According to Bazaz, 'No one in the history of Kashmir has enjoyed so much popularity with the masses as he'.[308]

While high-profile and popular, Abdullah was not the only Muslim political leader in Kashmir, nor the only political leader in J&K. Some other, but by no means all, Kashmiri political figures included: the secular Hindus, Prem Nath Bazaz and Pandit Shyam Lal Saraf; the Muslim religious leader Mirwaiz Yusuf Shah, and his religious rival in Srinagar, Mirwaiz Ahmadullah Hamadani, who supported Abdullah; and the moderate Muslims, Ghulam Mohiuddin Karra (or Qara) and Maulana Masoodi. Other senior figures in Abdullah's political party included Bakshi Ghulam Mohammed (or Ghulam Mohammed Bakshi), G. M. (Ghulam Mohammed) Sadiq, Mirza Afzal Beg, and Mir Qasim. Other J&K political leaders included various Jammuites: Ghulam Abbas, Chaudhri Hamidullah, Allah Rakha and Sardar Budh Singh, a Sikh who was a former official, the oldest politician in J&K,[309] and popularly was known as 'Mahatma Bud Singh'.[310] However, of all these J&K-ites, I now focus on Sheikh Abdullah, chiefly because he was the most significant, and contentious, politician over the longest term, both as a Kashmiri and in J&K. Abdullah also was highly significant in the 1940s because of his great popularity with Muslim Kashmiris, although he was not necessarily popular amongst other J&K-ites, some of whom were 'not even prepared to touch him with a barge pole'.[311] Similarly, his party lost support amongst J&K-ites on occasions because it allegedly engaged in '*goondaism* [thuggery] and gangsterism'.[312]

Apart from his high profile and popularity, Sheikh Abdullah was significant in J&K politics for other reasons. The first was because of his friendship with Jawaharlal Nehru, who the Kashmiri first met in 1937,[313] the same year Maharaja Hari Singh would grant a 'general amnesty to all political prisoners detained since the Jammu agitation and the Moslem [sic] agitation in Srinagar'.[314] Ten years later, Nehru would become one of independent India's leading political figures, chiefly in his role as (post-British) India's first Prime Minister. He became highly important in relation to J&K, certainly after Sardar Patel's death on 15 December 1950, after which Nehru, due to his standing, intellect and capabilities, essentially was unchallenged as India's most influential politician. Nehru had much antipathy for Mohammad Ali Jinnah, as did Abdullah. The Kashmiri felt that, apart from Jinnah being 'not in the least interested in observing even the basic tenets of Islam', that his political rival 'had a streak of misanthropy'[315] and 'a very high opinion of himself' for which the 'entire subcontinent had to suffer the consequences of his inflated ego'.[316] Equally, however, Abdullah grudgingly admired Jinnah's 'unexampled steadfastness' and noted that Congress leaders had, at times, insulted the Muslim League supremo.[317] These Congress leaders, of course, included Nehru, whose fraught relationship with Jinnah was a major factor contributing to the British decision to partition British India and create Pakistan.

Abdullah's local standing and popularity also were highly significant. Some saw him in almost divine terms. According to a Kashmiri scholar, in the 'years leading up to 1947', the most popular slogan for Abdullah among Kashmiris 'was "la ila ha ilal la Sheikh Mohammad Abdullah" (There is no God but Allah, and there is Sheikh Mohammad Abdullah)'.[318] Bakshi Ghulam Mohammad once stated that he had a sixth cardinal Islamic principle to which he personally adhered: 'complete faith in the leadership of Sheikh Mohammad Abdullah'.[319] There was also, to some extent, a perception that 'Sheikh Abdullah was Kashmir' and 'Kashmir was Sheikh Abdullah' (my terminology). Hari Singh, with some frustration, had similarly wondered 'whether Sheikh Abdullah is a synonymous term with the people of Kashmir'.[320] Problematically for his rivals but motivatingly for his supporters, Abdullah also spoke his mind.[321] This was because, according to his autobiography, the Kashmiri had a strong social conscience from early in his life. It also resulted partly from being relatively poor and partly from being discriminated against. A significant and often quoted statement about J&K Muslims that seemingly informed many Indians and motivated a lot of Muslim Kashmiris, including Sheikh Abdullah,[322] was Banerji's statement in 1929 about Kashmiris being 'practically governed like dumb-driven cattle'.[323] This was a major cause and motivating factor for disgruntled J&K-ites, including Abdullah, and their significant 1931 uprising that brought his name into prominence.

The perception of Sheikh Abdullah being 'the chief hero of the Kashmir movement … and primarily responsible for the politics of the State' was important to many people.[324] In particular, this included Jawaharlal Nehru, both before Maharajah Hari Singh's accession to India and in the early years of the post-accessional Kashmir dispute. Another was Maharaja Hari Singh, particularly before, but also after, his accession to India. Abdullah opposed, and disliked, the Maharaja – and vice versa. From the outset, their relationship was difficult. According to Saraf, 'Maharaja Hari Singh never had a friendly disposition towards Sheikh Mohammad Abdullah; on the contrary, he had reasons to be hateful of him'.[325] Equally, Abdullah's writings suggest that he clearly disliked the (non-Kashmiri) ruler whom he saw as elitist and exploitative. According to Sardar Patel, who conversed with the Maharaja a number of times, 'His Highness personally dislikes Sheikh Sahib' and his 'endeavours'.[326] From 1931 to 1946, however, Maharaja Hari Singh was formidable in J&K to the detriment of his political rivals including Sheikh Abdullah, whereas from late 1947 until 1953, Abdullah was redoubtable, ultimately to the detriment of both the Dogra ruler and Dogra rule. And, despite disliking the Hindu Maharaja, Abdullah ironically observed after his rival's death in 1961 that Maharaja Hari Singh's 'sense of personal dignity was praiseworthy'.[327]

Phases in the Hari Singh–Sheikh Abdullah relationship

The Singh–Abdullah relationship essentially had a pre-1946 aspect and a post-1946 aspect. In the pre-1946 aspect, a subservient Abdullah was trying to challenge the all-powerful Dogra ruler. In the post-1946 aspect, an increasingly assertive Abdullah started to succeed over a waning Hari Singh. Writing in 1946, an astute, unnamed but well-informed journalist stated that the pre-1946 Singh–Abdullah relationship developed in three phases. These mainly revolved around Abdullah's political development, not Hari Singh's.[328] Following Abdullah's groundbreaking role in the 1931 anti-Maharaja uprising, the first phase was a communal one from 1932 to around 1938. The second was a nationalist phase from around 1938 to 1944. The third phase, 1944–46 (and to a large extent thereafter) was the pursuit of 'full-fledged socialism'. Arguably, the journalist's labelling of the first two stages was accurate. However, while Abdullah would pursue socialism for many years after 1944, he also confronted some significant upheavals and challenges. In 1946, his highly significant Quit Kashmir call marked a watershed in the Singh–Abdullah relationship. In 1947, both the British departure from India and Maharaja Hari Singh's ultimate accession to India would irretrievably change the political dynamics in J&K and between J&K-ites.

From 1932, Sheikh Abdullah's communal phase saw him predominantly pursuing rights for Kashmiri Muslims. After the formation of the Muslim Conference in 1932, this party pursued a communal agenda that sought to defend 'Islam in danger', to advance Muslims' rights, such as securing jobs in the administration, and to obtain some minimal political rights, such as freedom of speech.[329] Around the same time, according to the J&K Government, 'Mir Waiz Mohammed Yusuf' (Shah) formed the 'Azad party, in consequence, it is presumed, of its dissociation from the Jammu and Kashmir Muslim Conference'.[330] The Government presumed correctly, with Yusuf Shah apparently affronted by Abdullah's election as President of the Muslim Conference in October 1933.[331] While Abdullah and Shah were different personalities with separate parties, both men through their earlier cooperation in the Reading Room and through their ability to motivate Muslims helped to sustain the anti-Maharaja agitation in 1931. Thereafter, Sheikh Abdullah's star, along with his secular credentials, would rise significantly. Conversely, Mirwaiz Yusuf Shah would move politically and inextricably to a strongly communal Muslim position, culminating in him being both pro-Pakistan in 1947 and physically moving to Azad Kashmir, which quickly came under Pakistan's control. Thereafter, Yusuf Shah would serve twice as President of Azad Kashmir: for seven months in 1951–52 and briefly for three months in 1956.

Around 1938, Sheikh Abdullah's second and 'J&K nationalist' phase started. It occurred because he and some leading Kashmiris, Hindu and Muslim, realised that many J&K-ites were politically and economically depressed and that people in all J&K communities needed to be uplifted and advanced. In 1938, in a sign of growing 'national' inclusivity and secularism, a group of twelve political activists comprising six Muslims, five Hindu Pandits and one Sikh, presented Maharaja Hari Singh with a 'National Demand' (*Qaumi Mutaliba*) manifesto.[332] The twelve signatories were: 'Sh. Mohammad Abdullah; M. M. Sayeed; G. M. Sadiq; Mian Ahmad Yar; M. A. Beg; Pt. Kashyap Bandhu; Pt. Prem Nath Bazaz; S. Budh Singh; Pt. Jia Lal Kilam; Ghulam Mohammad Bakshi; Pt. Sham Lai Saraf; Dr. Shamboo

Nath Peshin'.[333] By the 'nation', these activists were referring to J&K under Hari Singh's rule, not a free or independent Kashmir'. Indeed, the twelve activists sought responsible government 'subject to the general control and residuary powers of His Highness' and in which all members to the legislature would be elected on the basis of adult franchise and to which body the J&K Ministry would be responsible.[334] Hence, they did not seek a radical change in J&K or the dethroning of Maharaja Hari Singh. Rather, the twelve were at pains to state 'at the very outset that our loyalty to His Highness' person and throne is unswerving and needs no reiteration', while the 'ultimate political goal of this movement is the achievement of complete responsible government under the aegis of His Highness'.[335]

Essentially, the twelve activists wanted more freedom and wellbeing for J&K-ites under the current administration and regime. However, conservative Muslims and Hindus opposed their National Demand, partly as they considered that minorities were not sufficiently protected.[336] The Maharaja himself also reacted negatively. He imposed a fifteen-day curfew,[337] arrested 'hundreds of leaders and workers', including Sheikh Abdullah, Prem Nath Bazaz and Ghulam Abbas,[338] who had not actually signed the manifesto, and used his police and military to repress the 'widespread rioting' that followed.[339] The Hindu–Muslim collaboration had been significant. As Bazaz put it, 'Pandits fought shoulder to shoulder with Muslims and suffered equally with them. It was a glorious chapter in the history of the Freedom Movement of Kashmir.' The activists' cross-communal actions, coupled with the Maharaja's excessive repression, 'strengthened the forces of nationalism in the State'.[340]

Meanwhile, some leading Kashmiris, including Sheikh Abdullah and Mirza Afzal Beg, had become frustrated with the Maharaja-dominated Praja Sabha and its significant limitations. Consequently, in 1939, led by Sheikh Abdullah, the now more outwardly looking and inclusive Muslim Conference changed its name and its communal approach. On 11 June 1939, it became the secular and inclusive National Conference. Shortly before, Sheikh Abdullah and Jawaharlal Nehru, who had first met coincidentally in 1937, had seriously 'exchanged views' in January 1938.[341] Almost certainly, this included discussions about secularism. By that time, the increasingly politically influential Indian National Congress had been elected to power in eight (of eleven) Indian Provinces, including significantly in Muslim-majority NWFP.[342] The renamed National Conference's leadership expected that 'large numbers of non-Muslims would join the [National] Conference and take an active part in moulding the destinies of the country'.[343] Certainly, some non-Muslims did join the National Conference. Equally, however, Muslims led by

Ghulam Abbas who were dissatisfied with the name change, with the party's non-exclusive Muslim focus and with its perceived proximity to and alignment with Congress, re-formed the Muslim Conference in 1941. Thereafter, they would attempt to rival the National Conference. Strongest in Jammu, the Muslim Conference was much weaker in Kashmir, if only because the party had no high-profile leader who spoke Kashmiri.

For two years until 1941, Sheikh Abdullah and the renamed National Conference party that he dominated essentially had a free run in J&K politics. Their only rival, albeit a very significant one, was Maharaja Hari Singh. In October 1939, the National Conference ratified the National Demand document. By that stage, however, World War II had intervened. Nevertheless, the National Conference retained its National Demand until 1944. At the same time, the party cooperated with the Maharaja and 'as patriots', while seeking to 'save' Kashmiris 'from hunger at home', also added its 'strength to the anti-Fascist struggle of the people of India and the world'.[344] The National Conference's abovementioned talk of 'destinies of the country' – not of one 'destiny' for the 'country' – anticipated J&K's future problems and its division and disintegration into a fragmented state. Equally, its change of name was arguably not so much to do with perceived nationalism. Rather, it was about broadening the movement so that all J&K-ites living in the supposed 'nation' of J&K could join the party, regardless of their ethnicity, religion, province and, importantly, their class, and pursue their rights and better living conditions. No longer would the party solely represent the J&K Muslim community; rather, it would represent all J&K-ites. This reflected Sheikh Abdullah's political growth. This had occurred partially and quickly due to his increased involvement with secular Indian nationalists, both Muslim, such as Khan Abdul Gaffer Khan and Maulana Azad, and non-Muslim, such as Mahatma Gandhi, Jawaharlal Nehru and Sardar Patel. Arguably, while these Indians valued Abdullah's role as a leading J&K politician, they influenced him more than vice versa.

The 'Naya Kashmir' manifesto

In 1944, the Singh–Abdullah relationship entered its third phase. This involved a more assertive National Conference and the pursuit of socialism. A major political change occurred with the release by the National Conference of a socialist manifesto titled *Naya Kashmir* or 'New Kashmir'.[345] The document's full title was *New Kashmir – The Constitution and Outline Economic Plan for the State of Jammu and Kashmir including Ladakh and the Frontier Regions and the Poonch and Chinani Ilaquas.*

Inspired by J&K-ites' backwardness,[346] this document had been 'drafted ... at the invitation of the Maharaja's Government with a view to establishing a welfare state' and as a 'future Constitution of Kashmir'.[347] It was probably a response to a 'Commission of Enquiry' established by Maharaja Hari Singh in 1943–44 to 'ascertain whether the existing [J&K] constitution had worked well and with a view to formulating a policy for the future . . administration of the state'.[348] Originally, therefore, Naya Kashmir was 'submitted' to the J&K Government 'as a comprehensive memorandum on the economic, political, social and cultural reconstruction of the State'.[349] Later, the National Conference unanimously adopted the 'memorandum' at its annual session at Sopore in September 1944,[350] after which it was later published.[351] Naya Kashmir espoused 'Kashmiri socialism'[352] or 'fully-fledged socialism' for J&K.[353] The manifesto was inspired by Communism and Communist ideology, with much of its text and ideas apparently 'borrowed' from the constitution that Josef Stalin had imposed on the Soviet Union in 1936.[354] Sheikh Abdullah had clearly been inspired by the Soviet Union. Introducing Naya Kashmir in 1944, he stated that the 'mighty Soviet State that is throwing back its barbarous invaders with deathless heroism, is an unanswerable argument for the building of democracy on the cornerstone of economic equality'.[355]

The Naya Kashmir manifesto comprised two parts: political and economic. The political part proposed a new constitution for J&K; the economic part suggested a plan to deal with the state's 'agriculture, industry, transport, distribution, utility services and currency and finance'. In essence, Naya Kashmir sought 'a model State in which democratic and responsible Government is only a means to an end – the amelioration of the people "through freedom from all forms of economic exploitation"'.[356] Importantly, the manifesto clearly envisaged a role for the Maharaja: 'After the elections, the Ruler shall convene the newly elected National Assembly within a period of one month'.[357] The jurisdiction of the National Assembly was also 'Subject to the general control of H. H. the Maharaja Bahadur'. Paragraph 27 of Naya Kashmir further specifically stated that

> The ruler of Jammu and Kashmir shall: a. convene sessions of tile [sic: the] National Assembly twice a year; shall convene extraordinary sessions of the Assembly at his own wish or at the request of the speaker of the Assembly; and b. dissolve the National Assembly and fix new elections; c. conduct a referendum upon his own initiative or upon the demand of the majority of the legislators; d. declare general or partial mobilization; e. ratify international treaties after they have been approved by the National Assembly[;] f. summon the leader of the largest single party in the National Assembly to form the Ministry.[358]

Thus, the writers of Naya Kashmir were seeking economic and political freedom in J&K and for J&K-ites, but not independence for the state. Nor were they seeking freedom from British paramountcy, nor, indeed, freedom from Dogra rule. That latter demand would come later.

Possibly the New Kashmir manifesto was released because the National Conference felt under threat. Its major political opponents – those dissatisfied Muslims who had re-formed the Muslim Conference in 1941 – were 'busy in propaganda' and were making 'great efforts to supplant them in the valley ... [a factor that] alarmed the National Conference'.[359] Indeed, by 1944, 'the old differences' and political rivalry between both parties had become so 'acute' that restrictions had to be placed on their activities in Srinagar.[360] In 1945, there was aggressive rivalry between the two conferences, with Muslim Conference members engaging in 'hostile demonstrations' and disrupting a river procession that the National Conference had organised to honour Jawaharlal Nehru and Khan Abdul Ghaffar Khan, who were visiting Kashmir. National Conference members responded in kind to the Muslim Conference provocateurs.[361] By the time of the J&K elections held on 4 January 1947, when it 'was beastly cold in the Valley',[362] the Muslim Conference seemingly was the more popular party.[363] Consequently, the National Conference chose to boycott these polls, possibly because it feared electoral defeat by the Muslim Conference. Other political parties also then existed in J&K, with up to sixteen contesting the 1947 elections. In 1947, J&K's major political parties were the Akali Party; Hindu Rajya Sabha; Kashmir Pandit Conference; Kisan Mazdoor Conference; Muslim Conference; National Conference; Socialist Party; and, the loyalist State People's Conference formed by Ramchandra Kak from 'highly moral and incorruptible men'.[364]

Concurrently, however, the National Conference cooperated, seemingly happily, with Maharaja Hari Singh's regime in a 'diarchic experiment'. This involved the Praja Sabha choosing six members,[365] 'three from Jammu and three from Kashmir (including the Frontier District)'. Three of these six were to be Muslims, from whom the Maharaja would appoint two ministers, one of whom would be a Muslim.[366] The Maharaja made these appointments 'to give effect' to his policy of 'associating [his] subjects with the administration of the State'.[367] While the Muslim Conference boycotted this process, a factor that helped its popularity,[368] the National Conference participated. From October 1944 until 18 March 1946, therefore, its member, Mirza Afzal Beg, served as a cabinet minister, holding the Public Works portfolio.[369] Ganga Ram, 'an ultra-loyalist Dogra politician', served in the other, and more important, position of Home Minister.[370] The 'boon' of the diarchic experiment supposedly 'was welcomed by all sections of the public'.[371] For Beg, it was a 'real concrete step forward for the people of this country who can now associate themselves with the administration of the country' – although he clearly hoped that there would be further steps 'in the progressive career of the country lead [sic] by His Highness the Maharaja'. Similarly, Chaudhri Hamidullah, leader of the Muslim Conference in the Praja Sabha, called the Maharaja 'One of the most enlightened princes' for his 'definite progressive step of which any Indian State may well feel proud', although he still hoped for 'the establishment of full responsible Government in the State'.[372] In early 1946, both major political parties seemed content having Maharaja Hari Singh rule J&K.

Quit Kashmir

Naya Kashmir marks the end of the third J&K nationalist phase of the Singh–Abdullah rivalry during which there was no serious challenge to Dogra rule. In May 1946, things changed – dramatically. Maharaja Hari Singh had ignored the Naya Kashmir manifesto and was 'apathetic' about political change.[373] Therefore, possibly as 'a logical corollary', Sheikh Abdullah developed a provocative slogan, and fomented a movement called, Quit Kashmir.[374] The aim was to get Hari Singh to leave, or quit, Kashmir, the region that his great grandfather had purchased from the British 100 years previously in 1846. For one Kashmiri politician, this was not a new slogan, but a development of a slogan that Kashmiris 'consistently voiced … from 1931 to 1946': "*Kashmir chor do buynama tod do*" (Leave Kashmir, abrogate the British sale deed in which Kashmir was sold to Dogras for Rupees 75 lacs)'.[375] An easier translation might be 'Break (or renounce) the sale deed and leave Kashmir'.[376] Either way, this aggressive call by an increasingly emboldened Sheikh Abdullah marked a watershed in his relationship with Maharaja Hari Singh. One inspiration was the Indian freedom movement and its 1942 'Quit India' movement; another possibly was the 1945 'Quit Asia' movement that supported the Indonesians' struggle against 'Dutch Imperialism'.[377]

The abovementioned 'sale deed' is important. The 1846 Treaty of Amritsar between the British and Raja Gulab Singh ratified Singh's title to the lands that comprised his existing Jammu domain, the Kashmir Valley, and land located in what later was called J&K's Frontier Districts Province. In return, Gulab Singh paid the British Rs 7.5 million. Thereafter, the 'proprietary rights in all of [Jammu and] Kashmir belong[ed] to the Ruling Chief exclusively, for the simple reason that the territories of [Jammu and] Kashmir were purchased by … Maharaja Gulab

Singh' in 1846.[378] The key word, particularly for Kashmiris, was the word 'purchased'. Along with buying J&K, Raja Gulab Singh also obtained possession of the human beings who populated this territory and who thereby became his subjects. For the Kashmiris, this treaty transaction amounted to a sale deed. What they often omitted to say was that this 'deal' was not just solely about the Kashmir Valley. It was about all of J&K. That said, it is hard to imagine what the impact of what amounted to a real estate sale was on the psyche of Kashmiris, particularly peasants. The Dogras became 'the absolute owners or lords of the soil', plus they created 'a class of landed gentry comprising mainly Kashmiri Pandits and the Dogra Rajputs' that essentially reduced the 'peasants to a state close to "serfdom"'.[379] Significantly, the Dogras also had not captured Kashmir by military conquest, as had previous oppressors, but had obtained it by virtue of a cash transaction. Thereafter, Kashmiris became third-class citizens.

This sale was neither the first time, nor the only time, that entities have obtained 'sovereignty through purchase' without consulting the residents therein. In 1803, the United States paid 60 million francs to France to acquire Louisiana; in 1867, it paid $7.1 million to Russia to acquire Alaska.[380] In 1958, Pakistan purchased the strategically important Gwadar area in southwestern Baluchistan from the Sultan of Oman.[381] The difference in the case of Kashmir, however, was that sovereignty was transferred to an individual, not to a nation or to a state. Furthermore, some of the Kashmiris being 'sold' individually would have known Maharaja Gulab Singh, not necessarily positively, given that he had previously served in Kashmir as an employee of Ranjit Singh on at least two occasions. Certainly, some Kashmiris initially opposed Singh and his attempt to take control of his latest possession, Kashmir. The British official, Henry Lawrence, along with 10,000 Sikh and Kohistani troops, helped to subdue the Kashmiris' short uprising, after which Gulab Singh was installed as Maharaja in November 1846.[382] Thereafter, there was ongoing Kashmiri sullenness about Dogra rule. And, with long memories and a liking for anniversaries, the sale of Kashmir to the Dogras in 1846 was clearly a factor in Sheikh Abdullah's anti-Maharaja Quit Kashmir political agitation that this Kashmiri instigated one hundred years after the mercantile 'deal'. Kashmiri nationalism among ethnic Kashmiris had been powerfully re-awakened.

The build up to Quit Kashmir is interesting. In March 1946, Sheikh Abdullah's National Conference colleague, Mirza Afzal Beg, resigned from his ministerial position as Minister for Public Works. Beg felt administratively impotent, in part because of excessive interference by the J&K Prime Minister, Ramchandra Kak. Significantly, his resignation occurred just before the UK Cabinet Mission's visit to J&K from 19–24 April 1946. By May 1946, 'The pronouncements of the British leaders and the activities of the Cabinet Mission left little doubt in the mind of far-seeing men that India was to be divided'. For J&K-ites, the pressing question was 'Where will Kashmir go?'[383] Would Maharaja Hari Singh unite J&K with India or with Pakistan? Also significantly, Beg resigned two days after the centenary of the signing of the Treaty of Amritsar. Motivated by the 'tyranny of the Dogras' and stimulated by the Cabinet Mission's visit to Srinagar, Beg and his colleagues, including Sheikh Abdullah, saw a political opportunity. Hence, Quit Kashmir. They also may have been trying to generate some political support as the popularity of the Muslim Conference, with which the National Conference had tried to make a rapprochement, was increasing.[384] Additionally, they may have been staking a future post-British position for Kashmir.

Around this time, Sheikh Abdullah was agitated. Apparently, he was 'crestfallen' as Mahatma Gandhi had refused to instigate an agitation to ensure that 'The right of accession should rest with the people of the States'.[385] Possibly as a reaction to Gandhi's snub, Abdullah publicly appealed to the Cabinet Mission on 22 April 1946, which was then visiting Srinagar, to abrogate the Treaty of Amritsar. He stated that: 'No sale deed, however sacrosanct, can condemn more than four million men and women to the servitude of an autocrat when the will to live under this rule is no longer there. The people of Kashmir are determined to mould their own destiny, and we appeal to the Members of the Cabinet Mission to recognise the justice and strength of our cause.'[386] It was unclear then what Abdullah meant by the term 'mould their own destiny'. He also offered no specific alternative to autocratic rule.

In his autobiography, Sheikh Abdullah states that, between 19 and 24 April 1946, he sent a(nother?) telegram to the Cabinet Mission, stating that:

> The Kashmiris' national demand today is no longer limited to the establishment of a responsible government. They demand total freedom from the Maharaja's autocratic rule. ... The people of Kashmir wish to draw the Cabinet Mission's attention to the fact that after the British rule ends, they have a right to become independent. The 1846 sales [sic] deed, which is mistakenly called the Treaty of Amritsar[,] shows clearly that a sales document, no matter how hard one might try to make it sacrosanct, cannot subject over forty hundred thousand men and women to the slavery of an autocrat, especially when they are determined not to remain under his subjugation.[387]

Importantly, this was the first time that Abdullah spoke of an independent Kashmir. He would not mention this concept again until October 1947. Chiefly, this was because he was jailed soon after sending these telegrams.

By May 1946, Sheikh Abdullah was 'exasperated beyond measure' by the 'haughty' Ramchandra Kak, by a lack of popular support, and by Hari Singh, who had refused a request by Abdullah for an interview in Bombay.[388] He may also have been inspired, or provoked, by a call on 12 May 1946 by his rival, Bazaz, in Anantnag District for 'Azad Kashmir'.[389] While not specific, Bazaz presumably meant a future J&K entity free (*azad*) from Maharaja Hari Singh's autocratic control. In a speech or speeches on or around 15 May 1946,[390] Abdullah went even further than Bazaz:

> The tyranny of the Dorgas [sic] has lacerated our souls. ... It is time for action. To end your poverty, you must fight slavery and enter the field of Jahad [sic] as soldiers. The fight slogan of our struggle is not only for our State but for the whole of India. India is fighting against Imperialism. The slogan was given on the banks of River Ravi ... Then came the slogan of 'Quit India' [August 1942]. The British gained hold of India by the force of arms and by treachery. The rulers of the Indian States who possess one-fourth of India, have always played traitors to the cause of Indian freedom. The demand that the Princely Order should quit is a logical extension of the policy of 'Quit India'. When the Indian freedom movement demands the complete withdrawal of British power, logically enough the stooges of British Imperialism also should go and restore sovereignty to its real owners – the people. When we raise the slogan of 'Quit Kashmir', we naturally visualise that the Princes and Nawabs should quit all the States. I am sure this demand applies similarly to a State like Hyderabad where the people will, I am sure, raise their voice, 'Quit Hyderabad'. ... God will give us faith in victory. The voice of truth will prevail. Prophets have spoken for the truth, which has always triumphed finally. Sovereignty is not the birthright of a ruler. Every man, woman and child will shout 'Quit Kashmir'. The Kashmiri nation has expressed its will. I ask for a plebiscite on this question.[391]

This was Abdullah's contentious Quit Kashmir speech, for which he was soon after tried, fined and imprisoned. (Interestingly, his call for a plebiscite may have inspired calls by India for a plebiscite when accepting Hari Singh's accession in 1947.)

Abdullah's message with Quit Kashmir was clear, and important: Hari Singh should leave the Kashmir Valley and allow 'the people' to decide their post-British political status. Alternatively, Abdullah 'entreated people to contribute one rupee each towards a collection of seventy-five lakh [7,500,000] rupees so that we could ... buy back the independence of Kashmir' from Maharaja Hari Singh.[392] That is, each and every J&K-ite, of whom there were about 4 million, should contribute Rs 1.88 per head to reimburse Maharaja Hari Singh the sum of Rs 7.5 million paid by Maharaja Gulab Singh to acquire J&K – presuming, of course, that Gulab's great grandson would accept such a repayment. As Hari Singh's actions thereafter showed, he was not at all interested in satisfying Sheikh Abdullah's political demand or in Abdullah's pecuniary proposal. These did, however, mark a new phase in their confrontation. Had Dogra rule miraculously ended in 1946, presumably J&K-ites would have received some form of popular rule, possibly based on Naya Kashmir and probably based around Sheikh Abdullah – although Abdullah did not then propose these alternatives.

Abdullah's confrontational call provoked varying responses. Some Muslims were supportive, particularly given his references to 'Jehad', 'Prophets' and the 'Kashmiri nation'. The Muslim Conference thought his call was a 'counsel of despair'.[393] Kashmiri Pandits were 'bitterly opposed' to it.[394] For Mir Qasim, a future Chief Minister of (Indian) J&K, the slogan 'acquired a Muslim orientation because the Sheikh mainly confined himself to Muslim majority areas and ignored the people of Jammu'. Although Abdullah was later careful to use the inclusive term of 'the people of Jammu and Kashmir',[395] this partially explained why there was opposition in both Kashmir and Jammu to his call.[396] A similar slogan in Urdu to 'Quit Kashmir', 'Dogra raj murdabad' ('Down with/death to Dogra rule'), did not resonate with Hindus and Muslims in Jammu where Dogras of both religious persuasions comprised the majority ethnic community. Many were loyal to Maharaja Hari Singh and/or they disliked 'Kashmir-based leaders', potential 'Kashmiri raj'[397] and/or 'Abdullahism'.[398] Hari Singh's regime was displeased and acted quickly. It arrested Sheikh Abdullah and 'all important members of the National Conference',[399] imposed a curfew in Srinagar, brought out the military to reinforce the police patrolling, cut private telephone services, and had military pickets secure bridges, post offices and public spaces.[400] By 27 May, there was a 'big exodus' of visitors while, concurrently, 450 people had been arrested.[401]

Outsiders also disliked Abdullah's Quit Kashmir call. Jinnah rejected Abdullah's call, stating that his and the Muslim Conference's 'creed' was 'the attainment of responsible government under the aegis of the Maharaja'.[402] Nehru was unhappy with Abdullah, who he felt had acted alone: the 'new policy had not been endorsed by the National Conference or its executive',[403] a point that Mir Qasim later confirmed.[404] Personally, Nehru thought that Abdullah's policy was 'regrettable' and 'unfortunate' and a 'marked variation' in the policies of the States Peoples' Conference, of which Nehru was then President (Abdullah would become President in 1946–47),[405] as well as of the National Conference, which was affiliated with AISPC (until the latter's dissolution in 1948).[406] Abdullah would have been aware of AISPC policies, given that, as Vice-President, he had attended its annual session held in Udaipur in January 1946.[407] Not wanting to upset India's still influential princes, many of whom were Hindus like Maharaja Hari Singh, Nehru pragmatically reiterated AISPC policy for princely states: 'responsible Government under the aegis of the rulers' would continue. On 29 May, he further publicly 'assured the Princes that there was no intention to abolish them'.[408] Nehru tempered his disappointment by stating that it was Abdullah's right to raise this issue and, as long as this was 'done in a peaceful way, no state has the right to suppress it'.[409] In 1947, Congress President, Acharya Kripalani, was more forthright: Abdullah's call for the ruler to Quit Kashmir had been 'unjust and unreasonable'. Hari Singh was not a foreigner, but 'a son of the soil' who had 'every right to live in Kashmir'.[410] Legally, Kripalani was correct: Hari Singh was a native from J&K. How could he quit his own homeland?

Although Sheikh Abdullah's Quit Kashmir speech was impetuous and questionable, it was also significant. It marked the first time that Kashmiris had talked seriously of ending Dogra rule. As Abdullah stated in 1946: 'When the Indian freedom movement demands the complete withdrawal of British power, logically enough the stooges of British Imperialism also should go and restore sovereignty to its real owners – the people'.[411] The specific 'stooge' in this case was Maharaja Hari Singh; the people were J&K-ites. Despite such inclusivity, Abdullah seemingly decided to instigate his campaign unilaterally, or possibly after advice from some close associates, such as Beg. Certainly, it was unclear why he chose to seriously antagonise a leading Indian prince during India's changing, but sensitive, political circumstances. Perhaps he was proactively inserting an early bid for J&K's post-British status – although, until the British departed, they wanted stability in J&K, not political unrest. One allegation was that Communism or Communist mentors, with their anti-imperialist agendas, had motivated him.[412] A prime motivation appears to have been a desire to advance the wellbeing of backward ethnic Kashmiris. The thrust of Abdullah's Quit Kashmir speech suggests this: 'To end your poverty, you must ... enter the field of Jahad [sic] as soldiers'.[413] However, the concept of *jihad* only applied to J&K Muslims. Similarly, the use of socialist,[414] even Communist,[415] ideas and terms such as *bourgeois* and *bourgeoisie*, 'exploiters and the exploited', 'oppressor and oppressed', applied largely to J&K Muslims.[416] For one Kashmiri, Abdullah's use of such terminology changed him from being the 'Lion of Kashmir' to the 'Lenin of Kashmir'.[417]

By 10 June 1946, some were suggesting that Quit Kashmir had 'died a natural death'.[418] With Abdullah arrested on 20 May[419] and 'all important members of the National Conference' arrested soon after,[420] this possibly was so, although twenty-two people were arrested in Srinagar in November 'for shouting "Quit Kashmir" slogans' in 'observance of "Shaikh [sic] Abdullah Day"'.[421] However, Quit Kashmir did not seriously challenge Hari Singh or his regime. Furthermore, Abdullah, who had been 'venting his spleen' or was being opportunistic, was charged with sedition. In September, he was put on trial under Section 124-A of the Ranbir Penal Code. He was charged with making three speeches in May 'calculated to bring into hatred and contempt and excite disaffection towards' the ruler.[422] Abdullah's Defence Counsel, Asaf Ali, a friend of Nehru,[423] when asked by the Judge, Barkat Rai, 'to explain' Quit Kashmir, stated that: 'Here [in J&K] the ruler is not a foriegner [sic] and therefore 'Quit Kashmir' means that he should relinquish autocratic authority and transfer to the people the power to rule themselves with him as the symbol of authority'.[424] In a long and spirited defence of Abdullah, Ali later reiterated, in a 'shocking' and 'backsliding' way for some Kashmiris,[425] that Abdullah 'did not mean for a single second that he wanted Maharaja Bahadur to quit personally'.[426] Rather, the Quit Kashmir slogan meant that 'sovereignty belongs to the people of the State and that the Maharaja should rule as a constitutional monarch'. It did not involve 'the deposition of the ruler',[427] just the end of his autocratic rule. Later, Abdullah similarly stated that his 'fight … against the autocratic rule was not against the person of the ruler but against a system'.[428] This post-facto explanation was disingenuous.

On 10 September 1946, Judge Rai found Abdullah guilty and sentenced him 'to three years' simple imprisonment on each of three counts' and to a fine of Rs 1,500.[429] The sentences were to 'run concurrently'.[430] This ended any amity that existed between Singh and Abdullah. The sentence also perturbed Nehru, who Hari Singh's regime had arrested in June as the enraged Indian sought (unsuccessfully) to enter J&K in order to defend his friend, Abdullah. Nehru's 'quixotic intervention' and arrest by the 'harassed Durbar' occurred when Nehru was meant to be discussing India's post-British future with the Cabinet Mission in New Delhi.[431] The J&K Government was seen as being 'heavy-fisted' and 'self-righteous', particularly as another princely ruler, the Maharaja of Bikaner, was then devolving responsible government to his subjects.[432] Thereafter, the 'Kashmir dispute' as Nehru then called it and as he ominously predicted, 'ceased to be a "personal adventure" and was now a matter for negotiation between Congress, the Political Department and the Kashmir Government'.[433] For Karan Singh, Nehru's arrest marked the beginning of the end of Dogra rule: 'I have no doubt that his arrest was the turning point in the history of the State'.[434] Nehru apparently never forgave Hari Singh for sending Abdullah to prison for sedition, a factor that would later impair the ruler's efforts to deal with the leaders of post-British India, particularly with its new (by then) Prime Minister, Jawaharlal Nehru. As Nehru had noted in 1946: 'undoubtedly'

Hari Singh 'will have to suffer for the policy of his administration. ... The talks that we are having about India's future become pale and shadowy before this grim reality.'[435]

While Quit Kashmir called for an end to Dogra rule in J&K, a contradiction occurred sixteen months later. On 26 September 1947, Sheikh Abdullah wrote to Maharaja Hari Singh from jail and twice pledged his 'steadfast loyalty' to the ruler:

> I assure Your Highness the fullest and loyal support of myself and my organization. ... Before I close this letter I beg to assure Your Highness once again of my steadfast loyalty and pray that God under Your Highness' aegis bring [sic] such an era of Peace, Prosperity and Good Government that it may be second to none and be an ideal for others to copy.[436]

In other words, Abdullah would support the Maharaja and his continuing rule in J&K. While 'fulsome and obsequious',[437] Abdullah's letter also was extraordinary. As the *Pakistan Times* wryly noted, 'The author of the "Quit Kashmir" movement has suddenly been converted to the slogan "Don't Quit Kashmir".'[438] While true, circumstances were drawing Singh and Abdullah together, chiefly around the significant issue of J&K possibly joining India. For this to occur, Abdullah's support was needed. For Hari Singh, these pledges of loyalty were likely a pre-condition to enable Abdullah's release from jail, which Gandhi probably sought when he met the Maharaja in early August 1947.[439] On 29 September, *The Civil & Military Gazette* reported that the Kashmiri had been freed after one year, four months and ten days in jail. After this early release, Sheikh Abdullah offered his loyalty in person to the Maharaja via a traditional *nazrana* (conferral) ceremony.[440] Presumably, this was satisfying for Hari Singh and humiliating for Sheikh Abdullah. Ominously, however, in his 26 September letter the Kashmiri had informed the Dogra 'that any party, within or without the State which may attempt to create any impediments in our efforts to gain our goal, will be treated as our enemy.'[441] Had Hari Singh been paying attention, this was a serious warning for him.

Fluidity in India

As early as 1944, 'The partition of India had become a burning issue' for J&K-ites.[442] That year, the J&K State *Administration Report* saw J&K's political situation as follows:

> The National Conference, which is led by Mr. S. M. Abdullah and has the support of some Hindus and Sikhs, continued to be chiefly a Muslim organization. A section

of the Muslims both in Jammu and Kashmir, however, continued to distrust the party on the ground [sic] that it does not stand for Pakistan and that its programme is subordinate to the policy of the All-India Congress, a Hindu organization. The attitude of Hindus in general is also unfriendly to the party. They distrust the National Conference, which according to them was the Muslim Conference only a few years ago and has not undergone a real r[e]-orientation, in spite of the change of name. Reports were current for some time in the local Hindu Press that Mr. Abdullah was establishing contact with Mr. M. A. Jinnah, President of the All-India Muslim League. These reports added further to the distrust of the Hindus. Mr. Abdullah, however, kept aloof from t[h]e Muslim League and refused to lend his support to Pakistan.

The Muslim Conference succeeded in winning the support of the All-India Muslim League and its leader, Mr. Jinnah. ... The old differences between the Muslim Conference and the National Conference, became so acute at one time in Srinagar that restrictions had to be imposed on public meetings, processions etc., in the city. ...

The Congress party [sic] in the State had no definite programme of action before it. The party did not make any headway during the year. ... There is no representative body for all the Hindus of the State. All their parties, however, continued to criticize the Pakistan scheme severely.[443]

Clearly, the emerging issue for J&K-ites was the future of India, including the possible creation of Pakistan.

By mid-1946, India's political future was a pre-eminent concern for Indians, including J&K-ites. In January, the demand of many Muslims for Pakistan could no longer be ignored, as the showing of the Muslim League in elections held in Indian Provinces confirmed. While Congress won the majority of non-Muslim seats, the Muslim League won the majority of Muslim seats.[444] The Cabinet Mission's visit to India in April 1946 further confirmed that the British would soon be leaving and that the political future of India was to be negotiated, and decided. In January 1947, elections were held in J&K during the depths of winter. The National Conference, displeased with the ruler's treatment of its leaders, and believing that the elections might well be tampered with – i.e., rigged – boycotted them. The Muslim Conference, however, along with fifteen other parties, contested the polls and won sixteen of the twenty-one seats reserved for Muslims, including some in Kashmir where the National Conference supposedly was more popular.

While the J&K elections suggested that the pro-Pakistan Muslim Conference was more popular in J&K than the secular National Conference, there were other factors to consider. Voter turnout was low: only 182,800 voters out of a possible electorate of 607,419 people voted,[445] while in perhaps as many as half of the contestable seats independent candidates were returned unopposed.[446] The low turnout may have been due to political pressure, physical intimidation, or apathy. Equally, it simply may have been due to the cold weather, which generally deterred outside activity at that time of the year. Nevertheless, both political parties, as much as they could, claimed victory: for the Muslim Conference, it won seats; for the National Conference, the low turnout was due to its boycott of the polls. Equally, Prime Minister Pandit Ramchandra Kak believed his position had been strengthened. This may have been so in the short term. Longer term, however, Kak became politically expendable, as he would discover when Maharaja Hari Singh sacked him on 11 August 1947, after which Kak (inevitably) was jailed. His sacking occurred four days before the British departure from India, which suggested that Hari Singh had something in mind, although it wasn't then clear exactly what.

After the J&K elections, both major parties were relatively quiet. Apart from the weather, the major reason for this was because their leaders, Sheikh Abdullah of the National Conference and Ghulam Abbas of the Muslim Conference, who often were the chief enunciators of policy, were incarcerated in J&K jails. Abdullah would remain in jail until 19 September 1947; Abbas, who had been jailed in October 1946,[447] apparently without a trial,[448] would be there until 2 March 1948. When both went to prison, 'the subcontinent was one unified whole'. When they were freed, 'it [wa]s split in two', with both men missing the independence celebrations on 14–15 August. Although they received news and newspapers 'irregularly' and even though their 'bodies were in prison', supposedly their 'souls were at large [and] engaged with happenings in the world outside'.[449] This included contemplating J&K's 'fate'.[450] Abbas apparently was in touch with the Muslim Conference hierarchy and possibly was the person who suggested, by letter, that the party propose that J&K be independent, with the Maharaja as a constitutional figurehead.[451] This stance changed on 22 July 1947. Thereafter, the Muslim Conference strongly suggested that Maharaja Hari Singh should accede to Pakistan.[452] After Abbas's release from jail in early March 1948, he went to Azad Kashmir, where he would play a major role in local politics until his death in 1968.

While languishing in jail, Sheikh Abdullah apparently contemplated the three options for J&K: Pakistan, India, or independence. Initially, he had some 'subconscious sympathy for the slogan "Pakistan" because it was a Muslim reaction against Hindu communalism'. However, from as early as December 1945, Abdullah was trying 'to combat the Pakistan slogan'.[453] He considered Pakistan to be an 'escapist device' and 'an emotional response' to the British departure that was 'likely to harm Muslim interests'.[454] Furthermore, he considered that the Muslim League 'had a close ideological affinity with the rulers of the states',[455] and that it had 'never upheld the cause of emancipation nor sided with the forces of progress and that it [Pakistan] would always be influenced by a capitalist feudal ideology'. Indeed, 'if the Kashmiris opted for Pakistan, their dream of "New Kashmir" would be broken and we would have to put on the same [autocratic?] yoke that we had been trying to get rid of'.[456] Equally, Jinnah, Liaquat and company, would have limited the Kashmiris' ability to operate locally. Essentially, as Beg noted in 1952, joining Pakistan 'would have snuffed out', even 'crushed', their 'torch of progress', as had happened with the ostracised, non-Muslim League Pukhtoon politician, Khan Abdul Ghaffar Khan, in Pakistan's North-West Frontier Province.[457] As Abdullah also later noted, more Muslims would remain in India (40 million) than would join West Pakistan (25 million). Therefore, if 'one Muslim is as good as another, the Kashmiri Muslims … should choose the forty million living in India'.[458] In relation to India, the National Conference and the Congress also had identical principles: secularism, socialism and democracy.[459] Its 'perceptions tallied with our own. Therefore, it would be quite likely that our objectives would be fulfilled if we joined India.'[460] This seemingly left no reason to discuss the question of independence.

Despite their rivalry, it seems that Abdullah and Abbas seriously talked about J&K's future, including the 'question of Kashmir's independence', while incarcerated in jail. This was well before the Maharaja's accession to India. Abbas possibly thought that independence for J&K would be a good option; Abdullah thought that the Maharaja wanted to remain independent.[461] Both men also probably knew that, following Gaffar Khan's party's boycott of the referendum that enabled NWFP voters to narrowly determine to join their province with Pakistan, Khan was talking of a 'third option besides those of Pakistan and India'. The so-called 'Frontier Gandhi' wanted an independent 'Pakhtoonistan',[462] which may have inspired Abbas and Abdullah. According to Abdullah, however, they dismissed independence as an option for J&K:

> we were unanimous that in the existing global scenario it was impossible for the little territory of Kashmir, surrounded as it was by powerful states, to maintain [sic] its independence. It would certainly turn into a hotbed of conspiracies. However, if these powers ensured our development and stability, one could give thought to that option.[463]

Some time well after Abdullah's release from jail in September 1947, but while Abbas was still incarcerated, the two political rivals apparently met in an 'atmosphere highly charged with emotions of love and tenderness'. After 'a long conversation', they concluded 'that a plebiscite, if held at all, would lead to further bloodshed.

Of course, the situation might improve if India and Pakistan guaranteed the state's independence.' Abdullah asked Abbas to 'persuade Jinnah' when he got to Pakistan 'to agree to the proposal [of independence that] we had thought out'. Abbas apparently tried but Jinnah rejected the idea.[464] By then, too much had changed in relation to J&K.

The beginning of the end of Dogra rule

From 1931, the position and power of Maharaja Hari Singh, the autocrat who ruled J&K, began to be challenged by civilians and by civil unrest. This process coincided with the rise of Kashmiri political aspirations and the re-awakening of Kashmiri nationalism. Sheikh Abdullah was one of the Kashmiris responsible for these factors. Arguably, he was the most important Kashmiri politician after the significant anti-Maharaja uprising in 1931. Thereafter, J&K politics moved slowly from being communal under the Muslim Conference, newly formed in 1932, through a nationalist period during which J&K-ites actively cooperated with the Maharaja. In 1939, the Muslim Conference was re-named the National Conference, which made this party secular and more inclusive. The Muslim Conference re-emerged in 1941, thereby giving J&K a type of two-party system. For one later observer, these political changes provided the 'origins' of the Kashmir dispute: thereafter, more religious Jammu Muslims generally would be pro-Pakistan; more secular Kashmiri Muslims generally would be pro-India.[465] From 1944, National Conference politicians actively pursued their Naya Kashmir socialist agenda, which Maharaja Hari Singh seems largely to have ignored. From 1931 to 1946, J&K-ites' political focus was on obtaining political rights and better economic conditions under the Dogra administration. There was never any talk of independence for J&K or of the state being ruled by 'a son of the soil'.

This all changed in 1946. Exactly one hundred years after Raja Gulab Singh had purchased his princely state from the British, Sheikh Abdullah took the extraordinary step of calling on the current Dogra ruler to Quit Kashmir. Although he later repudiated his call for Maharaja Hari Singh to leave J&K, Abdullah's slogan was provocative and significant. It was the first time that a popular J&K politician had unequivocally called for an end to Dogra rule in J&K. Kashmiri nationalism, as espoused by Abdullah, was alive and active. His call also inspired people to seriously contemplate, or possibly to foresee, for the first time the end of Dogra rule. As the partition of British India came closer, various J&K-ites considered options for J&K's post-British future and their aspirations. Significantly, these included independence for J&K – which possibly was the first time this possibility had been seriously considered since Akbar captured Kashmir in 1586 or since Dogra rule began in J&K in 1846. Ironically, as the British departure from India in 1947 neared, the two old rivals, Hari Singh and Sheikh Abdullah, moved politically closer, chiefly because of their desire not to join Pakistan. In 1947, their power dynamic would change dramatically – and not in the Dogra's favour. Unleashed, assertive and supported by India, Kashmiri nationalism would triumph over Dogra rule. This did not bring independence, but it did result in a significant transfer of political and administrative power within J&K.

Ultimately, the British were the effective guarantors of Dogra rule in J&K. This autocratic regime's control of J&K gave the imperial power the stability that it desired in this strategic princely state, particularly in relation to securing J&K's sensitive northern and northeastern border areas with Afghanistan and China, with the aggressive Soviet Union just beyond. The British therefore were supportive of Maharaja Hari Singh and his regime, although Singh himself was distrustful of them, believing that they had been involved fomenting troubles in Kashmir in 1931. While the final decision to partition the subcontinent into India and Pakistan was only taken by Lord Mountbatten on 4 June 1947,[466] it was clear long beforehand that the British would be departing India. Indeed, the Cabinet Mission's visit to J&K in April 1946 had confirmed this possibility. The intended, then actual, British departure from India unleashed huge passions and forces throughout the subcontinent. The potential post-British possibilities encouraged perceptive and active Indians to start thinking and agitating, including those in the larger princely states where their future was both uncertain and to be determined by their respective autocratic ruler. Although Maharaja Hari Singh didn't then realise it, the British departure from India was the beginning of the end of Dogra rule in J&K.

5

Sheikh Abdullah's pursuit of independence for 'Kashmir', 1946–53

On 3 June 1947, the political future of India became significantly clearer when Lord Mountbatten announced his plan to partition the British Indian Empire into the new dominions of India and Pakistan. A major issue thereafter became what would happen to the Indian States, including J&K. While Maharaja Hari Singh was responsible for the decision on the accession, the National Conference's stance, building on its *Naya Kashmir* strategy, was to have the J&K citizenry empowered to allow them to decide J&K's international future. Ultimately, the tribal invasion of J&K on 22 October 1947 forced the hands of both Hari Singh and Sheikh Abdullah. Both became – in the short term, at least – in favour of J&K joining India. Thereafter, the Indian state of Jammu and Kashmir became the successor entity to the former princely state of Jammu and Kashmir. In due course, Hari Singh would become disenchanted with India as he quickly lost power, prestige and, indeed, his entire princely state. Similarly, Abdullah would become disenchanted with India, but for different reasons and timings.

From his political rise in the early 1930s until his death in 1982, Sheikh Abdullah was a towering personality in Kashmir. This was partly related to his height: Abdullah was six foot four inches tall (1.93 metres), which was atypically tall for Kashmiri males. Equally, many J&K-ites, although not all of them, considered him to be 'a precious jewel' who 'burns for the well-being, dignity, honour and self-respect of the people of Jammu and Kashmir'. Given Abdullah's presence and influence in J&K politics after 1947, and his challenging post-accessional relationship with India, this chapter might better be titled 'Centre-Shaikh [sic] relations'.[1] While this relationship started positively, by 1953 there were many – indeed, too many – negative aspects. The assertive Abdullah was trying to ensure that 'his' state had as much autonomy and administrative distance from New Delhi as he could secure. New Delhi wanted the total opposite: for J&K, including Kashmir, to be 'just another

Indian state' and for its residents, including Kashmiris, to be 'ordinary Indians'. The turning point for Abdullah occurred in mid-1953 when New Delhi and some colleagues in Srinagar feared that he was seriously contemplating independence for Kashmir. By then, Prime Minister Nehru, who also had become disenchanted with the J&K Prime Minister, allowed Abdullah to be dismissed from office.

This chapter discusses Sheikh Abdullah and his often contrary attitudes to independence for J&K between 1946 and 1953. It also discusses his challenging relationship with New Delhi, which at times caused him to waver in his support for India and to contemplate other options for J&K, particularly independence. For New Delhi, the relationship was equally as challenging.

1947: accession to India?

In the first nine months of 1947, many J&K-ites contemplated a serious question: should J&K join Pakistan or India or pursue independence? While Sheikh Abdullah had thought about independence for J&K in 1946, he could do little to pursue this option in 1947 until his incarceration ended in late September. He also considered that, in relation to J&K's international status, 'sovereign power must rest with the people of Kashmir'.[2] This was not a new policy. The National Conference's annual conference in Sopore in 1945, attended by some senior Congressmen, had adopted a resolution 'asserting the right of self-determination' for J&K-ites.[3] His controversial anti-Maharaja Quit Kashmir campaign in 1946 also had strongly proclaimed this position – although his opponents considered it a 'Quit Autocracy' campaign, given that Hari Singh had as much right to reside in J&K as Abdullah.[4] Nevertheless, Abdullah's primary message in late 1947 remained enabling the people.

Increasingly, Sheikh Abdullah talked of the people's need to get rid of Dogra rule before the J&K accession was decided. He also wanted J&K-ites to be involved in determining 'their' state's future. On 3 October 1947 at Srinagar, Abdullah spoke publicly about 'internal independence'.[5] This followed the Maharaja granting him 'royal clemency' on 29 September, thereby releasing him from jail.[6] Hari Singh had done so following pressure from the Viceroy and Indian politicians.[7] Abdullah publicly stated that J&K needed a 'responsible government ... at this crucial juncture. We cannot decide our accession without our internal independence. So our slogan is – "Freedom before accession".[8] At another public rally around the same time, he stated that the issue was 'Should we accede to India or to Pakistan or opt for independence? ... the most important criterion that will determine our accession is the interests of our people.' Equally, the 'foremost obligation' was 'to shake off'

Dogra rule.[9] A further consideration was the type of political system that post-partition India and Pakistan would each adopt. That aside, Abdullah said that he would accept whatever decision the people took, including if they chose for J&K to join Pakistan.[10]

Abdullah's stance, which he wrote about retrospectively, may have been disingenuous. On 29 September 1947, a press report noting his release from jail had stated that it was 'believed that a settlement with the National Conference is indicative of the State's decision to accede to the Indian Union, which it is understood Sheikh Abdullah will support'.[11] Two days later, however, Abdullah was again 'on message', stating that the National Conference 'would give the people a proper lead after mature consideration and would stick to it in the teeth of opposition from any quarter'.[12] On 9 October, he repeated a similar message.[13] On 20 October, he reiterated his and his party's position on J&K's political future: 'After the lapse of paramountcy, sovereignty passes to the people and it is for the people to decide the future of a State. We will take our decision [about J&K's future] after coolly and calmly considering [the] pros and cons of every decision we take.'[14] This was two days before the Pukhtoons' invasion of Kashmir Province.

The next day (21 October), speaking at a reception in New Delhi, Abdullah 'pleaded for time to consider which Dominion the State should join'. For him, the current political 'atmosphere was not conducive to calm thinking'. People were uncertain and apprehensive due to the violence enveloping northern parts of the subcontinent, including in J&K's Jammu Province. He 'would not brook dictation from Pakistan or coercion from India'. Abdullah's first concern was 'freedom from autocracy' and 'self-government so that the people, armed with authority and responsibility, could decide for themselves where their interests lay'. Abdullah also observed that the 'rights accruing from the sale deed [of 1846] lapsed with the end of British rule'. If the Maharaja 'wanted to continue' as ruler of J&K, he 'must negotiate afresh with his people on the basis of the people's right to rule'.[15] While this was an interesting observation, in the tumult of 1947, other matters were more important than Kashmiri interpretations of the longevity, or otherwise, of the British-Dogra 'sale deed' of 1846.

On 22 October 1947 in New Delhi, Abdullah again called for 'immediate responsible government' to be granted in J&K.[16] His message was: 'Until we are free ourselves, we cannot give you an answer' about J&K's accession.[17] Ironically, however, J&K was about to become inextricably bound with India. The Pukhtoons' invasion of Kashmir Province that day quickly forced Maharaja Hari Singh's hand. On 26 October, he acceded to India, with Sheikh Abdullah and the National

Conference supporting this accession.[8] Writing retrospectively, Sheikh Abdullah claimed that Maharaja Hari Singh had wanted independence for his state.[19] This option supposedly also was Abdullah's 'first preference'.[20] However, his and Hari Singh's 'anti-Pakistan' desires converged in 1947[21] and Abdullah supported Singh's accession to India. The Maharaja confirmed Abdullah's importance by naming 'Sheikh Abdulla [sic]' in his letter to Governor-General Mountbatten, which accompanied his formal accession to India.[22] Abdullah was the only J&K-ite specifically mentioned by Singh. So, while the Maharaja provided the legal basis for J&K to join India, Abdullah and his National Conference provided the moral justification.[23] In October 1948, this accession was unanimously confirmed at a special convention of the National Conference.[24]

The day after the accession, Indian military forces entered J&K and began to establish themselves. They have never left. Hari Singh's accession ended both the speculation about J&K's international status and J&K-ites' need to consider 'the advantages of Kashmir's joining one or the other Dominion'.[25] Had the Pukhtoon invasion not occurred, perhaps – and this is a big perhaps – there might have been a different future for J&K. Equally, by the time of his accession, Maharaja Hari Singh had lost control of 'his' state. There was a major ongoing anti-Maharaja, pro-Pakistan uprising in Poonch, serious and uncontrolled inter-religious violence in Jammu between pro-Pakistan Muslims and pro-India Hindus and Sikhs, and the Azad (Free) Kashmir entity had been established on 24 October in areas 'freed' from Hari Singh's control. A week later, Muslims in the Gilgit area would also rebel and ask to join Pakistan. Seemingly, Sheikh Abdullah never sought seriously to join Pakistan, despite Maharaja Hari Singh's claim in 1952 that, in 1947 'the top ranking leaders of Pakistan were continually approaching the Kashmir National Conference leaders ... [and] promised them something approaching independence if only they would agree to Kashmir acceding to Pakistan. They [the Pakistanis] were even prepared to give the right of secession [to J&K]'.[26] Given Abdullah and his colleagues' support for J&K's unification with India in 1947, they clearly had dismissed these alleged Pakistani approaches.

1947: immediately after the accession to India

On the day Maharaja Hari Singh acceded to India, Sheikh Abdullah, as leader of the National Conference, made a statement that denounced the Pukhtoon invasion but which again stated that he and J&K-ites had hoped for time to decide their political future.[27] He made a similar statement the next day, although, pragmatically, he noted that the accession question had become 'a secondary issue. The first duty of every Kashmiri is to defend his motherland against the intruder.'[28] Later, Abdullah wrote that the National Conference supported Hari Singh's accession to India, which position he told Nehru personally on 26 October 1947 while a guest at his home in New Delhi.[29] (Ironically, at this challenging time, Hari Singh and Sheikh Abdullah, intentionally or otherwise, were absent from the Kashmir Valley. For their personal safety, both left Srinagar on 25 October: Singh for Jammu; Abdullah for New Delhi, with V. P. Menon.[30] Despite accusing Singh of fleeing Srinagar, Abdullah also surreptitiously evacuated his family from Srinagar to Delhi on 28 October.)[31] Abdullah made his pro-India affirmation in the presence of Prime Minister Mahajan, who surprisingly had threatened to negotiate with Pakistan if India did not support J&K.[32] Abdullah's Government later reported that the accession had 'jointly been made by the Maharaja, as required by law and [by] Sheikh Mohammad Abdullah, in the name of the people'.[33] In November, Nehru stated that 'We were asked … both on behalf of the Maharaja and Sheikh Abdullah to accept the accession of the State to the Indian Union'.[34] Generously, India did so.

On 29 October 1947, Maharaja Hari Singh appointed Sheikh Abdullah as Chief Emergency Administrator of the J&K Emergency Government based in Srinagar.[35] Almost incredibly, certainly in retrospect, Abdullah concurrently started to equivocate – or perhaps clarify might be kinder – about J&K's accession to India. On the same day as his appointment, *The Times* in Srinagar suggested that Sheikh Abdullah desired independence for J&K. Its 'Special Correspondent', who had spoken with the Kashmiri leader the day before, reported that Abdullah was 'obviously the key man in the Kashmir political crisis'. He confronted many issues, including conducting 'a referendum, preferably under the joint supervision of India and Pakistan, to decide to which Dominion Kashmir should accede'. For Abdullah, there were 'three considerations' for 'Kashmir': its geo-economic dependence on Pakistan; its biggest markets being in India; and tourists from Britain and the United States being its 'main source of revenue'.[36] Then, Sheikh Abdullah said something startling. He said that he and the National Conference 'preferred to keep an open mind, but if India and Pakistan would jointly undertake the protection of Kashmir from foreign aggression the state might be well advised to accede to neither, but to retain neutral status and serve as a meeting-ground for Hindu and Muslim ideas'.[37] To 'accede to neither but to retain neutral status' amounted to J&K being independent, albeit if – and this was a huge, and unlikely, if – India and Pakistan would 'jointly' protect J&K 'from foreign aggression'. Presumably, the potential aggressors were the USSR and/or China, both of which would have been difficult to defend against.

Around the same time, Sheikh Abdullah privately told 'the top officers at the Srinagar Secretariat' that J&K's accession to India 'was conditional and subject to a plebiscite.'[38] While differing from what he told *The Times*, this private stance made to 'his' bureaucrats was not surprising. It reflected Governor-General Mountbatten's response on 27 October to Maharaja Hari Singh's accession that, after normalcy was restored in J&K, 'it is my Government's wish that ... the question of the State's accession should be settled by a reference to the people.'[39] Nehru 'readily agreed' with Mountbatten's position, as he had informed Mahajan the day before[40] and as he reiterated via a broadcast on 2 November.[41] This 'reference to the people' amounted to a plebiscite. For Abdullah, it also meant that Maharaja Hari Singh's 'act of necessity'[42] in joining India was 'temporary',[43] 'provisional' or 'conditional' until a plebiscite enabled J&K-ites to reaffirm it. J&K's accession to India was not fully settled.

Significantly, almost immediately after Maharaja Hari Singh's accession, Sheikh Abdullah was either equivocating about J&K's full unification with India, contemplating other international options for J&K apart from India, or was stating that the accession was conditional and subject to ratification by a plebiscite. Possibly, his equivocations were understandable, given J&K's fluid, uncertain, even dangerous, circumstances. However, Abdullah would continue to use, or would be accused of using, these 'themes' of independence and self-determination for J&K interchangeably, contrarily and persistently, in his political discourses about the state. He would also continue to state that J&K's accession to India was conditional, provisional or temporary and required a confirmatory plebiscite, a stance that irked India, Indians and, as we shall see, many Jammuites. While such talk may not have been popular with others, the plebiscite was not Abdullah's personal invention, unlike his desire for independence for 'Kashmir'. He was only calling for something initially promised by India, reiterated in 1948 by the UNSC and by India's *White Paper on Jammu & Kashmir*,[44] and agreed to by Pakistan. Until the mid-1950s, J&K-ites expected that this plebiscite would be held.

While popular politically, Abdullah lacked experience as an administrator. Nevertheless, in his role as Chief Emergency Administrator of the J&K Emergency Government, he had 'absolute power to deal with any emergency'.[45] Essentially, a new absolute ruler (Sheikh Abdullah) had replaced the former one (Hari Singh), certainly in Kashmir. (Mahajan, Singh's Prime Minister, was more influential in Jammu.) Arguably, Abdullah enjoyed more leeway than Hari Singh, given that

India had welcomed his appointment and supported him almost unconditionally.[46] Indeed, Nehru was responsible for Abdullah obtaining his new position after insisting that India would advance military help to J&K provided that Abdullah was 'taken in the administration and made responsible for it along with the [J&K] Prime Minister'.[47] Speaking on 3 November 1947, Nehru congratulated the Maharaja on his decision to elevate Abdullah 'at this critical juncture' because 'the struggle in Kashmir is a struggle of the people of Kashmir under popular leadership against the invader'. He then reiterated that 'as soon as Kashmir is free from the invader ... the fate of Kashmir will be left in the hands of the people of Kashmir'.[48] Both of Nehru's comments possibly displeased the supposed ruler of J&K, Maharaja Hari Singh. Nehru would maintain his stance that J&K-ites would decide J&K's 'fate' via a plebiscite until the early 1950s. Meanwhile, from late 1947, Abdullah was distracted by his newfound 'heavier responsibility'. Apart from a large administrative load, he was involved organising a volunteer people's militia to defend against the Pukhtoons, ending the inter-religious violence in Jammu Province, initiating a major reform agenda, and supporting India at the United Nations.[49]

Sheikh Abdullah was also constrained by the need to publicly adhere to India's policy positions, especially on J&K. Increasingly, this requirement would cause him problems. Despite the compulsion to be pro-India, Abdullah's push for pseudo independence for J&K continued. On 3 November 1947, in a statement released by the J&K State, the Kashmiri leader declared that 'We do not want to be slaves of either Pakistan or Hindustan but we want Kashmir to be free under His Highness the Maharaja so that every one of us is a sharer in the administration of this country'.[50] While not necessarily a push for independence, Abdullah's statement was not unequivocally pro-India. Unusually, he also publicly supported the retention of his old political foe, Hari Singh, as the head of the state. This was logical: both men then needed to have a working relationship to protect J&K from the dangerously close Pukhtoons. Their post-accession bonhomie continued. In late 1947, according to Mahajan, who was then still Prime Minister of J&K, Abdullah apparently suggested to Maharaja Hari Singh in a meeting in Jammu that India and Pakistan be made to recognise J&K 'as an independent unit like Switzerland'. The Maharaja apparently 'nodded assent'.[51]

Jawaharlal Nehru had other ideas, however. On 1 December, he informed Hari Singh that 'It has been suggested that Kashmir State ... might be more or less an independent entity with its integrity and defence guaranteed by India and Pakistan'. For Nehru, this was a bad idea that would be 'likely to give trouble in the future' and 'might well continue' the India–Pakistan conflict over J&K.[52] Indeed, both nations 'guaranteeing independence to Kashmir would probably mean … poor Kashmir would be faced with ascendency by both'. Nehru had 'no objection theoretically' to the concept of an independent J&K; practically, he did not see how it could work.[53] Nehru's pragmatism seemingly struck home. On 30 December in New Delhi, Sheikh Abdullah 'emphasised that [the] Kashmir people had decided once and for all that their future lay with India. … Kashmir would not go to Pakistan as long as a single Kashmiri was alive'. The Kashmiris' fight was 'against the autocratic rule', a fight that would continue as long as we are not in a position to control our own destinies'. The National Conference's demand was people's empowerment, not independent rule: 'Full responsible government with the Maharaja as constitutional head – no more and no less'. Abdullah was still prepared to involve Hari Singh, albeit only as a powerless titular head of J&K.[54]

While affirming that J&K's future lay with India, the idea of an independent J&K did not 'die' at the end of 1947. Sheikh Abdullah publicly supported J&K being with India but was more forthcoming privately. At the United Nations in January 1948, he allegedly informed three Pakistanis that, as a face-saving solution for both nations, 'Kashmir should be an independent state free both India and Pakistan'.[55] The Pakistanis were not then (or perhaps at all) receptive to this suggestion from this Indian 'stooge'. Other people also took up the issue. On 9 March 1948, the Canadian High Commissioner to India, John D. Kearney, 'put forward' a plan to Prime Minister Nehru 'for a plebiscite to be confined to the question of independence for Kashmir or not[,] with a joint guarantee by both Dominions of an independent Kashmir'. In response, Nehru told Kearney 'that the idea was a possible solution and although it would not be liked in India he [Nehru] thought he could put it across'.[56] Arguably, Nehru was being diplomatic, not pragmatic, and he does not appear to have done anything to try to 'put it across'.

In June 1949, Nehru felt compelled to write to Sheikh Abdullah, who he considered had 'little political insight',[57] to tell him not to 'throw out suggestions in the air'. This concerned Michael Davidson's interview of Abdullah published in *The Scotsman* in April.[58] Davidson stated that Abdullah had 'accepted the principle of independence for the Vale of Kashmir as perhaps the sole solution to the problem'. In response to a suggestion by Davidson, Abdullah 'declared' that 'accession to either side cannot bring peace'. Rather, Abdullah stated that 'We want to live in friendship with both Dominions. Perhaps a middle path between them, with economic co-operation with each, will be the only way of doing it. But an independent Kashmir must be guaranteed not only by India and Pakistan but also by Britain, the United States and other members of the United Nations'.[59] For Davidson, this (incorrectly) was Abdullah's first 'swerve' from J&K being with India – although, in his defence, Abdullah did say 'Perhaps'. For Davidson, Abdullah's 'unexpected espousal of … A neutral Vale of Kashmir would remove the bone of contention [between India and Pakistan]; there would be nothing left to squabble about'. Importantly, as Davidson also noted, Abdullah's real fight was against 'religious sectarianism and despotic exploitation', about which matters 'his sincerity is patent'. As Abdullah regularly noted, the 'first task' for all Kashmiris was 'to win internal liberation from exploitation'.

Surprisingly, in early May 1949, Nehru had 'a hunch' that the Kashmir issue would be 'settled before this year [1949] is out, and settled naturally largely in our favour'.[60] Not surprisingly, he was 'irritated' by Abdullah's interview with *The Scotsman* and by the Kashmiri's intemperance. For Nehru, Abdullah was 'an excellent man and a very effective popular leader, [but he] rather lacks political foresight and has a knack of saying the wrong thing'.[61] The inconsistent Abdullah again saw the error of his ways. On 17 May, he 'clarified the position by a subsequent statement':[62] 'the alternative of independence "may be and is a charming idea but on consideration [is] meaningless". Kashmir still thought of no alternative other than accession to India.'[63] This reflected the National Conference's official position 'unanimously ratified' on 12 October 1948 by more than 300 representatives via a resolution 'recommending the permanent accession of the State to the Indian Union'.[64] Nehru concurred: 'Let there be no doubt … [the] future [of J&K] is tied up with India and any other future for Kashmir is unthinkable for us'.[65] This established India's 'bottom line' that it would adhere to for the remainder of the Kashmir dispute.

The 'reign' of Sheikh Abdullah

29 October 1947 marks both the beginning of the end of Maharaja Hari Singh's official reign and the beginning of Sheikh Abdullah's unofficial 'reign' in J&K. (I use the term 'reign' because, interestingly, Abdullah's granddaughter used this regal term to describe her forebear's period in office in J&K.[66] Similarly, a Kashmiri political scientist talks about 'the de-throning of the Sheikh in 1953'.)[67] From 29 October, when Sheikh Abdullah became Chief Emergency Administrator of the J&K Emergency Government, until his dismissal as Wazir-i-Azam (Prime Minister) of J&K on 8 August 1953, the issue of J&K's international status became less important, at least initially. Chiefly, this was because Abdullah was compelled to focus on internal matters within J&K. He staffed his twenty-three-man Emergency

Administration regime with few, if any people who had been elected or who had obtained a popular mandate, although all were members of the National Conference.[68] Additionally, he did not seek to form an inclusive or coalition administration that included some of his rivals, which might then have been healing and helpful in the politically and physically divided state. While these factors suggested an autocratic tendency (informed by Dogra rule of Kashmiris), Abdullah had few other options given the actual emergency of the invading Pukhtoons and given that J&K had never had representatives elected by popular or inclusive elections. When he became Prime Minister of J&K on 5 March 1948,[69] Abdullah was the twenty-eighth person, and the first Kashmiri Muslim, to hold this position since 1846.[70] By that time, although Kashmir was far more militarily stable, he again formed a narrow-based, non-coalition government dominated by National Conference members.

I have used the term 'Indian J&K' throughout the text above because, although India claims to possess all of J&K as a result of 'winning' Maharaja Hari Singh's accession in 1947, this nation has only ever physically and administratively controlled Jammu, the Kashmir Valley and Ladakh. These areas comprise Indian-controlled J&K, or what I call, when clarity requires it, 'Indian J&K'. (Throughout the remainder of the book, unless otherwise stated, when I use the term 'J&K', I will be referring to the (now former) Indian state that India called, and which called itself, 'Jammu and Kashmir'.) Since 1947, Pakistan has been administering the other two populated areas of J&K (Azad Jammu and Kashmir; the Northern Areas, renamed Gilgit-Baltistan in 2009) until the UN plebiscite is conducted. However, this poll is never likely to be held. As the possibility of it receded in the mid-1950s, both nations concentrated on integrating their areas into their respective mainland. For India, this process would prove challenging, if only because Sheikh Abdullah had expected to operate autonomously within J&K – and was, indeed, largely doing so, particularly in the Kashmir Valley. Concurrently, two things happened. First, as India sought to curtail J&K's autonomy, coupled with serious communal challenges in Jammu, Abdullah became disenchanted and started to seriously contemplate J&K's ongoing international status. In a nutshell, India sought to assert itself while Abdullah sought to resist. Each became disenchanted with the other, as a result of which Abdullah ultimately was sacked. Second, with the plebiscite looking increasingly unlikely and with J&K effectively, but not legally, divided into Indian-controlled and Pakistan-Administered areas, the Kashmir dispute essentially became a dispute not over J&K as a whole but over the Kashmir Valley, which region Abdullah dominated.

Between 1947 and 1951, Sheikh Abdullah and his Government faced difficult and uncertain circumstances, in which democratic processes were not the order of the day. Strong and decisive leadership was needed to calm people's uncertainties, to ensure J&K remained with India militarily and politically, and to provide stability. From March 1948, as Prime Minister of J&K, Abdullah led a narrow-based 'National Interim Government' with seven National Conference members and, surprisingly, only one representative of Maharaja Hari Singh.[71] That was his Dewan, 'Col R. B. Thakore Baldevsingh Pathania', who also was the state's Chief Justice.[72] The Maharaja's Proclamation on 5 March, which replaced the Emergency Administration with a 'popular Interim Government',[73] also governed, at least for Hari Singh, 'the relations of the State with India' (although Singh hadn't mentioned India in his Proclamation).[74] His eight-member Ministry, or Cabinet, would exercise 'all administrative powers' and 'act on the principle of joint responsibility'; 'the Ruler on the advice of the Ministry' would enact legislation; the Praja Sabha would cease functioning;[75] and, the administration would operate using the 1939 J&K Constitution.[76] Essentially, the Proclamation's changes made Hari Singh a constitutional head who did what his Cabinet, 'led by the popular leader of [his] people', Sheikh Abdullah,[77] 'advised' him to do. In the post-accession hierarchy and confronting challenging times, Abdullah's significant powerbase made him superior. At that stage, he was very popular both with Kashmiris and Nehru.

This unelected National Interim Government continued in office until J&K's first election in 1951. According to an official report by 'Sheikh Abdullah's Government', it pledged itself to three tasks. First, restoring 'lawful Government' throughout 'the entire territory of the state' and liquidating its rival, the Azad Kashmir Government. Second, rehabilitating all J&K-ites who had 'left their places of residence after the [Pukhtoon] raids and consequent disturbances'. Third, establishing an 'Assembly set up on the basis of general adult suffrage which will draw up the Constitution for the people of Kashmir'.[78] While these tasks involved assistance from the 'Nationalist Government of India', this official report did not reaffirm the state's accessional links with India, nor did it mention the Indian Army. Rather, to all intents and purposes, the J&K Government had been operating autonomously.[79] Furthermore, rather than trying to liquidate its rival in Azad Kashmir, Abdullah may have been in touch with his old rival, Chaudhri Ghulam Abbas, to try to conclude an 'internal settlement' to the Kashmir dispute.[80] Apparently as early as April 1950, Abbas had made a 'sporting offer' to have both sides of the LOC demilitarised, after which a militia of Kashmiri Muslims could maintain law and order while the plebiscite was conducted.[81]

From 1948 until November 1952, Sheikh Abdullah also successfully oversaw the demise of the Dogra regime. In March 1949, he returned to a pet theme: the Maharaja. Interviewed in Amritsar on 26 March, Abdullah stated that J&K could not tolerate 'one-man rule', and the 'retention of the Maharaja was incompatible with the ideals of a new Kashmir. "A poor state can ill afford to reserve a substantial portion of its revenues for the comforts of one man".[82] It was time for 'despotic rule' to end in J&K. In June 1949, Abdullah helped to facilitate Hari Singh's departure from J&K for 'health reasons'. He would never return. Singh's rapid demise, which began with his accession to India, coupled with Abdullah's ongoing ascendency, meant that 'the rulers became the ruled'.[83] The balance of power shifted inextricably: Kashmiris from Kashmir Province now ruled Dogras from Jammu Province. More truthfully, the *Census of India, 1961* stated that Singh had been 'deposed'.[84] The conspirators were Abdullah and Nehru – although, ultimately, it was Sardar Patel who told Singh that he needed to leave J&K. Before departing, Hari Singh ensured the installation of his only son, Yuvraj Karan Singh, as his Regent. On 14 November 1952, when Dogra rule in J&K was officially terminated, the younger Singh became the Head of the State of J&K after Abdullah nominated him.[85] This was surprising, given Abdullah's dislike of Dogra rule. Perhaps Abdullah was being conciliatory, given his role manipulating the Dogra regime's demise. Jawaharlal Nehru, who had a developing friendship with Karan Singh, may also have influenced him. Singh's appointment would later be to Abdullah's detriment.

In his early years administering J&K, Sheikh Abdullah's regime operated without close supervision by New Delhi. This allowed him and his colleagues to implement some significant changes in the areas that India's militarily forces physically controlled. These changes often were made in undemocratic ways that emulated the Maharaja's previously autocratic and largely unaccountable practices. One of the first, and most significant, changes was land reforms. On 10 March 1951, Yuvraj Karan Singh signed an Order 'Published for general information' concerning the 'Resumption of Jagirs'.[86] On Martyr's Day (13 July), the Abdullah Government declared its intention to institute far reaching 'Land to the Tiller' reforms. These were designed to alleviate 'the conditions of poverty, misery and squalor in which the people of Kashmir lived' and to end 'the systematic oppression, repression and exploitation by the vested interests', particularly 'exploitative landlordism' and 'merciless moneylenders'.[87] A landholder would be able to retain a maximum of 182 kanals (22.75 acres) of land. This total could comprise twenty acres of agricultural land, one acre for residential use or vegetable gardening, half an acre for residential sites, and 1.25 acres for orchards.[88] Three months later, on 17 October, the 'Big Landed Estates Abolition Act' was enacted, after which over 400,000 acres of land from 396 big jagirs and nine thousand big landowners was redistributed to over 200,000 beneficiaries.[89] By the end of March 1953, some 189,000 acres of land had been transferred to some 153,000 'tillers', at an average of 1.23 acres of land to each 'peasant'. Collective farms had been established on 87,500 acres.[90]

While the land reforms were groundbreaking, so to speak, there were issues. The land distributed to a peasant in Jammu was not as productive as the land distributed to a peasant in Kashmir.[91] Contentiously, no compensation was paid to the forcefully dispossessed landowners, chiefly because, according to Sheikh Abdullah, neither the Government with its 'bankrupt treasury', nor the penniless tiller' were in a position to do so.[92] Legislatively, the J&K Constituent Assembly agreed unanimously, but retrospectively, on 31 March 1952 not to pay compensation.[93] This lack of compensation seriously disenchanted dispossessed landowners, both Dogras and Pandits, who possibly, as a reaction, helped to 'hatch' the plot that led to Abdullah's dismissal in 1953.[94] There was some corruption, with National Conference 'functionaries' being allocated 'more and better land', including amounts above the maximum of 22.75 acres of agricultural land.[95] Finally, Abdullah's Government was able to undertake its major land reforms as the state was, to a large extent, outside India's direct control. As Abdullah later noted, such 'people's welfare projects which ... changed the destiny of the state' would not have been possible had J&K then been under the jurisdiction of the Indian Supreme Court.[96]

Also, Sheikh Abdullah and his Government did not have an electoral mandate for land reforms, nor, controversially, did they consult New Delhi on this major change. When both Naya Kashmir and Quit Kashmir had been announced, these indicated that there would be changes in J&K, including socio-economic, when the National Conference finally obtained power. Nevertheless, J&K politicians had not received popular endorsement via an election for this major change. The first inclusive adult suffrage elections held in J&K were only conducted in September 1951 for the J&K Constituent Assembly. By the time of these elections, however, the land reforms were well under way. These reforms were also 'a source of much concern and embarrassment' for the Government of India, chiefly as no compensation would be paid, as the Indian Constitution required.[97] Conversely, many J&K-ites who benefitted from land reforms were not concerned by such a peripheral issue. Indeed, Abdullah and his colleagues' efforts were popular, particularly in the

Kashmir Valley, where land reforms benefitted many poorer Muslim Kashmiris. The 1951 elections therefore gave the National Conference a post facto mandate for land reforms.

The divide begins, then widens

For the Kashmiri politician, Mir Qasim, who was later the state's Chief Minister, J&K's 'land reforms were the beginning of the mistrust between New Delhi and Sheikh Abdullah'.[98] Nehru was irked by Abdullah's proactivity on land reform 'without any reference' to the Indian Government. On 4 July 1950, he told Sheikh Abdullah that he 'greatly regret[ted]' that Abdullah did 'not attach any value to any friendly advice that we might give and indeed, consider it as improper interference', of which he (Abdullah) took 'a very grave view'. Nehru wistfully informed Abdullah that 'I am rather at a loss how to act when the foundation of my thought and action has been shaken up'.[99] This was nine days before the National Interim Government in J&K introduced its Big Landed Estates Abolition Act.[100] Abdullah and his colleagues may have been acting unilaterally before New Delhi attempted to tie the state closer to India legally, administratively and stiflingly, as later happened. Nevertheless, up until mid-1951, Abdullah had no complaints about any Indian interference in J&K's internal autonomy, as he noted in his first major address to the Constituent Assembly in November 1951.[101]

Beforehand, on 26 January 1950, Sheikh Abdullah had witnessed India's 'relatively conservative' Constitution come into force.[102] It included the significant Article 370 that provided 'temporary provisions with respect to the State of Jammu and Kashmir'.[103] This Article supposedly, but ultimately impotently, guaranteed 'semi-independent status' for J&K within the Indian Union, giving the state autonomy in all matters except defence, foreign affairs and communication, as per the Maharaja's accession.[104] It was designed to preserve J&K's 'distinct identity', although Jammuites and Ladakhis did not concur with this identity or with Article 370, as we shall see. For Abdullah, Article 370 'secured' for J&K 'within India's suzerainty, the right to have our own constitution, flag and constituent assembly'.[105] This was not necessarily New Delhi's position. Indeed, thereafter, J&K-ites and Indians viewed the Indian Constitution differently. For J&K politicians, many of whom were Muslim Kashmiris, the Indian Constitution was 'federal'; for 'the Centre' (i.e. New Delhi), it was 'unitary'.[106] This was an important distinction. Kashmiris wanted to preserve their unique identity as a separate entity within the Indian Union. Indians, as well many Jammuites and Ladakhis, however, wanted J&K to become fully part of, and to be dissolved in, India, and for J&K-ites to become, and to be, Indians first and foremost. Presciently, Patel told Nehru that he (Nehru) would regret granting J&K a special status in the Indian Constitution.[107] The tension between Kashmiris and Indians over Article 370 would plague their relationship for years. Indeed, it has never been resolved (despite India abrogating Article 370 in 2019).

After India's Constitution came into operation, politicians in J&K felt the need, and the inclination, to develop a constitution for their own state. For Sheikh Abdullah, this was partly to safeguard the people's interests and partly to give them some certainty. It also flowed from, and was justified by, Maharaja Hari Singh's Proclamation of 5 March 1948 that appointed Abdullah as his Prime Minister and which called on the 'National Assembly' to frame a constitution for his 'accept-ance'.[108] According to Singh, the ubiquitous 'Shri Gopalaswami [Ayyangar]', whose past involvement with J&K made it appear that he liked and understood J&K, had drafted this Proclamation, while the Government of India and Sheikh Abdullah had approved it.[109] Mullik, writing in 1971, claimed that Ayyangar considered that establishing the Constituent Assembly would have provided a way to involve popular opinion in political processes, given the UNSC's inability to deliver a plebiscite for J&K-ites.[110] However, in March 1948, Ayyangar, even though he was India's Representative at the UN, was still awaiting that impediment.

By November 1949, all other empowered rulers of princely states that had joined India had made the Indian Constitution operative in their states. Maharaja Hari Singh 'chose to act differently'.[111] Based on Clause 7 of his Instrument of Accession, he apparently 'deemed' himself not to be committed 'in any way to acceptance of any future constitution of India', nor did it 'fetter' his 'discretion to enter into arrangements with the Government of India under any such future constitution'.[112] Supposedly, this meant that India was not entitled to interfere or intrude in J&K, including via its Constitution. Equally, as per Maharaja Hari Singh's 1948 Proclama-tion, J&K could develop its own constitution to realise 'the goal of full responsible ... constitutional government with a Council of Ministers, a Legislature with a majority of elected members and an independent judiciary'.[113] Consequently, the J&K Constituent Assembly was convened to frame this constitution.[114] J&K was the only state in India to take such a step.

Around 1950, Sheikh Abdullah had also 'concluded, however unwillingly', that it was beyond the capabilities of the UNSC 'to find a just solution to the Kashmir issue'.[115] In October, the National Conference's General Council had resolved 'to form a constituent assembly ... [to] take a decision with regard to the future relations of the state with the centre'.[116] The lack of faith in the UNSC was significant. For some Kashmiris, the 'beginning of the Kashmiri disappointment [with India] can be traced to the Indian Government's decision to go to the Security Council'.[117] With his accession, Maharaja Hari Singh clearly had ceded control of 'external affairs' to India.[118] Nevertheless, Abdullah had not supported India taking the Kashmir dispute to the UNSC, partly as this formalised Pakistan's status as a litigant in the dispute. Following Abdullah's visit to the United Nations in 1948, he 'became convinced that the big powers were not interested in resolving the [Kashmir] issue'. He became irritated with India's commitment to the Security Council, which 'treated the attacker and the attacked equally'.[119] Or, as he later put it: 'We set out as a plaintiff but were put in the dock.'[120] Rather than simply confirming Singh's accession to India and condemning Pakistan's aggression, the UNSC established its UNCIP. It investigated the issue, after which the Security Council obtained the commitment of India and Pakistan to conduct a plebiscite in J&K. This did not, of course, resolve the dispute.

The UN's involvement and the potential UN-supervised plebiscite created significant hope, as well as uncertainty, throughout J&K. The hope was that the plebiscite would soon be held and that this would resolve the issue of J&K's status once and for all. The uncertainty was that, should this poll ever be held, those parts of J&K then under India's control (Jammu, Kashmir, Ladakh) could end up with Pakistan – or, alternatively, those parts of J&K then under Pakistan's control (Azad Kashmir, the Northern Areas) could end up with India. For Sheikh Abdullah and the National Conference, this was problematic, almost treacherous. Any realignment with Pakistan would occur despite Singh's accession to India, despite the National Conference's support for this action, and despite the National Conference's volunteer militia helping 'to drive out' the Pukhtoon raiders 'sent by Pakistan' from the Kashmir Valley in 1947–48.[121] For Kashmiri politicians, unification with Pakistan would have been difficult, if only because this would have seriously diminished their status and standing. Feeling disenchanted with India and faced with the possibility of J&K possibly becoming part of Pakistan should the plebiscite be 'lost', Abdullah, according to a 'confidante' P. N. Jalali, 'projected the third option of independence'.[122] This had no impact on the UNSC, which has never offered the option of independence to J&K-ites.

Had India not taken the Kashmir dispute to the UNSC, Pakistan may have been sidelined from J&K matters, at least initially. India would have been responsible for all international matters to do with J&K, with no direct involvement of third parties. Consequently, J&K might have become just another bilateral issue between the two dominions. Instead, Pakistan quickly became empowered as a party to the dispute, while the UN plebiscite 'hung like a sword of Damocles' over J&K, terminology often used in relation to this poll.[123] To maximise what would later be called 'people power', Sheikh Abdullah wanted to get the accession to India 'duly approved by the Constituent Assembly'.[124] This would have suggested popular support for J&K to join India. Uniquely, the J&K Constituent Assembly and Constitution would have made the state 'an independent sub-system in the entire Indian political system'.[125] This also would have confirmed J&K's political identity within India's national political identity. Abdullah therefore had been keen to establish a Constituent Assembly as a first step towards 'achieving the maximum possible autonomy' of J&K in 'the Union of India'. This would 'safeguard the best interests of the people of the state'.[126]

On 20 April 1951, Yuvraj Karan Singh, as Regent of J&K, issued a Proclamation which directed that 'a Constituent Assembly, consisting of the representatives of the people selected [sic] on the basis of adult franchise shall be constituted forth-with'.[127] This body would develop a constitution for J&K. The development caused consternation in India, Pakistan and the UNSC. For India, if J&K had a constitution in place, this meant, in theory, that the state was ready to become independent, should this possibility ever arise. Nevertheless, under Nehru's leadership, India begrudgingly supported the convening of the Constituent Assembly, which first met on 31 October 1951.[128] In Pakistan, there were concerns that India might be trying to secure J&K by stealth, thereby contravening the UN resolutions and the requirement for a plebiscite.[129] The UNSC opposed the creation of the Constituent Assembly but it took this body six years to agree to a resolution that said so. Provoked by the J&K Constitution potentially coming into operation on 26 January 1957, and with this constitution reaffirming that J&K 'was an integral part of the Union of India',[130] the Security Council passed Resolution 122 on 24 January. (The USSR abstained.) The UNSC's resolution reaffirmed that 'the final disposition' of J&K would be made 'in accordance with the will of the peoples [sic]'. It also noted that the UN plebiscite was embodied in UNSC resolutions of 21 April 1948, 3 June 1948 and 14 March 1950, and in UNCIP resolutions of 13 August 1948 and 5 January 1949. Therefore, 'any action' taken by the Constituent Assembly to determine J&K's 'future shape and affiliation ... would not constitute a disposition of the State in accordance with the [plebiscite] principle'.[131] While India, Pakistan and the UNSC disagreed about the holding, or not holding, of this poll, they all agreed that independence for J&K was not an option.

The J&K Constituent Assembly

In September 1951, elections were held in J&K for the Constituent Assembly. Yuvraj Karan Singh's Proclamation of 20 April provided the legal basis and broad rules for these elections. The J&K Election Commission conducted these elections in September.[132] With the National Conference very popular after the events of 1947 and the 1948 India–Pakistan war,[133] it won all seats. Furthermore, of the Constituent Assembly's seventy-five representatives, a staggering seventy-three were elected unopposed.[134] Apart from the National Conference's popularity and some intimidation, its victory also occurred because many nomination papers of its opponents were summarily rejected. Therefore, there had been little or no genuine democratic electoral contests for Constituent Assembly seats. Later, the J&K Constitution reserved twenty-five seats for representatives from Pakistan-Administered J&K,[135] but no elections took place on the 'other' side of J&K in 1951.

The J&K Constituent Assembly, despite its contentiousness with India, Pakistan and the United Nations, was nevertheless established. After the September elections, the Assembly's first session was held in October 1951. In a session on 5 November,[136] Prime Minister Sheikh Abdullah spoke of the 'classical Kashmiri genius for synthesis'. Utilising his own 'genius for controversy' (my term), he raised the matter of J&K's accession. Abdullah either was again having second thoughts about being with India or he genuinely wanted to hear the opinions of the people's representatives. He gave Assembly members four tasks: 'to devise a Constitution for the future governance of the country' (i.e., J&K); to decide 'the future of the Royal Dynasty' (i.e., the Dogra regime); to determine if compensation should be paid to landowners dispossessed by the 'land-to-the-tiller policy' carried out with 'vigour and determination'; and, to 'declare [their] reasoned conclusion regarding [the] accession'. For this significant fourth matter, Abdullah asked members to make a determination about joining India, joining Pakistan, or being independent. This fourth task was troublesome, given the Maharaja's accession to India, which Abdullah's party had supported. Nevertheless, Abdullah wanted this reassessment done to 'help us to canalise our energies resolutely and with greater zeal in directions in which we have already started moving for the social and economic advancement of our country'.

On 31 October 1951, Sheikh Abdullah outlined to Constituent Assembly members the pros and cons of being with India, with Pakistan, or of being independent. He

> asserted that Kashmir had no alternative but to belong to India as an integral part … and listed seven arguments in favour of India: democracy, secularism, common

struggle for freedom, land reforms which were easier to implement in a democratic India than in 'landlord-ridden Pakistan', marketability of Kashmir's products, availability of consumer goods in the State, and expectation of greater assistance to Kashmir's development and administration. In favour of Pakistan, the arguments were: existence of an all-weather road, timber trade through State rivers, and the Muslim majority in Pakistan ... [although it also] was a theocratic State without a constitution, healthy political tradition and a progressive policy. As for Independence it was [an impractical] Utopia, for there was no security against aggression, no guarantee of the goodwill of its neighbours and no likely unanimity among the neighbours on the question of assistance against external danger.[137]

On 5 November, Sheikh Abdullah asked members 'to weigh all these ... and pronounce where the true well-being of the country lies in the future'.[138] In relation to independence, he stated that:

The third course open to us has still to be discussed. We have to consider the alternative of making ourselves an Eastern Switzerland, of keeping aloof from both States, but having friendly relations with them. This might seem attractive in that it would appear to pave the way out of the present deadlock. To us as a tourist country it could also have certain obvious advantages. But in considering independence we must not ignore practical considerations. Firstly, it is not easy to protect sovereignty and independence in a small country which has not sufficient strength to defend itself on our long and difficult frontiers bordering so many countries. Secondly, we do not find powerful guarantors among them to pull together always in assuring us freedom from aggression. I would like to remind you that from August 15 to October 22 [sic], 1947 our State was independent and the result was that our weakness was exploited by the neighbor with whom we had a valid standstill agreement. The State was invaded. What is the guarantee that in future too we may not be victims of a singular aggression?

This suggested that Abdullah's preference was for India.

Retrospectively, Sheikh Abdullah states that he told members of the Constituent Assembly that it was the 'best option for us to accede to India on the basis of the instrument of accession'.[139] However, in relation to the state being invaded, Abdullah presumably was thinking only of a military invasion, not a political or an administrative 'invasion', as later happened under India's control, despite the existence of Article 370. Nevertheless, Abdullah's speeches in 1951 to the Constituent Assembly were significant. By discussing options other than J&K being with India, he confirmed that he was not fully reconciled about J&K's international status. This made some Indians question Abdullah's loyalty to India, his role in J&K, and this state's possibly tenuous relationship with India. Such questioning had already started to cause Abdullah problems.

Praja Parishad agitation

From 1950, Prime Minister Abdullah had faced significant political challenges in Jammu, chiefly from disenchanted right-wing Hindus. This 'Jammu Agitation'[140] was a 'pernicious affair ... [and] a running sore'.[141] It may have 'played into Abdullah's hands'[142] by causing him, or giving him justification, to rethink the state's relationship with India. Abdullah's opponents, at least 800 of whom his Government jailed,[143] were engaging in 'Dogra nationalism'.[144] These included disgruntled landlords whose lands had been redistributed 'without compensation',[145] people unhappy with the Dogra regime's demise and Hari Singh's loss of status and power,[146] and displeased 'upper classes'.[147] Many Hindu Jammuites feared that the plebiscite would be held, after which J&K might unify with Pakistan, a doubly distasteful possibility given that 'their' ruler clearly had acceded to India in 1947. They would have preferred regional plebiscites to allow them to determine the fate at least of Jammu.[148] Many disenchanted Jammuites belonged to the Praja Parishad, a 'people's council' formed as early as November 1947 to 'safeguard the legitimate democratic rights' of Jammuites from Abdullah's 'anti-Dogra Government'.[149] Led by Prem Nath Dogra, a 'veteran champion of Dogra ascendency',[150] the Praja Parishad was 'a Jammu based communal organization closely allied to communal organizations in the rest of India'.[151] These allies included the Jana Sangh, Hindu Mahasabha and Ram Rajya Parishad. Less obvious support came from the Rashtriya Swayamsevak Sangh and the Sikhs' Akali Dal.[152]

The Praja Parishad began because many Jammuites, particularly Hindus, disliked Sheikh Abdullah's equivocating about J&K being with India. This movement wanted 'One legislature, one Prime Minister and only one flag'.[153] It opposed J&K's special constitutional status,[154] was against any special privileges for J&K,[155] and aggressively demanded the state's full integration into India and the full imposition of the Indian Constitution.[156] Such a 'full integration' may have diluted the Kashmiris' post-partition domination of Jammuites, a factor particularly disliked by many Hindu Jammuites. Conversely, many Muslim Kashmiris wanted 'maximum autonomy' for the state.[157] Basically, therefore, the contest was between autonomy for J&K or the state's full integration into India. In the early years of the Praja Parishad's agitation, there was a concurrent Jammu-Kashmir power struggle between Maharaja Hari Singh and Sheikh Abdullah. Singh was supported by his influential brother-in-law, Thakur Nachint Chand, and by Karan Singh.[158] Nehru was Abdullah's strongest supporter. An extremist section of the Praja Parishad also wanted Abdullah to 'Quit – Jammu'.[159] In other words, they wanted a non-Kashmiri in charge of their region.

The Praja Parishad had 'a mass following locally', particularly in eastern parts of Jammu where Hindus were more prevalent.[160] Additionally, Shyama (or Syama) Prasad Mookerjee, a high profile disenchanted former Congressman, supported the Praja Parishad's agitation. Mookerjee, a Bengali from Calcutta, had once 'thundered' that 'In one country two Constitutions, two Prime Ministers and two flags shall not be tolerated'.[161] He wanted national uniformity and integration, not special treatment for J&K. The issue of 'special treatment for J&K' would vex relations between India and J&K, with Indians wanting no such special treatment and Kashmiris striving to protect their (supposed) special status. Supported by external elements, the Praja Parishad's movement in Jammu threatened to go national and cause India major challenges to its policies of secularism and inclusion. Nehru told Karan Singh in early 1953 that the Praja Parishad's activities had become 'an all India situation' in which 'several communal organizations in India' were 'taking an important part' and to which 'we have to pay a great deal of attention'.[162] For Nehru, the greater danger to India then was from 'Hindu, right wing fundamentalism', not from influential, post-war Communism.[163] Indians did not harbour the same negativity about Communism as Westerners did.

In April 1952, Sheikh Abdullah reacted to what he considered communalism: 'political action motivated primarily by religious considerations'.[164] On 10 April, he stated publicly at Ranbirsinghpura, symbolically located midway between Jammu City and Pakistan's Sialkot, that J&K's accession to India 'would have to be of a restricted nature as the communal spirit still existed in India'.[165] For Abdullah, this 'communal spirit' was important: Muslims were second-class citizens in India, which was unacceptable. Some felt threatened by their minority status and were concerned that partition-type anti-Muslim activities may recommence. Consequently, two weeks after Ranbirsinghpura, Abdullah assertively reiterated that 'Kashmir was completely free to decide on matters other than defence, communications and external affairs'.[166] On Martyr's Day 1952 (13 July), he went further, telling a public gathering that 'If I find we can progress and prosper by remaining independent, I will not hesitate to raise that voice. If I realize that by acceding to Pakistan we can go forward no power can suppress me to say so.'[167] These mixed messages suggested that a concerned, even aggravated, Abdullah was reconsidering J&K's relationship with India. For Nehru, Abdullah's Ranbirsinghpura speech suggested that the Kashmiri had 'become very angry'.[168] Equally, Nehru saw Abdullah's 'hostility to the Hindus of Jammu' as communal.[169]

The impact of the Pukhtoons' invasion of Kashmir

In relation to communalism, the impact of the Pukhtoon invasion in 1947 on the Kashmiris' psyche should not be underestimated. It may partly explain why Sheikh Abdullah reacted so negatively to the Praja Parishad's agitation. The Pukhtoons' actions were a perverted form of anti-Kashmiri ethnic (as against religious) communalism. At a deeper level, this invasion reminded some Kashmiris of the brutal invasions of Kashmir by Sikhs and Afghans, many of which latter group also comprised Pukhtoons. Many Kashmiris also remembered the repression and harshness of the Hindu Dogra regime whose roots and powerbase were in Jammu and whose actions kept Muslims poor and underprivileged, socially, politically, economically and administratively. Maharaja Hari Singh 'had a poor reputation for the treatment of his Muslim subjects'.[170] Nevertheless, despite their religion, many Kashmiris, including many Muslim Kashmiris, supported Singh's accession to secular and Hindu-dominant (but not Hindu-dominated) India. They rejected, certainly in the short term, their religious 'brethren' in Muslim-dominated Pakistan and, instead, were happy for J&K to join the religiously inclusive Indian Union, even though there was a significant economic cost in doing so. The Pukhtoons' invasion therefore 'expedited' Congress attempts 'to incorporate Kashmir into the Indian Union'.[171]

For Kashmiris, the economic cost of 'the State's unnatural accession to India' concerned the closure of the all-weather Jhelum Valley Road.[172] The Pukhtoon invasion and fighting thereafter closed this all-weather route into Kashmir in late 1947. This was a major inconvenience and loss for Kashmiris, particularly those located in towns on this road, such as Baramulla. The closure ended easy access to Rawalpindi and its railhead, or to Lahore beyond that for leisure and work. Thereafter, Kashmiris were compelled to travel to India, with this route going through Jammu Province, then eastwards through the long, narrow and militarily vulnerable corridor to Pathankot, in (Indian) Punjab. This route was longer, slower, often closed in winter due to snow, and sometimes closed by landslides in upper Jammu. The Kashmiris' travel situation improved when India extended the railway to Jammu Tawi in 1971. However, the Srinagar–Jammu route was/is still far less efficient than the old Jhelum Valley Road route.

While Sheikh Abdullah didn't always say as much, the communal actions in Jammu by Hindu militants also made him nervous for Muslims' wellbeing, both in J&K and throughout greater India. So too, of course, had the general, and brutal, inter-religious violence throughout Punjab in 1947 that killed tens of thousands and forced many to flee to religiously safer areas. By the early 1950s, some Muslims, including Abdullah, were again concerned that they would endure the same 'communal' fate suffered by Muslims in Punjab during 1947, or, even worse, by Muslims religiously 'cleansed' – i.e., killed, expelled or 'encouraged' to leave – in the Indian princely states of Kapurthala, Alwar and Bharatpur,[173] as well as, indeed, from parts of J&K's own Jammu Province. On 18 April 1952 in Srinagar, Abdullah let his feelings be publicly known: the people wanting the full application of India's Constitution on J&K were 'weakening the accession'. They were also 'the same people who had massacred Muslims in Jammu'. Their actions were causing 'suspicion in the minds of Muslims of the state'. When these remarks upset Nehru, Abdullah claimed he had been 'quoted inaccurately'.[174]

Political opposition in J&K

For a time, the strongly pro-India Praja Parishad, which wanted closer ties with India, was the only effective political opposition to the National Conference in J&K.[175] Nehru was prepared to admit that Jammuites had some justification for their 'dissatisfaction and frustration' with the Abdullah Government in Srinagar.[176] However, as he informed Sardar Patel, 'the prize we are fighting for [in J&K] is the valley of Kashmir', not Jammu,[177] which region and its residents, it was clear, already wanted to be with India. Motivated by the Praja Parishad's agitation, which Nehru noted had 'produced strong reactions in the Kashmir Valley',[178] and by Sheikh Abdullah's increasing doubts about the relationship with India, Nehru sought to remedy this circumstance via a formal agreement between India and J&K. He pondered whether the Praja Parishad's 'objectionable, anti-social, reactionary and subversive' agitation[179] was actually assisting Pakistan's cause in J&K.[180]

Importantly, Sheikh Abdullah's response to the Praja Parishad movement, the increasing 'all India' nature of which concerned him, may have been the initial spark that caused Karan Singh, and possibly Jawaharlal Nehru, to start to question Abdullah's actions and intentions. Abdullah believed that the Praja Parishad's agitation was being 'financially fuelled by the Maharaja and also by those whose vested interests had been marred by our reformist measures'.[181] Nehru told Abdullah that Hari Singh was, indeed, helping the 'mischief makers', though he did not know to what extent.[182] Presumably, by that stage, Hari Singh was well over the idea of independence for J&K; instead, he wanted his share of power in the state. Consequently, Abdullah attacked Hari Singh's son, Karan Singh. In April 1951, the

Yuvraj complained to Nehru that he was 'deeply hurt' and 'insulted' by Abdullah who publicly stated in Jammu that Singh was 'frequently conferring with the reactionary communal leaders … plotting to bring back the Maharaja'. Abdullah threatened 'the young Prince' that if he persisted 'in seeking the advice of the reactionaries and the communalists … his future [would] not be far different from that of his father'.[183] In other words, Karan Singh would be forced to leave J&K, a warning that the young Regent seemingly took seriously, given his later dismissal of Abdullah in 1953.

In 1952, therefore, Prime Minister Abdullah faced a 'peculiarly delicate and difficult situation'.[184] In Kashmir, he had to placate Muslims afraid that rampant Hindus in Jammu and elsewhere would threaten them physically. In Jammu, he confronted frustrated Jammuites displeased that J&K was not being fully integrated into the Indian Union and that the Indian flag was not being flown in the state.[185] For Jammuites, the ending of Dogra rule later that year, 'the only link which bound them to Kashmir', meant their position would be even more 'precarious' unless J&K was fully integrated into India.[186] Some Ladakhis with separatist tendencies, who were often Buddhists, were similarly 'unhappy and discontented'.[187] They disliked Abdullah's 'centralizing tendencies', the lack of economic assistance being provided, and J&K's lack of integration into India.[188] Concurrently, the J&K Constitution was being finalised, with Karan Singh's position in doubt. It was proposed that the J&K Legislature would now elect the Head of the State for a five-year term.[189] The potential election to this position of Karan Singh, who had significant influence in Jammu and Ladakh, was possibly an attempt by Sheikh Abdullah to alleviate the concerns of people in both regions.[190] During this difficult period, Nehru encouraged Singh to accept the nomination. Presciently, Nehru stated that 'Grave decisions are being taken which will naturally affect the future of the State'.[191] His inference was that these decisions concerned Sheikh Abdullah. Nehru later told Singh that his 'principal' role was to secure J&K's link with the Indian Union: 'If that breaks down in any way … all kinds of difficulties come in'.[192] On 14 November, Singh's titular position was resolved when the J&K Constituent Assembly unanimously elected him Sadar-i-Riyasat (Head of the State).[193] He served in this position until 1965 when its designation changed to Governor of J&K, in which position he served until 1967.

Throughout 1952, the idea of an independent Kashmir remained alive. In January, Iran's Prime Minister, Dr Mossadeq, suggested to India's Ambassador that Kashmir should become 'independent and sovereign'.[194] Given the historical links between Kashmir and Iran and India and Iran, this was significant. In March, Mirza Afzal

Beg suggested the creation of a 'Republic of Kashmir but tied up to the Indian Union in regard to some subjects'. For Nehru, this was a change not so much in substance, although the name change had 'certain important consequences'.[195] Also in January, J&K became a part of the 'East-West cold war' when the Soviet Union accused the United Kingdom and the United States in the UNSC of being responsible for the plebiscite not being held in J&K. For the Soviet diplomat, Jacob Malik, this was a 'deliberate attempt to prevent the people of Kashmir from expressing their own will' and the imposition of an 'American *dictat* on them'. This claim was ironic, coming from the representative of a hardline, one-party authoritarian state.[196]

As early as August 1952, Sheikh Abdullah and Jawaharlal Nehru actually discussed independence for J&K, and other related matters. Indeed, on 25 August, Nehru sent Abdullah a long note titled the 'Impracticability of an Independent Kashmir'.[197] While only two of its twenty-nine paragraphs actually discussed independence for either J&K or the Kashmir Valley, Nehru stated that an 'independent State of Jammu and Kashmir' was 'inconceivable'. He perceptively noted that neither India nor Pakistan would allow the other nation to 'gain the upper hand' there. This meant that Kashmir would 'continue to be the scene of conflict between India and Pakistan, even though it might be called independent'.[198] As for an independent Kashmir comprising 'the Valley and some surrounding areas only', chiefly 'the Kashmiri language speaking areas', Nehru noted that this very small state would be politically and economically unviable.[199] Even if India, Pakistan and the United Nations guaranteed its independence, this would be 'completely unworkable'. Such a state had 'not a ghost of a chance' of surviving and 'would disappear with great rapidity'.[200] Nehru therefore told Abdullah that they could discuss 'the quantum of autonomy' for J&K, but he 'could not imagine an independent Kashmir'. Indeed, he would 'rather give Kashmir to Pakistan on a platter' than allow intrigues 'to dangle' like a sword of Damocles over the two nations.[201] For Abdullah, on the other hand, the main issue was that 'the central leadership desired our complete merger in the Union'.[202] For him, the choice was clear: it was either complete independence for Kashmir or complete subjugation.

The Delhi Agreement

In mid-1952, the Indian Prime Minister decided that he needed to formally 'define' the relationship between India and J&K 'precisely'.[203] For Nehru, the accession was 'complete in law and, in fact, Jammu and Kashmir [was] a constitutional unit [in India] like any other'. However, because the Maharaja had acceded only for the three subjects of defence, communications and external affairs, 'that fact', and the temporary Article 370 that Sheikh Abdullah considered 'secured a special status' for J&K,[204] was producing a 'misunderstanding' that J&K's accession to India had been 'partial'.[205] Additionally, for Abdullah, J&K's accession was provisional and subject to confirmation by a plebiscite 'under the United Nations auspices'.[206] According to Menon, however, the J&K ruler 'had executed an Instrument of Accession on the three subjects, in the same way as had [all] other rulers'.[207] In that sense, Hari Singh's accession was neither special nor unique – despite what J&K-ites may claim. Furthermore, by mid-1952, major administrative changes had taken place in India and no former princely state was operating autonomously. Indeed, as early as April 1950, the 'complete financial integration with the Centre of all the States and Unions of States, with the exception of Jammu and Kashmir, became an accomplished fact'.[208] The problem was the perception that J&K was an 'exception', not just in terms of its financial relations with India but also in terms of its political relations.

In July 1952, after 'long and sometimes rather exhausting' discussions,[209] Jawaharlal Nehru and his Foreign Affairs Committee concluded the short – it had eight points – but politically important 'Delhi Agreement' with Sheikh Abdullah and his J&K delegation.[210] Karan Singh called it the 'Indo-Kashmir agreement',[211] a title better reflecting the agreement's purpose of 'demarcating the Union and State jurisdiction[s]'.[212] Sheikh Abdullah's delegation comprised four (then) trusted colleagues: Bakshi Ghulam Mohammad, Mirza Afzal Beg, Girdharilal Dogra and D. P. Dhar.[213] Lengthy discussions took place in New Delhi during 12–20 June and 16–22 July. The resultant formal agreement was signed on 24 July.[214] It was tabled in India's Lok Sabha on 24 July and its Rajya Sabha on 5 August.[215] The J&K Constituent Assembly ratified the agreement on 14 August 1952.[216]

For Sheikh Abdullah, the Delhi Agreement was 'an important watershed in the formulation of … constitutional relations with the Indian Union'.[217] It was devised to clear 'misunderstandings [that] had developed on the two sides',[218] including those after Abdullah's speech about the accession in the Constituent Assembly on 5 November 1951. Supposedly, the agreement ensured J&K's special status within India, with this state enjoying greater local control than other Indian states. Article 356 of the Indian Constitution, which enabled the Centre to impose President's (or direct) rule on any state 'was not insisted upon'.[219] Rather, 'in the case of internal disturbances, action [was] to be taken only with the concurrence of the State'.[220] The Delhi Agreement also established how J&K and India, and their major bodies and symbols, would relate to, and work with, each other. For Nehru, the agreement made clear 'the position of the Kashmir State in the Union of India'.[221] 'Many things were decided ... which knit the Jammu and Kashmir State closer to India and which make our Constitution applicable in greater measure to the state'.[222] Critics saw things differently. For one analyst, the Delhi Agreement amounted to J&K having 'relative independence'.[223] Mookerjee accused Abdullah of creating 'a republic within a republic', of 'creating a new sovereignty' for J&K, and of 'developing a three-nation theory', the third nation being 'the Kashmiri nation'.[224] For many Indian newspapers and 'communal-minded groups', including the Praja Parishad, the agreement amounted to 'the accession of India to Kashmir!', not vice versa.[225] Part of their complaint was that J&K-ites enjoyed the same rights as all Indian citizens while Indian citizens had no right to purchase land in J&K.[226]

Sheikh Abdullah was also unhappy with the Delhi Agreement. Publicly, he called it 'an important milestone in our constitutional relations with the [Indian] Union'.[227] Privately, there had been coercion during the negotiations. When one clause was being 'hotly debated', Nehru apparently whispered to Abdullah that, if the Kashmiri was to 'waver in embracing us, we will put gold chains in [sic] your neck'.[228] Such 'enslavement', even if potentially benevolent, did not appeal to Abdullah. For much of his political career, he sought the opposite: maximum autonomy, if not independence, for J&K. This may have confused people. As one Kashmiri analyst put it, 'Abdullah desired complete internal autonomy for the State which others interpreted as independence'.[229] Nehru's challenge was to fully integrate the state into India; Abdullah's challenge was to resist this integration.

While it was significant, the Delhi Agreement did not resolve matters between India and J&K. Sheikh Abdullah, the eternal contrarian, was reluctant to implement it, despite obtaining some 'real concessions' and certainty from New Delhi.[230] His obstinacy marks the beginning of the political end for him. Nehru was already having serious doubts about 'his' leader in J&K. On the day the agreement was signed, he told a colleague that his 'difficulty' with Kashmir was that 'I just do not know what Shaikh [sic] Abdullah might or might not say or do'.[231] A week later, Nehru told the same colleague that Abdullah had given him 'more trouble in recent months than Pakistan', which was saying something about how good India–Pakistan relations then were and how challenging relations with J&K were. Nehru could not explain Abdullah's ambivalent attitude towards India 'except on the uncharitable assumption that he has lost grip of his mind'.[232] Certainly, Abdullah's behaviour was often difficult to predict. His actions and statements often were not considered or considerate. Equally, Nehru did not understand, or could not accept, two things: first, how important autonomy was for Sheikh Abdullah; second, the negative impacts of the Praja Parishad's agitation on Kashmiri Muslims, including Abdullah. These Muslims were concerned that India's secularism was being seriously challenged as hardline Hindus threatened Muslims and sought to 'Indianise', even Hinduise, them. And what if the genuine secularist, Jawaharlal Nehru, died or lost power? What would become of India's Muslims and other minorities under 'lesser' or less tolerant leaders? These were serious matters at the forefront of Abdullah's concerns.

1953: a year of great significance

For Sheikh Abdullah, and all concerned, 1953 was a year of great significance. Increasingly, J&K's titular head, Karan Singh, and his mentor and confidante, India's Prime Minister, Jawaharlal Nehru, came fully to distrust Sheikh Abdullah. So too did Abdullah's political colleagues. Abdullah became suspicious of those outside his immediate circle of advisors and friends. This mutual mistrust worsened as the year progressed. As early as January, Abdullah's close colleague and proxy, Mirza Afzal Beg, was reported to have declared himself in support of 'the demand for the separation of the Kashmir Valley and, eventually, for its demarcation into an "independent" State'.[233] Beg's statement would not have helped Abdullah, given that Nehru had 'a very poor opinion' of Beg, whom he considered 'largely responsible for many of the difficulties that arose in Kashmir'.[234] By March, however, Nehru was more concerned about Abdullah than Beg. He informed his sister that Abdullah was 'very unhappy, distressed and confused' about matters and was 'not prepared to accept our advice'.[235] Physically and emotionally, Abdullah was becoming isolated; politically, he was moving away from India.

Things happened quickly. From March to August 1953, Constituent Assembly members 'wrangled with the basic issues relating to the proposed Constitution'. This included determining their 'reasoned conclusion' to the 'accession'.[236] G. M. Sadiq, President of the Constituent Assembly, was not interested in independence. On 21 April, Karan Singh informed Nehru that there was 'much difference' between Nehru's interpretation of the Delhi Agreement and Sheikh Abdullah's.[237] Singh noted that it did not seem that Nehru would do anything to resolve these differences, partly because, for Nehru, 'the whole international case' of India 'rested upon Sheikh Abdullah'. Then Singh apparently asked Nehru: 'what happens after Sheikh Sahib is dead', which question about Abdullah's seeming indispensability supposedly 'shook' Nehru.[238] Possibly, it was this conversation that started India's Prime Minister thinking about options and personalities in J&K other than 'Sheikh Sahib' whose commitment and efficacy as a pro-India political force was becoming increasingly doubtful.

Sheikh Abdullah did little to assuage Nehru's growing doubts. In April 1953, he hinted publicly in Jammu and in Srinagar that communal incidents in Jammu and in India, and the central government's inability to quell these, were forcing him to reassess the Delhi Agreement.[239] He was serious. On 27 April, *The Hindu* reported that Abdullah wanted to convert J&K into 'a federal polity comprising five autonomous units of Jammu, Kashmir, Ladakh, Poonch and Gilgit'. Roughly, but not exactly, this 'federal polity' reflected J&K's post-1947 division into Indian-controlled and Pakistan-Administered areas. Abdullah stated that this state's name would be changed to the 'Autonomous Federated Unit of the Republic of India',[240] although he didn't say how he would get Pakistan to relinquish control of 'its' areas. This new 'federal polity' would have confronted challenges, particularly in relation to the numerically and politically dominant Kashmiris' willingness to devolve genuine autonomy to the other four units. Another challenge would have been a legal one. To change the legal status of J&K alone would have required amending both the Indian Constitution and the J&K Constitution.[241]

By mid-year, Sheikh Abdullah was under considerable personal duress and pressure. From mid-November 1952, the Praja Parishad's agitation in Jammu had gone from 'bad to worse'.[242] On 23 June 1953, Shyama Prasad Mookerjee died in mysterious circumstances after forty days of detention in Srinagar. He was only fifty-two years old.[243] Both events affected Abdullah negatively. Concurrently, he was enduring criticism of his regime within J&K and within India, rancor from Pakistanis who considered him to be an Indian puppet or stooge, and politicking behind his back by colleagues whom Abdullah believed were engaging in corruption and self-advancement. Not surprisingly, perhaps, Abdullah developed a 'new political line that the State's limited accession to India be resolved in favour of an independent Kashmir'. On 11 May 1953, *Dawn* reported requests made in the presence of Ghulam Abbas at a Muslim Conference gathering in Azad Kashmir for the Pakistan Government to 'make an early arrangement for the [sic] meeting of Chaudhry Ghulam Abbas and Sheikh Abdullah'.[244] This may have been to further discuss an 'internal settlement' to the Kashmir dispute,[245] with this possibly now involving independence for J&K. Soon after, however, *Dawn* also reported that Abdullah had talked secretly with Nehru about this meeting, but Nehru had told Abdullah 'not to indulge in such international affairs'.[246] On 18 May, Abdullah had presented his 'new political line' to the National Conference's Working Committee. However, 'a good majority' of members in the Constituent Assembly became 'upset by the pronounced change in their leader's attitude' that had 'happened suddenly in the middle of May when distinguished foreign visitors came to the valley'.[247] Abdullah was starting to lose the confidence of his National Conference colleagues.

By June 1953, correspondence confirms that Sheikh Abdullah had made up his mind: he wanted independence for Kashmir. Others sought to discourage, even to deter, him. From 23–25 May, he and Nehru had a 'long talk' in Srinagar. This was just before Nehru went to London in June for the Commonwealth Prime Ministers' Conference. For Nehru, Abdullah was 'not quite clear' about J&K's status. He asked Abdullah 'to keep any decision pending' till Nehru's return from London.[248] Conversely, Abdullah felt that Nehru had lost trust in him.[249] Some time in June, Abdullah's mind became clear. He spoke with Nehru's close colleague, Abul Kalam Azad, India's Education Minister. On 9 July, Azad reminded Abdullah by letter that in previous meetings respectively with Nehru in May and him in June Abdullah had stressed the need for independence for Kashmir. Azad informed Abdullah that India was prepared to declare that 'the special position of Kashmir was of a permanent nature', but independence was not possible or feasible. Azad's correspondence makes it clear: Abdullah wanted 'independence of the Kashmir Valley'.[250] Presciently, Nehru had earlier informed Azad from London on 11 June that 'I am afraid Shaikh [sic] Abdullah will give us a good deal of trouble. He is acting very irresponsibly. I hope your visit will check him.'[251] On the same day, Nehru told another colleague that 'nothing much will be done [about Abdullah] till I return. After that, we shall have to face this irritating problem.'[252] A plan was developing.

Other information confirms that Sheikh Abdullah wanted independence for Kashmir. By late 1952, displeased with the Praja Parishad's agitation, Abdullah stated that 'if any region wished to break away, the Government [of J&K] would not attempt to retain it by force'. Jammu was free to leave; Kashmir would stand alone, if needs be. (Abdullah apparently repeated this stance in 1978.)[253] In June 1953, a draft constitution for an independent Kashmir appeared in Indian newspapers. It included establishing 'independent Kashmiri armed forces' and with India having 'responsibility only for Kashmir's foreign policy'.[254] By mid-1953, according to G. M. Sadiq, Abdullah 'began the agonizing search for alternatives to our accession with India'. This involved a 'fascination for independence of a truncated State which would, more or less, include only the Valley of Kashmir'.[255] Sadiq later clarified this statement. He stated that Abdullah's idea was for J&K to be 'decimated', with the 'Jammu areas' being 'absorbed' into India, 'the Poonch, Muzaffarabad and Frontier areas' becoming part of 'West Pakistan', and 'the Valley of Kashmir declared Independent'. No mention was made of Ladakh.[256] Sadiq's statement confirms Sheikh Abdullah's desire for independence for Kashmir.

In June 1953, Sheikh Abdullah publicly propagated the idea that J&K should 'steer clear between the two extreme views of merger with India and merger with Pakistan'.[257] It should be independent. Shortly beforehand, he partially, but not wholly, confirmed to his political colleagues his desire for independence. The National Conference's Working Committee comprising himself, Maulana Masoodi, Mirza Afzal Beg, Bakshi Ghulam Mohammad, G. M. Sadiq, Sardar Budh Singh, Girdharilal Dogra and Shamlal Saraf,[258] had been considering three issues. The first was 'The political situation vis a vis [the] Indo-Pak dispute over Kashmir'. (The other two concerned 'fundamental rights' for J&K-ites and extending the Indian Supreme Court's jurisdiction to J&K.)[259] On 9 June, the minutes of the Working Committee's final session mentioned four proposals 'as possible alternatives for an honourable and peaceful solution of the Kashmir dispute'. These were:

a. Overall plebiscite …
b. Independence of the whole State.
c. Independence of the whole State with joint [India–Pakistan][260] control of foreign affairs and defence.
d. Dixon plan with independence for the plebiscite area.[261]

Options b and c clearly involved some sort of independence for J&K. This, seemingly, was Abdullah's preference, although he knew this was not possible 'under the circumstances' prevailing.[262] Abdullah believed that Bakshi favoured the Dixon plan and that Sadiq favoured the plebiscite.[263] Sadiq later stated that the Committee's minutes were not official. Rather, they reflected musings about 'fantastic alternatives' and the lack of unanimity among Committee members.[264] After some twenty days of deliberations, the Working Committee rejected Abdullah's alternatives 'by a decisive margin'.[265]

The fourth of the 'possible alternatives' needs some explanation. The Dixon plan was the plan formulated in 1950 by the United Nations Representative for India and Pakistan, Sir Owen Dixon, an Australian jurist. (Dixon, who 'had more than one interview with Sheikh Abdullah',[266] was apparently told by Abdullah that 'independence for Kashmir should be an option in any plebiscite'.)[267] Dixon envisaged India and Pakistan obtaining those areas that they already had, except Kashmir, where a 'partial plebiscite in a limited area including or consisting of the valley of Kashmir' would be conducted. Kashmir was the only area where people's views were uncertain and therefore a vote of residents' desires needed to be taken.[268] Importantly, Dixon was not offering the 'third option' of independence to these residents: their choice was to stay with India or to join Pakistan. Additionally, he considered that United Nations administrators would need to supervise polling to minimise the possibility that the 'inhabitants of the valley of Kashmir would vote under fear or apprehension of consequences and other improper influences'.[269] He was concerned 'to secure the integrity of the plebiscite' in the Kashmir Valley, which he considered was then 'ruled by a police state'.[270] Later, G. M. Sadiq suggested that representatives from India, Pakistan, Afghanistan, the Soviet Union and China create a body to supervise a plebiscite.[271] This had shades of a suggestion made in 1948 by Sheikh Abdullah to Josef Korbel from UNCIP that J&K be made independent under the joint guarantee of the same five nations.[272]

Importantly, neither Bakshi Ghulam Mohammad nor G. M. Sadiq, both of whom were influential locally, supported independence for either J&K or the Kashmir Valley. Bakshi described the slogan of 'independence' as 'misleading'.[273] He made speeches in Kashmir on 23 July and 28 July 1953 reaffirming the India–Kashmir relationship based on the Maharaja's accession and the Delhi Agreement.[274] On 29 July, he reiterated in Kulgam that 'nothing has happened to alter our faith in the correctness of our decision' to accede to India.[275] On 20 July, Sadiq discounted independence, stating that 'an independent Kashmir will always be exposed to foreign invasion'.[276] Shortly after, he ridiculed the 'idea of "independence"', describing it as 'childish and impracticable'.[277] Later, Sadiq told Abdullah that in his opinion the 'irrevocability of the State's partnership with the Indian Union has become an accepted fact'.[278] In another letter, Sadiq reiterated that 'independence of the Valley of Kashmir' would be 'impractical' and 'ruinous for the people of the State' and that it 'would not serve as a basis for bringing about a rapprochement between India and Pakistan but would be instrumental in throwing them farther away from each other'.[279] This partially reflected Nehru's thinking.

By mid-1953, India also had indicated that a plebiscite was now impossible, unnecessary and impracticable. Probably, it was also unwinnable. The plebiscite was impossible because US military aid to Pakistan had 'materially altered the context of the entire Kashmir problem'. It had become part of the 'Cold War' following the Soviet Union's verbal attack of the United States and the United Kingdom in the Security Council.[280] The plebiscite was unnecessary because 'the people of the State feel quite settled now and [are] determined to march ahead as part of India'.[281] (Nehru discounted those J&K-ites located in Azad Kashmir and the Northern Areas.) A plebiscite was impracticable because, as Nehru realised as early as late 1948, 'we would never get the conditions which were necessary ... so I ruled out the plebiscite for all practical purposes'.[282] The most difficult of these 'conditions' was a requirement, as per UNSC resolutions, that Pakistan found impossible: to withdraw its forces from J&K and allow minimal Indian forces to enter the vacated areas. At the same time, senior Indians began to think that a free and fair plebiscite was unwinnable. India lacked sufficient popularity throughout J&K, including in the numerically important Kashmir Valley, to win.

By early August 1953, with the political picture 'pretty confused' in J&K, and with Sheikh Abdullah seriously contemplating independence, his position as Prime Minister of J&K was no longer politically unassailable.[283] Indeed, he was now on very shaky political ground. In his bastion of Srinagar, Abdullah was losing the confidence of his political colleagues. In New Delhi, he was losing the support of Jawaharlal Nehru, India's most influential politician and its major powerbroker who previously had backed Abdullah unquestioningly. In J&K, with India disinterested in having the plebiscite held, Abdullah was no longer India's much needed 'trump card' whose leadership and popularity could help it 'win' the poll. Indeed, Prime Minister Nehru had started to seriously doubt that Abdullah was now his 'man' in J&K. Plebiscite or no plebiscite, Nehru seems to have decided that he needed, and wanted, an unequivocally pro-India surrogate in J&K to ensure that, first, the state remained with India and, second, that it became more integrated into India. This combination of factors meant that Sheikh Abdullah had become politically expendable. 'Whisperings in corners had started' and Abdullah became 'greatly disturbed at the changed attitude of Jawaharlal'.[284] Something, or someone, was about to give.

The last days of Sheikh Abdullah's initial 'reign'

On 10 June 1953, Karan Singh informed Jawaharlal Nehru, who was then in London, that the 'political situation' in the Kashmir Valley continued to be 'extremely fluid'. Divisions within the National Conference were 'causing considerable tension', while Sheikh Abdullah appeared to be renouncing 'the solemn agreements which he has concluded with India' and 'his clear commitments', which would be 'a grave blow to our national interests'. Singh informed Nehru that this 'problem will claim your immediate attention upon your return [from England] for a final and decisive solution'.[285] Two days later, writing from London to his Home Minister, K. N. Katju, Nehru thoughtfully – or perhaps, presciently – noted: 'I am afraid we are going to have plenty of trouble in Kashmir because of the internal conflicts there'.[286] By mid-June, Nehru knew that he had a major issue in Kashmir with Sheikh Abdullah and that this situation would need to be, and would be, resolved after he returned to India. He would then determine or agree a 'final and decisive solution'.

Singh's communication was significant for Nehru as J&K was clearly on his mind. On 5 and 6 June 1953, he had held 'vague and general' talks in London with Pakistan's Prime Minister,[287] the little known Mohammad Ali Bogra. These 'aroused great interest and much speculation' in J&K, including about whether the UN plebiscite would be held.[288] However, the Nehru–Bogra talks may not have been as 'vague' as Nehru claimed, given that he and Bogra jointly announced on 20 August 1953 that 'the Plebiscite Administrator would be appointed by the end of April 1954'.[289] Being pro-active, Nehru must already have been considering that, should this plebiscite be held, India would need a stable Indian J&K with strongly pro-India leaders in place to maximise India's chances of winning. Equally, Nehru had 'little doubt … that the final decision about Kashmir would be in our favour, however long it may take'.[290] Meanwhile, Abdullah was posing challenges. The Praja Parishad's agitation had 'made the Kashmir problem far more difficult than it ever was' and had 'weakened' India's 'position in Kashmir terribly'. On 23 June, the situation worsened after Mookerjee's 'sad and painful' death in detention in Srinagar.[291] (Ominously, Mookerjee had stated in August 1952 that he would 'secure' the Constitution of India for Jammuites 'or sacrifice' himself.)[292] As Nehru was aware, the fallout and pressure from these matters, particularly the Hindu 'communalism' in Jammu, further influenced Abdullah negatively and increased his serious questioning about whether India was the best place for Muslim-dominated J&K. They may also have made Nehru more amenable to talks with Pakistan, if only to gain some time while he resolved issues at home.

By 26 June 1953, Singh was telling Nehru that the situation in Srinagar had 'become still worse, and it is now very grave'.[293] Nehru agreed, noting that the 'situation' had 'to be taken in hand'[294] because 'I have had no greater trouble or burden than this feeling of our losing our grip in Kashmir'.[295] Nehru partially started to 'take things in hand' on 28 June via a long and poignant note to Sheikh Abdullah. This marks the beginning of the end of their political relationship. As Nehru told Abdullah, there were 'other middle courses' apart from Abdullah's extremes of 'full integration or full autonomy'. Significantly, Nehru also told Abdullah that 'the question of Kashmir' had 'a logical appeal' and 'a strong emotional one' for him, although he could 'suppress' his emotions 'if logic demands that'. Then

Nehru offered a sad explanation for their potential and 'painful' parting 'after long years of comradeship': 'if our conscience so tells us, or … an overriding national interest so requires, then there is no help for it' but to part.[296] Abdullah responded that he believed in 'justice for all sections of the people'. As for their possible parting, he stated that 'whatever lot may be in store for us, never can you expect me to abandon my respect and affection for you'.[297] Seemingly then, at the end of June 1953, both men knew that their relationship was about to alter dramatically. As Nehru logically put it, 'the time for lengthy argument is over. … The time for clear understanding has come'.[298]

Other events in J&K in 1953

In 1953, some Indians became nervous about nefarious 'foreign hand activity' in the form of US involvement in J&K. They feared that Sheikh Abdullah had taken 'the imperialist bait of the possibility of an independent existence' and that he wanted to satisfy 'his personal ambition of being a "Sheikh" in the real meaning of the term' (i.e., the ruler of a fiefdom).[299] This was significant, given the increasingly divisive 'Cold War' being waged between the Western-led 'Free World' and the Soviet-led Communist bloc in which nations were being made to take sides. India tried to buck this trend by remaining non-aligned. Part of the US strategy was to try to encircle, or contain, the USSR. For this reason, areas located near the USSR's southern periphery were of interest, such as Iran, Pakistan, and India, and particularly the Kashmir region, which was also close to the other Communist nation, the People's Republic of China. As early as September 1950, Abdullah had met the US Ambassador to India, 'Roy Henderson'[300] or 'Louis Anderson', who, along his wife, often went to Kashmir and 'dropped in' on him.[301] (His name was actually Loy W. Henderson.) In a cable sent to the State Department after meeting Sheikh Abdullah on 29 October 1950, Henderson stated that, in relation to a discussion about the 'future of Kashmir, Abdullah was vigorous in restating that in his opinion it should be independent'. Abdullah allegedly also stated that the 'Kashmir people could not understand why [the] UN consistently ignored independence as a possible solution for Kashmir'.[302]

In 1952–53, Abdullah met other dignitaries and talked of independence. In 1952, he apparently informed the Australian High Commissioner to India, Walter Crocker, that he favoured independence for J&K.[303] In 1953, he had a 'long meeting' with the former US Democratic Party Presidential candidate, Adlai Stevenson.[304] This influential politician visited Srinagar on 1–3 May 1953 and supposedly met with Abdullah more than once. Their final meeting allegedly lasted for seven hours, although this may have been due to inclement weather delaying Stevenson.[305] *The Manchester Guardian* confirmed Stevenson had 'visited Kashmir and seems to have listened to suggestions that the best status for Kashmir would be independence from both India and Pakistan'.[306] By early May, it was 'widely rumoured' that Abdullah had also met with a former US Ambassador to India, Chester Bowles, who supposedly 'encouraged him for an independent Kashmir'.[307] Some Indians feared that Abdullah was being promised 'an independent Kashmir to be guaranteed by the United Nations, i.e., the Americans'. (Such an incorrect connection of the UN and the US was then apparently commonplace in Kashmir.)[308] There also were rumours that Abdullah 'might be planning to enter into his own relations with Washington'.[309] A book published in 1954 claimed that Abdullah was under the 'illusion of an "Independent" Kashmir backed by American military and economic aid'.[310] If such speculations were true, then it explained why New Delhi was concerned.

However, it is difficult to verify what role the United States played in Kashmir or how US activities influenced Sheikh Abdullah. Apparently, Abdullah was led to believe that, after he had 'declared the independence of Kashmir' at Eid (around 21 August in 1953), 'American air force planes were ready to land in Kashmir', presumably to support Abdullah's newly independent regime. This was significant for India, given Abdullah's aspiration, not to mention neighbouring Pakistan's active involvement in two US-led defence pacts, SEATO and CENTO.[311] Concurrently, the Indian press reported that Abdullah was 'championing the cause of an independent Kashmir at the behest of the Americans and thus was reluctant to implement the Delhi Agreement in full'.[312] Whether true or not, US influence in Indian J&K ended quickly and dramatically. In December 1955, the leaders of the USSR, Nikita Khrushchev and Nikolai Bulganin, visited Srinagar. Their high-level visit 'cemented' India–USSR relations, after which the USSR used, or threatened to use, its veto in the UN Security Council to stifle discussion about 'The India–Pakistan Question', i.e., the Kashmir dispute. For Sheikh Abdullah, this Soviet action enabled India 'to put the Kashmir issue in cold storage'.[313] It also sidelined US efforts in Indian J&K.

June 1953 therefore marked 'the calm before the storm'. Nehru was away; Abdullah was experiencing turmoil; matters were becoming intensely interesting. On 10 and 13 July, Abdullah told some National Conference workers that Kashmir would have to guard its autonomy at all costs. On Martyrs' Day (13 July) 1953, he stated that J&K did not want to become an appendage of India or Pakistan.[314] At the same time, Mirza Afzal Beg was campaigning for the independence of the Kashmir Valley. At a meeting of the National Conference's Working Committee, Beg proposed that, should the plebiscite be held, all 'foreign troops' should be withdrawn and that there should be a coalition of the ruling parties operating in Indian J&K and Azad Kashmir.[315] (No mention was made of the Northern Areas, possibly because this region was under Pakistan direct, and tight, control and had no such parties.) Around the same time, the National Conference's Working Committee unanimously adopted an alternative to resolve the Kashmir dispute: 'complete independence with Indo-Pak [sic] joint control over foreign affairs'.[316] Seemingly, Abdullah then had the support of a significant section of 'his' party.

On 10 July 1953, *The Times of India* re-published a bothersome article by Robert Trumbull from *The New York Times* of 5 July.[317] Trumbull, a US journalist, had long covered subcontinental affairs, including in J&K.[318] He reported from New Delhi, without identifying his sources, that the Indian and Pakistan Governments were contemplating 'excluding a plebiscite' due to its political and physical challenges and the 'serious dissatisfaction that would inevitably follow' the result. Instead, they were 'considering' granting the Kashmir Valley independence and dividing the rest of J&K along the ceasefire line, with minor territorial adjustments in favour of Pakistan in Jammu and Ladakh. As part of the envisaged 'formula', India and Pakistan would retain those areas of J&K they already held, except 'the famous Vale of Kashmir ... [which] would be independent' and with both nations 'safeguard[ing] its defence and communications'. A map showed the 'proposed division of Kashmir', with the independent 'Vale of Kashmir' (surprisingly) extended southeast to the India–J&K border seemingly to include (unspecified) eastern parts of Jammu Province, chiefly Udhampur District's tehsils of Kishtwar, Ramban and Bhaderwah. The India–Pakistan border between Baltistan and Ladakh would run due north from the end of the ceasefire line.[319] A sub-heading in the article stated 'Mr. Abdullah For Independence',[320] with Trumbull noting that Abdullah was 'said to lean towards [an] independent status', although there were also 'political differences' within J&K and 'troublesome' issues between India and J&K. Trumbull noted that these issues 'seem to urge some kind of over-all settlement before greater disorganization complicates the problem'.[321]

The next day (11 July), *The Times of India* published an article titled 'Hands Off Kashmir'.[322] Seemingly chastened, it reported that, while independence for Kashmir held 'a certain attraction' for Sheikh Abdullah and others, there was 'nothing original' about the reported plan. The 'mischief of the despatch' was its suggestion that the 'New Delhi and Karachi governments' were 'considering' the plan. The article concluded by asking 'must we continue to brook the unasked for interference of mischievous third parties?'[323] Concurrently, Nehru informed India's UN Representative, Rajeshwar Dayal, that Trumbull's story had 'no basis except rumours', that the Indian and Pakistan Governments had not considered this matter 'formally or informally', and that 'probably ... leading Americans, including [Secretary of State] Dulles and Adlai Stevenson [had] privately put forward this proposal'. Nehru also told Dayal that 'independence of Kashmir State, and more especially of [the] Valley, would be completely unreal and cannot endure'. There was 'no question of our [i.e., India] guaranteeing an arrangement which must lead to friction'.[324]

While independence was being talked about in 1953, it is uncertain if Sheikh Abdullah actually wanted this. Despite the Delhi Agreement and his 'allergy to Delhi',[325] he may have been 'queer[ing] the pitch', or politicking.[326] Still chastened, *The Times of India* stated that Abdullah knew that an independent Kashmir was 'not worth a day's purchase' (or effort). He had been informed that India would 'wash her [sic] hands' of such an entity, if only because it could not make any 'military guarantee' to preserve such independence.[327] Rather, Abdullah was talking of independence to gain leverage 'to keep Kashmir as autonomous as possible',[328] particularly when India and Pakistan were then seriously talking about J&K with 'some real hope that there might be a friendly solution'.[329] On 17 July, *The Times of India* again reported that the Indian Government firmly denied that 'independence' of the Kashmir Valley was under consideration.[330] Its Srinagar reporter believed that the 'campaign in favour of independence may be kept up until the final outcome of the Indo-Pakistani talks is known'.[331] Quite possibly, Abdullah was posturing. Other Kashmiris also had different opinions about independence. For some 'Veteran workers of the National Conference', independence would amount to 'retreating tortoise like into the Kashmiri shell' when 'revolutionary methods' were needed 'to bring the Jammu and Ladakh intelligentsia' into the National Conference's fold.[332] For G. M. Sadiq, the 'only way' that Kashmir could prosper 'was on the present basis of the accession to India on certain subjects and internal autonomy on other subjects'.[333] Abdullah considered Sadiq's views to be personal and that 'he had no right to speak on behalf of the State'. For Sadiq, 'no one should get away with the impression that the only voice that comes out of Kashmir is Sheikh Abdullah's'. Their rift was a significant development.[334]

By 19 July 1953, events in Kashmir had reached 'a very critical stage'. Karan Singh, 'greatly upset' and visiting Nehru in New Delhi,[335] noted that the Prime Minister's attitude had changed. Nehru was 'as disturbed' as Singh about 'the way the situation was developing' in Kashmir and was no longer prepared to defend Abdullah.[336] He also was pondering whether US agents had instigated 'the Praja Parishad Movement in Jammu as well as the separatist movement in the National Conference in Kashmir',[337] speculations that proposed an extraordinary US ability to coordinate two groups in J&K with distinctly opposing agendas. By August, Nehru had 'no doubt that American agents have been the cause of some mischief in Kashmir'.[338] In October, he still had 'no doubt' that 'the American Embassy [was] not only deeply interested in Kashmir but … constantly tending to interfere'. He told his sister, though, that he did not think that Adlai Stevenson, who publicly denied on 14 August that he had suggested 'an independent Kashmir to Abdullah',[339] was 'to blame in any way'.[340] Later, Bakshi made similar claims about 'foreign interference' in Kashmir.[341] The following year, two authors detailed similar claims with many names of foreigners but with little actual evidence about what they saw as a 'conspiracy for [a] foreign-sponsored "Independent" Kashmir'.[342] Seemingly, it was easier to blame others for India's woes in Kashmir.

US involvement aside, public statements made in July–August 1953 suggested troubles in the New Delhi–Srinagar relationship. On 30 July, Nehru told Bakshi that Abdullah 'appears to have developed a particular animus against all of us in India'.[343] Abdullah was then still questioning J&K's international status. At a public gathering the same day, he told an audience of peasants that J&K was dependent on the goodwill of both India and Pakistan and that the state should not merge with either nation.[344] The next day, he declared that the accession to India 'must be ratified by the free will of the people'. More significantly, he doubted that the J&K–India relationship could work satisfactorily, suggesting that the people instead 'steer clear between the two extreme views of merger with India and merger with Pakistan'.[345] Essentially, this meant independence. On 7 August, Abdullah told some National Conference members that J&K's accession to India had been due to the 'force of circumstances'.[346] In other words, had the Pukhtoons not invaded in 1947, J&K may not necessarily have joined India. Meanwhile, Nehru was reiterating that, in 1947, 'Kashmir, by accession, became a part of the Indian Union'.[347]

In August 1953, political infighting suggested that Sheikh Abdullah was becoming isolated in Kashmir from his pro-India colleagues and rivals. There were 'dissensions' and a 'serious rift' in the National Conference, with Abdullah in a 'minority' position and no longer the party's undisputed leader.[348] There was disgruntlement because he had reduced the Cabinet from nine to five members.[349] He was clearly having doubts about the limitations imposed by the Delhi Agreement, particularly in relation to the Head of the State position.[350] 'He' now held office at 'the pleasure of the President', which effectively, and significantly, made the incumbent responsible to the President of India, not to the J&K Government.[351] The Delhi Agreement also gave the President of India and the Indian Supreme Court certain other responsibilities in relation to J&K. This included power for the President to 'proclaim a general emergency in the State' should there be 'war or external aggression' and possibly if there were 'internal disturbances' – although the 'State delegation was … averse to the President exercising the power'. Such vague and weak language would not prevent any such Presidential proclamation, of course, and all of the subsequent interventionist consequences.[352] Later known as 'President's Rule', this intervention technique became a 'device used by New Delhi to topple inconvenient state governments'.[353]

On reflection, Abdullah must have realised that, overall, the Delhi Agreement weakened his state's autonomy. This furthered his serious second thoughts about the relationship with New Delhi and he began 'to publicly repudiate the policies to which he, his colleagues and the whole National Conference were solemnly committed'.[354] This confounded and irked Nehru.[355] However, Abdullah refused to meet him in New Delhi and discuss their issues. Given that Nehru's national responsibilities and workload made him the far busier man, Abdullah's reluctance looked like avoidance or intransigence, not cooperation or conciliation.

'A Proposal for the Future of Jammu and Kashmir'

On 31 July 1953, Nehru wrote a significant 'statement' titled 'A Proposal for the Future of Jammu and Kashmir'. Essentially, this was a clear instruction or edict – indeed, a blueprint for action – that noted that the 'present drift and the resulting confusion cannot be allowed to go on' in J&K. Nehru stated that 'Members' of the J&K Government should support the policy of J&K's accession to India. 'If the minority refuse to abide by it', then the Head of the State 'should ask for the resignation of the Government', then 'call upon another person representing the majority view to form a new government'. More pointedly, Nehru suggested that the Head of the State 'should have an order ready for the dismissal of the Government because it cannot fulfil its functions properly', after which he should immediately 'entrust the formation of the new Government to the other person'.[356] Presumably, this 'other person' was Bakshi Ghulam Mohammad, who led 'the majority group' in favour of J&K having 'a more comprehensive relationship' with India.[357] Nehru wanted the 'change-over' to be 'as peaceful as possible'. It should include 'the removal of certain well-known corrupt officers, etc., suspension of others whose loyalty is doubted, and an appeal to the people for [the] maintenance of peaceful conditions'.[358] Soon after, the perceptive Head of the State, Yuvraj Karan Singh, having mentally digested Nehru's proposal, would do almost exactly what his senior and ultimate boss had 'suggested'.

In early August 1953, matters came to a head. The fateful day was 8 August. Sheikh Abdullah's 'anti-Indian attitude' had made his 'anti-Indian group' a minority within the National Conference, the Constituent Assembly and the Cabinet. Rumours existed that Abdullah would declare independence on 21 August, 'the day of the great Id Festival, following which he would seek the protection of the United Nations against "Indian aggression"'.[359] With Abdullah's political position becoming increasingly unpopular and untenable, and with his advocating of independence being unacceptable in New Delhi and with the majority of his colleagues, the regime asserted itself. On 8 August, Karan Singh, as the Sadar-i-Riyasat, dismissed Abdullah because his Government 'had lost the confidence of the people'[360] while its disunity 'gravely jeopardized' J&K.[361] Indeed, there was such disunity of 'policy and action' and such 'a complete breakdown' in the Cabinet that Singh had 'no alternative but to dissolve the Ministry forthwith'.[362] In a letter to Abdullah, the Head of the State sweetened this devastating and unexpected (for Abdullah, at least) blow by saying he was personally 'deeply distressed at having to take this action'. Singh's final sentence was breathtakingly audacious or incredibly naive: 'I trust that this [action] will in no way affect the mutual regard and cordial feelings we have for each other'.[363]

Having dismissed Sheikh Abdullah, the Sadar-i-Riyasat asked Bakshi Ghulam Mohammad to form a new Ministry, which he did. Bakshi was selected because of his 'prestige and regard ... among the people of the State'.[364] Bakshi confronted four tasks, the fourth of which was to implement the Delhi Agreement,[365] which had been a significant pre-dismissal issue. Indeed, three of Abdullah's four Cabinet colleagues, Bakshi, G. L. Dogra and Sham Lal Saraf, had charged on 7 August in a Memorandum sent to Abdullah, copied to Karan Singh, that Abdullah and Beg 'in utter disregard' were ignoring and not consulting their colleagues, were not fulfilling joint Cabinet responsibility, were delaying implementing the Delhi Agreement,[366] and were 'purposefully and openly' denouncing it.[367] This Memorandum followed Abdullah's unsuccessful attempt on 6 August to force Saraf to resign on the grounds of incompetency,[368] which action 'precipitated the crisis'.[369] However, Saraf stalled. This gave him and his co-conspirators time to institute their plan to depose the now unacceptable Abdullah whose views 'on basic issues ... affecting the vital interests of [J&K] ... sharply opposed' those held by the pro-India majority of Cabinet members and by the pro-India Yuvraj Karan Singh.[370] For them, Abdullah had become a pro-independence 'dictator', which was unacceptable.[371] He had to be removed – and he was.

Down, but not out

In 1947, part of Sheikh Abdullah's challenge was to assert himself and J&K-ites as the ultimate deciders of J&K's international status. The Pukhtoon invasion ended this process, as well as any aspirations that Abdullah and Maharaja Hari Singh may have had for an independent J&K. Nevertheless, the accession to India did not settle J&K's unification with India, which Governor-General Mountbatten and Prime Minister Nehru both publicly noted was provisional and subject to confirmation by a plebiscite. Equally and paradoxically, this invasion quickly led to Abdullah becoming the chief political figure in J&K, and to Singh, to his chagrin, quickly becoming redundant. Three factors empowered Abdullah. The first was his serious and undeniable popularity, particularly in the early years of his 'reign'. The second was the significant support that he received from his friend, Jawaharlal Nehru. This support became almost unequivocal after, and because, of India's promise to hold a confirmatory plebiscite. Due to his popularity, Abdullah was needed to help India win this prospective poll. The third factor was the need for political stability and strong leadership as Indian forces stabilised Kashmir and their presence there. For Nehru, Hari Singh was not up to these tasks. Only Abdullah could do the job. The Kashmiri was then almost unassailable.

For the first few years of his rule in J&K, Sheikh Abdullah was decisive and popular. His land reforms were liked by poorer J&K-ites, although not by disgruntled landlords, most of whom were Hindus and/or were from Jammu. Furthermore, with his land reforms and other activities, Abdullah had neither consulted Nehru sufficiently, nor taken his advice fully, or at all. They had differing agendas that reflected a bigger dynamic: how much autonomy could, and should, J&K be allowed? Given that New Delhi had allowed Abdullah to govern almost unhindered, he felt and believed that the state was entitled to have full autonomy; Nehru wanted the state and its people to fully integrate into India. Resolving this dynamic would pose the major, and ongoing, challenge in centre–state relations, certainly for Sheikh Abdullah. As he saw things, New Delhi wanted his 'uncompromising submission' as well as that of 'his' state.[372] In this, I think Abdullah was correct.

In 1952, Jawaharlal Nehru tried to tie Sheikh Abdullah down by concluding the Delhi Agreement. However, rather than restricting Abdullah, it provoked him to seriously question his relationship with Nehru and to doubt J&K's involvement with India. So too did the Praja Parishad's agitation in Jammu and, in 1953, the Nehru-Bogra talks with which Abdullah was not directly involved. These factors challenged Abdullah's role and position in J&K and made him begin to consider other options for 'his' state, particularly independence. Concurrently, Abdullah's pro-India colleagues became concerned by his heavy-handed leadership and international aspirations. By mid-1953, there were rumours that Abdullah was serious about instituting independence for Kashmir. This was dangerous, so he had to be deposed. This was now possible, and acceptable for India's leaders, as Abdullah was no longer needed to help India win the plebiscite – in which, by 1953, India was losing interest. Abdullah's dismissal could be, and was, justified as being in the (amorphous) 'national interest', in this case, the matter of keeping India unified.[373] The use of this concept created a dangerous (and still unrequited) practice. Indeed, as a political scientist from Jammu has noted, the '"national interest" assumed primacy over everything else in Kashmir and everything was justified in its name – whether it was the absence of democracy, suppression of civil liberties, or disregard of popular responses. The consequence has been the accumulated discontent that has been erupting from time to time'.[374] India, of course, is not the only nation to justify all manner of things in the 'national interest'. While its use of this term does not excuse Sheikh Abdullah's dismissal in 1953, it does partially explain it.

In 1953, Sheikh Abdullah was dismissed by the Head of the State, Karan Singh. Almost certainly, Singh took this action with Nehru's approval and support. For Abdullah, his dismissal was undemocratic: Singh had exceeded his powers while Abdullah was prevented from testing his popularity and majority in the J&K Constituent Assembly, as would have been the usual democratic procedure. Ironically, however, Karan Singh was the son of Abdullah's old political rival, Hari Singh, suggesting that Abdullah may have made a mistake appointing the younger Dogra in the first place. While Abdullah clearly had been pondering the possibility of independence for 'Kashmir', it was a moot point as to whether he actually wanted this or whether it was a ploy to extract benefits, particularly the maximum amount of autonomy possible, from New Delhi. Abdullah did not appear to have a serious plan in place for an independent Kashmir. It also was a moot point as to how popular Abdullah's aspiration for independence was with J&K-ites or, more particularly, among 'his' Kashmiri community. Ultimately, Sheikh Abdullah failed: J&K did not get independence while, post-Abdullah, each Prime (later Chief) Minister of J&K allowed, even enabled, the state to be tied closely to India. After his dismissal, Abdullah was politically sidelined for many years, chiefly by being detained under house arrest or incarcerated in jail. This did not, however, end his aspirations for, or his activities in relation to, J&K's international status.

6

Sheikh Abdullah's pursuit of independence for 'Kashmir', post-1953

After Sheikh Abdullah's dismissal on 8 August 1953, other Kashmiris came to the fore. Slowly but surely, New Delhi started to tie J&K politically, administratively and economically closer to, and into, the Indian Union. Part of this process involved having a suitably pro-India Kashmiri politician able and willing to do New Delhi's bidding in charge of J&K. The two most significant such Kashmiris were the capable, but allegedly corrupt, Bakshi Ghulam Mohammad (in power 1953–63) and G. M. Sadiq (in power 1964–71), who was 'pro-Soviet by faction and inclination.'[1] Until his death in 1964, Nehru and New Delhi were prepared to tolerate politicians such as Bakshi, chiefly because they were indisputably pro-India. Meanwhile, the politically doubtful Sheikh Abdullah languished in detention until 1968. In 1975, he finally came in from 'the political cold'. During his twenty-two years in the political wilderness, Abdullah often would use such terms as 'independence' and 'self-determination'. He was finally silenced on the issue of J&K's international status when he became Chief Minister of J&K in 1975. In order for him to take this position, Abdullah had to accept that J&K was with, and was an integral part of, India.

This chapter discusses Sheikh Abdullah and his often unclear, indeed contrary, attitudes to independence or autonomy or self-determination for J&K during the period 1953–82. During his periods of brief release from detention, and certainly after his final release in 1968, Abdullah continued to talk of self-determination for J&K-ites via the Plebiscite Front, a political body he was associated with, or finding 'a solution of the Kashmir issue', including via two important People's Conventions held in 1968 and 1970, which New Delhi surprisingly allowed to be held.[2] A major turning point came in 1971 when India conclusively defeated Pakistan in their war in East Pakistan, the result of which was the creation of Bangladesh. This war confirmed that Islam was not a monolith and that Pakistan could not liberate J&K

from Indian control. India's victory also made Prime Minister Indira Gandhi politically unassailable. These factors greatly moderated Sheikh Abdullah's behaviour and his aspirations for J&K's international status. Indeed, in 1975, he agreed the Kashmir Accord with Mrs Gandhi, which enabled him to return to power in J&K. Abdullah died in office in 1982.

After Abdullah's 1953 sacking

Sheikh Abdullah considered his dismissal as the Prime Minister of J&K on 8 August 1953 to be an 'armed coup … prepared in Delhi'.[3] Arrested under the Public Safety Act and incarcerated,[4] he 'was denied the basic human right to defend … [himself] against very grave charges',[5] as well as to test his popular support in the Constituent Assembly.[6] Due to him being a 'strong advocate for Kashmiri independence', there had been some serious plotting against Abdullah.[7] Allegedly, Rafi Ahmed Kidwai, a Muslim from Uttar Pradesh, was 'director of the conspiracy'. Kidwai struck before, and because, Abdullah supposedly intended to declare independence for J&K and make himself its 'hereditary sultan'.[8] Other possible plotters included: Brigadier B. N. Kaul, former commander of the Kashmiri militia that 'routed the Pakistani invaders' and was then in charge of the Indian Army elements that seized Abdullah; Ajit Prasad Jain, a political adviser in New Delhi; B. N. Mullik, serving in Kashmir with the Intelligence Bureau; and, D. W. Mehra, a senior policeman who 'made his mark quelling tribals in NWFP'.[9] According to Abdullah, 'the 9th [sic] August operation' against him occurred with Nehru's assent.[10] It was successful: Abdullah lost power and was quickly sidelined. He then became almost a non-person. In J&K's first official post-Abdullah report, he was only mentioned once. This mention, not surprisingly, concerned his dismissal.[11]

Following Abdullah's dismissal, Bakshi Ghulam Mohammad, Abdullah's deputy, formed a new Government. Bakshi had previously disagreed with Abdullah. On obtaining power, this new, suitably pro-India, leader of J&K stated that 'some of our former colleagues … [had been] contemplating [the] formation of an independent country … obviously backed by foreign powers with stakes in this state'.[12] These 'foreign powers' presumably were Pakistan or the United States, although the USSR or the People's Republic of China cannot be ruled out, given fears then about the aggressive 'double shadow' of Communism.[13] Such ideology had been popular in J&K, particularly Kashmir, in the 1940s. In 1953, it still influenced some Kashmiri politicians such as G. M. Sadiq. Korbel, the Czechoslovakian member of UNCIP who had been the victim of Communists taking over his nation, claims that three of Bakshi's five ministers were Communists or 'fellow travellers': Sadiq, Girdharilal Dogra and Mir Qasim.[14] Some also saw Abdullah as having 'Communist proclivities', particularly people in the (anti-Soviet) United Kingdom and United States.[15] It is difficult to determine the veracity of these claims. Given India's strong socialist inclinations and later significant relationship with the USSR, having Communist leanings may not necessarily have been a shortcoming.

In the early 1950s, however, J&K, given its strategic location, was increasingly becoming a pawn in the growing Cold War containment environment resulting from the two rival adversarial approaches to international relations. A further issue at that time was the Korean War, which saw UN forces in the south oppose Communist forces in the north. Essentially, this was a proxy war between the United States and its allies and the Soviet Union and its allies. Like J&K, Kashmir also was divided by fighting. In relation to J&K, the Soviet Union was concerned that the United States might be attempting to create 'an independent state of Kashmir, as desired by Abdullah'. Conversely, the British believed that the USSR desired 'an independent Kashmir under the leftist Abdullah'. Meanwhile, India and its leader, Nehru, were 'dead opposed to an independent Kashmir'.[16] Similarly, Bakshi considered that Abdullah's advocacy of an 'Independent State' was a 'betrayal of the country's interests'.[17] Interestingly, neither the UK, US nor USSR seemed concerned when Abdullah was removed from office.

On 5 October 1953, Bakshi Ghulam Mohammad's position as Prime Minister of J&K was confirmed by a 'unanimous vote of confidence' in the first Constituent Assembly session held after Sheikh Abdullah's dismissal. This vote was flawed: Abdullah and five pro-Abdullah members were kept in detention when it was taken.[18] Abdullah was not given an opportunity to confirm his support, or lack thereof, in the Constituent Assembly. These actions had been informed by the Maharaja's autocracy – and indeed, by Abdullah's own previous (and later) autocratic behaviour. Abdullah had not been an unblemished democrat, with his position unrivalled and unassailable as long as India, and Nehru in particular, supported him in their politically symbiotic relationship. As Hari Singh had ironically noted, power had not passed from him to the people but to 'an oligarchy backed by [the] Government of India'.[19] After his arrest, Abdullah was detained in 'a sumptuous house at Udhampur'.[20] Meanwhile, Bakshi made it 'a point of honour' to win the hearts of Jammuites 'estranged under Sheikh Abdullah'.[21] Helpfully, he also made his new Cabinet more 'broad-based' by including Sadiq, the leader of the National Conference's 'left wing', and representatives from Jammu and Ladakh, respectively Major Piare Singh and Kushak Bakula.[22] The fact that these two regions had been either under represented (Jammu) or had no representation (Ladakh) in the previous Cabinet reflected Sheikh Abdullah's almost total focus on the Kashmir Valley. This was one reason for the disgruntlement of Jammuites and Ladakhis with Kashmiris.

After Sheikh Abdullah's arrest and dismissal in August 1953, over one million people apparently protested in Srinagar. Abdullah claims that his arrest provoked 'an upheaval reminiscent of the mass demonstrations of 1931 ... Some three thousand people were gunned down', although, oddly, 'not a trace of these shroudless and graveless victims could be found later'.[23] One local politician, Maulana Iftikhar Ansari, stated that 'there was a bloodbath, 1,500 people were killed in one day' in Kashmir.[24] Other reports stated that 'state-wide violence resulted in 168 persons being injured and 36 being killed'.[25] According to Karan Singh, there was 'trouble at various places in the Valley', with 46 people killed and 148 people injured in 'police firing' as Kashmiris showed their displeasure with Abdullah's dismissal.[26] On 20 August, a small hiccup occurred when Bakshi temperamentally resigned after the Nehru-Bogra declaration that a Plebiscite Administrator would be appointed in April 1954.[27] For a 'stunned' Bakshi, the possibility that, post-plebiscite, J&K might end up with Pakistan represented a complete reversal of his pro-India stance.[28] Bakshi's reaction may also have been provoked by Nehru's earlier criticism that he did 'not like things done in the dark and in the middle of the night', by which Nehru was referring to the circumstances of Abdullah's dismissal, arrest and detention on 8–9 August.[29] Bakshi quickly withdrew his resignation after Nehru's harsh reaction and some positive persuasion by colleagues.[30]

Bakshi and his pro-India colleagues quickly brought the situation in J&K under control. By mid-October, Nehru was informing India's Chief Ministers that it was 'really astonishing' how Bakshi and his colleagues 'by their policy and hard work, changed the entire picture and outlook in the state within two months'. The situation had 'improved very greatly and might almost be said to be normal'.[31] While he was glowing in his praise of Bakshi, who was a very capable administrator, Nehru was still troubled by the Praja Parishad's activism in Jammu.[32] Additionally, there was some political fallout from Abdullah's dismissal. According to Qasim, it had 'no constitutional sanction: nowhere in the world had a head of Government been dismissed because his cabinet was believed to have lost faith in him'. For Kashmiris, including those who disagreed with Abdullah's 'attitudes and statements', his dismissal shook their 'faith in democracy and the sanctity of the Indian Constitution'. The 'trust lost' in 1953 'was never restored'.[33] Furthermore, New Delhi, particularly the Prime Minister of India, thereafter became the major power broker in J&K politics, not J&K-ites, with the prime, later chief, minister of J&K, appropriately accommodating to India. (In March 1965, the term 'Prime Minister' was changed to 'Chief Minister' in keeping with the Indianisation of J&K.) As Sheikh Abdullah noted in 1968: 'only that person who enjoys the confidence of India can be the Chief Minister of Kashmir'.[34]

Almost certainly, Karan Singh took his monumental decision to depose Abdullah with Nehru's concurrence.[35] As Singh noted in his 'semi-formal letter' to Nehru on 9 August 1953, he had 'attempted to act in a democratic and constitutional manner, keeping in mind what you said when we last met'.[36] Singh also closely followed Nehru's 'Proposal for the Future of Jammu and Kashmir' of 31 July,[37] which India's Prime Minister had written after meeting a 'greatly upset' Singh in New Delhi on 19 July.[38] Apart from his own observations, Nehru had also become concerned about Abdullah's activities from 'detailed reports' received from various sources, including India's Intelligence Bureau.[39] For New Delhi, the 'recent developments in Kashmir'[40] required 'the maintenance of security and internal order' in J&K.[41] Nevertheless, Abdullah's dismissal marked the end of an era. Nehru, who had previously supported and politically enabled Abdullah, now allowed and facilitated his political disablement and sidelining. As Abdullah later noted, Nehru 'seemed to have lost trust in him' and, increasingly, dealt with other colleagues, such as Bakshi.[42] The irony communally was that Abdullah, a Kashmiri Muslim, had been sacked by Singh, a Hindu Dogra from Jammu, supported by Nehru, a nominal Hindu whose forebears were Kashmiri Pandits.

Apart from seeing it as a coup, Sheikh Abdullah believed that his dismissal was 'the first act of [the] murder of democracy' in J&K as he had been 'unconstitutionally and illegally removed'.[43] (Actually, this was the second such act, given that the Abdullah-led National Conference had 'captured', figuratively and literally, '100 per cent [of] seats' in the 1951 Constituent Assembly elections.)[44] However, Abdullah had never been democratically elected, either to the J&K Legislative Assembly or as Prime Minister. Rather, Maharaja Hari Singh's Proclamation on 5 March 1948 appointed Abdullah 'by Royal Warrant' as Prime Minister of the Interim Government.[45] This edict did not indicate how long Abdullah would serve, nor how he could be dismissed. Presumably, or by tradition, Abdullah served at the ruler's 'pleasure' – although, in the challenging circumstances of 1948, Hari Singh essentially was doing his Cabinet's 'bidding'. In 1953, Karan Singh, as Sadar-i-Riyasat, added a popular dimension to this royal prerogative: 'functioning in the interests of the people of the State, who have reposed the responsibility and authority of the Headship of the State in me', he ordered the dismissal of Abdullah and the Council of Ministers.[46] Thereafter, Section 39 of 'The Constitution of

Jammu and Kashmir Constitution, 1956', which replaced both the 1954 'Constitution (Amendment) Act' and the 1939 Constitution, stated that the Sadar-i-Riyasat would appoint the prime minister, with the latter holding office at the former's pleasure.[47] Section 92 also granted the Sadar-i-Riyasat special powers to take over in the event of a crisis.[48] Given that Abdullah was charged with 'disruptionism, corruption, nepotism, maladministration and establishing foreign contacts of a kind dangerous to the peace and prosperity of the state',[49] this, indeed, had been a crisis. Arguably, therefore, Abdullah's dismissal, had it occurred in 1956, would have been constitutional and legal.

Despite the seriousness of 'certain events' that had taken place in J&K,[50] Jawaharlal Nehru seemed ambivalent about them and about Kashmir. He neither informed Parliament, nor his Chief Ministers, that Sheikh Abdullah had wanted independence for Kashmir. Rather, he stated that 'within the Kashmir Cabinet' there were 'rival policies' and 'serious differences' about J&K's status in the Indian Union.[51] Bakshi was more forthright. In a 'long speech' about 'recent developments',[52] he stated that 'Kashmir had indissoluble links with India' but that Abdullah and 'some of his colleagues' had been 'working for an independent State with the "connivance and support of interested foreign powers"'.[53] Nehru only made his first visit to Srinagar since Abdullah's dismissal in December 1957.[54] Although he was well received by Kashmiris,[55] Kashmir was politically disunified. The capable Bakshi and the so-called 'Bakshi Brothers Corporation' (BBC) were allegedly making financial 'hay while the sun shines'.[56] (Mr Justice Ayyangar would later find fifteen of thirty-eight charges brought against Bakshi for corruption and misuse of power to be proven.)[57] More positively, he was known as 'Bakshi the Builder' for his many public works.[58] Conversely, Sadiq was leaving the National Conference and forming his own 'Democratic National Conference'.[59] Nehru's visit was chiefly to reconcile the various warring factions. Part of the process of New Delhi starting to tie J&K politically, administratively and economically closer to the Indian Union involved having a suitably pro-India Kashmiri in charge of J&K. This was why Nehru and New Delhi tolerated politicians such as Bakshi: he was indisputably pro-India.

Nehru-Bogra talks

Amid concerns about Abdullah's stance of independence, Prime Minister Nehru held serious talks with Pakistan's Prime Minister, Mohammad Ali Bogra, in August 1953. They agreed to announce the appointment of a Plebiscite Administrator 'by the end of April 1954'.[60] Significantly, Nehru believed that the 'final outcome about the State was likely to be one of division', with the plebiscite providing 'the necessary data for this decision' and division.[61] In other words, for India, the plebiscite would not be a 'winner takes all' contest. Rather, people's votes would help determine whether their particular area or region would join India or Pakistan. There was also an issue about J&K refugees returning to J&K to vote, with Nehru considering they 'should be left out, as this was wholly impracticable, and, in any event, would delay matters tremendously'.[62] Already, Nehru thought that it would take 'about two years … or possibly more' to resolve all the issues and organise the poll.[63] Sorting out the refugee issue would further delay this process – although the issue was important for Pakistan, given that it accommodated most J&K refugees, particularly Muslim Jammuites, a large number of whom had left Jammu in 1947–48. Their participation in any plebiscite would have enhanced the vote for Pakistan, a negative factor that India was no doubt aware of. Nehru also informed Bogra about 'the question of an independent Kashmir' and how this 'would be a very small State, neither politically nor economically viable … [and] a source of discord' in India–Pakistan relations.[64] According to Nehru, Bogra had 'wholly' agreed with this analysis.[65]

While Bogra may have agreed with Nehru's analysis, there was little other agreement between the Prime Ministers. As early as 3 September 1953, Nehru became disenchanted with his Pakistani interlocutor over issues and different understandings such as who should be Plebiscite Administrator, the idea of regional plebiscites, the role of the belligerent (as Nehru saw things) Pakistani press, and foreign diplomatic and/or military involvement in the region, particularly by the United States.[66] Nehru was particularly keen 'to isolate' J&K from 'big power politics'.[67] In October, he became perturbed that Bogra was not answering his letters.[68] In December, he became more perturbed with Pakistan's proposed involvement in a US-led military pact[69] and with a US proposal to grant military assistance to Pakistan. For Nehru, these circumstances 'created an entirely new situation',[70] with concerns that Pakistan might try to militarily capture J&K. Equally, this military pact provided India with an excuse not to hold the plebiscite. Ultimately, and perhaps not surprisingly, nothing came of this poll.

One significant reason why nothing came of the plebiscite is because, by 1957, the J&K Constitution had come into being. After its first meeting in 1951, the Constituent Assembly finalised this important document five years later on 17 November 1956.[71] The J&K Constitution became effective on 26 January 1957, exactly seven years after India's Constitution had been instituted. On the same day, the J&K Constituent Assembly dissolved itself.[72] Importantly, the J&K Constitution reiterated via Section 3 that 'The State of Jammu and Kashmir is and shall be an integral part of the Union of India'.[73] Indians thereafter used this reiteration to justify their disinterest in having a plebiscite held in J&K, even though 'in strict law', the Constituent Assembly did not have the authority for its reiteration.[74] For example, speaking at the UN General Assembly in 1965,[75] Mir Qasim stated that, 'frustrated by Pakistan's intransigence' in implementing the UNSC resolutions, J&K-ites' wishes had been 'ascertained fully' by the Constituent Assembly elections in 1951, by the J&K Constitution's ratification of the accession to India in 1957, and 'twice within eighteen years' when people had to defend against Pakistani aggression. There was 'no justification for any further ascertainment of the wishes of the people' and 'There will be no plebiscite'. This was disingenuous, certainly in terms of the 1951 elections. Apart from the National Conference 'capturing' all seventy-five seats in the elections,[76] there was no voting in Pakistan-Administered J&K. Therefore, the 'wishes' of about a quarter of J&K-ites living in Azad Kashmir or the Northern Areas had not actually been 'ascertained fully'.

Significantly, by 1957, India also had changed its stance on the Constituent Assembly's ability to ratify the accession to India. On 9 March 1951, India's Permanent Representative to the United Nations, Sir Benegal Rau (Prime Minister of J&K in 1944–45),[77] had noted that the J&K Constituent Assembly could 'express an opinion' on the question of J&K's accession to India, but it could 'take no decision' about this matter.[78] On 29 March, Rau repeated this position: India could not prevent 'Kashmir' from 'expressing its opinion' on the accession, but 'this opinion will not bind my Government or prejudice the position of the [Security] Council'.[79] From around 1954, India reversed this stance. Possibly as early as May 1953, Nehru agreed that the Constituent Assembly should confirm the Maharaja's accession to India and that this confirmation would be binding.[80] The Constituent Assembly did so unanimously in February 1954. It also requested closer formal links with India.[81] When the J&K Constitution finally came into being in January 1957, it importantly reaffirmed J&K's accession to India. Supposedly, this ended the issue of J&K's international status.

For New Delhi, these factors meant that a UN plebiscite was no longer necessary – although, equally, India felt that it could lose this poll. Indeed, as early as 1950, Sir Owen Dixon, the United Nations Representative for India and Pakistan, apparently thought that 'Nehru knew that if a fair plebiscite were held for the whole territory [of J&K] India would lose'.[82] In July 1955, India's Home Minister, G. B. Pant, publicly stated that a plebiscite was unnecessary: 'Many things had happened since [1947], which ruled out the plebiscite'.[83] India used one of these 'many things' to justify its no-plebiscite stance. Strategically, Pakistan had joined some Western-led military pacts which India was concerned might try to militarily capture J&K for Pakistan. More significantly, by 1955, the seemingly pro-independence Sheikh Abdullah also had been politically sidelined and incarcerated. He was nowhere to be seen.

Sheikh Abdullah after August 1953

After his dismissal, Sheikh Abdullah was marginalised politically and physically, and disappeared from public view. Bakshi and his colleagues quickly stabilised J&K, implemented the Delhi Agreement, and kept Abdullah incarcerated for much of the next fifteen years. Abdullah also disappeared from official discourse, with Karan Singh not discussing him in written communications with Nehru after January 1956.[84] For his part, Nehru was concerned about Abdullah's imprisonment, welfare and access to relatives, particularly Begum Abdullah and their children. His ongoing detention was 'unfortunate' and Nehru hoped that Abdullah would 'not be long there' (i.e., in detention). Disingenuously, Nehru claimed that it was 'difficult' for him 'to deal with the matter' of Abdullah's release as 'the Kashmir state [sic] Government is fully autonomous and the responsibility lies with that Government'.[85] Thereafter, he and Abdullah would remain distant, with no direct communications until 8 April 1955, when Nehru relented and responded to some notes that Abdullah had sent to him.[86]

After his dismissal in 1953, the National Conference split into the Abdullah faction, which had grassroots support and little organisation, and the less popular Bakshi faction, which controlled the party's administration and was in government.[87] Because Abdullah and his political lieutenant, Mirza Afzal Beg, were both then on the political outer and needed their own political party, and possibly in response to Home Minister Pant's statement in July 1955 that a plebiscite was no longer needed for J&K,[88] Beg established the All J&K Plebiscite Front (*Mahaz-e-Raishumari*) on 9 August 1953.[89] It had three 'basic issues': the accession issue was unresolved; a decision about this issue needed to be taken 'at an early date'; only the people could decide and their decision would be 'final and irrevocable'.[90] Its stance was that the people of J&K should be allowed to exercise their right of self-determination via a plebiscite that neutral nations would supervise.[91] This would 'keep alive' India's promise that the accession needed to be confirmed by a reference to the people.[92] (In 1965, a body also called the Plebiscite Front was formed in Azad Kashmir. It was not connected with the Kashmiri organisation.)[93]

Mirza Afzal Beg was the Plebiscite Front's President; Sheikh Abdullah was not even a member of this party. This was because, after his dismissal, Abdullah 'was so disgusted with organizations'[94] that he 'stayed aloof'. Instead, he gave the Plebiscite Front 'political and moral support'.[95] In actuality, many considered that he was this party's patron[96] and its de facto leader.[97] According to Indian intelligence, the Plebiscite Front evolved out of a body called the 'War Council' established soon after, and because of, Abdullah's dismissal.[98] As Abdullah later interestingly put it: 'When the National Conference ceased to be owned by us', Beg founded the Plebiscite Front, after which we were 'committed to jail'.[99] According to Beg, he established the Plebiscite Front 'in protest' against the Constituent Assembly's decision in 1954 to have the constitution that they were developing confirm J&K's accession to India.[100] According to Karan Singh, there was 'incontrovertible evidence' that this 'anti-India organization' received 'large sums of money from Pakistan'.[101] All of these explanations were plausible.

Meanwhile, Sheikh Abdullah's incarcerations 'added a halo of martyrdom to him'.[102] Initially, he was detained in 1953 for two months, ironically in a house belonging to Hari Singh.[103] Later in 1953, his detention was extended for a further two months.[104] Thereafter, he would spend a total of thirteen of the next fifteen years in jail or under house arrest, a limitation that prevented him from making public statements or advocating for independence. Abdullah did receive two brief respites from political prison: in January–April 1958 and from April 1964 to May 1965. His first period of freedom started on 8 January 1958, after which he immediately began politicking, organising and making speeches. For him, the only way to end the Kashmir dispute was 'to concede [the] right of self-determination to the people of Kashmir'.[105] Whether this meant holding the UN plebiscite or giving independence to J&K was open to interpretation. On 13 January, five days after his release, Abdullah again provocatively stated at Srinagar's famous Hazratbal shrine that the accession had never been 'finalized and ratification by the people was still due'. He continued that 'one of the solutions was Independence for the valley guaranteed by [the] United Nations and he would not mind Ladakh and Jammu going to India'.[106] Abdullah's focus had again narrowed to independence for the Kashmir Valley.

Not surprisingly, a free and relatively unfettered Sheikh Abdullah caused problems in 1958. As Nehru told his sister in mid-February, Abdullah was in Kashmir and 'he is more than a hand full'.[107] Bakshi and some of his colleagues were also nervous about Abdullah, particularly as he was largely unbounded by past statements, party discipline, or the need to toe India's line.[108] Some officials were concerned that Abdullah, 'by the very power of [his] popular support', could 'oust Bakshi and seize power', despite the Indian Army's presence in J&K.[109] On 11 April, Abdullah informed Prime Minister Nehru by letter that the 'only correct way' of ending the ten-year dispute over J&K was to give the 'Kashmiris their right to self-determination'.[110] Shortly after, Abdullah was again detained, perhaps predictably. During the night of 29–30 April 1958, he was re-arrested in Srinagar, this time for making 'anti-India utterances'.[111] He had been free less than four months. In May, Abdullah's closest colleague, Mirza Afzal Beg and twenty-five others were charged with 'conspiracy against the state'. Abdullah himself was charged with the same offence in October.[112] In what became known as the 'Kashmir Conspiracy Case', the alleged conspirators faced trial 'for attempting to overthrow the Government by criminal force and for anti-State activities'. These were serious charges: if convicted, the penalty was a life sentence or death. Despite Nehru's desire for the case not to be delayed,[113] it dragged on for five years and cost the J&K Government Rs 46,366.[114] On 5 April 1964, the Prime Minister of J&K, G. M. Sadiq, announced that the charges against Abdullah and the others would be withdrawn immediately.[115] This withdrawal was made on 'political grounds',[116] seemingly at the behest of Jawaharlal Nehru who felt that, after such a long time, there was 'obviously nothing to be proved'.[117]

After his re-arrest in 1958, Abdullah was detained until 8 April 1964. This again curtailed his political activities. Abdullah's release was due to two factors. First, the democrat, libertarian and former freedom fighter, Jawaharlal Nehru, detested people being detained for their political beliefs, and pressured, shamed or finally compelled, the J&K Government to conclude the 'Kashmir Conspiracy Case' or release those charged. Second, Nehru was perturbed by the serious disturbances in Kashmir that occurred after the revered holy relic housed at Hazratbal, the *Moe-e-Muqaddas* (Hair of the Prophet), disappeared in late December 1963. Khwaja Shamsuddin had become the (ineffectual) Prime Minister after Bakshi, his puppetmaster, was 'Kamrajed'.[118] (The Kamaraj Plan aimed to bring younger blood into positions of power in India.)[119] The disturbances had a strong anti-Bakshi, pro-autonomy sentiment, partly organised by a new political party, the Awami Action Committee.[120] While the holy relic was quickly restored and its authenticity validated, this violent incident made Nehru think. He knew that Bakshi's effective, but exploitative and unpopular, rule had eroded J&K's autonomy but tied the state significantly closer to India.[121] He was aware of Abdullah's continuing popularity and influence and that, without Abdullah's involvement, 'Kashmir could not settle down' and become stable.[122] He was concerned that the Kashmiris' serious disenchantment with India after sixteen years of association and their serious protests

made during the depth of the Kashmiri winter suggested that 'a new approach …
[and] a radical change in our thinking about Kashmir' was needed.[123] Part of this
change involved having Abdullah freed from detention. By the time of Abdullah's
unconditional release in April 1964, the more circumspect but also pro-India
Kashmiri, G. M. Sadiq, had replaced the Bakshi regime's Shamsuddin as Prime
Minister of J&K. Nevertheless, Abdullah was still the most popular politician in
Kashmir. This was confirmed when he returned triumphantly to Kashmir shortly
after his release.

In 1964, Sheikh Abdullah and Jawaharlal Nehru were dramatically reconciled.
In the twilight of his life, Nehru was ailing. He was tired after his exertions consolidating, then building, post-British India, ill after a serious stroke, disappointed
by China's decisive defeat of India in 1962, and concerned by Kashmir's recent
disturbances over the holy relic. Wanting to set things right, Abdullah and Nehru
met again after eleven years.[124] Afterwards, with Nehru's 'blessing', Abdullah went
to Pakistan to discuss with its President, the military dictator General Ayub Khan,
an 'amicable' way to resolve the Kashmir dispute that gave 'neither party a sense
of defeat'.[125] Abdullah aimed to schedule a meeting between the ailing Nehru and
the 'magnetic' Ayub[126] to 'discuss all possible proposals'.[127] This included a 'confederation between India and Pakistan, with Kashmir as an autonomous enclave between
them, on the model of Andorra, between France and Spain'.[128] According to Ayub,
Abdullah suggested the creation of a confederation between India, Pakistan, and
Kashmir'. Abdullah, however, claimed that Ayub raised, then 'continued to harp
on [about a] Confederation'.[129] Either way, the Pakistani leader dismissed this
'absurd proposal'[130] that he thought would 'extend Indian hegemony'.[131] Overall,
this India–Pakistan engagement involved many 'imponderables': Ayub's motives
for wanting to engage in talks; Nehru's ability to deliver any solution; the viability
of a confederation; and, Abdullah's actual agenda.[132] According to Karan Singh,
what Abdullah 'really favoured was some sort of semi-independent status for the
[Kashmir] valley guaranteed both by India and Pakistan'.[133] That is, a 'special status
just short of independence'.[134] For Singh, Abdullah, who was 'endowed with an
ego to match his impressive physical appearance', was still not 'in a mood to accept
the reality of Jammu and Kashmir being part of India'. He wanted Pakistan involved
in some way 'to guarantee Kashmiri rights'.[135]

While in Pakistan in 1964, Sheikh Abdullah met many former political colleagues
and rivals, including the expatriate Jammuite, Chaudhri Ghulam Abbas, and the
expatriate Kashmiri, Mirwaiz Yusuf Shah. The Mirwaiz apparently told Abdullah
that he was 'firmly convinced now that the best solution for Kashmir lay in its

independence' and that Abdullah 'should work towards that end'.[136] Although Abdullah doesn't state how he responded to Shah or what his stance about Kashmir was in Pakistan, the idea of independence for J&K was clearly still on the agenda for some J&K-ites. However, according to Indian intelligence, Abdullah got no encouragement in Pakistan for his 'pet idea of an independent Kashmir'.[137] His visit ended suddenly on 27 May when Nehru died while Abdullah was in Muzaffarabad, the capital of Pakistan-Administered Azad Kashmir. Distraught, Abdullah returned to India the next day for his longstanding friend's funeral. For Abdullah, Nehru's death had been 'sheer bad luck for Kashmir' as the Indian had finally made up his mind 'to solve the Kashmir problem once and for all'.[138] On what specific terms, Abdullah either didn't know or wasn't saying. Presumably, it would have involved some degree of genuine autonomy or semi-independence for Indian J&K and some type of access for Pakistan to Kashmir.[139]

Abdullah: after Nehru

The death of Jawaharlal Nehru marked the beginning of the end of Sheikh Abdullah's attempts to try to provide his state with an international option other than being with India. After Nehru's death, Abdullah's mission to Pakistan quickly floundered due to a lack of high-level support. Thereafter, despite his best efforts, the combination of India, Indians and subcontinental circumstances would ensure that the Kashmir dispute continued. Increasingly, Abdullah confronted less Nehruvian, more obdurate Indians not able, or willing, to understand or discuss either J&K's geo-political circumstances or the aspirations of some J&K-ites not to be with India. Ultimately, Abdullah would have to compromise significantly on his desires for J&K's independence, and even on his desires for the state's genuine autonomy within India, as supposedly had been guaranteed by Article 370 of the Indian Constitution. Ironically, his compromise would be made with Nehru's daughter, Indira Gandhi.

In 1965, Sheikh Abdullah took some time out – a gap year, if you like. In February, he undertook the Haj, after which he travelled to various other places, including Egypt, Algeria, Paris and London. As a result of some political and diplomatic issues while he was overseas, Abdullah again displeased New Delhi. In particular, he met and conversed in Algeria with China's Prime Minister, Chou En-lai. For some Indians, this meeting was lamentable, given China's defeat of India in their short 1962 border war and given that 'feelings over the Chinese aggression were still fresh'.[140] Abdullah and Chou, along with Mirza Afzal Beg, discussed India–China relations and the China–Pakistan agreement 'over the Gilgit border'.[141] (In March 1963, Pakistan had ceded the Shaksgam tract in far northern J&K to China's control.)[142] Supposedly, Abdullah didn't discuss with Chou the Kashmir dispute or his political desires for J&K. He then gave a 'detailed report' of his meeting with Chou En-lai to the Indian Ambassador in Algeria for forwarding to the Ministry of External Affairs, New Delhi.[143] Later in London where he was meeting many Kashmiri communities, Abdullah was told to return to India or his passport would be cancelled. On his return to India on 8 May, Abdullah was arrested by the Indian Government – not the J&K Government, for a change – under the Defence of India Rules.[144] This occurred in the tense period of the build-up towards the 1965 India–Pakistan war. Abdullah was then detained at Kodaikanal in south India for almost three years.[145] As Bhattacharjea notes,[146] Abdullah could have taken 'official refuge' in a number of countries, including Pakistan, which might have caused India far more problems than re-incarcerating him.

Shortly before his return to India, the prestigious *Foreign Affairs* journal published an article by Sheikh Abdullah titled 'Kashmir, India and Pakistan'.[147] This also impacted negatively on him. The article confirmed that Abdullah was not reconciled to J&K being with India and that he was seriously seeking other options, mostly probably independence. In the article, Abdullah stated that Hari Singh had desired independence for J&K, with India and Pakistan to guarantee this. He repeated Ayyangar's 1948 statements about J&K's option to 'withdraw' from its accession to India and accede to Pakistan or stay independent and that independence was 'the best solution to the Kashmir issue'.[148] He restated four resolution options suggested by the National Conference's Working Committee in 1953: a plebiscite for all of J&K, but also with the option of independence; independence for J&K; independence for J&K, with India–Pakistan jointly controlling foreign affairs; and, the Dixon plan: a plebiscite only for Kashmir, but with an option for independence. Abdullah stated that three 'distinguished leaders of Indian public opinion' – Rajagopalachari, Jayaprakash Narayan and Shiva Rao, who were no longer part of the Congress establishment – suggested a negotiated settlement that might involve 'independence for Kashmir', with the United Nations guaranteeing its defence, or J&K becoming a UN trustee for ten years, followed by a UN plebiscite with options to join India, Pakistan or be independent, or an India–Pakistan confederation with Kashmir as a constituent unit. Significantly, Abdullah also stated that, as a result of Indian attempts to erode Article 370 and impose the Indian Constitution on J&K, there had 'been a demonstrable diminution of the faith which the people of Kashmir had pinned on India'.[149]

In his article, Abdullah did not state what status he personally wanted for J&K. He noted that dialogue was important, a mediator might prove useful, and that an open mind would help so that 'by a process of elimination' a solution acceptable 'by and large' to J&K-ites, Pakistan and India could be found. Should J&K-ites choose to leave India, which may have been Abdullah's inferred and preferred solution, he hopefully reiterated what Nehru had said on 26 June and 7 August 1952: J&K's accession to India had been 'complete in law and in fact' but if J&K-ites wanted to leave India, so be it: 'We [Indians] want no forced marriages, no forced unions like this'. This, of course, was no longer India's position by 1965: India was clearly not prepared to let J&K leave India. In Abdullah's final three sentences, he expressed a collective hope and prayer that, because J&K-ites had suffered so much, 'wiser counsels will prevail and that the two countries will speedily seek a way out of this impasse'.[150] This suggests that Abdullah knew that neither he, nor J&K-ites, could, or would resolve the Kashmir dispute – it was up to India and Pakistan. As for them doing this 'speedily', haste has never been a priority in this dispute.

After being detained at Kodaikanal for almost three years, the Indian Government finally and permanently released India's 'most famous political prisoner' unconditionally from detention on 2 January 1968. Sheikh Abdullah was freed partly because democratic India was embarrassed internationally by 'having to adopt such extraordinary measures to isolate the Kashmiri leader from his following'. A second reason was that India's Preventive Detention Act under which he had been detained was about to lapse.[151] A third reason was that, by 1968, India felt confident of its hold over, and control in, J&K. When interviewed post-release by the press, Abdullah refused to commit to any specific solution to the Kashmir issue. He was then asked a pointed question by a journalist about whether he had been 'going to declare Kashmir completely independent from India on August 21, 1953' but could not do so because he had been arrested and dismissed from office. Abdullah replied that the charge was 'completely baseless'. He added that his arrest fifteen years ago had been due to differences with the Indian Government which was 'going back on promises made to me and the people of Kashmir'. Later, Abdullah blamed his 1953 dismissal on communalists, corrupt colleagues and Communists, with the latter wanting their man, G. M. Sadiq, to be in control of J&K, rather than Bakshi Ghulam Muhammad.[152] Abdullah's interest in 'the people of Kashmir' would remain a theme that ran strongly throughout his political career, as would his dislike of 'obnoxious' communalism.[153]

The issue of 'self-determination'

By the time Sheikh Abdullah was released from detention in January 1968, much had happened both in India and J&K. In India, Nehru was dead, while the successor government appeared to be more interested in J&K's constitutional, not emotional, integration into India.[154] The 1965 India–Pakistan war had been fought and drawn, with Pakistan failing to capture J&K despite using covert means and with Muslim Kashmiris supporting India, not Pakistan, and with the USSR brokering the post-war Tashkent Agreement between both nations in January 1966. After the untimely death of India's Prime Minister, Lal Bahadur Shastri, in Tashkent, Indira Gandhi had become the new Prime Minister of India, although she was yet to consolidate her position. Post-war, India's position on the Kashmir dispute had hardened and the issue had been 'pushed to the background'.[155] Similarly, the UN Security Council, which had discussed the 'India–Pakistan Question' 110 times by 1964,[156] stopped trying to resolve this issue after 1965.[157] In 1967, General Ayub released his auto-biography *Friends not Masters* in which he dismissed as 'absurd' an India–Pakistan–Kashmir confederation discussed with Sheikh Abdullah in 1964.[158] Concurrently, Ayub's unpopularity started to increase, as did the popularity of the charismatic Pakistani politician, Zulfiqar Ali Bhutto, partly due to Ayub's duplicitous role in the disastrous 1965 India–Pakistan war that, if nothing else, lost Pakistan further 'moral high ground' to India. As for Sheikh Abdullah, he was again out of jail after 'two years, nine months and twenty-four days' of detention.[159]

Within J&K, there also had been changes. In 1967, Karan Singh had relocated to New Delhi and joined Mrs Gandhi's Cabinet. An Indian had replaced Singh as Governor of J&K, with this nomenclature having been changed from 'Sadar-i-Riyasat' to 'Governor' in March 1965. Politically, the pro-India *apparatchik* and Abdullah's former colleague, G. M. Sadiq, was Chief Minister of J&K. He led the state (*pradesh*) branch of the Congress Party, which was formally launched in J&K on 26 January 1965[160] and into which the National Conference had been merged.[161] Despite the locally popular stance of self-determination for J&K-ites, India had long reneged on its commitment to have a plebiscite held in J&K.[162] Similarly, India was totally opposed to independence for J&K and to the establishment of an India–Pakistan condominium. Instead, India wanted its part of J&K for itself – and to be fully integrated into itself.[163] New Delhi also felt confident of its control of Indian J&K, which Pakistani forces had been unable to wrest from it in 1965. Conversely, Abdullah was seriously disenchanted with India. Asked whether he accepted that his state was an integral part of India, he responded that it was only India's armed strength that was holding Kashmir, which meant that India had 'hold on the bodies only – not the souls' of Kashmiris. It was not 'a true accession – accession can only be attained by trust and friendship'.[164] This response was disconcerting, at least for Indians: Abdullah clearly was not an Indian by inclination. He also was on shaky ground: in 1967, the Indian Parliament had passed its 'Unlawful Activities Prevention Act', as a result of which 'anyone found guilty of questioning India's sovereignty over territory to which it has established official claim' could be imprisoned.[165] This Act apparently was one reason why New Delhi had agreed to allow Abdullah to be released – if he transgressed, he could quickly be rearrested and silenced.[166]

Sheikh Abdullah's release in 1968 meant that he was physically free and more able to make political statements. He again focused on 'the ideal of self-determination' for 'Kashmiris'.[167] Early in January, when a journalist bluntly stated that the people of Kashmir had already exercised the right of self-determination, Abdullah correctly answered that 'If that [right] had been exercised, then there would be no dispute'.[168] Addressing a group of 'Kashmiri traders' in New Delhi on 12 January, he told them that 'only Kashmiris can decide the future of Kashmir' and that Kashmiris were demanding rights they had been promised previously: 'Kashmir for the Kashmiris! Self-determination is the right of the Kashmir masses!' were their popular slogans. Surprisingly, Abdullah told the traders that Kashmiris had been denied this right 'long ago', which was why, in 1931, they had started their anti-Maharaja agitation.[169] On 4 March, he told a huge and emotional crowd in Srinagar that there was 'no question of a compromise on the right of self-determination for Kashmir'.[170] On 6 March, he stated at a press conference in Srinagar that 'The fundamental issue is that the people of Kashmir should be enabled to have a sense of participation'.[171] While Abdullah was revising history in relation to the events of 1931, his promotion of self-determination in 1968 was not new: it reflected the Plebiscite Front's stance which he had been unable to propagate while being detained. It had also been a longstanding policy of 'his' National Conference. In 1945, the first resolution at the party's annual session in Sopore concerned 'the right of self-determination': that the people of J&K needed to decide J&K's international status.[172]

Practically speaking, the Plebiscite Front had kept the issue of J&K's international status on the political agenda while Abdullah was mostly in, and sometimes out, of detention. However, there may have been more to this pursuit of self-determination than met the eye. For Bazaz, Abdullah pursued this option to atone for 'a sense of sin' because he had 'forced' J&K to join India, had 'mercilessly suppressed'

Muslims, and had 'invited non-Muslim armies to assist him in this atrocious task'.[173] Pursuing self-determination made Abdullah appear to be a man of the people and a democrat. Equally, he may simply have been trying to create problems for India internally and externally, particularly with the United Nations and member nations.[174] Either way, the Plebiscite Front quickly developed into a force to be reckoned with,[175] having nearly 700,000 'basic members'.[176] Bazaz, writing in 1965 after 'study tours' to J&K in 1962 and 1964, stated that the Plebiscite Front was the strongest opposition force in J&K, with its popularity due largely to people's 'frustration and … resentment' with the J&K Government.[177] It was 'generally believed' that the Plebiscite Front wanted 'an independent Kashmir but … the party … [was] not averse to the Valley joining Pakistan'.[178] The former 'belief' was likely, given Abdullah's seemingly unrequited desires for independence; the latter perception was rather odd, given Abdullah's long and general dislike of Pakistan. Another of Abdullah's rivals, Ghulam Mohiuddin Qara (Karra), founder of the Kashmir Political Conference in June 1953, was unequivocal: he preferred 'to see Kashmir achieving an independent status'.[179] Interestingly, while Abdullah, Beg and the Plebiscite Front promoted self-determination for J&K-ites, this party boycotted the 1967 J&K elections because of 'alleged harassment and interference' by the Government.[180] Such 'interference' may have been true, given Bakshi's double entendre about the 1962 elections: 'You will cast your votes; but we will count them'.[181]

On occasions throughout 1968, Sheikh Abdullah also mentioned the option of independence for J&K. At his *alma mater*, Aligarh Muslim University, he reiterated on 19 January that, in 1947, India's princely states had had the right 'to accede to India or Pakistan or stay independent'. He said twice that 'the people of Kashmir' could decide whether 'to accede to India or Pakistan or remain independent'.[182] On 10 March,[183] speaking at Hazratbal, he again mentioned independence as an option for J&K. Indeed, he used the term 'independent' on three occasions. The first related to 1947 when the subcontinent was being divided: Abdullah said he had 'pleaded' then that it was for J&K-ites to decide whether to accede to India or Pakistan, or to remain independent. He repeated Ayyangar's 1948 statement that Indians would have no objections 'if Kashmir decided to remain independent'. His third mention was the most provocative: 'Kashmir is our country, and … we have the right to decide its future': to join India, Pakistan, or be 'independent'. Assertively, even aggressively, Abdullah then said that no nation in the world, including India and Pakistan, 'can prevent us from deciding this matter as we deem fit'. Realistically, however, Abdullah knew that this would be difficult to achieve. Possibly inspired by Hazratbal's sanctity, 'May God make our task easy!', he beseeched.

But Abdullah was difficult to pin down. In January 1968, he gave confusing answers to a journalist's questions about the Kashmir dispute. Surprisingly, Abdullah felt that a plebiscite could resolve this issue if there was 'general agreement on it'.[184] This suggested that he was prepared for J&K to join 'feudal' Pakistan, then still in the 'box seat' to win, a position that may have satisfied younger Kashmiris but which would have put the Kashmiri identity and Abdullah's socialist programme in doubt.[185] Equally, Abdullah knew that the plebiscite was never likely to be held, so was on safe ground. Later, Abdullah was asked if he subscribed to possible international control of Kashmir involving India and Pakistan and with internal independence for Kashmir. Dismissively, he said that 'complete freedom' was not the 'proper solution'. Open discussions and 'mutual give and take' were needed, after which something would 'be forthcoming'.[186] Later again and still thinking about 'international control of Kashmir', Abdullah stated that he was 'not in favour of complete independence for Kashmir either, because Kashmir can't defend itself'. It was always a challenge to understand whether Abdullah said what he meant and meant what he said. He was 'a truly enigmatic figure'.[187]

By 1968, Sheikh Abdullah was keeping 'Kashmir experts ... guessing'.[188] One Indian commentator considered that Abdullah's lack of specificity was a tactic and that he really was a Kashmiri nationalist 'guided solely by the consideration of advancing the cause of Kashmir's independence'.[189] Later, a US journalist noted that Abdullah's 'ambiguity' was because he was trying to satisfy his 'sentimental following, revering him as something of a religious figure and a martyr' while appealing to younger, more militant Kashmiris who favoured joining Pakistan and would have voted to join it had a plebiscite been held in 1969.[190] For Abdullah, promoting self-determination was a useful populist device that enabled him to challenge democratic India while ensuring that he didn't need to directly state that he wanted J&K to be independent. And, when promoting self-determination, he was on reasonably safe ground with India and his followers; if he specifically suggested anything other than J&K being with India, he was on shaky ground. Possibly, J&K-ites could read between the lines, particularly those disenchanted with India – predominantly, those displeased comprised Muslim Kashmiris.

The Jammu and Kashmir State People's Conventions

In October 1968, Sheikh Abdullah was allowed to hold a remarkable event in Srinagar: the Jammu and Kashmir State People's Convention.[191] Its aim was 'to seek a solution of the Kashmir issue'.[192] However, 'Implicit in the declared objective of the convention', as Mir Qasim noted, 'was the rejection of the finality of Kashmir's accession to India'.[193] This made the broad-based convention extraordinary: Abdullah and the attendees were allowed to float ideas about J&K's international status other than this state being an integral part of India. Some of J&K's 'big names' attended: Bakshi Ghulam Mohammad; Mirwaiz Maulvi Mohammad Farooq; Balraj Puri; Prem Nath Bazaz; Mirza Afzal Beg; Mohi-ud-Din Karra; Maulana Masoodi.[194] Other delegates attended from the Plebiscite Front, National Conference, Political Conference, Awami Action Committee, Jammu Autonomy Forum, and the Communist Party of India.[195] Chief Minister Sadiq did not attend, considering the event to be 'wholly misconceived' and 'an exercise in futility'. National and local elements of the pro-India Congress and the rival Jana Sangh also avoided the Convention, as indeed did most Indians. Both groups publicly pronounced beforehand that the J&K's accession to India 'was final and irrevocable',[196] a proclamation prevalent among Indians and pro-India J&K-ites post-Nehru and the 1965 war. Similarly, Jayaprakash Narayan, who delivered the inaugural address, stressed, to Sheikh Abdullah's chagrin and despite their close friendship, the need to find a solution 'within the framework of the Indian Union', which similarly meant that J&K was part of India.[197] A later unanimous resolution regretted that India 'had not allowed delegates from across the cease-fire line to attend'.[198] Supposedly, forty-seven delegates had intended to come.[199] Abdullah had 'no doubt' that their participation would have helped deliberations.[200] Perhaps it didn't matter. For one J&K-ite then living in Karachi, Sheikh Abdullah was already 'representing the views of an overwhelming majority of the people of Jammu and Kashmir living on both sides of the cease-fire line'.[201] Equally, some saw him as acting 'in unison' with Pakistan.[202]

The People's Convention met for eight days during 10–17 October 1968.[203] On day one, Sheikh Abdullah was elected Chairman. While he continued to promote 'the importance of self-determination' for J&K-ites,[204] his proposed solution was that of independence, as suggested in his 1965 *Foreign Affairs* article, copies of which Abdullah circulated at the Convention. This proposal was reported as entailing 'a plebiscite on accession or independence with joint control (of India and Pakistan) on foreign affairs and defence and the Dixon plan for a limited plebiscite in the valley'.[205] Of the other 260 Convention delegates, sixty-four recommended solutions to the Kashmir problem: '30 speakers supported a plebiscite without pressing for a specific outcome, 18 stressed the need to find a solution within the framework of the Indian federation, 14 favored independence, and two called for the accession of Jammu and Kashmir State to Pakistan'.[206] Fazili claims there were 'fifty-one suggestions': eighteen favoured accession to India; sixteen wanted independence; six suggested being under UN supervision; eleven wanted accession to Pakistan.

Ultimately, with the People's Convention unable to agree a final resolution, there were 'no tangible results'.[207] The organisers decided that 'further time was needed to prepare the way'[208] and the Convention unanimously resolved that a second session would be held. Thereafter, a twelve-member Steering Committee deliberated.[209] On 7 December 1968, it established a Sub-Committee to scrutinise, summarise and tabulate the first session's various papers and speeches. Its high-powered members comprised Mirza Afzal Beg, a Kashmiri Muslim; Balraj Puri, a Jammu Hindu; and, Prem Nath Bazaz, a Kashmiri Hindu. On 17 February 1969, the Sub-Committee delivered its Evaluation Report.[210] It made interesting reading. The report divided into six categories the various 'Proposals and Suggestions' received at the first session of the People's Convention. Essentially, these categories comprised: 1) a plebiscite; 2) accession to India; 3) accession to Pakistan; 4) independence for J&K; 5) interim arrangements; 6) others.[211] The report did not provide any details about the number of proposals and suggestions received, nor the specific numbers in each category.

The Evaluation Report's fourth category, which was titled 'Independence for the State', revealed that some J&K-ites had been seriously considering independence for J&K. This category suggested four possibilities for this state. The first was a federal republic comprising six semi-autonomous units: Kashmir (i.e., Kashmir Valley), Azad Kashmir, Jammu Plains, Jammu Hills, Northern Territories and Ladakh. Apart from Kashmir, each unit would have the immediate right to secede and join India or Pakistan. Kashmir would be under UN supervision for ten to twenty years. If people then rejected independence in a plebiscite, they would vote on acceding to India or Pakistan. The second possibility was an independent J&K as it had existed before August 1947, that is, as it had existed under Maharaja Hari Singh's rule. The third was an independent state comprising Jammu, Kashmir and Ladakh – which regions already comprised Indian J&K. The fourth possibility was an independent state comprising Indian J&K but with a federal structure.[212] Presumably, this federal structure was included in order to dilute the existing Kashmiri domination of Indian J&K. These four possibilities provided a rare articulation of an envisaged independent J&K.

Additionally and significantly, however, the Sub-Committee of the Steering Committee produced a document that was a proposed internal constitution for an independent J&K as it had existed before August 1947.[213] This 'Internal Constitutional Set-up (Broad Outlines)' suggested that the 'State of Jammu and Kashmir' would comprise three administrative units: Kashmir; Jammu; Frontier *Illaqa* (Districts). It would have an independent judiciary, a Legislative Assembly and an advisory 'Upper House'. Each administrative unit would be divided into 'zones' (districts), 'blocks' (tehsils) and '*panchayat*' (village) levels, with elected representatives and functions designated for each level. Interestingly, the 'Broad Outlines' document did not detail any law and order or policing matters, nor mention defence, foreign affairs or inter-state relations. Nevertheless, this proposed constitution, coupled with the Evaluation Report's 'Independence for the State' category, confirmed there had been serious contemplations and discussions about an envisaged independent Jammu and Kashmir State by some senior J&K-ites.

The second session of the J&K State People's Convention was held in Srinagar during 8–10 June 1970. Again, no participants from Pakistan-Administered J&K were allowed to attend, although some delegates from 'the other side' sent papers, with one J&K-ite living in Rawalpindi suggesting that a 'supreme council' be established under Sheikh Abdullah's stewardship to administer J&K for ten years.[214] Seemingly, Abdullah enjoyed considerable popularity across the border. In between the two sessions, however, he had publicly ruled out an 'Independent Kashmir' in October 1969, noting that 'instead of guaranteeing the peace, [it] would only create more difficulties'.[215] Nevertheless, for the Indian press, Abdullah was 'still for independence'.[216] He was 'still publicly committed to self-determination',[217] although he also apparently 'admitted that he had made a mistake' by agreeing to J&K's accession to India in 1947.[218] As usual, what Abdullah actually wanted or meant were uncertain. The second session, as per the first, received little press coverage. Abdullah himself was still under 'immense suspicion', particularly for 'a little too consistently preaching friendship with Pakistan'.[219]

A major incident occurred at the second session when Abdullah was challenged by the respected Jammu-based journalist, Ved Bhasin. He accused Abdullah of 'staging a "volte face" on the Kashmir issue after having committed the State to accession to India in 1947'. Abdullah responded angrily that he had supported the accession 'in good faith', but Nehru had wanted to make 'Kashmir a colony of India', had gone back on his commitments to the UNSC, and had undemocratically jailed him. After telling delegates that Kashmir should have the right for independence', Abdullah stated: 'We will not get freedom by sitting on the laps of either India or Pakistan. No one will give it to us – we will have to wrest it. ... This we will do as India did from the British and as the Algerians did from France [eight years before in 1962].' Otherwise and rather dramatically, Abdullah said that 'India can rule over our dead bodies only – and not over our hearts'.[220] Seemingly, he had taken up the mood of younger, and increasingly more impatient, Kashmiri delegates who had demanded at the first session that 'It is the whole of Kashmir [we want] either by ballot or bullet'.[221]

Despite the work of the Convention's two sessions and of the high-powered Beg-Puri-Bazaz Sub-Committee, little was achieved, apart from some documents being produced. Sheikh Abdullah spoke of no positive or decisive outcomes, except insipidly stating that the Convention 'resulted in lessening the social and personal tensions prevalent among the people'.[222] As one newspaper editorial noted, the Convention 'largely' reflected his 'personal dilemma[s]' since his 1968 release: to keep himself in 'the public eye' without antagonising the authorities; to use the Plebiscite Front's platform while placating communal and pro-Pakistan elements; to contain the 'communal and disruptive forces' in Kashmir without engaging his secular former colleagues; and, to stem demands for Pakistan while not siding with India.[223] Not unexpectedly, a third session proposed for autumn 1970 did not occur.[224] Possibly, this was a reaction to general disinterest: the Congress governments in India and in J&K had not supported either previous session; Pakistan seemed disinterested; some J&K-ites had become disenchanted after their pro-India or pro-Pakistan views were stifled by 'dissatisfied' anti-India elements who comprised the bulk of attendees.[225] Additionally, there had been serious negativity in India where some Indians (unrealistically) had expected that Convention participants 'might opt for more autonomy within the Indian Union' and were angry when, instead, strong anti-India feelings emerged.[226] Finally, as Fazili noted, the People's Convention had 'neither any legal nor any political sanctity'. They seemingly weren't very important, given that his book didn't even mention the Convention's second session.[227]

In terms of altering J&K's international status, the J&K State People's Convention was a total failure. Its only achievements were to provide some indications of what J&K-ites desired for J&K's international status, and the very fact that its two sessions had actually gone ahead. Possibly, they were allowed to proceed because Indira Gandhi was then in a relatively weak political position, or because there was some Indian idealism to 'do the right thing', or because Jayaprakash Narayan was influential and outspoken. Possibly, Chief Minister Sadiq allowed the sessions to proceed to appease his former colleague, Sheikh Abdullah, who was still a 'formidable force' in Kashmir, and to allow people, including the many influential attendees, 'to let off steam'. This reflected Sadiq's 'liberalisation policy – a policy giving everyone freedom of speech and movement' which he had instituted in 1964 on attaining power, thereby ending Bakshi's 'reign of terror'.[228] Sadiq may also have been unwell, given that he died in office on 12 December 1971 aged fifty-nine,[229] or he may have been distracted by his ongoing 'power struggle' with Mir Qasim, which began in 1968.[230] After Sadiq's death, Qasim took over as Chief Minister of J&K.

The People's Convention marked the high point in Sheikh Abdullah's attempts to change J&K's international status. After its 1970 session, events compelled him to move slowly but surely into accepting New Delhi's dominance of J&K and of him. This process had started imperceptibly around 1968 after his release from detention; it peaked in 1971. Following the 1965 India–Pakistan war and Pakistan's failure to foment rebellion in Kashmir or to militarily capture this region, a resilient India more certain of its capabilities in J&K had become inflexible on the Kashmir dispute. By 1968, New Delhi had also consolidated India's position in J&K during Abdullah's detention by steadily integrating the state politically, administratively and economically into India. By 1970, Pakistan was distracted by serious internal problems, particularly with Bengalis in East Pakistan. Therefore, following the conclusion of the People's Convention's second session and with Abdullah still committed to self-determination, his focus returned to the Plebiscite Front. It wanted to contest Lok Sabha elections to be held in J&K in March 1971. Sadiq prevented this by declaring the Plebiscite Front to be an 'illegal organization'. It was formally banned on 12 January 1971.[231] Abdullah was not allowed to enter J&K, which kept him physically and somewhat politically remote from his constituents. Even so, he had sufficient influence in Kashmir to help a supposedly independent candidate, Shamim Ahmad Shamim, win a Lok Sabha seat from Kashmir against the Congress's sitting candidate, the high-profile Bakshi Ghulam Mohammad.[232]

Perhaps most significantly, by 1970 Sheikh Abdullah was (inevitably) aging. By then, the sixty-five-year-old had high blood pressure and diabetes; he had been struggling politically in, and for, J&K, for almost forty years; he had been incarcerated for most of the previous seventeen years. Almost certainly, he had also realised that J&K would never obtain independence, as it briefly had in 1947, or that India would limit its control to foreign affairs, defence and communications, as per the Maharaja's accession and Article 370 of the Indian Constitution, or that J&K would revert to pre-1953 times when he was the pre-eminent politician in a largely autonomous state. J&K's circumstances had changed – irrevocably. By 1970, the Plebiscite Front's 'third alternative' of self-determination was popular with moderates, partly because it provided a middle path between irreconcilable and strongly pro-India and pro-Pakistan parties.[233] However, if this alternative actually meant giving J&K-ites a vote on their state's international status, it was uncertain how many Kashmiris – or, indeed, if Abdullah himself – seriously wanted J&K to join Pakistan via such a plebiscite, particularly given Pakistan's negative role in 1947, and more recently in the 1965 war and with its increasing political problems in 1970. Equally, it was uncertain how many Kashmiris wanted to remain with India.

By 1970, Sheikh Abdullah also confronted political challenges within J&K. The Plebiscite Front, while popular in Kashmir, was disliked by New Delhi. J&K's adherence to secularism had been seriously questioned at the second People's Convention by 'a large number of delegates', mainly Muslims led by the Jamaat-e-Islami, particularly in the light of some anti-Muslim communalism in India.[234] There were 'disturbing signs' of the rise of impatient, militant Kashmiri youth,[235] and of pro-Pakistan groups appearing. These latter included the Awami Action Committee, formed in 1963 around the *Moe-e-Muqaddas* incident,[236] and the Jamaat-e-Islami, formed in 1953 and 'wielding great influence in the valley'.[237] They offered other possibilities – chiefly for J&K to join Pakistan – than mainstream Kashmiri politicians and their continuing support for, and dependence on, India. Since his release in 1968, Abdullah had wanted 'to act as a bridge between India and Pakistan',[238] which was partly why he had organised the People's Convention. The attempted bridge-building had gone nowhere, however. Given these various factors, Mrs Gandhi felt that it was 'conceivable' that Sheikh Abdullah might be 'willing to soften his stand' in relation to the matter of Kashmir's status.[239] Interestingly, her position strengthened as Abdullah's post-1968 political position weakened.

1971 and beyond

In 1971, two significant events ensured Indira Gandhi's dominance over Sheikh Abdullah and ended his pretensions of wanting independence for Kashmir. First, in March, her faction of the Congress Party won a conclusive election victory that changed many things in India. For a start, she completely and significantly sidelined the 'old guard' of Congress and ensured her position both as leader of her faction and as India's Prime Minister. Indeed, her party's victory temporarily made her politically unassailable. Later, in December, under her strong, patient and courageous leadership, India defeated Pakistan in their third war, the result of which was the loss to Pakistan of 'its' eastern wing, the creation of the new state of Bangladesh, and India's humiliation for Pakistan of capturing some 90,000 Pakistani prisoners of war. There was also some fighting in J&K in which India's forces apparently did better.[240] India's decisive victory in 1971 added to Gandhi's reputation and standing.

It gave her a strong mandate and motivation to take on various issues and personalities, including her father's friend, Sheikh Abdullah.

In relation to J&K, the 1971 India–Pakistan war marked three important watersheds. First, the post-war India–Pakistan Simla Accord, which Prime Minister Indira Gandhi and President Zulfiqar Ali Bhutto signed in July 1972, ensured that, thereafter, the Kashmir dispute would be a bilateral issue between both nations, only. There would be no third party involvement, including that of the UNSC. This created the second watershed: a plebiscite for J&K 'receded into history'.[241] (Possibly, India might have won a poll in 1972, given Muslim J&K-ites' shock at Pakistani brutalities against fellow Muslim Bengalis.)[242] Third, the 1971 war confirmed for many J&K-ites and Pakistanis that a now much weakened Pakistan could not militarily liberate, let alone capture, J&K, including the prized Kashmir Valley from India. Equally, many J&K-ites realised that India's resolve was such that it was not prepared to 'give an inch' of territory to Pakistan in those parts of J&K that India physically controlled, especially the Kashmir Valley. India was now pre-eminent, strategically and militarily. Therefore, the 1971 India–Pakistan war changed matters in the subcontinent significantly for many people, including for all J&K-ites. It was only after, and because of, this war that Abdullah finally began to accept 'the harsh realities of the situation' of both India's strategic and political dominance[243] and the irrelevance of the plebiscite.[244] In May 1972, an older and politically tired Sheikh Abdullah and a younger and politically empowered Indira Gandhi, through their respective intermediaries, began to negotiate their own agreement to resolve their differences. This would finally clarify their understandings of the Kashmir–India relationship.

With no whiff of independence now existing, Sheikh Abdullah developed a new and pragmatic stance. Seemingly, he had finally come to grips with the circumstance that Kashmir was unlikely to 'escape' from India's stranglehold. A former senior Indian civil servant, Yezdezard Dinshaw Gundevia, ably articulated Abdullah's post-1971 stance on the Kashmir dispute: 'Kashmir's accession to India stands, but it was based on the Instrument of Accession; and its subsequent ratification by the Kashmir Constituent Assembly was based on the Delhi Agreement, which limited the powers of the Government of India to three subjects, Defence, External Affairs and Communication'.[245] Similarly, Abdullah 'assured' New Delhi that there were no differences regarding J&K's accession. He 'only wanted Article 370 to be maintained in its original [less interventionist] form'.[246] Or 'I had no quarrel with the centre regarding the accession. My contention was over the extent of the accession.'[247] His hope was for J&K to enjoy full autonomy within the Indian

Union, a special status that Article 370 supposedly sanctified. By 1971, however, Abdullah's hope was purely aspirational. Article 370 had been slowly and steadily diluted, even negated, since the Indian Constitution first became operative in 1950. By 1975, it was largely symbolic: J&K had lost much of its autonomy and specialness and was now tied closely to India. Furthermore, for New Delhi and as per the Indian Constitution, this article was temporary, although Abdullah was 'assured', possibly by the morally powerful but politically unempowered Jayaprakash Narayan, that Article 370 would be 'permanently retained'.[248] Nevertheless, the ever increasing expectation of Indian politicians was (and still is) that J&K would be fully integrated into India.

While accepting that independence for J&K was now impossible, Sheikh Abdullah was nevertheless still keen to try and ensure the state's autonomy. Optimistically and ambitiously, he told Mir Qasim in 1972 that, in relation to restoring Article 370 in full, he would review, and possibly amend, the various changes made to the J&K Constitution and the laws passed by the 'Central Legislature' in New Delhi since 1953 that applied to J&K which he found 'repugnant to the interest of the State'.[249] Similarly, he would review the role of entities such as the (Indian) Supreme Court and the (Indian) Election Commission, whose jurisdiction now extended to J&K. These matters would require 'arduous' negotiations by Abdullah's close colleague, Mirza Afzal Beg, and the Indian official, G. Parthasarathy, who were negotiating on behalf of Abdullah and Mrs Gandhi and who later both signed the actual agreement. (Parthasarathy, a 'well-known intellectual with a liberal outlook', was the son of Gopalaswami Ayyangar.)[250] Presumably, their 'principals',[251] Abdullah and Gandhi, used interlocutors as Mrs Gandhi was a busy woman. Equally, Abdullah found her remote and uncommunicable, which was possibly because she was insistent that, constitutionally, 'the clock could not be put back' to 1953 when Abdullah had last been in power, but which Abdullah had been 'very anxious' should happen.[252] The successful outcome of their interlocutors' almost three-year negotiation from May 1972 to February 1975 was the Kashmir Accord,[253] popularly called 'the Indira-Sheikh Accord'.[254]

For Sheikh Abdullah, the 1975 Kashmir Accord 'marked the beginning of a new phase in our political movement'. Others were less positive. The Accord enabled Abdullah to return to J&K as its Chief Minister.[255] In February, the incumbent, Mir Qasim, graciously stood aside for the more senior Kashmiri leader. Abdullah agreed to the Kashmir Accord even though it did not satisfy all of his demands, particularly in relation to Article 370's full restoration, and despite having strong contrary views about J&K's involvement with India, and vice versa. Bigheartedly,

Abdullah again 'sacrificed' his political life 'for the public cause'.[256] He chose 'responsibility' over 'escape'.[257] However, the Kashmir Accord made him appear weak and opportunistic.[258] It 'dented' his reputation, with many of his supporters 'distancing themselves from his compromise' with Mrs Gandhi.[259] The 'chorus of protest' in Kashmir was that Abdullah had 'sold out' Kashmiris' interests in order to obtain the Chief Ministership.[260] Almost overnight, he went from supporting self-determination for Kashmiris to subordination to New Delhi. Meanwhile, Abdullah claimed that serving in such a position was 'only a means to implement convictions and not an end in itself'.[261] The issue was how much autonomy he could extract from, or assert against, New Delhi: 'the quantum of accession, not the accession itself'.[262] This was a post facto justification for the Kashmir Accord. Some of his rivals, like Mirwaiz Maulvi Farooq of the Awami Action Committee, opposed Abdullah's return to power. For them, New Delhi's excessive focus on Abdullah reflected Sadiq's earlier criticism that there was an 'impression that the only voice that comes out of Kashmir is Sheikh Abdullah's'.[263]

Sheikh Abdullah agreed to the Kashmir Accord, not because he necessarily craved fame and political power. Rather, he did so, as he then saw matters, because of the 'fast deteriorating condition of the State' and the need to save it 'from utter collapse'.[264] Equally, after Pakistan's defeat in 1971, Abdullah had few other options but to acquiesce, particularly as the Simla Agreement's stress on bilateralism had rendered the plebiscite unnecessary. On 24 February 1975, Abdullah was unanimously elected the leader of the Congress Party, which 'created a precedent in Indian legislative history': it was 'the first time that a party with an absolute majority in the legislature had elected a non-party man as its leader'.[265] On 25 February in Jammu, Abdullah and three others were sworn in: he as Chief Minister; Mirza Afzal Beg as Deputy Chief Minister; and Devi Dass Thakur, from Jammu, and Sonam Narboo, from Ladakh, as Ministers.[266] None was a member of the J&K Legislative Assembly, a factor that made some observers consider this 'transfer of power' to be 'as undemocratic and unparliamentary' as his dismissal in 1953.[267] Particularly 'sad and sullen' were those J&K-ites who had previously deserted Abdullah politically and/or who would be 'divested of their powers, their efficacy and the offices they had held for decades'[268] after the 'Sheikh's capture of power' in 1975.[269] Abdullah had returned to power, but not to unequivocal popularity.

As a result of the Kashmir Accord, Sheikh Abdullah 'accepted the finality of [the] accession'[270] and agreed that J&K was an integral part of India, to which nation and its leader he offered his 'whole-hearted co-operation'.[271] For Abdullah, the 'dialogue' with Mrs Gandhi and her colleagues had 'rendered' the need for a plebiscite in J&K 'irrelevant' and had re-established 'trust and confidence' in the J&K–India relationship 'born out of shared ideals and common objectives which were there all through until 1953'.[272] As Mrs Gandhi saw things: 'Sheikh Abdullah has started [sic] in clear terms that the future of Jammu and Kashmir lies with India', which nation and its ideals she was confident he would strengthen and sustain.[273] Equally and importantly for her, the Kashmir Accord had negated Kashmir as a trump card for Pakistan to play.[274] Possibly, a new Constituent Assembly was to be convened in 1975 to revise and update the J&K Constitution. However, the diabolical Emergency that Mrs Gandhi imposed on India from June 1975 to March 1977 and which, essentially, allowed her to rule by decree, suspend civil liberties and postpone elections, usurped this possibility.[275]

The first two points of the Kashmir Accord confirmed the India–J&K relationship. First, J&K was 'a constituent unit of the Union of India … [that will] continue to be governed by Article 370 of the Constitution of India. Second, J&K would retain 'residuary powers of legislation' while New Delhi could, essentially, make laws relating to preventing any and all anti-India activities, including secession. The Accord also confirmed that provisions of India's Constitution 'already applied' to J&K 'without adaptation or modification [we]re unalterable'.[276] These could not be challenged. Whether Kashmiris liked it or not, India was now supreme and in charge in J&K, while citizens in this state were indisputably with it. This, seemingly, was the end of the issue of J&K's sovereignty, at least for Sheikh Abdullah and, at that time, for India. Abdullah's compromise with Indira Gandhi, without New Delhi reciprocating very much, allowed him to return as the state's Chief Minister. Equally, the Kashmir Accord 'dented' his reputation.[277]

The Kashmir Accord did not lead to an improvement in India–J&K relations. To Mrs Gandhi's chagrin, Sheikh Abdullah re-established the National Conference in 1975. She had wanted the Plebiscite Front to merge into Congress so that her party could function unrivalled in J&K.[278] Abdullah instead perfunctorily extinguished the Plebiscite Front, which had been a rallying point for Kashmiris, a serious irritant for India, and a useful device for Pakistan to use against its bitter rival. He also revived the National Conference, even though many Kashmiris who had supported and suffered deprivations for the Plebiscite Front wanted this political entity to continue. However, it had totally failed to achieve any form of self-determination for J&K-ites. On 5 July, after much discussion, 1,500 delegates unanimously resolved that the Plebiscite Front would become the National Conference.[279] As Beg pragmatically noted, the Plebiscite Front's 'old objective and nomenclature were irrelevant in the changed circumstances'. Its new programme would be 'socialism, secularism and democracy', which had been the National Conference's programme. Beg also stressed that the re-formed National Conference must ban 'known opportunists' who had 'indulged in anti-people activities ... after 1953'.[280] Presumably, he was referring to former Kashmiri leaders like Bakshi or Sadiq and their operatives. Thereafter, other parties, such as the J&K People's League[281] or Mahaz Azadi (Freedom Front), which a disgruntled former member of the Plebiscite Front formed in 1977,[282] continued to support a plebiscite for J&K-ites.

After returning to power, Sheikh Abdullah confronted a number of issues. These included: factionalism and defections, with Abdullah seriously falling out with Mirza Afzal Beg, who seemingly wanted Abdullah's job; confronting 'old animosities',[283] particularly with India, which, under Gandhi's leadership, was more confrontational, intrusive and aggressive; economic challenges, including transport costs and high prices; dealing with the hostile Indian press; contemplating his political successor; and, the controversial Resettlement Bill. After two years in office and confronting difficulties with his Congress 'colleagues', the Governor of J&K dissolved the Legislative Assembly on 27 March 1977, as per Section 53B of the J&K Constitution, and called for fresh elections. During the election period, the state came under Governor's Rule, the first use of such control in J&K.[284] On 24 May, Abdullah threatened to secede from India unless Article 370 and its safeguards were honoured: 'There has been much watering down of article [sic] 370 since 1953. We have to strengthen it with all our might.'[285] However, Abdullah's threat was more to do with politicking, given that he made this statement at the launch of his electoral campaign. The next day, the new Janata Party-led Government said that Abdullah's charge was 'baseless'.[286] Later, in September, while talking at a *Janamashtami* celebration, Abdullah stated that Article 370 'was there for all times to come, no matter which party came to power at the Centre'.[287] Forty-two years later he would, of course, be proven wrong.

In July 1977, well-contested and genuinely free and fair elections were held in J&K. Surprisingly, this was only the second election in J&K that Sheikh Abdullah had ever directly participated in. The re-formed National Conference regained political power in its own right, despite some unpopularity with Abdullah for removing food subsidies and despite some perceived electoral favouritism for him.[288] During the campaign, Abdullah suffered a heart attack and was infirm for six weeks. While personally and politically debilitating, this also led to 'an upsurge in support', although some of Abdullah's opponents were suspicious that reports of his sickness had been exaggerated.[289] Two eminent specialists from New Delhi confirmed Abdullah's condition, however. Apart from people's sympathy, Abdullah had another advantage: he was still very popular with rural-based Kashmiris. They comprised three-quarters of the Kashmiri electorate.[290] On 9 July 1977, a victorious Sheikh Abdullah, whose party had won forty-seven of seventy-six seats in the J&K Legislative Assembly, was sworn in as Chief Minister. This gave his revived National Conference the chance to again 'determine the curse [sic] of politics in the State.' (While the author almost certainly meant 'course', not curse, the irony is delicious.)

Also by July 1977, his chief interlocutor in New Delhi, Indira Gandhi, and her Congress Party were out of power as a result of the negative consequences of the Emergency, which had ended in March. Instead, the Janata Party-led coalition was governing India. Significantly, this new government had put pressure on officials and politicians in J&K to ensure that the elections in that state were 'free and fair'. In the 1977 elections, Abdullah campaigned for, and believed that he had won a mandate for, the 'restoration of the pre-9th August 1953 position' for J&K.[291] However, politics, circumstances and time would curtail any such 'restoration'. Conversely, Abdullah's predecessor as Chief Minister, the pro-India and pro-Congress Mir Qasim, saw the 1977 elections as being 'a convincing ratification of the Kashmir Accord ... [and] the acceptance by the people of the finality of the fact of the State's accession to India', which seems too positive.[292] Abdullah would serve as Chief Minister of J&K until his death on 8 September 1982. Generally, the Kashmir Accord curtailed his enthusiasm for J&K's options other than being with India.

Of all the issues Chief Minister Abdullah confronted – or instigated – after 1977, the Resettlement Bill was arguably the most significant. It concerned whether it was Srinagar/Jammu or New Delhi that determined who could be a citizen of J&K.[293] 'The Jammu & Kashmir Grant of Permit for Resettlement in (or Permanent Return to) the State Act, 1982', involved the possible repatriation of J&K-ites (and their descendants) who had migrated to Pakistan or Pakistan-Administered J&K between 1 March 1947 and 14 May 1954 and who could prove their 'permanent residence' (or state subject) status.[294] Abdullah may have created this act as a reaction to being asked to grant state subject status to 'a few lakhs of Hindu refugees ... from West Punjab' who, because of partition, had settled in J&K.[295] While the J&K Legislative Assembly and Legislative Council passed the bill in March 1982, the J&K Governor, B. K. Nehru, refused, to Abdullah's decided chagrin, to give his assent to the bill due to its sensitive nature.[296] For Abdullah, it was a 'humanitarian problem'.[297] For Governor Nehru, the bill was 'infructuous' (pointless or unnecessary)[298] and he returned it to the legislatures in April 1982.[299] Both houses again passed the bill on 4 October 1982, after which Nehru had no choice but to assent.[300] Afterwards, in a face-saving agreement, the Indian President, Giani Zail Singh, referred the law to the Indian Supreme Court asking it to rule on the bill's constitutionality. Farooq Abdullah, Sheikh Abdullah's son, who was by then Chief Minister of J&K, and Indira Gandhi agreed with this process.[301] After languishing for almost twenty years with the Supreme Court, this body returned the reference unanswered on 8 November 2001.[302] Inaction and avoidance, it seemed, had been the best way to deal with this fractious issue. In 2019, the matter was fully and finally resolved when the Indian Government passed the 'Jammu and Kashmir Reorganisation Act'. It scrapped the Resettlement Bill, along with 152 other laws.[303]

The resettlement issue was Sheikh Abdullah's final attempt to assert himself and his state against what he perceived to be an overbearing central government. Locally, the issue was popular, with many National Conference opponents endorsing Abdullah's stand.[304] However, the issue was highly unpopular with India, Jammuites and the Indian press. New Delhi 'bitterly opposed' the bill, with its major concern being to ensure India's security against potential fifth columnists coming, or returning, to Indian J&K from Pakistan or Pakistan-Administered J&K. Jammuites' concern was that returning Muslims might claim vacated properties in which Jammuites were now living. (This was not an issue for Kashmiris, few of whom moved to Pakistan or Pakistan-Administered J&K.) The Indian press reflected the Indian Government's stance that a 'floodgate' would open 'for Pakistani spies, saboteurs, disruptors and trouble makers to operate with impunity in the country's most sensitive state'.[305] For Abdullah, these concerns overstated matters, given that 'in the post-partition period only 117 people' had ever returned to Indian J&K.[306] He did not expect a 'floodgate' to open. Perhaps fortunately for all parties concerned, Sheikh Abdullah died before the bill was passed again by the J&K legislature. Had he been alive and virile enough, he might have caused serious constitutional and political challenges to India by insisting on J&K's right to determine who was a citizen of J&K. His son lacked the same drive on this issue. For Alastair Lamb, the Resettlement Bill 'was as near to a formal declaration of the virtual independence' of J&K as Abdullah had made since September 1947.[307] It was possibly also the greatest political issue concerning J&K since Abdullah's sacking in 1953.

Seemingly, after the Kashmir Accord, at least in terms of the Kashmir dispute, Sheikh Abdullah became increasingly pro-India. Most interestingly, the National Conference Government released a White Paper in May 1982 that countered the 'contention' of General Zia, Pakistan's military dictator, that Gilgit, Skardu and Hunza were integral parts of Pakistan, not of J&K. Supposedly, this paper was written to assist India's 'external affairs ministry',[308] which, amongst other things, was opposing the construction by Pakistan and China of the Karakoram Highway through the Northern Areas. Abdullah had come a long way. Nevertheless, as late as 1976, he did make a reference, albeit historical, to independence being an option for J&K. Talking about the British departure from India in 1947, Abdullah stated that the British had 'conceded the right of decision to the Princes, rather than to the people, to accede to either India or Pakistan, or even to remain independent of the two'. He then returned to a familiar theme: We 'advised the Maharaja to consult the people before he said anything. Even before a decision [was taken], we raised our voice for absolute freedom.'[309] Herein lay the ongoing challenge: what, for Sheikh Abdullah, did 'absolute freedom' comprise?

Arguably, it may have been enough for Sheikh Abdullah had J&K been granted full and genuine political autonomy within the Indian Union to enable J&K-ites to develop and enjoy full 'socialism, secularism, and democracy'.[310] Around 1968, in answer to a question about whether, after the departure of the British, circumstances changed considerably, he responded that

> With the departure of the British the biggest change was that the entire defence system came into the hands of the centre while during British rule, the states had maintained their own armies for defence. I would say that all these Indian states without seceding from India could be independent. In the Soviet Union these states, if they like, can be independent of the centre but this right has seldom been exercised. It is the same with Puerto Rico and other states in the United States.[311]

Seemingly, Sheikh Abdullah was confused about the term 'independence' and what this concept actually comprised. However, the above dialogue suggests that what he really wanted for J&K was full autonomy, not full independence. Whatever the political set-up, his challenge was to protect the Kashmir 'nation'. Equally, for the contrarian who 'called into question Kashmir's accession to India when it has suited him and declared it to be a settled fact at other times',[312] this may not have been enough.

Securing Naya Kashmir; regaining honour and dignity

Sheikh Abdullah was heavily involved in J&K politics from 1931 until 1982. In many ways, he was a larger-than-life character, as well as an active and controversial leader. For half a century, he was J&K's highest profile, most provocative and most controversial politician. As a result of his political activities, he spent about thirty-three months in Maharaja Hari Singh's jails between 1931 and 1947. Post-partition, his detentions were more severe: in the fifteen years between 1953 and 1968, his political colleagues forcibly confined him for over thirteen years in jails in J&K, under house arrest, or in exile in India. According to Sheikh Abdullah,[313] his arrests and imprisonments were as follows: 1) arrested 21 September 1931, jailed for thirteen days; 2) arrested 23 January 1932, jailed for four months and thirteen days; 3) arrested 23 May 1933 for two months and eighteen days; 4) arrested 13 July 1934 for nineteen days; 5) arrested 25 August 1938, released after six months; 6) arrested 20 May 1946, in prison until 1 October 1947 [*The Civil & Military Gazette* reported that Abdullah was freed on 29 September,[314] which amounted to a period of one year, four months and ten days]; 7) arrested August 1953, in jail for four years and five months, released 8 January 1958; 8) arrested 29 April 1958, in jail for five years, eleven months and nine days, released 18 April 1964; 9) arrested 8 May 1965, released 2 January 1968. Maharaja Hari Singh's Government made the arrests numbered 1 to 6 above; the J&K Government made arrests 7 and 8; the Indian Government made his final detention, number 9. Additionally, the J&K Government banned Abdullah from entering J&K while the 1971 Lok Sabha elections were conducted there.[315] These incarcerations represented a life of considerable struggle and hardship.

In his fifty-one-year political career, Abdullah was an 'unpredictable politician' who was difficult to 'read' and deal with.[316] Put simply, he was a contrarian. It was never certain, nor stated consistently what he wanted for J&K. After supporting Hari Singh's accession to India in 1947, he developed 'a tendency to deaccession'.[317] Sometimes he 'clamoured for complete independence of Kashmir'; sometimes he 'declared that independence was not a practicable idea'.[318] After his dismissal in 1953, he was keen for a plebiscite to be held, although some of this stance was Abdullah trying to assert himself against New Delhi. Perhaps the only certain thing is that Abdullah wanted as much internal autonomy for his region as he could possibly obtain or retain. A further factor was Sheikh Abdullah's localness. Karan Singh, who knew him well, considered that 'Despite his undoubted stature and charisma among the Kashmiri masses, Sheikh Abdullah was never able to … become a truly national leader'.[319] The potential was there, given Abdullah's friendship with Nehru and given that he was a respected Muslim leader in Hindu-dominant but secular India with its large Muslim minority somewhat adrift after the bitter partition experience. However, Abdullah's popularity was restricted mostly to areas of J&K populated by Muslims, particularly ethnic Muslim Kashmiris.

The rise of Sheikh Abdullah to power in J&K in 1947 created a trend whereby Kashmiris have long dominated the politics of this Indian state. In his early years,

Abdullah's chief political opponents were not other J&K-ites but Indians, chiefly Jawaharlal Nehru, Sardar Patel for a time, then later Indira Gandhi. For Abdullah, Nehru 'proved more oppressive and dictatorial than the Maharaja'.[320] The Kashmiri leader believed that, because of Nehru's love for Kashmir, which Mountbatten once called 'pathological',[321] he was jealous of Abdullah's hold over J&K's people, provoking his 'taking action against me [i.e., Abdullah]' in 1953.[322] A further opponent was the Praja Parishad, whose activities in Jammu caused Abdullah considerable angst. This agitation made him question the genuineness and longevity of India's secularism, of which Nehru was a staunch advocate and supporter. Somewhat presciently (particularly in relation to India's current regime), Abdullah had fears that the Indian leaders who followed Nehru would not be as strongly secular or prepared to engage meaningfully with Indian Muslims. One consequence of Indians' empowerment of Sheikh Abdullah in 1947 has been that every Prime Minister or Chief Minister of J&K has been an ethnic Kashmiri. This included Ghulam Nabi Azad (Chief Minister from 2005–8) who, while he was not born in the Kashmir Valley (he was born in Doda, Jammu), had ethnic Kashmiri forebears from Kulgam.[323] (That said, Karan Singh was the only J&K-ite who ever served as Governor of J&K between 1965, when this position came into being, and 2019, when it was abolished due to Jammu and Kashmir being downgraded to territory status.)

As a result of his long incarcerations and exiles, Sheikh Abdullah became India's 'most famous political prisoner'. For India, a nation that claimed to be democratic and a respecter of people's human rights, this was a serious shortcoming. The restrictions on Abdullah's freedom were 'a tacit admission of New Delhi's failure to solve the problem of Kashmir's status'.[324] They also set a dangerous precedent for other Indian leaders less tolerant of Kashmiri dissent. According to Abdullah, his 'personal privations' did not leave him bitter.[325] He did, however, acknowledge in 1976 that he and the National Conference had endured a 'dark patch of twenty three years'.[326] The same year, he reiterated that his lifelong 'fight in the National Conference against the feudal system … was part of a clearly defined and a positive economic and political movement'. He had not merely wanted to terminate Dogra rule. His party's aim had been 'to build a democratic set-up, a new pattern of economy and social welfare'.[327] This reflected one of Abdullah's major and ongoing political aspirations: advancing and 'maintaining Kashmir's national honour and dignity'.[328] The challenge for him was to do so within the Indian polity, particularly after J&K's autonomy was significantly diluted and diminished after he was replaced in 1953 by the strongly pro-India leader, Bakshi Ghulam Muhammad, then G. M.

Sadiq. Indeed, post-Abdullah, all Prime Ministers or Chief Ministers needed to be unequivocally pro-India.

On 8 September 1982, Sheikh Abdullah died. This concludes the Sheikh Abdullah story, although not the story of people in J&K seeking independence. The (almost) final words in this chapter belong to Sheikh Abdullah himself. On 21 August 1981, he made a long speech in Urdu in Srinagar at the handing over of the Chairmanship of the National Conference to his son and 'heir', Dr Farooq Abdullah, albeit to the chagrin of his politically influential son-in-law, G. M. Shah.[329] In one of his final public utterances, the now aging and unwell Abdullah stated that

> The aim of our movement will be fulfilled only when we … realise the dream of 'Naya Kashmir', which is based on justice, equal opportunity, mutual love and respect, where exploitation is banished and justice will prevail; where economic betterment of people is accompanied by spiritual advancement.[330]

Securing Naya Kashmir and regaining 'Izzat-o-Abroo (honour and dignity)' for Kashmiris had always been Sheikh Abdullah's predominant aims,[331] not obtaining an independent Kashmir. Opposed to 'tyranny and oppression'[332] and 'the tyranny of despotism'[333] – although, equally, not greatly tolerant of dissent or divergent views – Abdullah wanted that 'no one can treat us as dumb-driven cattle and impose his will on us.'[334] This suggests the nub of the Kashmir dispute: how to make ethnic Kashmiris feel that they are not 'catttle [sic] or chattle' and that they and their lands are not mere real estate to be acquired and incorporated.[335] India and Pakistan would do well to understand this important point – and not seek to impose their respective will unilaterally, paternalistically or forcefully on J&K-ites. As one Indian commentator succinctly put it in 2019 after New Delhi's major changes to J&K's status: 'Those who seek to bind the nation by force may well unravel the constitutional fabric that holds its infinite diversity together.'[336]

7

Kashmiris and independence since 1988

After Sheikh Abdullah's death in September 1982, Jammu and Kashmir went through increasingly difficult times. Slowly, pervasively and irreversibly, the state slid into upheaval as local and Indian politicians sought to impose their wills, often insensitively. Mostly, they were in competition with each other; sometimes, they collaborated. Ultimately, their actions and manipulations, actual or attempted, disgruntled Muslim Kashmiris so much that, in 1988, some instigated an anti-India agitation.[1] It is unclear who actually started this.[2] It may have been spontaneous, although elements from the Jammu Kashmir Liberation Front (JKLF)[3] seem to be the most likely 'culprits'. Certainly, by 1988, Muslim Kashmiris had become frustrated and angry with India and with Indian or local pro-India politicians misunderstanding, mismanaging and manipulating them. The final indignity was the rigged 1987 state elections. Kashmiri Muslims had expected local candidates to do better against the 'unholy' duumvirate of India's Prime Minister, Rajiv Gandhi, and J&K's Chief Minister, Farooq Abdullah, than they ultimately did. Their disenchantment, coupled with the availability of angry, unemployed Kashmiri youth, some Indian ineptness and some Pakistani opportunism, were sufficient to spark an uprising. Seemingly, the Kashmiris' time had come.

Throughout 1988, the Kashmiris' anti-India agitation was relatively peaceful. There were incidents of violence but these were nothing compared with what was to come. In 1989, this agitation turned violent – ultimately at great and tragic cost to all involved. Young Kashmiris, having been trained and armed in or by Pakistan, returned to the Kashmir Valley. They instigated an armed uprising that was both savage and somewhat unexpected, chiefly as Kashmiris supposedly were resigned to being with India, were ambivalent about Pakistan, and were pacific people. The younger Kashmiris' use of violence suggested a generational change in attitudes, given that Kashmiris had 'always prided themselves on especially being non-violent'.[4]

As early as 1980, there had been a 'veiled threat' that Kashmiris might instigate an armed struggle to free J&K from 'India's illegal occupation'.[5] However, the anti-India militancy initially bewildered India, surprised Pakistan, and excited Kashmiris. Many of them were convinced that Kashmir would soon achieve a change of status. Their preferred options were full independence from India or unification with Pakistan, with either option seemingly, almost intoxicatingly, close at hand. The cry 'of over 90 percent [of] Kashmiri Muslims was spontaneous: "Awake, awake (freedom) has dawned".[6] Neither of these desired changes of status for Kashmir came to be, however. Chiefly, this was because India, after its early bewilderment, showed enormous resolve and capacity to suppress, then control, the insurgency, thereby ensuring that Kashmir remained with India. India's strong desire to retain Kashmir and, increasingly, to incorporate it into India, remain huge obstacles for Kashmiris.

Sheikh Abdullah's agreement with Indira Gandhi in 1975, and his death in 1982, suggested that Kashmiri desires for independence had ended. However, since 1988, many Kashmiris have been motivated by a desire for *azadi*, which, for some Kashmiris, means 'independence' and, for others, means 'freedom'. This motivation may have started as early as 1975 as a result of Abdullah's 'sell out' to Mrs Gandhi via the Kashmir Accord, after which some Kashmiris felt a sense of 'betrayal' and considered Abdullah to be a 'traitor'.[7] And although India is now largely in control of the anti-India insurgency in Kashmir, the concept of *azadi* amongst Kashmiris has neither died nor disappeared. What Kashmiris actually mean by *azadi* is challenging. Problematically, there are many translations and spellings of this Persian/Urdu term, and more than one meaning or interpretation also exist, as we shall see. Increasingly, however, Kashmiris appear to be giving *azadi* a strongly negative meaning or connotation: to be rid of, or free from, India and Indian control. Such anti-Indian sentiments have been prevalent since 1990. As Mir Qasim, former Chief Minister of J&K, noted as early as 1992: 'those who think that it is not good to remain in India are in the majority'.[8] Given the many interpretations of the term *azadi*, should Kashmiris ever rid, or free, themselves from Indian control, it is very unclear what this post-India circumstance would entail for them and their region.

This chapter focuses on *azadi*, particularly on aspects associated with its interpretation as 'independence'. After a scene-setting overview of the Kashmiris' anti-India uprising and its five phases, the chapter examines some of the meanings, interpretations and usages of this vexed term. It then discusses the significant constitutional and administrative changes that New Delhi imposed on J&K in

2019 which comprise a sixth, and uncertain, phase in the Kashmiris' uprising. Then, taking *azadi* specifically to mean independence, the chapter examines the feasibility of either an independent J&K or an independent Kashmir surviving as an independent state. There are now two 'realities' concerning J&K: the Indian reality that J&K is fully integrated into India and the Kashmiri reality that most Kashmiris want little to do with India: they want *azadi*.

The anti-India insurgency: an (incomplete) overview

In 1988 Kashmiris, disenchanted as a result of 'the cumulative effect of the injustices perpetrated on Kashmir during the last 40 years', began a political campaign against Indian rule in, and of, Kashmir.[9] The following year, their campaign morphed into a violent anti-India insurgency led chiefly by militants from the pro-independence JKLF. New groups quickly joined the fray, particularly those wanting J&K to join Pakistan. After overcoming some initial surprise, India's new National Front Government inserted large numbers of paramilitary into the Kashmir Valley to confront, control, kill or defeat the disunified anti-India insurgent groups. This short-lived Indian Government (2 December 1989–21 June 1991, which was replaced by a Congress Government) was inspired to act partly by the Kashmiris' widespread protests and violence and partly by some serious kidnappings. The most notable of these occurred on 8 December 1989, less than a week after the National Front Government had assumed office, when the JKLF kidnapped Dr Rubaiya Sayeed. In a significant sleight, Rubaiya was the daughter of the newly appointed Indian Home Minister, Mufti Mohammed Sayeed, himself a Kashmiri politician and a rival of Farooq Abdullah. In an 'abject surrender' to the militants,[10] India's new Government quickly gave in five days later and released five JKLF militants, an act with which Abdullah strongly disagreed. Soon after, the militants released Rubaiya Sayeed.[11] Motivated militants-cum-terrorists increasingly attacked, intimidated or killed mainstream politicians, officials and members of the security forces, including the murder of three 'key' officials from the Intelligence Bureau in January 1990. By mid-January, New Delhi realised that it confronted a serious challenge in Kashmir.

The uprising occurred because Kashmiris had significant grievances against India and Indian rule. Locally, these grievances included: severe political disenchantment with a series of rigged elections, or more correctly 'selections', the first of which occurred in September 1951 (prior to 1987, only the 1977 election in J&K was considered to be genuinely free and fair); strong dislike of administrative corruption, inefficiency and non-responsiveness; and frustration with economic unemployment and underemployment, a lack of development and 'metropolitan' exploitation, including the perceived underpayment for electricity generated in Kashmir but used in other Indian states Additionally, many Kashmiris were unhappy with J&K's loss of autonomy, which Article 370 of the Indian Constitution supposedly guaranteed. Since the political sidelining of Sheikh Abdullah in 1953, Indian intrusiveness in J&K had steadily increased. Local Muslim Kashmiri politicians facilitated this process. These pro-India 'supplicants' allowed New Delhi to impose its will in Kashmir politically (via actions such as the use of President's Rule, i.e., direct rule by New Delhi, or by allowing appeals to the Indian Supreme Court), administratively (via installing the Indian Administrative Service and its cadre in the state), and economically (by New Delhi providing loans to J&K, not grants).[12] Steadily and unrelentingly, J&K's autonomy had been eroded 'thanks to Delhi's misguided policies.'[13]

Various external factors also fueled, or inspired, the Kashmiris' anti-India actions. These included: the Islamic revolution of 1979 that overthrew the Pahlavi dynasty in Iran; the violent campaign during the 1980s by Sikhs in neighbouring Punjab to establish an independent Khalistan, including Operation Blue Star in 1984, when Indian Army forces stormed the Golden Temple to remove militants holed up inside; the consequential assassination of Indira Gandhi in October 1984; the Afghan *mujahideen's* tenacious fight during the 1980s against the Soviet Union's Red Army, which finally withdrew from Afghanistan in February 1989; the deaths and difficulties experienced by the Indian Peacekeeping Force that fought the Liberation Tigers of Tamil Eelam in Sri Lanka between 1987 and 1990; the death in 1988 of Pakistan's guileful military dictator, General Zia-ul-Haq, who had helped the Afghans run their anti-Soviet *jehad* and who had supported Islamist (i.e., pro-Islam) elements in Kashmir, particularly the Jamaat-e-Islami (from which body came its 'tanzeem or militant arm', the Hizbul Mujahideen (Party of Holy Warriors) militant group);[14] China's Tiananmen Square protests in June 1989 and the regime's harsh response; ongoing anti-state insurgencies by ethnic minorities in Burma (now Myanmar); the demise during the late 1980s of the Soviet Union, with fourteen new independent states emerging in Asia (Armenia, Azerbaijan, Georgia, Kazakhstan, Kirghizstan, Tajikistan, Turkmenistan, Uzbekistan) and in Europe (Belarus, Estonia, Latvia, Lithuania, Moldova, Ukraine); Russia, the dominant republic in the Soviet Union straddling Europe and Asia, also became independent; the associated disintegration of the Soviet Union's eastern European 'empire', including the ending of various Communist regimes, particularly Romania's brutal and overbearing Ceausescu regime in 1989; and finally, and powerfully, the reunification of Eastern and Western Germany after the Berlin Wall fell in early November 1989. For Kashmiris, Germany's reunification showed that long-held dreams and hopes could come true.[15] For believers in 'people's power', these tumultuous times of protests, uprisings, and changes of sovereignty were inspiring.[16] Kashmiris similarly got 'caught up in the heady sweep of liberation activities'.[17]

For Kashmiris, a further factor that occurred outside the Kashmir Valley was alienation. Problematically, many Indians seemingly mistrusted Kashmiris and questioned their loyalty to India. (Feasibly, some Kashmiris may not have been loyal to India.) According to the Indian journalist, Tavleen Singh, the 'first political remark' she 'ever remember[s] hearing about Kashmir' was that 'All Kashmiris are traitors'.[18] For many Indians, Kashmiris have long taken advantage of India's financial, economic and military generosity and/or they have refused to become fully-fledged Indians and/or they have wanted their region to join Pakistan. (Economically, however, J&K has been one of India's better performing states.)[19] For Singh, the Indian press was 'the main reason why the alienation of Kashmir began': 'the Indian press, out of misguided patriotism, has always chosen to tell the Indian public less than the whole truth about Kashmir. This has made it possible for governments in Delhi to get away with dangerously myopic policies.'[20] Little has changed since Singh wrote this in 1995, as confirmed by much of the India media's often scant reporting or uncritical analysis of the constitutional and administrative changes, and the subsequent tough curfew, imposed on J&K in August 2019. Indeed, in 2020, Kashmiris apparently prefer foreign radio broadcasts (BBC, Voice of America) as 'The Indian media is not a trusted source of news. It is repeating what their government says about what is happening here.'[21]

In my research, I have rarely seen the Indian press explain or discuss in any great detail the term *azadi*, and the Kashmiris' widespread usage of this highly popular term. This subject, it seems, is taboo. According to a 'veteran' journalist 'Masood' from *The Kashmir Times*, in Srinagar, only thirty-seven words are needed to be a reporter in Kashmir:

fear, arrest, prison, torture, death, Indian security forces, separatists, guerrillas/militants/terrorists, grenades, assault rifles, sandbag bunkers, army installations, hideouts, crackdowns, search-and-destroy operations, frustration, tension, anxiety, trauma, democracy, betrayal, self-determinations, freedom, peace talks, international community, mediation, breakdown, despair, and rage.[22]

Surprisingly, neither the terms *azadi* nor independence appear in this list (although the more amorphous term 'freedom' does). Similarly, apart from regularly reading about the deaths of militants killed in 'incidents' or 'encounters' in J&K, we rarely get to read what dissident Kashmiris want for their region or about their (invariably anti-India) aspirations. Rather, most, but not all, reporters working in the Indian press generally have toed India's strongly, often paternalistic, line on Kashmir and Kashmiris.

Despite a lack of objective reporting, there were some early warning signs of the Kashmiris' anti-India uprising. As early as 1971, incidents of violence and sabotage were occurring in Kashmir. That year, two 'Kashmiri nationalists' associated with the JKLF hijacked an Indian Airlines plane from Srinagar to Lahore.[23] On 11 February 1984, New Delhi hanged Maqbool Butt (or Bhat, Bhatt), a founder of the JKLF, ostensibly in revenge for the murder of Ravindra Mhatre, India's Deputy High Commissioner in Birmingham, England. By then, Butt was a popular figure in Kashmir. Indeed, he possibly had replaced Abdullah 'as the beloved leader of Kashmiris'.[24] Within two years, Kashmiris had lost two significant figures: Sheikh Abdullah and Maqbool Butt. With Butt's hanging, the situation in Kashmir deteriorated. Secession groups became a problem, with 400 people associated with such groups arrested to prevent trouble after Butt's hanging.[25] As early as March 1984, the Indian Government was 'closely watching' anti-national activities by 'secessionist and subversive elements' in J&K. These included J&K Jamaat-e-Islami, Islami Jamaat-e-Tulba, J&K People's League, Mahaz-e-Azadi and Awami Action Committee,[26] most of which groups Sheikh Abdullah had previously strongly opposed.[27] His physical demise created operating space for them. In February 1985, India arrested about fifty members of 'anti-national' organisations, and deployed extra 'contingents' from the Border Security Force and the Central Reserve Police Force to deal with the 'situation' in Kashmir.[28] Trouble was brewing.

With violence and disenchantment slowly, but clearly, increasing, in Kashmir, the 1987 elections marked a turning point. The local and newly established Muslim United Front (*Muslim Mutthahida Mahaz*)[29] had expected to do reasonably well at the polls, possibly winning as many as ten seats in the seventy-six to be contested. However, voting was clearly manipulated (i.e., rigged) by elements associated with, or directed by, Rajiv Gandhi and Farooq Abdullah, whose Congress and National Conference parties had formed an electoral alliance for the poll. Consequently, Muslim United Front candidates, who were forced to compete as independents, won only five seats. Their lack of success was surprising as independents had obtained 35 per cent of the popular vote in J&K.[30] Thereafter, disenchanted Kashmiri Muslims started taking action. In particular, young, educated and unemployed

Kashmiri males began to consider other options apart from Kashmir remaining with India, and other methods of operating apart from engaging in mainstream politics. The obvious option was to seek the support of the neighbouring nation, i.e., Pakistan. In those days, the Line of Control was difficult to cross, but easier than in later years after India fenced large sectors of it. Consequently, young Kashmiri men, initially led by JKLF elements, began to move to Azad Kashmir and seek Pakistani assistance and support there.

The act that some, including the JKLF, consider marks the 'formal onset' of the Kashmiris' anti-India uprising occurred on 31 July 1988 when the Srinagar Telegraph Office was bombed.[31] In September, there was 'a series of bomb explosions and other disturbances in Srinagar and elsewhere in the valley'. The challenge was to determine who was responsible for these explosions. The J&K police thought pro-Pakistan groups were responsible; Indian intelligence agencies felt it was Kashmiri youth recently returned from receiving training in Pakistan; 'another view' proposed that it was a new anti-India group, operating on its own and not having any links with Pakistan. This 'view' suggested (correctly) the JKLF. There was significant political tension and anti-government protests, with '16 persons killed in police firings since June' 1988.[32] Six months later, with the security situation clearly deteriorating, Rajiv Gandhi had India's Home Minister, Buta Singh, and its Defence Minister, K. C. Pant, 'rush to Kashmir' to review the security situation there with J&K's Chief Minister, Farooq Abdullah.[33] Seriously agitated Kashmiris were seriously agitating.

After the early upheavals of 1988–89 in the Kashmir Valley, things got worse when New Delhi re-appointed Jagmohan Malhotra ('Jagmohan') Governor of J&K on 19 January 1990. Concurrently, Farooq Abdullah resigned. This was Jagmohan's second term as Governor. During his first term (1984–89), he was renowned for doing Indira and Rajiv Gandhi's often nefarious bidding. Controversially, this included having Ghulam Mohammad Shah replace his popularly elected brother-in-law, Farooq Abdullah, as Chief Minister in July 1984. In his first ninety days of office, the unpopular Shah was forced to impose curfews for seventy-two days.[34] He and his compromised colleagues served until March 1986, after which Governor's Rule, then President's Rule, were instituted until the disastrous 1987 elections took place. Many of Jagmohan's various actions taken in J&K made India unpopular with Muslims, but popular with non-Muslims. Jagmohan's machinations also made him popular with New Delhi, which, arguably, was this apparatchik's major concern. By the time of his return in 1990, however, J&K 'was on the verge of disintegration'. There was widespread and volatile political unrest and Indian authority was waning.

To prevent potential anti-India protests occurring on Republic Day (26 January), the self-confident, even strident, Jagmohan re-imposed Governor's Rule, and 'formally requested' the Indian Army to take 'whatever means necessary to bring the situation under control' in Kashmir.[35] However, on 21 January 1990, India's position was further weakened when panicky Indian security forces 'massacred' twelve,[36] or possibly 'more than a hundred', *azadi*-seeking Kashmiris at Gawakadal (also Gawkadal or Gowkadal). For many Kashmiris, this was 'considered the worst massacre in Kashmiri history'.[37]

On 26 May 1990, New Delhi replaced the hardline and unpopular Jagmohan with Girish (Gary) Saxena as Governor of J&K. Saxena's aim, along with that of his successors, was to try and curb, suppress, then end, the anti-India uprising. Jagmohan's demise after a mere four months in office was probably prompted by the assassination of the hereditary and respected Kashmiri Mirwaiz, Maulvi Farooq, on 21 May. Given Farooq's stature and given that he was not always anti-establishment – in the politically troubled mid-1980s, he had politically teamed up with the other Farooq (Abdullah) – this was a tragedy of massive proportions. Thereafter, Maulvi Farooq became 'a national hero as well as Kashmir's most important martyr'.[38] His killers were unknown. They may have been members of the then 'shadowy' Hizbul Mujahideen who worked under the direct orders of Pakistan's Inter-Services Intelligence Directorate (ISI), which effectively is under the control of the Pakistan Army.[39] Significantly, few Kashmiris held India responsible for Farooq's death. However, whatever moral 'high ground' New Delhi had attained quickly disappeared when anxious Indian security forces again fired on a large Kashmiri crowd. This time, it was the massive procession traversing Srinagar after Maulvi Farooq's funeral. As many as fifty people were killed,[40] or massacred, to use the local parlance. Also around the time of Jagmohan's demise, fearful Hindu Pandit families were fleeing Kashmir for the safer climes of Jammu, Delhi or other parts of India. By June 1990, 'some 58,000 families had relocated'. (Haksar, more exactly, states that 75,343 Pandit families left Kashmir.)[41] Only 20,000 Pandits remained.[42] Some Muslim militants had been targeting the minority Pandit community, including some in the supposedly secular JKLF that then dominated the anti-India insurgency.[43] This included using violence, with perhaps 900 Pandits 'systematically and brutally targeted' and killed over twenty-four months.[44] Equally, some Kashmiris consider that Jagmohan encouraged the Pandits to migrate.[45] Certainly, in the volatile and uncertain early days of the Muslim Kashmiris' anti-India uprising, the pro-India Pandits felt estranged, isolated, threatened, neglected and insecure. Few of these feelings have altered for them since.

The Kashmiris' anti-India insurgency brought significant levels of violence to Kashmir. The militants were far from saints. They were diverse, dispersed and without recognisable internal rules to guide, or curtail, their various organisations' ethics and operations, including the use of intimidation and extortion. Seemingly, the desired end of attaining *azadi* justified their often unsavoury means. India's security forces, apart from conducting counter-insurgency operations, were used to protect, and increasingly to police, control and subdue ethnic Kashmiris. During the difficult early years of the anti-India insurgency, democracy was suspended throughout J&K for almost seven years while these forces dealt with this insurgency, often insensitively. (At the same time, Jammu and Ladakh were placed under direct rule, even though the insurgency was then limited to the Kashmir Valley.) However, unlike the militants, India's security forces were subject to external controls. Their operations and personnel were enabled, and, as it turns out, protected, from accountability by strong – opponents would say draconian – legal acts, such as the Jammu and Kashmir Public Safety Act 1978 and the Armed Forces (Jammu and Kashmir) Special Powers Act 1990. Such acts were effective. The highly used Public Safety Act, for example, allows 'detention without trial for up to 2 years'.[46] According to the 2018 and 2019 reports of the Office of the United Nations High Commissioner for Human Rights (OHCHR) about the human rights situation in J&K,[47] 'No [Indian] security forces personnel accused of torture or other forms of degrading and inhuman treatment have [ever] been prosecuted in a civilian court' in India.[48]

During the early years of the insurgency, Pakistan also overcame its early surprise about the Kashmiris' serious anti-India actions and quickly began to house, train, arm, support and indoctrinate various anti-India militants. Initially, these militants comprised Muslim Kashmiris, with the JKLF the major, and then pre-eminent, group that Pakistan's security forces first supported.[49] Much of this Pakistani assistance was provided at locations in Pakistan-Administered Azad Kashmir, whose leaders had long considered their region to be the 'base camp' for the liberation of Indian J&K,[50] or in Pakistan's adjacent North-West Frontier Province (renamed Khyber Pakhtunkhwa Province in 2010). The JKLF, which had a five-phase formula, or *Roadmap*, for political change in J&K, sought independence for all of the former princely state of Jammu and Kashmir.[51] This had been this group's intention since some overseas J&K-ites first formed the organisation in Birmingham in 1977.[52] The JKLF arose from the 1963 Jammu and Kashmir Independence Committee, which had 'demanded' independence for J&K.[53] Other insurgent groups did not appear to have a clear and enunciated strategy for political change in J&K. For religious reasons, chiefly, they simply wanted the state to join Pakistan.

Some JKLF elements apparently had commenced 'political planning' for an insurgency as early as 1986. JKLF operations then began in July 1988.[54] One challenge for this group was that its planners, such as Amanullah Khan, were located in Pakistan or Azad Kashmir, while its fighters, such as the famous HAJY group, which comprised Hameed Sheikh, Ashfaq Majid Wani, Javed Ahmad Mir and Yasin Malik, were in Kashmir. Arguably, the planning element was more concerned about J&K as a whole, while the HAJY faction represented Kashmiri nationalism.[55] (In 1995, JKLF members on either side of the LOC would fall out.) Either way, the JKLF's pro-independence stance did not make this militant group popular with Islamabad, as the JKLF was soon to discover. Nevertheless, Pakistan initially supported the JKLF, if only because its militants were then causing India significant problems. Someone clearly remembered the maxim: 'my enemy's enemy is my friend'. However, from as early as 1990, pro-Pakistan militant groups and/or India's security forces began attacking and killing JKLF militants. Up to 600 JKLF fighters may have been killed.[56] These aggressive actions reflected the commitment of India and Pakistan, directly or via proxies, to suppress the JKLF's pursuit of independence for Kashmir. While these anti-JKLF actions seemingly were uncoordinated, by around 1993, they had severely degraded this pro-independence militant group's operational capabilities.

Alongside the JKLF's debasement in the early 1990s, Pakistan's security forces, led by the powerful and secretive ISI, only provided assistance to militant groups that wanted to join J&K with Pakistan. With Pakistan's support and guidance, these pro-Pakistan militants slowly coalesced into three major groups: the 'local' Hizbul Mujahideen, which largely comprised Kashmiris, and the 'foreign' Lashkar-e-Toiba (Army of the Righteous) and Jaish-e-Mohammed groups (Army of Mohammad), which largely comprised non-Kashmiris.[57] This ended some serious factional issues, such as personality clashes, infighting, internecine rivalry, assassinations of rivals, and profiteering, which had limited the various militant groups' abilities to confront Indian security forces in Kashmir.[58] These three anti-India militant groups continue to exist and pose problems for India's security forces, mainly in the Kashmir Valley, but they also sometimes conduct operations in adjacent upland or border areas of Jammu. In 2020, these groups, along with Al-Badr (Full Moon), may have morphed into a new Pakistani-controlled entity called 'The Resistance Front', which has been formed supposedly to be less overtly Islamic and more secular, as well as to give Pakistan deniability as the international

Financial Action Task Force seriously scrutinises, and possibly sanctions, Pakistan's involvement in terrorism.[59] Attempts also have been made to establish al-Qaeda or Daesh (Islamic State) cells in Kashmir, often by fighters disenchanted with one of these three groups, but with no great success. Very few Kashmiris, Indians or Pakistanis want such bodies to operate in Kashmir, it seems.

Both Lashkar-e-Toiba and Jaish-e-Mohammed have also engaged in terrorist activities in other parts of India. Despite India's accusations that Pakistan was significantly helping the anti-India militants operating in Kashmir, Pakistan has consistently claimed that it has only been providing moral and diplomatic support to them. This is hard to believe. The activities and operations of the ISI and, indeed, of Pakistan's security forces, led and dominated by the Pakistan Army, have long been beyond civilian control or general scrutiny. In 2010, Pakistan's former president and military dictator from 1999 to 2008, General Pervez Musharraf, actually confirmed Pakistani involvement with anti-India militant groups. Musharraf said publicly that Pakistan had formed 'militant underground groups to fight India in Kashmir' and it was 'the Pakistani security forces that trained them'. It was Pakistan's 'right ... to promote its own interests when India is not prepared to discuss Kashmir at the United Nations and is not prepared to resolve the dispute in a peaceful manner'.[60] Little has changed since, either in relation to Pakistan's support for anti-India militants operating in Indian J&K or in its denial of this role.

As the anti-India insurgency raged after 1989, India–Pakistan relations also became strained. For New Delhi, Pakistan's support for anti-India militants operating in Kashmir amounted to Pakistan mounting a proxy war against India. Equally, Pakistan, due to irredentism, felt the need to help fellow Muslims in Kashmir who were being oppressed. As they had done intermittently since 1947, the armies of both nations engaged in bitter artillery and small arms 'duels', or exchanges, along, and across, either the heavy-militarised LOC in J&K or the more southerly border between Pakistani Punjab and Indian J&K's Jammu region (and which Pakistan calls the 'working boundary', as it considers the Kashmir dispute to be unresolved). For J&K-ites living nearby, these exchanges have invariably resulted in significant dislocation and damage to them, their dwellings and livestock. For Pakistan, one aim or benefit of these exchanges was to create diversions to enable the 'exfiltration or infiltration' of militants across the LOC. Muslim Kashmiri Gujjars, whose animals grazed areas around the LOC, played a 'key role' in this process.[61] India lessened this option by fencing large parts of the LOC. While New Delhi accused Pakistan of supporting anti-India militants, Islamabad accused India of gross human rights violations against Kashmiris in 'occupied Kashmir'. Both nations' claims had some veracity.

While the insurgency continued in Kashmir, India and Pakistan also engaged in other activities. In 1998, both nations confirmed their nuclear weapons capabilities via a series of tests in remote areas in each nation. Realising the need to improve relations, India's Prime Minister, Atal Behari Vajpayee, and Pakistan's Prime Minister, Nawaz Sharif, met at Lahore in February 1999 and declared their intention to do so. Soon after, however, both nations' military forces fought a bitter and difficult war in mountains in the Kargil area, east of the Kashmir Valley, an action the Pakistan Army may well have been planning while Vajpayee was actually in Pakistan. A resolute India ultimately cleared these highlands of what Indians called 'terrorists' but whom Pakistan dubiously claimed were pro-Pakistan 'militants'. Despite Islamabad's claims, the 'militants' fighting India's armed forces were actually members of the Northern Light Infantry, a unit from the Pakistan-Administered Gilgit-Baltistan region led, trained and armed by the Pakistan Army.[62] Thereafter, India–Pakistan relations remained difficult, with Pakistan's President Musharraf and India's Prime Minister Vajpayee holding an acrimonious summit in Agra in July 2001. Soon after, the '9/11' terrorist attacks occurred in the United States, which changed many factors worldwide, particularly in relation to militancy, with many 'militants' and 'freedom fighters' quickly and effectively rebranded as 'terrorists'. This rebranding weakened international support for terrorist activities, including financial assistance, and enabled governments to operate more aggressively against their rivals. In December 2001, India–Pakistan relations worsened after Jaish-e-Mohammed and Lashkar-e-Toiba terrorists attacked India's Parliament. Both nations almost went to war and relations were ominous for much of 2001–2. Thankfully, cooler heads, along with significant international pressure, prevailed.

Still seeking better India–Pakistan relations, President Musharraf and Prime Minister Vajpayee tried again in early 2004. Between 2004 and 2008, Musharraf and Vajpayee (until May 2004), then India's Prime Minister, Dr Manmohan Singh, enabled their respective officials to engage in a serious 'composite dialogue' about eight major matters, including J&K. This dialogue was surprising given that Musharraf, as Chief of the Pakistan Army, had organised Pakistan's Kargil fiasco. It was also surprising as both nations overcame some deep reluctance to discuss certain matters: India finally agreed to talk about J&K; Pakistan finally agreed to talk about India's other seven issues. Musharraf and Singh in their personal discussions apparently got close to resolving the Kashmir dispute. However, Musharraf's political demise in 2008 ended this process. On 26 November 2008, India halted the composite dialogue after Lashkar-e-Toiba terrorists from Pakistan attacked Mumbai, killing ore than 170 people and wounding over 300. Since then, an insistent New Delhi has only been prepared to engage in talks with Islamabad once Pakistan's involvement with anti-India terrorist activities and anti-India terrorist groups stops. As noted, Pakistan denies any direct links with anti-India terrorists and their actions. Meanwhile, India–Pakistan relations remain poor-to-abysmal.

As the insurgency continued in Kashmir, Kashmiris of all ages, locations, religions and genders suffered. They were caught in the middle of two powerful and repressive forces: Indian security forces ruled the streets by day; anti-India militants ruled them by night. Muslim Kashmiris, particularly, were subjected to the security forces' intrusive anti-insurgency cordon and search operations, harassment and often overbearing attitudes. Suppressing the insurgency was challenging for tense security personnel, almost all of whom were 'foreigners' usually a long way away from their homes, families and familiar cultures and with little knowledge of Kashmir, Kashmiris or the Kashmiri language. Reporting the insurgency was difficult for members of the media, particularly local journalists who 'walk[ed] the razor's edge', given the security situation, the security forces' tight control of the region, and the pressure to conform to the militants' and the Government's opinions.[63] Meanwhile, the various and veracious anti-India militants, genuine or 'fake',[64] intimidated, extorted or pressured Kashmiris, almost all of whom were fellow Muslims. (Most Kashmiri Pandits had fled to Jammu or to other parts of India where many were surviving in arduous circumstances as 'internally displaced persons'. Many wanted a separate 'Panun Kashmir' homeland created for their community within the Kashmir Valley.)[65] In the mid-1990s, Kashmiris confronted a difficult new third force: armed former militants who opposed, often brutally, pro-Pakistan militant groups and their alleged associates or supporters. India enabled these pro-India *Ikhwan* forces that often operated in an extra-legal way. For Indians, these surrendered militants who had switched loyalty were 'friendlies'; for their former militant opponents, they were 'renegades'.[66] For Kashmiris, they were difficult to deal with.

Phases of the Kashmiris' anti-India insurgency

The Kashmiris' anti-India insurgency has gone through some six phases since 1988.[67] (The sixth, and most recent phase, which started in 2019, will be discussed later in the chapter.) In the first phase (1988–93), Kashmiris were 'euphoric': they had great hopes and expectations that their anti-India struggle would quickly succeed. In the second phase (1993–99), Kashmiris came to realise the strength and resilience of India's security forces, their own isolation and inferiority vis-a-vis India, and that Pakistan, by only supporting pro-Pakistan militant groups, appeared to be more interested in Kashmiris' land than in their welfare or freedom. In 1993, twenty-six Kashmiri political groups established the All Parties Hurriyat [Freedom] Conference (APHC) to provide a unified front and to demand self-determination.[68] It has not proven to be terribly effective. In the third phase (1999–2003), the bogged-down insurgents got somewhat desperate, with Hizbul Mujahideen declaring a unilateral ceasefire in 2000 but, conversely, with other militants attacking non-Muslims in an attempt to communalise, spread or reinvigorate the insurgency.

Five other major events occurred in the third phase. First, the 1999 Kargil 'war' confirmed India's military strength and Pakistan's opportunism.[69] Second, in 2001, the United States instigated its 'War on Terror', which helped India's position and activities in J&K and put pressure on Pakistan to cease its support for anti-India elements there. This 'war' weakened, or paused, the anti-India armed struggle in Kashmir. Third, the first post-9/11 terrorist attack in the world occurred when Jaish-e-Mohammed suicide bombers attacked the J&K State Assembly in Srinagar and killed forty people. Fourth, shortly after, on 13 December 2001, Jaish-e-Mohammed and Lashkar-e-Toiba terrorists attacked India's Parliament in New Delhi. Fifth, in 2001, deaths in the Kashmir insurgency peaked, with 4,011 people killed. These comprised 1,024 civilians, 628 security forces, 2,345 militants and 14 unspecified.[70] Concurrently in this third phase, exhaustion set in for Kashmiris as they came to realise that they had lost control of 'their' insurgency and that victory was unlikely, as deaths increased, and as economic and social conditions became tougher. Some militants and security force personnel, however, were making money from 'payments'; suppliers providing goods and services to India's security forces were also doing relatively well. In 2002, the leader of the People's Conference, Abdul Ghani Lone, was assassinated, possibly because he had called on 'foreign militants' to leave Kashmir.[71] In 2003, New Delhi had talks with the APHC but little came of them, except that the APHC split into two factions: centrists, who favoured some sort of dialogue with Delhi, and rejectionists, who did not.[72]

The fourth phase of the Kashmiris' anti-India insurgency (2004–7) saw India and Pakistan engage in their relatively brief, but significant, Composite Dialogue in 2004, after which the insurgency's intensity lessened and a ceasefire came into place that kept the LOC quiet until 2007. After this time the insurgency entered a new, difficult and ongoing fifth phase. Two positive joint India–Pakistan initiatives allowed cross-LOC bus services in 2005 for J&K-ites and cross-LOC trade in 2008. A number of events confirmed that Kashmiris were still disenchanted with India.[73] In May 2008, Muslim Kashmiris reacted negatively by staging massive protests when the J&K Government (unsuccessfully) sought to transfer ninety-nine acres of land to the (Hindu) Shri Amarnath Shrine Board. Kashmiris were aggravated by the authorities' heavy response that involved force, curfews and detentions. They were further antagonised when disenchanted Hindu Jammuites imposed a retaliatory economic blockade that prevented Kashmiri exports from traversing Jammu. From around 2010, Kashmiris regularly used social media to organise 'spontaneous' anti-India rallies and engaged in stone throwing protests at such rallies. (There is a long tradition in Kashmir of stone pelting as a popular form of protest.)[74] In 2010, over 120 'unarmed' Kashmiris were killed by police in protests that followed the security forces' alleged staged killings of three Kashmiri civilians in Kupwara District.[75] (Six Army personnel were later court martialled and sentenced to life imprisonment, but were bailed in 2017 pending a retrial.)[76] One of the protesters was a young Kashmiri whose death further enraged Kashmiris. The next year, the J&K Chief Minister, Omar Abdullah, the grandson of Sheikh Abdullah, announced an amnesty for 1,200 young male stone throwers. By December 2013, the number of youths charged with 'stone throwing and disruption of the peace' offences had climbed to 'around 1800 cases'. However, it was unclear how many cases had been withdrawn as this could only occur after (slow-moving) police investigations had been completed.[77]

In 2013 and 2016, the 'assassinations' of two Kashmiris severely aggravated many Muslim Kashmiris. In 2013, Afzal Guru, who reputedly for many Indians was 'the most hated man in India', was hanged in New Delhi. Kashmiris, who saw him otherwise, seriously protested. Guru, a former militant, had been convicted and executed – wrongly, according to some – for his involvement in the terrorist 'conspiracy' to attack the Indian Parliament in 2001.[78] Guru's previous activities had involved a shadowy J&K police officer, Davinder Singh, who, in 2020, was suspended and investigated for allegedly assisting Hizbul Mujahideen militants.[79] In July 2016, severely agitated Kashmiris staged massive protests after the Indian security forces killed the young, high-profile and popular, Kashmiri militant, Burhan Wani, from the Hizbul Mujahideen. According to Indian Army officers, Wani was a 'Facebook fighter': he 'fought' using social media rather than in actual kinetic operations against India's security forces.[80] Kashmiris saw him otherwise: they considered him to be a more moderate and inclusive fighter, a 'poster boy' militant, even 'a phenomenon, the glamorous hero of an almost romantic anti-State rebellion'.[81] In response to massive protests by Kashmiris after Wani's death, security forces killed around a hundred protesters between July and December 2016. These forces' pellet gun firings, a weapon and tactic first used in Kashmir in 2010,[82] injured over 6,200 Kashmiri protesters between July 2016 and February 2017. Over 700 suffered eye injuries, with 54 suffering 'visual impairment'.[83] In the three years after Wani's death, there were 1,092 deaths recorded. These comprised 182 civilians, 256 security forces and a massive 654 militants.[84]

Since 1988, there have been some serious human rights violations in J&K. In 2018, OHCHR published a *Report on the Situation of Human Rights in Kashmir*.[85] In 2019, it published an update that discussed nine types of abuses of human rights in 'Indian-Administered J&K': civilian killings and excessive use of force; continued use of pellet-firing shotguns; cordon and search operations; arbitrary detentions; impunity for human rights violations; restrictions on freedom of expression, plus censorship and attacks on press freedoms; restrictions on freedom of assembly and association; torture; and, the targeting of Kashmiri Muslims outside J&K. The 2019 OHCHR report also discussed six types of abuses of human rights in 'Pakistan-Administered J&K': constitutional and legal structures impacting the enjoyment of human rights; restrictions on the rights to freedom of expression and association; exploitative and environmentally unfriendly business developments controlled nationally that are imposed on local people without consultation and which largely keep them impoverished; impacts of counter-terrorism; restrictions on the freedom of religion or belief; and, enforced or involuntary disappearances.[86] Additionally, the OHCHR report detailed some human rights abuses 'by armed groups'.[87] While both the 2018 and 2019 reports were significant, neither India nor Pakistan had allowed OHCHR 'unconditional access' to the regions that they controlled on their respective sides of the LOC. Petulantly, 'India rejected this request'; equally petulantly, Pakistan would only provide access 'should the Office [OHCHR] obtain access to Indian-Administered Kashmir'.[88] Such actions are not unusual in India–Pakistan relations.

Azadi in Kashmir

Since beginning their insurgency in 1988, many Kashmiri Muslims in Indian J&K clearly have wanted, and have hoped for, a change in their region's international status. While some want Kashmir to join Pakistan, many others, possibly a majority, want *azadi* (*azaadi/aazadi/aazaadi*)[39] for their homelands. However, as we shall now see, it is unclear what they mean by this term and this desire. Since 1988, many Muslim Kashmiris have vociferously agitated for *azadi* by protesting and sloganeering using chants such as '*Hame kya chahiye? Azaadi, Azaadi* [(]What do we want? Freedom, freedom [sic])',[90] or '*Hum Kya Chahte Hain? Aazaadi … Aazaadi … Allah-o-Akbar*: "(What do we want? Independence … [God is Great])"'.[91] More contemporaneously, Kashmiris deliver this slogan as '"Hum Kya Chahte? Azadi!" (What do we want? Freedom!)'.[92] Another slogan that reflects the JKLF's aim for an independent J&K was '"Kashmir banega Khudmukhtar" (Kashmir will be independent)'.[93] A pro-Pakistan slogan has been '*Kashmir banega Pakistan* (Kashmir will become Pakistan)'.[94] For Muslim Kashmiris, however, *azadi* seems to have been their most popular and persistently used slogan. Kashmiris can easily articulate their frustrations and motivations for wanting *azadi*. However, it has always been difficult to determine what they actually mean by this imprecise term. For Kashmiris, it can mean 'freedom', 'independence', 'liberty', 'autonomy' or even 'accommodation' with, or within, the Republic of India or, potentially, the Islamic Republic of Pakistan. It is therefore often uncertain what political end state Kashmiris actually want in relation to their anti-India uprising and *azadi*. Some may want independence for Kashmir, but this is far from clear.

According to a Kashmiri news reporter, 'The protest slogan is a political art form, and in Kashmir, they've been honing it for centuries'.[95] Both historically and more recently, when political activities occur in Kashmir, these often have involved Kashmiris seeking *azadi*. The first call by Kashmiris for *azadi* possibly was made soon after the Mughal Emperor, Akbar, captured Kashmir in 1586, after which he reincorporated this region administratively into northern India. Soon after, young Kashmiris, known as 'Dilawars' (brave or courageous ones), who were 'akin' to the current anti-India militants in Kashmir, raised slogans against the Mughal 'invaders'. These Kashmiris apparently chanted in Persian: 'Maa azadi, me khaim!' or 'We want freedom!'[96] Later, under Sikh rulers (1819–46), Kashmiris coined the slogan: 'Hum kya chahtay? Azadi [What do we want? Freedom]'. After Maharaja Gulab Singh purchased Kashmir in 1846, Kashmiris created a new slogan: 'Khalkov kertov tobh taqseer, Dogruv melheth mulki Kashmir! (Pray, people, pray. The Dogras have bought Kashmir!)'. This related to a Kashmiri perception that these new rulers would exploit them and their region. The Dogras didn't disappoint. As we have seen, things changed dramatically for the Dogra ruling dynasty, and for J&K, in 1947. Thereafter, the final Dogra ruler, Maharaja Hari Singh, seemingly wanted, and seriously contemplated, independence for J&K, although he didn't use the term *azadi* to describe his ambition.[97]

Soon after partition, the term *azad* (free), which is related to *azadi*, began to appear in J&K. From around mid-August, pro-Pakistan Muslims in the Poonch Jagir in southwestern J&K began an anti-Maharaja uprising. They wanted J&K to join Pakistan and were prepared to fight to ensure this. They created a liberation militia which they called the 'Azad [Freedom] Army'. It opposed the Maharaja's military forces. On 24 October 1947, the Poonchi rebels announced the forma- tion of the 'Provisional Azad Government' of J&K in the areas they had 'liber- ated'. Ambitiously, they claimed that this 'free' government was 'assuming the administration of the [entire] state'.[98] The area they controlled officially came to be called 'Azad Jammu and Kashmir', which was shortened popularly to 'Azad Kashmir'.[99] For Azad Kashmiris, their region was not free (*azad*) in the sense of being independent. Rather, it was free from Maharaja Hari Singh's actual control. After he acceded to India, Azad Kashmiris were free from India's control, a status that their region has enjoyed ever since. According to one British journalist who served in India, some Indians consider that the 'heinous' term 'Azad Kashmir' 'was coined by Pakistan only to annoy, to confuse, to beg the question' of freedom for J&K.[100] Azad Kashmir is not totally politically free, however. Pakistan dominates and controls this area tightly. All Azad Kashmiris wanting to stand for elections must confirm that they favour J&K joining Pakistan.[101] This bars JKLF members who favour *azadi* for all of the former princely state. The JKLF is popular with some Azad Kashmiris, but, being electorally untried, it is impossible to know how many.

The term *azadi* also appeared later in 1947 in the remote and strategically important northern Gilgit region of J&K that the British had administered on behalf of the Maharaja. They retroceded (i.e., returned) both the Gilgit Agency and the Gilgit Leased Area to Maharaja Hari Singh's direct control on 1 August 1947. He then sent a Governor, Brigadier Ghansara Singh, to administer the Gilgit region. In early November, pro-Pakistan Muslims in Gilgit rebelled against the Maharaja's administration. These Gilgitis asked Karachi to join their region with Pakistan and requested that it send an administrator to Gilgit. They called their 'freedom struggle ... the *jang āzādi*'.[102] The local Gilgit Scouts, who then were still officered by Britishers (who played a controversial role in the rebel- lion), and the rebellious Muslim companies of the J&K State Forces stationed in Gilgit were 'combined together as "*āzād* (freedom) forces"'.[103] (These Gilgit forces were not involved with the Azad Kashmiris' Azad Army, although they may have been inspired by their actions.) After freeing themselves from Maharaja Hari Singh's control, the Gilgit forces defended their area from attempts by the invading – as Gilgitis saw things – Indian Army to incorporate them and their region into India. Like Azad Kashmir, the Gilgit region, along with neighbouring Baltistan to Gilgit's immediate southeast, remained free (*azad*) from Indian control. Like Azad Kashmiris, the Gilgitis had no interest in their region being independent.

The Kashmiri activist, Prem Nath Bazaz, has made an important distinction about the term *azadi*. In a book published in 1954, he translated *azadi* as 'freedom' or 'independence'. By freedom, Bazaz meant having personal political rights and socio-economic wellbeing: a country is 'free only when the people living in it enjoy liberty in political, social, economic and intellectual spheres'. For Bazaz, independence meant Kashmir being ruled by a local Kashmiri ruler: 'A country is independent when it is ruled by the sons of the soil irrespective of the structure of the government'.[104] Arguably, freedom was the higher, broader or more beneficial concept for people, given that a 'son of the soil' might have, or impose, a structure of government that enabled him or her to act as a dictator with little interest in genuine liberty for people. However, as Bazaz saw things, the India–Pakistan war in and over J&K in 1948 suggested that there was 'no chance' of independence for Kashmir.[105] Both nations wanted Kashmir and neither would allow the establishment of an independent Kashmir, even if it was ruled by a 'son of the soil'. That said, it may have been possible for Kashmir to attain freedom within India.

In 1947 and in the early years of the Kashmir dispute, while some J&K-ites were calling for *azadi*, this was generally articulated as wanting *freedom from* something, not a desire *for* independence. Thereafter, the term *azadi* seemingly disappeared or took a lower profile. In 1953, it resurfaced after Karan Singh dismissed Sheikh Abdullah on 8 August. There followed various periods of protest against India between 1953 and 1975. Writing later, a Kashmiri claims that 'The streets of Kashmir were abuzz with the slogans of *azaadi ya maut* (freedom or death)'. In 1965, the Muttahida Mahaz-e-Azadi (United Movement for Freedom) apparently was 'distributing seditious posters' proposing *azadi*.[106] At the same time, the Plebiscite Front 'kept the aspiration of "azad and khudmukhtar Kashmir" (free and independent Kashmir) alive'.[107] Yet, despite its name, the Plebiscite Front possibly 'broadly favoured independence' until 1975 when Sheikh Abdullah agreed the Kashmir Accord with Indira Gandhi.[108] In 1977, a disenchanted senior Vice-President of the former Plebiscite Front, Sufi Akbar, who supposedly represented 'extremist elements', formed a new party, 'Mahaz Azadi (freedom front), to fight for self-determination in Kashmir'.[109] Otherwise, the term *azadi* does not appear to have had a high profile in J&K until 1988 when Muslim Kashmiris dramatically began their anti-India uprising.

Kashmiris' use of *azadi* in their anti-India uprising

After the unsatisfactory 1987 elections in J&K, many Muslim Kashmiris were disenchanted. As early as 20 August 1987, 'angry' Kashmiris chanted slogans such as "'*Jabri Nata Tod Do, Kashmir Hamara Chhod Do*" (Break the forced relationship, leave our Kashmir)'.[110] A further factor that inspired Muslim Kashmiris was the electoral defeat of the allegedly corrupt Rajiv Gandhi-led Congress Government in India in November 1989. The relatively raw and inexperienced National Front Government replaced it. The Press Council of India reported that this new Government's impact on Kashmiris was 'heady'. Already agitated Kashmiri 'Crowds chanting "azadi" took to the streets, especially under the banner of the Jammu and Kashmir Liberation Front. … Excitement mounted. Tensions escalated.' Volatile Kashmiris were widely using the term *azadi*. Conversely, and as a reaction, the term 'sedition' also appeared in despatches, with this serious nomenclature being used to label disgruntled and protesting anti-India elements in Kashmir. The Press Council stated that 'charges of over-reaction and excesses against the administration [were] being countered by reference to the compulsions of dealing with seditious violence backed by terrorists with trans-border support'.[111] According to one senior Indian jurist, 'Calling for Kashmir's Azadi is Not Sedition'.[112]

By 1990, the insurgency had become violent – and serious. Chief Minister Abdullah noted that there had been 170 'bomb explosions' in Kashmir in 1989.[113] By late December 1989, the 'principal secessionist group', the JKLF, 'had rendered … Srinagar, ungovernable', while JKLF-sponsored *hartals* (strikes) had 'largely paralysed' Kashmir, as had Government-imposed curfews.[114] On 18 June 1990, the JKLF leader, Amanullah Khan, announced that he had formed a 'provisional government … to represent Kashmiris living under Indian occupation'.[115] While the proposed twenty-four-member body was ambitious, many Kashmiris were anticipating that *azadi* was within their grasp. Following this change to Kashmir's international status, liberated Kashmiris would need a new administration to govern themselves. Concurrently, the new Indian Government and its security forces were rattled. Pakistan was assessing how to take advantage of India's dilemma while simultaneously controlling 'its' own agitated J&K-ites living in Azad Kashmir and the Northern Areas who had considerable sympathy for the Kashmiris and their anti-India cause. Kashmiris were significantly motivated.

However, in the early years of their anti-India uprising, Kashmiris' political desires were also not clearly articulated. The Indian journalist, Manoj Joshi, in his comprehensive book, noted that, in April 1989, members of the supposedly secular JKLF used the slogans '*Islam zindabad* and *Hum chahten hein azadi, azadi*'.[116] These 'interchangeable slogans' translate respectively as 'long live Islam' and 'we want freedom'.[117] In May 1990, a delegation member who had recently visited the Kashmir Valley 'observed that the demand for Azad Kashmir and/or [for a] plebiscite has captured the imagination of the majority of the vocal elements in the valley'.[118] Many Kashmiris then wanted, and expected, Kashmir to unify with Pakistan, although the number of pro-Pakistan supporters in Kashmir has always been difficult to quantify. Some Kashmiris are ostensibly pro-Pakistan simply to irk Indians.

Another Indian journalist, Praveen Swami, who did much reporting from Kashmir, noted that the 'anthem' of the 'Jammu and Kashmir National Liberation Front' was:

> Ek Haal, ek umang, guerilla jang, guerilla jang;
> Azadi ka ek hi dhang, guerilla jang, guerilla jang
> [Our one objective, our one desire, [is] guerilla war, guerilla war;
> There is only one way to freedom, guerilla war, guerilla war].[119]

This Front had been the militarised arm of the former (Azad Kashmir) Plebiscite Front.[120] In 1977, the JKLF emerged out of both organisations.[121] When JKLF militants instigated their anti-India uprising, they were not then focusing on the concept of freedom (*azadi*) per se. Rather, possibly inspired by successful resistance movements in neighbouring China in 1949, in Muslim-majority Algeria in 1962, and in Vietnam in 1975,[122] the JKLF wanted to instigate a 'guerilla war' to obtain freedom to win J&K-ites an independent J&K state.

As early as 1970, Amanullah Khan had proposed an armed struggle against India. He wanted the Azad (Free) Kashmir Government to be truly free, i.e., independent, and to take steps 'to free the remaining part of the State from [the] Indian yoke'. For Khan, the 'best way' to do this would be 'guerrilla-cum-commando warfare against India in Kashmir and a very strong propaganda drive abroad'.[123] By 1988, the JKLF, of which Khan was then Chairman, apparently 'had no alternative but to start [an] armed freedom struggle in Kashmir ... to attract world attention to its just cause'.[124] While supposedly wanting to create 'an independent, secular-democratic state', the JKLF nevertheless 'during the early 1990s, cast its agenda in expressly Islamist terms'. According to one Indian analyst, its cadre wanted to create 'an Islamic democracy, … [with] Islamic socialism, and the protection of minority rights as prescribed by the Quran and religious tradition'.[125] Later in the decade, a 1998 JKLF pamphlet stated that a 'requirement' for a solution to the Kashmir dispute was that 'It should safe-guard [sic] the rights of religious and cultural minorities of Kashmir'.[125] The JKLF's 2003 *Roadmap* makes no specific mention of Islam. A 2007 pamphlet talked of J&K being secular.[127] Nevertheless, JKLF militants on the ground in Kashmir employed Islamic terms in their anti-India struggle. This made sense as such terms would have resonated with Muslim Kashmiris, whose language and 'regional culture' has long been 'articulated in the universal language of Islam'.[128]

The JKLF's proposed 'guerrilla-cum-commando warfare against India' was ambitious. The militant group lacked a local safe haven in which it could plan, train, operate and, indeed, as later circumstances showed, physically and militarily survive. It was not motivated or guided by a strong ideology, nor led by battle-hardened guerilla strategists and tacticians, such as Mao Zedong or Ho Chi Minh. It did not operate in a country that was huge (China) or challenging (Vietnam) in which it could mount a protracted popular war and draw succour and protection from local sympathisers. It could not build on the destabilising effects of World War II, as China's Communists had done, nor on a major victory, such as the Vietnamese Communists' catastrophic defeat of the French at Dien Bien Phu in 1954. And, unlike the tough Communist guerillas, the JKLF's 'troops' were raw, inexperienced and relatively 'soft'. Perhaps most significantly, the JKLF did not have the long-term support of a powerful external power, as China and Vietnam had 'enjoyed' with the Soviet Union. The support of Pakistan, the only nation to which the JKLF could realistically turn for help and military assistance, was conditional. Otherwise, China was too difficult to physically access and too strategically close to Pakistan; the Soviet Union was in disarray; and the United States was not interested. Significantly, however, Islamabad would not support on a long-term basis a militant group that wanted Kashmir to be independent of Pakistan.

Kashmiris used other slogans in their insurgency, with many being less ambitious, more Islamic, or clearly against Indians and pro-India Kashmiris. These included: 'Indian pigs go home';[129] 'Indian dogs go home!',[130] and, '["] *Laillah-hailah* [sic] and *yahan kaya chalega – Nizame Mustafa*" (only Islamic rule will be permitted here)'.[131] (*Nizame Mustafa* can be translated as 'Islamic Rule'; Behera translates it as 'the Prophet's order of governance', or the Islamic way of life'.)[132] Some other slogans were clearly directed against pro-India Kashmiri Pandits. In September

1989, with 'militants and secessionists ... said to guarantee communal harmony – there [wa]s no Hindu-Muslim tension in the valley' – supposedly. Local Hindus could conduct their *Janamashtami* celebrations of Lord Krishna's birthday, provided they did not use slogans such as 'Bharat Mata Ki Jai (Hail Mother India)', which would not be tolerated.[133]

However, by 19–20 January 1990, according to one Pandit, the communal situation had worsened. Loudspeakers in Srinagar blared 'threatening' pro-Islamic, anti-India and anti-Pandit slogans before many of his intimidated community fled the Kashmir Valley.[134] These slogans included: 'Eliminate every Indian'; 'Pray to God for the elimination of Kafirs [non-believers]!'; 'Kashmir mein rahna hai to Allah, Allah Kahna hai' (one desirous of living in Kashmir will have to espouse Islam); 'Either mix or leave, otherwise we shall annihilate you'; ... 'Yahan kya Chalega – Nizam-e-Mustafa' (It will be only Nizam-e-Mustafa here).[135] The next day, 'Slogans denouncing the police, India and calling for "Azadi" were raised.'[136] 'Facing homelessness, the Hindu community regarded *aazadi* as an exclusory slogan.'[137]

Other Kashmiri Pandits endured similar slogans. In February 1990, a Pandit nurse heard a passing procession 'raising anti-national' and 'fundamentalist' slogans. These included: '*Kashmir mein agar rehna hoga, Allah ho Akbar kehna hoga*' (If you wish to live in Kashmir you have to say 'Allah ho Akbar' [God is Great]) and '*Dil mein rakho Allah ka khauf, haath mein rakho Kalashnikov*' (One must have fear of Allah in his heart and a Kalashnikov in his hand).[138] According to another Pandit, by the end of January 1990, loudspeakers in Srinagar mosques were broadcasting slogans like '*Kafiron Kashmir chhod do* [Infidels, leave our Kashmir]', 'Pakistan zindabad [Long live Pakistan]', '*Jiye jiye mujahideen* [Long live the mujahideen]', and '*Hindustani kutto Pakistan chhodo*' [Indian dogs leave Pakistan].'[139] In February, to hide his identity, a young Pandit joined other Kashmiris in Srinagar shouting slogans. He 'called for "azadi" for Kashmir' and 'hailed Pakistan and condemned the "Indian dogs" – [because] there was little else I could do if I had [wanted] to live that day'.[140] Such anti-Pandit sentiments and slogans while despicable, may have been overstated. According to one commentator, the 'available evidence' suggested that such 'allegations' were 'largely though not entirely, a potpourri of fabrication and exaggeration'.[141] This was not then, and is not now, the perception of many Kashmiri Pandits.

The significance of these various slogans is that they reflected the disparate nature of the Muslim Kashmiris' anti-India insurgency which, almost from its instigation in 1988, was disunified and with more than one aim. In 1990, there may have been 'about 32 militant groups',[142] although Behera has provided a 'select list' of a staggering 175 'militant groups of Jammu and Kashmir'.[143] Not surprisingly, as Ishaq Khan noted, with such an array of participating and competing groups, 'the mass movement became rudderless in no time, with many local, not national or truly Islamic revolutionary, leaders in the fray'.[144] While some militant groups favoured independence for Kashmir or joining Pakistan, some seemingly had no idea what they wanted, except to protest. The JKLF was clearly for an independent J&K. Newer groups 'like Allah Tigers, Al Jihad, Al Maqbool, Hizb-e-Allah, Hizb-e-Islam and Al Khomeini ... along with the "non-violent" People's League [we]re believed to be pro-Pakistan' and/or motivated by Islam.[145]

Over time, the Kashmiris' anti-India insurgency stabilised as militants coalesced or were eliminated by the Indian paramilitary, or by rival groups. Most insurgent actions came to be undertaken by the three major pro-Pakistan militant groups: Hizbul Mujahideen, Lashkar-e-Toiba and Jaish-e-Mohammed. The JKLF continued to exist, but members located in Kashmir (as against in Azad Kashmir or in Pakistan) renounced violence and the party joined the APHC.[146] In May 1994, Yasin Malik, a high-profile Kashmiri JKLF fighter and leader, 'declared a ceasefire and announced that he would pursue non-violent means for *azadi*'.[147] Shortly before, he, Syed Ali Shah Geelani, Shabbir Shah, Abdul Ghani Lone and some 176 other political prisoners had been released from detention in a good will gesture by India.[148] Despite ill health while being detained between 1990–94, Malik continued to be politically active thereafter. In 2003, for example, he was the main attraction of a mass *yatra* (journey; pilgrimage) called *Safar-e-Azadi* (Journey of Freedom) that travelled through Kashmir. This followed his party's collection of 800,000 signatures in support of 'an independent, secular, democratic country'. Problematically, however, Yasin Malik appeared to overwhelmingly and excessively control the JKLF.[149] In 2019, the Indian Government outlawed the Yasin Malik faction of the JKLF under the Unlawful Activities (Prevention) Act (UAPA). New Delhi accused Malik's faction of 'funnelling funds for fomenting terrorism' and the killing of Kashmiri Pandits in 1989 that led to their departure from Kashmir.[150] The Indian Government put Malik, along with Shabbir Shah and some other Kashmiris who India sees as being anti-India, in jail again in New Delhi. It is difficult to know how popular the JKLF is in Kashmir.

Apart from slogans such as 'Go India, Go Back',[151] *azadi* still appeared to be the term that most Kashmiris used in their agitations. According to the Kashmiri journalist, Gowhar Geelani, following the killing of the popular militant and supposed 'people's hero', Burhan Wani, in 2016, the *azadi* slogan was widely shouted by all segments of distraught and unhappy Kashmiri Muslim society throughout Kashmir, as well as by some Kashmiri Sikhs:

> 'Hum kya chahate, azadi,
> Hai haq hamara, azadi,
> Burhan, tere khoon se, inquilab aayega'
> ('We want freedom,
> freedom is our right,
> Burhan, your blood will bring forth the revolution')[152]

Reflecting the 'many fissures' in Kashmir, some Kashmiri Muslims also chanted 'Burhan bhai ka kya farman: Kashmir banega Pakistan' ('What is the order of brother Burhan: Kashmir will merge with Pakistan'). For Geelani, the mood around the time of Wani's funeral was similar to the mood when the uprising began in 1989. Amongst other things, Wani's death 'recharge[d] the sentiment of azadi'. Nevertheless, the challenge for outsiders – and, indeed, for Kashmiris themselves – was, and continues to be, to understand what Kashmiris mean, and what they actually want, when they use this term.

Meanings of azadi

There are many translations and meanings for this imprecise and confusing term azadi. In 2013, Dilip Padgaonkar, who led a committee of three official Indian interlocutors on J&K comprising himself, Radha Kumar and M. M. Ansari, also confronted this problem:

> People of Kashmir don't know the specific meaning of Azadi. They raise this slogan without knowing what they want. ... We asked people to be specific and describe the meaning of Azadi, but to our surprise they failed to describe the meaning of Azadi. They did not want Azadi from India but wanted that their social and economic issues should be addressed.

Padgaonkar claimed that 'not a single person' whom he met – and his committee apparently interacted with 700 delegations in 2010–11[153] – 'sought freedom from India'; equally importantly, 'those want[ing] Azadi from India did not bother to meet the team' that Padgaonkar led.[154] Padgaonkar is one in a long list of high-profile Indians who have engaged with Kashmiris as interlocutors or via various committees. These Indians include: K. C. Pant (2001), Arun Jaitley (2002), Ram Jethmalani (2002), N. N. Vohra (2003), Hamid Ansari (2007), M. K. Rasgotra (2007), L. K. Advani (2013), Yashwant Sinha (2016) and Dineshwar Sharma (2017).[155]

Another challenge with the term *azadi* is that, in some instances, a writer simply assumes that the reader knows what it is. For example, Tavleen Singh, in her informative book about Kashmir, notes that '*azadi* has always been something that has lurked in the background' in Kashmir. This seemingly inherent knowledge may explain why Singh neither discusses, nor explains, what *azadi* actually is, despite this term appearing some nineteen times in her book.[156] On the other hand, in a long book written by the Indian political commentator, A. G. Noorani, the term '*azaadi*' appeared twenty-five times. Noorani provided at least five differing explanations for this term: freedom; independence; secession from India; self-rule within India; and accession to Pakistan.[157] Essentially, these five explanations appear to represent the major aspirations of Kashmiris.

For scholars also, there appears to be little agreement about what *azadi* means. The Kashmiri, Mohammad Ishaq Khan, who lived through the early years of the Kashmiris' anti-India uprising, translated *azadi* as 'independence', which desire he says Kashmiris have nurtured since 1931, and possibly even since 1586.[158] Other scholars, such as Reeta Tremblay, have translated *azadi* as 'freedom'; 'Since 1953, … the nationalist discourse in the Kashmir Valley has incrementally progressed from the demand for *raishumari* (plebiscite), then for autonomy and, finally, for *azaadi* (freedom). Indeed, *azaadi* is now the operative discourse in the Valley.'[159] Another scholar, Shahla Hussain, who has analysed 'Kashmiri nationalism through the shifting meaning of the word *aazadi*',[160] has translated the term as 'freedom', although she also has concluded that, for Kashmiris, *azadi* 'has a much deeper meaning then mere political freedom'. It involves 'the desire to live freely with dignity in one's homeland, without constraints or impositions'. It 'envisions a society free from social hierarchies and economic disparities, a society based on faith and trust – and one that respects differences, allows criticism and values human dignity'.[161] Similarly, Maqbool Butt at his trial in Pakistan for collaborating with Indian intelligence agencies described *azadi* as 'not just getting rid of foreign occupation of our beloved motherland but also … remov[ing] hunger, poverty, ignorance and disease, and … overcome[ing] economic and social deprivation'.[162] Arguably, this explanation reflected what Sheikh Abdullah wanted for Kashmir and Kashmiris.

Pro-India elements generally have other explanations for the term *azadi*. For the late political activist, Balraj Puri, from Jammu, 'As far as the sentiment of *azadi* is concerned, it is the Urdu translation of two different concepts of independence and freedom'. According to Puri, in 1947, Sheikh Abdullah 'claimed that he achieved *azadi* for Kashmir after four centuries of slavery', although, thereafter, 'he did not provide freedom to the people. No opposition was allowed.'[163] In this case, *azadi* meant freedom from being ruled by non-Kashmiris. For India's former Home Minister, P. Chidambaram, *azadi* meant 'greater autonomy': 'when people of Jammu and Kashmir ask for "azadi", most of them mean greater autonomy'.[164] For a former chief of India's Research and Analysis Wing, Amarjit Singh Dulat, who served in J&K from 1988–90 during the early days of the insurgency, *azadi* for Kashmiris meant 'accommodation': 'The azadi (freedom) that they want … is accommodation. They want their honour, dignity and most of all, justice.'[165] As noted in Chapter 6, securing 'Izzat-o-Abroo (honour and dignity)' for Kashmiris has always been important.

The Indian scholar, Yoginder Sikand, has explained that *azadi* may mean 'accession to Pakistan' or even the establishment of an Islamic state. Sikand states that the respected Kashmiri political leader, Syed Ali Shah Geelani, gave *azadi* 'an entirely different twist' in his book, *Nava-e Hurriyat* [Voice of Freedom].[166] Geelani 'interprets it [*azadi*] to mean both accession to Pakistan as well as unrelenting opposition to an independent Jammu and Kashmir. It is as if only by joining Pakistan that Kashmir can find azadi, the term here being reduced simply to anti-Indianism or freedom from Indian rule.'[167] Furthermore, Geelani considers that it is Islam that motivates militants, not Kashmiri nationalism or anti-India sentiments, and that the aim is to establish an 'Islamic state'. This 'Islamist vision' for J&K had appeal for other Kashmiris.[168] The journalist, Riyaz Wani, quoting the former Hizbul Mujahideen commander, Zakir Musa (who left this organisation and was killed in May 2019), states that Musa said: 'I will not fight for Azadi for a secular state. I will fight for Azadi for Islam, for the establishment of an Islamic state'.[169] Arguably, then, *azadi* is in the eye of the beholder.

It is difficult to determine how many Kashmiris actually favour *azadi*, or independence, for their homelands. Some opinion polls have been conducted, although none has been fully representative of J&K-ites. In 2009, Robert Bradnock surveyed Jammu, Ladakh, most of Kashmir, and most of Azad Kashmir. However, his poll excluded some districts in Indian J&K (Doda, Kupwara, Pulwama), Azad Kashmir's Neelum District, and all of Gilgit-Baltistan. The sample group was small, with most respondents living in urban areas, both of which factors influenced the results. (Traditionally, urban dwellers are more inclined to want to change the status quo than rural dwellers.) Bradnock's results were interesting. Of the 1,400 Azad Kashmiris surveyed, 44 per cent favoured 'independence for the whole of Kashmir [sic]', that is independence for J&K. Surprisingly, this included 58 per cent of people surveyed in Poonch District, whose forebears had staged an anti-Maharaja, pro-Pakistan uprising in 1947. In Indian J&K, 43 per cent of the 2,374 people surveyed favoured independence. Specifically, in Ladakh, 30 per cent of people surveyed in Leh District and 20 per cent in Kargil District wanted independence. Conversely, there was zero support for independence in all Jammu districts except for Jammu, where a miniscule 1 per cent wanted independence. In the Kashmir Valley's districts, many of those surveyed favoured independence: 74 per cent in Anantnag; 75 per cent in Badgam; 95 per cent in Baramulla; and 82 per cent in Srinagar.[170] Overall, Bradnock's results supported the view that many J&K-ites want to be offered the third option of independence for their state or homelands.[171]

The final word to end this discussion about what the term *azadi* actually means belongs to Madhu Kishwar. For her, *azadi* means 'independence'. However, Kishwar also importantly notes that 'Azadi is no doubt a very powerful and emotive slogan but it has remained precisely that: a mere slogan'.[172] This factor, coupled with the term's imprecision, are the nub of the problem for Kashmiris.

The sixth phase: unilaterally, India has resolved the Kashmir dispute?

In 2019, the Indian Government took some highly significant actions in relation to J&K that mean the Kashmiris' anti-India uprising has now entered a sixth, and uncertain, phase. This phase reflects a hardening of attitudes by both Indians and Kashmiris. In recent years, the Kashmiris' lack of clarity about *azadi* appears to have changed. Increasingly, many 'ordinary' or 'average' Muslim Kashmiris – as against 'special' pro-India Kashmiri politicians or violent anti-India militants – now strongly seem to want Kashmir to be free from both India and Indian control, regardless of the costs that must be borne to obtain this freedom. Such strident Kashmiris are no longer inclined to toe the Indian line. Instead, they appear to be pursuing 'negative' *azadi* – strongly, blindly, even violently, wanting to be free from India – rather than 'positive' *azadi* – desiring and agitating, usually using peaceful means, for the creation of a new state independent from India. Such a deeply negative attitude among ordinary Muslim Kashmiris is a relatively recent phenomenon.

A significant turning point had been the killing of Burhan Wani in July 2016, followed by the security forces' tough response to the subsequent protests. Seemingly, such brutality was the final indignity for many ordinary Kashmiris. Post-Wani, their anti-India insurgency seemed to become wider and more inclusive, spreading to include urban and rural Kashmiris, northern and southern Kashmiris, and highly- and lesser-educated Kashmiris. They appeared to be prepared to confront

Indian security forces operating in the Kashmir Valley openly, even brazenly, whatever the consequences, including suffering serious injury or being killed. Indeed, for Kashmiris, *azadi* now seems to mean, simply and predominantly, 'opposing India' whenever they can and with whatever they have at their disposal, beginning with stones. It occurred to me after meeting a Kashmiri analyst in 2018 that, for Kashmiris, the term *azadi* might now be an acronym: Actively, Zealously, Always, Denying India. Independence, in the sense of establishing a self-governing state free from coerced subordination to another nation, does not seem to be uppermost in many Muslim Kashmiris' thoughts any more. Rather, *azadi* is now all about resisting India. Concurrently, however, India has also become more hardline and uncompromising. Similarly, its security forces have adopted 'hard and muscular' counter-insurgency measures in Kashmir.[173] In August 2019, the re-elected BJP-led Indian Government delivered the *coup de grace*: it imposed some legislative and administrative changes unilaterally 'in secrecy and stealth' on J&K with little direct consultation on this specific issue with either elected J&K representatives or J&K voters.

The year 2019 had started badly. On 14 February, a vehicle-borne suicide bomber who belonged to Jaish-e-Mohammed attacked a convoy of Central Reserve Police Force personnel travelling through the Pulwama District, south of Srinagar. This local Kashmiri Muslim, Adil Ahmed Dar, executed the 'worst ever terror attack' in J&K, killing forty-four people.[174] India–Pakistan relations plummeted, and India suspended both cross-LOC bus services for J&K-ites and cross-LOC trade. On 26 February, Indian Air Force planes bombed an alleged terrorist haven located near Balakot, in Pakistan's Khyber Pakhtunkhwa Province, in what appeared to be a retaliatory attack. India reviles the Jaish-e-Mohammed, partly because its founder, Masood Azhar, had been in an Indian jail during 1994–99. In 1999, the Indian Government released Azhar, who was then a member of the Harkat-ul-Mujahideen (Movement of Holy Warriors), as part of a deal to end the hijacking of an Indian Airlines plane to Kandahar.[175] While India claimed that the Balakot operation was a success, Pakistan denied that the Indian strike caused any damage.[176] Nevertheless, the Indian action satisfied a short term desire by many Indians for revenge, while also helpfully boosting the campaign rhetoric of the ruling Bharatiya Janata Party (BJP) for India's April-May general elections. In 2019, the BJP-led National Democratic Alliance Government was returned to office with an increased majority.

By the end of 2019, ceasefire violations, infiltration attempts across the LOC and the number of Kashmiris joining militant groups had all increased, but levels of violence had decreased, as had tourist numbers – dramatically. In 2018, 268,000 people visited J&K; in 2019, the figure was a mere 36,000.[177] These figures compared unfavourably with the 2011 figure of over 1 million Indian and 32,000 foreign tourists.[178] Indeed, the 2019 figure was almost back to the level seen in 1940 when 29,000 tourists comprising 21,000 Indians and 8,000 foreigners visited Kashmir (which then was a significant number).[179] Partly this decrease in tourism to Kashmir was due to political uncertainty and instability in the state after Governor's Rule was imposed for the eighth time in J&K on 20 June 2018. This followed the collapse of the People's Democratic Party–BJP Government after the BJP withdrew from this coalition.[180] The (final) Governor of J&K, Satya Pal Malik, then governed J&K himself, not a cabinet formed from elected members of the J&K Legislative Assembly, which body Malik also suspended. After Governor's Rule expired in December 2018, it was replaced by President's Rule (which was extended until 31 October 2019). In other words, New Delhi now directly controlled the state, albeit still through Governor Malik and his bureaucrats.

Tourist numbers were also affected after the Indian Government imposed a severe clampdown on Kashmir during the latter half of 2019 following some significant changes that were made to J&K's status and stature. On 5 August 2019, things changed dramatically for J&K when Home Minister Amit Shah took a well-planned and decisive set of actions that had clearly resulted after he and his colleagues had put in 'a lot of thought'.[181] Shah utilised two Presidential Orders to revoke J&K's 'special rights' and autonomy supposedly, but largely unsuccessfully, guaranteed by the 'temporary provisions' of Article 370 of the Indian Constitution.[182] Put simply, the first Presidential Order enabled the (suspended) J&K Legislative Assembly to supersede the defunct J&K Constituent Assembly, 'the recommendation' of which latter body, according to Article 370, was required to abrogate or amend this very article. The first Presidential Order also made clear that 'the Governor of Jammu and Kashmir' essentially equated to 'the Government of the said State'.[183] The second Presidential Order then revoked, or 'cease[d] to make operative', Article 370, which, in turn, immediately and consequentially annulled Article 35-A.[184] At the same time, the J&K Constitution was suspended.[185] Article 35-A had only allowed J&K State Subjects (i.e., locals) to purchase immoveable property (i.e., land) and/or to obtain government positions in J&K and/or to live in the state.[186] In a major change to the way that J&K has functioned, New Delhi would now determine who had the right to live and buy property in J&K, not J&K-ites.

For a non-lawyer like me, these Presidential Orders appeared to suffer from a serious flaw. Supposedly, in imposing them, the Indian President, Ram Nath Kovind, had acted with the J&K Government's 'concurrence'. However, he, of course, was essentially acting as the Government in that state following the instigation of President's Rule in December 2019. Essentially, therefore, the President of India, Ram Nath Kovind, concurred with himself, Ram Nath Kovind. The President may also have exceeded his constitutional powers, including in relation to J&K. His 'jugglery' also opened up many other questions, including whether the J&K Constituent Assembly, by its very dissolution without recommending abrogation, had ever intended that Article 370 be abrogated.[187] This Presidential process and the various legal and constitutional questions that it raised are one reason why petitioners have challenged these significant actions and their constitutionality in the Indian Supreme Court. At the time of writing, this Court had not made any rulings. This may take some time if the reference sent to the Supreme Court in 1982 about the contentious J&K Resettlement Bill, which it returned unanswered in 2001, is any guide.[188] It may be easier to stall and consider, over an extended time, the legalities of these serious, contentious changes and let matters settle down, than to address them immediately.

Shortly after Article 370's abrogation, large majorities in India's Rajya Sabha (5 August) and Lok Sabha (6 August) passed the 'Jammu and Kashmir Reorganisation Act, 2019'. The act received the President's (rapid) assent on 9 August.[189] This bill enabled the Indian Government to bifurcate J&K into two separate territories: Jammu and Kashmir, and Ladakh. The rationale for this significant change was buried in the act under a section titled 'Statement of Objects and Reasons':

> The Ladakh Division of the State of Jammu and Kashmir has a large area but is sparsely populated with a very difficult terrain. There has been a long pending demand of people of Ladakh, to give it the status of a Union Territory to enable them to realise their aspirations. The Union Territory of Ladakh will be without Legislature.
>
> Further, keeping in view the prevailing internal security situation, fuelled by cross border terrorism in the existing State of Jammu and Kashmir, a separate Union Territory for Jammu and Kashmir is being created. The Union Territory of Jammu and Kashmir will be with legislature.[190]

This significant demotion in status was to come into place on 31 October. It was a little odd that Ladakhis would be helped to 'realise their aspirations' without a legislature, while J&K would have a legislature seemingly due to their difficult 'prevailing internal security situation'. To ensure the creation of the new Union Territory, New Delhi appointed Girish Chandra Murmu as its Lieutenant Governor. Originally from Odisha, Murmu is a long-term bureaucrat who served as Narendra Modi's principal secretary when he was Chief Minister of Gujarat. Significantly, Murmu was trusted by both the Prime Minister and by the Home Minister, Amit

Shah,[191] an important factor given the major changes imposed on J&K and New Delhi's desire to integrate this state fully into India. On 7 August 2020, he was replaced by Manoj Sinha, a political figure from Uttar Pradesh.

The long and comprehensive Reorganisation Act, which had been drafted secretively, included other changes. It made 106 Central laws and seven State laws applicable to Jammu and Kashmir and to Ladakh; it repealed 164 State laws and Governor's Acts for both new territories; and it allowed a further 166 State Acts including Governor's Acts to remain in place for both new territories.[192] Similarly, the existing High Court will serve both territories. The Reorganisation bill also detailed a new Legislative Assembly for the new J&K territory, which would be largely advisory; the second J&K chamber, the Legislative Council, was abolished; Ladakh's Lieutenant Governor would directly administer this territory. J&K would receive a ninety-seat Legislative Assembly, with electorate boundaries to be based on the 2011 Indian Census. Essentially, the Assembly will 'aid and advise' the J&K Lieutenant Governor,[193] who appears to be far more powerful than either the Chief Minister, the Council of Ministers or the Legislature – based on the mention of each in the Reorganisation Act: the Lieutenant Governor is mentioned about fifty times; the Chief Minister only four times. New seats may be reserved for refugees, emigrants, women and some minority groups, with Kashmiris fearing that this delimitation process may tip the balance of seats in favour of Jammu. The major parties have boycotted this delimitation process. As the National Conference noted in May 2020, to do otherwise would be 'tantamount to accepting the events of August 5, 2019'.[194] With neither new territory being self-governing, this situation allows New Delhi to closely control both of these strategically important frontline border entities.

New Delhi also imposed severe security measures on Jammu and Kashmir. This 'comprehensive clampdown' included stringent curfews, intense security patrolling and total, followed by severe, limitations of access to telecommunications, including the internet. To aid these processes, New Delhi inducted 38,000 additional security forces into Kashmir shortly before Shah's actions. Some 8.8 million mobile phones were blocked. When internet services finally were restored after 'the longest internet shutdown ever imposed in a democracy', they were only at the 2G level, not 4G. This has posed serious challenges for businesses, health services and on-line schooling.[195] There is a long history of such curtailing, all-encompassing curfews in Kashmir. In the period 2012 to July 2018, the internet was blocked sixty-two times.[196] As a result of the most recent measures, the locked down Kashmiris did not live, but existed, in an 'open air prison'.[197] For people who weren't

Indian officials – which was most observers – it was impossible to know the Kashmiris' real situation, circumstances or wellbeing, as almost no news was coming out of Kashmir. Seemingly, Kashmiris had been effectively silenced. While Kashmiris quickly were made 'ordinary' Indians, India's security forces extraordinarily, rapidly and almost totally incarcerated them, a circumstance that was distinctly different from that of most other 'ordinary' Indians.

In 2020, two further significant changes were made concerning demography and the media. First, in April, the Ministry for Home Affairs issued a significant order for the 'adaptation and modification of State Laws … to further facilitate the application of Central Laws to the newly formed Union Territory of Jammu and Kashmir'.[198] Significantly, this order altered the 'conditions' of what was required for a person to attain 'domicile' for this territory. Under Item 14, 'The Jammu and Kashmir Civil Services (Decentralization and Recruitment) Act (Act No. XVI of 2010)', domicile was redefined, significantly, to include a person

> (a) who has resided for a period of fifteen years in the Union territory of Jammu and Kashmir or has studied for a period of seven years and appeared in Class 10th/12th examination in an educational institution located in the Union territory of Jammu and Kashmir; or (b) who is registered as a migrant by the Relief and Rehabilitation Commissioner (Migrants) in the Union territory of Jammu and Kashmir.[199]

Apart from causing 'anger and disillusionment among Kashmiris',[200] some Kashmiris – and, indeed, some Jammuites (and Ladakhis) – fear that this change will allow many non-J&K-ites to enter, and remain, in the newly formed Union Territory. For the Kashmiri political analyst, Siddiq Wahid, the new domicile laws will lead to demographic change in, or even 'demographic flooding' of, J&K.[201] Conversely, many Hindu Pandits, most of whom now reside outside the state, consider that demographic change has already occurred in Kashmir. Interestingly, early figures suggest that most 'residency certificates' were issued to applicants living in Jammu, not Kashmir. Of the 25,000 domicile certificates granted (out of 33,000 applications) between 18 May and 28 June 2020 via a 'fast-track' fifteen-day process, some 21,000 were issued to applicants living in Jammu's ten districts, particularly Doda (8,500), Rajouri (6,200) and Poonch (6,100). In Kashmir, only 435 certificates (of 720 applications) were issued.[202] Some Jammuites have reacted with alarm to this development.

A second significant change occurred in late April 2020 when the J&K Information and Public Relations Department released its revised 'Media Policy 2020'.[203] This 'fresh and pro-active media policy' noted that J&K had been 'through a transformative process'. Its long and incredibly detailed policy aimed to engage stakeholders and 'increase public awareness', to better and more widely disseminate information, to 'foster a genuinely positive image of the [J&K] Government' and 'to thwart mis-information, fake news and … any attempts to use [the] media to incite communal passions, preach violence, or to propagate any information prejudicial to the sovereignty and integrity of India'. To prevent 'the efforts of anti-social and anti-national elements to disturb the peace', each media outlet, whether print or online, and its 'publishers/editors/key personnel' and journalists would need to go through an 'empanelment' process that would include a 'robust background check including verification of antecedents of each journalist'. Each outlet would need to reapply every two years for re-empanelment. 'Any individual or group indulging in fake news, unethical or anti national activities' would be 'de-empanelled', 'proceeded against under law' and would not receive government advertisements, an important source of media revenue. A review committee comprising officers from the Information and Public Relations Department would hear any appeals against de-empanelment.

The aim of this excessively intrusive Media Policy 2020 and its myriad number of bureaucratic requirements appeared to be to rule out media outlets, rather than to rule them in. Even more pointedly, it aimed to disseminate, and ensure adherence to, the 'normalcy narrative': to ensure that a positive narrative about J&K is disseminated, both by the Department and by J&K's various media outlets.[204] Essentially, this policy will allow the J&K administration to indirectly 'influence' or directly control the J&K narrative and those attempting to report or discuss it. Presumably, this means that we will hear even less accurate reporting about what Kashmiris now want or are doing. Rather than fake news, it may now be 'flaky' news. Alternatively, if India can't extinguish the insurgency or the Kashmiris' desire for *azadi*, it will extinguish news of both. Freedom of speech and freedom of the press are the hallmarks of a vibrant, modern democracy, with regulations such as these currently becoming more prevalent in authoritarian regimes around the world. One of the factors that won the Cold War was openness and transparency, so something is being lost with these suppressions.

Seemingly, New Delhi's legal, administrative and communication changes since mid-2019 have resolved the issues of its former recalcitrant, once constitutionally different, state. Problem solved. Since 2019, the J&K state has ceased to exist and, rather than become 'just another Indian state', it has become 'just another two Indian territories'. Two Indian maps confirm these changes and show that all of J&K, including those areas 'occupied' by Pakistan and China, to the latter's chagrin, are part of India.[205] For New Delhi, all the areas of J&K unequivocally are now a part of India; all of the people in these areas are unequivocally now Indians! This means that the residents of the former state of J&K have not only lost their special status and privileges, but also non-J&K-ites can now purchase land anywhere in the former J&K state. This has made Kashmiris, Jammuites and Ladakhis wary lest wealthier outsiders purchase their land – although, equally, it will require these locals to agree to sell their land in the first place to any 'outsiders'. There is also uneasiness about bigger and better-resourced external companies chiefly from Punjab, Uttar Pradesh and Rajasthan, winning licenses in public auctions to lease and mine J&K's 554 mineral blocks, of which 261 are located in ten districts of Kashmir, including along the Jhelum River 'lifeline'. Most blocks contain sand deposits, a very important building resource, but other exploitable materials available in 'abundant supply' include coal, granite, marble, limestone, gypsum, bauxite and borax.[206]

Although these impositions were 'muscular', J&K-ites should not have been totally surprised that the BJP made them. The BJP-led Government justified them for two reasons. First, at the Lok Sabha elections in April-May 2019, the BJP had clearly sought a mandate for these changes, and had considered by its victory that it had obtained such a mandate. Item 14 in the 'Nation First' section of the BJP's electoral manifesto stated clearly that the party was committed to abrogating Article 370, reiterating that this has been a 'position [held] since the time of the Jan [sic] Sangh', and to annulling Article 35-A, which the BJP considered 'discriminatory' and 'an obstacle in the development of the state'. The 2019 manifesto also talked about the 'safe return of Kashmiri Pandits' and providing financial support for 'the resettlement of refugees from West [sic] Pakistan, Pakistan occupied Jammu and Kashmir (POJK) and Chhamb' – an issue that had caused Sheikh Abdullah major problems in the 1970s.[207] Interestingly, 'West Pakistan' has not existed since 1970, when India defeated Pakistan in the war that saw Bangladesh come into being. Presumably, New Delhi was referring to J&K-ites displaced during the 1965 India–Pakistan war.

While the BJP's 2019 electoral manifesto concerning J&K was stronger and more conclusive than its 2014 version, the older manifesto had also stated that the BJP was committed to abrogating Article 370, but that it would 'discuss this [issue] with all stakeholders'. It did not mention Article 35-A.[208] Ominously, the 2014 manifesto also had a prominent image of 'Dr Syama Prasad Mookerjee', the politician who had inspired the Praja Parishad's agitation in the 1950s and who had founded the Jana Sangh, a predecessor to the BJP. In 2014, some J&K-ites may also have been alerted, or alarmed, when Jitendra Singh, a 'powerful deputy in the Prime

Minister's Office' stated on his first day in office that the BJP had 'started discussions for revoking Article 370'. Singh, a Jammuite politician, had defeated former J&K Chief Minister, Ghulam Nabi Azad, for the Udhampur constituency in the 2014 Lok Sabha elections. Immediately after, Singh publicly stated that the BJP had started discussions to revoke Article 370, which it now had a state and national mandate to do. After this 'stirred up a hornet's nest', he later claimed to have been misquoted.[209] As a former medical professional, he may also have been 'feeling the (political) pulse'. Given how thorough the BJP's abrogation 'programme' was in 2019, arguably, their planning for the momentous legal and administrative changes that they imposed on J&K may well have started in 2014.

The second reason for the BJP-led Government justifying its changes in J&K concerned Mr Modi himself. In 2014, India's new Prime Minister had stated positively while visiting Kashmir that 'his aim was to win the hearts of the people of the state'.[210] By 2019, he had become more hardline, certainly in relation to Articles 370 and 35-A. As Mr Modi publicly put things immediately after both Articles had been abrogated, they had

> given nothing but secessionism, terrorism, nepotism and widespread corruption on a large scale to Jammu-Kashmir. Both these articles were used as a weapon by Pakistan to flare up the emotions of some people. ... I assure these friends of Jammu–Kashmir that the situation will gradually return to normal and all their troubles too will reduce.[211]

That remains to be seen, although Mr Modi quite possibly has now lost 'the hearts of the people of the state', albeit mainly Kashmiri hearts. That said, the abrogation of Article 35-A has also displeased some Jammuites and Ladakhis. Perhaps the next move for the BJP will be to bifurcate the Union Territory of Jammu and Kashmir into its two component parts, which might appeal to people in both places, then to make Srinagar and Jammu the respective capital of each part. The former action would end Kashmiris' post-1947 domination and diminution of Jammuites; the latter action would resolve the costly and inefficient durbar 'issue' whereby the administration, all of its files, and much of its staff, moves between government offices located in either city every six months. This move, which involves some 7,000 employees, roughly half of whom 'avail' themselves of government accommodation existing in either city (and therefore which possibly is idle for half a year), costs around 'Rs 80 crore' each year for the actual move.[212] This seems a large expense for a developing state.

The Kashmiris' response to these various changes has been hard to gauge as, concurrently, they had to endure a heavy and harsh security 'lockdown' imposed on them, their movements and their communications, including media. Surprisingly, this lockdown included placing most high-profile, pro-India or mainstream politicians under house arrest, which suggested that New Delhi was concerned that even India's pro-India Kashmiri 'allies' would dislike these impositions. After the 'events' of 5 August 2019, '5,164 persons' were detained, 'of whom 609 were [still] under detention' on 20 November 2019.[213] Those detained included three former Chief Ministers: Farooq Abdullah, Omar Abdullah and Mehbooba Mufti, about whom the BJP appeared to be spitefully miffed as her party had previously been in an uneasy coalition with the BJP. No elected BJP legislator was detained.[214] While many of those arrested were slowly released, in order for this to happen, each person released surprisingly 'had to pledge that they would not criticize government actions'. At the time of writing (July 2020), Mehbooba Mufti was still being detained under the all-powerful, all-encompassing and oppressive Public Safety Act. There was nowhere that dissatisfied citizens, or their relatives, could seek redress. The Indian Government had permanently shut down all statutory bodies, such as state commissions for human rights, women and child rights, anti-corruption, and the right to information.[215] Basically, Kashmiris were on their own – literally and figuratively.

A former Indian interlocutor on J&K, Radha Kumar, believed that Kashmiris' response to these various impositions would have been 'utter rage and despair',[216] particularly as, just prior to being detained, a number of political leaders had agreed the 'Gupkar Declaration' on 4 August 2019. It resolved to 'protect and defend' J&K's identity, autonomy and special status 'against all attacks and onslaughts whatsoever', and stated that abrogation of Articles 35-A and 370 or 'trifurcation' of J&K 'would be an aggression against the people of Jammu[,] Kashmir and Ladakh'.[217] However, before they could do anything positively protective or detrimentally defensive, these leaders were put under house arrested and effectively silenced for at least the next seven months. It was hard to fully determine, but Kashmiris seemed unhappy and surly. For a group of concerned citizens, the Indian Government's 'disastrous' actions and its 'prioritization of counter-insurgency concerns over human security' had caused 'a near-total alienation of the people of the Kashmir valley from the Indian state and people'.[218]

An independent J&K or an independent Kashmir

Seemingly, the changes imposed by the Indian Government on Indian J&K in 2019 mean that New Delhi has unilaterally resolved its dispute with J&K and extinguished the desires for *azadi* amongst J&K-ites, particularly Kashmiris. Nevertheless, if we presume that J&K-ites, including Kashmiris, mean independence when they use the term *azadi*, then how feasible is it that either Jammu and Kashmir or Kashmir could actually exist as independent entities?[219] This section examines either possibility. As per Table 7.1, by 'Jammu and Kashmir', I mean the entire former princely state as it existed on 15 August 1947: Jammu Province, Kashmir Province, and the Frontier Districts Province, which included the Gilgit Agency and Gilgit Leased Area. This comprises the seven regions listed in Table 7.1. By 'Kashmir', I mean the Kashmir Valley, which equates to the Kashmir Valley Division in Table 7.1.

Table 7.1   *Jammu and Kashmir: areas and population, July 2019*[a]

Region	Area (square km)[b]	Population
Jammu & Kashmir	222,236	17,517,037
Indian Jammu & Kashmir	101,387	12,548,925
Jammu Division	26,293	5,350,811
Kashmir Valley Division	15,948	6,907,622
Ladakh Division	59,146	290,492
Non-Indian Jammu & Kashmir		
Combined area administered by Pakistan	78,114	4,968,112
Azad Jammu & Kashmir		4,045,367
Gilgit-Baltistan (formerly the Northern Areas)		922,745
Areas under China's control		
Shaksgam area	5,180	Light?
Aksai Chin	37,555	Light?

Source: (1) 'Divisions & Districts', *Jammu & Kashmir: Official State Portal*, undated (based on 'Census of India 2011'), https://jk.gov.in/jammukashmir/?q=divisions; (2) 'Jammu & Kashmir Profile', *CensusInfo India 2011*, undated (based on 'Census of India 2011'), http://censusindia.gov. in/2011census/censusinfodashboard/stock/profiles/en/IND001_Jammu%20&%20Kashmir.pdf; (3) Azad Jammu & Kashmir Government, *Azad Kashmir at a Glance, 2018*, Muzaffarabad, Azad Jammu and Kashmir Government, 2019, www.pndajk.gov.pk/uploadfiles/downloads/Final%20AJK%20at%20 a%20Glance.pdf; (4) 'Gilgit Baltistan', *Information about Pakistan and Facts about Pakistan*, undated [2019?], www.pakinformation.com/gilgit-baltistan/index.html.
Notes: [a] That is, before India imposed its changes on Indian J&K. [b] As provided in Source 2. Significantly, Source 3, second (unnumbered) page, agrees that the area of J&K is 222,236 square km. However, it divides this area into: Azad Jammu & Kashmir, 13,297 sq km; Gilgit-Baltistan, 77,676 sq km; 'Indian Held Kashmir', 93,708 sq km; 'Area Under Control of China', 37,555 sq km.

New states since 1947

History shows that many new states have come into being since World War II ended in 1945. When the United Nations was founded that year, it had fifty-one members, including India.[220] Afghanistan joined in 1946; Pakistan in 1947. At the time of writing, the United Nations has 193 members, with the Vatican City State the only internationally recognised country not a member.[221] The entities of Taiwan and Palestine are also not members. The last nation to join the United Nations was South Sudan, which joined in 2011 as its 193rd member. The most recent Asian state to join the United Nations was Timor Leste, which joined in 2002. It is, of course, impossible to say if the post-war trend towards the creation of new states will continue. Nevertheless, compared with the 194 existing states, the data provided below suggest that, should either an independent J&K or an independent Kashmir come into being, such an entity could, by comparison, be feasible as a new international state.

Area and population

An independent country of Jammu and Kashmir amounting to a total area of 222,236 square kilometres would be larger in area than 112 of the 194 countries that currently exist in the world.[222] Some of the smaller countries in area to J&K that currently exist include five located in South Asia – Bangladesh, Bhutan, Maldives (the smallest country in Asia), Nepal and Sri Lanka; two nearby in Central Asia – Kyrgyzstan and Tajikistan; and Asia's newest state, Timor-Leste.[223] An independent country of Kashmir that comprised the 'Kashmir Valley Division' in Table 7.1 (which Division currently comprises the ten districts of Anantnag, Bandipora, Baramulla, Budgam, Ganderbal, Kulgam, Kupwara, Pulwama, Shopian and Srinagar)[224] and which amounted to a total area of 15,948 square kilometres in area would be larger than forty countries of the 194 countries that currently exist. One of these smaller countries in area would be Maldives.

Population-wise, an independent country of Jammu and Kashmir would have an approximated population of 17.5 million. It would be more populous than 132 countries of the 194 countries that currently exist. Some of these less populous countries would include: Bhutan and Maldives in South Asia; nearby Tajikistan in Central Asia; and Timor-Leste. An independent country of Kashmir with an approximated population of 6.9 million would be more populous than ninety-one countries that currently exist. Some of these less populous countries would include: Bhutan and Maldives in South Asia; and nearby Turkmenistan in Central Asia.

Comparison to other landlocked states

Either an independent Jammu and Kashmir or an independent Kashmir would be landlocked.[225] That is, either prospective entity would be totally surrounded by land, with no direct access to the sea, while Karachi would be the closest shipping port. Currently, there are forty-five landlocked countries in the world. These comprise about 20 per cent of the world's nations, 11 per cent of the world's total area, and around 7 per cent of the world's population. An independent Jammu and Kashmir comprising 222,236 square kilometres in area would be larger in area than twenty-five other landlocked countries that currently exist, including Bhutan, Nepal and Tajikistan. An independent country of Kashmir comprising 15,948 square kilometres in area would be larger in area than five other landlocked countries that currently exist, all of them located in Europe.

An independent Jammu and Kashmir with an approximated population of 17.5 million would be more populous than thirty-seven landlocked countries that currently exist, including Bhutan, Kyrgyzstan, Tajikistan and Turkmenistan. An independent country of Kashmir with an approximated population of 6.9 million would be more populous than eighteen landlocked countries that currently exist, including Bhutan, Kyrgyzstan and Turkmenistan. (There are five entities whose status in dispute and who are not members of the United Nations: Artsakh (Nagorno-Karabakh), Kosovo, South Ossetia, Transnistria and the West Bank. They may point the way for J&K-ites and/or Kashmiris as to the challenges of becoming an independent entity.)

International borders

Were it to exist now, an independent Jammu and Kashmir would have international borders with four neighbouring countries: Afghanistan, China, India and Pakistan. However, it would need to develop new roads in, and through, Gilgit-Baltistan in order to access Afghanistan's Wakhan region in J&K's far north, and possibly the five Central Asian nations beyond (which also could possibly be accessed via Pakistan or China). This would be a challenging task, given the mountainous terrain, particularly if independent J&K had to rely only on its own resources and capabilities to build such infrastructure. An independent Jammu and Kashmir would be able to access China via the existing Karakoram Highway that runs through Gilgit-Baltistan and possibly via the more southerly Karakoram Pass, should this route be available. It would be able to access India via the existing road and railway from Jammu to Pathankot in Indian Punjab and via the existing Kullu-Manali Road to/from Leh, Ladakh. It would be able to access Pakistan via various routes, including by the existing Karakoram Highway, by the (long closed, except for approved travel and trade) Jhelum Valley Road from Srinagar, via Muzaffarabad, to Rawalpindi, and by the (long closed) road and (former) railway to Sialkot in Pakistani Punjab.

Were it to exist now, an independent Kashmir would only have borders with India (Jammu Division; Ladakh Division) and with Pakistan (Azad Kashmir; Gilgit-Baltistan). It would be able to access India via some major roads (the National Highway from Srinagar to Jammu Tawi; the Mughal Road from Shopian to Poonch) and railway to Jammu (when the long-delayed line to the Kashmir Valley is finally completed, possibly in 2021), or via the road to Kargil, Ladakh. It would be able to access Pakistan via the Jhelum Valley Road, and Gilgit via the (long closed) Burzil Pass route.

Part of the challenge for either potential new independent entity would be securing its land and air communications and connectivity. Large parts of an independent Jammu and Kashmir, particularly areas not easily or directly accessible from the plains of Pakistan or India, would be snowbound for around six months each year. Similarly, an independent Kashmir would be snowbound for periods of time each year. As a result, this region could become heavily reliant on the only all-weather into Kashmir: the Jhelum Valley Road. In terms of air access, either prospective new country would need the permission of India and/or Pakistan for air traffic to overfly their respective territory. Obtaining, and retaining, this might be challenging. (Either nation sometimes denies overflights of its territory to the other, particularly when the India–Pakistan relationship is poor.) Either new entity would also need to establish customs and immigration services and border posts to regulate and control the entry and exit of people and goods into their state.

Also challenging for either new entity would be defending its borders. An independent Jammu and Kashmir would confront a politically unstable Afghanistan in the north, which nation has a large military, currently dependent on US financing and support, and radical Islamic elements, chiefly the resilient Taliban, but also elements associated with Islamic State (Khorasan). These elements are not located near the Wakhan region, however. An independent Jammu and Kashmir would be contiguous to China's Xinjiang Province where Beijing is dealing with separatist Muslim Uighurs. It also would confront three nuclear-armed nations, all with large, relatively potent, militaries: India, Pakistan and China.

An independent Kashmir would 'only' have to confront India and Pakistan. It would be almost totally dependent on either or both for a range of goods and services, including land communications. An independent Kashmir could project itself as a bridge between these two inimical nations. However, part of its ongoing challenge would be placating the desire of either or both nations to dominate, intrude and meddle in Kashmir and its internal affairs.

Economic opportunities

No economic modelling or analysis appears to ever have been done for all of post-1947 J&K, even though India claims J&K in its entirety. In 2017, the J&K Government completed its 'Economic Survey 2017',[226] which discussed matters for Indian J&K, but not specifically for its Kashmir component of this state.

The JKLF's *Roadmap* has one paragraph that discusses the 'economic potentials of Kashmir'. These

> are such that within a decade or two of its reunification and independence, it [J&K] can become the most prosperous country of the region. Kashmir is called 'Switzerland of Asia' and 'Nature's Show Window' for its fascinating natural beauty and climate most pleasant and full of health. Kashmir valley [sic] and Gilgit Baltistan [sic] in particular are famous the world-over also for dozens of sky high-peaks [sic] including K2 and Nanga Parbat. All this can invite millions of tourists every year. Kashmir is very rich in water resources and can generate electricity on a large scale that is badly needed by its neighbouring countries. Fruit, timber, minerals and herbs are found in abundance in different parts of the state. The handicrafts of Kashmir, famous the world-over, can prove a valuable asset. Watch making industry, already functioning in Srinagar on a small scale, can be developed.[227]

This was a broad and rather optimistic forecast.

One obvious major economic activity for either prospective new independent entity of Jammu and Kashmir or Kashmir would be tourism – domestic, international (including mountaineering, skiing, hiking, fishing, camping), or religious (e.g., Vaishno Devi in Jammu; Amarnath or Hazratbal in Kashmir; various Buddhist monasteries in Ladakh). However, many potential tourists would be from India and Pakistan and/or would need to traverse or overfly either nation's territory. Other potential or actual tradeable items apart from tourism include timber and timber products, agricultural products (including grains, fruits, nuts, etc.), horticultural products, livestock, various handcrafts, mineral products, services, water and, importantly, hydroelectricity (hydel), which offers enormous potential.

Feasibility

An independent Jammu and Kashmir or an independent Kashmir could, in terms of its size and/or its population, take its place as an independent nation in the world comity. In theory, this would be possible. In practice, obtaining independence would be very difficult to achieve and to sustain. India and Pakistan are not simply going to give either J&K or Kashmir independence, nor to happily allow either entity to remain independent. Finding, developing or securing sufficient resources, including overseas aid and assistance, to be able to survive economically would pose challenges. So too would be getting India and Pakistan to desist from paternalistically interfering. JKLF activists still seek 'complete independence of Jammu and Kashmir including reunification of both sides of Kashmir'.[228] While this ideal may be popular with some J&K-ites, this concept does not appear to have resonated widely throughout all of J&K. An independent J&K is therefore an elusive option and a very unlikely possibility. Nevertheless, according to the JKLF's *Roadmap*, India and Pakistan are both 'committed, through their declarations made on [the] national and international level, to concede independence to Kashmir'.[229] Specifically, the JKLF was referring to Gopalaswami Ayyangar's statement made at the United Nations on 15 January 1948 and to Mohammad Ali Jinnah's pre-partition statements that princely states would be independent after the British left India.[230] These are very dated and hardly conclusive, given both nations' numerous statements and actions opposing independence for J&K thereafter. These reflect the only point that I have ever discovered on which both India and Pakistan appear to agree in their entire dispute over J&K – that neither J&K, nor any part of it, can be independent. This suggests that the establishment of either an independent Jammu and Kashmir or an independent Kashmir will be exceedingly difficult, probably impossible.

Implications

Kashmiri Muslims desire *azadi*. In their live protests and on social media, Kashmiri protesters use 'popular slogans' such as '"Go Indian [sic], Go Back", "We Want *Azadi* ['Freedom'] [sic]", "Solve Kashmir Issue", "Free Kashmir", "O Tyrants! O

Tormentors! Quit Our Kashmir", and so on'.[231] Some Kashmiris also chant 'Pakistan zindabad', not necessarily because they want their region to join this nation, but more to antagonise Indians.[232] In November 2018, the elderly Syed Ali Geelani, when leaving his home town of Sopore after being allowed to visit it following eight years of house arrest in Srinagar, was 'bid goodbye with pro-Azadi and pro-Islam slogans'.[233] (Given his pro-Pakistan leanings, the 'pro-Azadi' slogan may have jarred.) Worryingly for India, in June 2018, some people in Kishtwar, a district that is part of Jammu region but whose people speak a dialect of Kashmiri, 'raised pro-Azadi slogans during [an] Eid procession'.[234] In August 2018, a crowd of Kashmiris at Srinagar's famous Hazratbal mosque heckled Farooq Abdullah. He had raised the pro-India slogans of 'Bharat Mata ki Jai' (Victory for Mother India) and 'Jai Hind' (Long Live India) at a ceremony to condole India's late Prime Minister, Atal Behari Vajpayee. In 2003, Vajpayee had stated that issues to do with Kashmir should be guided by the principles of *insaniyat* (humanism), *jamhooriyat* (democracy) and *kashmiriyat* (inclusivity).[235] Nevertheless, in response, younger Kashmiris chanted 'Farooq Abdullah go back' and 'Hum kya chahte, azaadi'.[236] The use of the term *azadi* was alive and well, it seemed.

Despite this, the concept of what *azadi* means still remains vague and amorphous. The clearest part of the Kashmiris' aspiration now appears to be that they want Indians to leave the Kashmir Valley. As things currently stand, therefore, Kashmiris are under the influence of negative *azadi*: they don't want India, not positive *azadi*, whereby they seek a different status for Kashmir. However, Kashmiris do not necessarily want independence; rather, they want to be free from India. This suggests that the constitutional, administrative and communication changes that New Delhi have made, or rather imposed, in relation to (the now former) J&K may have resolved issues for New Delhi. However, almost certainly, they have not resolved issues for Kashmiris, nor made them feel more content. On the contrary, for some Kashmiris, as they noted on Martyrs' Day 2020, 'the current political scenario in Kashmir' is 'worse than [Hari Singh's] monarchy'.[237] In other words, the current system's repressiveness is worse than when the authoritarian autocrat, Maharaja Hari Singh, ruled J&K. An example of this was Martyrs' Day itself. In late 2019, the Union Territory of J&K's Government abolished the annual 13 July Martyrs' Day public holiday, along with an annual 5 December holiday to commemorate Sheikh Abdullah's birthday, although a holiday was added for Accession Day on 26 October.[238] It would seem unlikely that the changes imposed on Kashmiris will have lessened their desire for either autonomy or *azadi*. Indeed, they almost certainly will have increased the Kashmiris' 'deep simmering unrest' and disenchantment with India.[239] As a result, I expect to see further cries and prolonged calls for *azadi*: Actively, Zealously, Always, Denying India.

Since 1947, India has successfully engaged in a process that has slowly, but insidiously, resulted in the integration or 'domestication of Kashmir'. For the Indian lawyer and legal anthropologist, Shrimoyee Nandini Ghosh,[240] this has involved 'constitutional processes, … political maneuvers and brutal and intensive militarization'. India's highest court, the Supreme Court, has constituted Kashmir 'as a legalized permanent emergency, where bureaucratic discretion and military jurisdiction is expanded and judicially authorized, whilst seemingly upholding the rule of law'. This comprises 'a grey zone of hyperlegality' where the ends of integrating the state into India justify the muscular or malleable means. Ghosh's conclusion is that the 'languages and jurisprudence of Indian constitutionalism and emergency powers serve to render invisible the existence of a protracted and brutal armed conflict and occupation in Jammu and Kashmir'. There are now two 'realities' concerning J&K: the Indian reality that J&K is fully integrated into India and the Kashmiri reality that most Kashmiris want little to do with India: they want *azadi*. Never the twain shall meet, it seems.

Conclusion: to be independent, or not to be independent? That is the question[1]

On 26 October 1947, a truly extraordinary event occurred: the large, prestigious, Muslim-majority princely state of Jammu and Kashmir joined secular India, with which it had few geo-economic links, not Muslim Pakistan, on which it was then geo-economically dependent. India's acquisition of J&K was a triumph of Indians' greater strategic acumen and of Jawaharlal Nehru's meaningful engagement with Kashmiris, particularly Sheikh Abdullah. The Indians had seriously outmaneuvered the Pakistanis with their lackadaisical, even myopic, expectation that J&K would fall into Pakistan's 'lap like a ripe fruit'.[2] The Pakistanis had failed to realise that, apart from needing Maharaja Hari Singh's accession to 'win' J&K politically, they also needed Abdullah's support to 'win' J&K emotionally. Indians grasped these matters much earlier than Pakistanis. Also extraordinary, at least in hindsight, was the fact that J&K existed as an independent entity for seventy-two days from 15 August until 26 October 1947. Seemingly, Maharaja Hari Singh wanted an independent J&K. Practically, he did nothing to build such an entity. Instead, during J&K's period of independence, this ineffectual ruler vacillated. Finally, the Pukhtoons' invasion forced Hari Singh to make a decision. He acceded to India, which both ended J&K's period of independence and made him redundant. For the ruler of such a prestigious princely state, Hari Singh disappeared quickly from the Indian political scene. Nevertheless, an independent J&K is not a new concept, but only a lapsed or a subsumed one.

India's acquisition of J&K should have ended the issue of the state's international status, but it didn't. Immediately, India made Pakistan a formal party to the Kashmir dispute by offering J&K-ites a plebiscite to decide whether their state would join India or Pakistan.[3] This was unnecessary. Had India followed the established decolonisation process for Princely India – the full integration of the princely state into the dominion to which the ruler acceded – this would have made Singh's

311

accession 'final and absolute'.[4] The only issue then would have been when Pakistan would vacate those parts of J&K that it was illegally 'occupying'. Instead, the plebiscite acknowledged that J&K was disputed territory and that Pakistan was a party to this dispute. Similarly, India erred by going to the UNSC in late 1947. (Arguably, had India not done so, Pakistan would have.)[5] To India's chagrin, the UNSC failed to condemn Pakistan's aggression in J&K while also confirming a plebiscite for J&K-ites. Another Indian mistake in 1950 was to enshrine J&K's 'specialness' into the Indian Constitution via the 'temporary' Article 370. This was done to placate Kashmiris, whose support India then needed to retain J&K and to help it win the plebiscite. Without the existence of Article 370, Indian J&K may – and this is a very big may – have become just another Indian state.

In 1947, India made a further mistake – to empower Sheikh Abdullah immediately after Hari Singh's accession as, essentially, the undisputed leader of Indian J&K. Given Abdullah's standing and popularity, New Delhi then had few other options. However, from the outset, Abdullah, who had been heavily informed by Singh's autocracy, 'ruled' J&K in an authoritarian way. Invariably, New Delhi condoned his actions. Generally, Kashmiris seemed happy with them, particularly with the significant land reforms instituted by Abdullah. This was his greatest achievement. Around mid-1953, Abdullah's usefulness ended when India determined that a plebiscite was no longer needed in J&K. He had also become unacceptable due to his 'tendency to deaccession': wanting J&K to be separate, or independent, from both India and Pakistan.[6] Like Hari Singh before him, Sheikh Abdullah lacked the skills to obtain independence for 'Kashmir'. Similarly, he didn't realise that he had become politically redundant. In a blight on India's democracy, Karan Singh sacked J&K's elected Prime Minister in 1953. Abdullah's Government supposedly 'had lost the confidence of the people'[7] and its disunity 'gravely jeopardized' J&K,[8] but its popularity was not allowed to be tested in the J&K Constituent Assembly. Informed by British authoritarian methods, a further blight was for J&K or India to almost permanently incarcerate Abdullah from 1953 until 1968.

After his sacking in 1953, Sheikh Abdullah wavered between wanting full autonomy, independence or self-determination for 'Kashmir' until 1972, when he finally acknowledged that J&K would be with India. Possibly, Abdullah's fluctuations occurred because he was trying to placate two different constituencies: Indians, including the Indian press; and, J&K-ites.[9] However, it is impossible to determine what status he definitely wanted for 'Kashmir'. The only things that I can say with any certainty about Sheikh Abdullah are that: he was a Kashmiri nationalist who felt strongly about his beloved Kashmir but had less interest in other parts of J&K;

he often operated in an authoritarian way; and, he wanted as much autonomy for Kashmir as he could possibly obtain. Seemingly, Abdullah pursued independence to limit Indian involvement with, or intrusion into, Kashmir. He didn't dislike India; indeed, he preferred it to Pakistan. He just did not want J&K to be fully integrated into India. Therefore, he may have settled for 'his' state, or at least the Kashmir part of it, being fully autonomous within the Indian Union – provided that this autonomy was genuine. In 1995, India's Prime Minister, Narasimha Rao, famously said that, in relation to autonomy for J&K, 'short of azadi ... [the] sky was the limit for it'.[10] Generally, however, Indians' expectations have been that J&K and J&K-ites would become part of India. This fundamental contradiction has never been satisfactorily resolved, with both parties at odds with each other basically since 1947. Furthermore, as J&K has become more integrated into India, Kashmiris' disenchantment has risen in equal and opposite proportions. Perhaps not surprisingly, the bigger, more powerful, party has 'won' this integration struggle. Given the Kashmiris' ongoing anti-India insurgency since 1988, India's victory has been pyrrhic.

For some Indians, a further Indian mistake was to agree a ceasefire with Pakistan in 1949. They believe that Nehru should have allowed the Indian Army to advance to the Pakistan–J&K border and evict all pro-Pakistan forces from J&K. This would have brought the entire former princely state under Indian control and ended the Kashmir dispute. Their proposition is questionable. India's extended military supply lines would have been vulnerable, while pro-Pakistan elements and the Pakistan Army would have opposed Indian forces. In 2020, some people still consider using the military option in J&K. For the current Chief of the Indian Army, General Manoj Naravane, the Indian Army would 'definitely take appropriate action of reclaiming Pakistan Occupied Kashmir if ... given an order for it'.[11] The Prime Minister of Azad Kashmir, Raja Farooq Haider, has 'called for the Pakistani government to act "militarily" in the Kashmir dispute with neighbouring India'.[12] Such military actions are always possible, given India's current 'muscular' Government and Pakistan's perennially military-dominated Governments. But their outcome would be uncertain, particularly if any conflict seriously escalated to involve nuclear weapons, a prospect some ethnic Kashmiris fear. As Sheikh Abdullah once noted, according to Kalhana's Rajtarangini, 'You can conquer Kashmir by spiritual power, not by weapons of war'.[13] Seemingly, some senior leaders in both nations are yet to understand this maxim.

Observing Sheikh Abdullah's actions between 1931 and 1982, it seems that the real challenge in relation to Kashmir is how to successfully accommodate the

Kashmir identity, particularly the Muslim Kashmiri identity, within India (or within Pakistan, should it ever obtain possession of Kashmir). The Kashmiri identity is strong, resilient and far older than either the post-British Indian or Pakistani identities. The Kashmiri people who hold this identity, along with their region, invariably have been the focus of the Kashmir dispute, particularly since they began their anti-India uprising in 1988. Indeed, the so-called 'Kashmir dispute' is now really only about who should control the real Kashmir, i.e., the Kashmir Valley, not about who should control J&K. In terms of preserving their unique identity, an independent Kashmir might be one way to resolve this issue. This also might resolve the three longstanding disputes involving J&K mentioned in the Introduction: the India–Pakistan dispute over possession of J&K; the vexed relationship between India and Indian J&K; and, Kashmiris' disunity over what international status they want for Kashmir. The establishment of an independent entity Kashmir might therefore be a good idea. If nothing else, its creation could provide a 'win-win' solution for India and Pakistan by, paradoxically, creating a 'lose-lose' situation for them: neither nation would have control of the prized Kashmir region. As *The Scotsman's* Michael Davidson aptly stated as early as 1949 in an article titled 'Kashmir: Independence a Possible Solution': 'A neutral Vale of Kashmir would remove the bone of contention; there would be nothing left [for India and Pakistan] to squabble about'.[14]

However, to obtain independence for J&K or for Kashmir will be difficult. The sole point that India and Pakistan currently agree on in the Kashmir dispute is that neither J&K, nor any part of it, can have independence. Furthermore, most J&K-ites are not interested in independence. In relation to an independent J&K, only members of the JKLF are interested in this possibility. While this political party has a presence in the Kashmir Valley and in Azad Kashmir, it is hard to determine its popularity as JKLF members are barred from contesting elections. It also is difficult to imagine J&K's five regions ever being reunified into a single 1947-style political entity as the JKLF desires, given that these regions have now been separated for almost seventy-five years. Most likely, a reunified J&K entity will only remain in people's imaginations. Additionally, the concept of an independent J&K has never been clearly articulated. In my research, I have found only two documents that describe in any detail what an independent J&K might comprise or how this entity might be achieved.[15] These are the 'Internal Constitutional Set-up (Broad Outlines)' for an independent J&K given to the J&K State People's Convention in 1969[16] and *The JKLF Roadmap for Peace & Prosperity in South Asia* in 2003.[17] Both documents are rudimentary. In 1951, Bazaz wrote a book titled *Azad Kashmir (Free Kashmir): A Democratic Socialist Conception*, which detailed what 'a free Kashmir' would entail. Seemingly, he was only talking about the Kashmir Valley. There has not been a lot of sustained political thought or effort put into securing an independent J&K. This concept can be dismissed as a possibility.

An independent Kashmir is another matter. The only region of J&K where people are severely disenchanted with their 'lot' is Kashmir. Seemingly, many Kashmiris, perhaps a majority, want *azadi*. Informed by Sheikh Abdullah's earlier desire for Kashmir to be free from Indian control, this may now be an entrenched Kashmiri attitude. In theory, an independent Kashmir entity is possible. In practice, it will be a great challenge for Kashmiris to obtain independence as long as Kashmir's immediate neighbours comprise two competitive, paternalistic, belligerent nations. Indeed, the India–Pakistan contest over Kashmir suggests that this region will never be free as long as these combative nations exist in their present structures: 'secular', but (increasingly) Hindu dominant, India and 'Islamic' Pakistan, with their intense geo-political rivalry and unrelenting desire to possess Kashmir. India also has some significant advantages. Its economy is larger and more dynamic; its security forces are capable, resilient and able to resist Pakistani forces and proxies; it has strategic depth, diversity and reach; it currently holds the 'moral high ground'; and, since 1947, Indians have tied J&K closely, almost irreversibly, to India politically, economically and administratively. Additionally, New Delhi has, in some ways, fenced Kashmir in and made it totally dependent on India. Much of the LOC to Kashmir's west and north is fenced, armed and alarmed. More significantly, since 1947, India has totally severed all of the major geo-economic links that Kashmir once had with other parts of J&K that now comprise Pakistan-Administered J&K, particularly the all-weather Jhelum Valley Road. Kashmir has no direct connections with Pakistan and no alternative but to be involved with India. This includes via roads that are regularly blocked by snows in winter or by landslides.

Meanwhile, the Kashmiris themselves confront serious challenges. Most importantly, they suffer from a telling lack of a unified desire for their region's international status. They cannot determine whether they want Kashmir to stay with India, join Pakistan, strive for independence, or be something else. This disunity allows India to 'divide and rule' Kashmiris, a method successfully used by New Delhi to deal with other insurgencies in India. Kashmiris also lack a liberation strategy or ideology, such as Gandhism or Maoism, that instructs them about how to free themselves from India and/or how to attain *azadi* or to join Pakistan.[18] Similarly, Kashmiris don't have a Mahatma Gandhi or Mao Zedong-type leader with the vision, capabilities and charisma to lead them to the 'promised land' in what would be a long, arduous and brutal campaign. All Indian governments have prevented such a leader from emerging, or operating, by detaining dissident Kashmiris, actual or potential. The dangerous contrarian, Sheikh Abdullah, was detained for long periods of time. After 5 August 2019, 6,605 people were taken into preventative custody (i.e., arrested) including 'miscreants, stone-pelters, over ground workers (OGWs), [and] separatists'. Amongst them were 144 children, one as young as nine years old.[19] At the time of writing (July 2020), India, surprisingly, was still detaining the pro-India Mehbooba Mufti, who was under preventative detention; the pro-independence Yasin Malik was in jail, albeit on criminal charges (possibly politically motivated); the pro-self-determination Shabbir Shah was in jail; and the up-and-coming Shah Faesel had recently been released from detention. Surprisingly, India had also previously detained Sheikh Abdullah's pro-India son, Farooq, and his pro-India grandson, Omar. To seriously challenge democratic India – even if you are pro-India – is to be compelled to languish in detention. As a significant recent report by concerned Indians about the 'lockdown' in Kashmir poignantly noted: 'Kashmir has in many ways been the litmus test of Indian democracy … we have failed miserably'.[20]

To ensure India's ongoing hold over Kashmir, large numbers of India's security forces will continue to be needed to suppress Kashmiris and keep them in their place, literally and figuratively. New Delhi will justify this by its need to better (i.e., more directly) govern the strategically important but frontline territory of J&K. Nevertheless, Kashmir may well go on being an 'open air prison',[21] with Kashmiris as open air prisoners – although we may not know their actual circumstances, given the new media regulations imposed on Kashmiri journalists in 2020 and the requirement to not report fake news, with this fakeness determined by New Delhi politicians and bureaucrats. Since being heavily suppressed since August 2019, 'caged' Kashmiris[22] now possibly have an entrenched 'siege mentality'. Conversely, however, from New Delhi's point of view, J&K has been normalised and the problems there made redundant. Kashmiris are well on the way to becoming 'ordinary' Indians, which is what New Delhi currently wants. 'Redundant', therefore, would seem to be the word that now best describes Kashmir, Kashmiris, Kashmiri issues and Kashmiris' aspirations. Nevertheless, New Delhi might do well to remember that, when Maharaja Pratap Singh allowed 'foreign' Punjabis to enter J&K, the subsequent agitations by J&K subjects, particularly Hindu Kashmiri Pandits – not Kashmiri Muslims – resulted in the cry of 'Kashmir for Kashmiris' and, ultimately, to State Subject status being instituted in 1927. As we saw in Chapter 7, some Jammuites are already concerned about negative demographic change occurring in Jammu. Fiddling with J&K's demography may have unforeseen consequences.

Currently, Kashmiris are uncertain what they want or what to do. The clearest part of their *azadi* aspiration seems to be that they want Indians to leave the Kashmir Valley. Overwhelming, therefore, *azadi* now appears to mean freedom *from* India, not necessarily a desire *for* independence. However, for Kashmiris to free Kashmir from India will continue to be incredibly difficult to achieve. In May 2018, the then Chief of the Indian Army, General Bipin Rawat, told Kashmiris that 'Azadi will never happen'. He highlighted the Indian Army's 'muscular policy': 'if you want to fight us, then we will fight you with all our force. ... Azadi isn't possible.' He continued: 'We will always fight those who seek Azadi, those who want to secede. (Azadi) is not going to happen, never.' He then wondered what made Kashmiris so angry and blamed Pakistan.[23] Rawat's martial message was insightful, if unreal. It was insightful as it confirmed India's resolve to retain Kashmir. It was unreal as he predictably blamed Pakistan for all of India's woes in J&K. Indeed, his statement displayed typical Indian ignorance, or disdain, about why Kashmiris became, and still are, angry and disenchanted with India. Conversely, Tavleen Singh has continued to argue – correctly, in my opinion – that it was Indians, not Pakistanis, who made the mistakes in Kashmir that provoked the Kashmiris' anti-Indian insurgency in 1988. Talking about Sheikh Abdullah's son, Farooq, she has stated that his popularity and the militancy 'grew exponentially' during Farooq's second term as Chief Minister of J&K between 1986 and 1990. This was 'because of mistakes made by Delhi and not Islamabad'. For Tavleen Singh, it was clear that both Pakistan and the ISI were 'fully involved in spreading jihadist violence' in Kashmir, 'but they did not create the problem. It was created by mistakes made by Indian prime ministers. Mistakes continue to be made today [2018].'[24] In my experience, Kashmiris find the Indians' paternalistic attitudes of 'do as I say' or 'I know what is best for you' or 'Pakistan is responsible for all of the problems in Kashmir' irksome – and false. The unrequited arrogance and certainty of some Indians that Kashmir must be with India reminds me of a rhyme I once heard and which now is even more applicable: 'Jammu and Kashmir: Damn you and come here'.

India's greatest challenges in relation to Kashmir are twofold and inter-related: to accommodate the Kashmiris' unique identity within India and to make Kashmiris renounce their anti-India sentiments and desires willingly, genuinely, and of their own accord. New Delhi could, if it wanted to, give special consideration again to J&K's unique situation in the way that the Indian Constitution still apparently does for up to ten other Indian states.[25] This would require the BJP-led Government to move beyond its rather unreal insistence that all Indians must be treated the same, with no consideration for difference or for special needs. Furthermore, the Kashmiris' disaffection, while significant, is not an irredeemable problem. As Farooq Abdullah noted in the 1990s: if the choice is between 'a democratic, secular India and an Islamic, military Pakistan', Kashmiris 'will always choose India'. Islam would only become a factor should India become 'repressive, communal'.[26] It is hard to know, but Abdullah's observation may still hold, given India's stronger economy, the fact that civilians control India's military, and India's complex and still pluralistic society. As India's 'master communicator', Prime Minister Narendra Modi, put it: 'unity in diversity is India's uniqueness'.[27] Nevertheless, as the Hindu Kashmiri political activist, Prem Nath Bazaz, observed as early as 1965, Kashmiri 'resentment' with India is a major factor. It has stemmed 'from the sulkiness, anger, and disaffection of the people' who, to some extent, feel uneasy being Indians.[28] Even earlier, Nehru noted in 1953 that 'ultimately it is those people [Kashmiris] who will decide. If we win them over well and good. Otherwise, well, we just do not succeed.'[29] Allowing Kashmiris to decide their own 'fate' is an important, unresolved issue, despite the dubious pro-India reaffirmations of the J&K Constituent Assembly and the J&K Constitution. (These are dubious as the 1951 elections that elected the Constituent Assembly were both rigged and included no candidates from Pakistan-Administered J&K.) Kashmiris – and, indeed all J&K-ites – have never been asked in any meaningful or inclusive way what international status they specifically want. India, Pakistan and the UNSC also have only ever given them the option of joining India or Pakistan. Clearly some J&K-ites want independence, with many, but not all, of them located in Kashmir. While this may not be possible, some serious dialogue and consultations with Kashmiris would be a useful, even beneficial, start.

As things currently stand, India is most likely to retain Kashmir. Pakistan and the anti-India/pro-Pakistan militant groups lack the capabilities to eject Indian forces from Kashmir, which region remains vital for India in terms of national pride and strategically in relation to resupplying Indian forces in Ladakh. Equally, for these very reasons, Pakistan will continue to try to cause India problems in Kashmir. Problematically, neither nation has any compelling need to resolve the Kashmir dispute. Each has survived since 1947 with few interactions and poor relations. (I am amazed that there is still only one border crossing between India and Pakistan, whose combined populations now amount to about 1.5 billion people.) There are few concerned citizens, voters or pressure groups in India or Pakistan demanding that the Kashmir dispute be resolved. There is little international interest, or pressure, to resolve this issue, apart from the odd offer to mediate by an ill-informed US President or an opportunistic Chinese President. The UNSC has not seriously addressed the Kashmir dispute since 1965. It did briefly talk about this matter in August 2019 and January 2020, but nothing came of these superficial mentions, with most nations, except China and Pakistan, considering that the Kashmir dispute is a bilateral issue for India and Pakistan to resolve. Things have changed since the early 1950s, when Kashmir seemingly was part of the Cold War and when the USSR either threatened to use its veto or actually did use its veto five times to keep the India–Pakistan Question out of the UNSC: February 1957; June 1962; December 1971 (three times).[30] Now, internationally speaking, J&K is a tepid backwater – although it could become 'hot' and boil over any time.

Seemingly, therefore, only when something happens to shatter the detrimental India–Pakistan dynamic will the Kashmir dispute be resolved. Then, Kashmir might again become free from control by non-Kashmiris, as it was before 1586. History suggests that eventually the India–Pakistan shibboleth will be shattered – although we don't know when, or how, or with what consequences. One possibility is for something unexpected, unanticipated and major to occur in the subcontinent that impacts on India, Pakistan and J&K: a so-called 'black swan' event.[31] Although by its very nature we will not know what, or when, such an event might be or will lead to, it always is possible. History also suggests that further border or territorial changes will occur in South Asia, including in relation to J&K. I say 'further' as boundary changes are not new events in the Indian subcontinent, or South Asia, as this 'region' has become known since British decolonisation. Before the British finally unified India around 1849, it had comprised various competing kingdoms and entities. Indeed, it was only the British who first unified all of India into a single political entity. Similarly, while Mughals captured Kashmir in 1586, this region later came under the control of Afghan, Sikh and Dogra rulers. History confirms that change is inevitable. Since 1947, fifteen major border changes have occurred in South Asia.[32] I expect to see more in my lifetime. It is possible that these will involve J&K. For example, India and Pakistan may agree to convert the LOC into the international border in J&K. Similarly, China and India may come to a formal agreement on their dispute in northeastern J&K/Aksai Chin.[33] Equally, there may be changes that we can't, or won't, foresee.

In summary, the Kashmiris' aspiration for *azadi* is incomplete in two ways: the desired end state and how to get there are unclear; and, the movement has not succeeded. The serious question for Kashmiris now, therefore, is 'Do we want

Kashmir to be independent or not?' If Kashmiris really want to obtain *azadi* for their homelands –meaning obtaining independence for Kashmir from India – then they are going to have to fight far more determinedly and effectively for this end result. No Indian Government will give them independence 'on a plate'. No insurgency in post-British India has ever succeeded in obtaining independence, while only two insurgencies have ever succeeded in South Asia: Bangladeshis in 1971; the Afghan Taliban in 1996. Few nations, high-profile individuals or significant pressure and lobby groups outside India (and Pakistan) openly support Kashmiris' independence. India continues to have the will, capabilities, resilience, economic power and the internal support of most Indians to control and suppress the disgruntled Kashmiris – and to ensure that Pakistan does not obtain Kashmir. Therefore, if Kashmiris still seriously aspire to obtaining independence for their homelands, they will need, firstly, to unify resolutely behind this aim and, secondly, to employ a new and more effective strategy to achieve it. (A third factor they will need is some good old fashioned luck.) After that, Kashmiris will need to be even more determined than India's General Rawat. Reworking his words, Kashmiris will need to 'fight India with all their force [moral and/or military] and make *azadi* happen'. They will need to be united, determined, resourceful, patient, and incredibly resilient in what will be a long and brutal campaign. History, including that associated with Gandhi and Mao, suggests that the Kashmiris *might* succeed and finally win their independence – but it's only a suggestion, not a guarantee.

Since beginning their anti-India uprising in 1988, Kashmiris have suffered, with many hardships imposed on them by India's security forces and by anti-India militants – and now legislatively and administratively by the Indian Government. Pakistan has also stirred these troubled waters. The Kashmiris' hardships, which are atypical for most 'ordinary' Indians, have included curfews, dislocation, economic losses, regular harassment, intimidation and torture, physical and psychological injuries, murders and deaths via 'encounters', people being 'disappeared', the denial of democracy, the imposition and re-imposition of direct rule, and being corralled in the Kashmir Valley. The most recent hardships involve the long-term deprivation of basic freedoms and communications, which have had a major economic and emotional cost, after New Delhi unilaterally abrogated Articles 370 and 35-A without any direct or serious consultation with voters or elected representatives in J&K. Added to these changes, Kashmiris (and Jammuites) have seen 'their' state downgraded to a Union Territory, which gives New Delhi enormous, and largely unaccountable, power and control in J&K. Eerily, the latest incarceration of Kashmiris reflects, or perhaps was inspired by, their forebears' situation in 1846 when Kashmiris were regularly 'kept in a kind of involuntary prison, none being allowed to go to or from [Kashmir] without a passport from the authorities'.[34] In some ways, little has changed in 175 years. This is lamentable.

The changes imposed by India in J&K since 2019 have put the Kashmiri identity under severe threat of further dilution within India, even of it being totally subsumed by India. Equally, however, it seems that India lacks the desire, and also the ability, to win Kashmiris' hearts and minds. Therefore, in attempting to make Kashmir issues redundant and in trying to seriously dilute, or assimilate, the Kashmiri identity, New Delhi has only suppressed and quarantined this identity, not accommodated – or obliterated – it. The Kashmiri identity is too old, entrenched and resilient to ever be fully suppressed. Therefore, like a phoenix, or a virus, I expect this identity to re-emerge strongly at a time and place of its own choosing, possibly instigated, provoked or even propelled, by a black swan event. Perhaps, Kashmir may then again become independent. This could be a good thing. Kashmiris could once more lead more normal, productive and happy lives. Kashmir might also then become a positive bridge between India and Pakistan, rather than an obstacle that they relentlessly compete and fight over.

Appendix I

Comparison of Jammu and Kashmir with other entities[1]

Extracts from the 1931 Census

'6. Comparison of area with other States and Countries'

A comparison of the recent area figures of the various Provinces and States ... shows that Jammu and Kashmir occupies the first place amongst the Indian States in respect of its territorial extent possessing an area of 84,471 square miles which is distinctly larger than Hyderabad State (82,698), about thrice as large as Mysore (29,469), ten times the area of Baroda (8,164), about four times that of Gwalior (26,367) and Bikaner (23,317). The States of Jaipur (11,459) and Mewar (12,694) reach only one-seventh while Travancore (7,625) has only one-eleventh of territory as compared to this State.

On a comparison with the Provinces of British India the State will be found larger than Bihar and Orissa (83,054), Bengal (77,521), Assam (55,014), N. W. F. Provinces (13,518), slightly smaller than Central Provinces including Berar (99,920), about ⅔rd of Bombay (123,679), about ⅗th of Madras (142,277), ¾ of United Provinces (112,191), ⅗th of Punjab (135,496).

Among the Foreign Asiatic countries, the State is 1½ times larger than Nepal (54,000), 4 times as big as Bhutan (20,000), and about 3½ times bigger than Ceylon (25,332). It is equal to ⅓ of Afghanistan (245,000), over one half of Japan (147,655) and is almost on par with Korea (86,000).

England and Wales combined (58,344) will go to make up only ⅔rd of the State while Scotland (30,405) and Ireland (32,360) are each a little more than one third. The State is about six times the size of Switzerland (15,940) and more than seven times the size of Belgium (11,755).

322

'7. Inter-District Comparisons'

... of the total area of 84,471 square miles, three fourths – 63,553 square miles – is absorbed by the Frontier Districts which are mostly covered by high mountains, vast deserts, and forests with very scanty population sheltered in valleys and other habitable spots. This region is not very important from the Census point of view at present unless further opening up of this difficult country attracts [a] larger population for which there are very little grounds to be optimistic in the near future.

This leaves us with the 1/4 of the total area [of] 20,917 square miles of which the Jammu Province (inclusive of Jagirs) occupies 12,375 square miles i.e. ⅗th; and the Kashmir Province shares the remaining ⅖th equal to 8,539 square miles in all.

Table I.1   *Areas, estimated populations and estimated revenues for some major Indian states in 1934*

State	Majority	Ruler	Area (square miles)	Population	Revenue
Hyderabad	Hindu	Muslim	82,000	13.5 million	£7 million
Mysore	Hindu	Hindu	29,464	6 million	£3 million
Baroda	Hindu	Hindu	8,135	2.5 million	£1.75 million
J&K	Muslim	Hindu	84,258	3.75 million	£2 million
Travancore	Hindu	Hindu	7,626	5 million	£1.75 million
Gwalior	Hindu	Hindu	25,382	1.5 million	£1.8 million
Patiala	Sikh	Sikh	5,932	1.5 million	£1.25 million
Indore	Hindu	Hindu	9,519	1.5 million	£1.1 million
Jodhpur	Hindu	Hindu	35,000	2 million	£1 million
Jaipur	Hindu	Hindu	15,600	2.5 million	£1 million
Junagadh	Hindu	Muslim	3,336	544,000	£600,000
Kalat	Muslim	Muslim	75,000	328,000	not available

Source: William Barton, *The Princes of India*, London, Nisbet & Co., 1934, pp. xiv, 83, 118, 138, 164, 186, 214.

Appendix I

In 1930, Gurmukh Nihal Singh graded forty-one of the larger princely states based on those with 'a revenue of Rs. 50 lakhs [5 million] a year or more' and/or 'whose rulers are entitled to a salute of not less than 15 guns each'. This table provides details of the top ten princely states, plus details of Junagadh and Kalat which were controversial in 1947–48.

Table I.2   Largest princely states in India, based on revenue

Order	State	Group/Agency	Area (square miles)	Population	Revenue (Rs)	Salute
1	Hyderabad	IPR with I[a]	82,698	12,472,000	65,351,000	21
2	Mysore	IPR with I	29,528	5,860,000	34,637,000	21
3	Baroda	IPR with I	8,135	2,127,000	23,707,000	21
4	J&K	IPR with I	80,000	3,332,000	22,777,000	21
5	Travancore	Madras	7,625	4,006,000	22,188,000	19
6	Gwalior	IPR with I	26,383	3,195,000	21,400,000	21
7	Patiala	Punjab States	5,932	1,500,000	12,850,000	17
8	Indore	Central India	9,519	1,152,000	12,400,000	19
9	Jodhpur	Rajputana	34,963	1,842,000	12,190,000	17
10	Jaipur	Rajputana	15,579	2,339,000	12,000,000	17
14	Junagadh	Western India States	3,337	465,000	8,193,000	13
35	Kalat	Baluchistan	73,278	328,000	1,649,000	19

Source: 'Appendix D: Bigger States: A Table', in Gurmukh Nihal Singh, *Indian States & British India: Their Future Relations*, Benares, Nand Kishore & Bros, 1930, pp. 272–4. The author's source, as stated at the bottom of p. 274, is the Government of India Publication *The Indian States* and the figures are correct up to 1 January 1927.
Note: [a] IPR with I = In Immediate Political Relations with the Government of India.

Appendix II

Kashmir Valley Muslims in J&K and their numerical dominance

In 1947, Jammu and Kashmir was religiously complex. Table II.1 provides details of the state's religious composition.

In 1947, Kashmir Province was J&K's smallest province but its second most populous. It comprised three districts: Anantnag, Baramulla and Muzaffarabad. This made the Kashmir Valley part of Kashmir Province. Specifically, the Kashmir Valley – i.e., Kashmir – consisted 'of the valley of the Jhelum from its source to Baramulla and the subsidiary valleys on both banks'.[1] More specifically, the following 'form[ed] what is usually known as the Kashmir Valley': the four tehsils in the southerly Anantnag District: Anantnag Khas (which included the city of Srinagar and was sometimes also called Srinagar),[2] Kulgam and Pulwama; and the three tehsils of the more northerly Baramulla District, comprising Baramulla, Sri Pratapsinghpura and Uttarmachhipura.[3]

The Kashmir Valley was approximately '84 miles long by 20 to 25 miles broad' (135 kilometres long by thirty-two to forty kilometres broad),[4] with an area of 6,131 square miles (15,879 square kilometres). This area was made up of 2,814 square miles in Anantnag District and 3,317 square miles in Baramulla District.[5] The population of these two districts was 1,464,034: Anantnag: 851,606; Baramulla: 612,428.

The 1941 Census of J&K stated that 77.11 per cent of J&K's population of 4,021,616 were Muslims.[6] This amounted to 3,101,247 people. Of these, 1,369,620 were located in Kashmir: 778,684 in Anantnag District; 590,936 in Baramulla District.

In relation to Muslims located in Kashmir Province, the Census noted that

> The Muslims living in the southern part of the Kashmir Province [i.e., not in Muzaffarabad District] are of the same stock as the Kashmiri Pandit community and are usually designated Muslims; those of the Muzaffarabad District are partly Kashmiri, partly Gujjar and the rest are of same stock as the tribes of the neighbouring Punjab and North-West Frontier Province districts.[7]

Table II.1   Religious composition of Jammu and Kashmir

Religious group	Number	% J&K	% J&K Muslims
Muslims:			
Kashmir Province	1,615,478	40.17	52.09
Kashmir Valley			
Anantnag District	*778,684*		
Baramulla District	*590,936*		
Total	*1,369,620*		
Muzaffarabad District	*245,858*		
Jammu Province	1,215,676	30.23	39.20
Frontier Districts Province	270,093	6.72	8.71
Total Muslims	3,101,247	77.11	
Hindus:			
Kashmir Province	85,580	2.13	
Jammu Province	722,835	17.97	
Frontier Districts Province	750	.02	
Total Hindus	809,165	20.12	
Sikhs:			
Kashmir Province	27,034	.67	
Jammu Province	38,566	.96	
Frontier Districts Province	303	.01	
Total Sikhs	65,903	1.64	
Buddhists:			
Kashmir Province	10	Negligible	
Jammu Province	522	.01	
Frontier Districts Province	40,164	1.00	
Total Buddhists	40,696	1.01	
Others[a]	4,605	0.12	
Total	4,021,616	100.00	100.00

Source: *Census of India 1941*, Volume XXII, Jammu & Kashmir State, Part I, pp. 13 and Part II, Tables, pp. 342–3, Srinagar R. G. Wreford, Editor, Jammu and Kashmir Government, 1942.
Note: [a] 'Others' = Indian Christians: 3,079; European and Anglo-Indian Christians: 430; Jains: 910; Parsis/Parsees: 29; Jews: 11; Primitive Tribes: 51; (Unspecified) Others: 95.

According to the 1941 Census, there were 1,270,261 people who were identified as Kashmiri Muslims living in the fourteen districts of J&K. This number included Shia Muslims. Table II.2 gives specific figures for each district. It is not possible to determine how many were Shia Muslims. However, according to the 1941 Census, most J&K Muslims were Sunnis (2,821,247 people). There also were 280,000 Shias

Table II.2   Kashmiri Muslims living in J&K

Locality/District[a]	Province	Persons
Jammu	Jammu	2,596
Kathua	Jammu	2,843
Udhampur	Jammu	58,989
Reasi	Jammu	21,761
Mirpur	Jammu	15,163
Poonch	Jammu	27,871
Chenani Jagir	Jammu	537
Kashmir Valley		
Baramulla	Kashmir	476,362
Anantnag	Kashmir	633,965
Total		1,100,327
Muzaffarabad	Kashmir	27,319
Ladakh	Frontier Districts	1,596
Astore	Frontier Districts	799
Gilgit (Leased Area)	Frontier Districts	460
Gilgit Agency[b]	Frontier Districts	(400 in 1931)
Total		1,270,261

Source: 'Imperial Table XIV: Variation in Population of Selected Tribes, Scheduled Castes and Important Elements', *Census of India 1941*, Volume XXII, Jammu & Kashmir State, Part II, Tables, Srinagar, R. G. Wreford, Editor, Jammu and Kashmir Government, 1942, p. 361.
Notes: [a] As in the order the 1941 Census listed these. [b] According to the Census, p. 353, figures were not available for the Gilgit Agency 'as the record was not sorted for this table'. Instead, figures from the 1931 Census were provided.

living in J&K, of whom 74,000 were located in the Gilgit Agency of the Frontier Districts Province.[8] J&K's Shia population therefore amounted to about 9 per cent of the princely state's total Muslim population. Presumably, there was a similar percentage of Shia Muslims in Kashmir.

Overall, there were 1,110,327 Kashmiri Muslims living in Kashmir. However, not all Muslims living in Kashmir were Kashmiri Muslims. The following table provides some figures for people who were identified as non-Kashmiri Muslims living in Kashmir. It is based on the 1941 Census's 'Imperial Table XIV: Variation in Population of Selected Tribes, Scheduled Castes and Important Elements'. The Census table only included groups of 'Castes with numbers exceeding 10000 in 1931' and 'whose social status, political importance or special character are such as to justify inclusion'.[9] The religion was given for each group or 'caste' (even if they were non-Hindus, the Census used this term for the various sub-groups); a population count was provided on a district basis. Therefore, these figures do not include all J&K-ites, or necessarily all J&K-ite Muslims. They do not total the

Table II.3   Extract from 'Tribes, Castes and Other Important Elements' in J&K, with a focus on Muslims in Kashmir

Category	Rel	Maj	Total J&K	Anantnag[a]	Baramulla[b]	Ms in KV
Arain	M	JP	23,368	10	36	46
Bafinda	M	JP	9,826	215	101	316
Bakarwal	M	JP	15,299	769	7	776
Balti	M	L	99,348	301	42	343
Dhund	M	JP	17,670	2	57	59
Gujjar	M	JP	381,457	28,170	32,447	60,617
Hajjam	M	KP	38,678	11,507	10,103	21,610
Hanjis	M	KP	7,403	5,172	2,231	7,403
Jat	M	JP	121,696	102	0	102
K Muslims	M	KP	1,270,261	633,965	476,362	1,110,327
Kumiar	M	KP	25,457	6,979	5,059	12,038
Lohar	M	JP	28,823	6,260	3,440	9,700
Machi	M	JP	248	0	102	102
Moghal	M	JP	42,256	1,337	1,109	2,446
Pathan	M	JP	22,399	3,044	3,420	6,464
Rajput	M	JP	226,404	2,826	1,608	4,434
Sheikh	M	KP	109,781	42,612	28,908	71,520
Sudhan	M	JP	78,412	8	16	24
Syed	M	JP	52,293	6,930	4,792	11,722
Tarkhan	M	KP	35,249	9,379	8,564	17,943
Teli	M	JP	28,134	7,458	5,006	12,464
Total			2,649,978	767,046	583,410	1,350,456
Minus KM				−633,965	−476,362	−1,110,327
Other Ms in KV				133,081	107,048	240,129

Source: 'Imperial Table XIV: Variation in Population of Selected Tribes, Scheduled Castes and Important Elements', *Census of India 1941*, Volume XXII, Jammu & Kashmir State, Part II, Tables, Srinagar, R. G. Wreford, Editor, Jammu and Kashmir Government, 1942, pp. 353–66.
Notes: [a] Living in Anantnag District, i.e., in the Kashmir Valley; [b] Living in Baramulla District, i.e., in the Kashmir Valley; JP = Jammu Province; K = Kashmiri; KP = Kashmir Province; L = Ladakh District; Maj = Locality where the majority (i.e., at least 50 per cent) of the element lived; M = Muslim; Ms in KV = Muslims living in Kashmir Valley: i.e., in Baramulla and Anantnag districts.

population figures given in Table II.1 above. However, they are a good indicator and confirmation of the dominance of Muslims in Kashmir and in J&K.

Based on Table 3, there were 1,270,261 people identified as Kashmiri Muslims living in J&K. Of these, 1,110,327 lived in Kashmir: 633,965 in Anantnag District; 476,362 in Baramulla District. There also were 240,129 people identified as other types of Muslims living in Kashmir: 133,081 in Anantnag; 107,048 in Baramulla. The total number of people identified as Muslims living in Kashmir therefore was 1,350,456: 767,046 in Anantnag District; 583,410 in Baramulla District. This was

19,164 people less than the total number of Muslims living in the Kashmir Valley, as per Table 1 above. The Census does not explain this shortfall. Presumably these 19,164 people did not belong to 'Castes with numbers exceeding 10000 in 1931', while their 'social status, political importance or special character [we]re [not] such as to justify inclusion'.[10] For example, such Muslims included 'offshoots of the Sunni sect' such as Wahabis and Qadianis, who were of 'comparatively recent growth and numerically un-important in the State'.[11]

Divisions among Kashmiri Muslims

In relation to some of the Muslims living in the Kashmir Valley listed above, *An Ethnohistorical Dictionary* notes that:

> Kashmiri society is fractured by profound divisions which in themselves constitute different ethnic groups. ... Caste lines also divide the Kashmiris, although they are not as rigid as those of Hindus. At the very top of the Kashmiri social structure are Sayyids [Syeds], who claim direct descent from the Prophet Muhammed and marry endogamously. Just below the Sayyids are the Shaikhs [Sheikhs], who claim descent from the Prophet's earliest disciples. Shaikhs also marry endogamously. Sayyids control the religious establishment, whereas Shaikhs are merchants and traders. At the very bottom of the social structure are the so-called occupational sub-castes. The Teli are oil pressers, the Lohars are blacksmiths, the Kumiar are potters, the Hanji are fishermen, the Hajjam are barbers, and the Machis are leather workers.[12]

Similarly, the *Census of India, 1931* noted that in relation to J&K Muslims 'Arains in the State are traditionally market gardeners and vegetable growers', Bafindas were 'weavers', 'the Balti is an inhabitant of Baltistan which is another name of Skardu, a tehsil of Ladakh district', Hajjams were 'barbers', a Jat was an 'agriculturalist by tradition', Jhiwars were 'water-bearers' and 'Palki-bearers' [palanquin or chair bearers], 'Mughal [Moghal] and Pathans are the relics of foreign invaders who have in course of time got mingled with the locals', the 'traditional occupation of the Rajputs is service (especially in the Army) and agriculture', 'Sheikh is a generic term applied to a convert to Islam which has crystallised into a caste name', Sudhan was 'a Muslim caste found mostly in the Poonch Jagir', and Tarkhan was 'an indispensable part of the village organisation like the Lohar [mechanic]'.[13]

Specifically in relation to Kashmiri Muslims, the *Census of India, 1931* noted that this community had various 'sub-castes'. The most important 'from the statistical point of view' were 'the Bat, the Dar, the Ganai, the Khan, the Lon, the Malik, the Mir, the Pare, the Rather, Shah, Sheikh and Wain'. Most were found in 'Kashmir

Table II.4 Extract from 'Tribes, Castes and Other Important Elements' in J&K, with a focus on Hindus in Kashmir Valley

Category	Baramulla	Anantnag	Total
Brahman	52	665	717
Jat	0	30	30
Jhiwar	0	218	218
Kashmiri Pandits	11,203	62,039	73,242
Khatris	925	875	1,800
Lohar	367	4	371
Mahajan	9	72	81
Rajput	166	1,862	2,028
14 Scheduled Castes	7	35	42
Total	12,729	65,800	78,529

Source: 'Imperial Table XIV: Variation in Population of Selected Tribes, Scheduled Castes and Important Elements', *Census of India 1941*,Volume XXII, Jammu & Kashmir State, Part II, Tables, Srinagar, R. G. Wreford, Editor, Jammu and Kashmir Government, 1942, pp. 353–66.

Province and Udhampur district of the Jammu Province.[14] The 1931 Census in its 'Table XVII. Race, Tribe and Caste' divided Kashmiri Muslims into twenty-six 'sub-castes': Aito, Akhoon, Bat, Chaupan, Dar, Gunai, Hajam, Hanji, Khan, Khauja, Lon, Magre, Malik, Mir, Pandit, Parai, Pirzada, Raina, Rather, Rishi, Syed, Shah, Sheikh, Tantrei, Wain, and Others.[15] The 1941 Census, however, listed (and counted) four of these sub-castes separately: Hajjam (Hajam), Hanjis, Sheikh, Syed.

Hindus in Kashmir

The 1941 Census shows that there were 78,529 Hindus living in Kashmir: 62,039 in Anantnag District; 11,203 in Baramulla Province. Over 90 per cent of these were Kashmiri Pandits: 73,242. The total figure of 78,529 was 7,051 less than the total number of Hindus living in Kashmir as per Table II.1: 85,580 people. The Census does not explain this shortfall. Presumably these 7,051 people did not belong to 'Castes with numbers exceeding 10000 in 1931', while their 'social status, political importance or special character [we]re such as to justify inclusion'.[16]

Border or territorial changes, actual or attempted, in South Asia since 15 August 1947

Over its long history, the Indian subcontinent and its various civilisations have had numerous empires and rulers. However, in terms of local rulers, only the Mauryan Empire and the later Mughal Empire controlled much, but not all, of the Indian subcontinent. One major achievement of the external British was to politically unite, then divide, this geographic entity. The East India Company's unification of India essentially was completed in 1849 with the defeat of the Sikhs in the second Anglo-Sikh war. After the Indians' 1856 uprising (or mutiny, as the British saw things) had very seriously challenged East India Company rule, the British Government took direct control of India. Thereafter, the British tightly controlled their Indian Empire, administering it directly via British India and indirectly via Princely India. The British Government's division of its Indian Empire occurred in 1947. This ended the first, and only, ever unified Indian political entity. In 1968, the British decolonised their last South Asian territory by granting independence to the Maldives. However, they did not totally leave the greater region. The British retained ownership of the significant British Indian Ocean Territory (also called Diego Garcia), which they had depopulated and severed from Mauritius in 1965 (and which Mauritius still claims). Diego Garcia sits strategically in the centre of the Indian Ocean. Given how long it is since the British left both India and the Maldives, it is now difficult for South Asians to blame the British for all of their post-decolonisation problems.

Since 1947, there have been some fifteen major changes to borders in South Asia. These are detailed below. While most of these changes occurred in the first thirty years of the existence of (post-British) India and Pakistan, two changes occurred as recently as 2014 and 2015. In July 2014, the Permanent Court of Arbitration, The Hague, resolved the Bangladesh–India maritime border. In 2015, Bangladesh and India successfully, and peacefully, exchanged 162 territorial enclaves.

Nevertheless, some significant and unresolved territorial and border issues still exist for some South Asian nations. Consequently, we may see – and, indeed, I expect to see – further border or territorial changes in South Asia, although not necessarily as a result of tumultuous or traumatic experiences. (I certainly do not wish violence on South Asians.) History shows that this is a real possibility, even an inevitability, in the diverse, disparate and sometimes disputed subcontinental 'region'. For example, China and India could peacefully resolve their longstanding border and territorial dispute, as could India and Pakistan, or India and Nepal. That said, aggressive statements by people such as the Chief of the Indian Army or the Prime Minister of Azad Kashmir, as discussed in Chapter 7, suggest that further changes against 'the other' may be externally instigated or supported. There is plenty of 'raw material' in South Asia to work with, including ongoing insurgencies in Afghanistan, in Pakistan's Balochistan Province, in India's northeast states, in its Kashmir territory, and in peninsula India (Maoists). Some of these insurgencies are old: the Baluchistan insurgency began in 1948 and is now in its fifth phase; the Naga insurgency began in the early 1950s, although, even in 1947, Nagas apparently did not want to join either India or Pakistan; the roots of the Maoists' struggle go back to the Naxalbari uprising in 1967, or even to the Telangana peasant rebellion in the last 1940s. Two insurgencies (Afghanistan and Kashmir) are in the International Crisis Group's '10 Conflicts to Watch in 2020'.[1] Apart from insurgencies, there are numerous other possibilities for territorial changes in South Asia, or for South Asians: a reunified Bengal 'nation' comprising Bangladesh and India's West Bengal state; a reunified Punjab 'nation' comprising all the areas that made up Punjab Province in 1947; a unified Pukhtoon/Pushtoon 'nation' that would comprise southeast Afghanistan and northwest Pakistan; a new Dravidian 'nation' in southern peninsula India consisting of Andhra Pradesh, Karnataka, Kerala, Tamil Nadu, Telangana, and possibly Goa; a new 'nation' of northeast Indian states, possibly in conjunction with greater Bengal; a new mercantile nation that comprised the Indian states of Maharashtra and Gujarat and the Pakistani province of Sind. The possibilities are endless.

I do not necessarily expect any of these boundary or territorial changes to occur soon; rather, I am speculating. However, they might. That said, it is worth noting that there have only ever been two successful insurgencies in South Asia since 1947. The first was the violent breakaway from Pakistan in 1971 by Bengalis who established Bangladesh in Pakistan's East Pakistan Province. The second was the Afghan Taliban, who won control of Afghanistan in 1996 (but lost it when US-led foreign forces invaded in 2001). Significantly, while Bengalis fought hard for their success, they also were helped by the support of an external third power: India and Indian military support. Other Bengali assets were: a large population; access to the sea; its cultural and physical remoteness from West Pakistan; a sanctuary to which fighters and refugees could retreat (India); and a capable, brave and inspiring leader who, when he finally decided to fight, knew exactly what he wanted to achieve. Similarly, the motivated Afghan Taliban received sanctuary, help and support from Pakistan. Not all of the above insurgencies share these factors. While Pakistan might help Kashmiris, for example, there is no guarantee that Islamabad would leave Kashmiris be should they ever free themselves from India's control. Border changes in South Asia may therefore seem unlikely. However, just as COVID-19 or the coronavirus sprang upon us silently, quickly and ruthlessly in 2020, so too could unexpected or unanticipated border changes. Should India ever disintegrate, Kashmiris may find it possible to regain the independence that Kashmir lost when the Mughal Emperor, Akbar, captured this region in 1586. Equally, should Pakistan ever disintegrate, Kashmir might find itself quickly and totally subsumed by a resurgent, all-encompassing India – or by some new, unforeseen entity. Some Indian Hindus also still talk of reconstituting Akhund Bharat: a mythical 'undivided India' comprising India, Pakistan, Bangladesh, Afghanistan, all of J&K, Tibet, Bhutan, Nepal, Sri Lanka, and Myanmar that has never actually existed.[2] Such a concept is totally unappealing for Muslim Pakistanis. Should China and India fight another war, this could offer significant time-critical liberation possibilities for either J&K or Kashmir. Once again, these thoughts are all speculative. The point is that the future is uncertain and unpredictable.

Table III.1 details the fifteen border or territorial changes, actual or attempted, that have occurred in South Asia since 15 August 1947. It also details some major events in India and/or Pakistan of relevance. At the end of the table, there is a list of outstanding border or territorial issues in, or involving, South Asia.

Table III.1   *Fifteen border or territorial changes, actual or attempted, in South Asia since 15 August 1947*

	Date	Event	Beneficiary
1	15 August 1947	British vacate their Indian Empire and partition directly-ruled British India into two dominions: India and Pakistan, with the latter having two wings: West Pakistan and East Bengal (later East Pakistan)	The new dominions of India and Pakistan; however, on 15 August 1947, borders between them unknown and uncertain

Table III.1 Fifteen border or territorial changes, actual or attempted, in South Asia since 15 August 1947 (Continued)

	Date	Event	Beneficiary
2	By 15 August 1947	Almost all princely rulers in indirectly British-ruled Princely India who are entitled to make an accession have done so	For geo-economic reasons, most rulers join India; nine join Pakistan
1	17 August 1947	Punjab and Bengal Boundary Commissions announce India–Pakistan borders; to Pakistanis' chagrin, three of Gurdaspur District's four tehsils awarded to India	India; it gets strategic land access from Pathankot to Jammu Province in Jammu and Kashmir (J&K)
3	18 August 1947	Accession of (Muslim) Nawab of (Hindu-majority) Junagadh to Pakistan	Pakistan; but, soon after, India's military forces enter
4	From August 1947–26 October 1947	Soon after partition, pro-Pakistan Muslims in Poonch and Mirpur areas of southwestern J&K begin an anti-Maharaja uprising in J&K	Pakistan; the 'freed' areas become part of Azad (Free) Kashmir
4	22 October 1947	Pukhtoon tribesmen from Pakistan invade J&K's Kashmir Province; their aim is to capture J&K, Princely India's largest and most strategic princely state, for Pakistan	India ultimately, as the invasion provoked the Maharaja of J&K to accede to India
4	24 October 1947	Pro-Pakistan Muslim 'rebels' in Poonch and Mirpur establish a Provisional Government of Azad (Free) Kashmir in their liberated areas; supposedly, it is to govern all of J&K	Pakistan; Azad Kashmir region quickly comes under Pakistan's administration
4	26 October 1947	(Hindu) Maharaja of (Muslim-majority) J&K accedes to India; Pakistan rejects accession as 'based on fraud and violence'	India; but, the so-called 'Kashmir dispute' begins
4	27 October 1947	Indian Army soldiers fly into Srinagar to defend India's newest acquisition: J&K; begin to repel anti-India elements	India, Kashmiris; the Pukhtoons' brutal violence and pillaging delays them
4	Early November 1947	Pro-Pakistan Muslims in the Gilgit area of northern J&K rebel and ask Pakistan to send an administrator to the region	Pakistan; the Northern Areas quickly come under Pakistan's administration

Table III.1   Fifteen border or territorial changes, actual or attempted, in South Asia since
15 August 1947 (Continued)

	Date	Event	Beneficiary
4	Early November 1947	Local rulers of Hunza and Nagar, in the Gilgit area but under the suzerainty of the Maharaja of J&K, try to accede to Pakistan	Pakistan; it acknowledges, but does not formally accept, these 'accessions'
4	27 October 1947–1 January 1949	Indian Army fights pro-Pakistan Muslims in J&K (Poonchis; Mirpuris; Pukhtoons; Gilgitis, Baltistanis); Pakistan Army officially enters J&K, and this fight, in May 1948	Pakistan 'wins' roughly one third of J&K: Azad Kashmir and the Northern Areas (Gilgit-Baltistan after 2009)
4	1 January 1948	India asks United Nations Security Council (UNSC) to condemn Pakistan's aggression in J&K under Article 35 of UN Charter; but UNSC sets up UN Commission for India and Pakistan (UNCIP) to investigate this issue	Not India; this broadens the dispute over J&K to formally include both Pakistan and UNSC
3	February 1948	Plebiscite in Junagadh; people vote overwhelmingly to join India	India, but Pakistan goes on claiming Junagadh as its own
5	March 1948	(Muslim) Khan of Kalat's princely state militarily incorporated into Pakistan	Pakistan; Kalat had sought to be independent
4	May 1948	Pakistan Army officially enters J&K; Karachi only informs UNCIP of this in June 1948	India; this furthers its hold of the 'moral high ground'
6	September 1948	(Muslim) Nizam of Hyderabad's (Hindu-majority) princely state, India's wealthiest, is militarily incorporated into India	India; the reclusive Nizam had wanted independence for his state
2	1947–48	Successful integration of all 562 princely states, except J&K, into India or Pakistan	Almost all integrated into India; ten into Pakistan
4	21 April 1948	UNSC reiterates that a plebiscite should be held to resolve the Kashmir dispute	People of J&K (J&K-ites)
4	1 January 1949	United Nations-brokered ceasefire ends first India–Pakistan war in disputed J&K	India, Pakistan, J&K, J&K-ites

*Table III.1   Fifteen border or territorial changes, actual or attempted, in South Asia since
15 August 1947 (Continued)*

	Date	Event	Beneficiary
4	July 1949	Indian, Pakistan militaries agree ceasefire line in J&K; demarcated to NJ 980 420, after which it heads 'north to the borders'	India, Pakistan
	[26 January 1950]	[India institutes its constitution; becomes a fully independent republic]	
4	[8 August 1953]	[Sheikh Abdullah dismissed as Indian J&K Prime Minister; thereafter detained but advocates for self-determination for J&K-ites]	[India; post-Abdullah, Indian J&K Prime/ Chief Ministers must be strongly pro-India]
4	[14 November 1952]	[Dogra rule officially ends in J&K]	[India; J&K-ites]
7	1954	Pondicherry and French India incorporated into India	India; becomes Indian territory
4	1954	Indian maps show Chinese-held Aksai Chin in J&K/Tibet as Indian territory because Raja Gulab Singh captured this region in 1843	India, cartographically only
	[23 March 1956]	[Pakistan institutes its constitution; becomes a fully independent republic]	
4	26 January 1957	Indian J&K Constitution comes into force; reiterates that 'J&K is and shall be an integral part of the Union of India'	India; constitution rejected by UNSC: people to decide J&K's 'final disposition'
8	1958	Pakistan enlarged after purchasing Gwadar enclave from Oman	Pakistan; becomes part of Baluchistan Province
9	1961	Goa and Portuguese India militarily incorporated into India	India; become Indian territories
4	1963	Pakistan cedes northern Shaksgam Valley of J&K to China; India objects to this loss of territory that is an 'integral part of India'	China; soon after, Pakistan and China become 'all weather friends'
10	April 1965	Pakistan seizes territory from India in Rann of Kutch, in western India	Pakistan; precursor to second India– Pakistan war

Table III.1   *Fifteen border or territorial changes, actual or attempted, in South Asia since 15 August 1947 (Continued)*

	Date	Event	Beneficiary
4	[August–September 1965]	[Second India–Pakistan war in J&K: Pakistan tries to foment Kashmiri uprising, then its forces seize territory in Jammu; Indian forces capture strategic Pir Panjal heights, then surround Lahore]	[Stalemate; Tashkent Declaration, January 1966, restores *status quo ante*]
10	1968	United Nations arbitration over Rann of Kutch incident in April 1965	To India's chagrin, Pakistan awarded 10% of Kutch
11	1971	Uprising by 'Pakistani' Bengalis in East Pakistan; they had convincingly won the 1970 elections but West Pakistanis would not allow power to be devolved to them	Bangladesh; with India's support, the Bengali 'rebels' bring this new nation into existence
11	1971	Third India–Pakistan war, with India aiding Mukti Banini guerrillas (freedom fighters); Pakistan loses East Pakistan/Bangladesh	India; captures 90,000 Pakistanis (56,000 military); weakens Pakistan
4	1972	India–Pakistan Simla Agreement; minor, but important, changes made to 1949 ceasefire line; it is renamed the Line of Control (LOC)	India; all India–Pakistan matters become bilateral; no third party involvement
12	1973	Incorporation of the protectorate of Sikkim into India	India
13	1976	India, Sri Lanka and Maldives agree their maritime borders, including the tri-junction point in the Gulf of Mannar	India, Sri Lanka, Maldives
4	[1984]	[India and Pakistan put military forces on Siachen Glacier, beyond NJ 980 420 in an area not demarcated by 1949 ceasefire line]	[India apparently has the superior tactical positions on Siachen Glacier]
4	[1988 – ongoing]	[Disenchanted Muslim Kashmiris wanting *azadi* (independence) for J&K, or for J&K to join Pakistan, begin anti-India uprising; this becomes violent in 1989; India accuses Pakistan of supporting terrorists/terrorism, and of mounting a proxy war in Kashmir]	[Pakistan; many problems in Kashmir are of India's making; Pakistan takes advantage of these by supporting anti-India elements]

Table III.1   *Fifteen border or territorial changes, actual or attempted, in South Asia since*
15 August 1947 (Continued)

	Date	Event	Beneficiary
	[1998]	[India and Pakistan confirm their nuclear capabilities via a series of tests]	[Pakistan?; makes conventional war difficult]
4	[1999]	[India fights 'militants' (actually Pakistan-officered, armed and trained Northern Light Infantry from Gilgit-Baltistan) in the mountainous Kargil sector of J&K]	[India wins this 'war' (over 1,000 soldiers killed); significant US pressure on Pakistan to desist]
4	[2004–8]	[India–Pakistan conduct their Composite Dialogue of eight items, including J&K; Dr Singh and General Musharraf apparently get close to resolving the Kashmir issue]	[India agrees to discuss J&K; Pakistan agrees to discuss the other seven items]
4	[2006]	[For the first time since 1947, India and Pakistan officially allow J&K-ites divided by LOC to access each other via five crossing points; trade also permitted for a limited number of items]	[J&K-ites, although the processes involved are difficult]
4	[26 November 2008]	[Lashkar-e-Taiba terrorists from Pakistan brutally attack Mumbai; India suspends India–Pakistan Composite Dialogue; this dialogue is never really resumed]	[India not prepared to engage with Pakistan until it ends its support for terrorists and terrorism]
14	7 July 2014	India–Bangladesh Maritime Delimitation made by the Arbitration Tribunal at the Permanent Court of Arbitration, The Hague	Bangladesh; seemingly, it gets the larger or better parts of the maritime areas
15	2015	Bangladesh–India exchange 162 enclaves of land: Bangladesh receives 111 Indian enclaves (6,940 hectares) located in Bangladesh; India gets fifty-one Bangladesh enclaves (2,880 hectares) located in India	Bangladesh, India; the exchanges resolve a longstanding issue that caused considerable inconvenience to people

Table III.1   *Fifteen border or territorial changes, actual or attempted, in South Asia since 15 August 1947 (Continued)*

	Date	Event	Beneficiary
4	[5 August 2019]	[India divides Indian J&K into two territories: J&K and Ladakh; Articles 35-A and 370 also abrogated; strict security measures essentially confine Kashmiris in an 'open jail']	[India: allows it to directly control both regions; Jammuites and Ladakhis, who have long disliked Kashmiri domination in Indian J&K]
4	[After August 2019]	[Pakistan tries to internationalise the Kashmir dispute. UNSC briefly discusses the issue in August 2019 and January 2020; few nations except China support Pakistan;]	[India; most nations agree that Kashmir is a bilateral issue that India and Pakistan must resolve]
4	20??	Independent J&K or independent Kashmir?	J&K-ites? Kashmiris?
	Outstanding border or territorial issues in, or involving, South Asia:	• Afghanistan–Pakistan re Kabul's non-acceptance of the 1894 British-imposed Durand Line border between Afghanistan and British India, now Pakistan • Bhutan–China border • China–India re Aksai Chin, re Arunachal Pradesh/'South Tibet', and re sections of the China-India border • India–Nepal re territory and border around Kalapari River area and Susta area • India–Pakistan re disputed J&K and re Sir Creek waterway near the Arabian Sea	

Note: The number in the first column refers to the Issue, of which there were fifteen. The Events are in date sequence. Some Issues only have single entries while others have recurring entries as the Issue has progressed. Information within square brackets relates to noteworthy events and/or to events of significance that relate to J&K but which have not led directly to border or territorial changes.

Notes

Introduction

1 Generally, I have used this spelling for 'Mohammad' throughout the book.
2 David E. Lockwood, 'Sheikh Abdullah and the Politics of Kashmir', *Asian Survey*, Vol. 9, No. 5 (May 1969), p. 382.
3 It is possible that the Indian Supreme Court may negate the actions taken by the Indian Government in 2019 in relation to Indian J&K (as discussed in Chapter 7), but at the time of writing (July 2020) this is uncertain.
4 Christopher Snedden, *The Untold Story of the People of Azad Kashmir*, London, Hurst & Co., 2012, Chapter 2.
5 *The Testament of Sheikh Abdullah*, New Delhi, Palit and Palit, 1974, p. 8.
6 Philip Ziegler, *Mountbatten: The Official Biography*, Glasgow, Fontana/Collins, 1985, p. 610.
7 I use the term 'Jammu Kashmir Liberation Front' (not Jammu & Kashmir Liberation Front), as per its 2003 manifesto: Amanullah Khan, *The JKLF Roadmap for Peace & Prosperity in South Asia*, Muzaffarabad, Jammu Kashmir Liberation Front, 2003.
8 Maria Abi-Habib, Jalaluddin Mughal and Salman Masood, 'In Pakistan-Held Kashmir, Growing Calls for Independence', *The New York Times*, 19 September 2019, www.nytimes.com/2019/09/19/world/asia/pakistan-kashmir-independence.html [accessed 6 April 2020]; Fayaz Bukhari, 'Indian Kashmir Hit by General Strike Called by Separatists', *Reuters*, 9 February 2020, www.reuters.com/article/us-india-kashmir/indian-kashmir-hit-by-general-strike-called-by-separatists-idUSKBN2030CH [accessed 6 April 2020].
9 Andrew Whitehead, *A Mission in Kashmir*, New Delhi, Viking, 2007, p. 31.
10 Navnita Chadha Behera, *State, Identity and Violence: Jammu, Kashmir and Ladakh*, New Delhi, Manohar, 2000, p. 229.
11 'Jammu and Kashmir Unfinished Agenda of Partition: Mamnoon', *Pakistan Today*, 2 February 2017, www.pakistantoday.com.pk/2017/02/02/jammu-and-kashmir-unfinished-agenda-of-partition-mamnoon/ [accessed 20 March 2017]; 'Kashmir is the "Unfinished Business of Partition", Says Pakistan Army Chief', *Scroll.in*, 8 September 2015, https://scroll.in/article/754127/kashmir-is-the-unfinished-business-of-partition-says-pakistan-army-chief [accessed 20 March 2017].
12 *Constitutional Relations Between Britain and India, The Transfer of Power 1942–7*, Volumes VI, VII, IX, X, XI, XII, London, Nicholas Mansergh, Editor-in-Chief, Her Majesty's Stationery Office, 1976–1983, deals with this process.

13 *Census of India, 1931*, Volume XXIV, Jammu & Kashmir State, Part I – Report, Rai Bahadur, Pt. Anand Ram, Census Commissioner, and Pt. Hira Nand Raina, Assistant Census Commissioner, [Jammu and Kashmir Government], Jammu, 1933, p. 15.

14 Mohammad Ishaq Khan, *Perspectives on Kashmir*, Srinagar, Gulshan Publishers, 1983, p. 18; G. M. D. Sufi, *Kashir* [sic]: *Being a History of Kashmir From the Earliest Times to Our Own*, Volume I, Lahore, The University of the Punjab, 1948.

15 My two previous books are: Christopher Snedden, *The Untold Story of the People of Azad Kashmir, London,* Hurst and Co., 2012/New York, Columbia University Press, 2012; republished in Pakistan by Oxford University Press, Karachi, 2013; republished in India by HarperCollins, New Delhi, 2013, as *Kashmir: The Unwritten History*; and Christopher Snedden, *Understanding Kashmir and Kashmiris, London,* Hurst and Co., 2015; republished in South Asia by Speaking Tiger Books, New Delhi, 2017.

16 Edward Thornton, *A Gazetteer of the Territories under the Government of the East India Company and of the Native States on the Continent of India*, London, Wm H. Allen & Co., 1854, Volumes I–IV.

17 *Census of India, 1901*, Volume XXIII [Jammu and] Kashmir, Part I. Report, by Khan Bahadur Munshi Ghulam Ahmed Khan, Revenue Member, State Council, and Superintendent of Census Operations, Jammu and Kashmir State, Lahore, The 'Civil and Military Gazette' Press, 1902.

18 Manzoor Fazili, *Kashmir Government and Politics*, Srinagar, Gulshan Publishers, 1982, p. 82.

Chapter 1 Decolonisation and the departure of the British from India

1   John Bew, *Citizen Clem*, London, Riverrun, 2016, p. 437.

2   *Ibid.*, p. 413.

3   *The Times*, 30 October 1947.

4   Frederick Sykes, 'The Indian States and the Reforms', *International Affairs*, Vol. 14, No. 1, Jan–Feb 1935, p. 49.

5   V. P. Menon, *The Story of the Integration of the Indian States*, Bombay, Orient Longman, 1961, p. 105.

6   *Report of the Indian States Committee, 1928–1929*, London, His Majesty's Stationery Office, 1929, p. 10.

7   K. R. R. Sastry, *Treaties, Engagements and Sanads of Indian States: A Contribution in Indian Jurisprudence*, Allahabad, self-published, 1942, pp. 3, 4 and various.

8   Reginald Coupland, *India: A Re-statement*, London, Oxford University Press, 1945, p. 301.

9   *Indian Independence Act 1947*, London, Parliament of the United Kingdom, 1947, www.legislation.gov.uk/ukpga/1947/30/pdfs/ukpga_19470030_en.pdf [accessed 27 June 2017], p. 1.

10 P. B. Gajendragadkar, *Kashmir – Retrospect and Prospect*, Bombay, University of Bombay, 1967, p. 134.

11 Alan Campbell-Johnson, *Mission With Mountbatten*, New York, Atheneum, 1986, p. 89.

Notes

12 Diana Mansergh, Editor, *Independence Years: The Selected Indian and Commonwealth Papers of Nicholas Mansergh*, New Delhi, Oxford University Press, 1999, p. 218.

13 'Rear-Admiral Viscount Mountbatten of Burma to the Earl of Listowel', in *The Transfer of Power*, Volume XI, p. 394.

14 'Member States', *United Nations*, undated, www.un.org/en/member-states/ [accessed 26 March 2019].

15 Robin Jeffrey, 'Introduction', in Robin Jeffrey, Editor, *People, Princes and Paramount Power*, Delhi, Oxford University Press, 1978, p. 24.

16 B. N. Mullik, *My Years with Nehru: Kashmir*, Bombay, Allied Publishers, 1971, p. 4.

17 Campbell-Johnson, *Mission*, p. 137.

18 R. Coupland, *Indian Politics 1936–1942*, London, Oxford University Press, 1943, p. 2.

19 Menon, *The Story*, p. 19.

20 Sastry, *Treaties*, pp. 17–18.

21 *White Paper on Indian States*, New Delhi, Government of India, revised edition, 1950, p. 21.

22 W. H. Morris-Jones, 'Thirty-Six Years Later: The Mixed Legacies of Mountbatten's Transfer of Power', *International Affairs*, Vol. 59, No. 4, Autumn 1983, p. 624.

23 *Report of the Indian States Committee*, p. 15.

24 *Ibid.*, p. 26.

25 Gajendragadkar, *Kashmir*, p. 20.

26 Publications Division, Ministry of Information and Broadcasting, *Indian States Today*, Delhi, Government of India, 1948, p. 16.

27 *White Paper on Indian States*, p. 33.

28 Campbell-Johnson, *Mission*, p. 140.

29 Section 1, *Indian Independence Act 1947*, p. 1.

30 Barney White-Spunner, *Partition: The Story of Indian Independence and the Creation of Pakistan in 1947*, London, Simon & Schuster, 2017, p. 72.

31 Menon, *The Story*, p. 33.

32 Sykes, 'The Indian States and the Reforms', pp. 53–4.

33 Part II, Chapter I, *Government of India Act, 1935*, London, Parliament of the United Kingdom, 1935, www.legislation.gov.uk/ukpga/1935/2/pdfs/ukpga_19350002_en.pdf, pp. 2–5 [accessed 27 June 2017].

34 Menon, *The Story*, pp. 33, 34.

35 Coupland, *Indian Politics*, p. 3.

36 *Report of the Indian States Committee*, p. 10.

37 *List of the Private Secretaries to the Governors-General and Viceroys from 1774 to 1908*, Calcutta, Superintendent Government Printing, India, 1908, p. 20.

38 Walter Roper Lawrence, *The India We Served*, London, Cassell and Company, 1928, p. 182.

39 *Ibid.*, p. 179.

40 Sastry, *Treaties*, pp. 17, 202.

41 George MacMunn, *The Indian States and Princes*, London, Jarrolds, 1936, pp. 256, 266.

42 *Report of the Indian States Committee*, cover page and p. 10.

43 *Ibid.*, p. 10.

44 Coupland, *India: A Re-statement*, p. 301.

45 Jeffrey, 'Introduction', in Jeffrey, *People, Princes*, p. 26.

46 Sastry, *Treaties*, p. 18.

47 Publications Division, *Indian States Today*, p. 8.

48 Sastry, *Treaties*, pp. 57–8.

49 Menon, *The Story*, p. 24.

50 Sir Francis Younghusband, *Kashmir*, London, Adam & Charles Black, 1911, p. 183.

51 Ian Copland, 'The Other Guardians: Ideology and Performance in the Indian Political Service', in Jeffrey, *People, Princes*, p. 276.

52 David Gilmour, *The Ruling Caste*, New York, Farrar, Straus and Giroux, 2005, p. 183.

53 John Collet, *Guide to Kashmir*, Calcutta, W. Newman and Co., 1898, p. 11.

54 The figures for the number of states for each division are from *Report of the Indian States Committee*, p. 10.

55 Menon, *The Story*, p. 17.

56 The Viceroy was entitled to a 31-gun salute; the King-Emperor to a 101-gun salute. According to Shashi Tharoor, *Inglorious Empire: What the British Did to India*, London, Hurst and Co., 2017, p. 49, footnote 6, J&K became a 21-gun Salute State in 1921 in appreciation of its soldiers' services to the British in World War I. Before then, it had been entitled to a 19-gun salute.

57 Publications Division, *Indian States Today*, p. 53.

58 MacMunn, *The Indian States*, pp. 195, 201, 202, 206, 215, 266.

59 *Report of the Indian States Committee*, p. 10.

60 Larry Collins and Dominique Lapierre, *Freedom at Midnight*, London, Panther, 1982, p. 154.

61 Publications Division, *Indian States Today*, p. 11.

62 *White Paper on Indian States*, p. 36.

63 *Report of the Indian States Committee*, p. 10.

64 *Ibid.*, pp. 11, 13.

65 Publications Division, *Indian States Today*, p. 11.

66 William Barton, *The Princes of India*, London, Nisbet & Co., 1934, p. xiii.

67 *Report of the Indian States Committee*, p. 10.

68 Menon, *The Story*, p. 102.

69 *Ibid.*, p. 16.

70 *Report of the Indian States Committee*, p. 20.

71 Sumanta K. Bhowmick, 'The Forgotten Chamber of Princes', *Live History India*, February 2019, www.livehistoryindia.com/cover-story/2019/02/18/the-forgotten-chamber-of-princes [accessed 12 October 2019].

72 Ishaq Khan, *Perspectives*, pp. 51, 53.

73 Bawa Satinder Singh, *The Jammu Fox*, Carbondale, Southern Illinois University Press, 1974, p. 129.

74 Lawrence, *The India We Served*, pp. 127, 128.

75 F. M. Hassnain, *Gilgit: The Northern Gate of India*, New Delhi, Sterling Publisher, 1975, p. 80.

76 Lawrence, *The India We Served*, p. 126.

77 *Census of India, 1931*, Part I – Report, pp. 34, 60.

78 *India in 1932–33*, Delhi, Manager of Publications, 1934, 34, p. 61.

79 Richard Leonard Park, 'India Argues with Kashmir', *Far Eastern Survey*, Vol. 21, No. 11, 2 July 1952, p. 114. The terms 'communal' and 'communalism' will appear many times throughout this book.

80 Lawrence, *The India We Served*, p. 199.
81 Sufi, *Kashir* [sic]: *Being a History of Kashmir*, p. 809.
82 Tharoor, *Inglorious Empire*, p. 84.
83 Jyoti Bhusan Das Gupta, *Jammu and Kashmir*, The Hague, Martinus Nijhoff, 1968, p. 59.
84 Barton, *The Princes of India*, pp. 272–4.
85 Menon, *The Story*, p. 82.
86 *Ibid.*, p. 105.
87 *Ibid.*, pp. 105–6.
88 L. F. R. W. [sic], 'The Indian Dominion and the States', *The World Today*, Vol. 5, No. 1, January 1949, p. 32.
89 'Notes by Sir C. Corfield and Rear-Admiral Viscount Mountbatten of Burma', 22 April 1947, in *The Transfer of Power*, Volume X, p. 463.
90 Sir Conrad Corfield, *The Princely India I Knew: From Reading to Mountbatten*, Madras, Indo British Historical Society, 1975, p. 4.
91 Barbara N. Ramusack, *The Indian Princes and Their States*, Cambridge, Cambridge University Press, 2004, p. 18.
92 Section 7 1b, *Indian Independence Act 1947*, p. 4.
93 Mehr Chand Mahajan, *Looking Back*, New Delhi, Har-Anand Publications, 1994 [first published 1963?], p. 132.
94 Corfield, *The Princely India*, p. 157, italics as per the original.
95 Lord Birdwood, 'Kashmir', *International Affairs*, Vol. 28, No. 3, July 1952, p. 301.
96 *Report of the Indian States Committee*, p. 26.
97 Corfield, *The Princely India*, p. 157, italics as per the original.
98 Publications Division, *Indian States Today*, p. 16.
99 S. M. Gokhale, *Indian States and the Cabinet Mission Plan*, Baroda, Mrs. M. S. Gokhale, 1947, p. 51.
100 P. J. G. [sic], 'The Indian Union and Pakistan: The Political Outlook', *The World Today*, Vol. 3, No. 12, December 1947, p. 525.
101 Campbell-Johnson, *Mission*, p. 105.
102 'History of the Commonwealth', *Commonwealth Network*, www.commonwealthofnations.org/commonwealth/history/ [accessed 12 March 2017].
103 Ziegler, *Mountbatten*, p. 381.
104 James Manor, 'The Demise of the Princely Order: A Reassessment', in Jeffrey, *People, Princes*, p. 318.
105 R. P. Bhargava, *The Chamber of Princes*, New Delhi, Northern Book Centre, 1991, p. 310.
106 S. M. Verma, *Chamber of Princes (1921–1947)*, New Delhi, National Book Organisation, 1990, p. xi.
107 Ziegler, *Mountbatten*, pp. 386–7.
108 Bhargava, *The Chamber*, p. 312.
109 Bhattacharjea, *Sheikh Mohammad Abdullah: Tragic Hero of Kashmir*, New Delhi, Roli Books, 2008, p. 96.
110 Menon, *The Story*, pp. 75–6.
111 Balraj Krishna, *Sardar Vallabhbhai Patel: India's Iron Man*, New Delhi, Rupa, 2013, p. 332.

112 *The Statesman*, 20 June 1947.

113 'Pandit Nehru to Rear-Admiral Viscount Mountbatten of Burma', 22 June 1947, in *The Transfer of Power*, Volume XI, pp. 556–7.

114 White-Spunner, *Partition*, p. 105.

115 *The Statesman*, 18 July 1947.

116 Menon, *The Story*, p. 87.

117 Corfield, *The Princely India*, p. 157.

118 'Government of India's approach to problem of States', in *White Paper on Hyderabad*, [Delhi], Government of India, 1948.

119 H. V. Hodson, *The Great Divide: Britain-India-Pakistan*, London, Hutchinson, 1969, pp. 367–8.

120 Jeffrey, 'Introduction', in Jeffrey, *People, Princes*, p. 15.

121 P. J. G. [sic], 'The Indian Union and Pakistan', p. 526.

122 Menon, *The Story*, p. 111–12.

123 P. J. G. [sic], 'The Indian Union and Pakistan', p. 526.

124 *White Paper on Indian States*, p. 113.

125 Menon, *The Story*, p. 358.

126 'Hyderabad Farman, Dated the 23rd November, 1949', in *White Paper on Indian States*, Appendix LVI, p. 369.

127 Jeffrey, 'Introduction', in Jeffrey, *People, Princes*, p. 15.

128 Ramusack, *The Indian Princes*, p. 273.

129 Menon, *The Story*, p. 105.

130 *White Paper on Indian States*, p. 36.

131 *Ibid.*, p. 6.

132 Krishna, *Sardar Vallabhbhai Patel*, p. 325.

133 'Appendix V Accession of States', Mohammad Ali Jinnah, *Quaid-i-Azam Mohammad Ali Jinnah Papers*, Volume V, Islamabad, Government of Pakistan, Cabinet Division, 2000, p. 534.

134 Yaqoob Khan Bangash, *A Princely Affair: The Accession and Integration of the Princely States of Pakistan, 1947–1955*, Karachi, Oxford University Press, 2015, pp. 166–7, 189.

135 Publications Division, *Indian States Today*, p. 121.

136 Charles Allen and Sharada Dwivedi, *Lives of the Indian Princes*, London, Arena, 1984, p. 246.

137 L. F. R. W. [sic], 'The Indian Dominion', p. 29.

138 Menon, *The Story*, pp. 416, 468.

139 Publications Division, *Indian States Today*, p. 8.

140 *Census of India, 1941*, Volume XXII, Jammu & Kashmir State, Part II, Tables, Srinagar, R. G. Wreford, Editor, Jammu and Kashmir Government, 1942, pp. 72–3.

141 *Dawn*, 18 June 1947.

142 'No. 108, Press Statement by M. A. Jinnah, F.788/33', Mohammad Ali Jinnah, *Quaid-i-Azam Mohammad Ali Jinnah Papers* Volume III, Islamabad, Government of Pakistan, Cabinet Division, 1997, pp. 298–9.

143 *Dawn*, 21 April 1947, quoted in Sisir Gupta, *Kashmir: A Study in India-Pakistan Relations*, Bombay, Asia Publishing House, 1966, p. 47.

144 'Sir W. Monckton to Mr W. Churchill, Lord Salisbury, Mr Eden and Mr R. A. Butler', 9 August 1947, in *The Transfer of Power*, Volume XII, p. 613.

145 Lord Mountbatten to Maharaja Hari Singh, 27 October 1947, in Jawaid Alam, Editor, *Jammu and Kashmir 1949–64: Select Correspondence between Jawaharlal Nehru and Karan Singh*, New Delhi, Penguin/Viking, 2006, p. 358.
146 Hodson, *The Great Divide*, p. 454.
147 'Statement of the Representative of India, Mr. G. Ayyangar, in the Security Council, 15 January 1948', in Sarwar K. Hasan and Zubeida Hasan, Editors, *Documents on the Foreign Relations of Pakistan: The Kashmir Question*, Karachi, Pakistan Institute of International Relations, 1966, p. 144.
148 Nisid Hajari, *Midnight's Furies: The Deadly Legacy of India's Partition*, Stroud, Amberley, 2017, p. 97.
149 *Dawn*, 18 June 1947.
150 'Enclosure to V. 26: Note by All-Jammu & Kashmir Muslim Conference, [25 August 1947]', in Jinnah, *Quaid-i-Azam*, Volume V, pp. 568, 570.
151 Bangash, *A Princely Affair*, pp. 166–7, 189.
152 William L. Richter, 'Traditional Rulers in Post-Traditional Societies: The Princes of India and Pakistan', in Jeffrey, *People, Princes*, p. 331.
153 Snedden, *Understanding Kashmir*, p. 180.
154 *Keesing's Contemporary Archives*, London, Longman, Volume VI (1947), p. 8931.
155 Snedden, *Understanding Kashmir*, pp. 110–11.
156 *The New York Times*, 7 October 1947.
157 Chaudhri Muhammad Ali, *The Emergence of Pakistan*, New York, Columbia University Press, 1967, pp. 287, 297.
158 Balraj Madhok, *Kashmir: Centre of New Alignments*, New Delhi, Deepak Prakashan [1963], p. 41.
159 Muhammad Yusuf Saraf, *Kashmiris Fight – For Freedom*, Volume I (1819–1946), Lahore, Ferozsons, 1977, p. 629.
160 Snedden, *Understanding Kashmir*, p. 178.
161 Ian Copland, 'The Princely States, the Muslim League, and the Partition of India in 1947', *The International History Review*, Vol. 13, No. 1, February 1991, p. 55.
162 Mir Qasim, *My Life and Times*, New Delhi, Allied Publishers, 1992, p. 31.
163 Amrik Singh, 'Kashmir: The Quest for Independence', in Gull Mohd. Wani, Compiler, *Kashmir: From Autonomy to Azadi*, Srinagar, Valley Book House, 1996, p. 199.
164 C. Sharma, 'The Accession of the J&K State and Maharaja Hari Singh', in M. L. Kapur, Editor, *Maharaja Hari Singh, 1895–1961*, New Delhi, Har-Anand Publications, 1995, p. 136, states that 'It is alleged by one [unnamed] scholar that the Maharaja paid an incognito visit to the Governor General of Pakistan and discussed with him the conditions under which the State could accede to Pakistan'. I have seen nothing to substantiate this allegation, nor to suggest that the two men ever met.
165 Mir Abdul Aziz, *Freedom Struggle in Kashmir*, Lahore, Research Society of Pakistan, University of the Punjab, 2000, p. 84.
166 Saraf, *Kashmiris Fight*, Volume I, pp. 619.
167 Sheikh Mohammad Abdullah, *The Blazing Chinar: An Autobiography* [Translated from Urdu by Mohammad Amin], Srinagar, Gulshan Books, second edition, 2013, p. 220, says Jinnah visited Kashmir in 1935.
168 Saraf, *Kashmiris Fight*, Volume I, pp. 622–37.
169 Abdullah, *The Blazing Chinar*, p. 227, says Jinnah visited Srinagar for one and a half months.

170 Saraf, *Kashmiris Fight*, Volume I, p. 624.

171 Khalid Hassan, Editor, *K. H. Khurshid: Memories of Jinnah*, Karachi, Oxford University Press, 1990, p. 13.

172 *The Times of India*, 22 June 1944.

173 *Ibid.*, 29 June 1944.

174 Mahajan, *Looking Back*, p. 265.

175 Corfield, *The Princely India*, p. 174.

176 Whitehead, *A Mission*, pp. 52, 57, 58.

177 Abdullah, *The Blazing Chinar*, pp. 223–9.

178 *Ibid.*, p. 327.

179 Muhammad Saeed Asad, *Wounded Memories of the Tribal Attack on Kashmir* [Translated from Urdu by Quayyum Raja and Tanveer Ahmed], Mirpur, National Institute of Kashmir Studies, 2010, pp. 10, 148.

180 Campbell-Johnson, *Mission*, p. 120.

181 *The Civil & Military Gazette*, 7 August 1947.

182 Menon, *The Story*, p. 105.

183 Sheikh Mohammad Abdullah, *Flames of the Chinar* [Translated by Khushwant Singh], New Delhi, Viking, 1993, p. 47.

184 Menon, *The Story*, pp. 33, 34.

185 Gajendragadkar, *Kashmir*, p. 46.

186 'Kashmir is Not an Internal Matter of India: Karan Singh', *The Hindu*, 11 August 2016, www.thehindu.com/news/national/Kashmir-is-not-an-internal-matter-of-India-Karan-Singh/article14562551.ece [accessed 27 September 2016].

187 Menon, *The Story*, pp. 37, 40, 41, 107–8.

188 Prithvi Nath Tikoo, *Story of Kashmir*, New Delhi, Light & Life Publishers, 1979, p. 88.

189 *Keesing's Contemporary Archives*, Volume VI (1947), p. 8931.

190 *The Civil & Military Gazette*, 30 September 1947.

191 *Dawn*, 4 March 1948.

192 *The Times*, 3 November 1947.

193 *Census of India, 1941*, Part I: Essay, pp. 28–9.

194 Bakshi Gulam [sic; Ghulam] Mohd., *Kashmir Today 'Thru' Many Eyes'*, Bombay, Bombay Provincial Congress Committee, [1946], pp. 3, 85, 98.

195 *Administration Report of the Jammu and Kashmir State for the Second Half of S. 1998 and for S. 1999 (18 months from 16th October 1941 to 12th April 1943)*, Jammu, Ranbir Government Press, 1944, p. 69.

196 Menon, *The Story*, p. 111.

197 Dewan Ram Prakash, *Fight for Kashmir*, New Delhi, Tagore Memorial Publications, 1948, pp. 277–8, 283.

198 Ian Stephens, *Horned Moon*, London, Chatto & Windus, 1953, pp. 139, 143.

199 Andrew Whitehead, 'The Rise and Fall of New Kashmir', in Chitralekha Zutshi, Editor, *Kashmir: History, Politics, Representation*, Cambridge, Cambridge University Press, 2018, p. 75.

200 A. G. Noorani, *The Kashmir Dispute 1947–2012*, Karachi, Oxford University Press, 2014, p. 32.

201 'Letter to Begum Abdullah', 4 June 1947, Jawaharlal Nehru, *Selected Works of Jawaharlal Nehru*, New Delhi, Jawaharlal Nehru Memorial Fund, Second Series, Volume 3, 1985, p. 197.

202 Noorani, *The Kashmir Dispute*, pp. 32–3.
203 Phillips Talbot, *An American Witness to India's Partition*, New Delhi, Sage Publications, 2007, p. 387.
204 *Ibid.*, p. 352.
205 *The Times*, 23 December 1947.
206 *The Civil & Military Gazette*, 18 August 1948.
207 Hajari, *Midnight's Furies*, p. 252.
208 Josef Korbel, *Danger in Kashmir*, Oxford, Oxford University Press, 1954, p. 147.
209 *The Civil & Military Gazette*, 20 August 1948.
210 *The Testament of Sheikh Abdullah*, p. 36.
211 Ziegler, *Mountbatten*, p. 451.
212 Hodson, *The Great Divide*, p. 472.
213 'Solution by Mediation', Press Conference 16 November 1949, *Selected Works of Jawaharlal Nehru*, Volume 14, 1992, p. 187.
214 A Study Group of the Pakistan Institute of International Affairs, 'An Examination of Suggestions for the Partition of Kashmir', *Pakistan Horizon*, Vol. 1, No. 4, December 1948, pp. 275, 292, 296. Despite the publication date, the article retrospectively discusses the UN-brokered ceasefire that came into place on 1 January 1949.
215 'Report submitted by the United Nations Representative for India and Pakistan, Sir Owen Dixon, to the Security Council, 15 September 1950', in Hasan and Hasan, *Documents*, p. 267.
216 *The Times of India*, 10 July 1953.
217 'Conversations with Mohammad Ali [Bogra]', 17 August 1953, *Selected Works of Jawaharlal Nehru*, Volume 23, 1998, pp. 334, 335.
218 Gupta, *Kashmir*, p. 303.
219 Pervaiz Iqbal Cheema, 'The Kashmir Cobweb: Can it be Resolved?', in Wani, Compiler, *Kashmir*, p. 276.
220 Karan Singh, *Autobiography*, New Delhi, Oxford University Press, revised edition, 1994 [first published 1989], p. 53.
221 Hodson, *The Great Divide*, pp. 471–2.
222 *Census of India, 1931*, Part I – Report, p. 289.
223 Snedden, *The Untold Story*, Appendix II, pp. 239–44.
224 *Ibid.*, p. 242.
225 Talbot, *An American Witness*, p. 352.
226 *The Civil & Military Gazette*, 2 November 1947.
227 Pervez Hoodbhoy 'Kashmir: From Nuclear Flashpoint to South Asia's Bridge of Peace', in Pervez Hoodbhoy, Editor, *Confronting the Bomb: Pakistani and Indian Scientists Speak Out*, Karachi, Oxford University Press, 2013, p. 117.
228 Menon, *The Story*, p. 113.
229 *Ibid.*, p. 394.
230 *Ibid.*
231 Rajmohan Gandhi, *Patel: A Life*, Ahmedabad, Navajivan Publishing House [1991], p. 439.
232 Pandit Jawaharlal Nehru, 'Introduction Essay on Kashmir', in D. P. Dhar, *Kashmir: Eden of the East*, Allahabad, Kitab Mahal, 1945, p. xvii, states that Iqbal 'was a Sapru'. Abdullah, *Flames*, p. 52, states that Iqbal was 'proud' that he was descended from a Kashmiri clan called Sapru.

233 Hector Bolitho, *Jinnah, Creator of Pakistan*, London, John Murray, 1954, p. 99.

234 Mohd Aslma Khan, Rahmat Ali, Sheikh Mohd Sadiq and Inayat Ullah Khan, *Now or Never: Are We to Live or Perish Forever?*, 28 January 1933, no original publication details, copy available at www.mediamonitors.net/nowornever.html [accessed 6 June 2017].

235 Until the Sikhs captured the northwest of India in 1834, this area had actually been part of Afghanistan, with Peshawar being Afghanistan's winter capital.

236 Abdullah, *The Blazing Chinar*, p. 387.

237 Khalid B. Sayeed, *The Political System of Pakistan*, Boston, Houghton Mifflin Company, 1967, p. 39, italics as per the original. His source is 'Choudhary Rahmat Ali, Pakistan the Fatherland of the Pak Nation (London: The Pak National Liberation Movement, 1947), p. 225'.

238 Hodson, *The Great Divide*, p. 322, footnote 1.

239 Anindita Dasgupta, 'Remembering Sylhet: A Forgotten Story of India's 1947 Partition', *Economic and Political Weekly*, 2 August 2008, p. 19.

240 Gupta, *Kashmir*, p. 46.

241 Stanley Wolpert, *Jinnah of Pakistan*, New York, Oxford University Press, 1984, pp. 184–5.

242 *Ibid.*, p. 185.

243 Gupta, *Kashmir*, p. 46. Gupta's source was '*Gandhi-Jinnah Talks*, published by the Hindustan Times Ltd., New Delhi, 1944'.

Chapter 2 Maharaja Hari Singh and his accession issue

1 See Appendix I: Comparison of Jammu and Kashmir with other entities.

2 Rosita Forbes, *India of the Princes*, London, The Right Book Club, 1939, p. 281.

3 Mark Tully and Zareer Masani, *India Forty Years of Independence*, New York, George Braziller, 1988, p. 20.

4 To 'The Hon'ble Pandit Jawaharlal Nehru', 8 October 1947, Sardar Patel, *Sardar Patel's Correspondence 1945–50,Volume I, New Light on Kashmir*, Ahmedabad, Navajivan Publishing House, 1971, p. 56.

5 Barton, *The Princes of India*, p. 126.

6 Five books specifically about Maharaja Hari Singh, listed by publication dates, are: Bhagwan Singh, *Political Conspiracies of Kashmir*, Rohtak, Light and Life, 1973; M. L. Kapur, Editor, *Maharaja Hari Singh, 1895–1961*, New Delhi, Har-Anand Publications, 1995; Surjit Singh Sooden, *Jammu under the Reign of Maharaja Hari Singh: A Study on Socio-economic Conditions* Jammu, Vinod Publishers & Distributors, 1999; Somnath Wakhlu, *Hari Singh: The Maharaja, The Man and the Times: A Biography of Maharaja Hari Singh of Jammu and Kashmir State (1895–1961)*, New Delhi, National Publishing House, 2004; and Harbans Singh, *Maharaja Hari Singh: The Troubled Years*, New Delhi, Brahaspati Publications, 2011. Malka Pukhraj, *Song Sung True: A Memoir* [Edited and translated by Saleem Kidwai], New Delhi, Kali for Women, 2003, is not specifically about Maharaja Hari Singh, but she mentions him a lot. All these books have limitations, particularly in relation to providing supporting references for their various claims about Maharaja Hari Singh.

7 'Memorandum [from Maharaja Hari Singh], August 1952, Poona, [to] Dr Rajendra Prasad, President of India, New Delhi', in Alam, *Jammu and Kashmir*, pp. 309–30.

8 'Excerpts from the speech of Dr. Karan Singh', in Singh, *Maharaja Hari Singh*, p. (a).

9 *Administration Report of the Jammu and Kashmir State for S. 2000 (13th April 1943–12th April 1944)*, Jammu, Ranbir Government Press, 1945, page immediately after title page with the heading 'Maharaja'.

10 [Resident in Kashmir], *Revised List of Ruling Princes, Chiefs and Leading Personages of the Jammu and Kashmir State and the Gilgit Agency*, New Delhi, The Manager of Publications, 1939, p. 3.

11 P. N. K. Bamzai, *Culture and Political History of Kashmir*, Volume III: Modern Kashmir, New Delhi, MD Publications, 1994, p. 722.

12 *The Times*, 27 March 1909.

13 *Ibid.*, 25 September 1925.

14 'Hari Singh of Kashmir', *The Argus*, Melbourne, 17 January 1925, https://trove.nla.gov.au/newspaper/article/2027200 [accessed 16 October 2019].

15 Bamzai, *History of Kashmir*, p. 721.

16 Publicity Department, *A Handbook of the Jammu and Kashmir State*, His Highness's Government, Jammu and Kashmir, Jammu, 1947, p. 31.

17 [Resident in Kashmir], *Revised List*, p. 3.

18 F. M. Hassnain, *British Policy Towards Kashmir (1846–1921) (Kashmir in Anglo-Russian Politics)*, New Delhi, Sterling Publishers, 1974, p. 95.

19 [Resident in Kashmir], *Revised List*, p. 3.

20 Singh, *Autobiography*, p. 2.

21 [Resident in Kashmir], *Revised List*, p. 3.

22 'Hari Singh, by One Who Knows Him', *The Herald*, Melbourne, 5 December 1924, https://trove.nla.gov.au/newspaper/article/243869655 [accessed 14 October 2019].

23 James Milne, *The Road to Kashmir*, London, Hodder and Stoughton, [1929], p. 140.

24 *The Times*, 25 September 1925.

25 'Hari Singh of Kashmir', *The Argus*, Melbourne, 17 January 1925.

26 C. E. Bechhofer Roberts, *The Mr. A Case*, London, Jarrolds, [1950].

27 'Mr. "A's" Name Revealed', *The Cairns Post*, Cairns, 5 December 1924, https://trove.nla.gov.au/newspaper/article/40496770 [accessed 14 October 2019].

28 Peter Gladwin, 'Sir Hari Singh (Mr. A)', *The Daily Telegraph*, Sydney, 1 November 1947, https://trove.nla.gov.au/newspaper/article/248176133 [accessed 14 October 2019].

29 *The New York Times*, 21 June 1946.

30 'Hari Singh of Kashmir', *The Argus*, Melbourne, 17 January 1925.

31 Gopalkrishna Gandhi, 'New J&K Governor Must Observe Vajpayee's Doctrine of Kashmiriyat', *Hindustan Times*, 23 August 2018, www.hindustantimes.com/columns/new-j-k-governor-must-observe-vajpayee-s-doctrine-of-kashmiriyat/story-W4sQMZxZ8OSrt3clcvV0YK.html [accessed 25 August 2018].

32 Singh, *Autobiography*. Singh states on p. vii that his *Autobiography* 'was originally published in two separate volumes' of twelve chapters each: *Heir Apparent, An Autobiography*, Delhi, Oxford University Press, 1982, and *Sadar-I-Riyasat, An Autobiography*, Volume II (1953–67), Delhi, Oxford University Press, 1985.

33 *Ibid.*, p. 7.

34 'Excerpts from the speech of Dr. Karan Singh', in Harbans Singh, *Maharaja Hari Singh*, p. (e).

35 Singh, *Autobiography*, pp. 30, 31, 40, 77.

36 *Ibid.*, p. 93.

37 *Ibid.*, pp. 93, 121.

38 *Ibid.*, pp. 39, 216.

39 *Ibid.*, p. 230.

40 [Pandit Ramchandra Kak], *Jammu and Kashmir State in 1946–47: Dilemma of Accession – The Missing Link in the Story*, [self published?], [1956?], p. 14. Rakesh Ankit, *The Kashmir Conflict: From Empire to the Cold War, 1945–66*, Abingdon, Routledge, 2016, p. 38, footnote 8, states he accessed Kak's report in 'Richard Powell Papers, MSS Eur D 862, IOR [India Office Records]'. On 13 June 2017, I accessed Kak's report at www.vigilonline.com. On 26 October 2019, this site was no longer available.

41 *The Times*, 2 June 1933.

42 *Ibid.*, 6 July 1946.

43 Mahajan, *Looking Back*, pp. 127, 172.

44 *Ibid.*, pp. 173, 174.

45 Tathagata Roy, *Syama Prasad Mookerjee*, Gurgaon, Penguin, 2018, p. 378.

46 Mahajan, *Looking Back*, p. 126.

47 *Ibid.*, pp. 126, 127.

48 Singh, *Autobiography*, pp. 38, 39, 40, 41.

49 James Manor, 'The Demise of the Princely Order: A Reassessment', in Jeffrey, *People, Princes*, pp. 320, 321.

50 'Field Marshall Viscount Wavell to Lord Pethick-Lawrence', 16 October 1945, in *The Transfer of Power*, Volume VI, p. 352.

51 Singh, *Autobiography*, pp. 38, 39.

52 *Report of the Indian States Committee* p. 6.

53 Ian Copland, *The Princes of India in the Endgame of Empire, 1917–1947*, Cambridge, Cambridge University Press, 1997, p. 84, footnote 37.

54 *Ibid.*, p. 78, footnote 15.

55 M. L. Kapur, 'From Maharaja Gulab Singh to Maharaja Hari Singh', in Kapur, Editor, *Maharaja Hari Singh*, p. 34.

56 W. Wedgwood Benn, 'The Indian Round Table Conference', *International Affairs*, Vol. 10, No. 2, March 1931, p. 148.

57 'Prefatory Note', *Administration Report of the Jammu and Kashmir State for the Second Half of S. 1998*, unnumbered page.

58 *Ibid.*, pp. 59–60.

59 *State versus Sheikh Abdullah, Kashmir on Trial*, Lahore, The Lion Press, 1947, p. 66.

60 Publicity Department, *A Handbook*, p. 61.

61 *Administration Report of the Jammu and Kashmir State for S. 2000*, pp. 2, 6. Saraf, *Kashmiris Fight*, Volume I, p. 581, states that, in World War II, J&K State provided '71,667 soldiers', with about 40,000 coming from 'Poonch district alone'.

62 Singh, *Autobiography*, p. 34.

63 Publicity Department, *A Handbook* p. 31.

64 As reported in 'Mr. "A's" Name Revealed', *The Cairns Post*, Cairns, 5 December 1924.

65 Larry Rue, 'Secret Empire Talks Begin in London Today', *Chicago Tribune*, 1 May 1944, http://archives.chicagotribune.com/1944/05/01/page/9/article/secret-empire-talks-begin-in-london-today [accessed 6 June 2017].

66 'Address of Welcome (22–7–1944) [by Maharaja Hari Singh]', in Gwasha Lal Kaul, *Kashmir Through the Ages (5000 B.C. to 1965 A.D.)*, Srinagar, Chronicle Publishing House, 1963, p. 273.

67 Publicity Department, *A Handbook*, p. 61.

68 'Field Marshall Viscount Wavell to Lord Pethick-Lawrence', 27 December 1945, in *The Transfer of Power*, Volume VI, p. 691.

69 *The Times*, 22 April 1946.

70 'Mr Turnbull to Sir C. Corfield', 29 April 1946, in *The Transfer of Power*, Volume VII, p. 378.

71 'H. H. of Kashmir's Draft re points from His Highness' talk with the Secretary of State', 22 April 1946, in *The Transfer of Power*, Volume VII, pp. 378–9.

72 Publicity Department, *A Handbook*, p. 64. The *Handbook*'s front cover has 'Printed at The Ranbir Government Press – 25-9-2003 – 500'. Translating what appears to be a Samvat date of 25 9 (Agrahayana) 2003, the *Handbook* possibly came out on 4 December 1946. See 'Hindu Calendar December 1946', Prokerala.com, www.prokerala.com/general/calendar/hinducalendar.php?year=1946&mon=december&sb=1 [accessed 19 November 2017].

73 *Ibid.*, p. 31.

74 *Ibid.*

75 Singh, *Autobiography*, p. 19.

76 *Ibid.*, p. 20; Wakhlu, *Hari Singh*, p. 153.

77 'Excerpts from the speech of Dr. Karan Singh', in Harbans Singh, *Maharaja Hari Singh*, p. (d).

78 Bhagwan Singh, *Political Conspiracies*, p. 8.

79 'Memorandum [from Maharaja Hari Singh], in Alam, *Jammu and Kashmir*, p. 309.

80 Singh, *Autobiography*, p. 20.

81 U. K. Zutshi, *Emergence of Political Awakening in Kashmir*, New Delhi, Manohar, 1986, pp. 100, 231.

82 Singh, *Autobiography*, p. 4.

83 Zutshi, *Emergence*, pp. 7–9.

84 'Memorandum [from Maharaja Hari Singh], in Alam, *Jammu and Kashmir*, p. 309.

85 *The Times*, 13 April 1944.

86 Singh, *Autobiography*, p. 8.

87 *Census of India, 1941*, Part I: Introduction, front page.

88 Singh, *Autobiography*, p. 10.

89 *Ibid.*, p. 10.

90 Mohammad Ishaq Khan, *History of Srinagar 1846-1947: A Study in Socio-cultural Change*, Srinagar, Aamir Publications, 1978, p. 176.

91 Singh, *Autobiography*, pp. 20–1.

92 *Administration Report of the Jammu and Kashmir State for the Second Half of S. 1998*, p. 70.

93 *Administration Report of the Jammu and Kashmir State for S. 2000*, pp. 10, 11, 12.

94 Prem Nath Bazaz, *The History of Struggle for Freedom in Kashmir*, New Delhi, Pamposh Publications, 1954, p. 216.

95 Saraf, *Kashmiris Fight*, Volume I, pp. 649–50.

96 Bazaz, *The History of Struggle*, p. 251.

97 Snedden, *The Untold Story*, p. 10.

98 *The Times of India*, 20 October 1947.
99 Rakesh Ankit, 'Forgotten Men of Kashmir', *Himal Southasian*, February 2010, http://old.himalmag.com/component/content/article/66-forgotten-men-of-kashmir.html [accessed 25 April 2019].
100 As quoted in Whitehead, *A Mission*, pp. 26–7, and p. 246, footnote 14.
101 Ankit, *The Kashmir Conflict*, p. 41.
102 Menon, *The Story*, p. 51.
103 *Ibid.*, p. 64.
104 *Ibid.*, p. 84.
105 *The Times*, 22 April 1946.
106 Ankit, *The Kashmir Conflict*, p. 17.
107 [Pandit Ramchandra Kak], *Dilemma of Accession*, p. 1.
108 Corfield, *The Princely India*, p. 171.
109 *Ibid.*
110 William A. Brown, *The Gilgit Rebellion 1947*, [no place of publication], Ibex, 1998, p. 124.
111 'To Rajendra Prasad', 7 September 1952, Jawaharlal Nehru, *Selected Works of Jawaharlal Nehru*, Volume 19, 1996, p. 334.
112 Prithvi Nath Kaula and Kanahaya Lal Dhar, *Kashmir Speaks*, Delhi, S. Chand & Co., 1950, p. 48.
113 Bazaz, *The History of Struggle*, pp. 243–4.
114 Singh, *Autobiography*, p. 31.
115 *The Times*, 27 April 1934.
116 [Resident in Kashmir], *Revised List*, p. 17.
117 *Administration Report of the Jammu and Kashmir State for the Second Half of S. 1998*, Appendix I, p. iv.
118 Bhattacharjea, *Abdullah*, p. 85.
119 Ankit, *The Kashmir Conflict*, p. 15.
120 'Field Marshall Viscount Wavell to Lord Pethick-Lawrence', 16 October 1945, in *The Transfer of Power*, Volume VI, p. 352.
121 Ankit, *The Kashmir Conflict*, p. 15.
122 *The New York Times*, 21 June 1946.
123 'Pandit Nehru to Rear-Admiral Viscount Mountbatten of Burma, … A Note on Kashmir', 17 June 1947, in *The Transfer of Power*, Volume XI, p. 446.
124 'To Lord Mountbatten', 31 December 1948, *Selected Works of Jawaharlal Nehru*, Volume 9, 1990, p. 227.
125 'Field Marshall Viscount Wavell to Lord Pethick-Lawrence', 27 December 1945, in *The Transfer of Power*, Volume VI, p. 691.
126 'Enclosure to No. 37 "C"', in *Transfer of Power*, Volume IX, pp. 71–2.
127 [Pandit Ramchandra Kak], *Dilemma of Accession*, pp. 2, 3.
128 *Ibid.*, p. 3.
129 Menon, *The Story*, p. 104.
130 Campbell-Johnson, *Mission*, pp. 120, 141–2.
131 Menon, *The Story*, p. 104.
132 Campbell-Johnson, *Mission*, p. 141.
133 Menon, *The Story*, p. 104.
134 *Ibid.*

135 Campbell-Johnson, *Mission*, p. 142.
136 'Minutes of the Meeting of the Viceroy with Members of the States negotiating Committee', 4 June 1947, in *The Transfer of Power*, Volume XI, p. 80.
137 Campbell-Johnson, *Mission*, p. 105.
138 *Ibid.*
139 Gokhale, *Indian States*, pp. 63–4.
140 *The Times of India*, 24 April 1947.
141 'The Maharaja of Kashmir to Rear-Admiral Viscount Mountbatten of Burma', 8 July 1947, in *The Transfer of Power*, Volume XII, p. 3.
142 *Ibid.*, p. 4.
143 [Pandit Ramchandra Kak], *Dilemma of Accession*, pp. 4–5.
144 *Ibid.*, pp. 5, 38, 39.
145 Menon, *The Story*, p. 377.
146 Lesley Brown, Editor, *The New Shorter Oxford English Dictionary*, Oxford, Oxford University Press, 1993, p. 1763.
147 Ishaq Khan, *Perspectives*, p. 63.
148 Publications Division, *Indian States Today*, pp. 17, 19.
149 'Pandit Jawaharlal Nehru's remarks in his presidential address at the Udaipur Session of the All-India States Peoples' Conference held in December, 1945', *State versus Sheikh Abdullah*, p. 222.
150 M. Ganju, *This is Kashmir (With Special Reference to U.N.O.)*, Delhi, S. Chand & Co., [1948], p. 15.
151 'Minutes of Viceroy's Sixth Miscellaneous Meeting', 22 April 1947, in *The Transfer of Power*, Volume X, p. 365.
152 Sheikh Mohammad Abdullah, *The Blazing Chinar: An Autobiography* [Translated from Urdu by Mohammad Amin], Srinagar, Gulshan Books, second edition, 2013, p. 162.
153 *The Times*, 10 October 1947.
154 Singh, *Autobiography*, pp. 41–2.
155 Zutshi, *Emergence*, p. 231.
156 Singh, *Autobiography*, p. 42.
157 [Pandit Ramchandra Kak], *Dilemma of Accession*, p. 10.
158 Singh, *Autobiography*, p. 48.
159 *The Civil & Military Gazette*, 7 August 1947.
160 Zutshi, *Emergence*, pp. 16, 231.
161 Singh, *Autobiography*, p. 44.
162 Walter R. Lawrence, *The Valley of Kashmir*, London, Oxford University Press, 1895, title page.
163 Lawrence, *The India We Served*, p. 192.
164 Lawrence, *The Valley*, p. 305.
165 *Census of India, 1941*, Part I: Essay, p. 12.
166 Shivnath Dogri, *Jammu Misecllany [sic]*, Kashmir Times Publications, [Jammu], 2005, http://shivnathdogri.com/images/aboutthebook/jammu%20in%20legends.pdf [accessed 9 November 2019], p. 9.
167 Singh, *Autobiography*, p. 41.
168 *Ibid.*, pp. 41–2.

169 Harbans Singh, *Maharaja Hari Singh*, p. 88. Harbans Singh provides no evidence to support his claim.

170 Stanley Wolpert, *Jinnah of Pakistan*, New York, Oxford University Press, 1984, p. 335.

171 'Mr Wakefield to Lieutenant-Colonel Webb', 2 December 1946, in *The Transfer of Power*, Volume IX, p. 238.

172 'Record of Interview between Rear-Admiral Viscount Mountbatten of Burma and Pandit Nehru', 24 June 1947, in *The Transfer of Power*, Volume XI, p. 592.

173 'Rear-Admiral Viscount Mountbatten of Burma to Mr Gandhi', 12 July 1947, in *The Transfer of Power*, Volume XII, p. 114.

174 Campbell-Johnson, *Mission*, p. 120.

175 'Viceroy's Personal Report No. 10', 27 June 1947, in *The Transfer of Power*, Volume XI, p. 688.

176 According to Ziegler, *Mountbatten*, p. 420, Mountbatten was, indeed, 'trying to ensure that the Maharaja of Kashmir acceded to Pakistan'.

177 'Memorandum [from Maharaja Hari Singh], in Alam, *Jammu and Kashmir*, pp. 312–13.

178 Alastair Lamb, *Kashmir, A Disputed Legacy, 1846–1990*, Karachi, Oxford University Press, second impression, 1994, p. 121.

179 'Memorandum [from Maharaja Hari Singh], in Alam, *Jammu and Kashmir*, p. 313.

180 'Chronology of Important Events 15 August to 30 September 1947', *Mohammad Ali Jinnah Papers*, Volume V, p. xxix.

181 'Memorandum [from Maharaja Hari Singh], in Alam, *Jammu and Kashmir*, p. 313.

182 Appendix XXI, 'Extracts from the Inaugural Address of Sheikh Mohammed Abdullah to the Jammu and Kashmir Constituent Assembly on 5 November 1951', in K. L. Bhatia, *Jammu and Kashmir: Article 370 of the Constitution of India*, New Delhi, Deep & Deep Publications, 1997, p. 127.

183 V. Shankar, *My Reminiscences of Sardar Patel*, Delhi, Macmillan, 1974, p. 115.

184 Campbell-Johnson, *Mission*, p. 177.

185 'Memorandum [from Maharaja Hari Singh], in Alam, *Jammu and Kashmir*, pp. 313–14.

186 *Ibid.*, pp. 312–13.

187 Menon, *The Story*, Dedication page.

188 Shankar, *My Reminiscences*, p. 115.

189 Madhok, *Kashmir: Centre of New Alignments*, p. 122.

190 Menon, *The Story*, p. 392.

191 'Memorandum [from Maharaja Hari Singh], in Alam, *Jammu and Kashmir*, p. 315.

192 Campbell-Johnson, *Mission*, p. 177.

193 'Memorandum [from Maharaja Hari Singh], in Alam, *Jammu and Kashmir*, p. 312.

194 Snedden, *Understanding Kashmir*, p. 131.

195 'Memorandum [from Maharaja Hari Singh], in Alam, *Jammu and Kashmir*, pp. 328–9.

196 *The Civil & Military Gazette*, 4 November 1948.

197 *The Times of India*, 3 August 1947.

198 *The Civil & Military Gazette*, 7 August 1947.

199 'Jawaharlal Nehru to Maharaja Hari Singh, 5 July 1952', in Alam, *Jammu and Kashmir*, p. 347.

200 Jawaharlal Nehru to Karan Singh, 5 September 1952, in Alam, *Jammu and Kashmir*, p. 54; 'To Rajendra Prasad', 7 September 1952, *Selected Works of Jawaharlal Nehru*, Volume 19, 1996, p. 334.

201 Singh, *Autobiography*, pp. 18–19.

202 *Ibid.*, p. 30.

203 'Field Marshall Viscount Wavell to Lord Pethick-Lawrence', 16 October 1945, in *The Transfer of Power*, Volume VI, p. 352.

204 'Jawaharlal Nehru's Note on his Visit to Kashmir', 12 August 1946, Sumit Sarkar, Editor, *Towards Freedom: Documents on the Movement for Independence in India 1946*, New Delhi, Oxford University Press, 2009, pp. 1046–7.

205 'Memorandum [from Maharaja Hari Singh], in Alam, *Jammu and Kashmir*, p. 318.

206 Christopher Snedden, 'Would a Plebiscite Have Resolved the Kashmir Dispute?', *South Asia: Journal of South Asian Studies*, Vol. 28, No. 1, April 2005, pp. 71–2.

207 Singh, *Autobiography*, pp. 310, 311.

208 'Memorandum [from Maharaja Hari Singh], in Alam, *Jammu and Kashmir*, p. 312.

209 Bhagwan Singh, *Political Conspiracies*, pp. 80–1.

210 *Ibid.*, pp. 50–1.

211 *Ibid.*

212 Ganju, *This is Kashmir*, p. ix.

213 Mahajan, *Looking Back*, p. 265.

214 *The Civil & Military Gazette*, 29 July 1947.

215 *Census of India, 1941*, Part I: Essay, p. 22.

216 *The Civil & Military Gazette*, 14 September 1947.

217 C. Sharma, 'The Accession of the J&K State and Maharaja Hari Singh', in Kapur, Editor, *Maharaja Hari Singh*, p. 136.

218 Shankar, *My Reminiscences*, p. 116.

219 'Mr. V. P. Menon to Mr C. P. Scott', 17 July 1947, in *The Transfer of Power*, Volume XII, pp. 212–13.

220 Menon, *The Story*, p. 89.

221 'Viceroy's Personal Report No. 17', 16 August 1947, in *The Transfer of Power*, Volume XII, pp. 757, 769.

222 *Ibid.*, p. 758.

223 *Census of India, 1941*, Volume VI, Punjab, Tables, Delhi, Khan Bahadur Sheikh Fazl-i-Ilahi, Superintendent of Census Operations, Punjab, 1941, pp. 53, 60–61. Non-Muslims in Pathankot Tehsil comprised 'Hindus (Scheduled castes other than Ad-Dharmis [Untouchables]; Other Hindus), Ad-Dharmis, Jains, Sikhs, Indian Christians, and Others'.

224 Ziegler, *Mountbatten*, p. 420.

225 Victoria Schofield, *Wavell: Soldier & Statesman*, Barnsley, Pen & Sword Military, 2010, pp. 346 and 465–6, footnote 67.

226 Lucy P. Chester, *Borders and Conflict in South Asia: The Radcliffe Boundary Commission and the Partition of Punjab*, Manchester, Manchester University Press, 2009, p. 109.

227 Mahajan, *Looking Back*, p. 142.

228 Lamb, *Kashmir*, p. 122.

229 Amanullah Khan, *Free Kashmir*, [No Publisher Details], 1970, p. 60.

230 Singh, *Autobiography*, p. 37.

231 *Ibid.*, p. 38; Kaul, *Kashmir Through the Ages*, p. 132.

232 Snedden, *Understanding Kashmir*, p. 152.

233 [Pandit Ramchandra Kak], *Dilemma of Accession*, p. 15.

234 *Ibid.*

235 *Ibid.*

236 *The Statesman*, 18 July 1947.

237 'Viceroy's Personal Report No. 15', 1 August 1947, in *The Transfer of Power*, Volume XII, p. 455.

238 Bawa Satinder Singh, 'Raja Gulab Singh's Role in the First Anglo-Sikh War', *Modern Asian Studies*, Vol. 5, No. 1, 1971, p. 36.

239 Prem Nath Bazaz, *Inside Kashmir*, Srinagar, The Kashmir Publishing Company, 1941, p. 399.

240 *State versus Sheikh Abdullah*, pp. 137, 138.

241 Mullik, *My Years*, p. 199.

242 *Census of India, 1941*, Part III: Village Tables, p. 2.

243 Singh, *Autobiography*, pp. 2, 5, 38, 43–4.

244 *A Brief Note on the Administration of the Jammu and Kashmir State for the Year 1934*, Srinagar, Pratap Press, 1935, p. 2.

245 P. N. Chopra, Chief Editor, *India's Struggle for Freedom: Role of Associated Movements*, Delhi, Agam Prakashan, 1985, p. 754.

246 *The Civil & Military Gazette*, 12 August 1947.

247 [Resident in Kashmir], *Revised List of Ruling Princes*, p. 10.

248 Bazaz, *Inside Kashmir*, p. 100.

249 Singh, *Autobiography*, p. 3.

250 'Memorandum [from Maharaja Hari Singh], in Alam, *Jammu and Kashmir*, p. 314.

251 Singh, *Autobiography*, p. 55.

252 [Pandit Ramchandra Kak], *Dilemma of Accession*, p. 15.

253 Lockwood, 'Sheikh Abdullah', p. 382.

254 [Pandit Ramchandra Kak], *Dilemma of Accession*, p. 15.

255 *State versus Sheikh Abdullah*, p. 194.

256 [Pandit Ramchandra Kak], *Dilemma of Accession*, p. 16.

257 *Ibid.*, p. 3.

258 *Ibid.*, pp. 4, 5.

259 *Dawn*, 4 August 1947.

260 'The Resident at Kashmir to Sir G. Abell', 13 August 1947, in *The Transfer of Power*, Volume XII, pp. 696–7.

261 [Pandit Ramchandra Kak], *Dilemma of Accession*, p. 6.

262 Abdullah, *Flames*, pp. 87, 91; Mahajan, *Looking Back*, p. 131.

263 'Enclosure to Appendix V. 26: Note by All-Jammu & Kashmir Muslim Conference, [25 August 1947]', *Mohammad Ali Jinnah Papers*, Volume V, p. 563; Madhok, *Kashmir: Centre of New Alignments*, p. 42. Madhok claims he 'discussed the question [of independence for J&K] at length with him [Kak]'.

264 Narayan Sitaram Phadke, *Birth-pangs of New Kashmir*, Bombay, Rind Kitabs, [1948], pp. 9–10.

265 Balraj Puri, 'Neglected Regional Aspirations in Jammu and Kashmir', *Economic & Political Weekly*, 5 January 2008, p. 13.

266 Balraj Puri, *Simmering Volcano: Study of Jammu's Relations with Kashmir*, New Delhi, Sterling Publishers, 1983, p. 11.

267 Bamzai, *History of Kashmir*, pp. 679, 691, 719.

268 Singh, *Autobiography*, p. 37.

269 *Dawn*, 22 June 1947.

270 Puri, 'Neglected Regional Aspirations', p. 14.

271 Bazaz, *The History of Struggle*, p. 322.

272 'Memorandum [from Maharaja Hari Singh], in Alam, *Jammu and Kashmir*, p. 310.

273 *Dawn*, 11 May 1947.

274 *Ibid.*, 22 May 1947.

275 Saraf, *Kashmiris Fight*, Volume I, p. 707.

276 *Dawn*, 22 June 1947.

277 *Ibid.*, 4 July 1947.

278 'Whither Kashmir?', *Dawn*, 29 July 1947.

279 *Dawn*, 30 July 1947.

280 *The Civil & Military Gazette*, 24 July 1947.

281 *Dawn*, 22 July 1947.

282 Snedden, *The Untold Story*, pp. 37–63.

283 'Whither Kashmir?', *Dawn*, 29 July 1947.

284 *The Civil & Military Gazette*, 3 July 1947.

285 Collins and Lapierre, *Freedom at Midnight*, p. 239. This book has two errors in relation to J&K, both on p. 171: Maharaja Hari Singh was not 'a Hindu of a high Brahman sub-caste': he was a Jamwal Rajput, which is a Kshatriya sub-caste; Jawaharlal Nehru was not born in J&K: he was born in Allahabad.

286 *The New York Times*, 4 August 1947. The same article noted that 'Apparently it does not seem remarkable here [in New Delhi] that Mr. Gandhi might exert his efforts to bring a predominantly Moslem state into Hindu affiliation while he himself – the greatest of present-day Hindus – is reported to have said the other day that he might become a citizen of Pakistan'.

287 Gokhale, *Indian States*, p. 25. The Preface (p. 2) and p. 93 state the book was published on '4th August 1947'.

288 *White Paper on Jammu & Kashmir*, [Delhi], Government of India, [1948], pp. 7, 11, 12.

289 'Document', in Kapur, Editor, *Maharaja Hari Singh*, p. 195.

290 Menon, *The Story*, pp. 376–7.

291 'Maharaja Hari Singh to Lord Mountbatten', 26 October 1947, in Alam, *Jammu and Kashmir*, p. 356, emphasis added.

292 'Note of a Discussion with Mr. Jinnah in the Presence of Lord Ismay at Government House, Lahore, on 1 November 1947', *Sardar Patel's Correspondence*, p. 77.

293 Whitehead, *A Mission*, p. 98 and p. 253, endnote 1.

294 [Pandit Ramchandra Kak], *Dilemma of Accession*, pp. 6–8.

295 Brahma Singh, *History of Jammu and Kashmir Rifles 1820–1956*, New Delhi, Lancer International, 1990, p. 169.

296 [Pandit Ramchandra Kak], *Dilemma of Accession*, p. 8.

297 Ankit, *The Kashmir Conflict*, provides a well-researched discussion that puts the Kashmir dispute into the international historical security scene.

298 Abdullah, *The Blazing Chinar*, p. 273.

299 *The Civil & Military Gazette*, 3 July 1947.

300 *Ibid.*, 2 July 1947.

301 *Ibid.*, 3 July 1947.

302 Stephens, *Horned Moon*, p. 107.

303 'Pandit Nehru to Rear-Admiral Viscount Mountbatten of Burma, … A Note on Kashmir', 17 June 1947, in *The Transfer of Power*, Volume XI, pp. 446–7.

304 *The Civil & Military Gazette*, 12 August 1947.

305 [Pandit Ramchandra Kak], *Dilemma of Accession*, p. 5.

306 Discussion with Mir Abdul Aziz, 24 March 1999, Rawalpindi.

307 'The Resident of Kashmir to Sir G. Abell', 13 August 1947, in *The Transfer of Power*, Volume XII, p. 696.

308 *Ibid.*

309 Lamb, *Kashmir*, p. 121.

310 [Pandit Ramchandra Kak], *Dilemma of Accession*, pp. 5, 19.

311 Singh, *Autobiography*, p. 55.

312 Muhammad Yusuf Saraf, *Kashmiris Fight – For Freedom*, Volume II (1947–78), Lahore, Ferozsons, 1979, p. 769.

313 Bazaz, *The History of Struggle*, p. 274.

314 *The Civil & Military Gazette*, 12 August 1947; *Dawn*, 13 August 1947.

315 Singh, *Autobiography*, p. 12.

316 Saraf, *Kashmiris Fight*, Volume II, p. 769.

317 Mahajan, *Looking Back*, p. 1; Singh, *Autobiography*, p. 55.

318 'Copy of Note by R. C. Kak, Jammu and Kashmir State in 1946–47', p. 16, *Powell Collection, Papers and Correspondence*, dated 1947–60, of Richard Powell (1889–1961), Indian Police Force 1908–1947, Inspector-General of Police Jammu and Kashmir 1946–47, Indian Office Records, MSS EUR D862 [accessed at National Document Centre, Islamabad, December 2004].

319 *The Civil & Military Gazette*, 15 October 1947.

320 Saraf, *Kashmiris Fight*, Volume II, p. 755.

321 *The Civil & Military Gazette*, 12 August 1947.

322 Bazaz, *The History of Struggle*, p. 275.

323 Singh, *Autobiography*, p. 43.

324 [Pandit Ramchandra Kak], *Dilemma of Accession*, p. 6.

325 *The Civil & Military Gazette*, 12 August 1947.

326 *The Times of India*, 20 October 1947.

327 [Pandit Ramchandra Kak], *Dilemma of Accession*, pp. 6, 7.

328 *Times of India*, 20 October 1947.

329 *Ibid.*, p. 10.

330 *Census of India, 1941*, Part III: Village Tables, p. 181.

331 Singh, *History of Jammu and Kashmir Rifles*, p. 215.

332 *White Paper on Jammu & Kashmir*, pp. 6–12.

333 Prakash, *Fight for Kashmir*, pp. 27–8.

334 Saraf, *Kashmiris Fight*, Volume II, p. 771.

335 *The Civil & Military Gazette*, 17 September 1947.

336 *Ibid.*, 14 September 1947.

337 *Ibid.*, 3 July 1947.

338 *The Times*, 2 August 1947.

339 *The Civil & Military Gazette*, 20 September 1947.

340 'Chronology of Important Events 15 August to 30 September 1947', *Mohammad Ali Jinnah Papers*, Volume V, pp. xxxi, xxxii.

341 *The Times of India*, 7 September 1947.

342 Hajari, *Midnight's Furies*, p. 104.

343 Lawrence, *The India We Served*, p. 142.

344 'V. 23: Publicity Secretary, Muslim Conference, Kashmir, to Liaquat Ali Khan, 23 August 1947', *Mohammad Ali Jinnah Papers*, Volume V, p. 558. This was followed by a longer detailed report on 25 August 1947.

345 *The Civil & Military Gazette*, 3 October 1947.

346 *The Sunday Statesman*, 12 October 1947.

347 *Hindustan Times*, 14 October 1947.

348 *The Civil & Military Gazette*, 17 October 1947; *The Times of India*, 21 October 1947.

349 Singh, *Autobiography*, p. 81.

350 *Ibid.*, p. 41.

351 *Ibid.*, p. 42.

352 Menon, *The Story*, p. 113.

353 Calculated from figures for 'Marwar' (i.e., Jodhpur), M. W. M. Yeatts, *Census of India, 1941*, 'Volume I, India, Part I, Tables', Delhi, Manager of Publications, 1943, pp. 134–5.

354 Korbel, *Danger*, p. 59.

355 *The Times*, 8 August 1947.

356 Sharma, 'The Accession of the J&K State', in Kapur, Editor, *Maharaja Hari Singh*, p. 136.

357 Shashi Tharoor, *Why I Am a Hindu*, New Delhi, Aleph, 2018, p. 146.

358 Sharma, 'The Accession of the J&K State', in Kapur, Editor, *Maharaja Hari Singh*, pp. 135–6.

359 Letter from Vallabhbhai Patel to Maharaja Hari Singh, 2 October 1947, *Sardar Patel's Correspondence*, p. 42.

360 Gandhi, *Patel: A Life*, p. 445.

361 Singh, *Autobiography*, p. 38.

362 Jawaharlal Nehru, *Selected Works of Jawaharlal Nehru*, New Delhi, Orient Longman, First Series, Volume 15, 1982, p. 414.

363 Sharma, 'The Accession of the J&K State', in Kapur, Editor, *Maharaja Hari Singh*, p. 136.

364 Singh, *Autobiography*, p. 38.

365 Mahajan, *Looking Back*, p. 264.

366 Bhattacharjea, *Abdullah*, p. 105.

367 *Hindustan Times*, 14 October 1947.

368 Bhattacharjea, *Abdullah*, pp. 105, and 111, footnote 3.

369 Mahajan, *Looking Back*, pp. 273–4.

370 *Sardar Patel's Correspondence*, pp. 45–7.

371 Jawaharlal Nehru, *India's Foreign Policy, Selected Speeches, September 1946 – April 1961*, New Delhi, Publications Division, Ministry of Information and Broadcasting, Government of India, 1961, p. 443.

372 Letter from Vallabhbhai Patel to Maharaja Hari Singh, 2 October 1947, *Sardar Patel's Correspondence*, p. 42.

373 *Selected Works of Jawaharlal Nehru*, Volume 3, 1985, p. 265.

374 Enclosure, 'Nehru to Patel', 5 October 1947, *Sardar Patel's Correspondence*, p. 54.

375 *The Times*, 21 June 1946.

376 Sardar Patel to Sardar Baldev Singh, 7 October 1947, *Sardar Patel's Correspondence*, p. 59.

377 'Copy of a Telegram, Dated 6th October 1947, from Foreign, Karachi, to Prime Minister, Srinagar', *White Paper on Jammu & Kashmir*, p. 8.

378 Whitehead, *A Mission*, pp. 102–3. Whitehead has a photo of this letter opposite p. 147. On p. 254, footnote 13, he states that 'historians who have researched in the maharaja's [sic] archives' and he consider that the letter 'is likely to be genuine'.

379 Mahajan, *Looking Back*, p. 142.

380 Whitehead, *A Mission*, p. 61.

381 Ganju, *This is Kashmir*, p. 21.

382 *The Times*, 25 October 1947.

383 *Ibid.*, 7 November 1947.

384 *Ibid.*, 10 November 1947.

385 Whitehead, *A Mission*, pp. 40–1.

386 *The Times*, 28 October 1947.

387 Whitehead, *A Mission*, pp. 191–2.

388 *Ibid.*, p. 192.

389 *Ibid.*, p. 62.

390 *The Times*, 30 December 1947.

391 Whitehead, *A Mission*, p. 243.

392 Lord Birdwood, 'Kashmir', *International Affairs*, Vol. 28, No. 3, July 1952, pp. 302, 303.

393 Ziegler, *Mountbatten*, p. 445.

394 Hodson, *The Great Divide*, p. 454.

395 Hajari, *Midnight's Furies*, p. 201.

396 Sher-i-Kashmir Sheikh Mohd. Abdullah, *Speeches & Interviews*, Series 2, [Srinagar?], G. M. Shah, [1968], p. 35.

397 Prakash, *Fight for Kashmir*, Appendix IV, p. 178, states that Ayyangar was Chairman of the five-man Indian Delegation that attended the United Nations in 1948.

398 'Statement of the Representative of India, Mr. G. Ayyangar, in the Security Council, 15 January 1948', in Hasan and Hasan, *Documents*, 1966, p. 144.

399 B. D. Basu, 'Rise of the Christian Power in India', in Bakshi, *Kashmir Today*, p. 69.

400 *The Times*, 1 November 1947.

401 Balraj Krishna, *Sardar Vallabhbhai Patel: India's Iron Man*, New Delhi, Rupa, 2013, p. 362.

402 Hajari, *Midnight's Furies*, p. 233.

403 Puri, *Simmering Volcano*, p. 24.

404 *The Times*, 10 October 1947.

405 *The Economist*, 11 October 1947.

406 Singh, *Autobiography*, pp. 41–2.

407 Das Gupta, *Jammu and Kashmir*, p. 81.

408 Singh, *Autobiography*, p. 30.

409 Menon, *The Story*, p. 465.

410 Snedden, *Understanding Kashmir*, pp. 170–1, 299.

Chapter 3 The significance of Kashmir and Kashmiri identity in J&K

1 Graham Evans and Jeffrey Newnham, *Dictionary of International Relations*, London, Penguin, 1998, p. 343.

2 Brown, Editor, *The New Shorter Oxford*, p. 1887.
3 Sunil Khilnani, *Incarnations: A History of India in Fifty Lives*, New York, Farrar, Straus and Giroux, 2016, p. 304. While Khilnani was actually writing about Jinnah and Muslim identity in the Indian subcontinent, his statements can also be applied to Muslim Kashmiri nationalism.
4 Nicholas Abercrombie, Stephen Hill and Bryan S. Turner, *Dictionary of Sociology*, London, Penguin, second edition, 1988, p. 162.
5 Ishaq Khan, *Perspectives*, p. 160, footnote 93.
6 Abdullah, *The Blazing Chinar*, p. 21.
7 *Ibid.*, p. 299.
8 *The Times*, 25 September 1925.
9 *Ibid.,* 23 March 1937.
10 Snedden, *Understanding Kashmir*, pp. 170-1, 299.
11 Both treaties are contained in Justice Syed Manzoor Hussain Gilani, *The Constitution of Azad Jammu & Kashmir*, Islamabad, National Book Foundation, 2008, pp. 583-8. Despite its title, this book includes seventy documents in appendices of relevance re J&K.
12 David Stacton, *A Ride on a Tiger: The Curious Travels of Victor Jacquemont*, London, Museum Press, 1954, p. 149.
13 Snedden, *Understanding Kashmir*, p. 63.
14 W. L. McGregor, *The History of the Sikhs*, London, James Madden, 1846, p. 29.
15 Snedden, *Understanding Kashmir*, p. 313, footnote 1.
16 Letter from Herbert Edwardes to Sir Henry Lawrence, 12th October, 1846, in Herbert B. Edwardes and Herman Merivale, *Life of Sir Henry Lawrence*, London, Smith, Elder & Co., third edition, 1873, p. 398.
17 Not to be confused with Walter Lawrence, Settlement Commissioner in J&K from 1889–1895.
18 Undated [1846?] letter by Henry Lawrence, in Edwardes and Merivale, *Life of Sir Henry Lawrence*, pp. 387-9.
19 Snedden, *Understanding Kashmir*, pp. 74-5.
20 Hassnain, *British Policy*, p. 106.
21 'Amritsar Treaty, 1846', K. M. Panikkar, *The Founding of the Kashmir State: A Biography of Maharaja Gulab Singh, 1792-1858*, London, George Allen & Unwin, 1953, pp. 111-15.
22 Sastry, *Treaties*, p. 66.
23 Abdullah, *Flames*, p. 78.
24 Bhagwan Singh, *Political Conspiracies*, p. 38.
25 Edwardes and Merivale, *Life of Sir Henry Lawrence*, p. 387.
26 David Gilmour, *The Ruling Caste*, New York, Farrar, Straus and Giroux, 2005, pp. 223-6.
27 Frederic Drew, *The Jummoo and Kashmir Territories: A Geographical Account*, London, Edward Stanford, 1875, p. 24. Drew refers to Jammu as 'Jummoo' and to Srinagar as 'Sirinagar'.
28 Explanations for 'charas' and 'namadas' from *Census of India, 1941*, Part I: Essay, p. 29.
29 Inter-provincial trade from Sooden, *Jammu*, p. 274.
30 *Administration Report ... for the Second Half of S. 1998 and for S. 1999*, pp. 18-19.

Notes

31 Publicity Department, *A Handbook*, pp. 19, 21.

32 Mridu Rai, *Hindu Rulers, Muslim Subjects: Islam, Rights and the History of Kashmir*, London, Hurst & Company, 2004, pp. 7, 80.

33 Abdullah, *Flames*, p. 91.

34 *Administration Report ... for S. 2000*, Appendix I, 'List of Chief Officers at the end of S. 2000', pp. iii–viii.

35 The rest of this paragraph is based on Publicity Department, *A Handbook*, p. 33.

36 *A Brief Note on the Administration of the Jammu and Kashmir State for the Year 1936*, Srinagar, Pratap Press, 1937, p. 5. When he commenced, Scott was a brigadier.

37 Based on figures in *A Brief Note on the Administration of the Jammu and Kashmir State for the Year 1935*, Srinagar, Pratap Press, 1936, p. 4.

38 MacMunn, *The Indian States*, p. 130.

39 Bazaz, *Inside Kashmir*, p. 200.

40 Brahma Singh, *History*, pp. 145, 169.

41 *The Times*, 20 November 1947.

42 Bazaz, *The History of Struggle*, pp. 127, 140.

43 Henny Sender, *The Kashmiri Pandits: A Study of Cultural Choice in North India*, Delhi, Oxford University Press, 1988, pp. 22, 28.

44 Zutshi, *Emergence*, p. 108.

45 Sender, *The Kashmiri Pandits*, p. 20.

46 Tikoo, *Story of Kashmir*, p. 107.

47 *Ibid.*, p. 223.

48 Bazaz, *The History of Struggle*, p. 145.

49 Prem Nath Bazaz, *Kashmir in Crucible*, New Delhi, Pamposh Publications, 1967, p. 29.

50 *Kashmir*, General Secretary, All India States' People's Conference, Bombay, 1939, p. 6.

51 *Census of India*, 1941, Part I: Essay, Part II: Tables, and Part III: Village Tables, various pages.

52 *Ibid.*, Part II: Tables, pp. 341–3.

53 *Census of India*, 1931, Part I – Report, pp. 10, 291.

54 Abdullah, *Flames*, p. 68.

55 Saraf, *Kashmiris Fight*, Volume I, p. 655.

56 Lawrence, *The India We Served*, pp. 180–1.

57 Balraj Puri, 'Kashmiriyat: The Vitality of Kashmiri Identity', *Contemporary South Asia*, March 1995, Vol. 4, No. 1, p. 57.

58 Abdullah, *The Blazing Chinar*, p. 250.

59 Qasim, *My Life*, pp. vi, 31.

60 *Census of India*, 1941, Part II: Tables, p. 73.

61 *Ibid.*, Part I: Essay, p. 14.

62 *Ibid.*, Part I: Essay, pp. 3, 7.

63 *Ibid.*, Part I: Essay, p. 7.

64 *Census of India*, 1931, Part I – Report, p. 58.

65 Hugh Whistler, 'Some Aspects of Bird Life in Kashmir', *The Himalayan Journal*, Vol. 1, No. 1, April 1929, p. 32.

66 *Census of India*, 1941, Part I: Essay, p. 1.

67 R. E. De Bourbel, *Routes in Jammu and Kashmir*, Calcutta, Thacker, Spink and Co, 1897, p. 6.

68 *Census of India*, 1941, Part I: Essay, p. 2.

69 *Papers on Indian States Development*, London, East and West, 1931, p. 47.

70 Dhar, *Kashmir*, p. 19.

71 *Census of India, 1941*, Part I: Essay, p. 24.

72 *Ibid.*, p. 7.

73 *Census of India, 1931*, Part I – Report, p. 59.

74 *Census of India, 1941*, Part I: Essay, p. 61.

75 *Ibid*: Essay, pp. 8, 23.

76 *Ibid.*, Part I: Essay, p. 7.

77 *Ibid.*, Part II: Tables, p. 74.

78 *Ibid.*, Part I: Essay, p. 40.

79 *Ibid.*, pp. 7–8.

80 *Ibid.*, p. 24.

81 'Karan Singh on Accession of Kashmir to India', *Outlook*, 19 September 2011, www.outlookindia.com/newswire/story/karan-singh-on-accession-of-kashmir-to-india/735445 [accessed 28 September 2018].

82 *Census of India, 1931*, Part I – Report, p. 5.

83 Officers in the Council of Ministers, as at 1 January 1945, *Administration Report ... for S. 2000*, p. [iii].

84 *Census of India, 1941*, Part I: Essay, p. 14.

85 *Ibid.*, Part III: Village Tables, p. 481.

86 *Census of India, 1931*, Part I – Report, p. 5.

87 *Ibid.*, p. 10.

88 *Census of India, 1941*, Part I: Essay, p. 4.

89 *Ibid.*, Part II: Tables, p. 304.

90 Snedden, *The Untold Story*, pp. 29–30, 234–8.

91 *Census of India, 1941*, Part III: Village Tables, p. 229.

92 *Ibid.*, Part II: Tables, p. 304.

93 *Census of India, 1931*, Part I – Report, p. 6, notes that J&K had another four jagirs until 1925, when Maharaja Hari Singh amalgamated his two personal jagirs of Bhadarwah and Langet, and his late uncle's personal jagirs of Natipura and Khousa, with state territories.

94 Brown, *The Gilgit Rebellion*, p. 5.

95 Snedden, *The Untold Story*, p. 243.

96 *The Times*, 1 August 1935.

97 *A Brief Note ... 1935*, p. 1.

98 Publicity Department, *A Handbook*, p. 16, italics as per the original.

99 Bazaz, *Inside Kashmir*, p. 396.

100 *The Civil & Military Gazette*, 29 July 1947, announced the 'Retrocession of Gilgit to Kashmir'; *The Civil & Military Gazette*, 2 August 1947, confirmed this action: 'Gilgit Retroceded to Kashmir'.

101 Publicity Department, *A Handbook*, p. 11.

102 Brown, *The Gilgit Rebellion*, pp. 52–3.

103 *The Civil & Military Gazette*, 25 October 1947.

104 The High Court of Judicature, Azad Jammu and Kashmir, *Verdict on Gilgit and Baltistan (Northern Area)*, Mirpur, Kashmir Human Rights Forum, [1993?], pp. 134–9.

105 'Resolution Adopted by the UNCIP [United Nations Commission for India and Pakistan], 13 August 1948 (S/1100, Para 75)', Hasan and Hasan, *Documents*, p. 182.

106 Brown, *The Gilgit Rebellion*. Brown details his role in this anti-Maharaja, pro-Pakistan uprising.
107 *Census of India, 1941*, Part II: Tables, p. 73.
108 *Ibid.,* Part 1: Essay, p. 9.
109 See Appendix II: Kashmir Valley Muslims in J&K and their numerical dominance.
110 Abdullah, *The Blazing Chinar*, p. 191.
111 *Census of India, 1941*, Part 1: Essay, p. 9.
112 Puri, 'Kashmiriyat', p. 62.
113 Calculated from figures at *Census of India, 1941*, Part I: Essay, p. 12.
114 *Census of India, 1931*, Part I – Report, p. 298.
115 I. S. Jehu, Editor, *The India and Pakistan Year Book 1948*, Bombay, Bennett, Coleman & Co., 1948, p. 25.
116 Ganju, *This is Kashmir*, p. ix.
117 Jehu, *The India and Pakistan Year Book 1948*, p. 25.
118 *Census of India, 1941*, Part III: Village Tables, p. 2.
119 *Census of India, 1931*, Part I – Report, pp. 13, 92.
120 Ishaq Khan, *History of Srinagar*, p. 42.
121 Rekha Chowdhary, *Jammu and Kashmir: Politics of Identity and Separatism*, New Delhi, Routledge, 2016, p. 178.
122 Puri, 'Kashmiriyat', p. 56.
123 *Ibid.,* p. 57.
124 *Administration Report … for S. 2000*, p. 12.
125 Snedden, *The Untold Story*, p. 10.
126 Rekha Chowdhary, 'Kashmir in the Indian Project of Nationalism', in Nyla Ali Khan, Editor, *The Parchment of Kashmir: History, Society, and Polity*, Houndmills, Palgrave Macmillan, 2012, p. 155.
127 Martijn Van Beek, 'True Patriots: Justifying Autonomy for Ladakh', *Himalaya*, Vol. 18, No. 1, Article 9, 1998, p. 38.
128 'Excerpts from the Memorandum Submitted by Shri Chhewang Rigzin; President Buddhist Association Ladakh to the Prime Minister of India on behalf of the People of Ladakh in 1949', in Bal Raj Madhok, *Jammu Kashmir and Ladakh: Problem & Solution*, New Delhi, Reliance Publishing, 1987, Appendix V, pp. 68–71.
129 Balraj Puri, 'Unfolding History', *India International Centre Quarterly*, Vol. 37, No. 3/4, Winter 2010–Spring 2011, pp. 147, 148.
130 Singh, *Autobiography*, p. 139.
131 'Excerpts from the speech of Dr. Karan Singh', in Harbans Singh, *Maharaja Hari Singh*, p. (c).
132 Singh, *Autobiography*, Appendix I, p. 329.
133 *Census of India, 1941*, Part I: Essay, p. 33.
134 Bazaz, *Inside Kashmir*, p. 255.
135 Copland, 'The Abdullah Factor: Kashmiri Muslims and the Crisis of 1947', in D. A. Low, Editor, *The Political Inheritance of Pakistan*, Basingstoke, Macmillan, 1991, p. 226.
136 *Kalhana's Rajatarangini: A Chronicle of the Kings of Kasmir* [sic] [Translated by M. A. Stein, Translator], Mirpur, Verinag Publishers, 1991 [First published by M/s A. Constable & Co., London, 1900], p. 6.
137 Bazaz, *Inside Kashmir*, p. 255.

138 Ishaq Khan, *Perspectives*, p. 38, states that the Sultanate was actually established in 1320 when the first Muslim, Rinchana, became ruler of Kashmir. However, Rinchana was a convert to Islam. The first 'true' Muslim was Shah Mir, who established his dynasty in 1339.

139 *Ibid.*, pp. 18, 43.

140 *Ibid.*, p. 43.

141 Saifuddin Soz, *Kashmir: Glimpses of History and the Story of Struggle*, New Delhi, Rupa, 2018, p. 136.

142 Ishaq Khan, *Perspectives*, p. 47.

143 E. F. Knight, *Where Three Empires Meet*, London, Longmans, second edition, 1893, p. 26.

144 Ishaq Khan, *Perspectives*, p. 2.

145 C. E. Tyndale Biscoe, *Kashmir in Sunlight & Shade*, London, Seeley Service, second edition, 1925, [First published 1921?], pp. 78–9.

146 'Report submitted by ... Sir Owen Dixon', in Hasan and Hasan, *Documents*, p. 273.

147 Bazaz, *The History of Struggle*, p. 124.

148 Ishaq Khan, *Perspectives*, p. 127.

149 Sufi, *Kashir* [sic]: *Being a History of Kashmir*, pp. 69, 132–3.

150 Abdullah, *The Blazing Chinar*, p. 110.

151 'Sheikh Mohammad Abdullah's View Explained: Second Plenary Session, J&K People's Convention, June 8–13, 1970', in Nyla Ali Khan, *Sheikh Mohammad Abdullah's Reflections on Kashmir*, Cham, Switzerland, Palgrave Macmillan, 2018, pp. 101, 103.

152 Gupta, *Kashmir*, p. 29.

153 Wajahat Habibullah, *My Kashmir: Conflict and the Prospects for Enduring Peace*, Washington D.C., United States Institute of Peace, 2008, p. 19.

154 [Resident in Kashmir], *Revised List of Ruling Princes*, p. 1.

155 Barbara D. Metcalf and Thomas R. Metcalf, *A Concise History of India*, Cambridge, Cambridge University Press, 2002, p. 17.

156 Ishaq Khan, *Perspectives*, p. 45.

157 Singh, *The Jammu Fox*, p. 120.

158 Patwant Singh and Jyoti M. Rai, *Empire of the Sikhs: The Life and Times of Maharaja Ranjit Singh*, London, Peter Owen Publishers, 2008, p. 134.

159 Publicity Department, *A Handbook*, p. 19.

160 *Census of India, 1901*, p. i. This Census mostly used the spelling 'Jammu', but occasionally called the region 'Jammoo'.

161 *Ibid.*, front cover.

162 Lawrence, *The India We Served*, pp. 126, 154.

163 Publicity Department, *A Handbook*, p. 23.

164 For example, Algernon Durand, *The Making of a Frontier*, London, Thomas Nelson & Sons, 1900.

165 Lawrence, *The Valley*, title page.

166 Lawrence, *The India We Served*, Introduction, footnote 11 and p. 123.

167 *The Civil & Military Gazette*, 7 August 1947.

168 *The Times*, 11 February 1936. This possibly was 'Sir B. Dalal', who according to *The Times*, 5 November 1931, was a 'Parsee Chief Justice of Kashmir'.

169 *Ibid.*, 5 April 1939.

170 Thornton, *A Gazetteer of the Territories*, Vol I, p. 272.

171 *Ibid.,* Vol II, pp. 256–7.

172 Drew, *The Jummoo and Kashmir Territories,* 1875, p. 2.

173 *Ibid.*

174 Frederic Drew, *The Northern Barrier of India: A Popular Account of the Jummoo and Kashmir Territories,* London, Edward Standford, 1877, p. 1.

175 Thornton, *A Gazetteer of the Territories,* Vol I, p. 276.

176 'A Voyage to Kachemire, the Paradise of Indostan', in Ros Ballaster, Editor, *Fables of the East: Selected Tales 1662–1785,* Oxford, Oxford University Press, 2005, p. 141.

177 Francois Bernier, *Travels in the Mogul Empire, AD 1656–1668,* Westminster, Archibald Constable and Company, 1891, pp. 400–1, italics as per the original.

178 Sir Francis Younghusband, *Kashmir,* London, Adam and Charles Black, 1911, pp. vii, 1.

179 *Census of India, 1901,* Part I. Report, p. 9.

180 Lawrence, 'The Valley of Kashmir', *Times of India,* 18 February 1930. For Lawrence, unlike the garden-building Mughals, 'the English, who have wisely left no tracks in Kashmir, have added something … the brown trout of England'.

181 J. Hutchison and J. Ph. Vogel, *History of the Panjab Hill States,* Lahore, Superintendent, Government Printing, 1933, Volume I pp. 46, 514. There is a Bahu Fort located in what now is known as Jammu City.

182 *Census of India, 1931,* Part I – Report, p. 138.

183 Publicity Department, *A Handbook,* p. 19.

184 Singh, *The Jammu Fox,* p. 120.

185 O. H. K. Spate, *India and Pakistan: A General and Regional Geography,* London, Methuen, 1954, pp. 18–19.

186 *Census of India, 1941,* Part II: Tables, p. 140.

187 *Ibid.,* Part I: Essay, p. 2.

188 *Census of India, 1931,* Part I – Report, p. 55.

189 *Ibid.,* Part I – Report, p. 282.

190 Bazaz, *Inside Kashmir,* p. 4.

191 Publicity Department, *A Handbook,* p. 2.

192 Lala Ganeshi Lal, *Siyahat-i-Kashmir (Kashmir Nama or Tarikh-i-Kashmir), being An Account of a Journey to Kashmir, March–June 1846* [Translated into English and Annotated by Vidya Sagar Suri, 1954, [Simla?], The Punjab Government, 1955, p. 32.

193 *Census of India, 1941,* Part 1: Essay, p. 21.

194 Zahid G. Muhammad, *Kashmir in War and Diplomacy,* Srinagar, Gulshan Books, 2007, p. 68.

195 *The Times,* 11 August 1928.

196 *Census of India, 1901,* Part I. Report, p. 10.

197 *Census of India, 1911,* Volume XX [Jammu and] Kashmir, Part I Report, Lucknow, Md. Matin-Uz-Zaman Khan, Superintendent of Census Operations, Jammu and Kashmir State, 1912, Part I Report, p. 55.

198 *Administration Report … for S. 2000,* p. 108.

199 All road distances in this paragraph are from Dhar, *Kashmir,* pp. 3–4, 120–5: Appendix C.

200 Abdullah, *The Blazing Chinar,* p. 235.

201 *A Brief Note … 1935,* pp. 1–2.

202 *Census of India, 1931*, Part I – Report, pp. 33–5.

203 *Selected Works of Jawaharlal Nehru*, Volume 24, 1999, p. 389, footnote 2, notes that, in 1956, India opened a tunnel '1.5 miles long tunnel and located at an altitude of 7,200 feet under the Bannihal [sic] pass' that was supposed to keep open the Jammu-Srinagar road 'throughout the year'.

204 *Census of India, 1941*, Part I: Essay, p. 21.

205 Publicity Department, *A Handbook*, p. 27.

206 *Papers Connected with the Re-organization of the Army in India, Supplementary to the Report of the Army Commission*, London, Her Majesty's Stationery Office, 1859, p. 6.

207 *Census of India, 1911*, Part I – Report, p. 55.

208 Robert C. Mayfield, 'A Geographic Study of the Kashmir Issue', *Geographical Review*, Vol. 45, No. 2, April 1955, p. 188.

209 *Administration Report ... for S. 2000*, p. 108.

210 F. S. Stanton, *Administration Report on the Railways in India for 1883–1884*, Simla, Government Central Branch Press, 1884, Part II, p. 133.

211 *Census of India, 1901*, Part I. Report, p. 5.

212 R. E. De Bourbel, *Jammu & Kashmir Railway: Proposed Western Routes Report*, Jammu, Ranbir Prakash Press, 1902, pp. 1–2.

213 [H. A. Rose], *Imperial Gazetteer of India, Provincial Series, North-West Frontier Province*, Calcutta, Superintendent of Government Printing, 1908, p. 106.

214 De Bourbel, *Jammu & Kashmir Railway*, pp. 9, 10.

215 *Census of India, 1911*, Part I Report, p. 55.

216 Ishaq Khan, *History of Srinagar*, p. 40.

217 Ishaq Khan, *Perspectives*, p. 20.

218 De Bourbel, *Routes in Jammu and Kashmir*, pp. 6–7.

219 Abdullah, *The Blazing Chinar*, p. 29.

220 *Ibid.*, p. 163.

221 *Census of India, 1931*, Part I – Report, pp. 107, 114. No figures were available in the 1941 Census.

222 *Ibid.*, p. 106.

223 *Ibid.*, p. 97.

224 *Census of India, 1921*, Volume XXII, [Jammu and] Kashmir, Part I, Lahore, Khan Bahadur Chaudhri Khushi Mohammed, Director of Census Operations, 1923, p. 26.

225 *Census of India, 1931*, Part I – Report, p. 114.

226 Jehu, *The India and Pakistan Year Book 1948*, p. 25.

227 *The Civil & Military Gazette*, 29 July 1947.

228 *Papers on Indian States Development*, p. 45.

229 Whitehead, *A Mission*, p. 29.

230 Sooden, *Jammu*, p. 268.

231 Sachchidananda Sinha, *Kashmir: 'The Playground of Asia'*, Allahabad, Ram Narain Lal, 1943, p. 115.

232 Tikoo, *Story of Kashmir*, p. 88.

233 *Census of India, 1941*, Part I: Essay, p. 33.

234 Tikoo, *Story of Kashmir*, p. 92.

235 Publicity Department, *A Handbook*, p. 34.

236 *Administration Report ... for S. 2000*, p. 5.

237 Mridu Rai, 'To "Tear the Mask off the Face of the Past"', in Zutshi, *Kashmir*, p. 35.
238 Bhattacharjea, *Abdullah*, p. 47.
239 *Administration Report ... for S. 2000*, pp. 4–6.
240 Publicity Department, *A Handbook*, p. 12.
241 *Administration Report ... for the Second Half of S. 1998*, pp. 12–13.
242 *Report of the Educational Reorganisation Committee*, His Highness' Government of Jammu & Kashmir, Srinagar, 1939, p. 1.
243 *Census of India*, 1931, Part I – Report, p. 254.
244 *Ibid.*, p. 256.
245 *Report of the Educational Reorganisation Committee*, pp. 65–7.
246 Saraf, *Kashmiris Fight*, Volume I, p. 360.
247 Sir Walter R. Lawrence, 'The Valley of Kashmir', *Times of India*, 18 February 1930.
248 *Census of India*, 1931, Part I – Report, p. 54.
249 *Ibid.*, pp. 54–5.
250 Surgeon H. W. Bellew, 'Cashmir' [sic]. *The Indian Medical Gazette*, 1 January 1870, p. 6, available at www.ncbi.nlm.nih.gov/pmc/articles/PMC5165417/?page=1 [accessed 3 February 2019].
251 *Administration Report ... for S. 2000*, p. 5.
252 *Census of India, 1941*, Part I: Essay, p. 27.
253 Tavleen Singh, *Kashmir: A Tragedy of Errors*, New Delhi, Viking, 1995, pp. 42–3.
254 *Census of India, 1941*, Part I: Essay, p. 27.
255 *Ibid.*, p. 33.
256 *Census of India, 1931*, Part I – Report. p. 54.
257 Vijay K. Sazawal, 'A Kashmiri Perspective II', *Asian Affairs*, Vol. 22, No. 1 (Spring, 1995), p. 31.
258 Abdullah, *Flames*, p. 171.
259 Martin Sökefeld, 'Jang Āzādi: Perspectives on a Major Theme in Northern Areas' History', in Irmtraud Stellrecht, Editor, *The Past in the Present: Horizons of Remembering in the Pakistan Himalayas*, Cologne, Köppe, 1997, p. 76, footnote 27.
260 Sökefeld, '"Not Part of Kashmir, but of the Kashmir Dispute": The Political Predicaments of Gilgit-Baltistan', in Zutshi, *Kashmir*, p. 133.
261 Bazaz, *The History of Struggle*, p. 182.
262 Snedden, *The Untold Story*, pp. 128–33.
263 *Census of India, 1931*, Part I – Report, p. 315.
264 W. Wakefield, *The Happy Valley: Sketches of Kashmir & the Kashmiris*, London, Sampson et al., 1879, p. 88.
265 Arthur Neve, *Thirty Years in Kashmir*, London, Edward Arnold, 1913, p. 44.
266 Tharoor, *Inglorious Empire*, p. 114.
267 *Census of India, 1941*, Part II: Tables, p. 337.
268 *Ibid.*, Part I: Essay, p. 14.
269 *Ibid.*, Part II: Tables, p. 338.
270 Singh, *Autobiography*, p. 121.
271 Sökefeld, 'The Political Predicaments of Gilgit-Baltistan', in Zutshi, *Kashmir*, p. 140.
272 *Ibid.*, pp. 141–2.
273 'Official Spokesperson's response to a query whether India has taken up the use of the term "Indian-administered Jammu and Kashmir"', *Ministry of External Affairs*,

29 June 2017, www.mea.gov.in/media-briefings.htm?dtl/28571/official+spokespersons+response+to+a+query+whether+india+has+taken+up+the+use+of+the+term+indianadministered+jammu+and+kashmir [accessed 21 March 2018].

274 One possible exception is Skardu, southeastern Gilgit-Baltistan, where non-Muslims in the J&K State Forces, who nominally became Indians after Maharaja Hari Singh acceded to India, endured a siege thereafter until they surrendered to, and then seemingly were killed by, pro-Pakistan forces on 14 August 1948. However, the presence of these 'Indians' in Skardu was by circumstance, not by design. See Harbans Singh, *Maharaja Hari Singh*, p. 212.

275 'Appendix 1: "Id SPEECH"', Mridula Sarabhai, *Sheikh-Sadiq Correspondence (August to October 1956)* [New Delhi], [Mridula Sarabhai], [1958], p. 46.

276 Chowdhary, 'Kashmir in the Indian Project of Nationalism', in Khan, *The Parchment*, p. 154.

277 Abdullah, *The Blazing Chinar*, p. 268.

278 Nyla Ali Khan, 'Introduction', in Khan, *The Parchment*, p. 7.

279 Alexander Evans, 'Kashmiri Exceptionalism', in Aparna Rao, Editor, *The Valley of Kashmir: The Making and Unmaking of a Composite Culture?*, New Delhi, Manohar, 2008, p. 716, italics as per the original.

280 *Ibid.*, p. 739.

281 Navnita Chadha Behera, 'Re-framing the Conflict', *India International Centre Quarterly*, Vol. 37, No. 3/4, Winter 2010–Spring 2011, p. 81.

282 Abdullah, *The Blazing Chinar*, p. 73.

283 Nandita Haksar, *The Many Faces of Kashmiri Nationalism: From the Cold War to the Present Day*, New Delhi, Speaking Tiger Books, 2015, p. 224.

284 Evans, 'Kashmiri Exceptionalism', in Rao, Editor, *The Valley of Kashmir*, 2008, p. 721.

285 *Census of India, 1931*, Part I – Report, p. 280.

286 Sir George Abraham Grierson, *The Languages of India: Being a Reprint of the Chapter on Languages*, Office of the Superintendent of Government Printing, Calcutta, 1903, p. 64.

287 *Census of India, 1931*, Part I – Report, p. 280.

288 Publicity Department, *A Handbook*, p. 13.

289 *Census of India, 1941*, Part III: Village Tables, p. 345.

290 Yoginder Sikand, 'Jihad, Islam and Kashmir: Syed Ali Shah Gilani's Political Project', *Economic & Political Weekly*, 2 October 2010, Vol. 45, No. 40, p. 126.

291 Bazaz, *The History of Struggle*, p. 81.

292 Evans, 'Kashmiri Exceptionalism', in Rao, Editor, *The Valley of Kashmir*, p. 721.

293 Mohammad Ishaq Khan, *Experiencing Islam*, New Delhi, Sterling Publishers, 1997, pp. 92–3.

294 Abdullah, *The Blazing Chinar*, p. 386.

295 Bazaz, *The History of Struggle*, p. 85.

296 Chitralekha Zutshi, *Languages of Belonging: Islam, Regional Identity, and the Making of Kashmir*, London, Hurst & Co., 2004, pp. 19, 21.

297 Bazaz, *The History of Struggle*, pp. 85–90.

298 Ishaq Khan, *Perspectives*, p. 129.

299 Abdullah, *The Blazing Chinar*, p. 73.

Notes

300 *A Brief Note on the Administration of the Jammu and Kashmir State for the Year 1933*, Srinagar, Pratap Press, 1934, p. 1.

301 *Census of India, 1931*, Part I – Report, pp 298, 308. Ahmadi/Ahmadiyya and Qadiani are now generally considered to be the same sect. However, *The Constitution of the Islamic Republic of Pakistan* (Islamabad, National Assembly of Pakistan, 2012, Chapter 5, Section 260, Sub-section 3b, pp. 155–6, http://na.gov.pk/uploads/documents/1333523681_951.pdf [accessed 2 March 2018]) considers Ahmadis to be non-Muslims. So do many Pakistanis. See Mohammed Hanif, 'Pakistan, Land of the Intolerant', *The New York Times*, 19 October 2017, www.nytimes.com/2017/10/19/opinion/pakistan-muslims-ahmadis.html [accessed 2 March 2018].

302 See Appendix II: Kashmir Valley Muslims in J&K and their numerical dominance.

303 Publicity Department, *A Handbook*, p. 26.

304 Abdul Jabbar Ganai, *Kashmir National Conference and Politics (1975–1980)*, Srinagar, Gulshan Publishers, 1984, p. 77.

305 Ishaq Khan, *Perspectives*, p. 18.

306 Puri, 'Kashmiriyat', p. 56.

307 Behera, *State, Identity and Violence*, p. 66, italics as per the original.

308 Abdullah, *The Blazing Chinar*, p. 533

309 Puri, 'Kashmiriyat', p. 62.

310 Abdullah, *The Blazing Chinar*, p. 215.

311 Mayfield, 'A Geographic Study of the Kashmir Issue', p. 195.

312 Lawrence, *The India We Served*, p. 161.

313 *Census of India, 1911*, Part I Report, p. 102.

314 Lawrence, *The Valley*, p. 285.

315 *Ibid.*, pp. 1, 2.

316 Lawrence, *The India We Served*, p. 157.

317 Bazaz, *The History of Struggle*, p. 91.

318 Habibullah, *My Kashmir*, pp. 24–5.

319 Haksar, *The Many Faces*, p. 200.

320 Zutshi, *Languages of Belonging*, pp. 55, 245.

321 Bazaz, *The History of Struggle*, p. 91.

322 Rattan Lal Hangroo, 'Kashmiriyat: The Voice of the Past Misconstrued', in Khan, *The Parchment*, pp. 37, 43.

323 Gull Mohammad Wani, 'Political Assertion of Kashmiri Identity', in Khan, *The Parchment*, p. 146.

324 Raju G. C. Thomas, 'Reflections on the Kashmir Problem', in Raju G. C. Thomas, Editor, *Perspectives on Kashmir: The Roots of Conflict in South Asia*, Boulder, Westview Press, 1992, p. 39.

325 Ishaq Khan, *Perspectives*, p. 22.

326 Haksar, *The Many Faces*, p. 275.

327 Ishaq Khan, *History of Srinagar*, pp. 119–20.

328 Bazaz, *Inside Kashmir*, p. 177.

329 Ishaq Khan, *Perspectives*, p. 6.

330 *Ibid.*, p. 25.

331 Haksar, *The Many Faces*, p. ix.

332 Lawrence, *The Valley*, p. 215.

333 Lawrence, *The India We Served*, pp. 133–4.
334 Abercrombie, Hill and Turner, *Dictionary of Sociology*, p. 162.
335 *Census of India, 1941*, Part I: Essay, p. 9.
336 Bazaz, *Inside Kashmir*, p. 263.
337 Bazaz, *The History of Struggle*, pp. 127, 140.
338 Wakefield, *The Happy Valley*, pp. 19, 120.
339 Bazaz, *Inside Kashmir*, p. 401.
340 *Ibid.*, p. 61.
341 Knight, *Where Three Empires Meet*, p. 62.
342 Bazaz, *Inside Kashmir*, pp. 195–7.
343 Rai, *Hindu Rulers*, pp. 154–6.
344 Bamzai, *History of Kashmir*, pp. 672, 708.
345 Bazaz, *Inside Kashmir*, p. 250.
346 *Ibid.*, p. 107.
347 Fazili, *Kashmir Government*, pp. 131–3.
348 Bhattacharjea, *Abdullah*, p. 49.
349 Bhagwan Singh, *Political Conspiracies*, p. 49.
350 Jagmohan [Malhotra], 'The Logic of History', *Business Standard*, 14 June 2013, www.business-standard.com/article/beyond-business/the-logic-of-history-106112301093_1.html [accessed 30 September 2018].
351 Abdullah, *Flames*, 1993, p. 92.
352 Ganai, *Kashmir National Conference*, pp. 39–40.
353 Gupta, *Kashmir*, p. 36.
354 Pandit Jawaharlal Nehru, 'Introduction Essay on Kashmir', in Dhar, *Kashmir*, p. xiii.
355 'Nehru to Mountbatten', 17 June 1947, in *The Transfer of Power*, Volume XI, pp. 442–8.

Chapter 4 The rise of Kashmiri aspirations, 1924–47

1 Puri, *Simmering Volcano*, pp. 134–5.
2 *The Times*, 27 May 1946.
3 'Ale Ahmad Suroor's "Foreword"', in Abdullah, *The Blazing Chinar*, p. 15.
4 Abdullah, *The Blazing Chinar*, p. 25.
5 *Ibid.*, p. 27.
6 *Ibid.*, p. 50.
7 *Census of India, 1931*, Part I – Report, p. 254.
8 Abdullah, *The Blazing Chinar*, p. 36.
9 *Ibid.*, p. 47.
10 *Ibid.*, pp. 45–6.
11 *Ibid.*, p. 48.
12 *Ibid.*, p. 50.
13 *Ibid.*, p. 51.
14 Saraf, *Kashmiris Fight*, Volume I, p. 359.
15 Discussion with Mir Abdul Aziz, Rawalpindi, 23 January 1998.
16 Abdullah, *The Blazing Chinar*, pp. 63, 70.
17 *Ibid.*, p. 70.

18 Saraf, *Kashmiris Fight*, Volume I, p. 367.
19 Chopra, Chief Editor, *India's Struggle*, p. 728.
20 Abdullah, *The Blazing Chinar*, p. 155.
21 *Ibid.*, p. 182.
22 Bakshi, *Kashmir Today*, p. 3.
23 Hassnain, *British Policy*, p. 44.
24 Bazaz, *The History of Struggle*, p. 124.
25 Robert A. Huttenback, *Kashmir and the British Raj, 1847–1947*, Karachi, Oxford University Press, 2004, p. 133.
26 Ishaq Khan, *Perspectives*, p. 134.
27 Ishaq Khan, *History of Srinagar*, p. 171, footnote 6.
28 Ian Copland, 'Islam and Political Mobilization in Kashmir, 1931–34', *Pacific Affairs*, Vol. 54, No. 2, 1981, p. 235.
29 Bhattacharjea, *Abdullah*, p. 27.
30 Puri, 'The Era of Sheikh Mohammed Abdullah', p. 188.
31 Bhattacharjea, *Abdullah*, p. 27.
32 Abdullah, *Flames*, p. 13.
33 *Census of India, 1931*, Part I – Report, p. 216.
34 Publicity Department, *A Handbook*, p. 23.
35 Hassnain, *British Policy*, pp. 44, 46.
36 *Ibid.*, pp. 44, 45.
37 *The Times*, 13 July 1865.
38 Ishaq Khan, *Perspectives*, pp. 134–5.
39 Publicity Department, *A Handbook*, p. 47.
40 Bazaz, *Inside Kashmir*, p. 234.
41 Ishaq Khan, *Perspectives*, p. 77.
42 Abdul Gani, *Labour-management Relations: A Study of Textile Industry in Jammu and Kashmir*, New Delhi, Deep & Deep Publications, 1995, p. 70.
43 Sufi, *Kashir* [sic]: *Being a History of Kashmir*, p. 809.
44 Saraf, *Kashmiris Fight*, Volume I, pp. 336–7.
45 Ishaq Khan, *Perspectives*, p. 137.
46 Huttenback, *Kashmir*, p. 136.
47 Saraf, *Kashmiris Fight*, Volume I, p. 336.
48 Abdullah, *Flames*, p. 14.
49 Abdullah, *The Blazing Chinar*, pp. 42–4.
50 Bamzai, *History of Kashmir*, p. 719.
51 Abdullah, *The Blazing Chinar*, p. 374.
52 Bhattacharjea, *Abdullah*, p. 28.
53 Parvez Dewan, *A History of Kashmir*, New Delhi, Manas, 2014, p. 137.
54 Ishaq Khan, *Perspectives*, p. 135.
55 Henny Sender, *The Kashmiri Pandits: A Study of Cultural Choice in North India*, Delhi, Oxford University Press, 1988, p. 31.
56 *Census of India, 1931*, Part I – Report, p. 45.
57 Interview with Dr Karan Singh, Raja Amar Singh's grandson, 1 March 2013, New Delhi.
58 Snedden, *The Untold Story*, pp. 229–38.
59 Publicity Department, *A Handbook*, pp. 31–2.
60 Sufi, *Kashir* [sic], Volume II, pp. 819, 821.

61 'The following report on Kashmir situation was cabled by Mr. Norman Cliff, Foreign Editor, "News Chronicle", on June 21, 1946, to "News Chronicle", London', in Bakshi, *Kashmir Today*, p. 44.
62 Bazaz, *Inside Kashmir*, pp. 224–5.
63 *Report on the Administration of the Jammu and Kashmir State for Samvat 1993–94*, Jammu, The Ranbir Government Press, 1938, pp. 93, 94.
64 *Census of India, 1941*, Part I: Essay, pp. 20, 32.
65 *The Times*, 10 October 1935.
66 Bechhofer Roberts, *The Mr. A Case*, pp. 9, 10, 35.
67 'Proclamation of Maharaja Hari Singh, July 9, 1931, in Wakhlu, *Hari Singh*, Appendix 2, p. 271.
68 Huttenback, *Kashmir*, p. 137.
69 A. N. Sudarisanam, Editor, *Indian States Register and Directory 1929*, Madras, Indian States Register & Directory Office, 1929, p. 367.
70 Bamzai, *History of Kashmir*, p. 701.
71 Fazili, *Kashmir Government*, p. 63.
72 *Census of India, 1931*, Part II, Imperial & State Tables, p. 333.
73 Saraf, *Kashmiris Fight*, Volume I, p. 328.
74 Figures and details for J&K Army and J&K Police from *A Brief Note ... 1934*, pp. 2–3.
75 MacMunn, *The Indian States*, p. 130.
76 Bazaz, *Inside Kashmir*, p. 200.
77 *A Brief Note ... 1936*, p. 1.
78 Bazaz, *The History of Struggle*, p. 145.
79 'Report of the Srinagar Riot Enquiry Committee (1931–1988)', in Mirza Shafique Hussain, Compiler, *History of Kashmir: A Study in Documents 1916–1939*, Islamabad, National Institute of Historical and Cultural Research, 1992, p. 90. Hussain provides the entire 'Report' on pp. 72–130.
80 The four classes of a 'Hereditary State Subject' were provided in Chapter 3.
81 Fazili, *Kashmir Government*, p. 132.
82 Quoted in *Kashmir*, Bombay, General Secretary, All India States' People's Conference, 1939, pp. 6–7.
83 Bhattacharjea, *Abdullah*, p. 24.
84 'Report of the Srinagar Riot Enquiry Committee', in Hussain, Compiler, *History of Kashmir*, p. 91.
85 William Moorcroft and George Trebeck, *Travels in the Himalayan Provinces of Hindustan and the Panjab; in Ladakh and Kashmir; in Peshawar, Kabul, Kunduz, and Bokhara*, Volume II, London, John Murray, 1841, p. 293.
86 *Census of India, 1941*, Part I: Essay, pp. 18, 19.
87 'Report of the Srinagar Riot Enquiry Committee', in Hussain, Compiler, *History of Kashmir*, p. 91.
88 Bazaz, *Inside Kashmir*, p. 101.
89 Saraf, *Kashmiris Fight*, Volume I, p. 354.
90 Bazaz, *Inside Kashmir*, p. 101.
91 Abdullah, *The Blazing Chinar*, p. 167.
92 'Report of the Srinagar Riot Enquiry Committee', in Hussain, Compiler, *History of Kashmir*, p. 90.

93 Chowdhary, 'Kashmir in the Indian Project of Nationalism', in Khan, *The Parchment*, p. 155.

94 Aparna Rao, 'A Tortuous Search for Justice: Notes on the Kashmir Conflict', *Himalaya*, Vol. 19, No. 1, 1999, p. 10.

95 Pir Gias-ud-Din, 'Main Trends of the History of [the] Kashmir National Movement', in *Studies of Kashmir Council of Research, Special Number: Struggle for Freedom in Jammu and Kashmir*, Srinagar, Kashmir Council of Research, Volume III, 1978, p. 32.

96 Rao, 'A Tortuous Search for Justice', p. 10, footnote 2.

97 Special Correspondent, *The Statesman*, 11 June 1946, in Bakshi, *Kashmir Today*, p. 9.

98 'Report of the Srinagar Riot Enquiry Committee', in Hussain, Compiler, *History of Kashmir*, p. 96.

99 *Census of India, 1931*, Part I – Report, p. 60. The uprising occurred before the 1931 Census report was actually published.

100 Puri, 'Kashmiriyat', p. 56.

101 Bazaz, *The History of Struggle*, p. 155.

102 'Report of the Srinagar Riot Enquiry Committee', in Hussain, Compiler, *History of Kashmir*, pp. 72–3.

103 *Ibid.*, pp. 97–9, 113.

104 *Ibid.*, p. 110.

105 *Ibid.*, p. 93.

106 Bazaz, *The History of Struggle*, pp. 152, 175.

107 Bolitho, *Jinnah*, p. 99.

108 Copland, 'Islam and Political Mobilization', p. 235.

109 Bazaz, *Inside Kashmir*, p. 119.

110 Saraf, *Kashmiris Fight*, Volume I, p. 359.

111 Bazaz, *Inside Kashmir*, p. 107.

112 Bazaz, *The History of Struggle*, pp. 147–9.

113 Saraf, *Kashmiris Fight*, Volume I, p. 354.

114 Bhatia, *Jammu and Kashmir: Article 370*, p. 13.

115 *Kashmir*, Bombay, General Secretary, p. 7.

116 Santosh Bakaya, 'Kashmiri's [sic] Struggle for Freedom Movement', in *Studies of Kashmir Council*, p. 110.

117 N. N. Raina, '"Hegemony of the Working People"', in *Studies of Kashmir Council*, p. 7.

118 Saraf, *Kashmiris Fight*, Volume I, pp 361–3.

119 *The Times*, 15 July 1931.

120 *The Statesman* [weekly edition], 16 July 1931.

121 'Report of the Srinagar Riot Enquiry Committee', in Hussain, Compiler, *History of Kashmir*, p. 94.

122 Abdullah, *The Blazing Chinar*, pp. 75–6.

123 Saraf, *Kashmiris Fight*, Volume I, p. 372.

124 *Ibid.*, p. 373.

125 Bazaz, *Inside Kashmir*, p. 125.

126 *Ibid.*, p. 126.

127 Saraf, *Kashmiris Fight*, Volume I, p. 372.

128 'Report of the Srinagar Riot Enquiry Committee', in Hussain, Compiler, *History of Kashmir*, p. 76.

129 *A Brief Note … 1933*, p. 1.

130 Saraf, *Kashmiris Fight*, Volume I, pp. 378–9, provides the names, ages and residential location of the twenty-two Kashmiri 'martyrs'.

131 'Report of the Srinagar Riot Enquiry Committee', in Hussain, Compiler, *History of Kashmir*, pp. 79, 82–3.

132 Copland, 'Islam and Political Mobilization', p. 233.

133 *The Times*, 15 July 1931.

134 *The Statesman* [weekly edition], 16 July 1931.

135 *Ibid.*, 23 July 1931.

136 Abdullah, *Flames*, pp. 24–5.

137 Copland, 'Islam and Political Mobilization', p. 239.

138 *The Statesman* [weekly edition], 1 October 1931.

139 'Presidential Address at the All-India States' Peoples' Conference, February, 1939, Ludhiana', in Jawaharlal Nehru, *The Unity of India: Collected Writings 1937–1940*, London, Lindsay Drummond, 1942, p. 37, footnote 1.

140 Copland, 'Islam and Political Mobilization', p. 239.

141 Abdullah, *Flames*, p. 51.

142 L. Middleton, 'Report on an Inquiry into Disturbances at Jammu and its Environments During the First Week of November 1931', in Hussain, Compiler, *History of Kashmir*, p. 131. Hussain provides the entire 'Report' on pp. 131–209.

143 *Ibid.*, p. 190.

144 Abdullah, *The Blazing Chinar*, pp. 96, 116.

145 *The Times*, 13 November 1931.

146 *The Statesman*, 18 February 1932.

147 *The Times*, 4 March 1932.

148 Bazaz, *The History of Struggle*, pp. 159–60.

149 Middleton, 'Report', in Hussain, Compiler, *History of Kashmir*, p. 131.

150 Harbans Singh, *Maharaja Hari Singh*, p. 20.

151 *A Brief Note … 1933*, p. 2.

152 Abdullah, *Flames*, p. 33.

153 *The Statesman* [weekly edition], 21 January 1932.

154 Barton, *The Princes of India*, p. 292.

155 *The Times*, 9 November 1931.

156 *Ibid.*, 13 November 1931.

157 *The Statesman* [weekly edition], 28 January 1932.

158 *Ibid.*, 11 February 1932.

159 *Ibid.*, 18 February 1932.

160 Special Correspondent, *The Statesman*, Gulam [sic] Mohd., *Kashmir Today*, p. 9.

161 *A Brief Note … 1933*, p. 3.

162 Middleton, 'Report', in Hussain, Compiler, *History of Kashmir*, pp. 190–1, 202.

163 *The Times of India*, 2 June 1933.

164 *Ibid.*, 1 June 1933.

165 *The Times of India*, 1 July 1933.

166 *The Testament of Sheikh Abdullah*, p, 33.

167 Copland, 'Islam and Political Mobilization', p. 248.

168 Bazaz, *Inside Kashmir*, p. 185.

169 *A Brief Note … 1934*, p. 1.

170 Bazaz, *Inside Kashmir*, p. 186.

171 Altaf Hussain Para, *The Making of Modern Kashmir: Sheikh Abdullah and the Politics of the State*, Abingdon, Routledge, 2019, pp. 50, 274.

172 Copland, 'Islam and Political Mobilization', pp. 248–50.

173 *Ibid.*, p. 253.

174 *A Brief Note ... 1935*, p. 1.

175 Copland, 'Islam and Political Mobilization', p. 257.

176 *A Brief Note ... 1936*, p. 2.

177 Bazaz, *The History of Struggle*, p. 154.

178 Copland, 'Islam and Political Mobilization', pp. 231, 233, 236.

179 *The Times*, 5 November 1931.

180 *India in 1932–33*, Delhi, Manager of Publications, 1934, p. 61.

181 Copland, 'Islam and Political Mobilization', p. 243.

182 *India in 1932–33*, Delhi, Manager of Publications, 1934, p. 61.

183 *The Times*, 5 November 1931.

184 *The Statesman* [weekly edition], 5 November 1931.

185 Marquess of Zetland, 'After the Indian Conference', *Foreign Affairs*, Vol. 10, No. 3, April 1932, p. 375.

186 *The Statesman* [weekly edition], 25 February 1932.

187 Tikoo, *Story of Kashmir*, p. 110.

188 Abdullah, *The Blazing Chinar*, p. 185

189 Sumit Hakhoo, 'Pandits Observe "Black Day" in Memory of 1931', *The Tribune*, 13 July 2016, www.tribuneindia.com/news/jammu-kashmir/community/pandits-observe-black-day-in-memory-of-1931/265554.html [accessed 4 June 2018].

190 'Memorandum [from Maharaja Hari Singh]', in Alam, *Jammu and Kashmir*, pp. 309, 311.

191 Singh, *Autobiography*, p. 4.

192 Tikoo, *Story of Kashmir*, p. 108.

193 Harbans Singh, *Maharaja Hari Singh*, pp. 18–20, italics as per the original.

194 *Ibid.*, pp. 11–12.

195 Gilmour, *The Ruling Caste*, pp. 194–5.

196 *A Brief Note ... 1933*, p. 1.

197 *The Times of India*, 1 June 1933.

198 *A Brief Note ... 1933*, pp. 1–2.

199 Abdullah, *Flames*, p. 32.

200 Saraf, *Kashmiris Fight*, Volume I, p. 488.

201 Copland, 'Islam and Political Mobilization', pp. 236, 237, 250.

202 Middleton, 'Report', Hussain, Compiler, *History of Kashmir*, pp. 139–40, 201.

203 Central Publication Branch, *India in 1931–32*, Calcutta, Government of India, 1933, p. 14.

204 *Ibid.*, pp. 30–1.

205 *Ibid.*, pp. 31–2.

206 *A Brief Note ... 1935*, p. 1. The report calls it 'Shahidgunj'.

207 *Report on the Administration of the Jammu and Kashmir State for Samvat 1993–94*, p. 17.

208 'Report of the Srinagar Riot Enquiry Committee', in Hussain, Compiler, *History of Kashmir*, p. 75.

209 *Ibid.*, pp. 72, 73, 75, 130.

210 *Ibid.*, p. 108.

211 R. C. Kak, 'The Trouble In Kashmir', *The Times*, 9 November 1931.

212 'Report of the Srinagar Riot Enquiry Committee', in Hussain, Compiler, *History of Kashmir*, p. 110.

213 *The Times*, 9 November 1931. The information about Glancy was from a note 'To the Editor of The Times' written by 'R. C. Kak, Political Secretary, Kashmir State', London.

214 Bazaz, *Inside Kashmir*, pp. 171–2.

215 *The Times*, 12 April 1932.

216 *The Statesman* [weekly edition], 20 October 1931.

217 B. J. Glancy, *Report of the Commission Appointed under the Order of His Highness, the Maharaja Bahadur dated 12th November, 1931 to Enquire into Grievances and Complaints*, Jammu, Ranbir Govt. Press, 1933.

218 Special Correspondent, *The Statesman*, in Bakshi, *Kashmir Today*, p. 9.

219 *The Times*, 18 November 1931.

220 *Ibid.*, 21 April 1932.

221 Van Beek, 'True Patriots', pp. 37–8.

222 Bazaz, *The History of Struggle*, p. 162.

223 Saraf, *Kashmiris Fight*, Volume I, pp. 324–5.

224 Copland, 'Islam and Political Mobilization', p. 245.

225 *A Brief Note ... 1933*, p. 2, italics as per the original.

226 Bazaz, *Inside Kashmir*, pp. 187, 213.

227 *Ibid.*, p. 229.

228 *The Times*, 24 January 1934.

229 *Ibid.*

230 *Ibid.*

231 *Ibid.*, 15 December 1936.

232 Maharaja Hari Singh, 'A Proclamation, 11th February 1939' [Jammu?], *The Jammu & Kashmir Government Gazette*, 1939, p. 71.

233 Saraf, *Kashmiris Fight*, Volume I, p. 481.

234 *A Brief Note ... 1934*, p. 1.

235 *A Brief Note ... 1933*, p. 2.

236 The rest of this paragraph is based on Sudarisanam, *Indian States Register*, p. 368.

237 Publicity Department, *A Handbook*, p. 35.

238 Maharaja Hari Singh, 'A Proclamation, 11th February 1939', p. 72.

239 *Ibid.*

240 *The Times*, 18 October 1934.

241 Maharaja Hari Singh, 'A Proclamation, 11th February 1939', p. 74.

242 *Ibid.*

243 Publicity Department, *A Handbook*, p. 35.

244 *A Brief Note ... 1934*, p. 1.

245 'Glancy Report of the Kashmir Constitutional Reform Conference 1932', in Harbans Singh, *Maharaja Hari Singh*, p. 276.

246 *A Brief Note ... 1934*, p. 1.

247 Special Correspondent, *The Statesman*, in Bakshi, *Kashmir Today*, p. 11.

248 Saraf, *Kashmiris Fight*, Volume I, p. 502.

249 *Ibid.*, pp. 504–5.

250 Korbel, *Danger*, p. 19.
251 Saraf, *Kashmiris Fight*, Volume I, p. 50₂.
252 Bazaz, *Inside Kashmir*, p. 345.
253 *Ibid.*, pp. 190–1.
254 *Ibid.*, p. 191.
255 Saraf, *Kashmiris Fight*, Volume I, p. 51₂.
256 Korbel, *Danger*, p. 19.
257 Saraf, *Kashmiris Fight*, Volume I, pp. 556–7.
258 *A Brief Note ... 1935*, pp. 1–2.
259 *Ibid.*, pp. 2–3.
260 Publicity Department, *A Handbook*, p 37.
261 *Census of India, 1941*, Part I: Essay, p. 6.
262 Publicity Department, *A Handbook*, p. 13.
263 *Ibid.*, p. 37.
264 Madhok, *Kashmir: Centre of New Alignments*, p. 30, translates the term 'sher' as 'tiger'.
265 Copland, 'Islam and Political Mobilization', p. 235.
266 *The Times*, 4 March 1932.
267 *Ibid.*, 23 March 1932.
268 *The Testament of Sheikh Abdullah*, p. 29, italics as per the original.
269 Bazaz, *Inside Kashmir*, p. 183.
270 Saraf, *Kashmiris Fight*, Volume I, p. 432.
271 Abdullah, *Flames*, p. 150.
272 Saraf, *Kashmiris Fight*, Volume I, p. 514.
273 Special Correspondent, *The Statesman*, in Bakshi, *Kashmir Today*, p. 10.
274 Saraf, *Kashmiris Fight*, Volume I, p. 504.
275 Bazaz, *Inside Kashmir*, p. 184.
276 Tikoo, *Story of Kashmir*, pp. 107, 223.
277 Abdullah, *The Blazing Chinar*, p. 169.
278 Gias-ud-Din, 'Main Trends of the History', in *Studies of Kashmir Council*, p. 38.
279 Chowdhary, 'Kashmir in the Indian Project of Nationalism', in Khan, *The Parchment*, p. 155.
280 *Kashmir*, Bombay, General Secretary, pp. 9–10.
281 Tikoo, *Story of Kashmir*, p. 125.
282 Ishaq Khan, *History of Srinagar*, p. 132.
283 Bhatia, *Jammu and Kashmir: Article 370*, p. 14.
284 Habibullah, *My Kashmir*, pp. 24–5.
285 Bazaz, *The History of Struggle*, p. 164.
286 Abdullah, *The Blazing Chinar*, p. 125.
287 Special Correspondent, *The Statesman*, in Bakshi, *Kashmir Today*, p. 11.
288 *Ibid.*
289 Abdullah, *Flames*, p. 51.
290 Abdullah, *The Blazing Chinar*, pp. 175, 178.
291 Bazaz, *The History of Struggle*, p. 150.
292 'Memorandum [from Maharaja Hari Singh]', in Alam, *Jammu and Kashmir*, p. 309.
293 Bazaz, *The History of Struggle*, p. 185.
294 *A Brief Note ... 1933*, p. 3.

295 *Laws of Jammu and Kashmir, Volume II: 1977–1989*, Jammu, The Ranbir Government Press, 1941, pp. 815–24.
296 *Ibid.*, pp. 830–47.
297 *Ibid.*, pp. 873–1016.
298 *Ibid.*, p. 816.
299 *Ibid.*, pp. 817.
300 *Ibid.*, pp. 817–20.
301 *Ibid.*, p. 821.
302 *Ibid.*, p. 821.
303 *Ibid.*, p. 823.
304 'The Press and Publications Act, 1989', *Laws of Jammu and Kashmir*, p. 833.
305 *Ibid.*, p. 837.
306 'The Ranbir Penal Code, 1989', *Laws of Jammu and Kashmir*, p. 906.
307 'Report of the Srinagar Riot Enquiry Committee', in Hussain, Compiler, *History of Kashmir*, pp. 75, 83, 107.
308 Bazaz, *Inside Kashmir*, p. 344.
309 *Ibid.*, p. 343.
310 Soz, *Kashmir*, p. 137.
311 Harbans Singh, *Maharaja Hari Singh*, p. 188.
312 Bazaz, *The History of Struggle*, pp. 243, 257.
313 Abdullah, *Flames*, p. 47.
314 *The Times*, 1 October 1937.
315 Abdullah, *The Blazing Chinar*, pp. 228, 244.
316 Abdullah, *Flames*, p. 47.
317 Abdullah, *The Blazing Chinar*, p. 244.
318 Farrukh Faheem, 'Interrogating the Ordinary: Everyday Politics and the Struggle for Azadi in Kashmir', in Haley Duschinski, Mona Bhan, Ather Zia and Cynthia Mahmood, Editors, *Resisting Occupation in Kashmir*, Philadelphia, University of Pennsylvania Press, 2018, p. 232. Faheem does not state from where he got this slogan or any information about it.
319 Bazaz, *The History of Struggle*, p. 669.
320 'Memorandum [from Maharaja Hari Singh]', in Alam, *Jammu and Kashmir*, p. 325.
321 Abdullah, *Flames*, various pages.
322 Bhattacharjea, *Abdullah*, p. 24; Abdullah, *Flames*, p. 17.
323 Quoted in *Kashmir*, Bombay, General Secretary, pp. 6–7. There are various versions of Banerji's comments. Gurmukh Nihal Singh, *Indian States & British India: Their Future Relations*, Benares, Nand Kishore & Bros, 1930, p. 82, states that Banerji was interviewed by an Associated Press representative at Lahore on 15 March 1929, and that he uses slightly different words, including that 'They [Muslims] were governed almost like dumb driven cattle'. Abdullah, *Flames*, p. 16, states that 'The Muslims, who form an overwhelming majority, are illiterate, steeped in poverty, and driven like dumb cattle'.
324 Bazaz, *Inside Kashmir*, p. 344.
325 Saraf, *Kashmiris Fight*, Volume I, p. 666.
326 Gandhi, *Patel: A Life*, p. 445.
327 Abdullah, *The Blazing Chinar*, p. 475.
328 Special Correspondent, *The Statesman*, in Bakshi, *Kashmir Today*, pp. 6–14.

329   Chopra, Chief Editor, *India's Struggle*, p. 728.
330   *A Brief Note ... 1933*, p. 2.
331   Abdullah, *Flames*, p. 150.
332   Abdullah, *The Blazing Chinar*, p. 172.
333   Bazaz, *Inside Kashmir*, p. 196.
334   Special Correspondent, *The Statesman*, in Bakshi, *Kashmir Today*, p. 13.
335   'Appendix A, National Demand', in *Kashmir*, Bombay, General Secretary, p. 36.
336   Bhattacharjea, *Abdullah*, p. 63.
337   *The Times*, 24 May 1946.
338   Bazaz, *The History of Struggle*, p. 170.
339   *The New York Times*, 21 June 1946.
340   Bazaz, *The History of Struggle*, p. 170.
341   Bhattacharjea, *Abdullah*, p. 55.
342   Madhok, *Kashmir: Centre of New Alignments*, p. 33.
343   Bazaz, *Inside Kashmir*, p. 315.
344   Special Correspondent, *The Statesman*, in Bakshi, *Kashmir Today*, p. 13.
345   Gupta, *Kashmir*, p. 55.
346   Abdullah, *The Blazing Chinar*, p. 218.
347   Fazili, *Kashmir Government*, pp. 10, 76.
348   *Administration Report ... for S. 2000*, p. 3.
349   Gias-ud-Din, 'Main Trends of the History', in *Studies of Kashmir Council*, p. 38.
350   Bazaz, *The History of Struggle*, p. 217.
351   Ganai, *Kashmir National Conference*, p. 9.
352   Ruth Fischer, 'The Indian Communist Party', *Far Eastern Survey*, Vol. 22, No. 7 (June 1953), p. 83.
353   Special Correspondent, *The Statesman*, in Bakshi, *Kashmir Today*, p. 13.
354   Andrew Whitehead, 'The Rise and Fall of New Kashmir', in Zutshi, *Kashmir*, p. 75.
355   Raina, '"Hegemony of the Working People"', in *Studies of Kashmir Council*, p. 13.
356   Special Correspondent, *The Statesman*, in Bakshi, *Kashmir Today*, pp. 13–4.
357   Sheikh Mohammed Abdullah, *Naya Kashmir: The New Kashmiri Manifesto (1944)*, Oxford Islamic Studies Online, www.oxfordislamicstudies.com/article/doc/ps-islam-0320?_hi=0&_pos=5942 [accessed 1 May 2018].
358   *Ibid*.
359   *Administration Report ... for the Second Half of S. 1998*, p. 70.
360   *Administration Report ... for S. 2000*, p. 11.
361   *The Times of India*, 18 August 1945.
362   Bazaz, *The History of Struggle*, p. 267.
363   Zaheer Masood Quraishi, *Elections & State Politics of India (A Case-Study of Kashmir)*, Delhi, Sundeep Prakashan, 1979, pp 45–6.
364   Bazaz, *The History of Struggle*, pp. 257–8.
365   'Sheikh Mohd. Abdullah's statement on the ministerial crisis in the Kashmir State on April 22, 1946', in Bakshi, *Kashmir Today*, p. 15.
366   Publicity Department, *A Handbook*. p. 37.
367   *Ibid*., p. 31.
368   Bazaz, *The History of Struggle*, p. 223.
369   Bhattacharjea, *Abdullah*, p. 81.
370   Bazaz, *The History of Struggle*, p. 222.

371   Publicity Department, *A Handbook*, p. 37.

372   *Ibid.*, p. 39.

373   Fazili, *Kashmir Government*, p. 76.

374   Special Correspondent, *The Statesman*, in Bakshi, *Kashmir Today*, p. 14.

375   'Interview with Syed Ali Shah Geelani [31 July 1997]', in Omkar Razdan, *The Trauma of Kashmir*, New Delhi, Vikas, 1999, p. 206. It is unclear but the words in brackets appear to be Razdan's, not Geelani's.

376   Email communication on 16 March 2019 with a Kashmiri who wishes to remain anonymous.

377   *The Times of India*, 27 December 1945.

378   'Pratap Singh to his Chief Minister in a letter dated Dec. 14, 1918. File No. 191/H. 75 K. G. R. [Kashmir Government Records]', in Hassnain, *British Policy*, p. 117, footnote 53.

379   Ishaq Khan, *Perspectives*, pp. 131, 132.

380   Sastry, *Treaties*, pp. 67–8.

381   Snedden, *Understanding Kashmir*, p. 287.

382   J. J. McLeod Innes, *Sir Henry Lawrence, the Pacificator*, Oxford, Clarendon, 1898, pp. 68–9.

383   Bazaz, *The History of Struggle*, p. 252.

384   Korbel, *Danger*, p. 22.

385   Abdullah, *Flames*, p. 77.

386   'Sheikh Mohd. Abdullah's statement', in Bakshi, *Kashmir Today*, p. 16.

387   Abdullah, *The Blazing Chinar*, pp. 256–7.

388   Bazaz, *The History of Struggle*, pp. 253–4.

389   Prem Nath Bazaz, *Azad Kashmir: A Democratic Socialist Conception*, Lahore, Ferozsons, 1951, p. 11.

390   Abdullah, *The Blazing Chinar*, p. 257.

391   'Speech delivered by Sheikh Abdullah before his recent arrest as reported by the "Tribune" on May 26, 1946', in Bakshi, *Kashmir Today*, pp. 16–17.

392   Abdullah, *Flames*, p. 79.

393   *The Times of India*, 30 July 1946.

394   Abdullah, *Flames*, p. 171.

395   '"Not Guilty". The statement of Sher-i-Kashmir in the Court of the Sessions Judge, Srinagar', in *State versus Sheikh Abdullah*, pp. 23, 25, 26, 32, 38.

396   Qasim, *My Life*, p. 33.

397   Balraj Puri, 'Neglected Regional Aspirations in Jammu and Kashmir', *Economic & Political Weekly*, 5 January 2008, p. 14.

398   Abdullah, *Flames*, p. 123.

399   *The Times*, 27 May 1946.

400   *Ibid.*, 22 May 1946.

401   *Ibid.*, 28 May 1946.

402   *The Times of India*, 13 July 1946.

403   'Pandit Jawaharlal Nehru's [undated] statement to the press on the happenings in Kashmir after the arrest of Sheikh Mohd. Abdullah', in Bakshi, *Kashmir Today*, pp. 26–7.

404   Qasim, *My Life*, p. 34.

405   Abdullah, *The Blazing Chinar*, p. 279.

406 'Appendix I: Answers by the Government of the State of Jammu and Kashmir to the Questionnaire Submitted by the Economic and Political Mission', *United Nations Commission for India and Pakistan*, New York, Unpublished Restricted Document: S/AC.12/66 [9 September 1948], p. 28.

407 *The Times of India*, 4 January 1946.

408 'The "Bombay Sentinel" on May 29, 1946', in Bakshi, *Kashmir Today*, p. 62.

409 'Pandit Jawaharlal Nehru's [undated] statement', in Bakshi, *Kashmir Today*, pp. 26–7.

410 *The Times of India*, 26 May 1947.

411 'Speech delivered by Sheikh Abdullah', in Bakshi, *Kashmir Today*, p. 16.

412 *The Times of India*, 5 August 1946; Madhok, *Kashmir: Centre of New Alignments*, p. 36.

413 'Speech delivered by Sheikh Abdullah' in Bakshi, *Kashmir Today*, pp. 16–17.

414 Zutshi, *Languages of Belonging*, pp. 244–5.

415 Andrew Whitehead, 'The People's Militia: Communists and Kashmiri Nationalism in the 1940s', *Twentieth Century Communism: A Journal of International History*, Issue 2, 2010, pp. 141–68.

416 Abdullah, *The Blazing Chinar*, p. 217.

417 Kaul, *Kashmir Through the Ages*, p. 139.

418 *The Times of India*, 11 June 1946.

419 *Ibid.*, 11 September 1946.

420 *The Times*, 27 May 1946.

421 *The Times of India*, 12 November 1946.

422 *State versus Sheikh Abdullah*, pp. 15, 19.

423 Jawaharlal Nehru to Karan Singh, 6 April 1953, in Alam, *Jammu and Kashmir*, p. 109.

424 *State versus Sheikh Abdullah*, pp. 79–80.

425 Qasim, *My Life*, pp. 33, 34.

426 *State versus Sheikh Abdullah*, p. 129.

427 *The Sunday Statesman*, 12 October 1947.

428 Abdullah, *The Blazing Chinar*, p. 343.

429 *The Times of India*, 11 September 1946.

430 *State versus Sheikh Abdullah*, p. 215.

431 *The Times*, 22 June 1946.

432 *The Times of India*, 22 June 1946.

433 *The Times*, 11 July 1946.

434 Singh, *Autobiography*, p. 40.

435 'Pandit Jawaharlal Nehru's [undated] statement', in Bakshi, *Kashmir Today*, pp. 29, 30.

436 Singh, *Autobiography*, p. 82.

437 Bhattacharjea, *Abdullah*, p. 103.

438 *Pakistan Times* editorial, 29 October 1947, quoted in C. Bilqees Taseer, *The Kashmir of Sheikh Muhammad Abdullah*, Lahore, Ferozsons, 1986, p. 160.

439 Taseer, *The Kashmir*, p. 157.

440 Bazaz, *The History of Struggle*, p. 319.

441 Singh, *Autobiography*, p. 82.

442 Bazaz, *The History of Struggle*, p. 215.

443 *Administration Report ... for S. 2000*, pp. 10–12.

444 Ian Stephens, *Pakistan*, Ernest Benn Limited, 1963, p. 138.

445 Korbel, *Danger*, p. 23.

446 *The Statesman*, 9 January 1947.

447 Saraf, *Kashmiris Fight*, Volume II, p. 712.

448 *The Times of India*, 12 July 1947.

449 *The Statesman*, 18 October 1947.

450 Abdullah, *The Blazing Chinar*, pp. 268, 275.

451 Mir Abdul Aziz, 'Internal Kashmir Affairs – A Practicable Solution, Kashmiristan?', p. 2, in a proposal attached to a letter to 'The Hon'ble Minister for Kashmir Affairs, Pakistan (Rawalpindi)', by Mir Abdul Aziz, 'Member General Council, All Jammu and Kashmir Muslim Conference', 5 May 1950, pp. 53–61, contained in File No. 13 (5) PMS/50,Volume 10', Government of Pakistan, Prime Minister's Secretariat, All Jammu & Kashmir Muslim Conference', held at the National Documentation Centre, Cabinet Building, Islamabad, Pakistan.

452 *The Civil & Military Gazette*, 24 July 1947.

453 *The Times of India*, 27 December 1945.

454 Abdullah, *Flames*, pp. 56–7.

455 Abdullah, *The Blazing Chinar*, p. 234.

456 *Ibid.*, p. 268.

457 *Jammu & Kashmir 1968*, Jammu and Kashmir Department of Information [Srinagar?], [1969?], p. 9.

458 'Sheikh Abdullah's Speech in the Constituent Assembly, Jammu and Kashmir, on 5 November, 1951, Calling upon People to Perform their Duties', quoted in Qasim, *My Life*, Appendix II, p. 188.

459 Abdullah, *The Blazing Chinar*, p. 386.

460 *Ibid.*, p. 268.

461 *The Testament of Sheikh Abdullah*, p. 36; Abdullah, *Flames*, pp. 89, 91.

462 Abdullah, *The Blazing Chinar*, p. 249.

463 *Ibid.*, p. 268.

464 *Ibid.*, pp. 312–13.

465 Korbel, *Danger*, p. 20.

466 Campbell-Johnson, *Mission*, p. 105.

Chapter 5 Sheikh Abdullah's pursuit of independence for 'Kashmir', 1946–53

1 Mohammed Yasin, 'Understanding Sheikh Mohd. Abdullah', in *Studies of Kashmir Council*, pp. 1–3.

2 Narayan Sitaram Phadke, *Birth-pangs of New Kashmir*, Bombay, Rind Kitabs [1948], pp. 9–10.

3 Abdullah, *Flames*, p. 66.

4 'Enclosure to Appendix V. 26 [G. Mohamed to Liaquat Ali Khan]: Note by All-Jammu and Kashmir Muslim Conference, FAO, SA (4)-6/2', in *Mohammad Ali Jinnah Papers*, Volume V, p. 564.

5 Abdullah, *The Blazing Chinar*, p. 275.

6 *The Civil & Military Gazette*, 30 September 1947.

7 'Record of interview between Rear-Admiral Viscount Mountbatten of Burma and Mr V. K. Menon', 22 April 1947, in *The Transfer of Power*, Volume X, p. 374.

8   Abdullah, *The Blazing Chinar*, p. 275.

9   *Ibid.*

10 *Ibid.*, pp. 275, 278.

11 *The Civil & Military Gazette*, 30 September 1947.

12 *Ibid.*, 1 October 1947.

13 *The Sunday Statesman*, 12 October 1947.

14 'Abdulla [sic] speaks, New Delhi, 21st October 1947', in Dewan Ram Parkash, *Fight for Kashmir*, New Delhi, Tagore Memorial Publications, 1948, pp. 273–4.

15 *The Statesman*, 22 October 1947.

16 *The Civil & Military Gazette*, 23 October 1947.

17 Abdullah, *Flames*, p. 89.

18 *Ibid.*, p. 95.

19 *Ibid.*, pp. 89, 91.

20 Soz, *Kashmir*, p. 161.

21 *The Times*, 10 October 1947.

22 *White Paper on Jammu & Kashmir*, p. 47.

23 Qasim, *My Life*, p. 39.

24 Mullik, *My Years*, p. 7, footnote, p. 182.

25 *The Civil & Military Gazette*, 23 October 1947.

26 'Memorandum [from Maharaja Hari Singh]', in Alam, *Jammu and Kashmir*, pp. 315–16.

27 *The Statesman*, 28 October 1947.

28 *The Times of India*, 28 October 1947.

29 Abdullah, *The Blazing Chinar*, pp. 291–2.

30 *Ibid.*, pp. 288, 297.

31 Whitehead, *A Mission*, p. 147.

32 Abdullah, *Flames*, p. 95.

33 *Administration Report of the Jammu and Kashmir State for S. 2006 (13th April 1949–12th April 1950)*, Jammu, Ranbir Government Press, 1952, p. 3.

34 'Events in Kashmir, Statement in Legislative Assembly', 25 November 1947, *Selected Works of Jawaharlal Nehru*, Volume 4, 1986, p. 342.

35 *The Times*, 1 November 1947.

36 *Ibid.*, 29 October 1947.

37 *Ibid.*

38 Abdullah, *The Blazing Chinar*, p. 301.

39 'Appendix 4: Reply of 27 October 1947, from Lord Mountbatten to Maharaja Hari Singh', in Singh, *Autobiography*, p. 333.

40 'Note by Jawaharlal Nehru to Mehr Chand Mahajan 26 October 1947', in Alam, *Jammu and Kashmir*, p. 353.

41 Menon, *The Story*, pp. 381, 387.

42 Norman D. Palmer, 'The Changing Scene in Kashmir', *Far Eastern Survey*, Vol. 22, No. 12, November 1953, p. 157.

43 'Memorandum [from Maharaja Hari Singh], in Alam, *Jammu and Kashmir*, p. 321.

44 *White Paper on Jammu & Kashmir*, p. 3.

45 *The Civil & Military Gazette*, 1 November 1947.

46 'Appendix 4: Reply of 27 October 1947', in Singh, *Autobiography*, p. 333.

47 Mahajan, *Looking Back*, p. 155.

48 *The Civil & Military Gazette*, 4 November 1947.

49 'Jawaharlal Nehru's [speech], March 5, 1948', in Parkash, *Fight for Kashmir*, p. 272.

50 *The Civil & Military Gazette*, 4 November 1947.

51 Mahajan, *Looking Back*, p. 162.

52 'To the Maharaja of Kashmir', 1 December 1947, *Selected Works of Jawaharlal Nehru*, Volume 4, 1986, p. 352.

53 'Solution by Mediation', Press Conference 16 November 1949, *Selected Works of Jawaharlal Nehru*, Volume 14, Part 1, 1992, p. 187.

54 *The Civil & Military Gazette*, 31 December 1947.

55 Taseer, *The Kashmir*, p. 51.

56 'Report of an Interview with John D. Kearney', 9 March 1948, *Selected Works of Jawaharlal Nehru*, Volume 5, 1987, p. 254.

57 'To V. K. Krishna Menon', 2 June 1949, *Selected Works of Jawaharlal Nehru*, Volume 11, 1991, p. 146.

58 This paragraph is based on Michael Davidson, 'Kashmir: Independence a Possible Solution', *The Scotsman*, 14 April 1949.

59 *Ibid.*

60 'To S. M. Abdullah', 10 May 1949, *Selected Works of Jawaharlal Nehru*, Volume 11, 1991, p. 115.

61 'To V. K. Krishna Menon', 14 May 1949, *Ibid.*, p. 125, footnote 3.

62 Note on 'Integration of Kashmir', 21 May 1949, *Ibid.*, p. 125.

63 *Ibid.*, p. 125, footnote 3.

64 *Ibid.*, Volume 8, 1989, p. 81, footnote 2.

65 Note on 'Integration of Kashmir', *Ibid.*, Volume 11, 1991, p. 125.

66 Khan, *Abdullah's Reflections*, pp. xxvi, 3. On p. 5, Khan states that Abdullah, her 'maternal grandfather', was 'imprisoned by the Indian government for the next 22 years, from 1953 until 1972', which period, arithmetically, was only 19 years (which, nevertheless, was bad enough).

67 Fazili, *Kashmir Government*, p. 26.

68 *The Times*, 1 November 1947.

69 Abdullah, *The Blazing Chinar*, p. 301.

70 *Ibid.*

71 'Introduction', *Jammu & Kashmir 1947–50: An Account of Activities of [the] First Three Years of Sheikh Abdullah's Government*, Jammu [Government of Jammu and Kashmir], The Ranbir Government Press, 1951, pp. i–ii.

72 'His Highness' Government, Jammu and Kashmir Orders, 4th March 1948', in Jaswant Singh, *Jammu and Kashmir: Political and Constitutional Development*, New Delhi, Har-Anand Publications, 1996, p. 197.

73 'His Highness' Government, Jammu and Kashmir Notification Proclamation of Shreeman Inder Mohinder Rajrajeshwar Maharajadhiraj Shree Harisingh Ji Ruler of Jammu and Kashmir and Dependencies', [5 March 1948]', in Singh, *Jammu and Kashmir*, pp. 195–6.

74 'Memorandum [from Maharaja Hari Singh]', in Alam, *Jammu and Kashmir*, p. 327.

75 'Appendix I: Answers', *United Nations Commission for India and Pakistan*, p. 2.

76 Abdullah, *The Blazing Chinar*, p. 357.

77 'His Highness' Government, Jammu and Kashmir Notification', in Singh, *Jammu and Kashmir*, p. 195.

78 *Jammu & Kashmir 1947–50*, p. ii.

79 'Introduction', *Ibid.*, p. i.
80 Lamb, *Kashmir*, p. 189.
81 *Dawn*, 19 April 1950.
82 *The Civil & Military Gazette*, 26 March 1949.
83 Palmer, 'The Changing Scene', p. 158.
84 *Census of India 1961*, Volume VI, *Jammu and Kashmir*, Part I-A (i), *General Report*, Srinagar, M. H. Kamili, Superintendent of Census Operations Jammu and Kashmir, Census of India, 1968, p. 35.
85 Abdullah, *The Blazing Chinar*, p. 366.
86 'Resumption of Jagirs. Order No. 6-H of 1951, 10th March 1951', in Singh, *Jammu and Kashmir*, pp. 192–4.
87 *The Civil & Military Gazette*, 26 March 1949.
88 Josef Korbel, 'The National Conference Administration of Kashmir 1949–1954', *Middle East Journal*, Vol. 8, No. 3, Summer 1954, p. 284.
89 Abdullah, *Flames*, p. 108.
90 Korbel, 'The National Conference Administration', p. 284.
91 'Situation in Jammu', in Alam, *Jammu and Kashmir*, p. 79.
92 Konrad Bekker, 'Land Reform Legislation in India', *Middle East Journal*, Vol. 5, No. 3, Summer 1951, p. 328.
93 *Selected Works of Jawaharlal Nehru*, Volume 21, 1997, p. 187, footnote 2.
94 Ishaq Khan, *Perspectives*, p. 9.
95 Abdullah, *Flames*, p. 108.
96 Abdullah, *The Blazing Chinar*, pp. 366–7.
97 Mullik, *My Years*, p. 20.
98 Qasim, *My Life*, p. 45.
99 'To Shaikh Abdullah', 4 July 1950, *Selected Works of Jawaharlal Nehru*, Volume 14, Part 2, 1993, pp. 155, 157.
100 'Introduction', *Jammu & Kashmir 1947–50*, p. iii.
101 'Sheikh Abdullah's Speech in the Constituent Assembly, Jammu and Kashmir, on 5 November, 1951, Calling Upon People To Perform Their Duties', in Qasim, *My Life*, p. 186.
102 Abdullah, *The Blazing Chinar*, p. 367.
103 *The Constitution of India*, Contents, New Delhi, Government of India, 2007, pp. 243–5, www.india.gov.in/my-government/constitution-india/constitution-india-full-text [accessed 5 June 2020].
104 Mayfield, 'A Geographic Study of the Kashmir', p. 195.
105 Abdullah, *The Blazing Chinar*, p. 345.
106 Qasim, *My Life*, p. 56.
107 Gandhi, *Patel: A Life*, p. 517.
108 'His Highness' Government, Jammu and Kashmir Notification', in Singh, *Jammu and Kashmir*, pp. 195–6.
109 'Memorandum [from Maharaja Hari Singh]', in Alam, *Jammu and Kashmir*, p. 319.
110 Mullik, *My Years*, pp. 11, 21. Mullik calls him 'Iyengar'.
111 Soz, *Kashmir*, p. 148.
112 'Instrument of Accession of Jammu and Kashmir, 26 October 1947', in Hasan and Hasan, *Documents*, p. 59.

113 'His Highness' Government, Jammu and Kashmir Notification', in Singh, *Jammu and Kashmir*, p. 195.

114 Abdullah, *The Blazing Chinar*, p. 364.

115 *Ibid.*, p. 363.

116 *Ibid.*, p. 364.

117 Qasim, *My Life*, p. 171.

118 Mahajan, *Looking Back*, p. 172.

119 Qasim, *My Life*, p. 171.

120 Abdullah, *The Blazing Chinar*, p. 328.

121 Bhattacharjea, *Abdullah*, p. 140.

122 *Ibid.*, pp. 140, 147, footnote 2.

123 Qasim, *My Life*, p. 171; Z. G. Muhammad, 'Kashmir, Damocles Sword', *Greater Kashmir*, 12 September 2016, www.greaterkashmir.com/news/opinion/kashmir-damocles-sword/ [accessed 15 September 2016].

124 Qasim, *My Life*, p. 171.

125 Fazili, *Kashmir Government*, p. 121.

126 Soz, *Kashmir*, p. 147.

127 'Proclamation', in Singh, *Jammu and Kashmir*, pp. 203–4.

128 *Ibid.*

129 Abdullah, *The Blazing Chinar*, p. 369.

130 Alam, *Jammu and Kashmir*, p. 39, footnote 1.

131 'Resolution Adopted by the Security Council, 24 January 1957', Hasan and Hasan, *Documents*, pp. 298–9.

132 'Proclamation' in Singh, *Jammu and Kashmir*, pp. 203–4.

133 'Mir Qasim Press Statement on the Situation in Kashmir During March 1989', in Qasim, *My Life*, p. 292.

134 Abdullah, *Flames*, p. 115.

135 'Clause 48, The Jammu and Kashmir Constitution (Amendment) Act, 2011', in S. R. Bakshi, *Kashmir: Political Problems*, New Delhi, Sarup & Sons, 1997, p. 142.

136 This paragraph is based on 'Sheikh Abdullah's Speech', in Qasim, *My Life*, pp. 182, 188–9.

137 Jawaharlal Nehru, 'Impracticability of an Independent Kashmir', 25 August 1952, *Selected Works of Jawaharlal Nehru*, Volume 19, 1996, p. 322, footnote 2.

138 'Sheikh Abdullah's Speech', in Qasim, *My Life*, pp. 188–9.

139 Abdullah, *The Blazing Chinar*, p. 366.

140 'Jammu Agitation' [16 May 1953], *Selected Works of Jawaharlal Nehru*, Volume 22, 1998, p. 186.

141 'To Govind Ballabh Pant', 12 May 1953, *Ibid.*, p. 184.

142 *The Times of India*, 16 July 1953.

143 *Ibid.*, 9 July 1953.

144 Ganai, *Kashmir National Conference*, p. 17.

145 *Selected Works of Jawaharlal Nehru*, Volume 21, 1997, p. 187, footnote 2.

146 G. R. Najar, *Kashmir Accord (1975): A Political Analysis*, Srinagar, Gulshan Publishers, 1988, p. 26.

147 *Selected Works of Jawaharlal Nehru*, Volume 21, 1997, p. 176, footnote 8.

148 Puri, *Simmering Volcano*, p. 26, footnote 201.

149 Madhok, *Kashmir: Centre of New Alignments*, pp. 37–8.

150 Palmer, 'The Changing Scene', p. 159.
151 'Editor's Note', in Alam, *Jammu and Kashmir*, p. xi.
152 Alam, *Jammu and Kashmir*, p. 93, footnote 1.
153 Fazili, *Kashmir Government*, p. 41.
154 'Appendix IV: Founder of the Bharatiya Jana Sangh (BJP) [sic] Shyama Prasad Mookherjee's Correspondence with Jawaharlal Nehru, first Prime Minister of India, January 9, 1953, and Sheikh Mohammad Abdullah, Prime Minister of Jammu and Kashmir, February 4, 1953', in Khan, *Abdullah's Reflections*, p. 195.
155 *Selected Works of Jawaharlal Nehru*, Volume 10, 1990, p. 238, footnote 3.
156 Lockwood, 'Sheikh Abdullah', p. 386.
157 Puri, 'The Era of Sheikh Mohammed Abdullah', p. 189.
158 'To Vallabhbhai Patel', 17 April 1949, *Selected Works of Jawaharlal Nehru*, Volume 10, 1990, p. 238.
159 P. S. Verma, 'Jammu and Kashmir Politics: Religion, Region and Personality Symbiosis', *The Indian Journal of Political Science* Vol. 48, Oct–Dec 1987, p. 568.
160 Tathagata Roy, *Syama Prasad Mookerjee*, Gurgaon, Penguin, 2018, p. 359.
161 *Ibid.*, p. 347.
162 Jawaharlal Nehru to Karan Singh, 14 February 1953, in Alam, *Jammu and Kashmir*, p. 93.
163 Y. D. Gundevia, 'On Sheikh Abdullah', *The Testament of Sheikh Abdullah*, p. 110.
164 Richard Leonard Park, 'India Argues with Kashmir', *Far Eastern Survey*, Vol. 21, No. 11, 2 July 1952, p. 114.
165 *Selected Works of Jawaharlal Nehru*, Volume 18, 1996, p. 383, footnote 2.
166 *Ibid.*, p. 387, footnote 3.
167 Ganai, *Kashmir National Conference*, p. 35.
168 'To Abul Kalam Azad', 25 April 1952, *Selected Works of Jawaharlal Nehru*, Volume 18, 1996, p. 389.
169 Mullik, *My Years*, pp. 34, 102.
170 Whitehead, *A Mission*, p. 46.
171 Khan, *The Parchment*, p. 174, footnote 27.
172 Saraf, *Kashmiris Fight*, Volume II, p. 1228.
173 Abdullah, *Flames*, p. 90.
174 Para, *The Making of Modern Kashmir*, p. 181.
175 Korbel, 'The National Conference Administration', p. 287.
176 'To Shaikh Abdullah, 14 December 1952, *Selected Works of Jawaharlal Nehru*, Volume 20, 1997, p. 373.
177 'To Vallabhbhai Patel', 17 April 1949, *Ibid.*, Volume 10, 1990, p. 238.
178 'To Bhimsen Sachar', 31 July 1953, *Ibid.*, Volume 23, 1998, p. 306.
179 'Agitation in Jammu and Kashmir [Statement in Parliament]', 12 December 1952, *Ibid.*, Volume 20, 1997, p. 369.
180 'To Raghu Vira', 4 August 1949, *Ibid.*, Volume 11, 1991, p. 357.
181 Abdullah, *The Blazing Chinar*, p. 375.
182 'To Shaikh Abdullah', 5 January 1953, *Selected Works of Jawaharlal Nehru*, Volume 22, 1998, p. 199.
183 Karan Singh to Jawaharlal Nehru, 12 April 1951, in Alam, *Jammu and Kashmir*, pp. 19, footnote 1, 20.
184 Karan Singh to Jawaharlal Nehru, 7 August 1952, in *Ibid.*, p. 40.

185 'Situation in Jammu', in *Ibid.*, p. 77.
186 Karan Singh to Jawaharlal Nehru, 8 September 1952, in *Ibid.*, p. 49.
187 *Selected Works of Jawaharlal Nehru*, Volume 19, 1996, p. 340, footnote 2.
188 Korbel, *Danger*, pp. 228–9.
189 Bhatia, *Jammu and Kashmir: Article 370*, pp. 133–4.
190 Korbel, *Danger*, p. 225.
191 Jawaharlal Nehru to Karan Singh, 8 August 1952, in Alam, *Jammu and Kashmir*, p. 44.
192 Jawaharlal Nehru to Karan Singh, 2 November 1952, in *Ibid.*, p. 66.
193 *Ibid.*, p. 67, footnote 1. 'Sadar' is sometimes also spelt 'Sadr'.
194 'To Tara Chand', 27 January 1952, *Selected Works of Jawaharlal Nehru*, Volume 17, 1995, p. 440.
195 'Partition or Independence of Kashmir', 26 March 1952, *Ibid.*, p. 454.
196 'To S. M. Abdullah', 19 January 1952, *Ibid.*, p. 438.
197 Nehru, 'Impracticability of an Independent Kashmir', pp. 322–30.
198 *Ibid.*, p. 327.
199 'Conversations with Mohammad Ali', 17 August 1953, *Selected Works of Jawaharlal Nehru*, Volume 23, 1998, p. 336.
200 Nehru, 'Impracticability of an Independent Kashmir', p. 328.
201 Qasim, *My Life*, p. 61.
202 Abdullah, *The Blazing Chinar*, p. 357.
203 'To Rajendra Prasad', 19 June 1952, *Selected Works of Jawaharlal Nehru*, Volume 18, 1996, p. 405.
204 Abdullah, *Flames*, p. 110.
205 "'India's Relations with Kashmir", Statement in House of the People', 24 July 1952, *Selected Works of Jawaharlal Nehru*, Volume 19, 1996, p. 238.
206 Abdullah, *The Blazing Chinar*, p. 357.
207 Menon, *The Story*, p. 454.
208 *Ibid.*, p. 440.
209 'Letter to Chief Ministers', 25 July 1952, *Selected Works of Jawaharlal Nehru*, Volume 19, 1996, p. 685.
210 Bhatia, *Jammu and Kashmir: Article 370*, pp. 132–5.
211 Alam, *Jammu and Kashmir*, pp. 74, 84, 96.
212 Ganai, *Kashmir National Conference*, p. 17.
213 'Constitutional Relationship of Kashmir with India' [20 July 1952], *Selected Works of Jawaharlal Nehru*, Volume 19, 1996, p. 211.
214 *Ibid.*, Volume 23, 1998, p. 292, footnote 3.
215 *Ibid.*, Volume 21, 1997, p. 175, footnote 5.
216 *Ibid.*, Volume 19, 1996, p. 336, footnote 8.
217 Abdullah, *The Blazing Chinar*, p. 368.
218 'BJP Approach Will Alienate the Kashmiris ... January 20, 1992', in Qasim, *My Life*, p. 306.
219 'Mir Qasim Press Statement', in Qasim, *My Life*, p. 294.
220 Fazili, *Kashmir Government*, p. 137.
221 'Status of Kashmir in the Indian Union', Note, 19 June 1952, *Selected Works of Jawaharlal Nehru*, Volume 18, 1996, p. 402.
222 Jawaharlal Nehru to Karan Singh, 26 July 1952, in Alam, *Jammu and Kashmir*, p. 34.

223 Palmer, 'The Changing Scene', p. 160.
224 'Dr Syama Prasad Mookerjee to Sheikh Mohammad Abdullah' (February 13, 1953)', in Qasim, *My Life*, p. 208.
225 Abdullah, *The Blazing Chinar*, p. 375.
226 Korbel, *Danger*, p. 224.
227 Abdullah, *Flames*, p. 116.
228 Abdullah, *The Blazing Chinar*, p. 368.
229 Kaul, *Kashmir Through the Ages*, pp. 148–9.
230 Palmer, 'The Changing Scene', p. 160.
231 'To G. S. Bajpai', 24 July 1953, *Selected Works of Jawaharlal Nehru*, Volume 23, 1998, p. 424.
232 'To G. S. Bajpai', 30 July 1953, *Ibid.*, p. 453.
233 *Ibid.*, Volume 21, 1997, p. 174, footnote 3.
234 'To Lanka Sundaram', 11 April 1955, *Ibid.*, Volume 28, 2001, p. 356.
235 'To Vijayalakshmi Pandit', 3 March 1953, *Ibid.*, Volume 21, 1997, p. 243.
236 'Sheikh Abdullah's Speech', in Qasim, *My Life*, pp. 182, 188–9.
237 Karan Singh's 'Notes for Talks with Jawaharlal Nehru' on 21 April 1953, in Alam, *Jammu and Kashmir*, p. 113.
238 *Ibid.*
239 *Ibid.*, p. 115, footnote 1.
240 *Selected Works of Jawaharlal Nehru*, Volume 22, 1998, p. 213, footnote 6.
241 Gajendragadkar, *Kashmir*, p. 115. After the events of 2019, I may stand corrected on this point.
242 Karan Singh to Jawaharlal Nehru, 4 January 1953, in Alam, *Jammu and Kashmir*, p. 83.
243 *Ibid.*, p. 116, footnote 2.
244 *Dawn*, 11 May 1953.
245 Lamb, *Kashmir*, p. 189.
246 *Dawn*, 21 May 1953.
247 *Times of India*, 8 August 1953.
248 'To Shaikh Abdullah', 28 June 1953, *Selected Works of Jawaharlal Nehru*, Volume 22, 1998, p. 194.
249 Abdullah, *The Blazing Chinar*, p. 371.
250 *Selected Works of Jawaharlal Nehru*, Volume 23, 1998, p. 287 (the first) footnote 3.
251 'To Abul Kalam Azad', 11 June 1953, *Ibid.*, Volume 22, 1998, p. 291.
252 'To G. S. Bajpai', 11 June 1953, *Ibid.*, p. 191.
253 Puri, *Simmering Volcano*, pp. 29, 135
254 Korbel, *Danger*, p. 235.
255 'G. M. Sadiq's Reply – Dated 11th Sept. '56' in Sarabhai, *Sheikh-Sadiq Correspondence*, p. 10.
256 'G. M. Sadiq's Reply – Dated 22nd Oct. '56' in *Ibid.*, p. 28.
257 *Selected Works of Jawaharlal Nehru*, Volume 23, 1998, p. 304, footnote 2.
258 Sheikh Abdullah, 'Kashmir, India and Pakistan', *Foreign Affairs*, April 1965, p. 533.
259 'Sheikh Abdullah's Reply – Dated 26th Sept. '56' in Sarabhai, *Sheikh-Sadiq Correspondence*, p. 18.
260 *Selected Works of Jawaharlal Nehru*, Volume 21, 1997, p. 191, footnote 3, states re point c that it would be 'joint India-Pakistan control over foreign affairs and defence'.

261 'Sheikh Abdullah's Reply – Dated 26th Sept. '56' in Sarabhai, *Sheikh-Sadiq Correspondence*, p. 18.

262 Soz, *Kashmir*, p. 161.

263 Abdullah, *Flames*, p. 117.

264 'G. M. Sadiq's Reply – Dated 22nd Oct. '56' in Sarabhai, *Sheikh-Sadiq Correspondence*, p. 28.

265 Palmer, 'The Changing Scene', p. 160.

266 'Report submitted by ... Sir Owen Dixon', in Hasan and Hasan, *Documents*, p. 253.

267 Philip Ayres, *Owen Dixon*, Carlton, The Miegunyah Press, 2003, p. 202.

268 'Report submitted by ... Sir Owen Dixon', in Hasan and Hasan, *Documents*, pp. 253, 270.

269 *Ibid.,* pp. 273–4.

270 Ayres, *Owen Dixon*, pp. 209–10.

271 *Selected Works of Jawaharlal Nehru*, Volume 17, 1995, p. 429, footnote 2.

272 Korbel, *Danger*, p. 147.

273 *The Times of India*, 10 August 1953.

274 *Selected Works of Jawaharlal Nehru*, Volume 23, p. 302, footnote 5.

275 Bazaz, *The History of Struggle*, p. 669.

276 *Times of India*, 21 July 1953.

277 *Ibid.,* 2 August 1953.

278 'G. M. Sadiq's Reply – Dated 11th Sept. '56' in Sarabhai, *Sheikh-Sadiq Correspondence*, p. 14.

279 'G. M. Sadiq's Reply – Dated 22nd Oct. '56' in *Ibid.,* p. 28.

280 'To. S. M. Abdullah', 19 January 1952, *Selected Works of Jawaharlal Nehru*, Volume 17, 1995, p. 438.

281 'G. M. Sadiq's Reply – Dated 22nd Oct. '56' in Sarabhai, *Sheikh-Sadiq Correspondence*, pp. 28, 30–1.

282 Nehru, 'Impracticability of an Independent Kashmir', p. 323.

283 *Times of India*, 8 August 1953.

284 Abdullah, *Flames*, p. 117.

285 Karan Singh's Message to Jawaharlal Nehru, 10 June 1953, on the 'Political Situation in Kashmir', in Alam, *Jammu and Kashmir*, pp. 114–15.

286 'To K. N. Katju', 12 June 1953, *Selected Works of Jawaharlal Nehru*, Volume 22, 1998, p. 192.

287 Jawaharlal Nehru to Karan Singh, 29 June 1953, in Alam, *Jammu and Kashmir*, p. 118.

288 Karan Singh's Message to Jawaharlal Nehru, 10 June 1953, on the 'Political Situation in Kashmir', in *Ibid.,* p. 115.

289 *Ibid.,* p. 130, footnote 2.

290 'To B. C. Roy', 29 June 1953, *Selected Works of Jawaharlal Nehru*, Volume 22, 1998, p. 203. Roy was Chief Minister of West Bengal State.

291 'Appeal for Ending the Praja Parishad Agitation', 2 July 1953, *Ibid.,* Volume 23, 1998, p. 276.

292 Roy, *Syama Prasad Mookerjee*, p. 356.

293 Karan Singh to Jawaharlal Nehru, 26 June 1953, in Alam, *Jammu and Kashmir*, p. 116.

294 'To Karan Singh', 29 June 1953, *Selected Works of Jawaharlal Nehru*, Volume 22, 1998, p. 201.

295 'To B. C. Roy', 29 June 1953, *Ibid.,* p. 205.

296 'To Shaikh Abdullah', 28 June 1953, *Ibid.*, pp. 195–6, 199.
297 *Ibid.*, p. 199, footnote 15.
298 'To Shaikh Abdullah', 8 April 1955, *Ibid.* Volume 28, 2001, p. 352.
299 Mullik, *My Years*, p. 195.
300 Taseer, *The Kashmir*, p. 148.
301 Abdullah, *The Blazing Chinar*, p. 412.
302 Bhattacharjea, *Abdullah*, p. 155.
303 *Ibid.*, p. 156.
304 'Americans in Kashmir History', *Kashmir Life*, 1 November 2010, https://kashmirlife.net/americans-in-kashmir-history-958/ [accessed 29 May 2018].
305 *Selected Works of Jawaharlal Nehru*, Volume 23, 1999, p. 388, footnote 6.
306 'Kashmir', *The Manchester Guardian*, 17 August 1953.
307 *Selected Works of Jawaharlal Nehru*, Volume 22, 1998, p. 197, footnote 10.
308 Palmer, 'The Changing Scene', p. 162.
309 'Kashmir', *The Manchester Guardian*, 17 August 1953.
310 Ghulam Mohammad Rajpori and Manohar Nath Kaul, *Conspiracy in Kashmir*, Srinagar, Social & Political Study Group, 1954, p. 2.
311 Abdullah, *The Blazing Chinar*, pp. 417, 442. SEATO was the South East Asia Treaty Organization; CENTO was the Central Treaty Organization.
312 *Selected Works of Jawaharlal Nehru*, Volume 22, 1998, p. 195, footnote 6.
313 Abdullah, *Flames*, pp. 442–3.
314 Schofield, *Kashmir in the Crossfire*, p. 184.
315 *Selected Works of Jawaharlal Nehru*, Volume 23, 1998, p. 294, footnote 2.
316 Reeta Chowdhari Tremblay, 'Nation, Identity and the Intervening Role of the State: A Study of the Secessionist Movement in Kashmir', *Pacific Affairs*, Vol. 69, No. 4, Winter, 1996–97, p. 483.
317 *The Times of India*, 10 July 1953; *The New York Times*, 5 July 1953. The articles were the same except for the headings and some minor Indian changes re spelling, e.g., changing 'recognizing' to 'recognising'.
318 Trumbull was one of the first journalists to report the Pukhtoons' devastation of Baramulla in 1947, doing so via a report in *The New York Times* on 11 November 1947.
319 *The Times of India*, 10 July 1953.
320 *Ibid.* The sub-heading in *The New York Times* was 'India and Pakistan near Kashmir Pact'.
321 *Ibid.*
322 *Ibid.*, 11 July 1953.
323 *Ibid.*
324 'Cable to Rajeshwar Dayal', 9 July 1953, *Selected Works of Jawaharlal Nehru*, Volume 23, 1998, p. 287.
325 *The Times of India*, 16 July 1953.
326 *Ibid.*, 17 July 1953.
327 *Ibid.*, 16 July 1953.
328 Mullik, *My Years*, p. 24.
329 *The Times of India*, 16 July 1953.
330 *Ibid.*, 17 July 1953.
331 *Ibid.*
332 *Ibid.*

333 *Ibid.*, 21 July 1953.

334 *Ibid.*, 2 August 1953.

335 'To Abul Kalam Azad', 19 July 1953, *Selected Works of Jawaharlal Nehru*, Volume 23, 1998, p. 291.

336 Singh, *Autobiography*, p. 157.

337 'The Role of American Agents', Note 23 July 1953, *Selected Works of Jawaharlal Nehru*, Volume 23, 1998, p. 293.

338 'To Mohan Sinha Mehta', 28 August 1953, *Ibid.*, p. 353.

339 *Ibid.*, p. 388, footnote 6.

340 'To Vijayalakshmi Pandit', 3 October 1953, *Ibid.*, pp. 387, 388.

341 *Ibid.*, p. 387.

342 Rajpori and Kaul, *Conspiracy in Kashmir*, p. 1.

343 'To Bakshi Ghulam Mohammad', 30 July 1953, *Selected Works of Jawaharlal Nehru*, Volume 23, 1998, pp. 302–3.

344 Palmer, 'The Changing Scene', p. 160.

345 *Selected Works of Jawaharlal Nehru*, Volume 23, 1998, p. 304, footnote 2.

346 Palmer, 'The Changing Scene', p. 160.

347 *The Times of India*, 31 July 1953.

348 *Ibid.*, 8 August 1953.

349 Abdullah, *The Blazing Chinar*, p. 360.

350 'For Karan Singh', 30 October 1952, *Selected Works of Jawaharlal Nehru*, Volume 20, 1997, p. 390.

351 Bhatia, *Jammu and Kashmir: Article 370*, p. 134.

352 *Ibid.*, p. 135.

353 Bhattacharjea, *Abdullah*, p. 213.

354 Karan Singh to Jawaharlal Nehru, 9 August 1953, in Alam, *Jammu and Kashmir*, p. 118 and footnote 2.

355 'To Shaikh Abdullah', 28 June 1953, *Selected Works of Jawaharlal Nehru*, Volume 22, 1998, pp. 196–7.

356 'A Proposal for the Future of Jammu and Kashmir', 31 July 1953, *Ibid.*, Volume 23, 1998, p. 304.

357 *Ibid.*, p. 304, footnote 2.

358 'A Proposal for the Future of Jammu and Kashmir', 31 July 1953, *Ibid.*, p. 305.

359 Ramachandra Guha, 'Opening a Window in Kashmir', *World Policy Journal*, 1 September 2004, p. 81.

360 *Times of India*, 10 August 1953.

361 Singh, *Autobiography*, p. 162.

362 Karan Singh to Jawaharlal Nehru, 9 August 1953, in Alam, *Jammu and Kashmir*, p. 119.

363 'Sadar-i-Riyasat's letter to Sheikh Abdullah', 8 August 1953, in Bakshi, *Kashmir: Political Problems*, p. 107.

364 Karan Singh to Jawaharlal Nehru, 9 August 1953, in Alam, *Jammu and Kashmir*, pp. 119–20.

365 Karan Singh to Jawaharlal Nehru, 16 August 1953, in *Ibid.*, p. 125.

366 'Joint Memorandum submitted by Cabinet Members of the Sheikh Abdullah Ministry to the Sadar-i-Riyasat, 8th August, 1953', in Singh, *Jammu and Kashmir*, pp. 103–6.

367 Karan Singh to Jawaharlal Nehru, 9 August 1953, in Alam, Editor, *Jammu and Kashmir*, p. 118 and footnote 2.

368 Abdullah, *The Blazing Chinar*, p. 396.

369 Alam, *Jammu and Kashmir*, p. 118, footnote 1.

370 Singh, *Autobiography*, p. 162.

371 Abdullah, *The Blazing Chinar*, p. 355.

372 *Ibid.*, p. 391.

373 'To Shaikh Abdullah', 28 June 1953, *Selected Works of Jawaharlal Nehru*, Volume 22, 1998, pp. 195–6, 199.

374 Chowdhary, 'Kashmir in the Indian Project of Nationalism', in Khan, *The Parchment*, p. 172.

Chapter 6 Sheikh Abdullah's pursuit of independence for 'Kashmir', post-1953

1 Whitehead, 'The People's Militia', pp. 143, 163.

2 Gundevia, 'On Sheikh Abdullah', *The Testament of Sheikh Abdullah*, pp. 139–42.

3 Abdullah, *The Blazing Chinar*, p. 382.

4 *Selected Works of Jawaharlal Nehru*, Volume 23, 1998, p. 310, footnote 3.

5 Abdullah, *The Blazing Chinar*, p. 435.

6 Nyla Ali Khan, 'The Events of 1953 in Jammu and Kashmir: A Memoir of Three Generations', *Race & Class*, Vol. 56, No. 2, Oct–Dec 2014, p. 17.

7 Khan, *Abdullah's Reflections*, p. 5.

8 Durga Das, *India: From Curzon to Nehru & After*, London, Collins, 1969, p. 410.

9 Abdullah, *The Blazing Chinar*, pp. 382-3.

10 *Ibid.*, p. 383.

11 *Administration Report of Jammu and Kashmir for the years, 2011* [sic] *(13th April 1954–12th April 1955)*, [Srinagar?], Jammu and Kashmir Government, [1955?], p. 4.

12 Abdullah, *The Blazing Chinar*, p. 402.

13 Korbel, *Danger*, p. 272.

14 *Ibid.*, p. 267.

15 Ankit, *The Kashmir Conflict*, p. 54.

16 *Ibid.*, pp. 61, 112.

17 *Crisis in Kashmir Explained (Text of Policy Speech Broadcast by Bakshi Ghulam Mohammad, Prime Minister of Jammu and Kashmir on August 9, 1953)*, Srinagar, Lalla Rookh, [1953], pp. 2–3.

18 Balraj Puri, *Jammu and Kashmir: Triumph and Tragedy of Indian Federalisation*, New Delhi, Sterling Publishers, 1981, p. 130.

19 'Memorandum [from Maharaja Hari Singh]', in Alam, *Jammu and Kashmir*, pp. 326–7.

20 'To Vijayalakshmi Pandit', 3 October 1953, *Selected Works of Jawaharlal Nehru*, Volume 24, 1999, p. 388.

21 Publications Division, *Elections in Kashmir*, [New Delhi], Ministry of Information & Broadcasting, Government of India, 1957, p. 22.

22 *Selected Works of Jawaharlal Nehru*, Volume 24, 1999, p. 395, footnote 2.

Notes

23 Abdullah, *The Blazing Chinar*, p. 416.

24 Singh, *Kashmir: A Tragedy*, pp. 69, 78.

25 *Selected Works of Jawaharlal Nehru*, Volume 27, 2000, p. 250, footnote 5.

26 Karan Singh to Jawaharlal Nehru, 16 August 1953, in Alam, *Jammu and Kashmir*, p. 124 and footnote 3.

27 *Ibid.*, p. 130, footnote 2.

28 *Selected Works of Jawaharlal Nehru*, Volume 23, 1998, p. 346, footnote 2.

29 'To Bakshi Ghulam Mohammad', 15 August 1953, *Ibid.*, p. 327.

30 Alam, Editor, *Jammu and Kashmir 1949–64*, p. 130, footnote 3.

31 'Letters to Chief Ministers I', 7 October 1953, *Selected Works of Jawaharlal Nehru*, Volume 24, 1999, p. 657.

32 'To Karan Singh', 21 November 1953, *Ibid.*, p. 399.

33 Qasim, *My Life*, p. 172.

34 Gundevia, 'On Sheikh Abdullah', *The Testament of Sheikh Abdullah*, p. 88.

35 Singh, *Autobiography*, pp. 156–7, 165.

36 Karan Singh to Jawaharlal Nehru, 9 August 1953, in Alam, *Jammu and Kashmir*, p. 121.

37 'A Proposal for the Future of Jammu and Kashmir', 31 July 1953, *Selected Works of Jawaharlal Nehru*, Volume 23, 1998, p. 304.

38 *Ibid.*, p. 317, footnote 2.

39 Singh, *Autobiography*, p. 157.

40 'Recent Developments, Statement in Parliament', 10 August 1953, *Selected Works of Jawaharlal Nehru*, Volume 23, 1998, p. 316.

41 'Prime Minister's Statement on Kashmir Developments', *Kashmir (August 7–September 17, 1953)*, New Delhi, Current Affairs Publications, [1954], p. 27.

42 Abdullah, *The Blazing Chinar*, p. 371.

43 'Sheikh Abdullah's Letter – Dated 16th August '56' Sarabhai, *Sheikh-Sadiq Correspondence*, p. 1.

44 Abdullah, *Flames*, p. 115.

45 'His Highness' Government, Jammu and Kashmir Notification Proclamation', in Singh, *Jammu and Kashmir*, pp. 195–6.

46 'Order Issued by the Sadar-i-Riyasat on August 8, 1953', in Bakshi, *Kashmir: Political Problems*, p. 108.

47 'The Jammu and Kashmir Constitution (Amendment) Act, 2011', in Bakshi, *Kashmir: Political Problems*, p. 139.

48 *Ibid.*, pp. 165–7.

49 Palmer, 'The Changing Scene', p. 161.

50 'Recent Developments, Statement in Parliament', 10 August 1953, *Selected Works of Jawaharlal Nehru*, Volume 23, 1998, p. 312.

51 *Ibid.*, pp. 314, 315.

52 *Ibid.*, p. 316.

53 *Ibid.*, p. 316, footnote 5.

54 Abdullah, *Flames*, p. 447.

55 Kaul, *Kashmir Through the Ages*, p. 164.

56 *Ibid.*, p. 156.

57 Schofield, *Kashmir in the Crossfire*, p. 189.

58 Taseer, *The Kashmir*, p. 139.

59 Qasim, *My Life*, p. 84.
60 Alam, *Jammu and Kashmir*, p. 130, footnote 2.
61 'Conversations with Mohammad Ali', 17 August 1953, *Selected Works of Jawaharlal Nehru*, Volume 23, 1998, p. 335.
62 *Ibid.*
63 'To Bakshi Ghulam Mohammad, 18 August 1953, *Ibid.*, p. 341.
64 'Conversations with Mohammad Ali', 17 August 1953, *Ibid.*, p. 336.
65 *Ibid.*, p. 335.
66 'To Mohammad Ali', 3 September 1953 *Ibid.*, pp. 361–8.
67 'Continuity in Policy, Statement in the House of the People', 17 September 1953, *Ibid.*, p. 406.
68 'To Bakshi Ghulam Mohammad', 26 October 1953, *Ibid.*, Volume 24, 1999, p. 402.
69 'To Bakshi Ghulam Mohammad', 9 December 1953, *Ibid.*, p. 407.
70 'To D. P. Dhar', 27 December 1953, *Ibid.*, p. 401.
71 Fazili, *Kashmir Government*, pp. 90–1.
72 Publications Division, *Elections in Kashmir*, p. 7.
73 Gilani, *The Constitution of Azad Jammu & Kashmir*, p. 852. 'The Constitution of Jammu & Kashmir, 1957' is provided in its entirety on pp. 851–905.
74 'Note to Secretary, Kashmir Affairs, M. H. A. [Ministry of Home Affairs]', 15 November 1950, *Selected Works of Jawaharlal Nehru*, Volume 15, Part 2, 1993, p. 270.
75 'Syed Mir Qasim's Statement in the General Assembly on Pakistani Aggression Against India on 5 October 1965', in Qasim, *My Life*, pp. 245–6. Qasim was a 'Member of the Indian Delegation and Minister without Portfolio, Government of Jammu and Kashmir'.
76 Abdullah, *Flames*, p. 115.
77 *Administration Report for S. 2000*, pp 10, 11, 12.
78 'Statement of the Permanent Representative of India, Sir Benegal Rau, in the Security Council, 9 March 1951', in Hasan and Hasan, *Documents*, p. 294.
79 *Ibid.*, pp. 296–7.
80 Abdullah, *The Blazing Chinar*, pp. 373, 377.
81 *Administration Report for the years, 2011*, pp. 4–5.
82 Ayres, *Owen Dixon*, p. 206.
83 Qasim, *My Life*, p. 76.
84 Alam, *Jammu and Kashmir*, pp. 184–8.
85 'National and International Issues', 6 July 1956, *Selected Works of Jawaharlal Nehru*, Volume 34, 2005, p. 431.
86 'To Shaikh Abdullah', 8 April 1955, *Ibid.*, Volume 28, 2001, p. 352.
87 Fazili, *Kashmir Government*, p. 79.
88 Qasim, *My Life*, p. 76.
89 Abdullah, *The Blazing Chinar*, p. 438.
90 Ganai, *Kashmir National Conference*, p. 38.
91 Fazili, *Kashmir Government*, p. 79.
92 Bhattacharjea, *Abdullah*, p. 199.
93 Snedden, *The Untold Story*, p. 194.
94 Abdullah, *Flames*, p. 132.
95 Abdullah, *The Blazing Chinar*, p. 433.
96 Ganai, *Kashmir National Conference*, pp. 20, 38.

97 Prem Nath Bazaz, *The Shape of Things in Kashmir*, New Delhi, Pamposh Publications, 1965, p. 31; Balraj Puri, *Kashmir: Towards Insurgency*, Hyderabad, Orient Longman, 1993, p. 30.

98 Mullik, *My Years*, pp. 72–4.

99 'Speech at Hazratbal, Srinagar, March 15, 1968', in Khan, *Abdullah's Reflections*, p. 64.

100 Abdullah, *Flames*, p. 132, footnote.

101 Singh, *Autobiography*, pp. 221, 226.

102 Muhammad, *Kashmir in War and Diplomacy*, p. 23.

103 'Sheikh Abdullah Speaks', *The Testament of Sheikh Abdullah*, pp. 46–7.

104 *Selected Works of Jawaharlal Nehru*, Volume 23, 1998, p. 328, footnote 4.

105 *Ibid.*, Volume 42, 2010, p. 567, footnote 3.

106 Kaul, *Kashmir Through the Ages*, p. 167.

107 'To Vijaya Lakshmi Pandit', 17 February 1958, *Selected Works of Jawaharlal Nehru*, Volume 41, 2010, p. 364.

108 Najar, *Kashmir Accord (1975)*, p. 30.

109 Mullik, *My Years*, p. 78.

110 Abdullah, *The Blazing Chinar*, pp. 463–4.

111 *Selected Works of Jawaharlal Nehru*, Volume 42, 2010, p. 580, footnote 3.

112 Abdullah, *The Blazing Chinar*, pp. 465–6.

113 *Selected Works of Jawaharlal Nehru*, Volume 42, 2010, p. 571, footnote 2.

114 *Dawn*, 3 April 1947.

115 Mullik, *My Years*, p. 171.

116 Singh, *Autobiography*, p. 226.

117 Gundevia, 'On Sheikh Abdullah', *The Testament of Sheikh Abdullah*, p. 121.

118 Fazili, *Kashmir Government*, p. 46.

119 Singh, *Autobiography*, p. 253.

120 Fazili, *Kashmir Government*, p. 81.

121 Kaul, *Kashmir Through the Ages*, p. 156.

122 Bhattacharjea, *Abdullah*, p. 216.

123 Mullik, *My Years*, p. 172.

124 Abdullah, *The Blazing Chinar*, p. 498.

125 *Ibid.*, p. 502.

126 Abdullah, *Flames*, p. 155.

127 Abdullah, *The Blazing Chinar*, p. 504.

128 Bhattacharjea, *Abdullah*, p. 219.

129 Abdullah, *Flames*, p. 154.

130 Mohammad Ayub Khan, *Friends Not Masters*, London, Oxford University Press, 1967, p. 128.

131 Bhattacharjea, *Abdullah*, p. 221.

132 Ramachandra Guha, 'Opening a Window in Kashmir', *World Policy Journal*, 1 September 2004, p. 92.

133 Singh, *Autobiography*, p. 284.

134 Bhattacharjea, *Abdullah*, p. 186.

135 Singh, *Autobiography*, p. 285.

136 Abdullah, *The Blazing Chinar*, p. 506.

137 Mullik, *My Years*, p. 176.

138 Abdullah, *The Blazing Chinar*, p. 507.

139 This is my speculation.
140 Najar, *Kashmir Accord (1975)*, p. iii.
141 Abdullah, *The Blazing Chinar*, p. 514.
142 Snedden, *Understanding Kashmir*, pp. 238–9.
143 Abdullah, *The Blazing Chinar*, p. 515.
144 'Sheikh Abdullah Speaks', *The Testament of Sheikh Abdullah*, p. 17.
145 Abdullah, *Flames*, p. 161.
146 Bhattacharjea, *Abdullah*, p. 227.
147 Sheikh Abdullah, 'Kashmir, India and Pakistan', *Foreign Affairs*, April 1965, pp. 528–35.
148 Abdullah, *The Blazing Chinar*, p. 333.
149 Abdullah, 'Kashmir, India and Pakistan', *Foreign Affairs*, p. 534.
150 *Ibid.*, pp. 534, 535.
151 David E. Lockwood, 'Resolving the Problem of Kashmir', *World Affairs*, Vol. 133, No. 3 (December 1970), p. 202.
152 Gundevia, 'On Sheikh Abdullah', *The Testament of Sheikh Abdullah*, p. 127.
153 Abdullah, *The Blazing Chinar*, p. 532.
154 Puri, *Kashmir: Towards Insurgency*, p. 51.
155 Abdullah, *Flames*, p. 157.
156 Schofield, *Kashmir in the Crossfire*, p. 196.
157 This was/is the name that the UNSC uses for the Kashmir dispute.
158 Ayub Khan, *Friends Not Masters*, p. 128.
159 'Sheikh Abdullah Speaks', *The Testament of Sheikh Abdullah*, p. 18.
160 Singh, *Autobiography*, p. 293.
161 Peter Lyon, 'Kashmir', *International Relations: Journal of David Davies Memorial Institute of International Studies*, Vol. 3, No. 2, October 1966, p. 116.
162 Abdullah, *Flames*, p. 135.
163 Lockwood, 'Sheikh Abdullah', p. 393.
164 'Sheikh Abdullah Speaks', *The Testament of Sheikh Abdullah*, p. 70.
165 Lockwood, 'Sheikh Abdullah', p. 385.
166 *The Times*, 3 January 1968.
167 Lockwood, 'Sheikh Abdullah', pp. 393, 395.
168 'Interviews On Release, 2nd January 1958', G. M. Shah, Editor, *Interviews & Speeches by Sher-i-Kashmir Sheikh Mohd. Abdullah*, [Srinagar], [All Jammu and Kashmir Plebiscite Front], 1968, p. 10.
169 'Sheikh Abdullah Speaks', *The Testament of Sheikh Abdullah*, pp. 50–1.
170 Lockwood, 'Sheikh Abdullah', p. 393.
171 'Press Conference at a Reception Held in Sheikh Mohammad Abdullah's Honor [sic] by the Kashmir Press Club at Amar Singh Club, Srinagar, March 6, 1968', in Khan, *Abdullah's Reflections*, p. 123.
172 Abdullah, *Flames*, pp. 65–6.
173 Bazaz, *The Shape of Things*, p. 32.
174 Ganai, *Kashmir National Conference*, p. 48.
175 Fazili, *Kashmir Government*, p. 78.
176 Para, *The Making of Modern Kashmir*, p. 224. His source for membership numbers was '*Mahaz*, Srinagar, 10 October 1964, p. 5'.
177 Bazaz, *The Shape of Things*, pp. 1, 30.
178 *Ibid.*, p. 34.

179 *Ibid.*, p. 30.
180 Lockwood, 'Sheikh Abdullah', pp. 384, 388, 390.
181 Haksar, *The Many Faces*, p. 43.
182 Sher-i-Kashmir Sheikh Mohd. Abdullah, *Speeches & Interviews*, Series 2, [Srinagar?], G. M. Shah, [1968]. pp. 46, 48.
183 This remainder of this paragraph is based on 'Speech at Hazratbal, Srinagar, March 15, 1968', in Khan, *Abdullah's Reflections*, pp. 62–5.
184 'Sheikh Abdullah Speaks', *The Testament of Sheikh Abdullah*, p. 86.
185 Najar, *Kashmir Accord (1975)*, p. 31.
186 'Sheikh Abdullah Speaks', *The Testament of Sheikh Abdullah*, pp. 87–8.
187 'Publisher's Preface', *Ibid.*, p. 12.
188 *The Times of India*, 25 March 1968.
189 Girilal Jain, 'Sheikh Abdullah's Dilemma', *Ibid.*, 24 October 1968.
190 Sydney H. Schanberg, 'Sheik [sic] in Kashmir Remains Key to Pakistani-Indian settlement', *The New York Times*, 5 October 1969.
191 Lockwood, 'Resolving the Problem', p. 208.
192 Gundevia, 'On Sheikh Abdullah', *The Testament of Sheikh Abdullah*, pp. 139–42.
193 Qasim, *My Life*, p. 118.
194 Abdullah, *The Blazing Chinar*, p. 526.
195 Lockwood, 'Resolving the Problem', p. 209.
196 *Ibid.*
197 *The Times of India*, 11 October 1968.
198 *Ibid.*, 18 October 1968.
199 B. L. Sharma, *Kashmir Awakes*, Delhi, Vikas Publications, 1971, p. 165.
200 Abdullah, *The Blazing Chinar*, p. 527.
201 Amanullah Khan, 'Sheikh Abdullah', *The Times of India*, 10 February 1968.
202 Sharma, *Kashmir Awakes*, p. 169.
203 Ganai, *Kashmir National Conference*, p. 28.
204 Abdullah, *The Blazing Chinar*, pp. 527, 528.
205 *The Times of India*, 11 October 1968.
206 Lockwood, 'Resolving the Problem', p. 209.
207 Fazili, *Kashmir Government*, p. 54.
208 Lockwood, 'Resolving the Problem', p. 209.
209 *The Times of India*, 9 December 1968.
210 'Appendix II (Document B): Evaluation Report by the Sub-Committee', in Khan, *Abdullah's Reflections*, pp. 181–8.
211 *Ibid.*, p. 182.
212 *The Times of India*, 8 June 1970.
213 'Appendix III (Document "C"): Internal Constitutional Set-up (Broad Outlines)', in Khan, *Abdullah's Reflections*, pp. 189–93.
214 *The Times of India*, 11 June 1970.
215 *Ibid.*, 16 October 1969.
216 *Ibid.*, 13 June 1970.
217 Bhattacharjea, *Abdullah*, p. 228.
218 Lamb, *Kashmir*, p. 285. Lamb provides no supporting reference for this significant claim.

219 Gundevia, 'On Sheikh Abdullah', *The Testament of Sheikh Abdullah*, pp. 139–42.
220 *Times of India*, 13 June 1970.
221 *The Times*, 14 October 1968.
222 Abdullah, *Flames*, p. 162.
223 *The Times of India*, 11 June 1970.
224 *Ibid.*, 14 June 1970.
225 Balraj Puri, 'State People's Convention: An Assessment', *Economic and Political Weekly*, 12 September 1970.
226 *The Times*, 14 October 1968.
227 Fazili, *Kashmir Government*, p. 54.
228 *The Times of India*, 7 October 1969.
229 *The New York Times*, 13 December 1971.
230 *The Times of India*, 20 April 1968.
231 Ganai, *Kashmir National Conference*, p. 65.
232 *Ibid.*, p. 59.
233 Lockwood, 'Sheikh Abdullah', pp. 395–6.
234 *The Times of India*, 9 June 1970.
235 Bhattacharjea, *Abdullah*, p. 228.
236 Haksar, *The Many Faces*, p. 307, footnote 45.
237 *The Times of India*, 14 June 1970.
238 *Ibid.*, 15 January 1968.
239 Lockwood, 'Sheikh Abdullah', p. 395.
240 Brian Cloughley, *A History of the Pakistan Army*, Oxford, Oxford University Press, second edition, 2000, pp. 222–38.
241 Bhattacharjea, *Abdullah*, p. 229.
242 Tariq Ali *et al.*, *Kashmir: The Case for Freedom*, London, Verso, 2011, p. 44.
243 Singh, *Autobiography*, pp. 284–5.
244 Qasim, *My Life*, p. 292.
245 Gundevia, 'On Sheikh Abdullah', *The Testament of Sheikh Abdullah*, pp. 145–6.
246 Abdullah, *Flames*, p. 164.
247 Abdullah, *The Blazing Chinar*, p. 536
248 Bhattacharjea, *Abdullah*, p. 229.
249 Qasim, *My Life*, p. 134.
250 Abdullah, *The Blazing Chinar*, p. 537.
251 Bhatia, *Jammu and Kashmir: Article 370*, p. 143.
252 'Appendix IV: The Kashmir Accord; Statement of Smt. Indira Gandhi, Prime Minister, in Parliament on Jammu & Kashmir on February 24, 1975', Fazili, *Kashmir Government*, p. 141.
253 'Presidential Address, Delivered by Sheikh Mohammad Abdullah at the Annual Session of All Jammu and Kashmir National Conference, held at Idgah Grounds, Jammu, April 24, 1976', in Khan, *Abdullah's Reflections*, p. 81.
254 Haksar, *The Many Faces*, p. 84.
255 Abdullah, *Flames*, p. 164.
256 D. D. Thakur, *My Life and Years in Kashmir Politics*, Delhi, Konark Publishers, 2005, p. 175.
257 Abdullah, *The Blazing Chinar*, p. 541.

Notes

258 Aditya Sinha, *Farooq Abdullah: Kashmir's Prodigal Son*, New Delhi, UBSPD, 1996, p. 96.

259 Bhattacharjea, *Abdullah*, pp. 236–7.

260 Qasim, *My Life*, p. 141.

261 Abdullah, *The Blazing Chinar*, p. 449.

262 Bhattacharjea, *Abdullah*, p. 229.

263 *The Times of India*, 2 August 1953.

264 'Presidential Address … 1976', in Khan, *Abdullah's Reflections*, p. 81.

265 *The Times of India*, 25 February 1975.

266 *Ibid.*, 26 February 1975.

267 Suresh Chander, 'Kashmir Accord, To the Editor', *Ibid.*, 1 March 1975.

268 Thakur, *My Life and Years*, p. 191.

269 Fazili, *Kashmir Government*, p. 24.

270 Bhattacharjea, *Abdullah*, p. xvii.

271 'Appendix IV: The Kashmir Accord', in Fazili, *Kashmir Government*, p. 145.

272 Qasim, *My Life*, p. 142. Qasim provides no reference for this quote by Sheikh Abdullah.

273 'Appendix IV: The Kashmir Accord', in Fazili, *Kashmir Government*, p. 142.

274 *The Times of India*, 14 March 1975.

275 Ganai, *Kashmir National Conference*, p. 81.

276 'Appendix IV: The Kashmir Accord', Fazili, *Kashmir Government*, pp. 142, 143.

277 Bhattacharjea, *Abdullah*, p. 236.

278 Ganai, *Kashmir National Conference*, p. 71.

279 *Ibid.*, pp. 31, 69.

280 *The Times of India*, 6 July 1975.

281 Fazili, *Kashmir Government*, p. 85.

282 *The Times of India*, 1 June 1977.

283 Ganai, *Kashmir National Conference*, p. 129.

284 *Ibid.*, p. 76.

285 *The Times of India*, 24 May 1977.

286 *Ibid.*, 25 May 1977.

287 *Ibid.*, 8 September 1977.

288 Abdullah, Flames, p. 169.

289 Habibullah, *My Kashmir*, p. 39.

290 Ganai, *Kashmir National Conference*, pp. 81, 89.

291 *Ibid.*, p. 83.

292 'Mir Qasim to Indira Gandhi (June 18, 1983)', in Qasim, *My Life*, p. 272.

293 Lamb, *Kashmir*, p. 320.

294 Muzamil Jaleel, 'J&K Resettlement Law: Who it is For, Why it Has Been Challenged in Supreme Court', *The Indian Express*, 11 December 2018.

295 Para, *The Making of Modern Kashmir*, p. 272.

296 *The Times of India*, 3 June 1982.

297 *Ibid.*, 16 September 1981.

298 Nasir A. Naqash and G. M. Shah, *Kashmir: From Crisis to Crisis*, New Delhi, APH Publishing Corporation, 1997, pp. 126, 131.

299 *The Times of India*, 5 October 1982.

300 Naqash and Shah, *Kashmir: From Crisis to Crisis*, p. 130.

301 *The Times of India*, 6 October 1982.

302 Jaleel, 'J&K Resettlement Law', *The Indian Express*, 11 December 2018.

303 'Centre Scraps Jammu And Kashmir Resettlement Law Which Allowed Return of Residents Who Emigrated to Pakistan', *Swarajya*, 17 December 2019, https://swarajyamag.com/insta/centre-scraps-jammu-and-kashmir-resettlement-law-which-allowed-return-of-residents-who-emigrated-to-pakistan [accessed 2 June 2010].

304 Naqash and Shah, *Kashmir: From Crisis to Crisis*, p. 131.

305 Inder Malhotra, *The Times of India*, 3 June 1982.

306 Ganai, *Kashmir National Conference*, p. 105.

307 Lamb, *Kashmir*, p. 320.

308 Ganai, *Kashmir National Conference*, pp. 152–3.

309 'Presidential Address ... 1976', in Khan, *Abdullah's Reflections*, p. 77.

310 *Ibid.*, p. 74.

311 *The Testament of Sheikh Abdullah*, pp. 38–9. The date that he was asked the question is unclear, but it was probably 1968.

312 Malhotra, *The Times of India*, 3 June 1982.

313 'Sheikh Abdullah Speaks', *The Testament of Sheikh Abdullah*, pp. 29, 33.

314 *The Civil & Military Gazette*, 30 September 1947.

315 Abdullah, *The Blazing Chinar*, p. 528.

316 Bazaz, *The Shape of Things*, p. 34

317 Fazili, *Kashmir Government*, p. 2.

318 Mullik, *My Years*, p. 195.

319 Singh, *Autobiography*, p. 221.

320 Abdullah, *The Blazing Chinar*, p. 188.

321 'Viceroy's Personal Report No. 10', 27 June 1947, in *The Transfer of Power*, Volume XI, p. 687.

322 Abdullah, *Flames*, p. 76.

323 Snedden, *Understanding Kashmir*, p. 192.

324 Lockwood, 'Sheikh Abdullah', pp. 382, 384.

325 'Sheikh Abdullah Speaks', *The Testament of Sheikh Abdullah*, p. 20.

326 'Presidential Address ... 1976', in Khan, *Abdullah's Reflections*, p. 75.

327 'Sheikh Abdullah's Presidential Address (24 April 1976), Qasim, *My Life*, p. 258.

328 Bhattacharjea, *Abdullah*, p. 235.

329 *The Times of India*, 17 May 1982.

330 Taseer, *The Kashmir*, p. 101.

331 *Ibid.*, pp. 131–2, 134, quoting from her interview with Pandit Jayalal Kaul, a long-term Kashmiri observer of Sheikh Abdullah.

332 'Inaugural Address of Sheikh Mohammad Abdullah Delivered at the Convention of Delegates, Jammu and Kashmir: August 11, 1974, Mujahid Manzil, which was the rallying point of Kashmiri nationalist and resistance politics, Srinagar', in Khan, *Abdullah's Reflections*, p. 67.

333 'Presidential Address ... 1976', in *Ibid.*, p. 69.

334 'Sheikh Mohammad Abdullah's View Explained: Second Plenary Session, J&K People's Convention, June 8–13, 1970', in *Ibid.*, p. 103.

335 Bakshi, *Kashmir: Political Problems*, p. 271.

336 Ajai Sahni, 'India: J&K: A New Reality, South Asia Terrorism Review', *South Asia Terrorism Portal*, 12 August 2019, www.satp.org/south-asia-intelligence-review-Volume-18-No-7#assessment1 [accessed 15 August 2019].

Chapter 7 Kashmiris and independence since 1988

1 Manoj Joshi, *The Lost Rebellion*, New Delhi, Penguin, 1999, pp. 1–11.

2 *Ibid.*, p. 53.

3 As noted in my Introduction, this is the correct name for this group.

4 Singh, *Kashmir: A Tragedy*, p. 206.

5 *Times of India*, 9 August 1980.

6 Mohammad Ishaq Khan, 'Evolution of My Identity vis-a-vis Islam and Kashmir', in Khan, *The Parchment*, p. 29.

7 Faheem, 'Interrogating the Ordinary', in Duschinski *et al.*, *Resisting Occupation*, p. 241.

8 Qasim, *My Life*, pp. 298–9.

9 N. Y. Dole, 'Kashmir: A Deep-rooted Alienation', *Economic and Political Weekly*, 5–12 May 1990, p. 978.

10 Navnita Chadha Behera, *Demystifying Kashmir*, Brookings, Washington D.C., 2006, p. 48.

11 Joshi, *The Lost Rebellion*, pp. 33–5.

12 Christopher Snedden, *Paramountcy, Patrimonialism and the People of Jammu and Kashmir, 1947–1991*, PhD dissertation, Melbourne, La Trobe University, 2001, various pages.

13 Singh, *Kashmir: A Tragedy*, p. 204.

14 Joshi, *The Lost Rebellion*, p. 17.

15 *The Times of India*, 20 November 1981.

16 The Press Council of India, *Crisis and Credibility*, New Delhi, Lancer International, 1991, p. 61.

17 Behera, *Demystifying Kashmir*, p. 146.

18 Singh, *Kashmir: A Tragedy*, p. 1.

19 *Jammu and Kashmir: The Impact of Lockdowns on Human Rights: August 2019– July 2020 Report*, The Forum for Human Rights in Jammu and Kashmir, 2020, p. 45.

20 Singh, *Kashmir: A Tragedy*, pp. xii, 38.

21 *Jammu and Kashmir: The Impact of Lockdowns on Human Rights*, p. 56.

22 Basharat Peer, *Curfewed Night: A Frontline Memoir of Life, Love and War in Kashmir*, London, Harper Press, 2010, pp. 75–6.

23 Joshi, *The Lost Rebellion*, p. 13.

24 Faheem, 'Interrogating the Ordinary', in Duschinski *et al.*, *Resisting Occupation*, pp. 241–2.

25 *The Times of India*, 9 February 1984.

26 *Ibid.*, 2 March 1984.

27 Haksar, *The Many Faces*, p. 108.

28 *The Times of India*, 11 February 1985.

29 Haksar, *The Many Faces*, p. 119.

30 Snedden, *Understanding Kashmir*, p. 202.
31 Joshi, *The Lost Rebellion*, p. 23.
32 Askari H. Zaidi, 'Doubts over groups behind Kashmir blasts', *The Times of India*, 13 September 1988.
33 *Ibid.*, 15 April 1989.
34 Haksar, *The Many Faces*, p. 110.
35 Joshi, *The Lost Rebellion*, pp. 41–2.
36 *Ibid.*, p. 42.
37 Singh, *Kashmir: A Tragedy*, p. 132.
38 *Ibid.*, p. 154.
39 Joshi, *The Lost Rebellion*, pp. 73–4.
40 *Ibid.*, p. 73.
41 Haksar, *The Many Faces*, p. 161.
42 Soz, *Kashmir*, p. 181.
43 Behera, *Demystifying Kashmir*, pp. 150-1.
44 Ramachandra Guha, 'The Many Tragedies of the Kashmiri Pandits', *Hindustan Times*, 8 September 2019, www.hindustantimes.com/columns/the-many-tragedies-of-the-kashmiri-pandits/story-8QKwlRf8ZrsfxhXlqwUEMM.html [accessed 25 July 2020]. Guha is quoting Sonia Jabbar in her essay 'The Spirit of Place'.
45 Joshi, *The Lost Rebellion*, p. 65.
46 *Jammu and Kashmir: The Impact of Lockdowns on Human Rights*, p. 24.
47 Office of the United Nations High Commissioner for Human Rights [OHCHR], *Report on the Situation of Human Rights in Kashmir: Developments in the Indian State of Jammu and Kashmir from June 2016 to April 2018, and General Human Rights Concerns in Azad Jammu and Kashmir and Gilgit-Baltistan*, Geneva, United Nations Human Rights: Office of the High Commissioner, 14 June 2018; OHCHR, *Update of the Situation of Human Rights in Indian-Administered Kashmir and Pakistan-Administered Kashmir from May 2018 to April 2019*, Geneva, United Nations Human Rights: Office of the High Commissioner, 8 July 2019.
48 OHCHR, *Update … May 2018 to April 2019*, p. 5.
49 Joshi, *The Lost Rebellion*, p. 46.
50 Snedden, *The Untold Story*, pp. 101, 347, footnote 200; Behera, *Demystifying Kashmir*, p. 149.
51 Khan, *The JKLF Roadmap*.
52 *Ibid.*, p. 13.
53 Khan, *Free Kashmir*, p. 224.
54 Behera, *Demystifying Kashmir*, p. 148.
55 Haksar, *The Many Faces*, p. 141.
56 Mudasir Ahmad, 'A Brief History of the J&K Liberation Front, Now Banned Under UAPA', *The Wire*, 23 March 2019, https://thewire.in/security/kashmir-jklf-ban-yasin-malik [accessed 27 September 2019]. UAPA is the acronym for the Unlawful Activities (Prevention) Act, 1967.
57 'India – Terrorist, Insurgent and Extremist Groups Jammu & Kashmir', *South Asia Terrorism Portal*, www.satp.org/terrorist-groups/india-jammukashmir.htm [accessed 10 February 2020].
58 Iffat Malik, *Kashmir: Ethnic Conflict, International Dispute*, Oxford, Oxford University Press, 2002, pp. 293–4, 298.

59 Manu Pubby and Dipanjan Roy Chaudhury, 'The Resistance Front: New Name of Terror Groups in Kashmir', *The Economic Times*, 29 April 2020, https://economictimes. indiatimes.com/news/defence/the-resistance-front-new-name-of-terror-groups-in-kashmir/articleshow/75440416.cms [accessed 4 May 2020].

60 'Pakistan is Always Seen as the Rogue: SPIEGEL Interview with Pervez Musharraf (Interview conducted by Susanne Koelbl)', *Spiegel*, 4 October 2010, www.spiegel.de/international/world/0,1518,721110,00.html [accessed 10 February 2020].

61 Joshi, *The Lost Rebellion*, p. 140.

62 Cloughley, *A History of the Pakistan Army*, pp. 376–7.

63 Singh, *Kashmir: A Tragedy*, pp. 216–17.

64 Soz, *Kashmir*, p. 175.

65 Behera, *State, Identity and Violence*, p. 229.

66 *Ibid.*, p. 199.

67 Christopher Snedden, 'Kashmir: Placating Frustrated People', in Edward Aspinall, Robin Jeffrey and Anthony J. Regan, Editors, *Diminishing Conflicts in Asia and the Pacific: Why Some Subside and Others Don't*, Abingdon, Routledge, 2013, pp. 235–49.

68 Whitehead, *A Mission in Kashmir*, p. 15.

69 It is considered a war as more than 1,000 people died in this India–Pakistan military engagement.

70 'Fatalities in Terrorist Violence 1988–2019', *South Asia Terrorism Portal*, 19 November 2019, www.satp.org/satporgtp/countries/india/states/jandk/data_sheets/annual_casualties.htm [accessed 10 February 2020].

71 Ramesh Vinayak, 'Mujahideen Can't Drive Away or Defeat Indian Army: Abdul Ghani Lone', *India Today*, 3 June 2002.

72 Praveen Swami, 'Danger Signals from the Valley, *Frontline*, 10 October 2003.

73 My list of major events is not exhaustive. For further information, see: Jammu Kashmir Coalition of Civil Society's website: http://jkccs.net, or South Asia Terrorism Portal's website: www.satp.org.

74 *A Brief Note ... 1933*, p. 1.

75 Zahid Rafiq, 'Macchil Fake Encounter: Life Term for 5 Army Men', *The Hindu*, 13 November 2014, www.thehindu.com/news/national/other-states/Macchil-fake-encounter-life-term-for-5-Army-men/article11008202.ece/amp/ [accessed 7 June 2020].

76 'Macchil "Fake" Encounter: Tribunal Stays Life Term to Soldiers, Gives Them Bail', *Hindustan Times*, 26 July 2017, www.hindustantimes.com/india-news/machil-fake-encounter-tribunal-stays-life-term-to-five-soldiers-gives-them-bail/story-bea8T1JsYv86diYm5dvERJ_amp.html [accessed 7 June 2020].

77 Shabir Ibn Yusuf, 'Amnesty Announced by Omar in 2011 Awaits Implementation', *Greater Kashmir*, 14 August 2014, www.greaterkashmir.com/news/kashmir/amnesty-announced-by-omar-in-2011-awaits-implementation/ [accessed 7 June 2020].

78 See Haksar, *The Many Faces*, pp. 186–8, and various other pages.

79 'Davinder Singh's Custody Extended Till June 16', *The Hindu*, 18 May 2020, www.thehindu.com/news/national/davinder-singhs-custody-extended-till-june-16/article31616218.ece/amp/ [accessed 7 June 2020].

80 In various conversations with Indian Army officers in recent years, a number have informed me that they called Wani and the like 'Facebook fighters' because Indian security forces rarely, if ever, encountered them in direct confrontations.

81 Gowhar Geelani, *Rage and Reason*, New Delhi, Rupa Publications, 2019, pp. xv, 2.

82 *Annual Human Rights Review 2019, A Review of Human Rights Situation in Jammu and Kashmir*, Jammu Kashmir Coalition of Civil Society & Association of Parents of Disappeared Persons, Srinagar, 31 December 2019, p. 6.

83 OHCHR, *Report on the Situation of Human Rights in Kashmir*, pp. 17, 22.

84 'Datasheet – Jammu & Kashmir: Yearly Fatalities', *South Asia Terrorism Portal*, www.satp.org/datasheet-terrorist-attack/fatalities/india-jammukashmir [accessed 7 June 2020].

85 OHCHR, *Report on the Situation of Human Rights in Kashmir*.

86 OHCHR, *Update ... May 2018 to April 2019*, pp. 2, 30–3.

87 *Ibid.*, pp. 3, 9.

88 OHCHR, *Report on the Situation of Human Rights in Kashmir*, p. 6.

89 There are various spellings of the term *azadi*. In my research, I have found it written as *azadi, azaadi, aazadi* and *aazaadi*. The most frequent spelling appears to be *azadi*. Throughout this chapter, I use the spelling *azadi*, unless quoting. All quotations appear exactly as they were in the version from which I have extracted them, including with their original punctuation.

90 Meera Sharma, 'Why is Kashmir Burning?', *The Indian Express*, 20 February 1990.

91 P. S. Verma, *Jammu and Kashmir at the Political Crossroads*, New Delhi, Vikas, 1994, p. 243.

92 Khan Ansur, '"Hum Kya Chahte? AZADI" – The Slogan Which Always Reverberates in Kashmir', *Khan Ansur blog*, 26 August 2016, https://khanansur.wordpress.com/2016/08/26/hum-kya-chahte-azadi-the-slogan-which-always-reverberates-in-kashmir/ [accessed 20 November 2018].

93 Haksar, *The Many Faces*, p. 216.

94 Sumantra Bose, *Kashmir: Roots of Conflict, Paths to Peace*, New Delhi, Vistaar, 2003, p. 130.

95 All quotations in this paragraph are from Safeena Wani, 'Kashmir's Anthems of Azadi', *Arré*, 25 April 2017, www.arre.co.in/politics/kashmir-india-pakistan-burhan-wani-protests-slogans-kashmir-conflict/ [accessed 15 November 2018].

96 Wani states that her source for this chant is 'Zareef Ahmed Zareef, a Kashmiri historian and poet'.

97 'Appendix 2: Text of letter dated 26 October 1947 from Sir Hari Singh, the Maharaja of Jammu and Kashmir to Lord Mountbatten, the Governor-General of India', in Singh, *Autobiography*, p. 330.

98 *The Civil & Military Gazette*, 25 October 1947.

99 *Ibid.*, 1 November 1947.

100 Ian Stephens, *Horned Moon*, London, Chatto & Windus, 1953, pp. 116–17. Stephens was a former British editor of the respected Indian newspaper, *The Statesman*. I have met Indians who cannot bring themselves to utter the 'heinous' term 'Azad Kashmir'.

101 Syed Manzoor H. Gilani, *Constitutional Development in Azad Jammu & Kashmir*, Lahore, National Book Depot, 1988, 'The Azad Jammu and Kashmir Government Act, 1970', Appendix VIII, Appendixes Section, pp. 201–3.

102 Martin Sökefeld, '*Jang Āzādī*', in Stellrecht, *The Past in the Present*, p. 62.

103 *Ibid.*, p. 66.

104 Bazaz, *The History of Struggle*, p. 124.

105 Bazaz, *Azad Kashmir*, p. 58.

106 Praveen Swami, *India, Pakistan and the Secret Jihad: The Covert War in Kashmir, 1947–2004*, London, Routledge, 2007, p. 79.

Notes

107 Farrukh Faheem, 'Three Generations of Kashmir's Azaadi: A Short History of Discontent', *Economic and Political Weekly*, Vol. 51, No. 35, 27 August 2016, www.epw.in/journal/2016/35/web-exclusives/three-generations-kashmirs-azaadi-short-history-discontent.html [accessed 27 October 2017].

108 Joshi, *The Lost Rebellion*, p. 2.

109 *The Times of India*, 1 June 1977.

110 Verma, *Jammu and Kashmir*, p. 219.

111 Press Council of India, *Crisis and Credibility*, pp. 61–2.

112 Markandey Katju, 'Calling for Kashmir's Azadi is Not Sedition, Even if it's Illogical and Reactionary', *The Wire*, 20 August 2016, https://thewire.in/rights/calling-for-kashmirs-azadi-is-not-sedition-even-if-its-illogical-and-reactionary [accessed 14 May 2020].

113 *Keesing's Record of World Events*, Volume 36, No. 3, March 1990, p. 37348.

114 *Ibid.*, Volume 36, No. 1, January 1990, p. 37183.

115 *Ibid.*, Volume 36, No. 6, June 1990, p. 37530.

116 Joshi, *The Lost Rebellion*, p. 28.

117 Swami, *India, Pakistan and the Secret Jihad*, p. 167.

118 Dole, 'Kashmir: A Deep-rooted Alienation', p. 978. The delegation was from the Rashtra Seva Dal (Organisation to Serve the Nation).

119 Swami, *India, Pakistan and the Secret Jihad*, p. 104.

120 Victoria Schofield, *Kashmir in Conflict*, London, I. B. Taurus, 2000, p. 114.

121 Khan, *The JKLF Roadmap*, p. 13.

122 Schofield, *Kashmir in Conflict*, p. 114;

123 Khan, *Free Kashmir*, p. 208.

124 Khan, *The JKLF Roadmap*, pp. 2, 13.

125 Swami, *India, Pakistan and the Secret Jihad*, pp. 182–3.

126 Amanullah Khan, *Kashmir: Who and How to Bell the Cat*, Rawalpindi, Jammu Kashmir Liberation Front, 1998, p. 5.

127 Amanullah Khan, *The Best & Easiest Solution of Kashmir Issue*, Rawalpindi, Jammu Kashmir Liberation Front, 2007, p. 13.

128 Zutshi, *Languages of Belonging*, p. 27.

129 William Dalrymple, 'Kashmir Massacre Turns Hell into Heaven', *Sunday Correspondent*, 2 February 1990, in Shafi Khan, 'Extracts from Foreign Press', *Focus on Kashmir*, after p. 30.

130 Susan H. Greenberg with Sudip Mazumdar, 'A Bloody Challenge for Singh', *Newsweek*, 5 February 1990.

131 Sharma, 'Why is Kashmir Burning?'

132 Behera, *State, Identity and Violence*, p. 158.

133 Kuldip Nayar, 'Terrorists Call Shots in Srinagar', *India Abroad*, 8 September 1989.

134 M. K. Dhar, 'That Fateful Night', in Devendra Swarup and Sushil Aggarwal, *The Roots of [the] Kashmir Problem*, New Delhi, Manthan Prakashan, 1992, pp. 17, 19.

135 *Ibid.*, p. 17.

136 *Ibid.*, p. 19.

137 Shahla Hussain, 'Kashmiri Visions of Freedom', in Zutshi, *Kashmir*, p. 105.

138 'The Refugees Speak Out', in Swarup and Aggarwal, *The Roots of [the] Kashmir Problem*, p. 34.

139 *Ibid.*, p. 35.

140 *Ibid.*, p. 36.

141 Sumantra Bose, *The Challenge in Kashmir: Democracy, Self-determination, and a Just Peace*, New Delhi, Sage, 1997, p. 72.

142 Sharma, 'Why is Kashmir Burning?'

143 Behera, *State, Identity and Violence*, Appendix VI, pp. 326–8.

144 Ishaq Khan, 'Evolution of My Identity', in Khan, *The Parchment*, p. 31.

145 Sharma, 'Why is Kashmir Burning?'

146 Whitehead, *A Mission in Kashmir*, p. 15

147 Ahmad, 'A Brief History of the J&K Liberation Front, Now Banned Under UAPA'.

148 Malik, *Kashmir: Ethnic Conflict*, p. 323.

149 Haksar, *The Many Faces*, pp. 210–11, 218.

150 Rahiba R. Parveen, 'What is the JKLF, the Organisation Banned by the Modi Government?', *The Print*, 23 March 2019, https://theprint.in/india/what-is-the-jklf-the-organisation-banned-by-the-modi-government/210560/ [accessed 11 February 2020].

151 'Kashmir: Pro-freedom Leaders Update "Go India Go Back" Program', *Kashmir Watch*, 30 July 2016, http://kashmirwatch.com/kashmir-pro-freedom-leaders-update-go-india-go-back-program/ [accessed 17 November 2018].

152 Geelani, *Rage and Reason*, pp. 4–5. Geelani provides an interesting discussion about how Kashmiris felt about Wani and his death.

153 Rahul Tripathi, 'Before Dineshwar Sharma: What Earlier Panels to Reach Out to J&K Tried, What They Achieved', *The Indian Express*, 14 November 2017, https://indianexpress.com/article/explained/what-earlier-panels-to-reach-out-toJK-tried-what-they-achieved-jammu-kashmir-interlocutor-dinsehwar-sharma-burhan-wani-dialogue-valley-4936140/ [accessed 27 June 2020].

154 'Kashmiris Failed To Describe "Azadi Term": Padgaonkar', *Kashmir Times*, 9 November 2013, www.kashmirtimes.in/newsdet.aspx?q=16018/ [accessed 5 March 2020].

155 '"Deceit" of Dialogue', *Kashmir Life*, 24 October 2011, https://kashmirlife.net/deceit-of-dialogue-1846/ [accessed 27 June 2020]; and Tripathi, 'Before Dineshwar Sharma'.

156 Singh, *Kashmir: A Tragedy*, p. 124.

157 A. G. Noorani, *The Kashmir Dispute 1947–2012*, Karachi, Oxford University Press, 2014, pp. 2, 81, 118, 224, 421.

158 Ishaq Khan, 'Evolution of My Identity', in Khan, *The Parchment*, pp. 30, 31, 32.

159 Reeta Chowdhari Tremblay, 'Contested Governance, Competing Nationalisms and Disenchanted Publics: Kashmir Beyond Intractability?' in Zutshi, *Kashmir*, p. 221.

160 Chitralekha Zutshi, 'Introduction: New Directions in the Study of Kashmir', in Zutshi, *Kashmir*, p. 8.

161 Shahla Hussain, 'Kashmiri Visions of Freedom', in Zutshi, *Kashmir*, p. 107.

162 Mona Bhan, Haley Duschinski and Ather Zia, '"Rebels of the Streets": Violence, Protest, and Freedom in Kashmir', in Duschinski *et al.*, *Resisting Occupation*, p. 23.

163 Balraj Puri, 'Unfolding History', p. 149.

164 'Smriti Irani on Chidambaram's Kashmir comment: Disgusting That he Speaks About Breaking India into Pieces', *India Today*, 28 October 2017, http://indiatoday.intoday.in/story/smriti-irani-chidambaram-kashmir-comment-greater-autonomy-jammu-and-kashmir/1/1077492.html [accessed 17 November 2018].

165 Shalaka Shinde, 'Former RAW Chief A S Dulat's Surprise Take on Kashmir', *Hindustan Times*, 23 April 2018, www.hindustantimes.com/pune-news/former-raw-chief-a-s-dulat-s-surprise-take-on-kashmir/story-Xwg09nOO3ck6JP2vYhaXfK.html [accessed 28 April 2018].

166 Syed Ali Shah Geelani, *Kashmir: Nava-e Hurriyat* [*Kashmir: Voice of Freedom*], Srinagar, Mizan Publications, 1995.

167 Sikand, 'Jihad, Islam and Kashmir: Syed Ali Shah Gilani's Political Project', p. 128.

168 *Ibid.*, pp. 133, 134.

169 Riyaz Wani, 'How Al-Qaeda Came to Kashmir', *The Diplomat*, 20 December 2017, https://thediplomat.com/2017/12/how-al-qaeda-came-to-kashmir/ [accessed 24 December 2017].

170 Robert W. Bradnock, *Kashmir: Paths to Peace*, London, Chatham House, 2010, pp. 1, 15, 16, 19.

171 *Ibid.*, p. 30.

172 Madhu Kishwar, 'Why Fear People's Choice? Calling Pakistan's Bluff on Plebiscite in J and K', *Economic and Political Weekly*, 6 September 2003, pp. 3773, 3775.

173 *Jammu and Kashmir: The Impact of Lockdowns on Human Rights*, p. 15.

174 'Jammu & Kashmir: Timeline (Terrorist Activities) – 2019', *South Asia Terrorism Portal*, www.satp.org/terrorist-activitity/india-jammukashmir-Feb-2019 [accessed 5 June 2020].

175 Malik, *Kashmir: Ethnic Conflict*, p. 302.

176 'Pak Suffered "No Damage" in Balakot Air Strike: Pak Army', *Business Standard*, 29 April 2019. www.business-standard.com/article/pti-stories/pak-suffered-no-damage-in-balakot-air-strike-pak-army-119042900881_1.html [accessed 1 May 2019].

177 *Census of India, 1941*, Part III: Village Tables, p. 346.

178 'Jammu & Kashmir: Assessment – 2020', *South Asia Terrorism Portal*, www.satp.org/terrorism-assessment/india-jammukashmir [accessed 5 June 2020].

179 Amar Grover, 'Postcard from … Kashmir: Still a hotspot – but for the right reasons', *Financial Times*, 3 February 2011, www.ft.com/intl/ cms/s/2/9abef77e-4819-11e1-b1b4-00144feabdco.html#axzz1lf489NCY [accessed 7 February 2011].

180 'Governor's Rule Imposed in J&K After BJP Withdraws from Alliance With PDP', *The Wire*, 20 June 2018, https://thewire.in/politics/governor-rule-bjp-pdp-jammu-kashmir-government [accessed 5 June 2020].

181 'English Rendering of PM's Address to the Nation', *Prime Minister's Office*, 8 August 2019, https://pib.gov.in/PressReleaseDetail.aspx?PRID=1581598 [accessed 10 August 2019].

182 'The Constitution of India', Parts I to XXII, *National Portal of India*, New Delhi, Government of India, undated, pp. 243–4, www.india.gov.in/sites/upload_files/npi/files/coi_part_full.pdf [accessed 5 June 2020].

183 Ministry of Law and Justice, 'The Constitution (Application to Jammu and Kashmir) Order, 2019 C. O. 272', *The Gazette of India*, Controller of Publications, Delhi, 2019, http://egazette.nic.in/WriteReadData/2019/210049.pdf [accessed 6 August 2019].

184 Ministry of Law and Justice, 'Declaration Under Article 370(3) of the Constitution "C. O. 273"', *The Gazette of India*, Controller of Publications, Delhi, 2019, http://egazette.nic.in/WriteReadData/2019/210243.pdf [accessed 6 August 2019].

185 *Jammu and Kashmir: The Impact of Lockdowns on Human Rights*, p. 8.

186 'The Constitution of India', Appendix I & II, *National Portal of India*, pp. 360–1 www.india.gov.in/sites/upload_files/npi/files/coi_part_full.pdf [accessed 5 June 2020].

187 Jeet H. Shroff, 'Four Reasons Why the Presidential Order on Kashmir is Not Kosher, Yet', *The Hindu Business Line*, 6 August 2019, www.thehindubusinessohline.com/opinion/three-reasons-why-the-presidential-order-on-kashmir-is-not-kosher-yet/article28836245.ece/amp/ [accessed 7 August 2019].

188 Jaleel, 'J&K Resettlement Law', *The Indian Express*, 11 December 2018.

189 Ministry of Law and Justice, 'The Jammu and Kashmir Reorganisation Act, 2019 No. 34 of 2019', *The Gazette of India*, Controller of Publications, Delhi, 9 August 2019, http://egazette.nic.in/WriteReadData/2019/210407.pdf [accessed 10 August 2019].

190 *Ibid.*, p. 28.

191 Sana Shakil, 'Girish Chandra Murmu Appointed as New L-G of Jammu Kashmir, Satya Pal Malik Moved to Goa', *The New Indian Express*, 25 October 2019, https://newindianexpress.com/nation/2019/oct/25/girish-chandra-murmu-appointed-as-new-governor-of-jammu-and-kashmir-satya-pal-malik-moved-to-goa-2052937.html [accessed 5 June 2020].

192 Auriol Wiegold, 'The Jammu and Kashmir Reorganisation Act 2019 – Progress on the BJP's Election Manifesto', *Future Directions International*, www.futuredirections.org.au/publication/the-jammu-and-kashmir-reorganisation-act-2019-progress-on-the-bjps-election-manifesto/ [accessed 5 June 2020].

193 'The Jammu and Kashmir Reorganisation Act, 2019', p. 14.

194 Peerzada Ashiq, 'Won't Participate in J&K Delimitation Commission: NC', *The Hindu*, 30 May 2020, www.thehindu.com/news/national/other-states/wont-participate-in-jk-delimitation-commission-nc/article31706534.ece [accessed 2 July 2020].

195 *Jammu and Kashmir: The Impact of Lockdowns on Human Rights*, pp. 8, 12, 14.

196 Geelani, *Rage and Reason*, p. 3.

197 Riyaz Wani, 'Life Under Siege in Kashmir', *The Diplomat*, 21 January 2020, https://thediplomat.com/2020/01/life-under-siege-in-kashmir/ [accessed 23 January 2020].

198 Ministry of Home Affairs, 'Jammu and Kashmir Reorganisation (Adaptation of State Laws) Order, 2020', *Press Information Bureau*, 1 April 2020, https://pib.gov.in/PressReleaseIframePage.aspx?PRID=1609804 [accessed 5 June 2020].

199 'Ministry of Home Affairs (Department of Jammu, Kashmir and Ladakh Affairs) Order New Delhi, the 31st March, 2020', *The Gazette of India*, Controller of Publications, Delhi, 2019, http://164.100.117.97/WriteReadData/userfiles/218978.pdf [accessed 5 June 2020].

200 Naseer Ganai and Bhavna Vij-Aurora, 'After Revocation of Article 370, Has China Become A "Third Party" To Kashmir Dispute?', *Outlook*, 15 June 2020, www.outlookindia.com/magazine/story/india-news-after-revocation-of-article-370-has-china-become-a-third-party-to-kashmir-dispute/303297 [accessed 5 June 2020].

201 '"Demographic Flooding": India Introduces New Kashmir Domicile Law', *Al Jazeera*, 1 April 2020, www.aljazeera.com/news/2020/04/flooding-india-introduces-kashmir-domicile-law-200401100651450.html [accessed 5 June 2020].

202 'Kashmir Muslims Fear Demographic Shift as Thousands get Residency', *Al Jazeera*, 28 June 2020, www.aljazeera.com/news/2020/06/kashmir-muslims-fear-demographic-shift-thousands-residency-200627113940283.html [accessed 29 June 2020].

203 It was almost impossible to find this policy on the internet. A copy of 'GDC-89/CM/2020 dated May 12, 2020' and approved by 'Administrative Council Decision No. 61/8/2020 on 29 April 2020' is available at 'Jammu and Kashmir Media Policy 2020', *Kashmir Life*, 11 June 2020, https://kashmirlife.net/jammu-and-kashmir-media-policy-2020-236330/ [accessed 28 June 2020].

204 *Jammu and Kashmir: The Impact of Lockdowns on Human Rights*, p. 52.

205 'Maps of Newly Formed Union Territories of Jammu Kashmir [sic] and Ladakh, with the Map of India', *Press Information Bureau*, 2 November 2019, www.mha.gov.in/sites/

default/files/PressRelease_NoteonUTofJ&K%26Ladakh_04112019.pdf [accessed 7 June 2020].

206 Azaan Javaid, 'Outside Firms Enter Mining Race in J&K, Lease Earnings Touch Crores From Lakhs', *The Print*, 6 February 2020, https://theprint.in/india/outside-firms-enter-mining-race-in-JK-lease-earnings-touch-crores-from-lakhs/360175/ [accessed 7 February 2020].

207 *Sankalp Patra Lok Sabha 2019*, Bharatiya Janata Party, New Delhi, 2019, p. 12.

208 *Ek Bharat – Shreshtha Bharat 2014*, Bharatiya Janata Party, New Delhi, 2014, p. 8.

209 'Jitendra Singh Says Government Has Started Discussions to Revoke Article 370; Backtracks Later', *The Economic Times*, 28 May 2014, https://economictimes.indiatimes.com/news/politics-and-nation/jitendra-singh-says-government-has-started-discussions-to-revoke-article-370-backtracks-later/articleshow/35642188.cms?utm_source=contentofinterest&utm_medium=text&utm_campaign=cppst [accessed 1 June 2020].

210 'Narendra Modi's First Visit to Kashmir as PM Triggers Shutdown', *The Guardian*, 4 July 2014, www.theguardian.com/world/2014/jul/04/narendra-modi-visit-kashmir-shutdown-protest [accessed 1 June 2020].

211 'English Rendering of PM's address to the Nation', *Prime Minister's Office*, 8 August 2019, https://pib.gov.in/PressReleseDetail.aspx?PRID=1581598 [accessed 10 August 2019].

212 Gowhar Bhat, 'Durbar Move Cost: Rs 80 Crore/Year', *Greater Kashmir*, 14 March 2015, www.greaterkashmir.com/news/more/news/durbar-move-cost-rs-80-crore-year/%3famp [accessed 5 June 2020].

213 *Annual Human Rights Review 2019*, Jammu Kashmir Coalition of Civil Society, p. 6.

214 *Jammu and Kashmir: The Impact of Lockdowns on Human Rights*, p. 8.

215 *Ibid.*, pp. 8–9.

216 Mehak Mahajan, 'Making Kashmir a Union Territory is Bogus and Pointless: Former Interlocutor Radha Kumar', *The Caravan*, 7 August 2019.

217 'After All-party Meeting, Gupkar Declaration Issued', *Kashmir Life*, 4 August 2019, https://kashmirlife.net/after-all-party-meeting-gupkar-declaration-issued-217172/ [accessed 20 June 2020].

218 *Jammu and Kashmir: The Impact of Lockdowns on Human Rights*, pp. 8, 9, 58.

219 I am not advocating for or against an independent Jammu and Kashmir or an independent Kashmir being established. For my stance on resolving the Kashmir dispute, see Snedden, *The Untold Story*, pp. 222–7.

220 All figures in this paragraph for the growth of the United Nations are from 'Growth in United Nations Membership, 1945–present', *United Nations*, undated, www.un.org/en/sections/member-states/growth-united-nations-membership-1945-present/index.html [accessed 6 April 2020].

221 'Member States', *United Nations*, undated, www.un.org/en/member-states/ [accessed 26 March 2019].

222 Based on information contained in 'Popular Statistical Tables, Country (Area) and Regional Profiles', *UNdata*, 2015, http://data.un.org/en/index.html [accessed 8 July 2019], and 'List of Countries and Dependencies by Area', *Wikipedia*, undated [2018?], https://en.wikipedia.org/wiki/List_of_countries_and_dependencies_by_area [accessed 9 July 2019].

223   Analysed from data at 'Popular Indicators', *World Bank*, [2015?], https://databank.
      worldbank.org/indicator/SP.POP.TOTL/1ff4a498/Popular-Indicators# [accessed 28
      July 2019].

224   'Divisions & Districts', *Jammu & Kashmir: Official State Portal*, undated [based on
      2011 Census of India?], https://jk.gov.in/jammukashmir/?q=divisions [accessed 8 July
      2019].

225   This paragraph is based on 'Landlocked Countries 2020', *World Population Review*,
      http://worldpopulationreview.com/countries/landlocked-countries/ [accessed 7 March
      2020].

226   Directorate of Economic & Statistics J&K, *Economic Survey 2017*, Srinagar/Jammu,
      Government of Jammu & Kashmir, no date [2018?].

227   Khan, *The JKLF Roadmap*, p. 12.

228   Parveen, 'What is the JKLF?', *The Print*, 23 March 2019, https://theprint.in/india/
      what-is-the-jklf-the-organisation-banned-by-the-modi-government/210560/ [accessed
      11 February 2020].

229   Khan, *The JKLF Roadmap*, p. 12.

230   Khan, *The Best & Easiest Solution of Kashmir Issue*, p. 11.

231   Aamir Ali Bhat, 'October 27, 1947: The Day Kashmir's Conflict was Born', *TheNewArab*,
      26 October 2018, www.alaraby.co.uk/english/indepth/2018/10/26/October-27-1947-The-
      day-Kashmirs-conflict-was-born [accessed 17 November 2017].

232   Interview with a Kashmiri (who wished to remain anonymous), New Delhi, 16 August
      2018.

233   Altaf Baba, 'Geelani in Sopore after 8 Years: Struggle Will Continue till Goal Achieved',
      Greater Kashmir, 16 November 2018, https://greaterkashmir.com/news/front-page/
      geelani-in-sopore-after-8-years-struggle-will-continue-till-goal-achieved/303132.html
      [accessed 17 November 2018].

234   'J&K: Pro-Azadi Slogans Raised in Kishtwar on Eid, Case Registered', *The Indian
      Express*, 16 June 2018, https://indianexpress.com/article/india/jk-pro-azadi-slogans-
      raised-in-kishtwar-on-eid-case-registered-5220406/ [accessed 17 November 2018].

235   'Atal Bihari Vajpayee's "Insaniyat, Jamhuriyat, Kashmiriyat" is the Foundation for Peace
      in Kashmir', *Firstpost*, 16 August 2018, www.firstpost.com/india/atal-bihari-vajpayees-
      insaniyat-jamhuriyat-kashmiriyat-is-the-foundation-for-peace-in-kashmir-4976011.html
      [accessed 3 July 2020].

236   'Former J&K CM Farooq Abdullah Heckled During Eid Prayers for Chanting
      "Bharat Mata ki Jai" at Vajpayee meet', *The Indian Express*, 22 August 2018, https://
      indianexpress.com/article/india/farooq-abdullah-heckled-eid-prayers-bharat-mata-ki-
      jai-5319287/ [accessed 11February 2020].

237   Naseer Ganai, 'On "1931 Martyrs Day', J-K Political Parties Say Present Govt "Worse Than
      Monarchy"', *Outlook*, 13 July 2020, www.outlookindia.com/website/story/india-news-
      on-1931–martyrs-day-j-k-political-parties-say-present-govt-worse-than-monarchy/356601
      [accessed 14 July 2020].

238   'Kashmir Martyrs' Day Dropped rom Public Holidays: Accession Day Included', *Outlook*,
      28 December 2019, www.outlookindia.com/website/story/india-news-kashmir-martyrs-
      day-dropped-from-public-holidays-accession-day-included/344787 [accessed 14 July
      2020].

239   Soz, *Kashmir*, p. 187.

240 This paragraph is based on Shrimoyee Nandini Ghosh, 'Crisis Constitutionalism, Permanent Emergency and the Amnesias of International Law in Jammu and Kashmir', *Kashmir Times*, 6 January 2020, www.kashmirtimes.com/newsdet.aspx?q+102660 [accessed 5 June 2020].

Conclusion: to be independent, or not to be independent? That is the question

1 With apologies to William Shakespeare.
2 Ali, *The Emergence of Pakistan*, pp. 287, 297.
3 'Note by Jawaharlal Nehru to Mehr Chand Mahajan 26 October 1947', in Alam, *Jammu and Kashmir*, p. 353.
4 Mahajan, *Looking Back*, pp. 280–1.
5 *The Times of India*, 10 September 1982.
6 Fazili, *Kashmir Government*, p. 2.
7 *Times of India*, 10 August 1953.
8 Singh, *Autobiography*, p. 162.
9 *The Times of India*, 10 September 1982.
10 Soz, *Kashmir*, pp. 205–6. Oddly, Rao made that statement while abroad in Burkina Faso.
11 Shaurya Karanbir Gurung, 'Will Take Action to Reclaim PoK if Ordered, Says Army Chief General Naravane', *The Economic Times*, 12 January 2020, https://economictimes.indiatimes.com/news/defence/will-take-action-to-reclaim-pok-if-ordered-says-army-chief-mukund-naravane/articleshow/73201632.cms?utm_source=contentofinterest&utm_medium=text&utm_campaign=cppst [accessed 22 January 2020].
12 Asad Hashim, 'Pakistan-administered Kashmir's PM Calls For "Military" Action', *Al Jazeera*, 26 February 2020, www.aljazeera.com/news/2020/02/pakistan-administered-kashmir-pm-calls-military-action-200226113022856.html?fbclid=IwAR3X1S_t2xZQh-KYZ5JT9cHVOdROzKQql89mrMt68YINy_LMTqpfD5DQLI3g [accessed 28 February 2020].
13 Abdullah, *The Blazing Chinar*, p. 391. At the start of this book (no page number), this appears as '*Kashmir can be conquered by the power of spirit, not by the sword*. Kalhana, Rajatarangini (1149 CE)'.
14 Michael Davidson, *The Scotsman*, 14 April 1949.
15 There may be other documents, but I have not located any.
16 'Appendix III (Document "C"): Internal Constitutional Set-up (Broad Outlines)', in Khan, *Abdullah's Reflections*, pp. 189–3.
17 Khan, *Free Kashmir*. Two other documents by Amanullah Khan were in a similar vein: *Kashmir: Who and How to Bell the Cat*, 1998; *The Best & Easiest Solution of Kashmir Issue*, 2007.
18 Katju, 'Calling for Kashmir's Azadi is Not Sedition', *The Wire*, 20 August 2016.
19 *Jammu and Kashmir: The Impact of Lockdowns on Human Rights*, pp. 12, 24.
20 *Ibid.*, p. 60.
21 Wani, 'Life Under Siege in Kashmir'.

22 '"Caged Like Animals," Mehbooba Mufti's Daughter Writes To Amit Shah', *NDTV*, 16 August 2019, www.ndtv.com/india-news/mehbooba-mufti-daughter-iltija-javed-writes-to-amit-shah-says-caged-like-animals-2085742 [accessed 23 January 2020].

23 'Need to Tell Youth Azadi Will Never Happen, You Can't Fight Us: Army Chief General Bipin Rawat', *The Indian Express*, 10 May 2018, https://indianexpress.com/article/india/indian-army-general-bipin-rawat-kashmir-unrest-burhan-wani-encounter-azadi-will-never-happen-you-cant-fight-us-5170701/ [accessed 17 November 2018].

24 Tavleen Singh, 'Fifth Column: Between Myth and History', *The Indian Express*, 6 May 2018, https://indianexpress.com/article/opinion/columns/fifth-column-between-myth-and-history-jammu-and-kashmir-5164935/ [accessed 17 November 2018].

25 The Wire Staff, 'Not Just J&K, India's Constitution Provides Special Powers to 10 States', *The Wire*, 5 August 2019, https://thewire.in/government/jammu-kashmir-constitution-special-powers-10-states [accessed18 July 2020].

26 Singh, *Kashmir: A Tragedy*, p. 87.

27 Nirmala Ganapathy, 'Modi Reaches Out to Muslims, Speaking of "Unity in Diversity"', *The Straits Times*, 23 December 2019. www.straitstimes.com/asia/south-asia/modi-reaches-out-to-muslims-speaking-of-unity-in-diversity [accessed 25 December 2019].

28 Bazaz, *The Shape of Things*, p. 35.

29 'To Karan Singh', 30 October 1953, *Selected Works of Jawaharlal Nehru*, Volume 23, 1999, p. 393.

30 'Security Council – Veto List', *Dag Hammarskjöld Library*, undated [2019], https://research.un.org/en/docs/sc/quick [accessed 12 July 2020].

31 Nassim Nicholas Taleb, *The Black Swan: The Impact of the Highly Improbable*, London, Penguin, 2010.

32 Appendix III: Border and/or territorial changes, actual or attempted, in South Asia since 15 August 1947.

33 None of the censuses of J&K that I accessed (1901, 1911, 1921, 1931, 1941) use the term 'Aksai Chin' nor do they specifically discuss what would comprise this region, although their maps do clearly show Ladakh as extending into what is now called Aksai Chin. Only the map in the 1931 Census labels this extension, which it calls the 'Lingzi Thang Plains'. See *Census of India, 1931*, Part I, map between p. 6 and p. 7.

34 Lala Ganeshi Lal, *Siyahat-i-Kashmir*, p. 32.

Appendix I

1 *Census of India, 1931*, Part I – Report, pp. 8–9.

Appendix II

1 *Census of India, 1931*, Part II: Tables p. 2.

2 *Ibid.*, Part II: Tables, p. 140.

3 *Ibid.*, Part I: Essay, p. 2.

4 Dhar, *Kashmir: Eden of the East*, p. 19.

5 *Census of India, 1941*, Part II: Tables, p. 72.

6 *Ibid.*, Part I, p. 8.

7   *Ibid.*, Part I, p. 9.
8   *Ibid.*, Part I: Essay, p. 9.
9   *Ibid.*, Part II, p. 354.
10 *Ibid.*
11 *Ibid.*, Part I, p. 9.
12 James Stuart Olson, *An Ethnohistorical Dictionary of China*, Westport, Greenwood Publishing Group, 1998, p. 170.
13 *Census of India, 1931*, Part I – Report, pp. 315–17.
14 *Ibid.*, Part I – Report, p. 316.
15 *Ibid.*, Part II Imperial & State Tables, pp. 281–3.
16 *Census of India, 1941*, Part II, p. 354.

Appendix III

1   Robert Malley, '10 Conflicts to Watch in 2020', *International Crisis Group*, 27 December 2019, wwww.crisisgroup.org/global/10-conflicts-watch-2020 [accessed 6 April 2020]. The list is 1. Afghanistan; 2. Yemen; 3. Ethiopia; 4. Burkina Faso; 5. Libya; 6. The US, Iran, Israel, and the Persian Gulf; 7. US–North Korea; 8. Kashmir; 9. Venezuela; 10. Ukraine.
2   '"Akhand Bharat" or "Undivided India" as Dreamed by Nationalist Indian Partys [sic]', *Reddit*, 2017, www.reddit.com/r/MapPorn/comments/55vizx/akhand_bharat_or_undivided_india_as_dreamed_by/ [accessed 28 March 2020].

Bibliography

Official documents

Administration Report of the Jammu and Kashmir State for the Second Half of S. 1998 and for S. 1999 (18 months from 16th October 1941 to 12th April 1943), Jammu, Ranbir Government Press, 1944.

Administration Report of the Jammu and Kashmir State for S. 2000 (13th April 1943–12th April 1944), Jammu, Ranbir Government Press, 1945.

Administration Report of the Jammu and Kashmir State for S. 2006 (13th April 1949–12th April 1950), Jammu, Ranbir Government Press, 1952.

Administration Report of Jammu and Kashmir for the years, 2011 [sic] *(13th April 1954–12th April 1955)*, [Srinagar?], Jammu and Kashmir Government, [1955?].

Annual Human Rights Review 2019, A Review of Human Rights Situation in Jammu and Kashmir, Jammu Kashmir Coalition of Civil Society & Association of Parents of Disappeared Persons, Srinagar, 31 December 2019.

'Appendix I: Answers by the Government of the State of Jammu and Kashmir to the Questionnaire Submitted by the Economic and Political Mission', *United Nations Commission for India and Pakistan*, New York, Unpublished Restricted Document: S/AC.12/66, [9 September 1948].

Azad Kashmir at a Glance, 2018, Azad Jammu and Kashmir Government, 2018, www.pndajk.gov.pk/uploadfiles/downloads/Final%20AJK%20at%20a%20Glance.pdf [accessed 28 July 2019].

Aziz, Mir Abdul, 'Internal Kashmir Affairs – A Practicable Solution, Kashmiristan?', p. 2, in a proposal attached to a letter to 'The Hon'ble Minister for Kashmir Affairs, Pakistan (Rawalpindi)', by Mir Abdul Aziz, 'Member General Council, All Jammu and Kashmir Muslim Conference', 5 May 1950, pp. 52–61, contained in File No. 13 (5) PMS/50, Volume 10', Government of Pakistan, Prime Minister's Secretariat, All Jammu & Kashmir Muslim Conference', held at the National Documentation Centre, Cabinet Building, Islamabad, Pakistan.

A Brief Note on the Administration of the Jammu and Kashmir State for the Year 1933, Srinagar, Pratap Press, 1934.

A Brief Note on the Administration of the Jammu and Kashmir State for the Year 1934, Srinagar, Pratap Press, 1935.

A Brief Note on the Administration of the Jammu and Kashmir State for the Year 1935, Srinagar, Pratap Press, 1936.

417

A Brief Note on the Administration of the Jammu and Kashmir State for the Year 1936, Srinagar, Pratap Press, 1937.

Census of India, 1901, Volume XXIII [Jammu and] Kashmir, Khan Bahadur Munshi Ghulam Ahmed Khan, Revenue Member, State Council, and Superintendent of Census Operations, Jammu and Kashmir State, Lahore, The 'Civil and Military Gazette' Press, 1902.

Census of India, 1911, Volume XX [Jammu and] Kashmir, Lucknow, Md. Matin-Uz-Zaman Khan, Superintendent of Census Operations, Jammu and Kashmir State, 1912.

Census of India, 1921, Volume XXII, Kashmir, Lahore, Khan Bahadur Chaudhri Khushi Mohammed, [Government of India], 1923.

Census of India, 1931, Volume XXIV, Jammu & Kashmir State, Rai Bahadur, Pt. Anand Ram, Census Commissioner, and Pt. Hira Nand Raina, Assistant Census Commissioner, [Jammu and Kashmir Government], Jammu, 1933.

Census of India, 1941, Volume VI, Punjab, Tables, Delhi, Khan Bahadur Sheikh Fazl-i-Ilahi, Superintendent of Census Operations, Punjab, 1941.

Census of India, 1941, Volume XXII, Jammu & Kashmir State, Srinagar, R. G. Wreford, Editor, Jammu and Kashmtir Government, 1942.

Census of India, 1961, Volume VI, *Jammu and Kashmir*, Part I-A (i), *General Report*, Srinagar, M. H. Kamili, Superintendent of Census Operations Jammu and Kashmir, Census of India, 1968.

Central Publication Branch, *India in 1931-32*, Calcutta, Government of India, 1933.

The Constitution of India, New Delhi, Government of India, 2007, www.india.gov.in/my-government/constitution-india/constitution-india-full-text [accessed 5 June 2020].

The Constitution of the Islamic Republic of Pakistan, Islamabad, National Assembly of Pakistan, 2012, http://na.gov.pk/uploads/documents/1333523681_951.pdf [accessed 2 March 2018].

Constitutional Relations Between Britain and India, The Transfer of Power 1942-7, London, Nicholas Mansergh, Editor-in-Chief, Her Majesty's Stationery Office, 1976–1983:

- Volume VI, 1 August 1945–22 March 1946; published 1976;
- Volume VII, 23 March–29 June 1946; published 1977;
- Volume IX, 4 November 1946–22 March 1947; published 1980;
- Volume X, 22 March–30 May 1947; published 1981;
- Volume XI, 31 May–7 July 1947; published 1982;
- Volume XII, 8 July–15 August 1947; published 1983.

'Copy of Note by R. C. Kak, Jammu and Kashmir State in 1946–47', in *Powell Collection, Papers and Correspondence*, dated 1947–60, of Richard Powell (1889–1961), Indian Police Force 1908–47, Inspector-General of Police Jammu and Kashmir 1946–47, Indian Office Records, MSS EUR D862 [accessed at National Document Centre, Islamabad, December 2004].

Crisis in Kashmir Explained (Text of Policy Speech Broadcast by Bakshi Ghulam Mohammad, Prime Minister of Jammu and Kashmir on August 9, 1953), Srinagar, Lalla Rookh, [1953].

Directorate of Economic & Statistics J&K, *Economic Survey 2017*, Srinagar/Jammu, Government of Jammu & Kashmir, no date [2018?].

'Divisions & Districts', *Jammu & Kashmir: Official State Portal*, undated, https://jk.gov.in/jammukashmir/?q=divisions [accessed 8 July 2019].

Ek Bharat - Shreshtha Bharat 2014, Bharatiya Janata Party, New Delhi, 2014.

Glancy, B. J., *Report of the Commission Appointed under the Order of His Highness, the Maharaja Bahadur dated 12th November, 1931 to Enquire into Grievances and Complaints*, Jammu, Ranbir Govt. Press, 1933.

Government of India Act, 1935, London, Parliament of the United Kingdom, 1935, www. legislation.gov.uk/ukpga/1935/2/pdfs/ukpga_19350002_en.pdf [accessed 27 June 2017].

'Growth in United Nations membership, 1945–present', *United Nations*, undated, www.un.org/ en/sections/member-states/growth-united-nations-membership-1945-present/index.html [accessed 6 April 2020].

Hasan, Sarwar K. and Zubeida Hasan, Editors, *Documents on the Foreign Relations of Pakistan*: *The Kashmir Question*, Karachi, Pakistan Institute of International Relations, 1966.

The High Court of Judicature, Azad Jammu and Kashmir, *Verdict on Gilgit and Baltistan (Northern Area)*, Mirpur, Kashmir Human Rights Forum, [1993?].

India in 1932–33, Delhi, Manager of Publications, 1934.

Indian Independence Act 1947, London, Parliament of the United Kingdom, 1947, www.legislation.gov.uk/ukpga/1947/30/pdfs/ukpga_19470030_en.pdf [accessed 27 June 2017].

Information about Pakistan and Facts about Pakistan, undated [2019?], www.pakinformation.com/ gilgit-baltistan/index.html [accessed 28 July 2019].

Jammu and Kashmir: The Impact of Lockdowns on Human Rights: August 2019–July 2020 Report, The Forum for Human Rights in Jammu and Kashmir, 2020.

Jammu & Kashmir 1947–50: An Account of Activities of [the] First Three Years of Sheikh Abdullah's Government, Jammu, [Government of Jammu and Kashmir], The Ranbir Government Press, 1951.

Jammu & Kashmir 1968, Jammu and Kashmir Department of Information, [Srinagar?], [1969?].

'Jammu & Kashmir Profile', *CensusInfo India 2011*, undated (based on 'Census of India 2011'), http://censusindia.gov.in/2011census/censusinfodashboard/stock/profiles/en/ IND001_Jammu%20&%20Kashmir.pdf [accessed 8 July 2019].

Jawaharlal Nehru's Speeches 1949–1953, The Publications Division, Ministry of Information and Broadcasting, Government of India, Delhi, 1954.

Jinnah, Mohammad Ali, *Quaid-i-Azam Mohammad Ali Jinnah Papers*, Volumes III and V, Islamabad, Government of Pakistan, Cabinet Division, 1997, 2000.

Kashmir (August 7–September 17, 1953), New Delhi, Current Affairs Publications, [1954].

Lal, Lala Ganeshi, *Siyahat-i-Kashmir (Kashmir Nama or Tarikh-i-Kashmir), being An Account of a Journey to Kashmir, March–June 1846* [Translated into English and Annotated by Vidya Sagar Suri], 1954, [Simla?], The Punjab Government, 1955.

Laws of Jammu and Kashmir, Volume II: 1577–1989, Jammu, The Ranbir Government Press, 1941.

List of the Private Secretaries to the Governors-General and Viceroys from 1774 to 1908, Calcutta, Superintendent Government Printing, India, 1908.

'Maps of Newly Formed Union Territories of Jammu Kashmir [sic] and Ladakh, with the map of India', *Press Information Bureau* 2 November 2019, www.mha.gov.in/sites/default/ files/PressRelease_NoteonUTofJ&K%26Ladakh_04112019.pdf [accessed 7 June 2020].

'Member States', *United Nations*, undated, www.un.org/en/member-states/ [accessed 26 March 2019].

Ministry of Law and Justice, 'The Constitution (Application to Jammu and Kashmir) Order, 2019 C. O. 272', *The Gazette of India*, Controller of Publications, Delhi, 5 August 2019, http://egazette.nic.in/WriteReadData/2019/210049.pdf [accessed 10 August 2019].

Ministry of Law and Justice, 'Declaration Under Article 370(3) of the Constitution "C. O. 273"', *The Gazette of India*, Controller of Publications, Delhi, 6 August 2019, http:// egazette.nic.in/WriteReadData/2019/210243.pdf [accessed 10 August 2019].

Ministry of Law and Justice, 'The Jammu and Kashmir Reorganisation Act, 2019 No. 34 of 2019', *The Gazette of India*, Controller of Publications, Delhi, 9 August 2019, http://egazette.nic.in/WriteReadData/2019/210407.pdf [accessed 10 August 2019].

Nehru, Jawaharlal, *India's Foreign Policy, Selected Speeches, September 1946–April 1961*, New Delhi, Publications Division, Ministry of Information and Broadcasting, Government of India, 1961.

Nehru, Jawaharlal, *Selected Works of Jawaharlal Nehru*, New Delhi, Orient Longman, First Series, Volume 15, 1982.

Nehru, Jawaharlal, *Selected Works of Jawaharlal Nehru*, New Delhi, Jawaharlal Nehru Memorial Fund, Second Series: Volumes 3, 1985; 4, 1986; 5, 1987; 8, 1989; 9, 1990; 10, 1990; 11, 1991; 14, Part 1, 1992; 14, Part 2, 1993; 15, Part 2, 1993; 17, 1995; 18, 1996; 19, 1996; 20, 1997; 21, 1997; 22, 1998; 23, 1998; 24, 1999; 27, 2000; 28, 2001; 34, 2005; 41, 2010; 42, 2010.

Office of the United Nations High Commissioner for Human Rights, *Report on the Situation of Human Rights in Kashmir: Developments in the Indian State of Jammu and Kashmir from June 2016 to April 2018, and General Human Rights Concerns in Azad Jammu and Kashmir and Gilgit-Baltistan*, Geneva, United Nations Human Rights: Office of the High Commissioner, 14 June 2018.

Office of the United Nations High Commissioner for Human Rights, *Update of the Situation of Human Rights in Indian-Administered Kashmir and Pakistan-Administered Kashmir from May 2018 to April 2019*, Geneva, United Nations Human Rights: Office of the High Commissioner, 8 July 2019.

'Official Spokesperson's response to a query whether India has taken up the use of the term "Indian-administered Jammu and Kashmir"', *Ministry of External Affairs*, 29 June 2017, www.mea.gov.in/media-briefings.htm?dtl/28571/official+spokespersons+response+to+a+query+whether+india+has+taken+up+the+use+of+the+term+indianadministered+jammu+and+kashmir [accessed 21 March 2018].

Papers Connected with the Re-organization of the Army in India, Supplementary to the Report of the Army Commission, London, Her Majesty's Stationery Office, 1859.

Patel, Sardar, *Sardar Patel's Correspondence 1945–50, Volume I, New Light on Kashmir*, Ahmedabad, Navajivan Publishing House, 1971.

Prime Minister's Statement on Kashmir Developments', *Kashmir (August 7–September 17, 1953)*, New Delhi, Current Affairs Publications, [1954].

Publications Division, Ministry of Information and Broadcasting, *Indian States Today*, Delhi, Government of India, 1948.

Publications Division, *Elections in Kashmir*, [New Delhi], Ministry of Information & Broadcasting, Government of India, 1957.

Publicity Department, *A Handbook of the Jammu and Kashmir State*, His Highness's Government, Jammu and Kashmir, Jammu, 1947.

Report of the Educational Reorganisation Committee, His Highness' Government of Jammu & Kashmir, Srinagar, 1939.

Report of the Indian States Committee, 1928–1929, London, His Majesty's Stationery Office, 1929.

Report on the Administration of the Jammu and Kashmir State for Samvat 1993–94, Jammu, The Ranbir Government Press, 1938.

[Resident in Kashmir], *Revised List of Ruling Princes, Chiefs and Leading Personages of the Jammu and Kashmir State and the Gilgit Agency*, New Delhi, The Manager of Publications, 1939.

Bibliography

'Resolutions', *United Nations Security Council*, www.un.org/securitycouncil/content/resolutions-o [accessed 28 July 2019].

[Rose, H. A.], *Imperial Gazetteer of India, Provincial Series, North-West Frontier Province*, Calcutta, Superintendent of Government Printing, 1908.

Sankalp Patra Lok Sabha 2019, Bharatiya Janata Party, New Delhi, 2019.

Singh, Maharaja Hari, 'A Proclamation, 11th February 1939', [Jammu?], *The Jammu & Kashmir Government Gazette*, 1939.

Stanton, F. S., *Administration Report on the Railways in India for 1883–1884*, Simla, Government Central Branch Press, 1884.

Sudarisanam, A. N., Editor, *Indian States Register and Directory 1929*, Madras, Indian States Register & Directory Office, 1929.

White Paper on Hyderabad, [Delhi], Government of India, 1948.

White Paper on Indian States, New Delhi, Government of India, revised edition, 1950.

White Paper on Jammu & Kashmir, [Delhi], Government of India, [1948].

Yeatts, M. W. M., *Census of India 1941*, 'Volume I, India, Part I, Tables', Delhi, Manager of Publications, 1943.

Books and chapters in books

Abdullah, Sheikh Mohammad, *The Blazing Chinar: An Autobiography* [Translated from Urdu by Mohammad Amin], Srinagar, Gulshan Books, second edition, 2013.

Abdullah, Sheikh Mohammad, *Flames of the Chinar* [Translated by Khushwant Singh], New Delhi, Viking, 1993.

Abdullah, Sheikh Mohammed, *Naya Kashmir: The New Kashmiri Manifesto (1944)*, Oxford Islamic Studies Online, www.oxfordislamicstudies.com/article/doc/ps-islam-0320?_hi=0&_pos=5942 [accessed 1 May 2018].

Abercrombie, Nicholas, Stephen Hill and Bryan S. Turner, *Dictionary of Sociology*, London, Penguin, second edition, 1988.

Alam, Jawaid, Editor, *Jammu and Kashmir 1949–64: Select Correspondence between Jawaharlal Nehru and Karan Singh*, New Delhi, Penguin/Viking, 2006.

Ali, Chaudhri Muhammad, *The Emergence of Pakistan*, New York, Columbia University Press, 1967.

Ali, Tariq et al., *Kashmir: The Case for Freedom*, London, Verso, 2011.

Allen, Charles and Sharada Dwivedi, *Lives of the Indian Princes*, London, Arena, 1984.

Ankit, Rakesh, *The Kashmir Conflict: From Empire to the Cold War, 1945–66*, Abingdon, Routledge, 2016.

Asad, Muhammad Saeed, *Wounded Memories of the Tribal Attack on Kashmir* [Translated from Urdu by Quayyum Raja and Tanveer Ahmed], Mirpur, National Institute of Kashmir Studies, 2010.

Ayres, Philip, *Owen Dixon*, Carlton, The Miegunyah Press, 2003.

Aziz, Mir Abdul, *Freedom Struggle in Kashmir*, Lahore, Research Society of Pakistan, University of the Punjab, 2000.

Bakshi Gulam [sic; Ghulam] Mohd., *Kashmir Today 'Thru' Many Eyes'*, Bombay, Bombay Provincial Congress Committee, [1945].

Ballaster, Ros, Editor, *Fables of the East: Selected Tales 1662–1785*, Oxford, Oxford University Press, 2005.

421

Bibliography

Bakshi, S. R., *Kashmir: Political Problems*, New Delhi, Sarup & Sons, 1997.

Bamzai, P. N. K., *Culture and Political History of Kashmir, Volume III: Modern Kashmir*, New Delhi, MD Publications, 1994.

Bangash, Yaqoob Khan, *A Princely Affair: The Accession and Integration of the Princely States of Pakistan, 1947–1955*, Karachi, Oxford University Press, 2015.

Barton, William, *The Princes of India*, London, Nisbet & Co., 1934.

Bazaz, Prem Nath, *Azad Kashmir: A Democratic Socialist Conception*, Lahore, Ferozsons, 1951.

Bazaz, Prem Nath, *Inside Kashmir*, Srinagar, The Kashmir Publishing Company, 1941.

Bazaz, Prem Nath, *The History of Struggle for Freedom in Kashmir*, New Delhi, Pamposh Publications, 1954.

Bazaz, Prem Nath, *Kashmir in Crucible*, New Delhi, Pamposh Publications, 1967.

Bazaz, Prem Nath, *The Shape of Things in Kashmir*, New Delhi, Pamposh Publications, 1965.

Bechhofer Roberts, C. E., *The Mr. A Case*, London, Jarrolds, [1950].

Behera, Navnita Chadha, *Demystifying Kashmir*, Brookings, Washington D.C., 2006.

Behera, Navnita Chadha, *State, Identity and Violence: Jammu, Kashmir and Ladakh*, New Delhi, Manohar, 2000.

Bernier, Francois, *Travels in the Mogul Empire, AD 1656–1668*, Westminster, Archibald Constable and Company, 1891.

Bew, John, *Citizen Clem*, London, Riverrun, 2016.

Bhargava, R. P., *The Chamber of Princes*, New Delhi, Northern Book Centre, 1991.

Bhatia, K. L., *Jammu and Kashmir: Article 370 of the Constitution of India*, New Delhi, Deep & Deep Publications, 1997.

Bhattacharjea, Ajit, *Sheikh Mohammad Abdullah: Tragic Hero of Kashmir*, New Delhi, Roli Books, 2008.

Bolitho, Hector, *Jinnah, Creator of Pakistan*, London, John Murray, 1954.

Bose, Sumantra, *Kashmir: Roots of Conflict, Paths to Peace*, New Delhi, Vistaar, 2003.

Bose, Sumantra, *The Challenge in Kashmir: Democracy, Self-determination, and a Just Peace*, New Delhi, Sage, 1997.

Bradnock, Robert W., *Kashmir: Paths to Peace*, London, Chatham House, 2010.

Brata, Sasthi, *India: Labyrinths in the Lotus Land*, New York, William Morrow, 1985.

Brown, Lesley, Editor, *The New Shorter Oxford English Dictionary*, Oxford, Oxford University Press, 1993.

Brown, William A., *The Gilgit Rebellion 1947*, [no place of publication], Ibex, 1998.

Campbell-Johnson, Alan, *Mission With Mountbatten*, New York, Atheneum, 1986.

Chester, Lucy P., *Borders and Conflict in South Asia: The Radcliffe Boundary Commission and the Partition of Punjab*, Manchester, Manchester University Press, 2009.

Chopra, P. N., Chief Editor, *India's Struggle for Freedom: Role of Associated Movements*, Delhi, Agam Prakashan, 1985.

Chowdhary, Rekha, *Jammu and Kashmir: Politics of Identity and Separatism*, New Delhi, Routledge, 2016.

Cloughley, Brian, *A History of the Pakistan Army*, Oxford, Oxford University Press, second edition, 2000.

Collet, John, *Guide to Kashmir*, Calcutta, W. Newman and Co., 1898.

Collins, Larry and Dominique Lapierre, *Freedom at Midnight*, London, Panther, 1982.

Copland, Ian, *The Princes of India in the Endgame of Empire, 1917–1947*, Cambridge, Cambridge University Press, 1997.

Corfield, Sir Conrad, *The Princely India I Knew: From Reading to Mountbatten*, Madras, Indo British Historical Society, 1975.

Coupland, Reginald, *India: A Re-statement*, London, Oxford University Press, 1945.

Coupland, R., *Indian Politics 1936–1942*, London, Oxford University Press, 1943.

Das, Durga, *India: From Curzon to Nehru & After*, London, Collins, 1969.

Das Gupta, Jyoti Bhusan, *Jammu and Kashmir*, The Hague, Martinus Nijhoff, 1968.

De Bourbel, R. E., *Jammu & Kashmir Railway: Proposed Western Routes Report*, Jammu, Ranbir Prakash Press, 1902.

De Bourbel, R. E., *Routes in Jammu and Kashmir*, Calcutta, Thacker, Spink and Co, 1897.

Deora, M. S. and R. Grover, Editors, *Documents on Kashmir Problem*, Volume X, New Delhi, Discovery Publishing House, 1991.

Dewan, Parvez, *A History of Kashmir*, New Delhi, Manas, 2014.

Dhar, D. P., *Kashmir: Eden of the East*, Allahabad, Kitab Mahal, 1945:
- Pandit Jawaharlal Nehru, 'Introduction Essay on Kashmir'.

Dhar, M. K., 'That Fateful Night', in *Devendra Swarup and Sushil Aggarwal, The Roots of [the] Kashmir Problem*, New Delhi, Manthan Prakashan, 1992.

Drew, Frederic, *The Jummoo and Kashmir Territories: A Geographical Account*, London, Edward Stanford, 1875.

Drew, Frederic, *The Northern Barrier of India: A Popular Account of the Jummoo and Kashmir Territories*, London, Edward Standford, 1877.

Durand, Algernon, *The Making of a Frontier*, London, Thomas Nelson & Sons, 1900.

Duschinski, Haley, Mona Bhan, Ather Zia and Cynthia Mahmood, Editors, *Resisting Occupation in Kashmir*, Philadelphia, University of Pennsylvania Press, 2018:
- Mona Bhan, Haley Duschinski and Ather Zia, '"Rebels of the Streets": Violence, Protest, and Freedom in Kashmir';
- Farrukh Faheem, 'Interrogating the Ordinary: Everyday Politics and the Struggle for *Azadi* in Kashmir'.

Edwardes, Herbert B. and Herman Merivale, *Life of Sir Henry Lawrence*, London, Smith, Elder & Co., third edition, 1873.

Evans, Alexander, 'Kashmiri Exceptionalism', in Aparna Rao, Editor, *The Valley of Kashmir: The Making and Unmaking of a Composite Culture?*, New Delhi, Manohar, 2008.

Evans, Graham and Jeffrey Newnham, *Dictionary of International Relations*, London, Penguin, 1998.

Fazili, Manzoor, *Kashmir Government and Politics*, Srinagar, Gulshan Publishers, 1982.

Forbes, Rosita, *India of the Princes*, London, The Right Book Club, 1939.

Gajendragadkar, P. B., *Kashmir – Retrospect and Prospect*, Bombay, University of Bombay, 1967.

Ganai, Abdul Jabbar, *Kashmir National Conference and Politics (1975–1980)*, Srinagar, Gulshan Publishers, 1984.

Gandhi, Rajmohan, *Patel: A Life*, Ahmedabad, Navajivan Publishing House, [1991].

Gani, Abdul, *Labour-management Relations: A Study of Textile Industry in Jammu and Kashmir*, New Delhi, Deep & Deep Publications, 1995.

Ganju, M., *This is Kashmir (With Special Reference to U.N.O.)*, Delhi, S. Chand & Co., [1948].

Geelani, Gowhar, *Rage and Reason*, New Delhi, Rupa Publications, 2019.

Geelani, Syed Ali Shah, *Kashmir: Nava-e Hurriyat [Kashmir: Voice of Freedom]*, Srinagar, Mizan Publications, 1995.

Gilani, Justice Syed Manzoor Hussain, *The Constitution of Azad Jammu & Kashmir*, Islamabad, National Book Foundation, 2008.

Gilani, Syed Manzoor H., *Constitutional Development in Azad Jammu & Kashmir*, Lahore, National Book Depot, 1988.

Gilmour, David, *The Ruling Caste*, New York, Farrar, Straus and Giroux, 2005.

Gokhale, S. M., *Indian States and the Cabinet Mission Plan*, Baroda, Mrs. M. S. Gokhale, 1947.

Grierson, Sir George Abraham, *The Languages of India: Being a Reprint of the Chapter on Languages*, Office of the Superintendent of Government Printing, Calcutta, 1903.

Gupta, Sisir, *Kashmir: A Study in India-Pakistan Relations*, Bombay, Asia Publishing House, 1966.

Habibullah, Wajahat, *My Kashmir: Conflict and the Prospects for Enduring Peace*, Washington D.C., United States Institute of Peace, 2008.

Hajari, Nisid, *Midnight's Furies: The Deadly Legacy of India's Partition*, Stroud, Amberley, 2017.

Haksar, Nandita, *The Many Faces of Kashmiri Nationalism: From the Cold War to the Present Day*, New Delhi, Speaking Tiger Books, 2015.

Hassan, Khalid, Editor, *K. H. Khurshid: Memories of Jinnah*, Karachi, Oxford University Press, 1990.

Hassnain, F. M., *British Policy Towards Kashmir (1846-1921) (Kashmir in Anglo-Russian Politics)*, New Delhi, Sterling Publishers, 1974.

Hassnain, F. M., *Gilgit: The Northern Gate of India*, New Delhi, Sterling Publisher, 1975.

Hodson, H. V., *The Great Divide: Britain-India-Pakistan*, London, Hutchinson, 1969.

Hoodbhoy, Pervez, 'Kashmir: From Nuclear Flashpoint to South Asia's Bridge of Peace', in Pervez Hoodbhoy, Editor, *Confronting the Bomb: Pakistani and Indian Scientists Speak Out*, Karachi, Oxford University Press, 2013.

Hussain, Mirza Shafique, Compiler, *History of Kashmir: A Study in Documents 1916-1939*, Islamabad, National Institute of Historical and Cultural Research, 1992:
- L. Middleton, 'Report on an Inquiry into Disturbances at Jammu and its Environments During the First Week of November 1931';
- 'Report of the Srinagar Riot Enquiry Committee (1931-1988)'.

Hutchison, J. and J. Ph. Vogel, *History of the Panjab Hill States*, Lahore, Superintendent, Government Printing, 1933.

Huttenback, Robert A., *Kashmir and the British Raj, 1847-1947*, Karachi, Oxford University Press, 2004.

Jayakar, Pupul, *Indira Gandhi: A Biography*, Gurgaon, Penguin, 1995, revised edition (first published 1992).

Jeffrey, Robin, Editor, *People, Princes and Paramount Power*, Delhi, Oxford University Press, 1978:
- Ian Copland, 'The Other Guardians: Ideology and Performance in the Indian Political Service';
- Robin Jeffrey, 'Introduction';
- James Manor, 'The Demise of the Princely Order: A Reassessment';
- William L. Richter, 'Traditional Rulers in Post-traditional Societies: The Princes of India and Pakistan'.

Jehu, I. S., Editor, *The India and Pakistan Year Book 1948*, Bombay, Bennett, Coleman & Co., 1948.

Joshi, Manoj, *The Lost Rebellion*, New Delhi, Penguin, 1999.

[Kak, Pandit Ramchandra], *Jammu and Kashmir State in 1946-47: Dilemma of Accession – The Missing Link in the Story*, [self published?], [1956?].

Kalhana's Rajatarangini: A Chronicle of the Kings of Kasmir [sic] [Translated by M. A. Stein], *Mirpur, Verinag Publishers*, 1991, [First published by M/s A. Constable & Co., London, 1900].

Kapur, M. L., Editor, *Maharaja Hari Singh, 1895–1961*, New Delhi, Har-Anand Publications, 1995:

- M. L. Kapur, 'From Maharaja Gulab Singh to Maharaja Hari Singh';
- C. Sharma, 'The Accession of the J&K State and Maharaja Hari Singh'.

Kashmir, Bombay, General Secretary, All India States' People's Conference, 1939.

Kaul, Gwasha Lal, *Kashmir Through the Ages (5000 B.C. to 1965 A.D.)*, Srinagar, Chronicle Publishing House, 1963.

Kaula, Prithvi Nath and Kanahaya Lal Dhar, *Kashmir Speaks*, Delhi, S. Chand & Co., 1950.

Khan, Amanullah, *The Best & Easiest Solution of Kashmir Issue*, Rawalpindi, Jammu Kashmir Liberation Front, 2007.

Khan, Amanullah, *Free Kashmir*, [No Publisher Details], 1970.

Khan, Amanullah, *Kashmir: Who and How to Bell the Cat*, Rawalpindi, Jammu Kashmir Liberation Front, 1998.

Khan, Amanullah, *The JKLF Roadmap for Peace & Prosperity in South Asia*, Muzaffarabad, Jammu Kashmir Liberation Front, 2005.

Khan, Mohammad Ayub, *Friends Not Masters*, London, Oxford University Press, 1967.

Khan, Mohammad Ishaq, *Experiencing Islam*, New Delhi, Sterling Publishers, 1997.

Khan, Mohammad Ishaq, *History of Srinagar 1846–1947: A Study in Socio-cultural Change*, Srinagar, Aamir Publications, 1978.

Khan, Mohammad Ishaq, *Perspectives on Kashmir*, Srinagar, Gulshan Publishers, 1983.

Khan, Nyla Ali, *Sheikh Mohammad Abdullah's Reflections on Kashmir*, Cham, Switzerland, Palgrave Macmillan, 2018.

Khan, Nyla Ali, Editor, *The Parchment of Kashmir: History, Society, and Polity*, Houndmills, Palgrave Macmillan, 2012:

- Rekha Chowdhary, 'Kashmir in the Indian Project of Nationalism';
- Rattan Lal Hangroo, 'Kashmiriyat: The Voice of the Past Misconstrued';
- Mohammad Ishaq Khan, 'Evolution of My Identity vis-a-vis Islam and Kashmir';
- Nyla Ali Khan, 'Introduction';
- Gull Mohammad Wani, 'Political Assertion of Kashmiri Identity'.

Khan, Brig. (Retd.) M. Shafi, 'Extracts from Foreign Press', *Focus on Kashmir*, Islamabad, Institute of Policy Studies, 1990.

Khilnani, Sunil, *Incarnations: A History of India in Fifty Lives*, New York, Farrar, Straus and Giroux, 2016.

Knight, E. F., *Where Three Empires Meet*, London, Longmans, second edition, 1893.

Korbel, Josef, *Danger in Kashmir*, Oxford, Oxford University Press, 1954.

Krishna, Balraj, *Sardar Vallabhbhai Patel: India's Iron Man*, New Delhi, Rupa, 2013.

Lamb, Alastair, *Kashmir, A Disputed Legacy, 1846–1990*, Karachi, Oxford University Press, second impression, 1994.

Lawrence, Walter R., *The Valley of Kashmir*, London, Oxford University Press, 1895.

Lawrence, Walter Roper, *The India We Served*, London, Cassell and Company, 1928.

Low, D. A., Editor, *The Political Inheritance of Pakistan*, Basingstoke, Macmillan, 1991.

MacMunn, George, *The Indian States and Princes*, London, Jarrolds, 1936.

Madhok, Balraj, *Kashmir: Centre of New Alignments*, New Delhi, Deepak Prakashan, [1963].

Bibliography

Madhok, Bal Raj, *Jammu Kashmir and Ladakh: Problem & Solution*, New Delhi, Reliance Publishing, 1987.

Mahajan, Mehr Chand, *Looking Back*, New Delhi, Har-Anand Publications, 1994 [first published 1963?].

Malik, Iffat, *Kashmir: Ethnic Conflict, International Dispute*, Oxford, Oxford University Press, 2002.

Mansergh, Diana, Editor, *Independence Years: The Selected Indian and Commonwealth Papers of Nicholas Mansergh*, New Delhi, Oxford University Press, 1999.

McGregor, W. L., *The History of the Sikhs*, London, James Madden, 1846.

McLeod Innes, J. J., *Sir Henry Lawrence, the Pacificator*, Oxford, Clarendon, 1898.

Menon, V. P., *The Story of the Integration of the Indian States*, Bombay, Orient Longman, 1961.

Metcalf, Barbara D. and Thomas R. Metcalf, *A Concise History of India*, Cambridge, Cambridge University Press, 2002.

Milne, James, *The Road to Kashmir*, London, Hodder and Stoughton, [1929].

Moorcroft, William and George Trebeck, *Travels in the Himalayan Provinces of Hindustan and the Panjab; in Ladakh and Kashmir; in Peshawar, Kabul, Kunduz, and Bokhara*, Volume II, London, John Murray, 1841.

Muhammad, Zahid G., *Kashmir in War and Diplomacy*, Srinagar, Gulshan Books, 2007.

Mullik, B. N., *My Years with Nehru: Kashmir*, Bombay, Allied Publishers, 1971.

Najar, G. R., *Kashmir Accord (1975): A Political Analysis*, Srinagar, Gulshan Publishers, 1988.

Naqash, Nasir A. and G. M. Shah, *Kashmir: From Crisis to Crisis*, New Delhi, APH Publishing Corporation, 1997.

Nehru, Jawaharlal, *An Autobiography*, London, John Lane The Bodley Head, 1947 (first published 1936; reprinted with additional chapter, 1942).

Nehru, Jawaharlal, *The Unity of India: Collected Writings 1937–1940*, London, Lindsay Drummond, 1942.

Neve, Arthur, *Thirty Years in Kashmir*, London, Edward Arnold, 1913.

Noorani, A. G., *The Kashmir Dispute 1947–2012*, Karachi, Oxford University Press, 2014.

Olson, James Stuart, *An Ethnohistorical Dictionary of China*, Westport, Greenwood Publishing Group, 1998.

Panikkar, K. M., *The Founding of the Kashmir State: A Biography of Maharaja Gulab Singh, 1792–1858*, London, George Allen & Unwin, 1953.

Papers on Indian States Development, London, East and West, 1931.

Para, Altaf Hussain, *The Making of Modern Kashmir: Sheikh Abdullah and the Politics of the State*, Abingdon, Routledge, 2019.

Parkash, Dewan Ram, *Fight for Kashmir*, New Delhi, Tagore Memorial Publications, 1948.

Peer, Basharat, *Curfewed Night: A Frontline Memoir of Life, Love and War in Kashmir*, London, Harper Press, 2010.

Phadke, Narayan Sitaram, *Birth-pangs of New Kashmir*, Bombay, Rind Kitabs, [1948].

Pillai, G. R., *Co-operation in Indian States*, Quilon, Sree Rama Vilas Press, 1933.

Pukhraj, Malka, *Song Sung True: A Memoir* [Edited and translated by Saleem Kidwai], New Delhi, Kali for Women, 2003.

Puri, Balraj, *Jammu and Kashmir: Triumph and Tragedy of Indian Federalisation*, New Delhi, Sterling Publishers, 1981.

Puri, Balraj, *Kashmir: Towards Insurgency*, Hyderabad, Orient Longman, 1993.

Puri, Balraj, *Simmering Volcano: Study of Jammu's Relations with Kashmir*, New Delhi, Sterling Publishers, 1983.

Qasim, Mir, *My Life and Times*, New Delhi, Allied Publishers, 1992.

Quraishi, Zaheer Masood, *Elections & State Politics of India (A Case-Study of Kashmir)*, Delhi, Sundeep Prakashan, 1979.

Rai, Mridu, *Hindu Rulers, Muslim Subjects: Islam, Rights and the History of Kashmir*, London, Hurst & Company, 2004.

Raina, Pramathesh, *Kashmir: Towards Demilitarisation*, New Delhi, Pentagon Press, 2016.

Rajpori, Ghulam Mohammad and Manohar Nath Kaul, *Conspiracy in Kashmir*, Srinagar, Social & Political Study Group, 1954.

Ramusack, Barbara N., *The Indian Princes and Their States*, Cambridge, Cambridge University Press, 2004.

Rao, Aparna, Editor, *The Valley of Kashmir: The Making and Unmaking of a Composite Culture?*, New Delhi, Manohar, 2008.

Razdan, Omkar, *The Trauma of Kashmir*, New Delhi, Vikas, 1999.

Roy, Tathagata, *Syama Prasad Mookerjee*, Gurgaon, Penguin, 2018.

Sarabhai, Mridula, *Sheikh-Sadiq Correspondence (August to October 1956)*, [New Delhi], [Mridula Sarabhai], [1958].

Saraf, Muhammad Yusuf, *Kashmiris Fight – For Freedom*, Volume I (1819–1946), Lahore, Ferozsons, 1977.

Saraf, Muhammad Yusuf, *Kashmiris Fight – For Freedom*, Volume II (1947–78), Lahore, Ferozsons, 1979.

Sarkar, Sumit, Editor, *Towards Freedom: Documents on the Movement for Independence in India 1946*, New Delhi, Oxford University Press, 2009.

Sastry, K. R. R., *Treaties, Engagements and Sanads of Indian States: A Contribution in Indian Jurisprudence*, Allahabad, self-published, 1942.

Sayeed, Khalid B., *The Political System of Pakistan*, Boston, Houghton Mifflin Company, 1967.

Schofield, Victoria, *Kashmir in Conflict*, London, I. B. Taurus, 2000.

Schofield, Victoria, *Kashmir in the Crossfire*, London, I. B. Taurus, 1996.

Schofield, Victoria, *Wavell: Soldier & Statesman*, Barnsley, Pen & Sword Military, 2010.

Sen, Lt. General L. P., *Slender was the Thread*, Hyderabad, Orient Longman, 1988 [first published 1969].

Sender, Henny, *The Kashmiri Pandits: A Study of Cultural Choice in North India*, Delhi, Oxford University Press, 1988.

Shah, G. M., Editor, *Interviews & Speeches by Sher-i-Kashmir Sheikh Mohd. Abdullah*, [Srinagar], [All Jammu and Kashmir Plebiscite Front], 1968.

Shankar, V., *My Reminiscences of Sardar Patel*, Delhi, Macmillan, 1974.

Sharma, B. L., *Kashmir Awakes*, Delhi, Vikas Publications, 1971.

Sher-i-Kashmir Sheikh Mohd. Abdullah, *Speeches & Interviews*, Series 2, [Srinagar?], G. M. Shah, [1968].

Singh, Bawa Satinder, *The Jammu Fox*, Carbondale, Southern Illinois University Press, 1974.

Singh, Bhagwan, *Political Conspiracies of Kashmir*, Rohtak, Light and Life, 1973.

Singh, Major K. Brahma, *History of Jammu and Kashmir Rifles 1820–1956*, New Delhi, Lancer International, 1990.

Singh, Gurmukh Nihal, *Indian States & British India: Their Future Relations*, Benares, Nand Kishore & Bros, 1930.

Singh, Harbans, *Maharaja Hari Singh: The Troubled Years*, New Delhi, Brahaspati Publications, 2011.

Singh, Jaswant, *Jammu and Kashmir: Political and Constitutional Development*, 1996, New Delhi, Har-Anand Publications, 1996.

Singh, Karan, *Autobiography*, New Delhi, Oxford University Press, revised edition, 1994 [first published 1989].

Singh, Patwant and Jyoti M. Rai, *Empire of the Sikhs: The Life and Times of Maharaja Ranjit Singh*, London, Peter Owen Publishers, 2008.

Singh, Tavleen, *Kashmir: A Tragedy of Errors*, New Delhi, Viking, 1995.

Sinha, Aditya, *Farooq Abdullah: Kashmir's Prodigal Son*, New Delhi, UBSPD, 1996.

Sinha, Sachchidananda, *Kashmir: 'The Playground of Asia'*, Allahabad, Ram Narain Lal, 1943.

Snedden, Christopher, 'Kashmir: Placating Frustrated People', in Edward Aspinall, Robin Jeffrey and Anthony J. Regan, Editors, *Diminishing Conflicts in Asia and the Pacific: Why Some Subside and Others Don't*, Abingdon, Routledge, 2013.

Snedden, Christopher, *Paramountcy, Patrimonialism and the Peoples of Jammu and Kashmir, 1947–1991*, PhD dissertation, La Trobe University, Melbourne, 2001.

Snedden, Christopher, *The Untold Story of the People of Azad Kashmir, London, Hurst and Co., 2012/New York*, Columbia University Press, 2012; republished in Pakistan by Oxford University Press, Karachi, 2013; republished in India by HarperCollins, New Delhi, 2013, as *Kashmir: The Unwritten History*.

Snedden, Christopher, *Understanding Kashmir and Kashmiris*, London, Hurst & Co., 2015; republished in South Asia by Speaking Tiger Books, New Delhi, 2017.

Sökefeld, Martin, '*Jang Āzādi*: Perspectives on a Major Theme in Northern Areas' History', in Irmtraud Stellrecht, Editor, *The Past in the Present: Horizons of Remembering in the Pakistan Himalayas*, Cologne, Köppe, 1997.

Sooden, Surjit Singh, *Jammu under the Reign of Maharaja Hari Singh: A Study on Socio-economic Conditions*, Jammu, Vinod Publishers & Distributors, 1999.

Soz, Saifuddin, *Kashmir: Glimpses of History and the Story of Struggle*, New Delhi, Rupa, 2018.

Spate, O. H. K., *India and Pakistan: A General and Regional Geography*, London, Methuen, 1954.

Stacton, David, *A Ride on a Tiger: The Curious Travels of Victor Jacquemont*, London, Museum Press, 1954.

State versus Sheikh Abdullah, Kashmir on Trial, Lahore, The Lion Press, 1947.

Stephens, Ian, *Horned Moon*, London, Chatto & Windus, 1953.

Stephens, Ian, *Pakistan*, Ernest Benn Limited, 1963.

Studies of Kashmir Council of Research, Special Number: Struggle for Freedom in Jammu and Kashmir, Srinagar, Kashmir Council of Research, Volume III, 1978:
- Santosh Bakaya, 'Kashmiri's [sic] Struggle for Freedom Movement';
- Pir Gias-ud-Din, 'Main Trends of the History of [the] Kashmir National Movement';
- N. N. Raina, '"Hegemony of the Working People"';
- Mohammed Yasin, 'Understanding Sheikh Mohd. Abdullah'.

Sufi, G. M. D., *Kashir [sic]: Being a History of Kashmir From the Earliest Times to Our Own*, Volume II, Lahore, The University of the Punjab, 1949.

Swami, Praveen, *India, Pakistan and the Secret Jihad: The Covert War in Kashmir, 1947–2004*, London, Routledge, 2007.

Swarup, Devendra, and Sushil Aggarwal, *The Roots of [the] Kashmir Problem*, New Delhi, Manthan Prakashan, 1992.

Talbot, Phillips, *An American Witness to India's Partition*, New Delhi, Sage Publications, 2007.

Bibliography

Taleb, Nassim Nicholas, *The Black Swan: The Impact of the Highly Improbable*, London, Penguin, 2010.

Taseer, C. Bilqees, *The Kashmir of Sheikh Muhammad Abdullah*, Lahore, Ferozsons, 1986.

Thakur, D. D., *My Life and Years in Kashmir Politics*, Delhi, Konark Publishers, 2005.

Tharoor, Shashi, *Inglorious Empire: What the British Did to India*, London, Hurst and Co., 2017 (first published as *An Era of Darkness: The British Empire in India*, New Delhi, Aleph Book Company, 2016).

Tharoor, Shashi, *Why I Am a Hindu*, New Delhi, Aleph, 2018.

The Press Council of India, *Crisis and Credibility*, New Delhi, Lancer International, 1991.

The Testament of Sheikh Abdullah, New Delhi, Palit and Palit, 1974:
- 'Publisher's Preface';
- 'Sheikh Abdullah Speaks';
- Y. D. Gundevia, 'On Sheikh Abdullah';
- Y. D. Gundevia, 'Postscript'.

Thomas, Raju G. C., Editor, *Perspectives on Kashmir: The Roots of Conflict in South Asia*, Boulder, Westview Press, 1992.

Thornton, Edward, *A Gazetteer of the Territories under the Government of the East India Company and of the Native States on the Continent of India*, London, Wm H. Allen & Co., 1854.

Tikoo, Prithvi Nath, *Story of Kashmir*, New Delhi, Light & Life Publishers, 1979.

Tully, *Mark and Zareer Masani, India: Forty Years of Independence*, New York, George Braziller, 1988.

Tyndale Biscoe, C. E., *Kashmir in Sunlight & Shade*, London, Seeley Service, second edition, 1925, [First published 1921?].

Verma, P. S., *Jammu and Kashmir at the Political Crossroads*, New Delhi, Vikas, 1994.

Verma, S. M., *Chamber of Princes (1921–1947)*, New Delhi, National Book Organisation, 1990.

Wakefield, W., *The Happy Valley: Sketches of Kashmir & the Kashmiris*, London, Sampson et al., 1879.

Wakhlu, Somnath, *Hari Singh: The Maharaja, The Man and the Times: A Biography of Maharaja Hari Singh of Jammu and Kashmir State (1895–1961)*, New Delhi, National Publishing House, 2004.

Wani, Gull Mohd., Compiler, *Kashmir: From Autonomy to Azadi*, Srinagar, Valley Book House, 1996:
- Pervaiz Iqbal Cheema, 'The Kashmir Cobweb: Can it be Resolved?';
- Amrik Singh, 'Kashmir: The Quest for Independence'.

Webb, Matthew J., *Kashmir's Right to Secede*, Abingdon, Routledge, 2012.

Whitehead, Andrew, *A Mission in Kashmir*, New Delhi, Viking, 2007.

White-Spunner, Barney, *Partition: The Story of Indian Independence and the Creation of Pakistan in 1947*, London, Simon & Schuster, 2017.

Wolpert, Stanley, *Jinnah of Pakistan*, New York, Oxford University Press, 1984.

Younghusband, Sir Francis, *Kashmir*, London, Adam & Charles Black, 1911.

Ziegler, Philip, *Mountbatten: The Official Biography*, Glasgow, Fontana/Collins, 1985.

Zutshi, Chitralekha, Editor, *Kashmir: History, Politics, Representation*, Cambridge, Cambridge University Press, 2018:
- Shahla Hussain, 'Kashmiri Visions of Freedom';
- Martin Sökefeld, '"Not Part of Kashmir, but of the Kashmir Dispute": The Political Predicaments of Gilgit-Baltistan';

Bibliography

- Reeta Chowdhari Tremblay, 'Contested Governance, Competing Nationalisms and Disenchanted Publics: Kashmir Beyond Intractability?';
- Andrew Whitehead, 'The Rise and Fall of New Kashmir';
- Chitralekha Zutshi, 'Introduction: New Directions in the Study of Kashmir'.

Zutshi, Chitralekha, *Languages of Belonging: Islam, Regional Identity, and the Making of Kashmir*, London, Hurst & Co., 2004.

Zutshi, U. K., *Emergence of Political Awakening in Kashmir*, New Delhi, Manohar, 1986.

Journal and other articles

Abdullah, Sheikh, 'Kashmir, India and Pakistan', *Foreign Affairs*, April 1965.

Ankit, Rakesh, 'Forgotten Men of Kashmir', *Himal Southasian*, February 2010, http://old.himalmag.com/component/content/article/66forgotten-men-of-kashmir.html [accessed 25 April 2019].

Behera, Navnita Chadha, 'Re-framing the Conflict', *India International Centre Quarterly*, Vol. 37, No. 3/4, Winter 2010–Spring 2011.

Bekker, Konrad, 'Land Reform Legislation in India', *Middle East Journal*, Vol. 5, No. 3, Summer 1951.

Bellew, Surgeon H. W., 'Cashmir' [sic], *The Indian Medical Gazette*, 1 January 1870, p. 6, www.ncbi.nlm.nih.gov/pmc/articles/PMC5165417/?page=1 [accessed 3 February 2019].

Birdwood, Lord, 'Kashmir', *International Affairs*, Vol. 28, No. 3, July 1952.

Blank, Jonah, 'Kashmir: Fundamentalism Takes Root', *Foreign Affairs*, Vol. 78, No. 6, November/December 1999.

Copland, Ian, 'Islam and Political Mobilization in Kashmir, 1931–34', *Pacific Affairs*, Vol. 54, No. 2, 1981.

Copland, Ian, 'The Princely States, the Muslim League, and the Partition of India in 1947', *The International History Review*, Vol. 13, No. 1, February 1991.

Dasgupta, Anindita, 'Remembering Sylhet: A Forgotten Story of India's 1947 Partition', *Economic and Political Weekly*, 2 August 2008.

Dole, N. Y., 'Kashmir: A Deep-rooted Alienation', *Economic and Political Weekly*, 5–12 May 1990.

Faheem, Farrukh, 'Three Generations of Kashmir's Azaadi: A Short History of Discontent', *Economic and Political Weekly*, Vol. 51, No. 35, 27 August 2016, www.epw.in/journal/2016/35/web-exclusives/three-generations-kashmirs-azaadi-short-history-discontent.html [accessed 27 October 2017].

Fischer, Ruth, 'The Indian Communist Party', *Far Eastern Survey*, Vol. 22, No. 7, June 1953.

Furber, Holden, 'Constitution-making in India', *Far Eastern Survey*, Vol. 18, No. 8, 20 April 1949.

Ganai, Naseer and Bhavna Vij-Aurora, 'After Revocation of Article 370, Has China Become A "Third Party" To Kashmir Dispute?', *Outlook*, 15 June 2020, www.outlookindia.com/magazine/story/india-news-after-revocation-of-article-370-has-china-become-a-third-party-to-kashmir-dispute/303297 [accessed 5 June 2020].

Guha, Ramachandra, 'Opening a Window in Kashmir', *World Policy Journal*, 1 September 2004.

'Kashmir: The View from New Delhi', *International Crisis Group*, New Delhi/Brussels, 4 December 2003.

Bibliography

Katju, Markandey, 'Calling for Kashmir's Azadi is Not Sedition, Even if it's Illogical and Reactionary', *The Wire*, 20 August 2016, https://thewire.in/rights/calling-for-kashmirs-azadi-is-not-sedition-even-if-its-illogical-and-reactionary [accessed 14 May 2020].

Khan, Nyla Ali, 'The Events of 1953 in Jammu and Kashmir: A Memoir of Three Generations', *Race & Class*, Vol. 56, No. 2, Oct–Dec 2014.

Kishwar, Madhu, 'Why Fear People's Choice? Calling Pakistan's Bluff on Plebiscite in J and K', *Economic and Political Weekly*, 6 September 2003.

Korbel, Josef, 'The National Conference Administration of Kashmir 1949–1954', *Middle East Journal*, Vol. 8, No. 3, Summer 1954.

L. F. R. W. [sic], 'The Indian Dominion and the States', *The World Today*, Vol. 5, No. 1, January 1949.

Lockwood, David E., 'Resolving the Problem of Kashmir', *World Affairs*, Vol. 133, No. 3, December 1970.

Lockwood, David E., 'Sheikh Abdullah and the Politics of Kashmir', *Asian Survey*, Vol. 9, No. 5, May 1969.

Lyon, Peter, 'Kashmir', *International Relations: Journal of David Davies Memorial Institute of International Studies*, Vol. 3, No. 2, October 1966.

Mayfield, Robert C., 'A Geographic Study of the Kashmir Issue', *Geographical Review*, Vol. 45, No. 2, April 1955.

Morris-Jones, W. H., 'Thirty-Six Years Later: The Mixed Legacies of Mountbatten's Transfer of Power', *International Affairs*, Vol. 59, No. 4, Autumn 1983.

P. J. G. [sic], 'The Indian Union and Pakistan: The Political Outlook', *The World Today*, Vol. 3, No. 12, December 1947.

Palmer, Norman D., 'The Changing Scene in Kashmir', *Far Eastern Survey*, Vol. 22, No. 12, November 1953.

Park, Richard Leonard, 'India Argues with Kashmir', *Far Eastern Survey*, Vol. 21, No. 11, 2 July 1952.

Puri, Balraj, 'Independence, Autonomy and Freedom in Kashmir?', *Economic & Political Weekly*, 22 March 2008.

Puri, Balraj, 'Kashmiriyat: The Vitality of Kashmiri Identity', *Contemporary South Asia*, March 1995, Vol. 4, No. 1.

Puri, Balraj, 'Neglected Regional Aspirations in Jammu and Kashmir', *Economic & Political Weekly*, 5 January 2008.

Puri, Balraj, 'The Era of Sheikh Mohammed Abdullah', *Economic and Political Weekly*, Vol. 18, No. 6, 5 February 1983.

Puri, Balraj, 'Unfolding History', *India International Centre Quarterly*, Vol. 37, No. 3/4, Winter 2010–Spring 2011.

Rao, Aparna, 'A Tortuous Search for Justice: Notes on the Kashmir Conflict', *Himalaya*, Vol. 19, No. 1, 1999.

Sazawal, Vijay K., 'A Kashmiri Perspective II', *Asian Affairs*, Vol. 22, No. 1, Spring, 1995.

Sikand, Yoginder, 'Jihad, Islam and Kashmir: Syed Ali Shah Gilani's Political Project', *Economic & Political Weekly*, 2 October 2010, Vol. 45, No. 40.

Singh, Bawa Satinder, 'Raja Gulab Singh's Role in the First Anglo-Sikh War', *Modern Asian Studies*, Vol. 5, No. 1, 1971.

Snedden, Christopher, 'Would a Plebiscite Have Resolved the Kashmir Dispute?', *South Asia: Journal of South Asian Studies*, Vol. 28, No. 1, April 2005.

Bibliography

A Study Group of the Pakistan Institute of International Affairs, 'An Examination of Suggestions for the Partition of Kashmir', *Pakistan Horizon*, Vol. 1, No. 4, December 1948.

Sykes, Frederick, 'The Indian States and the Reforms', *International Affairs*, Vol. 14, No. 1, Jan–Feb 1935.

Tremblay, Reeta Chowdhari, 'Nation, Identity and the Intervening Role of the State: A Study of the Secessionist Movement in Kashmir', *Pacific Affairs*, Vol. 69, No. 4, Winter, 1996–97.

Van Beek, Martijn, 'True Patriots: Justifying Autonomy for Ladakh', *Himalaya*, Vol. 18, No. 1, Article 9, 1998.

Verma, P. S., 'Jammu and Kashmir Politics: Religion, Region and Personality Symbiosis', *The Indian Journal of Political Science*, Vol. 48, Oct–Dec 1987.

Wani, Riyaz, 'How Al-Qaeda Came to Kashmir', *The Diplomat*, 20 December 2017, https://thediplomat.com/2017/12/how-al-qaeda-came-to-kashmir/ [accessed 24 December 2017].

Wani, Riyaz, 'Life Under Siege in Kashmir', *The Diplomat*, 21 January 2020, https://thediplomat.com/2020/01/life-under-siege-in-kashmir/ [accessed 23 January 2020].

Wani, Safeena, 'Kashmir's Anthems of Azadi', *Arré*, 25 April 2017, www.arre.co.in/politics/kashmir-india-pakistan-burhan-wani-protests-slogans-kashmir-conflict/ [accessed 15 November 2018].

Webb, Matthew J., 'Grievance and the Kashmiri Diaspora', *Defense & Security Analysis*, Vol. 30, No. 3, 2014.

Wedgwood Benn, W., 'The Indian Round Table Conference', *International Affairs*, Vol. 10, No. 2, March 1931.

Whistler, Hugh, 'Some Aspects of Bird Life in Kashmir', *The Himalayan Journal*, Vol. 1, No. 1, April 1929.

Whitehead, Andrew, 'The People's Militia: Communists and Kashmiri Nationalism in the 1940s', *Twentieth Century Communism: A Journal of International History*, Issue 2, 2010.

Zetland, Marquess of, 'After the Indian Conference', *Foreign Affairs*, Vol. 10, No. 3, April 1932.

Newspapers, magazines, news services

Al Jazeera
The Argus, Melbourne
Business Insider
Business Standard
The Cairns Post
The Caravan
Chicago Tribune
The Civil & Military Gazette
The Daily Telegraph, Sydney
Dawn
Dissent
Economic and Political Weekly
The Economic Times
The Economist
Financial Times
Firstpost
Frontline

Bibliography

Greater Kashmir
The Guardian
The Herald, Melbourne
Himal Southasian
The Hindu
The Hindu Business Line
Hindustan Times
India Abroad
India Today
The Indian Express
Kashmir Life
Kashmir Times
Kashmir Watch
Keesing's Contemporary Archives
TheNewArab
The New York Times
Newsweek
Outlook
Pakistan Today
The Print
Reddit
Reuters
The Scotsman
Scroll.in
The Statesman, daily or weekly editions
The Straits Times
Swarajya
Tehelka Magazine
The Times
The Times of India
The Wire

Websites, blogs, (non-official) articles on websites

Ahmad, Mudasir, 'A Brief History of the J&K Liberation Front, Now Banned Under UAPA', *The Wire*, 23 March 2019, https://thewire.in/security/kashmir-jklf-ban-yasin-malik [accessed 27 September 2019].

'Americans in Kashmir History', *Kashmir Life*, 1 November 2010, https://kashmirlife.net/americans-in-kashmir-history-958/ [accessed 29 May 2018].

Ansur, Khan, '"Hum Kya Chahte? AZADI" – The Slogan Which Always Reverberates in Kashmir', *Khan Ansur blog*, 26 August 2016, https://khanansur.wordpress.com/2016/08/26/hum-kya-chahte-azadi-the-slogan-which-always-reverberates-in-kashmir/ [accessed 20 November 2018].

Bhowmick, Sumanta K., 'The Forgotten Chamber of Princes', *Live History India*, February 2019, www.livehistoryindia.com/cover-story/2019/02/18/the-forgotten-chamber-of-princes [accessed 12 October 2019].

Bibliography

Dogri, Shivnath, *Jammu Misecllany [sic; Miscellany]*, Kashmir Times Publications, [Jammu], 2005, http://shivnathdogri.com/images/aboutthebook/jammu%20in%20legends.pdf [accessed 9 November 2019].

'Hindu Calendar December 1946', Prokerala.com, www.prokerala.com/general/calendar/hinducalendar.php?year=1946&mon=december&sb=1 [accessed 19 November 2017].

'History of the Commonwealth', *Commonwealth Network*, www.commonwealthofnations.org/commonwealth/history/ [accessed 12 March 2017].

'Jammu & Kashmir', *South Asia Terrorism Portal*, www.satp.org/.

'Landlocked Countries 2020', *World Population Review*, http://worldpopulationreview.com/countries/landlocked-countries/ [accessed 7 March 2020].

'List of Countries and Dependencies by Area', *Wikipedia*, undated [2018?], https://en.wikipedia.org/wiki/List_of_countries_and_dependencies_by_area [accessed 9 July 2019].

Malley, Robert, '10 Conflicts to Watch in 2020', *International Crisis Group*, 27 December 2019, www.crisisgroup.org/global/10-conflicts-watch-2020 [accessed 6 April 2020].

'Member States', *United Nations*, undated, www.un.org/en/member-states/ [accessed 26 March 2019].

Mohd Aslma Khan, Rahmat Ali, Sheikh Mohd Sadiq and Inayat Ullah Khan, *Now or Never: Are We to Live or Perish Forever?*, 28 January 1933, no original publication details, copy available at www.mediamonitors.net/noworrnever.html [accessed 6 June 2017].

'Pakistan is Always Seen as the Rogue: SPIEGEL Interview with Pervez Musharraf (Interview conducted by Susanne Koelbl)', *Spiegel*, 4 October 2010, www.spiegel.de/international/world/0,1518,721110,00.html [accessed 10 February 2020].

'Popular Indicators', *World Bank* website, [2015?], https://databank.worldbank.org/indicator/SP.POP.TOTL/1ff4a498/Popular-Indicators# [accessed 28 July 2019].

'Popular statistical tables, country (area) and regional profiles', *UNdata*, 2015, http://data.un.org/en/index.html [accessed 8 July 2019].

Sahni, Ajai, 'India: J&K: A New Reality, South Asia Terrorism Review', *South Asia Terrorism Portal*, 12 August 2019, www.satp.org/south-asia-intelligence-review-Volume-18-No-7#assessment1 [accessed 8 July 2019].

'Security Council – Veto List', *Dag Hammarskjöld Library*, undated [2019], https://research.un.org/en/docs/sc/quick [accessed 12 July 2020].

Wiegold, Auriol, 'The Jammu and Kashmir Reorganisation Act 2019 – Progress on the BJP's Election Manifesto', *Future Directions International*, www.futuredirections.org.au/publication/the-jammu-and-kashmir-reorganisation-act-2019-progress-on-the-bjps-election-manifesto/ [accessed 5 June 2020].

Index

EU authorised representative for GPSR:
Easy Access System Europe, Mustamäe tee 50,
10621 Tallinn, Estonia
gpsr.requests@easproject.com

www.ingramcontent.com/pod-product-compliance
Lightning Source LLC
Chambersburg PA
CBHW020340100426
42812CB00029B/3199/J